Outlook 2000:
The Complete Reference

Tom E. Barich

Osborne/McGraw-Hill

Berkeley   New York   St. Louis   San Francisco
Auckland   Bogotá   Hamburg   London   Madrid
Mexico City   Milan   Montreal   New Delhi   Panama City
Paris   São Paulo   Singapore   Sydney
Tokyo   Toronto

Osborne/**McGraw-Hill**
2600 Tenth Street
Berkeley, California 94710
U.S.A.

For information on translations or book distributors outside the U.S.A., or to arrange bulk purchase discounts for sales promotions, premiums, or fundraisers, please contact Osborne/McGraw-Hill at the above address.

Outlook 2000: The Complete Reference

1234567890 DOC DOC 019876543210

Book P/N 0-07-212434-2 and CD P/N 0-07-212435-0
parts of
ISBN 0-07-212436-9

Publisher	**Copy Editor**
Brandon A. Nordin	Lunaea Weatherstone
Vice President and Associate Publisher	**Proofreader**
Scott Rogers	Stefany Otis
Acquisitions Editor	**Indexer**
Megg Bonar	Jack Lewis
Project Editor	**Computer Designers**
Jody McKenzie	Jani Beckwith
	Lucie Ericksen
Acquisitions Coordinator	Jim Kussow
Cindy Wathen	Kelly Stanton-Scott
Technical Editor	**Illustrators**
Virginia Anderson	Michael Mueller
	Beth E. Young

This book was composed with Corel VENTURA™ Publisher.

This book is dedicated
to the memory
of Esther Rojeski,
one of my favorite aunts,
and maker of the
world's best brownies.

About the Author...

Thomas E. Barich is a computer consultant, CD-ROM developer, and author of a number of titles on a variety of computer software applications, including Microsoft Outlook, Microsoft Office, Symantec's ACT!, and others.

Contents at a Glance

Contents

Part I
Outlook Basics

Part II

Communicating with E-mail

Part IV

Managing Time and Details

Part VII

Building Outlook Applications

Part VIII

Appendixes

Acknowledgments

The fact that this has been one of the most satisfying book writing projects I've ever undertaken is due, in no small part, to the exceptionally talented people involved. The original cast of Osborne characters included Joanne Cuthbertson and Stephanie Thomas, both of whom moved on to other things midway through the book. While they were there, they did a great job. I was fortunate that their replacements were equally qualified and talented. Megg Bonar, acquisitions editor, was on hand when I needed her and provided the support that got me through this book with most of my sanity intact. Cindy Wathen, acquisitions coordinator, did a great job of keeping things on track, with only an occasional crack of the whip. Virginia Anderson is an author's dream technical editor. She kept an eagle eye out to ensure the book's technical accuracy and offered great suggestions for enhancing the coverage. Jody McKenzie, project editor, kept us on the straight and narrow, and provided lots of good insights. Thanks to the valiant efforts of Lunaea Weatherstone, our copy editor, you'll probably never even suspect that I'm among the punctuationally challenged.

I also want to thank Ken Slovak for providing the first-rate chapter on VBA. He stepped in to help out at the last minute and saved the day.

Last, but not least, I want to thank Andrea Golden for the much needed support and the excellent research she provided.

Introduction

Computer book introductions usually attempt to convey three things to the reader: what that book is about, for whom the book is written, and how to understand the conventions used in the book. While I think these objectives are worthy, the typical approach generally falls short of the mark. Therefore, I propose to make this introduction less typical and more helpful.

To give the reader a sense of what the book is about, the typical computer book introduction provides a synopsis of what each part covers. There's nothing wrong with that, but it's no match for the table of contents. If you really want to know what kind of coverage this book contains, head there. It's clear, concise, informative, and to the point.

Who is this book written for? That's easy. It's written for the reader who wants to learn about Outlook, and who wants a good reference book handy to help solve problems when they arise. Other than that, the onus of deciding whether this book is right for you falls, naturally, on your shoulders. The only way you can decide is by making sure the coverage is appropriate and the style is easy to read and understand. Therefore, I recommend that you review the table of contents, read random sections of the book, and skim through the index.

The third thing most computer book introductions explain is the conventions used throughout the book. Since the icons and text formatting used in this book to mark special items, such as tips, notes, and MOUS coverage, are clear and unambiguous, there's no reason to belabor the issue. I'm sure you know that each time you see an icon that says Tip, it means the associated text is actually a bit of helpful advice.

Now on to the really important stuff. If you haven't already purchased this book, do so now. If you own the book, stop wasting time and get to work.

The
Complete
Reference

Part I

Outlook Basics

The Complete Reference

Chapter 1

Exploring Outlook

Outlook 2000 can greatly enhance your productivity by helping you get organized and keeping you organized. Unfortunately, as good as Outlook is, it can't do it alone, so you're going to have to roll up your sleeves and do some of the work yourself. Since the first order of business is to become familiar with the program and the way it functions, this chapter is going to take you on a tour of Outlook 2000. Here you'll get a good look at what exactly Outlook 2000 is and what it can do for you. You'll discover the convenience and flexibility Outlook provides in helping you communicate, delegate, schedule, track, and otherwise organize your day, your work, and your life. You'll learn about the program's main features and tools, how to open, close, and get around in the program, and how to get additional help when you need it.

Introducing Outlook

Outlook 2000 is the Swiss army knife of personal information managers (PIMs). It provides you with all the tools you need to send and receive e-mail, keep track of your schedule, stay in touch with your contacts, and even manage your to-do lists. In addition, it integrates with other applications to enable you to compose form letters, send faxes, access the Internet, and more.

Send and Receive E-mail, Faxes, and Documents

Although Outlook is a full-featured PIM, its e-mail management feature is, by far, its most popular. Some folks use Outlook for nothing else. Not only can you send and receive e-mail from any number of corporate or Internet mail addresses, you can also send documents and files, sort messages in a variety of ways, and even organize your messages automatically with the Outlook Rules Wizard. Because Outlook is Internet-savvy, you can send messages in the HTML format, which enables you to include colorful text and graphics. Depending on your configuration, you also can send faxes directly from Outlook. As you can see in Figure 1-1, the Inbox holds all your incoming mail, shown in the right pane, until you either store or delete it.

Schedule Meetings and Appointments

For keeping track of your schedule, Outlook provides a powerful set of features to ensure you never miss another appointment or important engagement (unless, of course, you want to!). Corporate users on a network running Microsoft Exchange Server can schedule complex meetings with ease down to the last detail. Just enter the names of everyone you want to invite to the meeting, then ask Outlook to find a time at which everyone is available. You can even include a conference room or a resource (such as an overhead projector) by inviting the resource just as you would another

Figure 1-1.   *The Outlook Inbox helps you manage all your e-mail*

meeting participant. Of course, the resource must have its own mailbox set up on the server before it will appear in the Select Attendees and Resources dialog box.

Need an online meeting instead? No problem—Outlook works with Microsoft NetMeeting to connect you with users anywhere on the planet for a live, real-time conference.

Even home users will find dozens of ways to use the Calendar folder: you can keep track of birthdays, holidays, and other special occasions; plan trips and vacations; or be reminded about next week's doctor's appointment (see Figure 1-2).

Figure 1-2. *The Calendar folder provides all the tools you need to stay on schedule*

Manage Your Contact List

After you learn to use Outlook's contact management features, you can throw away your Rolodex, your little black book, *and* that unruly stack of business cards (not to mention the cocktail napkins and matchbook covers scribbled with names and numbers). The Outlook Contacts folder (shown in Figure 1-3) provides the room to store virtually any kind of information about each and every important person in your life, whether it's the company CEO, the potential client you met at a trade show last month, or your long-lost nephew in Sheboygan. However, the best part of using the Contacts folder is the ability to retrieve your contact information with just a click of your mouse.

Figure 1-3.   *Accessing contact information is a breeze with the Outlook Contacts folder*

Track and Delegate Tasks and Projects

As you can see in Figure 1-4, the Tasks feature in Outlook provides everything you've always wanted in a to-do list, and more. In addition to managing your own to-do lists, you can assign tasks to other users, set due dates and reminders, even get automatic progress reports at specific intervals. You can also use the Tasks feature for personal reminders, such as paying bills, remembering the kids' games, and *not* forgetting to pick up an anniversary present for your spouse.

Figure 1-4.   *Managing your to-do list was never this easy*

Log Journal Entries and Keep Notes

The Journal is a convenient way to keep track of what you did, when you did it, and how long it took (see Figure 1-5). If you bill hourly for your work, you'll certainly appreciate this feature. Start the timer before beginning work on a task to log time spent. Jot down notes from your phone call while it's happening (and use the timer to track the length of the call). Use contacts and categories to sort journal entries by clients or jobs. While not designed for complex project management, the Journal can handle everyday projects with ease.

Figure 1-5. *Use the Journal feature to log project activities, phone calls, and documents*

Access Web Sites and Newsgroups

Outlook makes your Internet access complete by acting as a Web browser and by working with Outlook Express to give you access to newsgroups (see Figure 1-6). You can even configure Outlook to open a particular Web page each time you click a folder. Of course, in order to take advantage of the Web and newsgroup features you must have an Internet connection, either through your network or a modem.

Figure 1-6.   *Outlook integrates with Outlook Express to give access to Internet newsgroups*

> **Tip**   *If you select View | Go To | News, and Outlook Express opens instead of the Microsoft Outlook Newsreader, it means that Outlook Express and not Outlook is designated as your default newsgroups software. To use the Outlook Newsreader, Outlook must be your default newsgroups program. See Chapter 21 for details on how to make Outlook your default newsgroups software.*

Is Your Computer on a Network?

If you're using Outlook at work, you're probably connected to a network. A network consists of two types of computers: servers and workstations. The servers are those computers, locked in the closet on the fourth floor, that receive, warehouse, and distribute information to the workstations, or clients. The workstations are the computers sitting on everyone's desk (including yours).

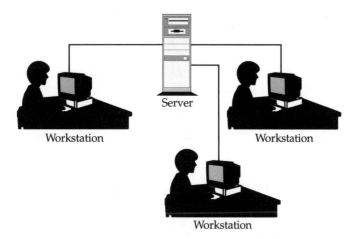

It's also likely that a program called Microsoft Exchange Server is running on that network. Exchange Server is a popular network server-based messaging and groupware system that manages and distributes large volumes of mail to a multitude of users. Microsoft Outlook is a client mail program that runs on individual users' computers (workstations). You may have another mail system, such as Lotus cc:Mail or Microsoft Mail instead of Exchange Server. No problem—Outlook works with those too. If you're not sure about which mail system your company uses, check with your network administrator.

The details of how networks and Exchange Server work are not necessary for an understanding of Outlook. The main things you need to know are whether or not you're on a network and, if so, whether it is running Exchange Server.

Note   *You'll learn more about the benefits you get from using Outlook with Exchange Server in Part V.*

How Is Outlook Configured?

Depending on your network status, Outlook 2000 may be installed in one of three basic configurations:

■ **Internet Only**   If you aren't connected to a network or if your network isn't running a server-based mail application, but you do have access to the Internet through a modem or through the network, choose this configuration. Be advised that the option is called Internet Only, but the actual configuration is called Internet Mail Only (IMO). You won't be able to use some of Outlook's networking features, but you'll still have access to a vast array of basic e-mail and information management features.

■ **Corporate or Workgroup**   If you're attached to a network, you'll want to use the Corporate or Workgroup configuration. In addition to messages from your corporate mail system, you can send and receive mail from the Internet, use LDAP Internet directories (global e-mail address listings), plan meetings and appointments over the network, delegate tasks and scheduling to others, and much more. For faxing, you'll get Microsoft at Work Fax, a free program you install separately. You don't have to be on a network to use this configuration. You might use the Corporate or Workgroup (C/W) configuration, for example, when more than one person uses your computer to access Internet e-mail via a dial-up connection.

■ **No E-mail**   If you have no plans to use e-mail of any kind, choose this option. You should also use this configuration if you use e-mail that cannot be downloaded into Outlook, such as AOL. Even without the e-mail features, Outlook is an excellent personal information manager, especially for keeping track of contacts and appointments.

Tip   *When Outlook is running, you can determine which way it is configured by clicking Help | About Microsoft Outlook. The current configuration appears in the About Microsoft Outlook dialog box.*

Some Outlook features work differently or aren't available at all in the Internet Mail Only configuration, or without Exchange Server, or under other specific conditions. In addition, some features may work similarly in either configuration, but the menu commands or dialog boxes may be different. It's not possible to anticipate every possible configuration; thus, to offer the most value to the widest range of users, this book assumes that:

■ Outlook is installed on your computer using the C/W configuration.

■ You are attached to a network running Microsoft Exchange Server.

When a feature differs significantly or is not available in other configurations, this book uses an icon in the margin to point out those situations. Since the No E-mail configuration is identical to the Internet Mail Only configuration except for the lack of an e-mail account, the icon used will refer to IMO:

Your dialog box may be different if you're using the Internet Mail Only configuration.

Changing Your Configuration

You can change your configuration after Outlook is installed; just remember that you'll reconfigure Outlook for all users on that computer, not just yourself. To reconfigure

Outlook, choose Tools | Options from the menu bar to open the Options dialog box. Click the Mail Services tab to view the options for your mail services (see Figure 1-7). Then click Reconfigure Mail Support and follow the onscreen directions.

 The Options dialog box found in the Internet Mail Only configuration does not contain a Mail Services tab. You'll find the Reconfigure Mail Support button on the Mail Delivery tab.

If this is the first time you're changing to this configuration, you may be prompted to insert your Office 2000 CD so Office can install the files needed for the new configuration.

Figure 1-7.   *Switching between Outlook configurations is easy as long as you have your CD handy*

Starting Outlook

Outlook, like most Windows programs, plants a shortcut on the Start menu during installation. And as is the case with other Windows programs, you can count on having more than one way to do the same thing. With that in mind, here are a few ways you can launch Outlook:

- **From the Start menu**   Click Start | Programs | Microsoft Outlook.

- **From the desktop**   Double-click the Outlook icon on the desktop.

- **From the Quick Launch bar (Windows 98/2000)**   By default, Outlook does not put a shortcut on the Quick Launch bar. Therefore, you'll have to do it yourself. The easiest method is to click Start | Programs and locate the Outlook shortcut. Right-click the shortcut and drag it to the Quick Launch bar. Move your mouse pointer to a place on the bar to the right or left of an existing shortcut and release the right mouse button when your cursor turns into a dark I bar. After that, all you have to do is click the icon to launch Outlook.

- **From the Office Shortcut bar**   If you regularly use the Office Shortcut bar, you'll find the variety of Outlook-related buttons here useful. You can use the shortcut bar to go directly to a new message, appointment, task, contact, journal entry, or note. Outlook will open (if it isn't already) and present you with the blank item you requested.

If you have multiple profiles set up in the C/W configuration and you enable the Prompt For A Profile To Be Used option in the Mail Services Startup Settings, Outlook asks you to select the profile you want to use each time you start the program. With the option disabled, Outlook starts with the profile selected in the Always Use This Profile option. Profiles are groups of individualized settings that determine which services are available to each user and how those services are configured. You'll learn more about creating your own profile in Chapter 2.

After you choose which profile to use, Outlook will begin loading the files and settings last used in that profile. Unless you've changed the default settings, Outlook opens to the Inbox (see Figure 1-8).

Figure 1-8.   *If you're like most users, you'll be a frequent visitor to the Inbox*

Exploring the Outlook Interface

In order to harness the power Outlook offers, you must understand the different components, how they work, and how they integrate with each other. To make that task a little easier, familiarize yourself with some of the basic features common to all Outlook components.

Figure 1-9 identifies the main Outlook screen items. You'll recognize some of them from other Microsoft or Windows applications; others will be discussed in more detail later in this chapter:

■ **Title bar**   Check here if you forget where you are. Click here and drag to move the window on the screen, or double-click to maximize or restore the window size.

Figure 1-9.   *The Outlook interface is easy to use and easy to navigate*

- **Menu bar**   Click a menu topic to reveal a list of available commands and submenus, then click the desired command.

- **Status bar**   Look here for statistics on the current view, such as total number of items in the selected folder.

- **Toolbars**   Toolbars are the button bars at the top of the window, containing a variety of common commands. The toolbars and the buttons they include vary depending on which component you are using.

- **Folder List**   The Folder List provides a Windows Explorer-like view of your Outlook folders. To activate the Folder List, select View | Folder List from the menu bar. You can also open the Folder List by clicking the current folder's title in the Folder banner.

- **Folder banner**   The Folder banner displays the name of the folder in which you're currently working.

- **Outlook Bar**   The Outlook Bar provides a quick and easy way to navigate around Outlook. You'll find shortcuts to the main Outlook components as well as your system files on the Outlook Bar. Click a shortcut to switch to the associated folder. As you can see in Figure 1-9, the Outlook Bar is comprised of three shortcut groups—Outlook Shortcuts, My Shortcuts, and Other Shortcuts. You'll learn how to add and remove shortcuts and shortcut groups from the Outlook Bar in Chapter 23.

- **Information viewer**   The Information viewer is the main viewing area of the Outlook window. It displays the contents of the currently selected folder. For example, in the Inbox, the Information viewer displays a list of your received e-mail messages. Switch to Calendar, and the Information viewer displays today's appointments along with the Date Navigator and the TaskPad.

What Is Outlook Today?

As you can see in Figure 1-10, Outlook Today is a handy one-screen summary of your day. At a single glance, you can see today's date, your upcoming appointments, the number of unread messages in your Inbox, and the current items on your Tasks list.

If you need a little more detail, simply click an item to display the form (appointments and tasks) or the folder (messages) associated with it. You can even mark tasks as completed by checking them off in the Outlook Today view.

If you like the idea of getting a quick overview of your day each morning, you can elect to have Outlook open to Outlook Today each time you start the program. See Chapter 24 for details.

Using the Information Viewer

Since the Information viewer is the display area for the currently selected folder, your options for manipulating it are limited to those involving the viewing of information. You can resize it by changing the size of (or hiding) the Outlook Bar. Depending on the folder you're in, you can split the Information viewer by activating the Preview Pane,

Figure 1-10.   *Outlook Today provides a quick overview of appointments and tasks*

and you can open the Folder List by clicking the folder name in the Folder banner. You can also access shortcut menus by right-clicking the Folder banner or the display area of the Information viewer itself.

To allow more room in the Information viewer, keep the Folder List closed. You can click the folder's title on the Folder banner to briefly reveal the Folder List. Choose the folder you want to see next; the Folder List will close again, leaving your Information viewer uncluttered.

Getting Around in Outlook

  There are a number of ways to move around in Outlook, but you'll find there are two methods that provide the easiest and most flexible means of navigating the program. They are the Outlook Bar and the Folder List.

Using the Outlook Bar

The Outlook Bar shown in Figure 1-11, is the primary navigation tool in Outlook. It's loaded with shortcuts to the main Outlook components as well as your system files and folders. Click a shortcut icon to open the associated folder.

Figure 1-11.   *After using the Outlook Bar you'll wish every Windows program had one*

By default, the Outlook Bar contains three shortcut groups:

■ **Outlook Shortcuts** This group contains shortcuts to the most commonly used Outlook folders.

■ **My Shortcuts** Here you'll find some of the less frequently used Outlook shortcuts.

■ **Other Shortcuts** The Other Shortcuts group provides access to your system files and folders as well as My Computer and your Favorites folder.

Navigating with the Outlook Bar

Now that you understand the theory, it's time for a little practical application. Why not take the Outlook Bar for a test drive and see what it can do? To begin with, click any shortcut and open the associated folder. You'll note that not only does the content of the Information viewer change, but also the commands on the toolbar. If you check the menus, you'll find differences there as well. Spend a little time moving around Outlook using the Outlook Shortcuts. Here's a list of the places you can go using the shortcuts found in the Outlook Shortcuts group:

■ **Outlook Today** As discussed earlier in this chapter, Outlook Today provides a quick overview of your daily activities and unread messages.

■ **Inbox** The Inbox is the heart of your e-mail system. It's where all your incoming mail resides until you decide what to do with it.

■ **Calendar** The Calendar folder contains the appointment calendar, the Date Navigator, and the TaskPad. You can schedule appointments and meetings, look up dates, and even record tasks on your to-do list.

■ **Contacts** The Contacts folder is the receptacle for all your contact information. In addition to storing and manipulating your contact data, the Contacts folder can also double as an Outlook address book.

■ **Tasks** The Tasks folder is a to-do list on steroids. It provides all the tools you need to track and manage your past (in case you're just a little behind), present, and future tasks.

■ **Notes** Can't figure out what to do with a miscellaneous scrap of information you know you should hold on to? Create an Outlook note! The electronic equivalent of sticky notes, Outlook notes let you record and organize bits and pieces of data that don't seem to fit anywhere else.

■ **Deleted Items** When you delete an Outlook item, it gets dumped in the Deleted Items folder. However, be sure not to confuse Deleted Items with the

Windows Recycle Bin. They have nothing to do with one another, and they do not collaborate. Items moved to the Deleted Items folder remain there until you empty the folder, at which time they are removed permanently from your hard disk. They do *not* go to the Windows Recycle Bin.

Depending on your screen resolution and the state of your Outlook window, you may not be able to view all the shortcuts in My Shortcuts at one time. If you see a down arrow button in the bottom right corner of the Outlook Bar it indicates the presence of additional shortcuts.

Click the down arrow button to bring the additional buttons into view. Once you do that, you'll notice that the shortcuts at the top of the Outlook Bar have now disappeared, and an up arrow button appears in the top right corner. As you've undoubtedly figured out by now, the buttons are scroll buttons and you simply click them to move the missing shortcuts into view.

If you're ready to move on and try something new, click the My Shortcuts button to display the secondary set of Outlook shortcuts (see Figure 1-12).

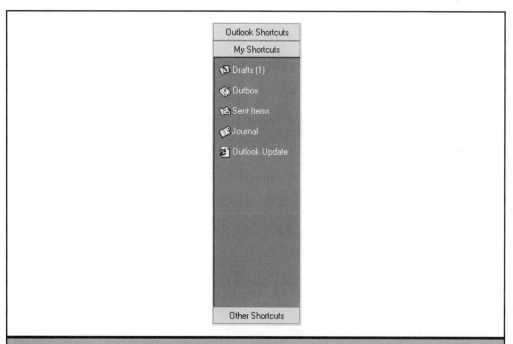

Figure 1-12.   *The My Shortcuts group provides access to some of the less frequently used Outlook folders*

Even if you don't use these shortcuts often, it's nice to know where they are when you need them:

- **Drafts**   Did you ever write an e-mail in haste and hit the Send button, only to realize that you forgot something, or even worse, that you never should have sent the message at all? Use the Drafts folder to save unfinished or questionable messages for later review.

- **Outbox**   The Outbox is a way station for messages you send. On a Microsoft Exchange Server network the server sweeps the Outbox at regular intervals and picks up your outgoing mail automatically, so messages spend little time there when you're logged on to the network. If, however, you're working offline, messages stay in the Outbox until you log back on. The Outbox also gets used if you have an Internet e-mail account and choose not to have outgoing messages sent automatically. They are stored in the Outbox until the next time you manually send mail using your Internet account.

- **Sent Items**   When you get the urge to review messages you've sent (or when a question arises that may be answered in a previously sent message), you'll find the Sent Items folder quite helpful. By default, Outlook is configured to save a copy of all outgoing messages in the Sent Items folder.

- **Journal**   The Outlook Journal provides a place for you to track phone calls, e-mail messages, tasks, and even Office documents.

- **Outlook Update**   If you're connected to the Internet, either through your network or through a modem, the Outlook Update shortcut opens the Outlook section of the Microsoft Office Update Web site right in your Information viewer.

The third and final shortcut group, Other Shortcuts, provides access to your computer and your system files:

- **My Computer**   This shortcut is identical to the My Computer icon on your Windows desktop. It displays your Windows environment in the Outlook Information viewer.

- **My Documents**   For quick and easy access to the My Documents folder on your hard disk, click this shortcut icon. The contents of your My Documents folder appears in the Outlook Information viewer.

- **Favorites**   The Favorites shortcut, as you've probably guessed, opens your Favorites folder and displays the contents in the Outlook Information viewer.

Tip   *You can add your own groups and shortcuts to the Outlook Bar, which you'll learn more about in Chapter 23.*

Drag and Drop Items on the Outlook Bar

Not only is the Outlook Bar a great tool for getting around in Outlook, it also provides a quick and easy way to move and copy information. In addition, it enables you to easily create one kind of Outlook item from another. You can create messages from notes, contacts from appointments, and even appointments from tasks.

For example, suppose you've got a task on your to-do list to make a doctor's appointment. Once you stop procrastinating and get around to making the appointment, there are a couple of ways you can add it to your calendar. You can delete the task from the Tasks list (or mark it completed), open the Calendar folder, and finally create a new appointment—or you can save yourself some trouble and use the Outlook Bar. Simply drag the item from your Tasks list and drop it on the Calendar shortcut on the Outlook Bar. A new appointment form opens immediately with all the available information from the Tasks list already included. All you have to do is fill in the date and time, set a reminder, and click Save and Close.

Note *For more information on working with tasks and appointments, see Chapters 11 and 13.*

Hiding and Restoring the Outlook Bar

One nice thing about the Outlook Bar is that if you don't like it you don't have to look at it. Even if you do like it, you may decide you need more room for the Information viewer. In either case, you can hide and display the Outlook Bar at will. You can even change its size if you like.

If the Outlook Bar is visible, you can hide it by opening the View menu and clicking Outlook Bar to remove the checkmark that appears to the left. To display a hidden Outlook Bar simply return to the View menu and click Outlook Bar to add a checkmark.

Using the Folder List as a Navigational Tool

The Folder List is a tree-like structure that provides you with a simple way to view, navigate through, and utilize your Outlook folders. If you're at all familiar with the Windows Explorer you'll feel right at home using the Folder List (see Figure 1-13).

Using the Folder List to make your way around Outlook is easy. From any folder, choose View | Folder List to display the Folder List in the Information viewer. You can also display the Folder List by clicking the folder name, which assumes the appearance of a button as soon as you move your mouse pointer over it. The folder name is located at the left side of the Folder banner and contains a small down arrow indicating the presence of a drop-down window.

Note *Clicking the folder name only opens the Folder List temporarily. As soon as you make a selection in the Folder List, or take any other action in Outlook, the Folder List closes automatically. You can keep it open permanently (or at least until you elect to close it) by clicking the yellow pushpin icon located in the top right corner of the Folder List.*

Figure 1-13. *The Folder List provides the same ease of use found in the Windows Explorer*

Once you've got the Folder List open, all you have to do is click the folder to which you want to move. Immediately you're transported to the selected folder. If you used the Folder List command on the View menu, or if you clicked the yellow pushpin, the Folder List remains open, enabling you to keep moving whenever the urge strikes.

In addition to providing you with another navigation tool, the Folder List also gives you another means of creating Outlook items by dragging the item and dropping it on a folder in the list. As soon as you drop the item, a new form of the type used in the folder on which you dropped the original item opens, containing the data from the dropped item. For example, if you drop an appointments item in the Notes folder, a new Notes form opens, containing the appointment information. It's the same as dropping items on the Outlook Bar shortcuts, except that you have more options (unless you've customized the Outlook Bar) with the Folder List.

MOUS EXAM PRACTICE

In this section, you discovered the two main methods of getting around in Outlook: (1) using the Outlook Bar to move from folder to folder and (2) displaying and using the Folder List. Move through each of your existing folders using the Outlook Bar. Keep in mind that the Outlook Bar may or may not contain a shortcut for every folder you have. Next, open the folder by using both methods: by accessing the Folder List command on the View menu, and by clicking the folder name. When you use the folder name method, be sure to take the necessary step to keep the Folder List open until you decide to shut it. After you have the Folder List open, use it to move around all your Outlook folders.

Using the Toolbars

Toolbars are those handy little devices that you find hanging out on most Windows programs. They contain buttons for accessing the most commonly used features of the program. Outlook follows the tradition and has a great set of toolbars (see Figure 1-14), and a wealth of toolbar options. In addition to providing you with four main toolbars (three if you're using Internet Mail Only) and four subsidiary toolbars (found only in certain Outlook forms), Outlook also enables you to modify existing toolbars and even create your own custom toolbars.

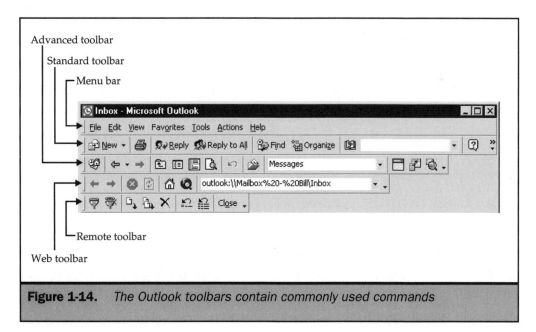

Figure 1-14.   *The Outlook toolbars contain commonly used commands*

When you open the Customize dialog box, you'll see the Menu bar listed under toolbars. Technically this is accurate, since the Menu bar is nothing more than a toolbar that contains menus instead of command buttons. However, for the sake of clarity, this book treats toolbars and menus as different devices.

The primary Outlook toolbars include the following:

- **Standard**   This is your "meat and potatoes" toolbar. It contains the standard commands you find in most Windows programs, such as New, Print, and Find, plus the basic commands for the Outlook component you currently have open.

- **Advanced**   The Advanced toolbar sports a collection of command buttons that let you perform Outlook tasks such as changing views, showing and hiding the Folder List, undoing the last command, and so on. As with the Standard toolbar, the Advanced toolbar changes depending on the Outlook folder that is currently open.

- **Remote**   If you use the Exchange Server Remote Mail feature, you'll notice the Remote toolbar appears. It contains command buttons to connect to and disconnect from the remote server as well as some commands for setting message retrieval criteria. See Chapter 17 for more information on using Remote Mail.

The Remote toolbar is available only to users running the C/W configuration of Outlook 2000. It does not appear on the Toolbars tab of the Customize dialog box in the Internet Mail Only configuration.

- **Web**   When you use Outlook to view Web pages on the Internet or your company's intranet, the Web toolbar appears. If you understand Back, Home, Refresh, and Stop, you shouldn't have much trouble figuring out this one. (See "Using Outlook as a Web and File Browser," later in this chapter.)

The secondary toolbars are found only in Outlook forms, such as the appointment form, the message form, the contact form, and so on:

- **Formatting**   If you use a word processor, the Formatting toolbar should be a familiar sight. It provides the basic commands for manipulating and dressing up your text. The Formatting toolbar is available in any form that accepts text in a message or note field.

- **Clipboard**   This Office Clipboard, which Outlook uses, enables you to cut and paste up to 12 different items in any one session. The Clipboard toolbar gives the option to select which item to paste, to paste all items on the clipboard, or to clear the entire Office Clipboard. Like the Formatting toolbar, the Clipboard toolbar is available in all forms that accept text entry in a message or notes field.

- **Form Design**   This toolbar provides you with commands used in designing and customizing forms. Although the Form Design toolbar appears on the Toolbars tab of the Customize box when accessed from any form, it can only be activated in the design mode.

- **Response**   This toolbar is available only when viewing e-mail messages you receive that contain voting buttons.

Showing and Hiding Toolbars

The first time you run Outlook, the Standard toolbar is the only one that appears in most Outlook folders. You can access additional toolbars by right-clicking anywhere on a visible toolbar and selecting from the shortcut menu that appears. Toolbars with checkmarks are already visible. Toolbars without checkmarks are currently hidden. To hide a visible toolbar, right-click and deselect the toolbar you want to eliminate.

   You can open the Customize dialog box by double-clicking a blank area to the right of any toolbar.

Repositioning Toolbars

Since not everyone works the same way, you'll be pleased to discover that you're not locked into using the Outlook toolbars where they fall. Each toolbar can be moved from its original position and placed anywhere in the Outlook window that pleases your fancy. While you can locate the toolbars anywhere you want, there are two toolbar states that you should be aware of: docked and floating. As you can see in Figure 1-15, a docked toolbar is one that is securely planted along one of the four edges (or adjacent to a toolbar on the edge) of the Outlook window. A floating toolbar, on the other hand, is one that is just hanging out in any random spot on the window.

To move a docked toolbar, grab its handle (the raised vertical bar at the left edge of the toolbar), drag it to the new location and drop it. To move a floating toolbar, grab it by the title bar, drag it to a new location and drop it. To dock any toolbar, move it to the desired edge of the Outlook window until it automatically positions itself against the window edge or against an existing docked toolbar. To float a toolbar, move it into

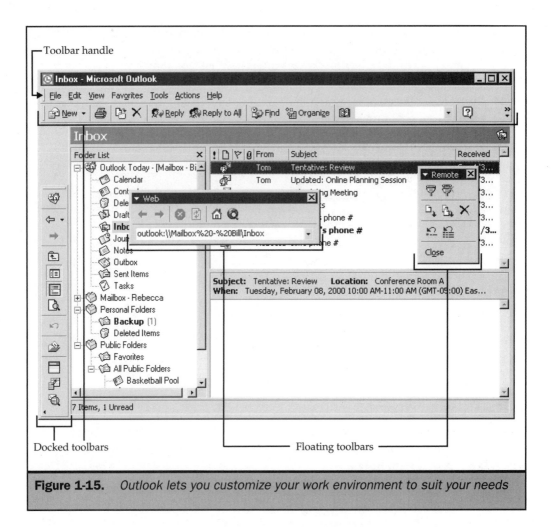

Figure 1-15. *Outlook lets you customize your work environment to suit your needs*

the Outlook window and drop it wherever you want it. You can also resize floating toolbars by dragging either of the four sides to enlarge or reduce the length or width of the toolbar.

If you double-click the title bar of a floating toolbar, it will automatically return to its last docked location.

Customizing Toolbars

You can add and remove buttons on existing toolbars, change the order in which the buttons appear, and even create your own toolbar from scratch. For more information on these procedures see Chapter 23.

Working with Multiple Outlook Windows

Despite its power and flexibility, there are a few things Outlook can't do that many users wish it could. You can't, for example, view different components at the same time in the same session of Outlook. So what do you do if you're responding to a ton of e-mail requests to set up meetings over the next several months and you want to view both your Inbox and your Calendar window at the same time? Simple enough: start a new Outlook session, then position both windows so you can see as much as you can of both. If you have a large monitor (17 inches or more) and run at a high screen resolution, you can really pack a lot of information on one screen.

You can run as many sessions of Outlook or any other application(s) as your computer can handle. If performance deteriorates, it's probably because your computer is running low on available memory (RAM). You may have to close one or more open windows, documents, or sessions before proceeding.

To run multiple sessions of Outlook and arrange them neatly onscreen, follow these steps:

1. With one Outlook session already running in any view, minimize all open windows. If you're using Windows 98 or later, just click the Desktop button on the Quick Launch bar. Otherwise, right-click anywhere on a blank area of the Windows taskbar and choose Minimize All Windows.

2. Double-click the Outlook icon on the Windows desktop to open a second session.

3. Click the original Outlook session's taskbar button to restore it. You now have two Outlook sessions visible; if any other applications are running, they are minimized.

4. Right-click the taskbar and choose Tile Windows Vertically. The windows will be evenly sized, the currently selected window filling the left half of the screen, the other filling the right half, as shown in Figure 1-16.

5. If you'd prefer to have the windows lined up one on top of the other, right-click the taskbar and choose Tile Windows Horizontally. The windows will be evenly sized, the currently selected window filling the top half of the screen, the other filling the lower half.

Figure 1-16.   *Placing both Outlook sessions side by side makes working in two folders at the same time a snap*

Most of the interior borders within the Outlook window can be adjusted by dragging them elsewhere (see Figure 1-17). With a large monitor, a speedy computer, and some creative resizing, you can view several Outlook components at once and still have room to work on a word processing document or other window on the desktop. Don't overdo it though—it doesn't take much to drain your computer's memory resources.

Using Outlook as a Web and File Browser

Because the Office 2000 suite of applications is so closely integrated with the Internet, it's no surprise that the "don't use a hammer to drive a screw" rule doesn't always apply: now you can create Web pages with Excel, you can create graphics in Word, and you can use Outlook as a browser.

Border handle

Figure 1-17.   *Drag interior and exterior borders to make the Outlook environment fit your needs*

The rising popularity of corporate intranets has made this feature even more popular. Employees now can use a single application to access e-mail, schedule meetings, manage files, order supplies, update their personnel information, receive company news and information, and more, all from the same application. What's more, Outlook reads and creates electronic forms in HTML (Hypertext Markup Language, the language used to compose Web pages), so gathering information from employees, customers, and others is now as simple as sending e-mail. Home users might like to view their favorite Web page while their e-mail downloads. Because of this nearly seamless integration, the possibilities are endless.

Technically, Outlook Today is a Web page too—it's just one that's built into Outlook rather than posted on the Net. When you view Outlook Today, you're really using Outlook as a browser.

Setting a Home Page for an Outlook Folder

If you have a particular Web site or intranet page you visit frequently, you can tell Outlook you want to view that page each time you go to a particular folder. A Web or intranet page designated in this way is called a folder home page. In fact, your network administrator may have already set a home page for some or all of your folders. To designate a home page for a folder, follow these steps:

1. Right-click the desired folder shortcut in the Outlook Bar and choose Properties from the shortcut menu that appears. The Properties dialog box is displayed.

2. Click the Home Page tab to display the setting for the folder Home Page (see Figure 1-18).

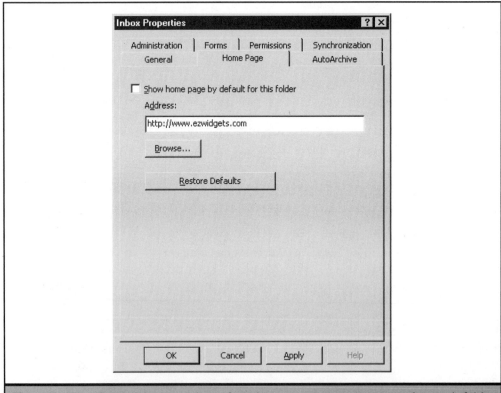

Figure 1-18.   *Outlook has a variety of settings you can use to customize each folder*

The folder properties dialog boxes in the Internet Mail Only (IMO) configuration contain fewer tabs than the folder properties dialog boxes in the C/W configuration.

3. Enter the URL of the page you want to set as the folder home page. The address can be a Web page on the Internet or your corporate intranet, a file on your local hard drive, or even another folder within Outlook.

4. If you want the page to display automatically every time you open that folder, click Show Home Page By Default For This Folder.

5. Click OK to save the settings.

If you opted to have the home page appear automatically, all you have to do now is click the folder to see the home page. Otherwise, to see the folder's home page, click the folder on the Folder List or Outlook Bar, then choose View | Show Folder Home Page. The page will appear in the Information viewer.

 If you set a Web page as the folder Home Page, you must be connected to the Internet to view it.

Using Outlook to Browse System Folders

The Outlook programmers at Microsoft have been diligently working to make Outlook an all-encompassing work environment. To that end they've provided the functionality of the Windows Explorer within Outlook. The Other Shortcuts group on the Outlook Bar contains three shortcuts that give you complete access to your system folders, files, and drives without ever having to leave Outlook. Click the Other Shortcuts button in the Outlook Bar to display the available shortcut icons. Then click the desired shortcut, and the associated windows environment (My Computer) or system folder (My Documents or Favorites) appears in the Information viewer. As you can see in Figure 1-19, the Information viewer adopts the Windows Explorer appearance by displaying drives and folders in the left pane and their contents in the right pane.

Getting Help

 Whether you're a novice or an expert, there are going to be times when you run up against something in Outlook that has you totally stumped. When that time comes, don't panic, there's plenty of help at hand. Fortunately, Outlook has a very thorough Help system that offers information on a variety of Outlook subjects and features.

Figure 1-19.   *You may never have to stray from the Outlook environment again*

You'll even find troubleshooting guides that walk you through some of the frequently encountered problems and offer solutions.

Using the Office Assistant

The Office Assistant was first introduced in Office 97 as a way to make the Help system more user-friendly. The Office Assistant is an animated onscreen character that interacts with the user. You tell it, in plain English, what you want to know, and it offers several Help topics it thinks may help you out.

OUTLOOK BASICS

The Office Assistant works fairly well and can be helpful if you're new to the program. It can also be customized, enabling you to change the way it works and the way it looks (by selecting a different animated character). If, as you become more experienced, the little critter starts to drive you crazy, you can always hide it or terminate it permanently by uninstalling it.

By default, the Office Assistant will appear any time you open Outlook or another Office application. If you don't see the Office Assistant, click Help | Show the Office Assistant. (You may need to expand the menu first by clicking the down arrow at the bottom of the menu.) If the option is not available on the extended menu, the Office Assistant is not installed.

To get help from the Office Assistant, follow these steps:

1. Click the Microsoft Outlook Help button (the question mark) on the Standard toolbar to activate the Office Assistant. The animated character (Clippit, by default) appears on the screen and asks you what you'd like to do (see the previous illustration).

2. Enter a question or keywords that are related to the subject. The current text in the text box is highlighted so you can start typing immediately. You can enter keywords (**print**, **contacts**, and so on) or complete questions, such as **How do I a print a contact?** There's no need to worry about proper casing or punctuation, since the Assistant ignores both.

3. Click Search. The Office Assistant presents a short list of topics that match your sentence or your keywords.

4. Click the topic that seems most likely to supply the answer to your question. The Outlook Help application opens to the appropriate page and provides detailed information on the topic (see Figure 1-20).

5. When you're finished with Help, click the Close button.

Customizing the Assistant

By default, the Office Assistant appears in the guise of Clippit, an animated and (according to some users) cute paper clip. However, there's no accounting for taste, and consequently some folks find him more annoying than cute. If you're among that number, you might want to select a different character, also referred to as an *actor*. You can choose another actor at any time, however, you may need your Office 2000 discs if the optional actors were not installed during the initial installation. Each assistant has a unique look and personality, but you always get the same information. In addition to changing the actors, you can also set a variety of other options.

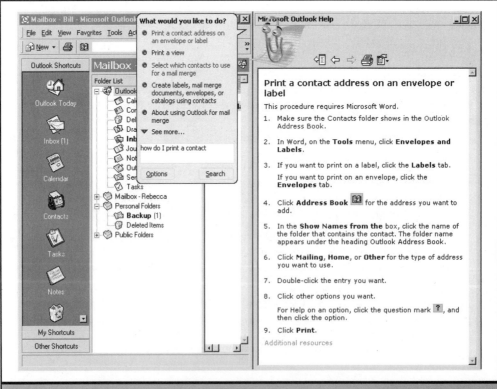

Figure 1-20.   *The Office Assistant is your guide through the Outlook Help system*

Choosing a new actor is easy:

1. Right-click the Office Assistant and click Choose Assistant from the shortcut menu to display the Office Assistant dialog box.

2. Click the Gallery tab to view the available actors. Unless you've changed actors before, the first actor you see is Clippit.

3. Click Next to see the next actor, The Dot.

4. Continue clicking Next until you find the actor of your choice. Click Back if you want to review earlier actors. Click OK when you find one you want to use.

5. If the additional actors are installed, you're returned to the active window and the new actor replaces Clippit. If, however, the actor you've chosen is not available, Clippit informs you and asks if you would like to install it now.

6. If you want to install the other actors, insert the Office 2000 CD in your CD-ROM drive and click Yes; otherwise click No to return to Outlook and stick with Clippit.

Tip   *You also can download new actors from Microsoft's Web site at http:// officeupdate.microsoft.com/.*

Thankfully, the Office Assistant's actors are not the only thing you can customize. You can also change a variety of settings that control the way the Office Assistant operates.

To set the Office Assistant options, follow these steps:

1. Right-click the Office Assistant and choose Options to display the Office Assistant dialog box.

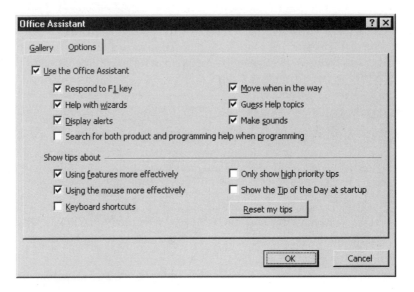

2. Set the Office Assistant options. To enable an option, click it to add a checkmark. To disable an option, click it to remove the checkmark. The options are:

   ■ **Use The Office Assistant** This is the option to use if you want to turn the Office Assistant off. Clear this option, and Clippit and his little buddies will stay out of your hair while you're working. To bring the Office Assistant back to life, return to the Options dialog box and check this option, or select Help | Show the Office Assistant from the menu bar.

   ■ **Respond To F1 Key** In most Windows programs, pressing the F1 key brings up the Help system. With this option enabled, the Office Assistant appears in Outlook when you press F1.

   ■ **Help With Wizards** If you want the Office Assistant to offer unsolicited help when you use the Rules Wizard, check this option.

   ■ **Display Alerts** To display messages from the Office Assistant, enable this option.

- **Search For Both Product And Programming Help When Programming**
If you're using Visual Basic for Applications (VBA), enabling this option causes the Office Assistant to search both the Outlook Help system and the VBA Help system when responding to a Help question.

- **Move When In The Way**   Always keep this option enabled when using the Office Assistant. Since he's programmed to stay on top of all windows, he'll get in your way when you open a form or dialog box unless you check this option and tell him to move out of the way while you work.

- **Guess Help Topics**   In an effort to anticipate your needs, the Office Assistant will attempt to guess which Help topics you'll need, depending on the task you're working on. While this can be helpful occasionally, it can also be very annoying to have the Office Assistant constantly popping up and offering his two cents without having been asked.

- **Make Sounds**   If you'd like the Office Assistant to use sounds, check this option.

- **Show Tips About**   The remaining options determine the type of tips the Office Assistant offers. Enable the tips you think will be helpful and disable those you don't need.

- **Reset My Tips**   After you've been using Outlook for a while, you may exhaust the supply of tips, since they're not repeated. Click the Reset My Tips button to start over and enable the Office Assistant to display previously viewed tips.

3. Click OK to save your new settings and return to the active window.

Tip   *If hiding the Office Assistant isn't enough, you can permanently disable it by uninstalling it. You'll need your Office 2000 CD (or Outlook 2000 CD) to perform the uninstall. If you're using Outlook at work, you may have to talk to your network administrator about removing the Office Assistant.*

The Office 2000 Help System

As the name implies, the Office Assistant is not an essential part of the Outlook Help system, merely an "assistant." Therefore, if you decide to hide or uninstall the Office Assistant you can still use all the features of the Help system. Outlook Help includes five different components to ensure you get the help you need quickly and easily:

- **Microsoft Outlook Help**   Here you'll find definitions, step-by-step instructions, and cross-references to related topics. After you disable the Office Assistant, you can access Outlook Help by clicking the Microsoft Outlook Help button on the Standard toolbar, pressing F1, or selecting Help | Microsoft Outlook Help from the menu bar.

- **Troubleshooting Wizards** When something isn't going right and you can't figure out why, you can call on a Troubleshooting Wizard to walk you through the problem, asking specific questions, and providing interactive instructions for the solution.

- **ScreenTips** Not quite sure what that button does? Just point to it and wait a moment—a brief description appears in a text bubble.

- **What's This?** For those times when all you need is a quick description or explanation of an item, use the What's This? feature. To use What's This? choose Help | What's This? from the menu bar. When your mouse pointer turns into a question mark, point to the item you want more information on and click. An information box pops up with an explanation of the item unless there is no Help on that particular item, in which case a message displays informing you of that fact. Press ESC to close the box when you're finished.

- **Office on the Web** If you're connected to the Internet, this Help feature whisks you away to the Outlook section of the Microsoft Office Update Web site, where you'll find information, updates, and news items about Outlook.

Browsing Microsoft Outlook Help

Microsoft Outlook Help provides access to a large store of useful information regarding the use and troubleshooting of most of the Outlook features. As you can see in Figure 1-23, Microsoft Outlook Help provides three methods of locating the information you need:

- **Contents** A hierarchical listing of Help topics, each of which can be expanded by clicking the plus sign to the left.

- **Answer Wizard** Enter keywords or questions and search for related information.

- **Index** An alphabetical listing of topics covered in the Help file.

To view the Help contents with the Office Assistant disabled (or the Respond to F1 Key option disabled), follow these steps:

1. Press F1 to open the Microsoft Office Help window, seen in Figure 1-21. If the Contents pane is not visible, click the Contents tab to display it.

Tip *If you think you've disabled the Office Assistant, but it still appears when you press the F1 key, it's probably only hidden, not disabled. To disable the Office Assistant, show it, click Options, and deselect Use The Office Assistant. If you want to keep the Office Assistant, but still be able to access the Microsoft Outlook Help window, only disable the Respond to F1 Key option.*

Figure 1-21.   *The Contents tab provides an easy-to-navigate table of contents of the available Help topics*

Note   *If only one pane of the Help window is visible, click the Show button on the toolbar to display both panes.*

2. Click the plus sign to the left of a topic to display its subtopics. Book icons represent topic headings and question mark icons represent the actual topics.

3. Find and click the topic on which you need help to display the topic contents in the right pane.

4. When you're finished, click the close button (the small X in the upper-right corner of the Help window) to close the Help file and return to the active window.

As you're viewing Help information in the right pane of the Help window, you may notice blue, underlined text which resembles links you see on Web pages. It just so happens that they are links—not to Web pages, but to other, related Help topics. To view the related topic, click the link.

Using the Answer Wizard

The Answer Wizard provides the same type of assistance as that offered by the Office Assistant, without the antics. It works pretty much the same way. Type your question or enter keywords in the What Would You Like To Do? text box, click Search, and then click the topic that looks like it will provide the help you're looking for. The topic appears in the right pane.

Using the Help Index

The third component of the Microsoft Outlook Help window is the Index. Like any other index, it contains an alphabetical listing of the most commonly sought-after words and phrases in the body of the document. To make it even easier to use, a search option is provided so you don't have to scroll through the list looking for a particular topic.

1. Press F1 to open the Microsoft Outlook Help window. Remember, this only works if you've disabled the Office Assistant.

2. Click the Index tab to display the Index page.

3. Enter a keyword in the Type Keywords text box and click Search to display a list of topics related to the keyword. You can also scroll through the keyword list and click a keyword to display the associated topics.

4. Click the desired topic in the Choose a Topic list to display the topic contents in the right pane.

5. Click Close to exit the Microsoft Outlook Help window.

Unfortunately, the Microsoft Outlook Help system no longer contains a full text search that includes every word in the Help files. Therefore, any searches you perform must be done using the Answer Wizard or the Index. Since the Index is rather limited, you may get better results using the Answer Wizard to search for keywords.

MOUS

MOUS EXAM PRACTICE

In this section, you've learned everything you need to know to master the Outlook Help system. Whether you decide to stick with the Office Assistant or ban the pesky little critter from your desktop altogether, you'll be able get help when you need it. To confirm you've got it down pat, try using the Office Assistant to search for Help on specific topics, such as hiding the Outlook Bar, docking toolbars, or setting a folder Home Page. Next, disable the Office Assistant and use the standard Help system to locate the same information. Try using both the Index and the Answer Wizard to find the information. When you find a topic that fits the bill, switch to the Contents tab to see which heading it appears under.

Finding an Outlook 97 Menu Command in Office 2000

If you've used a previous version of Outlook, you may find that some of the tools and features you've become accustomed to seem to be missing. Don't worry—in most cases, they've simply been moved or renamed. Using the Help system, it's easy to find them.

1. Press F1 to open Help (assuming you've disabled the Office Assistant or its Respond to F1 Key option), then click the Contents tab.

2. Double-click the Getting Started heading. The list of related topics will appear.

3. Click the Find Outlook 97 menu commands in Outlook 2000. The topic page displayed in the right pane contains a number of links to specific Outlook 97 commands covered (see Figure 1-22).

4. Click the desired link to view a table of all the related commands and their Outlook 2000 counterparts.

5. When you're finished, press ALT-F4 to exit the Microsoft Outlook Help window.

Figure 1-22.   *With these tips, Outlook 97 users will be breezing around Outlook 2000 in no time*

Getting Help Online

If you can't find what you're looking for in the Microsoft Outlook Help files, there's another Help feature you can try. It's called Office on the Web. Here you'll find important security updates, general announcements, technical support pages, a searchable information database, and more. To visit the Office Update Web site, click Help | Office on the Web. After establishing a connection, Outlook will open your default Web browser and display the Outlook section of the Microsoft Office Update Web site (see Figure 1-23). From there, you're free to explore all of the tools available.

One of the most useful resources on the Microsoft Web site is the Knowledgebase. It contains a vast database of questions (and answers) posed to the Microsoft technical support department.

Figure 1-23.   *The Microsoft Office Update Web site contains an array of information and Help resources*

Web pages change frequently, so don't be concerned if the page you open doesn't match the one shown here.

Closing Outlook

If you can afford the RAM, you may want to launch Outlook as part of your daily startup and leave it open the entire time you're at your computer. If you use reminders for meetings and tasks, this is even more important, since Outlook can't remind you unless it's running. When you decide to shut down the program, be sure to save any unfinished work and close any open items. (If an individual message or other item is still open, Outlook can't finish shutting down until you close that item.)

To close Outlook, just click the Close button on the title bar. If you want to switch profiles or let another user log on, click File | Exit and Log Off.

 MOUS Exam Objectives Explored in Chapter 1

Objective	Activity	Heading
OL2000.4.1	Use Outlook Help and Office Assistant components	"Getting Help"
OL2000.4.3	Navigate between Outlook Components	"Getting Around in Outlook"

The
Complete
Reference

Chapter 2

Working with Profiles

One of the nice things about running Outlook in the C/W configuration is the ability to create and use multiple profiles. Profiles are the basic settings that enable each user to save his or her customizations of Outlook. In addition to making it easy for different users to share the same machine, profiles enable a single user to establish different Outlook configurations containing different services and different settings. This chapter takes you through the necessary steps to create and customize profiles. You'll also learn to add information services to a profile as well as set delivery and addressing preferences.

Profiles are only available in the Corporate/Workgroup (C/W) configuration.

Creating a Profile

Profiles are Outlook's way of remembering the services, preferences, and option settings for individual users. No matter how a user customizes Outlook 2000, all changes made to the settings are retained in the profile being used at the time the changes are effected.

Users who log on from different computers can have their profiles available no matter which computer they're using. However, the profiles must be created by the network administrator and stored on the server. Each time the user makes a change, it's saved before logging off the server.

By default, a profile called MS Exchange Settings is created when Outlook C/W is installed. You can either customize that profile or create your own. If you're going to create your own profile, you can start from scratch, or you can copy an existing profile, then modify it to suit your needs.

Creating a New Profile from Scratch

If there are no existing profiles in your Outlook configuration, or you need to create one considerably different from the existing ones, you'll need to start from the beginning. To create a new profile from scratch, follow these steps:

1. Choose Start | Settings | Control Panel to open the Control Panel window.

2. Double-click the Mail (Mail and Fax if you have faxing installed) applet icon to open the Properties dialog box for the default profile, as seen in Figure 2-1. Keep in mind that your settings may be different than those in Figure 2-1.

3. Click Show Profiles to display the Mail dialog box, which displays all existing profiles on this computer.

4. Click Add to start the Inbox Setup Wizard, seen in Figure 2-2.

5. Select the information service(s) to use or click Manually Configure Information Services to add them after you name the profile.

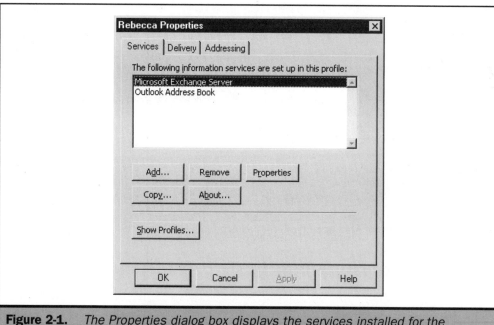

Figure 2-1.   *The Properties dialog box displays the services installed for the default profile*

Figure 2-2.   *The Inbox Setup Wizard makes creating a new profile as easy as breaking a New Year's resolution*

Tip   *If the service(s) you want to add don't appear on this screen, or if you want to see a listing of all services available, use the manual configuration option. After naming the profile, the profile properties dialog box appears, in which you get a complete listing of all available information services by clicking the Add button.*

6. Click Next and enter a name for the profile. The name is used for descriptive purposes only and should be something that enables users to easily identify the profile (for example, the user's name on a computer with multiple users, or something like "Traveling" for a profile used while on the road).

Note   *The screens that follow depend on the information service(s) selected in the opening Inbox Setup Wizard. The remainder of the steps in this exercise cover the installation of the MS Exchange Server information service. For any other service, follow the instructions on the screens that appear, clicking Next until you reach the end.*

7. Click Next to display the Microsoft Exchange Server screen.

8. Enter the name of the Microsoft Exchange server (the computer that is running Microsoft Exchange Server software). If you don't know the name, ask your network administrator.

   Check the properties of existing profiles to see if any have Microsoft Exchange Server services installed. If so, select Microsoft Exchange Server and click the Properties button to find the Microsoft Exchange server name.

9. Enter the name of the Microsoft Exchange Server mailbox you want to use for this profile. Unless you know it, you'll have to get this name from your network administrator, since each user has a unique mailbox.

Caution   *The Inbox Setup Wizard will accept any name you enter without balking. However, when you attempt to use the profile, you will be unable to connect to the Microsoft Exchange server unless the mailbox actually exists on the server. This also applies to the Microsoft Exchange server name in the previous step.*

10. Click Next and let the wizard know whether or not you travel with this computer.

11. Click Next to display the final Inbox Setup Wizard screen, which lists the information services installed.

12. Click Finish to complete the profile setup and return to the Mail dialog box.

OUTLOOK BASICS

You can modify the properties of the new profile at any time by returning to the Mail dialog box, selecting the profile and clicking Properties. However, you cannot change the Microsoft Exchange server name or the mailbox name of a profile that is in use. Once you switch profiles or close Outlook you can change either.

Copying an Existing Profile

When several users access the same computer, it's likely that the services and settings for one user's profile will be similar to others'. You can save a lot of time by making a copy of an existing profile, and then making the necessary adjustments for the new user.

Caution *When you copy a profile that contains personal folders, the new profile inherits the personal folders file of the original profile, including all existing contents. To make matters worse, there's no way to change the target personal folders' .pst file, which means both profiles share the original personal folders (and any changes made by either user) forever. The only way to remedy this situation is to delete the personal folders service in the new profile and then re-add personal folders, specifying a new personal folders file.*

Follow these steps to create a new profile from an existing profile:

1. Open the Control Panel and double-click the Mail (Mail and Fax) icon to open the properties dialog box of the default profile.
2. Click Show Profiles to display the Mail dialog box.
3. Select the existing profile to use as the basis for the new profile, and click Copy. Outlook will prompt you to name the new profile.
4. Enter a name for the new profile and click OK. The profile is added to the list.
5. Select the profile you just created and click Properties to view the properties dialog box for the new profile. All of the services that were included in the original profile are listed here.

Tip *You can display a profile's properties dialog box by double-clicking the profile name in the list of existing profiles.*

6. Open each service by selecting it and clicking Properties, and make the necessary changes for the new user. Delete any services that aren't needed, such as the original user's personal folders, address books, or Internet e-mail account.

Tip *If Microsoft Exchange Server is one of the information services in the copy, be sure to verify the server name and change the mailbox name to match the new user. The new user will not be able to log on to Microsoft Exchange Server if the server and mailbox name do not match his or her user profile on the network server.*

7. Click OK to return to the Mail dialog box.

Adding profiles by copying existing profiles is quick and easy. However, the ability to copy personalized information means that care should be taken to ensure that the feature is not abused. One way is to password-protect personal folders on all profiles. That way, even if the personal folders are copied, they cannot be accessed unless the new user knows the password.

Adding an Information Service to an Existing Profile

Information services are groups of settings that control how your messages are sent, received, stored, and addressed. Each profile can have a variety of information services installed. The standard information services available in Outlook 2000 include:

- **Internet E-mail**   If you have an Internet connection through your network or through a modem, you can add Internet e-mail accounts when this information service is added to your profile.

- **Microsoft Exchange Server**   The Microsoft Exchange Server service enables you to connect to a Microsoft Exchange server on your network as long as you have a user profile and a mailbox set up on the server.

- **Microsoft LDAP Directory**   The Lightweight Directory Access Protocol (LDAP) service provides access to public Internet directories containing address information.

- **Microsoft Mail**   The Microsoft Mail service provides access to a Microsoft Mail post office. If you use Microsoft Mail, be sure to also add Personal Folders, since Microsoft Mail messages are stored on the local computer rather than the server.

- **MS Outlook support for Lotus cc:Mail**   Installing this service enables Outlook users to send to and receive e-mail from a cc:Mail post office.

- **Outlook Address Book**   This information service, which uses your Contacts folder as an address book, is automatically added when you add the Microsoft Exchange Server service.

- **Personal Address Book**   To maintain a Personal Address Book (PAB) of addresses that is separate from your Outlook Address Book and your Global Address List, add this service.

- **Personal Folders**   The Personal Folders service creates a .pst file in which you can store Outlook items locally on your computer. Personal folders are handy for storing information you want available even when you're not logged on to the server. They're also useful for saving Outlook items that may get deleted from the server periodically due to storage limits imposed by the network administrator.

Additional information services may be available depending on other software installed on your computer.

Note   *When adding some services you may be prompted to insert your Microsoft Office 2000 CD.*

You can add services from within Outlook or from the Mail applet in the Control Panel. To use the Control Panel Mail applet, choose Start | Settings | Mail to open the properties dialog box for the default profile. Click Show Profiles to open the Mail dialog box. Then select the profile you wish to modify, and click Properties to open the properties dialog box for the selected profile. From this point you can jump to step 2 in the next sequence and follow the remaining steps.

To add information services to your profile from within Outlook, follow these steps:

1. Choose Tools | Services to open the Services dialog box.

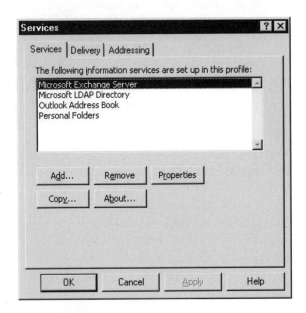

2. Click Add to display the Add Service to Profile dialog box, which contains a list of available information services.

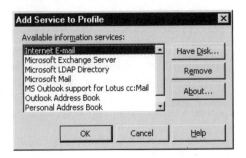

3. Select the desired service.

Note *If the service you're looking for does not appear on the list and you have a disk containing the service, insert the disk, click Have Disk, and follow the instructions that appear.*

4. Click OK to add the service. If the service you select requires additional information, a dialog box appears. Enter the appropriate information and click OK to proceed.

Note *You can only add some services, such as Microsoft Exchange Server, once in each profile. Attempting to add a second instance of the service results in an error message informing you that the service has already been added.*

5. Continue adding information services until you're through.

6. Click OK to return to the active Outlook window.

7. Since most information services will not be available until you exit and reopen Outlook, choose Exit and Log Off from the File menu to close Outlook.

8. Restart Outlook.

As soon as you return to Outlook, the new information services should be available to you.

Editing and Removing Information Services

As you've probably discovered, the one thing in life that remains constant is that things always change. After adding a service there's bound to come a time when you need to modify it, or perhaps no longer need it at all and want to eliminate it. When that time arrives, you can either change the service or remove it quickly by following these steps:

1. Select Tools | Services from the menu bar to open the Services dialog box.

Note *You can also use the Control Panel Mail applet to make the changes. See the previous section on adding services for details on using the Mail applet.*

2. Select the service you want to modify or remove.

3. To delete the service from the selected profile, click Remove, then click OK when asked if you're sure (unless, of course, you're not sure).

4. To modify the selected service, click Properties to display the properties dialog box associated with the service.

5. Click OK to return to the Services dialog box.

6. Repeat the process until you've modified or removed all the desired services.

7. Click OK to return to the active Outlook window.

Choosing a Start-Up Profile

Each time Outlook loads, it uses one profile that has been designated as the default profile. If you only have one profile on your computer, it automatically becomes the default profile. If, however, you have multiple profiles on a single computer, you have to decide which profile is loaded by default when Outlook starts. Obviously, you will choose the profile you use most frequently.

To select a default profile, follow these steps:

1. Choose Start | Settings | Control Panel to open the Control Panel.

2. Double-click the Mail applet to open the properties dialog box for the current default profile.

3. Click Show Profiles to display the Mail dialog box.

4. From the When Starting Microsoft Outlook, Use This Profile drop-down list, select the profile to use as the default.

5. Click Close to save the new setting and return to the active Outlook window.

Unfortunately, this presents a problem when the user logged on to the network is not the owner of the default profile. Each time a user logs on to the network, he signs on with his logon name, which is associated with a specific mailbox on the Microsoft Exchange server. If the mailbox associated with the default profile isn't the same as the one associated with the logon name, Outlook will not start. There are two solutions to this problem: change the default profile to match your logon name before launching Outlook, or override the default profile setting and have Outlook ask which profile to use each time you start the program. The second solution is, by far, cleaner since there's nothing to remember (except the name of your profile) every time you log on, and it requires fewer steps than changing the default profile.

Overriding the default profile setting and instructing Outlook to prompt for a profile each time it starts is simple:

1. Choose Tools | Options from the menu bar to open the Options dialog box, seen in Figure 2-3.

2. Click the Mail Services tab to display the mail services options (see Figure 2-4).

3. Select Prompt for a Profile to Be Used. The Always Use This Profile option is automatically disabled.

4. Click OK to save the new settings and return to the active Outlook window.

OUTLOOK BASICS

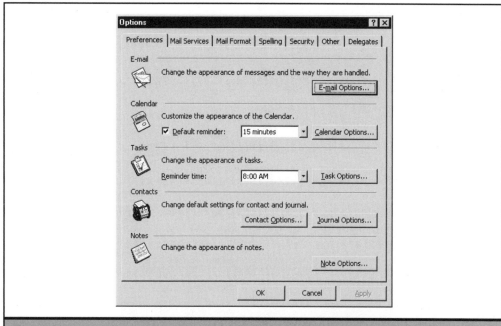

Figure 2-3.   *Outlook 2000 has a wealth of optional settings*

Figure 2-4.   *The Mail Services options enable you to customize the way the mail services function*

The next time *any* user starts Outlook, the Choose Profile dialog box appears, asking for the name of the profile to be used for the current session of Outlook.

In addition to providing a choice of profiles to use, the Choose Profile dialog box contains several options. Clicking the New button launches the Inbox Setup Wizard, which enables you to create a new profile on the spot. For more options, click the Options button to expand the Choose Profile dialog box.

The last two options in the Choose Profile dialog box are:

- **Set as default profile** This sets the currently selected profile name as the default profile. Don't worry, it does not return Outlook to the practice of automatically opening with the default profile. It simply makes the currently selected profile the one that appears in the Profile Name box each time the Choose Profile dialog box is displayed.

- **Show Logon screens for all information services** With this option enabled, the properties dialog box for each information service in the selected profile appears, and must be approved (click OK) before Outlook opens. It ensures that you have, indeed, selected the correct profile, and it offers an opportunity to make changes to each service before you start Outlook. However, unless you can't remember your profile name or you modify your information services constantly, this is a bit of overkill and should probably be left unchecked.

After you set the desired options, click OK to launch Outlook. If at some point in the future you find yourself with a single profile and no need for the Choose Profile dialog box, return to the Outlook Options dialog box and enable the Always Use This Profile setting on the Mail Services tab.

Deleting a Profile

If you've been using multiple profiles and one of the profiles is no longer necessary, you can do a little housekeeping and remove the unneeded profile. The truth of the matter is, anyone with access to your computer can delete any of the profiles on the computer. However, that's not quite as bad as it sounds since none of your data is lost. But, on the other hand, it can be annoying if you've done extensive customization of your Outlook settings and options. They, unfortunately, *will* be lost.

 If your profile is deleted accidentally or intentionally before you're ready to give it up, you may be able to avoid recustomizing the new profile you create by copying an existing profile that has the same or similar settings to those in the deleted profile. See the section on copying profiles earlier in this chapter.

If you're bound and determined to delete an existing profile, here's all you have to do:

1. Choose Start | Settings | Control Panel to open the Control Panel window.
2. Double-click the Mail (Mail and Fax) applet to open the properties dialog box for the default profile.
3. Click Show Profiles to display the Mail dialog box (see Figure 2-5).
4. Select the profile you want to delete.
5. Click Remove and the profile is deleted.
6. Click Close to exit the Mail dialog box and return to the active window.

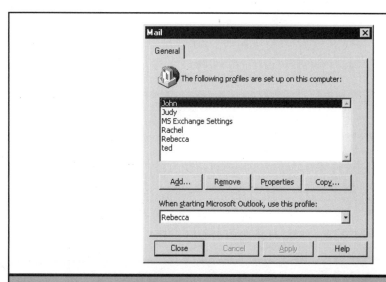

Figure 2-5.   *The Mail dialog box enables you to add, copy, and remove profiles as well as view their properties*

In the event that you change your mind after you click the Remove button, you'll have no recourse but to create a new profile to replace it. Deleted profiles are *not* placed in the Windows Recycle Bin or any other place from which they can be resurrected.

Setting Delivery Preferences

If you have both a server-based mailbox and personal folders added to your profile, you can choose one or the other as the delivery location for your e-mail. Actually, "delivery location" is somewhat misleading since it includes both the incoming and outgoing messages. If you select the server-based mailbox as your delivery location, all incoming mail is deposited in the Inbox subfolder of the main Mailbox folder, and copies of sent mail (if you have enabled the Save Copies of Sent Mail option) are retained in the Sent subfolder of the main Mailbox folder. If you choose Personal Folders as your delivery location, the Inbox and Sent Items subfolders of Personal Folders are used.

> **Tip** *Unless you meticulously back up your personal folders every day, you should set the delivery location to the server-based mailbox even if you have personal folders. The reason is simple: most administrators back up all the information stored on the server nightly.*

The best use of personal folders is to store messages you want to retain if your network administrator imposes any size limitations on the server-based mailbox. When your mailbox on the server reaches the maximum capacity, you may lose some of your e-mailing privileges until you clean up your mailbox. When that time comes, you'll want to transfer the more important messages to your Personal Folders.

To set the delivery options, follow these steps:

1. Choose Tools | Services to display the Services dialog box for the currently logged-on profile.

2. Click the Delivery tab to view the delivery options.

3. From the Deliver New Mail to the Following Location drop-down list, select the location to which you want your mail delivered.

4. Set the processing order for the available information services by selecting the service and moving up or down with the arrow buttons to the right.

Note   *The processing order is important only if you have added two services that support the same mail type. If, for example, you have Internet e-mail and Microsoft Exchange Server, both of which support Internet addresses (Simple Mail Transfer Protocol, or SMTP), you could elect to have the SMTP mail processed by either of the installed information services—Microsoft Exchange Server or Internet E-mail. The order of the processing list determines which service takes precedence.*

5. Click OK to save the new settings and return to the active Outlook window.

You can also set the delivery options by accessing the profile properties dialog box from the Control Panel Mail (Mail and Fax) applet.

Setting Addressing Preferences

Outlook address books are the electronic equivalents of the old paper-based address books and Rolodexes that have populated desktops for eons. They contain the basic information you need to get in touch with those individuals with whom you communicate regularly. Although all the Outlook address books can hold a variety of information, for the purposes of this discussion the only important piece of information is the e-mail address. Fortunately, all three of the different Address Book types available in Outlook are capable of handling e-mail addresses:

■ **Outlook Address Book**   The Outlook Address Book is installed automatically when you add the Microsoft Exchange Server information service to a profile. It utilizes the e-mail information found in the Contacts folder. However, contact information is not stored directly in the Outlook Address Book, but rather in folders displayed as e-mail address books. By default the Contacts folder appears as an Outlook Address Book. If you open the Contacts Outlook Address Book, you'll see a listing of all your contacts and their respective e-mail addresses and/or fax numbers. Contacts that have neither do not appear in the Contacts Outlook Address Book.

■ **Global Address List**   This is the company-wide listing of internal e-mail addresses maintained on the Microsoft Exchange server. If most of your e-mail communication is internal, you'll probably want to use this as your default address book.

■ **Personal Address Book (PAB)**   If you communicate with people you don't want to add to your Contacts database, you can create a Personal Address Book that is stored locally on your computer and contains only those names you choose to enter.

For more information on creating and using address books, see Chapter 7.

Outlook enables you to customize the way address books are used. You set a default address book to use when you employ the Address Book command or each time you address an e-mail. You can also indicate the address book in which you want to keep your personal addresses, and set the order in which address books are used to check names added as recipients to e-mail messages.

To set the addressing options, follow these steps:

1. Choose Tools | Services from the menu bar to open the Services dialog box for the current profile.

2. Click the Addressing tab to display the addressing options.

3. From the Show This Address List First drop-down list, select the address book you want designated as the default address book. This is the address book that appears automatically when you use the Address Book command, or when you click the To, Cc, or Bcc buttons on a new e-mail message form.

4. From the Keep Personal Addresses In drop-down list, select the address book in which you want names you add to the address book stored. By default, Outlook uses the Outlook Address Book.

Note   *Since only administrators can add names to the Global Address List, your choices are going to be limited to the Outlook Address Book and the Personal Address Book, even if you have all three address books installed.*

5. Set the order in which you want the name-checking feature to search the installed address lists. Use the arrow buttons to the right to move the address lists up or down on the list.

6. If the address book you want to use for name checking doesn't appear on the list, click Add to open the Add Address List dialog box.

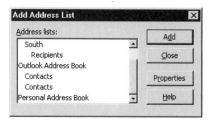

7. Select the address book from the list and click Add.

8. Click Close to return to the Addressing tab of the Services dialog box.

9. If necessary, adjust the position of the newly added address book in the list.

10. Click OK to save your settings and return to the active Outlook window.

The next time you send an e-mail message or select the Check Names command, Outlook will search your address books for the recipient(s) name(s) in the order designated in the list. You can also remove address books from the Check Names list or view their properties by highlighting them in the Check Names list and clicking either the Remove button or the Properties button.

OUTLOOK BASICS

The
Complete
Reference

Part II

Communicating with E-mail

The
Complete
Reference

Chapter 3

Composing and Sending Messages

While Outlook can help you with any number of organizational tasks, its primary and most popular function is handling e-mail. Outlook includes a full-featured e-mail client that can create, format, spell check, and even grammar check (if you use Microsoft Word as your e-mail editor) your e-mail before sending it on its way. This chapter provides you with everything you need to harness the power of the Outlook e-mail engine for composing and sending e-mail messages.

Navigating Outlook E-mail

Getting around the Outlook e-mail component is actually pretty easy. The first thing to do is familiarize yourself with the various folders that make up the e-mail component and the way they work.

The mail folders include:

- **Inbox**   The Inbox folder is the receptacle for all incoming mail. As mail arrives, it is deposited in the Inbox where it remains until you move it or delete it, either manually or by applying a pre-established message-handling rule. For more information on automating message handling, see Chapter 19.

- **Outbox**   The Outbox folder is a way station for outgoing mail. In a Microsoft Exchange Server environment, messages you send are held in the Outbox only until the Microsoft Exchange server makes its periodic sweep to pick up mail. Outlook users with the Internet Mail Only (IMO) configuration installed have the option to send messages immediately or store them in the Outbox until the Send command is issued.

- **Sent Items**   By default, a copy of each message you send is stored in the Sent Items folder. Any time you need to verify that information was sent, just check this folder.

- **Drafts**   When the phone rings or somebody knocks on your door while you're in the middle of composing an e-mail message, the Drafts folder provides a safe haven for the partially completed message. Rather than risk losing it, you can click the Save button to send it to the Drafts folder. If you forget to save it, don't worry, you'll probably still be okay. Every three minutes, Outlook automatically saves unsent messages to the Drafts folder (unless you've disabled the default setting).

Once you've got the hang of which folder does what, the rest is a snap. Use the Outlook Bar or Folder List to open the desired mail folder and display any messages it contains in the Information viewer (see Figure 3-1).

To use the Outlook Bar, click the shortcut associated with the mail folder you want to open. The folder opens and its contents appear in the Information viewer. By default, you'll find the Inbox shortcut in the Outlook Shortcuts group, and the Outbox, Drafts, and Sent Items shortcuts in the My Shortcuts group.

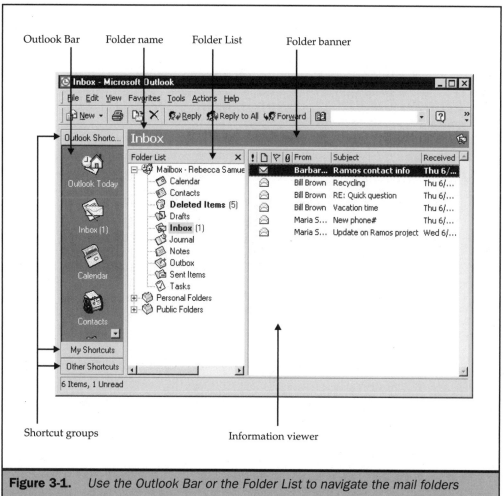

Outlook Bar   Folder name   Folder List   Folder banner

Shortcut groups   Information viewer

Figure 3-1.   *Use the Outlook Bar or the Folder List to navigate the mail folders*

COMMUNICATING WITH E-MAIL

Tip

If you only use Outlook for e-mail, or if you find yourself accessing the Outbox, Drafts, or Sent Items folders frequently, you may want to move their shortcuts from the My Shortcuts group to the Outlook Shortcuts group. See Chapter 23 for more information on modifying the Outlook Bar.

The Folder List displays a tree-like listing of all your Outlook folders, enabling you to navigate between mail folders the same way the Windows Explorer enables you to navigate your system folders. To display the Folder List, click the folder name that appears in the Folder banner or choose View | Folder List. Then click the folder you want to open. Folders designed to hold mail items (Inbox, Outbox, and so on) that contain unread or unsent mail appear in bold with a number in parentheses to the right of the folder name. The number indicates how many unread or unsent messages the folder contains.

By default, the Folder List closes after you select a folder. If you want it to stay open permanently (or at least until you decide to close it), click the pushpin in the top right corner of the Folder List window. When you're tired of looking at it, click the X in the top right corner of the Folder List to close it.

After you open the desired mail folder, the next step is to open and read the messages. Nothing could be simpler. Double-click a message to open it in its own window.

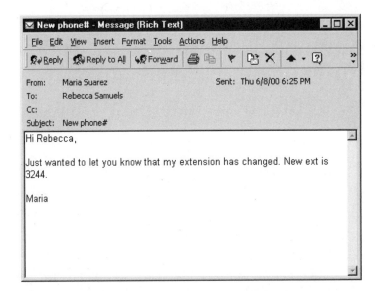

There are a couple of viewing options that make it even easier to read your e-mail. As a matter of fact, if you use them you don't even have to open your messages. These options are AutoPreview and Preview Pane, seen in Figure 3-2.

- **AutoPreview**   As you can see, AutoPreview displays the message header information and the first line or two of the message. This comes in handy for quickly reviewing an onslaught of incoming mail to see which messages should be read immediately, and which ones can languish in the Inbox until you have nothing better to do.

AutoPreview   Preview Pane

Figure 3-2. *If opening messages is too strenuous for you, take advantage of the preview options Outlook affords*

■ **Preview Pane** The Preview Pane creates a small window within the Information viewer in which the contents of the selected messages are displayed. Using the Preview Pane is rather convenient since, unlike opening each message in its own window, there's nothing to close after you read the message. As trivial as it may sound, you'll actually save a noticeable amount of time and energy by taking advantage of these productivity aids Outlook offers—especially if you receive a lot of e-mail each day.

After you've mastered getting around the Outlook mail components, the next step is to actually start putting them to work for you.

COMMUNICATING WITH E-MAIL

MOUS

MOUS EXAM PRACTICE

In this section, you became familiar with the various Outlook e-mail folders and their functions. Now try them for yourself. Use the Outlook Bar to move between the mail folders. Don't forget there are mail folder shortcuts in the My Shortcuts group. Next, open the Folder List and use it to jump from mail folder to mail folder. Take note of whether or not the folders contain unread or unsent mail items, and if so, how many. Finally, turn on the AutoPreview feature and see how it works, then turn it off and try the Preview Pane. If you're feeling adventurous, try them both at the same time.

Choosing an E-mail Editor

Outlook is a standalone program, which means it needs no other software application (other than the operating system) to function. However, it is also part of the Microsoft Office suite, and as such takes advantage of the relationship. One of the ways in which Outlook uses the other Office applications is by integrating Microsoft Word as an optional e-mail editor.

By default, Outlook uses its own built-in editor. However, if you have Microsoft Word installed on your computer, you can choose it as your editor. The advantage of using Microsoft Word is the simple fact that you get almost all the additional functionality Word offers, including the thesaurus, the grammar checker, AutoCorrect, a wealth of formatting options, and a lot more.

To select Microsoft Word as your e-mail editor, follow these steps:

1. Choose Tools | Options to open the Options dialog box.

2. Click the Mail Format tab to view the options for formatting e-mail messages (see Figure 3-3).

3. Click Use Microsoft Word To Edit E-mail Messages to enable the option. A checkmark appears in the box to the left. If the box is already checked, Word is currently your e-mail editor.

Note   *If the Use Microsoft Word To Edit E-mail Messages option is unavailable, you don't have Microsoft Word installed.*

4. Click OK to save the change and return to the active Outlook window.

Using Word as your editor causes a number of changes to the new message form used to compose e-mail messages. The message window title bar now indicates that Microsoft Word is the editor. The Actions menu is gone and in its place are the Table and Window menus. Some new toolbar buttons have been added, and some existing buttons have been relocated (see Figure 3-4).

Where you'll really notice the difference is in the menu commands available to you. Open a few of the menus and you'll see the difference. Any time you decide to return

Figure 3-3.   *Outlook gives you a variety of options for changing the way your e-mail messages appear*

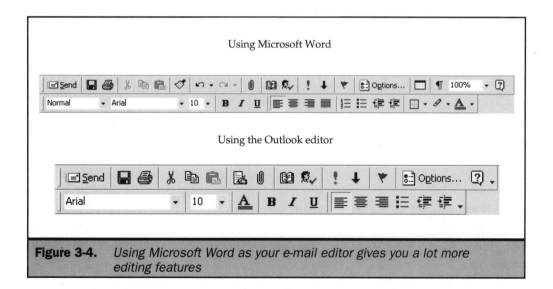

Figure 3-4.   *Using Microsoft Word as your e-mail editor gives you a lot more editing features*

to Outlook as your e-mail editor, simply open the Options dialog box and deselect the Use Microsoft Word To Edit E-mail Messages option.

Creating a New Message

Composing e-mail messages is what this chapter is all about, so roll up your sleeves and get ready to go to work. The first order of business is to open a new e-mail message form and understand what makes it tick (see Figure 3-5).

Regardless of whether you use the default editor or Microsoft Word, the basic elements of the message form remain the same:

- **Menu and toolbars**   The menu and toolbars in a message form contain commands for formatting, viewing, adding attachments, sending, and otherwise manipulating the message.

- **To**   The one thing every message must have is a recipient in the To field, which makes perfectly good sense, since it's impossible to deliver a message (or anything else, for that matter) if you don't know where it's going. A message can have multiple recipients. Clicking the To button displays the Select Names dialog box containing the listing from the default address book. Select as many recipients as you need.

- **Cc**   The Cc field is used for sending copies to recipients other than the primary recipient(s) named in the To field. Cc is a holdover from the pre-electronic memo days when you would send a carbon copy. If you're sending a note to the leader of a project, you might want to keep all the team members in the loop by including them in the Cc field. Clicking the Cc button displays the Select Names dialog box.

- **Bcc**   For those times when you want to send a copy of a message to someone other than the primary recipient, but you don't want the primary recipient to know about it, use the Bcc field (blind carbon copy). You might use it to send a message to a team member who has a lot on his plate and occasionally forgets things, and a blind copy to the project leader to ensure that your note doesn't get lost in the shuffle. Clicking the Bcc field brings up the well-known (if you read the last two items) Select Names dialog box.

- **Subject**   This all-important field should not be taken lightly. Its main purpose in life is to induce the recipient to open and read your message. Since priority flags are often misused or overused, people who receive a lot of mail frequently decide which messages to open first based on the Subject line. Therefore, you should make yours brief, informative, and accurate.

- **Message body**   The message body window in which you type your message is actually a text editor. As soon as you begin typing your message here, all the text editing functions of your selected editor (Outlook or Microsoft Word) become available.

Message header

Message body

Figure 3-5. *This is what a new e-mail message form looks like when you use the default Outlook e-mail editor*

 Tip

One of the drawbacks of sending e-mail to multiple recipients is that when you use the To or Cc fields you expose the addresses of all recipients to everyone who receives a copy of the message. To keep all e-mail addresses confidential, address the message to yourself and include all your recipients in the Bcc field. This way yours is the only address visible.

Once you understand the components of an e-mail message, you're ready to create one of your own.

Composing the Message

 Creating an e-mail message in Outlook is a simple task. The most complicated thing about composing a message is deciding which of the various methods you want to use to open a new message form. As you can see in Table 3-1, Outlook offers you a number of ways to start your new message.

From This Outlook Folder	Use This Action
Any folder	Press CTRL-SHIFT-M
Any folder	Click the down arrow to the right of the New button and select Mail Message
Any folder	Click File | New | Mail Message
Inbox, Outbox, Drafts, Sent items	Press CTRL-N
Inbox, Outbox, Drafts, Sent items	Click the New button on the Standard toolbar
Inbox, Outbox, Drafts, Sent items	Right-click a blank spot in the Information viewer and select New Mail Message

Table 3-1.   *Methods Used to Open a New E-mail Message Form*

There are actually a number of other ways to open a new e-mail message form, as you'll discover throughout this book. However, each of those methods utilizes an existing Outlook item and incorporates specific information from the item into the new e-mail message form. The methods presented in Table 3-1 simply open a blank e-mail message form. Now, on to actually creating an e-mail message:

1. Press CTRL-SHIFT-M (or your preferred method) to open a new e-mail message form (as shown in Figure 3-5).

2. Enter the name(s) of the recipient(s) in the To, Cc, and Bcc fields using one of the following methods:

   ■ **Type the full e-mail address**   If you know the recipient's e-mail address (for example, bsmith@iquest.net), you can type it in directly. Be sure to type it correctly, since a single mistake will prevent the message from ever reaching its intended destination.

   ■ **Enter an address book name**   If you know (or think you know) the recipient's name as it's listed in one of your address books, type it in. To be sure it's accurate, you can use the Check Names feature by choosing Tools \| Check Names from the Menu bar in the mail message form.

■ **Open the Select Names dialog box**   Click the To button to display the
Select Names dialog box. Double-click the name(s) of the individual(s) to
whom you want to address the message to add them to the Message
Recipients list on the right. When you close the Select Names dialog box,
they appear in the To field. To display names from other address books,
open the Show Names From The drop-down list and select the desired
address book.

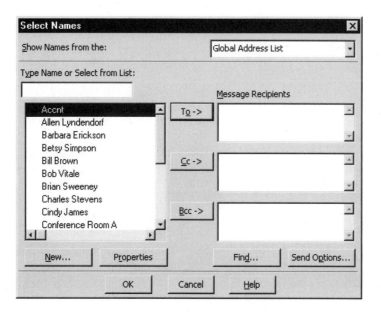

COMMUNICATING
WITH E-MAIL

Tip   *Instead of opening and closing the Select Names dialog box for each of the recipient fields
(To, Cc, and Bcc) you can select names from the list and click the appropriate button
(To ->, Cc ->, or Bcc ->) to add all three in one operation.*

Tip   *You can select multiple nonadjacent names by holding down the* CTRL *key as you click
each name. To select multiple adjacent names, hold down the* SHIFT *key, click the first
name, and then click the last name.*

3. If you used the Select Names dialog box to add recipients, click OK to close it
   and return to the e-mail message form, which should look something like this
   one if you've added the three different types of recipients.

4. Fill in the Subject line with a concise, informative word or phrase that describes the message contents. In other words, don't write "Quick question" when you need directions to the meeting site. Enter "Need directions to the meeting" instead. The more information your Subject line imparts (without going overboard), the more likely you'll get a quick response.

5. Type your message in the message body window. Again, it's important to remember that most people receive a lot of e-mail. Try to be as concise and informative as possible when composing business-related messages. At this point your message should resemble the one here.

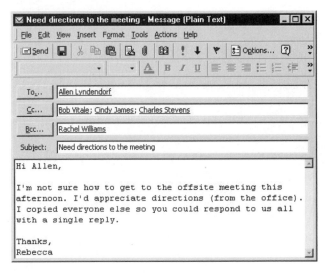

6. Click the Send button to transmit the message.

Tip   *You can add a frequently used e-mail address to a toolbar by assigning the address to a command button as a hyperlink. See Chapter 23 for details.*

MOUS   **MOUS EXAM PRACTICE**
In this section, you learned the basic elements that comprise an e-mail message, as well as the means to utilize those elements. Now might be a good time to write to all those friends and family members who've been wondering for years if you're still alive. Open a new message form and send them each a single message. Then select a group of them and send the message to one, and copy the others. Try addressing the messages by selecting names from your various address books. Then enter some addresses manually. By the time you're done, your friends and relatives will be longing for the good old days, and you'll be an expert at composing and addressing e-mail.

Formatting Messages

 If you're exchanging e-mail with others who use an e-mail application that supports text formatting, you can add verve, flair, and emphasis to your messages by including formatting. If you're exchanging e-mail with another Outlook user whose default editor is Microsoft Word, you can even include things like tables and bullet lists. To use the formatting features of your Outlook editor, whether it's Microsoft Word or the standard Outlook editor, you first must create an e-mail message or open a message saved in the Drafts folder. Next, move to the body of the message. The formatting features do not work in any area of the message except the body. If you place your cursor in any of the recipient fields or the Subject field, you'll notice that the formatting commands on the toolbars and menus are grayed out, which means they're unavailable.

Selecting the Message Format

The first and most basic formatting option is the overall message format. Your choices include Plain Text, HTML, and Microsoft Outlook Rich Text. Each provides a different level of formatting:

- **Plain Text**   There's not much more to be said about this than it's plain text. No-frills, mono-spaced type with absolutely no formatting options is what you'll get when you select this format. As grim as that may sound, it's often the best choice, especially if the bulk of your e-mail is sent to recipients over the Internet. Not all e-mail software supports text formatting. Therefore, unless you know that your recipients are using e-mail software that supports text formatting, it's a good idea to stick with Plain Text.

- **HTML**   The HTML format, which provides a variety of formatting options, is available when you use Outlook 2000 or Microsoft Word 2000 as your e-mail editor, but not if you use Microsoft Word 97. The features you get with the HTML format include text formatting (font and paragraph), bullets, numbering, HTML styles, and Web pages, as well as the ability to use stationery and signatures.

If you use Word 2000 as your default e-mail editor, you'll have to specify the stationery and signature options in Word rather than in Outlook.

■ **Microsoft Outlook Rich Text**   The Microsoft Outlook Rich Text format provides basic text formatting features, such as font and paragraph formatting, bullets, and alignment, as well as the use of signatures.

If you send HTML or Rich Text messages to people whose e-mail software doesn't support formatting, they may get the message, but lose the formatting. Even those recipients whose e-mail programs support these formats may receive something different from what you send, since other factors, including their installed fonts and option settings, may influence the way your message appears.

Font Formatting

When the word "formatting" pops up in cocktail chatter, as it tends to do from time to time, most peoples' minds turn to thoughts of font formatting. This makes sense since font formatting is the most visual and the most easily identified type of formatting. Font formatting is all about dressing up your text in a manner fitting the occasion. Using a wacky, slanted font when e-mailing jokes to your golfing buddies makes sense. However, using that same font when e-mailing the budget report to your CEO would probably not be a smart move. Then again, if your company makes practical joke novelties, it might be the perfect font to send the CEO.

Text that is red, bold, and underlined commands immediate attention. A script font presented in silver or gold implies pomp and sophistication, while a straight, sans serif (no frills), black font has a businesslike quality. The bottom line is that in addition to dressing up the appearance of your text, font formatting can also help convey your message.

Applying font formatting to text is a simple and straightforward task, as you'll see if you follow these steps:

1. Press CTRL-SHIFT-M to open a new mail message form.

2. Choose Format | HTML from the message form menu bar.

Note *Depending on your default setting for the basic message format (Plain Text, HTML, or Microsoft Outlook Rich Text), HTML may not be a choice on the Format menu. In that case, select Rich Text.*

3. Enter the desired recipients in the To, Cc, and Bcc fields.

4. Enter an appropriate description of the message contents in the Subject field.

5. Type your message in the message body window.

6. Format the text by highlighting the characters, words, or blocks of text you want to dress up and use the appropriate toolbar button (see Figure 3-6) to apply the formatting.

   ■ **Style** If you're using the Outlook e-mail editor, this button appears only if you've selected HTML as the message format. If Microsoft Word is your default e-mail editor, the Style button appears in all message formats. Styles are groups of font settings that are applied all at once. A style can include one or more of the following: font type, font size, font style (bold or italic), font color, and font effects such as underlining. For example, when you apply the Heading 1 style to a block of text in an HTML message, it changes the font to Times New Roman, the font size to 24pt, and the font style to bold.

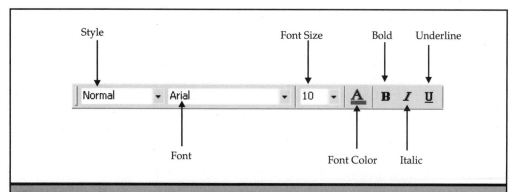

Figure 3-6. *The Formatting toolbar contains all the font options you'll need*

- **Font**   Whether you wear formal attire or your favorite Hawaiian shirt and shorts, it's still you underneath it all. The same goes for your text. No matter how you dress it up, it's still the same combination of characters; it just looks different. That's where the font comes in—it's the basic attire for your text. Click the down arrow to the right of the Font field to display a drop-down list of available fonts.

- **Font Size**   When composing an e-mail for the visually impaired, you might want to increase the size of the font to ensure they don't miss anything. If, on the other hand, you want to include some fine print in the hopes the recipients miss it, you can decrease the font size. Click the down arrow to the right of the Font Size field and choose a size from the drop-down list to apply to the selected text.

- **Font Color**   You can use color in your text to add emphasis or just to liven up the appearance of your e-mail. Click the Font Color button to display a color palette, then click the color of your choice to apply to the selected text.

- **Bold**   There's not much more to say. Highlight the text and click the Bold button to make the selected text **bold**.

- **Italic**   Italic is the *slanted font style* used in this sentence. Highlight the text and click the Italic button to apply the italic style to the selected text.

- **Underline**   You're on your own with *this* one!

7. Click Send to transmit the message.

If you want one-stop shopping for font formatting options, there's another way to apply font formatting to selected text. Highlight the text and choose Format | Paragraph from the Menu bar to display the Font dialog box.

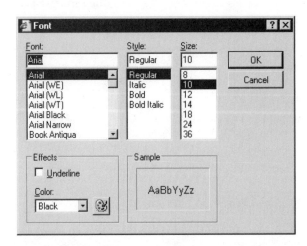

Select the font, the font style, the font size, the font color, and even whether or not to underline the selected text, and click OK to apply the formatting.

Remember, no matter how you apply the formatting, what your recipients see depends on their e-mail software, installed fonts, and so on.

Paragraph Formatting

Paragraph formatting is the less glamorous of the two main formatting features, but no less important. As with font formatting, paragraph formatting is restricted to HTML or Microsoft Outlook Rich Text. Before moving on to the techniques and features available for paragraph formatting, it's important to understand how Outlook defines a paragraph. A paragraph is everything that precedes a hard return. A hard return is an invisible formatting character that is embedded in the document every time you press the ENTER key while composing the message body. This means that as far as Outlook is concerned, a paragraph can be a blank line, a single character, a word, a sentence, or even an entire novel, as long as you don't press the ENTER key. Once you press the ENTER key you've started a new paragraph.

HTML messages can take advantage of what is called a soft return. By holding down the SHIFT key when pressing the ENTER key, you can start a new line that is considered part of the same paragraph as the preceding line. As a matter of fact, both HTML and Microsoft Outlook Rich Text automatically add soft returns to the end of the line, and word wrap takes over and creates a new line. This is what makes it possible to have a paragraph as long as a novel.

Putting paragraph formatting to work is even easier than using font formatting. Try it for yourself and see (remember, formatting is only available in HTML or Rich Text messages):

1. Press CTRL-SHIFT-M to open a new e-mail message form.

2. Enter the desired recipients in the To, Cc, and Bcc fields.

3. Type a brief description of the message contents in the Subject field.

4. Type your message in the message body window.

5. Select the paragraph(s) you want to format. Don't forget that Outlook considers a paragraph anything that precedes a hard return.

> **Tip** *You can select a single paragraph by placing your cursor anywhere in the paragraph. To select multiple paragraphs, highlight the text in the paragraphs you want to format. As long as you highlight some text from each paragraph the formatting will apply to all the paragraphs selected.*

6. Click the appropriate button on the Formatting toolbar, seen in Figure 3-7, to apply the paragraph formatting.

   ■ **Left** This is the default paragraph alignment. It lines the paragraph flush against the left margin of the message body window.

   ■ **Center** If you want the paragraph contents centered in the middle of the message body window, use the Center command.

■ **Right**   To line a paragraph flush against the right margin, use the Right command. This is frequently used to format a column of numbers to ensure they line up correctly.

■ **Bullets**   To create a list of bulleted items, use the Bullets command. It indents the line and places a bullet at the beginning of the line.

■ **Numbering**   If you're creating an HTML message, you can create a numbered list with the Numbering command. It is similar to Bullets in that it indents the line and places the character (a number, in this case) at the beginning of the line. What's nice is that if you apply the numbering format to the first line before creating additional lines, every time you press the ENTER key a new line is created with the next number in the sequence. Unfortunately, numbering is not available in Rich Text messages.

■ **Decrease Indent**   This command moves the selected paragraph to the left a predetermined number of spaces. One thing to note is that Decrease Indent will not move an aligned paragraph beyond the left margin determined by the alignment setting. In other words, a center-aligned paragraph will not move any further to the left than it is, even though it is far to the right of the left margin of the message body window. If, however, you move it to the right using the Increase Indent command you can then return it to its original position using the Decrease Indent command.

■ **Increase Indent**   This command moves the selected paragraph to the right a predetermined number of spaces.

■ **Insert Horizontal Line**   The Insert Horizontal Line command is a handy device that does just what its name states: it inserts a horizontal line at the place in the message body where the cursor happens to be when you click the Insert Horizontal Line button. As with the Numbering command, the Insert Horizontal Line command is available only in HTML messages.

Note

A new paragraph, created when you hit the ENTER key, inherits the paragraph formatting of the previous paragraph. This means that if you are typing a paragraph that is right-aligned and you press the ENTER key to start a new paragraph, the new paragraph will automatically be right-aligned as well.

7. Click Send to transmit the message.

As with font formatting, what your recipient sees of the paragraph formatting you apply is dependent upon a number of things that are out of your control—the recipient's e-mail software, installed fonts, and so on.

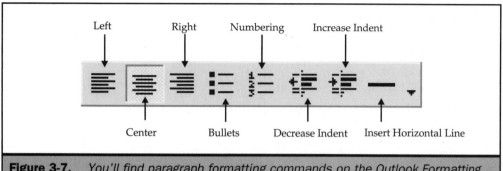

Figure 3-7. *You'll find paragraph formatting commands on the Outlook Formatting toolbar for quick access*

In addition to using the toolbar buttons, there are two additional ways to apply paragraph formatting. You can select the paragraph(s) to format and choose Format | Paragraph to display the Paragraph dialog box.

However, as you can see, the paragraph formatting options are limited to Bullets and Left, Center, or Right alignment.

An alternative method of applying paragraph formatting entails selecting the paragraph(s) and right-clicking anywhere on the selected paragraph(s) to display the shortcut menu that contains formatting commands.

Note *The shortcut menus for HTML and Rich Text messages are not identical. The HTML shortcut menu just shown contains more formatting commands than the Rich Text shortcut menu. In addition, it works a little differently.*

From the shortcut menu, select the formatting you want to apply to the selected paragraph(s). Point to Align to display the Align submenu containing Left, Center, and Right.

MOUS ***MOUS EXAM PRACTICE***
In this section, you learned how to customize the look of outgoing e-mail. Now try it yourself. Open the Outlook Options dialog box (choose Tools | Options), and switch to the Mail Format tab. See what your basic message format is set to, and change it to a different format. Then save the change and return to Outlook. Open a new message form and see how the form has changed. Take a look at the Format menu and see what menu items appear. Next, type some text in the message body window and apply font formatting. Change the font, the font style, the font size, the font color, and so on. After font formatting, try some paragraph formatting. Make sure your message has at least five paragraphs, and apply different paragraph formatting to each. Align one to the left, another to the center, and a third to the right. Then make a bullet list and a numbered list. Finally, try moving them left and right by decreasing and increasing the indent.

Flagging Outgoing Messages

 Sometimes just sending a message isn't enough. For example, suppose you're sending a message requesting that a co-worker remain available for a conference call the following day. Wouldn't it be nice if the message would also tap her on the shoulder tomorrow and remind her about the call? If you use a flag on the message it can. Flagging messages enables you to add an information bar to the top of the message that includes a comment indicating the type of flag and, if you set a reminder, the date and time it will go off.

To flag an outgoing message, follow these steps:

1. Press CTRL-SHIFT-M to open a new mail message form.

2. Enter the desired recipients in the To, Cc, and Bcc fields.

3. Type a brief description of the message contents in the Subject field.

4. Type your message in the message body window.

5. Click the Flag For Follow Up button on the Standard toolbar to display the Flag For Follow Up dialog box.

Note *You can also access the Flag For Follow Up dialog box by pressing CTRL-SHIFT-G or by choosing Actions | Flag For Follow Up from the message form menu bar.*

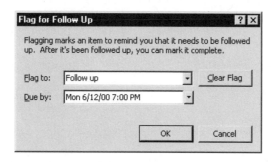

6. From the Flag To drop-down list, select the comment you want to include in the information bar added to the top of the message.

7. If you want to include a reminder, select the reminder date from the Due By drop-down calendar. When you select a date, the day, date, and time are included in the reminder.

Tip *When you include a reminder, the time is automatically set for the end of the selected workday (by default 5:00 PM). You can change the time by placing your cursor in the Due By line and editing the time manually. In addition, you can change the default time setting by changing the end time for your workday in the Calendar options. See Chapter 10 for more information on setting Calendar options.*

8. Click OK to save the flag and return to the mail message form. As you can see in Figure 3-8, the information bar appears at the top of the message and includes the comment and reminder (if you added one).

Note *If you change your mind about flagging a message, you can reopen the Flag For Follow Up dialog box and click the Clear Flag button.*

9. If your message is ready to go, press Send to send it on its way.

As with many Outlook features, flagging may appear differently to your recipients, depending on the e-mail software they use. Only other Outlook users will see the information bar with the comment and reminder information. In addition, only other Outlook users will have a reminder set to go off at the designated date and time. Non-Outlook users will have two additional lines added to the header of the message they receive—one that includes the comment, and another that includes Reply-By followed by the date and time.

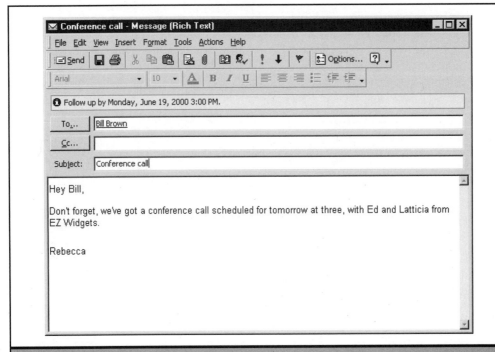

Figure 3-8. *Flagging a message is a good way to let the recipient know of any subsequent action that needs to be taken*

MOUS EXAM PRACTICE

In this section, you learned how to flag outgoing e-mail messages to provide additional information as well as reminders to the recipients. Now try creating and sending several flagged messages. Send one with a comment only and another with a comment and a reminder. Change the time on the reminder to something other than the default. Send flagged messages to recipients using Outlook and to recipients using e-mail software other than Outlook. Ask the recipients to reply to the flagged messages and include a copy of the header information from the original message so you can see how a flagged message appears to non-Outlook recipients.

Setting Message Options

One thing you can't fault Outlook for is a lack of options. It seems no matter where you turn there are tons of settings you can adjust to make things work your way. This is certainly the case with outgoing e-mail messages. Outgoing message options include message settings, voting and tracking options, delivery options, and even the ability to assign specific messages to contacts and categories.

Using the Message Options

The Message Options dialog box, seen in Figure 3-9, includes a variety of options that enable you to set delivery, tracking, and voting options as well as some message settings. These options are especially handy if you exchange e-mail with other Outlook users on a Microsoft Exchange Server network.

Voting buttons and delivery receipts are only available in the C/W configuration. However, if you have multiple Internet e-mail accounts, the IMO configuration contains a Send Message Using option that enables you to choose the Internet account to use.

Setting message options is easy if you follow these steps:

1. Press CTRL-SHIFT-M to open a new mail message form.

2. Add the desired recipients to the To, Cc, and Bcc fields.

3. Enter a brief description of the message contents in the Subject field.

4. Type the message in the message body window.

5. Click the Options button on the Standard toolbar to display the Message Options dialog box.

6. Set the desired options from among those available:

   - **Importance**   From the Importance drop-down list select the importance setting to attach to this message. Recipients can use this setting to determine how urgent the message is, and how quickly they need to deal with it. However, use the High setting judiciously. If you overuse it, it will quickly lose its impact, and recipients may begin to ignore it, even when you send a message that really is important. You can relax now—I have no intention of making any reference to the boy who cried wolf.

   - **Sensitivity**   When you're sending sensitive or confidential information in a message, you may want to alert the recipient to that fact by selecting a sensitivity setting from the drop-down list. However, keep in mind that no e-mail is entirely secure unless you employ the security measures available by using digital signatures and encryption.

   - **Security**   The two options found here enable you to keep your message safe from prying eyes. However, the options are unavailable unless you first set the Outlook security options to use digital signatures and encryption.

   - **Use voting buttons**   If you're on a Microsoft Exchange Server network, you'll love the voting buttons feature. It enables you to send a message to other users on the network, asking a simple question (such as, "Do you want to go out for lunch today?") and enabling them to respond by clicking a Yes,

Figure 3-9. *The Message Options dialog box gives you a great deal of control over outgoing messages*

No, or Maybe button in the message. You can determine the response buttons that appear by making your selection from the Use Voting Buttons drop-down list.

■ **Request a delivery receipt for this message** If you want to be notified when the recipient receives the message, enable this option.

■ **Request a read receipt for this message** If you want to be notified when the recipient opens the message, enable this option. Obviously there's no way to know if the recipient actually reads the message, so opening the message is as close as you can get.

■ **Have replies sent to** If you want someone else to receive replies to the message, enter the individual's e-mail address in the text box, or use the Select Names button to choose a name from your address book.

■ **Save sent message to** By default this option is enabled and set to the Sent Items folder. You can disable the option by removing the checkmark. You can also choose a different folder by clicking the Browse button and selecting a folder from the Select Folder dialog box.

- **Do not deliver before**   Enable this option to specify the earliest time at which you want the message delivered. Use the drop-down calendar to select a delivery date. To change the delivery time, edit it manually. When you hit the Send button, the message is deposited in your Outbox, where it remains until the specified time. One thing to note is that the delivery time is determined by the clock on the Microsoft Exchange server, not on your desktop computer. Therefore, if the clock on the server is five minutes slower than the clock on your desktop computer, the message will appear to be sitting in your Outbox an extra five minutes before being delivered.

- **Expires after**   If your message is time-sensitive, enable the Expires After option and set the date and time after which the message becomes invalid. When the time passes, the message is automatically deleted from the user's Inbox unless it has been opened, in which case a line is drawn through the message information making it appear to be crossed out.

- **Contacts**   To assign the message to one or more contacts, click the Contacts button and select the names. You might use this feature to link a message concerning a project update to all team members working on the project. It's like tossing a hard copy in each person's file folder.

- **Categories**   To enable quick and easy organizing of sent messages, you can assign them to categories (such as Business, Personal, and so on). Click the Categories button and make your selection from the Categories dialog box that appears.

7. Click Close to apply the message options to the message.

8. Click Send to transmit the message.

If you are sending the message to another user on the Exchange Server network, all the options will work as advertised. If you are sending the message to someone over the Internet, the results will vary depending on the e-mail software used by the recipient(s).

Spell Checking Messages

No matter how great your spelling skills may be, you're bound to make mistakes sooner or later. They may only be typographical errors, but the party who receives your e-mail won't know that. Therefore, you'll probably want to take advantage of the Outlook spell checker, especially on your business correspondence. The spell checker is so good, it will make everyone you exchange e-mail with think you actually stayed awake during your high school English classes.

Using the spell checker is a breeze:

1. Press CTRL-SHIFT-M to create a new mail message.

2. Enter the desired recipients in the To, Cc, and Bcc fields.

3. Enter a brief description of the message contents in the Subject field.

4. Type your message in the message body window.

5. With the cursor still in the message body, press F7 or choose Tools | Spelling to start the spell checker. When it encounters a misspelled word, it displays the Spelling dialog box. The Spelling dialog box indicates the word it thinks is misspelled and generally offers one or more suggestions.

Note   *The spell checker considers any word not found in its dictionary a misspelled word. Therefore, you'll probably encounter a number of correctly spelled words coming up as misspelled. When that happens, just add them to the dictionary. However, be careful not to add misspellings or they'll never be caught again.*

6. Select the way you want Outlook to deal with the misspelled word. Your choices include:

- ■ **Ignore**   Click this button to move on to the next misspelled word without making any change to the current misspelled word.

- ■ **Ignore All**   This command is similar to the Ignore command except it automatically ignores every instance of the currently selected word, not just the current instance.

- ■ **Change**   After you've selected the correct word from the Suggestions list or typed your own in the Change To field, click this button to replace the misspelled word with the selected word.

- ■ **Change All**   Use this command to replace every instance of the misspelled word with the selected word.

- ■ **Add**   The Outlook dictionary is by no means complete. Therefore, you're bound to encounter correctly spelled words that the spell checker thinks are misspelled simply because they are not in the dictionary. When you run across such words, add them to the dictionary. The next time the spell checker encounters them it will recognize them as properly spelled words. You can also use this command to add proper names, abbreviations, or other shorthand you use regularly.

Tip   *If you accidentally add a misspelled word to the dictionary you can remove it by opening the Custom.dic file found in C:\Windows\Application Data\Microsoft\Proof folder. Use Notepad or some other text editor to open the file, then delete the misspelled word. Save and close the Custom.dic file and return to Outlook. The next time you run the spell checker, it will catch the misspelling.*

- ■ **Suggest**   If you type a word in the Change To field, the Suggest button becomes available. When you click the button, a list of suggested spellings for the word you typed appears in the Suggestions window.

- ■ **Options**   Click this button to display the Spelling tab of the Options dialog box. Here you can set general options as well as add custom and international dictionaries.

- ■ **Undo Last**   After you've made a correction, you can undo it by clicking Undo Last.

7. Repeat the process for each misspelled word. After you deal with the last misspelled word, an information box appears and informs you that the spell check is complete.

8. Click OK to return to the e-mail message.

9. Click Send to close and send the message on its way.

If you move too fast and sometimes forget to spell check your messages, you can have Outlook do it automatically before sending messages. All you have to do is enable the Always Check Spelling Before Sending option located on the Spelling tab of the Options dialog box (Tools | Options).

Adding Attachments

The e-mail revolution did for 20th century communication what the telephone did for 19th century communication: reduce the time and cost of communicating with others no matter where on the planet they may be, while at the same time increasing the ease with which it's done. However, unlike the telephone, e-mail also enables users to send more than just words. By taking advantage of the attachments feature of e-mail, you can send not only messages, but also documents, spreadsheets, artwork, software programs, and anything else that comes in the form of a computer file.

Outlook users have one advantage over other e-mail software users, in that in addition to regular computer files, they can also attach Outlook items to e-mail messages. You can attach tasks, appointments, notes, and so on. This, of course, is only useful when exchanging such information with another Outlook user who can then utilize the item within Outlook.

Inserting Files

Since so much modern work is done on computers, the ability to transmit computer files along with e-mail messages is a phenomenal time and money saver. Authors can send completed manuscripts to publishers, programmers can send computer programs, financial analysts can send entire spreadsheets. The uses are seemingly endless. What used to require a special courier or an hour-long fax call can now be accomplished with the push of a button.

Adding file attachments to Outlook e-mail messages is quite easy:

1. Create a new e-mail message using the method described earlier in this chapter.

2. Click the Insert File button on the Standard toolbar to open the Insert File dialog box shown in Figure 3-10.

3. Click the down arrow to the right of the Look In field to display the drop-down tree view of your computer system.

4. Use the tree view to locate the file you want to attach.

5. Double-click the file to attach it to your e-mail message (see Figure 3-11). You can also click the down arrow next to Insert and choose Insert As Attachment.

Note *You can also insert the contents of a text file in an e-mail message rather than attaching the text file itself. In other words, all the text from the document is simply tagged on to the message you've already typed in the message body window. This is useful when sending to a recipient who is having difficulty receiving your attachments. Follow the preceding procedure and click the down arrow to the right of the Insert button and select Insert As Text.*

Figure 3-10.   *The Insert File dialog box enables you to search your hard disk(s) to locate the file you want to attach*

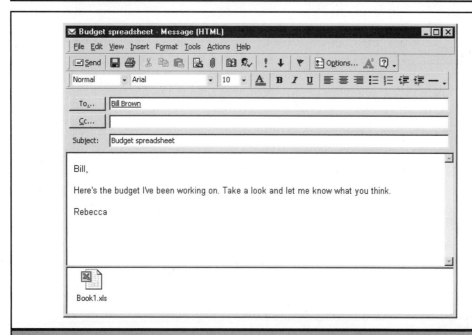

Figure 3-11.   *The file appears in your message as an icon with the filename*

6. Repeat the process to add all the attachments you want to include with the e-mail.

7. Click Send to transmit the message.

As powerful as the file attachment feature is, it does have some limitations. Network administrators and Internet service providers (ISPs) frequently put a size limit on the messages that are allowed to pass through their servers. Consequently, some messages with extremely large attachments may not make it. Check with your administrator to find out if there's a limit on the size of messages you can send and receive.

One way to reduce the size of file attachments is through the use of file compression software such as WinZip. Depending on the file type, compression software can reduce the size of a file by 50 percent or more. You can find file compression shareware and trialware on many of the download sites on the Internet, such as ZDNet and CNET. However, be sure that the recipients also have file compression software to restore the file to its original state, or they will be unable to access the file.

Including Outlook Items

The ability to exchange Outlook items such as contacts, meetings, notes, and more comes in quite handy at times. If you have contact information in your Contacts folder that you want to share with a number of other Outlook users, all you have to do is insert the contact(s) in an e-mail message and send it to everyone with whom you want to share the data. When they receive the message, they simply drag the attached contacts to their respective Contacts folders and drop them. The contacts are automatically added to each user's Contacts database.

Unfortunately, Outlook items do not travel well except on a Microsoft Exchange Server network. Attaching Outlook items to Internet e-mail, even if the recipient is using Outlook, is a waste of time. The items disappear in transit and the recipients receive nothing but the message.

Tip
Although you can't attach an Outlook item to an Internet e-mail, you can include the information from the item by inserting it as text only. See the steps that follow for more information.

To attach an Outlook item to an e-mail message, follow these steps:

1. Create an e-mail message using the method described earlier in this chapter.

2. Choose Insert | Item from the message form menu bar to display the Insert Item dialog box, seen in Figure 3-12.

3. From the Look In pane, choose the folder containing the item(s) you want to insert. The folder's contents are displayed in the Items list below the Look In pane.

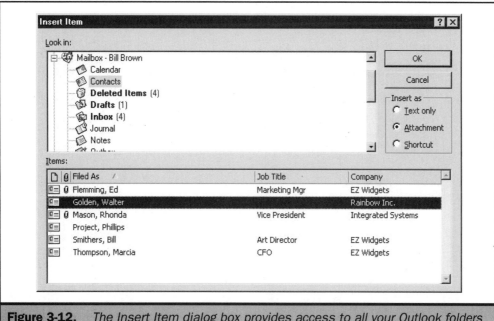

Figure 3-12.   *The Insert Item dialog box provides access to all your Outlook folders and items*

4. Select the appropriate Insert As option:

- ■ **Text Only**   To include the information only from the Outlook item, choose this option. This adds the data from the selected item to your message as text. Therefore, it becomes part of the message itself and has no trouble traveling over the Internet (see Figure 3-13).

- ■ **Attachment**   Select this option to include the Outlook item itself. Remember, this only works if you're sending the e-mail to someone connected to your network.

- ■ **Shortcut**   Rather than send any of the information, you can choose to send a shortcut or pointer to the information. However, to be of any use, the recipient must have permission to access your folders.

Tip   *You can insert multiple Outlook items from the same folder by holding down the CTRL key and selecting adjacent or non-adjacent items. To select a series of adjacent items, select the first item, hold down the SHIFT key and then select the last item.*

5. Click OK to insert the item(s) in the e-mail message.

6. Click Send to transmit the message.

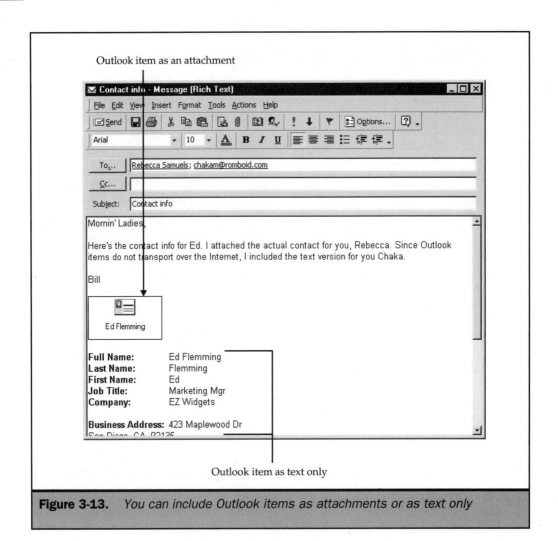

Figure 3-13. *You can include Outlook items as attachments or as text only*

Once the recipients receive your message, all they have to do is drag the Outlook item to the appropriate folder and drop it to add it to the folder.

Attaching Objects to Messages

If you select Microsoft Outlook Rich Text as your message format, you can also include objects in your messages. Objects can be documents, charts, worksheets, graphics, controls or just about any other type of file. You can either embed or link the objects you include in messages. Embedded objects become part of the message and retain no connection with the original file from which they were taken. Linked objects, on the other hand, remain connected (as long as the connection is open).

For example, if you insert a linked Excel spreadsheet in a message, double-clicking the spreadsheet launches Excel and opens the original document. In addition, when the original spreadsheet is modified, the linked spreadsheet is also modified. An embedded spreadsheet does not change no matter what happens to the original.

To insert an object, follow these steps:

1. Create an e-mail message using the method described earlier in this chapter.

2. Choose Format | Rich Text to change the message format to Microsoft Outlook Rich Text. If Rich Text is not an option, change the default message format on the Mail Format tab of the Options dialog box (Tools | Options) to either Microsoft Outlook Rich Text or Plain Text.

3. Place the cursor in the message body window and choose Insert | Object from the Menu bar to open the Insert Object dialog box.

4. To create a new object, select Create New and then the kind of object you want to create from the Object Type list. The program associated with the object type opens and you can create the new object.

Note *Objects you create are embedded in the message, since there is no existing file with which to link them.*

5. To embed an existing object or to create a link to an existing object, select Create From File to display the File text box, the Browse button, and the Link option.

COMMUNICATING
WITH E-MAIL

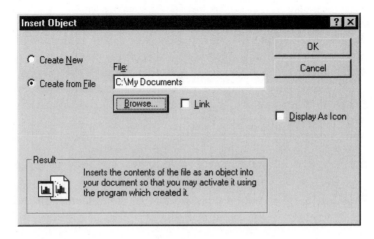

6. Click the Browse button to locate the file you want to insert in the message.

7. To link the file rather than embed it, click the Link option. This links the entire file.

To link or embed only part of the file in your message, open it in the associated program and copy the portion you want to link or embed. Next, move to the Outlook message form and place the cursor in the message body window. Then choose Edit | Paste Special from the Menu bar. To embed the information, select Paste. To link the information, select Paste Link.

8. Click Send to transmit the message.

Linking and embedding objects works as advertised when the e-mail is sent to recipients on the network. When sending e-mail with embedded objects to Internet mail recipients, the objects arrive as attachments. Linked objects, on the other hand, are lost entirely when transmitted to Internet mail recipients.

MOUS EXAM PRACTICE

In this section, you learned to attach everything but the kitchen sink to an Outlook e-mail message. Now try your hand at creating messages and attaching various files, items, and objects to them. Begin by inserting a computer file from your hard disk into an e-mail. Next, create a message and include an Outlook item. Try using both methods—inserting the item as an attachment and as text only. Send both items to someone with an Internet e-mail account and ask them what they actually receive. Finally, create a message and use embedding and linking of objects to include additional information in your e-mail.

Saving Drafts of Messages

During a busy workday, it's not uncommon for a number of things to interrupt you while you're in the process of composing an e-mail message—a co-worker knocking on your door, the phone ringing, an urgent e-mail requiring an immediate response, or a hundred other distractions. While you're distracted, your unfinished message is hanging out in RAM limbo. Therefore, it's a good idea to save your message to ensure it doesn't get lost in the event of a computer crash, a power surge, or some other minor calamity.

Outlook provides a separate folder just for this purpose: the Drafts folder. As a matter of fact, by default, Outlook saves unsent messages to the Drafts folder every three minutes. However, to be on the safe side you should probably save unfinished messages yourself by pressing CTRL-S. When you're ready to finish the e-mail, pick up where you left off. If you've closed the message since you saved it, you can reopen it by opening the Drafts folder and double-clicking the message.

Recalling Sent Messages

Did you ever dash off one of those e-mails that you know you shouldn't send, but in the heat of the moment you lose the ability to think rationally and send it anyway? Usually what happens next is that about three nanoseconds after it disappears your brain returns and you realize that you just did something you wish you hadn't. Well, if you're on a Microsoft Exchange Server network, there may be hope. Under certain circumstances, you can actually recall the message after you send it.

The Recall Messages feature, although available in the IMO configuration, does not work as expected. Rather than recalling a sent message, it merely sends a second message stating that the sender wants to recall the original message.

Before you get too excited, however, be advised that for it to work, the stars, moon, and planets have to be properly aligned, and you must have a little bit of good karma stored up. Okay, that may be a slight exaggeration, but there are a number of factors that influence the effectiveness of the Recall Message feature:

- **Recipient's e-mail system**   The recipient must be using Outlook and be on the Microsoft Exchange Server network for the feature to work. Do yourself a favor, and do *not* try to recall a message sent to an Internet mail recipient. You'll only make matters worse. All that happens is the original message stays intact and the recipient receives a follow-up message that says you would like to recall the original message.

- **Message status**   Only unread messages can be recalled. If the recipient has opened the message, you're out of luck. Of course, if the recipient has read the message, it no longer matters whether you can recall the message.

■ **Message location**   The message must still be in the recipient's Inbox. If the message has been moved, the message recall fails. This is true even if the moved message is still unread. If your recipient employs the Rules Wizard to automatically sort incoming mail, your message may never see the Inbox.

■ **Network status**   The user must be logged on to the Microsoft Exchange Server network for a recall to work. If you attempt to recall a message and the user is not logged on, the recall will not be attempted until the next time the user logs on. At that time, all the other factors come into play.

To recall a sent message, follow these steps:

1. Open your Sent Items folder and locate the message you want to recall.
2. Open the message you want to recall.
3. Choose Actions | Recall This Message from the Menu bar to display the Recall This Message dialog box.

4. Select the appropriate options for the recall.

■ **Delete unread copies of this message**   To simply remove the unread message from the recipient's Inbox, select this option.

■ **Delete unread copies and replace with a new message**   If you want to send a new message to replace the original, use this option. It creates a new message that is an exact duplicate of the original, which you can edit and send.

■ **Tell me if recall succeeds or fails for each recipient**   Unless you check this option, you'll never know whether the recall has succeeded. With this option enabled, you receive an e-mail response informing you of the success or failure of your recall attempt.

5. Click OK to recall the original message. If you selected Delete Unread Copies And Replace With A New Message, the new message form opens with all the original message information included. Modify it and send it on its way.

If the recipient is logged on to the network, you'll get an e-mail response informing you of the success or failure of your recall attempt within a short while. That's assuming, of course, you enabled the Tell Me If Recall Succeeds Or Fails For Each Recipient option. However, if the recipient is not logged on to the network, you'll hear nothing until the next time the user logs on.

One more thing to be aware of is the fact that even when message recall works, it sends a second message that appears in the recipient's mailbox for a brief time. The header of the second message says Recalling followed by the subject line of the original message. Both the original and Recalling messages remain in the recipient's Inbox until the Microsoft Exchange server makes the next sweep for a mail pickup. If the recipient happens to open the Inbox while the recall is taking place, he or she may be alerted to the fact that you've recalled a message.

MOUS

MOUS EXAM PRACTICE

In this section, you learned to recall or replace a sent message. In addition, you learned that a number of factors are required for the feature to work properly. Create several test messages and send them to both Microsoft Exchange Server recipients and Internet mail recipients. Alert the recipients that the messages are coming, and ask them to let you know what happens on their end. Try replacing messages as well as recalling them. So you can see for yourself what happens, ask one of your coworkers to send you test messages, and then recall them.

Resending Sent Messages

Occasionally e-mail messages start off on their journey as usual, but whether the result of happenstance, foul play, or a blip in the electronic ether, they never arrive at their intended destination. If the message requires no response from the recipient, you may never know. However, if you're expecting a response and don't get one, or someone asks you to send information and it never arrives, you'll probably want to send the message again. When you encounter a situation involving an errant e-mail message, you can use the Resend This Message command.

Here's all you have to do to resend a previously sent message:

1. Open the Sent Items folder and locate the message you want to resend.

2. Double-click the message to open it.

3. Choose Actions | Resend This Message to create a new message containing all the information of the original, including the recipients, subject line, contents, and attachments.

COMMUNICATING WITH E-MAIL

4. Make any changes to the new e-mail that you feel are necessary.

5. Click Send to send it on its way.

From this point forward, the resent message behaves like every other sent message, and a copy is saved in your Sent Items folder (unless you've changed the default settings).

Exam ▾ | MOUS Exam Objectives Explored in Chapter 3

Objective	Activity	Heading
OL2000.1.2	Send mail	All
OL2000.1.3	Compose mail by entering text	"Composing the Message"
OL2000.1.5	Address mail by entering text	"Composing the Message"
OL2000.1.6	Use mail features (recall)	"Recalling Sent Messages"
OL2000.1.7	Use address book to address mail	"Composing the Message"
OL2000.1.8	Flag mail messages	"Flagging Outgoing Messages"
OL2000.1.9	Navigate within mail	"Navigating Outlook E-mail"
OL2000.1.12	Work with attachments	"Adding Attachments"
OL2000.1.14	Customize the look of mail	"Formatting Messages"

The
Complete
Reference

2000
Outlook

Chapter 4

Reading and Replying to Messages

As important as writing and sending e-mail is, the flip side of the coin—receiving and replying to incoming e-mail—is equally important. So much of today's communication, both personal and business, is conducted via e-mail that dealing with incoming e-mail is a skill everyone must master.

While it's true that receiving e-mail requires no effort if you're on a Microsoft Exchange Server network, and very little if you use an Internet e-mail account, there are quite a few things you can do with incoming e-mail after it lands in your Inbox. You can open it, read it, discard it, reply to it, store it, flag it, or even ignore it if you choose. That's what this chapter is all about: providing you with the skills to dispatch your incoming e-mail quickly and effectively.

Configuring the Inbox

The first thing you'll want to do is set up the Inbox to suit your work habits and needs. Fortunately, Outlook provides a number of options that enable you to customize the Inbox so that managing your incoming e-mail will be a breeze.

AutoPreview

For a sneak peek at the contents of each incoming message, you can turn on AutoPreview. It's a handy feature that displays, in the Information viewer, the first line or two of each message in addition to the usual header information.

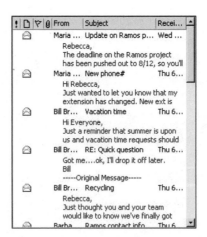

It's especially helpful if you're pressed for time and receive a lot of e-mail every day. You can take a quick look and decide for yourself the importance of the message, without even opening it.

To activate the AutoPreview feature, follow these steps:

1. Click the Inbox shortcut on the Outlook Bar to open the Inbox folder.

2. Choose View | AutoPreview from the Menu bar to enable AutoPreview.

Tip   *You can also activate AutoPreview by right-clicking a blank spot (below the last message) in the Inbox Information viewer and selecting AutoPreview from the shortcut menu that appears.*

3. Scroll through the Information viewer to scan the messages in the Inbox. The message contents appear with a blue background.

4. Choose View | AutoPreview a second time to turn off the AutoPreview feature.

The only downside to AutoPreview is that it utilizes a lot of Information viewer real estate. If you have a large number of incoming messages, you may find it easier to turn AutoPreview off and rely on the Subject line to determine the importance of each message.

Preview Pane

The Preview Pane offers another means of viewing the message contents without actually opening the message. Unlike AutoPreview, the Preview Pane displays the entire message, not just the first line or two. However, Preview Pane actually splits the Information viewer into two panes. The top pane retains the standard header information, while the bottom pane displays the message contents (see Figure 4-1).

Figure 4-1.   *The Preview Pane enables you to read a message without opening it*

Activating the Preview Pane is as simple as choosing View | Preview Pane from the Menu bar. This immediately splits the Inbox Information viewer into two panes, with the Preview Pane inhabiting the bottom pane. After the Preview Pane is activated, select a message in the Inbox Information viewer to display it in the Preview Pane. Scroll through the message to read the entire contents. If the message has one or more attachments, a paperclip icon appears on the right side of the header information (see Figure 4-1). Click the paperclip to display a list of attachments. Select an attachment from the list to open it. Of course, you must have the associated program installed to open the attached file.

Unless the sender uses Rich Text as the message format, the attachments themselves will not appear in the Preview Pane. To do anything except read the attachment in a non-Rich Text message, you'll have to open the message, right-click the attachment, and select the appropriate command from the shortcut menu that appears.

The Preview Pane is no different from other Outlook features in that it has several options you can set to customize the way it works. To change the Preview Pane settings, right-click the Preview Pane header and choose Preview Pane Options from the shortcut menu.

The available choices include hiding the Preview Pane itself, hiding the Preview Pane header information and setting Preview Pane options.

The Preview Pane options available in the Preview Pane dialog box shown in Figure 4-2 include the following:

- **Mark messages as read in preview window** This option works in conjunction with the next option to give you a chance to preview messages or move quickly through them without necessarily marking them as read. Once you select this option you have the amount of time specified in the next option to display the message in the Preview Pane before it is automatically marked as read.

- **Wait ___ seconds before marking item as read** Only available if the preceding option is checked, this option indicates the amount of time a message can be viewed in the Preview Pane before it is marked as read. This is handy if you want to search for a particular message by skimming the contents of the Inbox, without marking each message as read. When you return to view your

Figure 4-2. *The Preview Pane options let you change the way the Preview Pane looks and works*

unread e-mail at a later time, you won't mistakenly think you've read everything you skimmed.

■ **Mark item as read when selection changes**   The default setting for the Preview Pane, this option causes a viewed message to be marked as read when the next message is selected.

■ **Single key reading using SPACEBAR**   With this option enabled, you can move through the messages (sequentially) by pressing the SPACEBAR. To move forward, press the SPACEBAR. To move backward, hold the SHIFT key down while pressing the SPACEBAR. If a message has more information than fits in the Preview Pane, pressing the SPACEBAR scrolls through the message until the end is reached, at which time the next message is displayed.

■ **Preview header**   Click the Font button to select the font, font style, and font size used in the Preview Pane header.

Note   *The Preview Pane has a couple of idiosyncrasies. Comments and reminders in flagged messages do not appear in the Preview Pane header information. So be sure to open flagged messages to view the comments and reminders. Also, don't be surprised if you get a message recall (success or failure) notification, and you're unable to view the contents in the Preview Pane. While both contain information when the message is opened, neither displays it in the Preview Pane.*

One last thing. If you like the Preview Pane but don't like the amount of space it takes, you can resize it by dragging its top border up or down to increase or decrease its height. You can also change its width by dragging the left border left or right. Just be aware that this resizes the Information viewer at the same time.

MOUS

MOUS EXAM PRACTICE

In this section, you discovered different Outlook features that enable you to customize the Inbox to make it a more effective work environment. You can increase your productivity by cutting down the amount of time spent opening and closing messages when you employ either the AutoPreview feature or the Preview Pane. Since AutoPreview is relatively simple, the only thing you need to do is remember there are two ways to activate it: by right-clicking a blank spot in the Inbox Information viewer and selecting AutoPreview from the shortcut menu, or by choosing View | AutoPreview from the Menu bar. The Preview Pane offers a few more challenges, so try your hand at opening and closing it, hiding and displaying the Preview Pane header, and setting the options.

Receiving E-mail

If you're on a Microsoft Exchange Server network, all you have to do is log on to the Microsoft Exchange server and sit back and wait for mail to come to you. It's that easy. The server handles receipt and distribution of all incoming as well as outgoing mail. This means that the Microsoft Exchange server intercepts all messages addressed to you, whether from other users on the network or from the Internet (except those addressed to any Internet mail accounts you have added to your profile), and places them in your mailbox.

When you "receive" mail, you're not actually receiving the messages on your computer, but rather being notified that mail has been placed in your mailbox on the server. When you open, read, delete, or otherwise perform an action on individual pieces of e-mail it is all taking place on the Microsoft Exchange server, not on your computer.

Tip

You can have your mail delivered to and stored on your computer rather than on the server. You do this by adding personal folders to your profile and changing the delivery location in the Deliver New Mail To The Following Location option found on the Delivery tab of the Services dialog box (Tools | Services). However, be advised that most network administrators make daily backups of everything on the server, including e-mail. Once you change the delivery location to your personal folders, your e-mail will no longer be stored on the server, and consequently will not be backed up regularly unless you do it yourself.

If the only mail service you have installed is Microsoft Exchange Server, there's little you need to do to receive mail except log on to the server. One thing to remember is that when the server goes down, so does your mail service. Until it comes back up, you won't be able to receive (or send) mail unless you have an Internet mail account with an outside connection.

No matter which mail services you use, all your incoming e-mail is, by default, deposited in your Inbox. When new messages arrive you may or may not receive notification, depending on how you've set up your mail receipt options.

Receiving Notification of New Mail

There are several ways you can tell when new mail arrives in your Inbox. The first telltale sign is the melodious sound emanating from your speakers (of course, you must have a sound card installed and speakers attached). By default, Outlook is programmed to emit the Windows New Mail Notification sound, which you can change by opening the Sounds applet in the Control Panel and selecting a different sound file (see Figure 4-3).

Adding Visual Notification

Ah, but what if you don't have sound on your system, or you want double insurance you don't miss new mail? No problem. You can also instruct Outlook to display a message informing you of the fact that new mail has arrived. To add a visual notification follow these steps:

1. Choose Tools | Options to display the Options dialog box.

2. Click the E-mail Options button on the Preferences tab to open the E-mail Options dialog box shown in Figure 4-4.

3. Check the Display A Notification Message When New Mail Arrives check box.

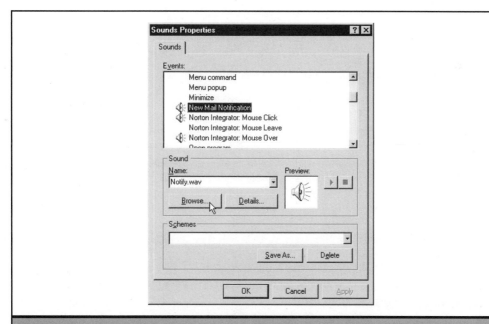

Figure 4-3.   *Use the Sounds Properties dialog box to customize the Outlook e-mail notification sound*

Figure 4-4.   *You can customize the way Outlook handles e-mail by taking advantage of the large selection of e-mail options*

4. Click OK to save the change and return to the Options dialog box.

5. Click OK to return to the active Outlook window.

Now each time a new message arrives, Outlook interrupts whatever you're doing and presents you with a notification dialog box. Of course, Outlook must be running and you must be connected to the Microsoft Exchange server to receive notification.

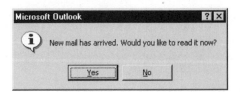

Click Yes to open the new message immediately. Click No to return to the task at hand. You can then return to Outlook at a later time and open it at your convenience. If you elect to click Yes and open the message immediately, the Previous Item and Next Item buttons do not work. You'll have to close the message and return to the Inbox to open your other messages. According to Microsoft, this is not a bug, but rather a design feature. In spite of this declaration, most users have a difficult time grasping the benefit derived from disabling the buttons.

In theory, there's another default setting that alerts you to the fact that new mail has arrived. Your mouse pointer momentarily changes shape, resembling a small envelope. However, unless you spend an inordinate amount of time staring at your mouse pointer, you'll probably miss this one.

There is another way that Outlook indicates the presence of new mail. The Inbox shortcut on the Outlook Bar sports a number in parentheses next to the word Inbox, indicating how many unread messages are in your Inbox. Each time a new piece of e-mail arrives, the number is increased by one until you open the e-mail, which then decreases the number by one. The same is true of the Folder List. If you generally read all your messages when they come in, or if you have an idea of how many unread messages are in your Inbox, you can generally tell by the number in parentheses whether or not you have new mail.

Creating Customized Notifications

Perhaps you're not concerned about getting e-mail from the majority of the folks with whom you correspond, but there are probably a few, such as your boss, her boss, and the CEO, that you don't want to keep waiting for a reply. If this is the case, don't bother setting a general notification alert. Instead, set an alert to go off each time you receive e-mail from any of those three individuals.

In order to do it, all you have to do is fire up the Rules Wizard and create a special notification rule. Here's how:

1. Choose Tools | Rules Wizard from the Menu bar to open the Rules Wizard dialog box, shown in Figure 4-5.

2. Click the New button to begin creating a new rule.

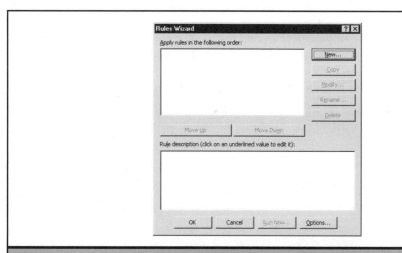

Figure 4-5.   *You can use the Rules Wizard to customize the way Outlook handles both incoming and outgoing messages*

3. From the Which Type Of Rule Do You Want To Create list, select Check Messages When They Arrive, and then click Next to view the conditions screen.

4. From the Which Condition(s) Do You Want To Check list, select From People Or Distribution List.

 If you want to create a custom message that notifies you of any new mail, regardless of the sender, click Next without checking an option. Then answer Yes when you're informed the rule will be applied to every message you receive.

5. Click the blue, underlined "people or distribution link list" in the Rule description below the list to open the Rule Address dialog box seen in Figure 4-6.

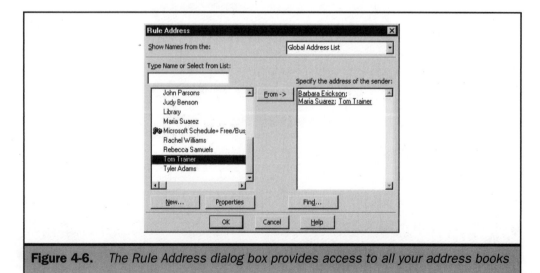

Figure 4-6.   *The Rule Address dialog box provides access to all your address books*

If you're using the IMO configuration, your Rule Address dialog box may appear slightly different.

6. Select the names of those individuals to whom this rule will apply. In other words, choose those people whose e-mail is important enough to trigger a special notification when it arrives.

7. Click OK to close the Rule Address dialog box and return to the Rules Wizard. The description window now contains the names you selected.

8. Click Next to move to the action screen, scroll down the list of possible actions to take and check Notify Me Using A Specific Message.

9. Click the "a specific message" link in the Rule description box to display the Notification Message dialog box.

10. Enter the text for the notification message that will appear when you receive mail from any of the individuals selected in step 6.

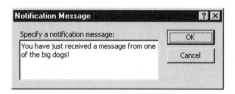

11. Click OK to save the message and return to the Rules Wizard. Once again, the new information you entered now appears in the Rule Description pane.

12. Click Next to view the exceptions screen. If there are any circumstances under which you don't want to be notified of incoming mail from any of the selected

COMMUNICATING WITH E-MAIL

individuals, check that option here. For example, you may not care unless you're the only recipient.

13. Click Next to view the final screen. Give the new rule an appropriate name and set the final option. If you want to apply the new rule to messages already received, check Run This Rule Now On Messages Already In "Inbox." Leave Turn On This Rule checked to ensure the rule actually works. If you remove the checkmark, the rule will not run.

14. Click Finish to activate the rule. An information dialog box appears, informing you this rule is client-only and will not work unless Outlook is running.

15. Keep that in mind, and click OK to return to the opening screen of the Rules Wizard, where your new rule now appears in the Apply Rules In The Following Order list.

16. Click OK to save the new rule and return to the active Outlook window.

The next time you receive an e-mail message from any of the individuals named in the new rule, the custom message you created appears. As you can see, not only is your custom message included, but also the sender's name and the message subject.

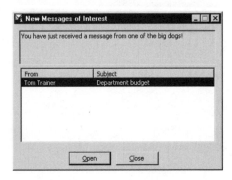

By the way, if you have created a custom notification rule *and* you have the Display A Notification Message When New Mail Arrives option enabled, you'll get a standard notification message and a custom message each time new mail arrives from one of the individuals named in the custom notification rule.

Receiving Internet Mail Automatically

If you're running the C/W configuration of Outlook and have one or more Internet mail services installed, you can have Outlook check your Internet mail account(s) automatically by setting a couple of options.

To enable automatic mail checking in the C/W configuration, follow these steps:

1. Choose Tools | Options to open the Options dialog box.

2. Click the Internet E-mail tab to display the available options for your Internet mail service, as shown in Figure 4-7.

The IMO configuration also enables you to set automatic mail-checking options. However, the Mail Delivery tab of the Options dialog box contains a number of differences from the Mail Delivery tab in the C/W configuration.

3. Put a checkmark in the Check My Local Network Connection(s) For New Mail Every __ Minute(s) check box.

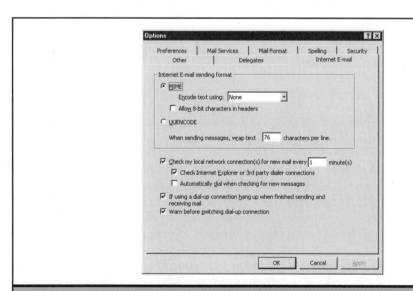

Figure 4-7.   *The Internet E-mail options let you control how and when Outlook checks your Internet e-mail account*

4. Enter the number of minutes you want Outlook to wait before checking for new mail on your Internet mail account.

5. Check the appropriate option for making the connection. Your choices are:

- **Check Internet Explorer or 3rd party dialer connections**   Use this option if you're connected to the Internet through your local area network (LAN) or if you have a connection set up for dialing out when you use Internet Explorer to surf the Web.

- **Automatically dial when checking for new messages**   Check this option if you have a dial-up networking (DUN) connection set up to connect to the Internet. When the time interval set in the previous option expires, Outlook automatically dials the DUN connection to check your Internet mail.

- **If using a dial-up connection hang up when finished sending and receiving mail**   Check this option if you want the connection terminated after Outlook sends and receives e-mail.

- **Warn before switching dial-up connection**   Use this option to instruct Outlook to give you the opportunity to use a different DUN connection if the designated connection isn't working.

6. Click OK to save the new settings and return to the active Outlook window.

If you have multiple Internet mail services installed, Outlook will check all accounts when you enable the options for automatic Internet mail checking. Unfortunately, you cannot set the automatic checking options for individual Internet e-mail accounts. It's all or nothing.

   Don't be fooled into thinking the Check For New Mail On option, found on the Mail Services tab of the Options dialog box, will enable you to set the automatic mail checking for individual Internet e-mail accounts. This option affects the mail services checked only when you use the Send or Send and Receive commands. It has no effect on automatic mail checking at all.

Checking Internet Mail Manually

If you have a network connection to the Internet that remains open all the time, using automatic checking is probably a good idea. However, if you have to dial out to get your Internet e-mail each time, you may prefer to check it manually. Having a dial-up connection launch itself and start dialing unexpectedly, especially if you're in the middle of another task, can be rather annoying, to say the least.

To check your Internet e-mail manually, open the Inbox (or any folder that holds mail items) and choose Tools | Send and Receive. In addition to checking for incoming mail, this also sends any messages sitting in the Outbox. If you take a look at the Tools menu, you'll notice that your only choices are Send, and Send and Receive. There is no

Receive-only command. If you want to be able to receive mail without sending at the same time, there is a way, however: use Remote Mail. For information on setting up and using Remote Mail, see Chapter 17.

Opening and Reading E-mail

MOUS

For the most part, you'll probably open and read (or at least scan) most e-mail you receive. The process is simple: double-click the message you want to open, and just like magic, it appears in its own message window, as shown in Figure 4-8.

Just for the record, there are a couple of other ways you can open a message:

- Right-click the message and choose Open from the shortcut menu that appears
- Highlight the message and press CTRL-O
- Highlight the message and choose File | Open | Selected Items

Once you're done reading the message, you can close it, delete it, reply to it, forward it, move it, or just pretend it's not there. Oh yes, there's one more thing you can do: read other messages without closing the current message. Simply click the appropriate arrow on the Standard toolbar in the message window. The up arrow opens the previous message, the down arrow opens the next message. Using this method you can cycle through all your messages without opening and closing each one individually.

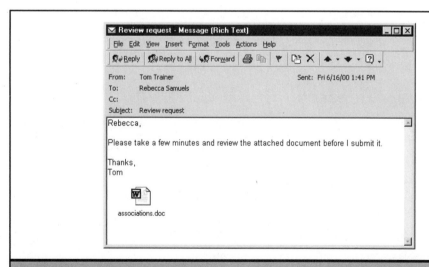

Figure 4-8.   *Opening a message makes it easy to view the entire contents at a glance*

If you prefer not to open any messages, you can use one of the two methods described earlier in this chapter for previewing messages—AutoPreview or the Preview Pane.

Changing the Formatting of Received Messages

Occasionally you may receive messages that are difficult to read, either because the type is too small or the formatting is too extravagant. Or perhaps someone has gone overboard with colors and the whole thing is giving you flashbacks to the psychedelic Sixties. Whatever the reason, you can modify the contents of received messages. Rich Text messages are editable as they arrive. All you have to do is highlight the offending text and choose Tools | Font to change the font formatting, or Tools | Paragraph to change the paragraph formatting. You can even add or delete text from the message.

You can also change HTML messages, but you must choose Edit | Edit Message before Outlook lets you do any editing. Plain Text messages are a little trickier. First you must choose Edit | Edit Message to make the message editable. However, since Plain Text accepts no formatting, the only thing you can do at this point is add or delete text. To apply formatting to a Plain Text message, you have to next change it to a different format. Choose Format and select either Rich Text or HTML. The message text immediately assumes the default font of the selected format. You can now apply font and paragraph formatting.

If you make any changes to the message, Outlook asks if you want to save those changes when you close the message. Click Yes to save the changes or No to return it to its original state.

 If you find reading Plain Text messages difficult due to the 10-point Courier font Outlook uses by default, you can change the settings so all Plain Text messages you receive are automatically displayed with a different font. See Chapter 6 for details on changing default fonts in e-mail messages.

Viewing Message Headers

You can view or hide the header information on mail you receive from other users on the Microsoft Exchange server, including the To, Cc, and Subject information. Although the header also contains the From information (the sender), that remains visible even when you hide header information. To hide or display the header information, open the message and choose View | Message Header. If the header information is already visible, this command hides it. If, however, the header information is hidden, this command displays it.

Right about now, you're probably yawning and thinking "What's the big deal about headers?" Truthfully, hiding the message header is no big deal with Microsoft Exchange Server mail except that it may give you a little extra room to read the message itself. Where header information does become important is when it comes to Internet e-mail. Here, the message header provides a host of information, including the exact path the message took in getting to you. While you may not care, your

Figure 4-9.   _The Internet headers information lets you track the e-mail to its source_

network administrator will want that information to track down any bulk mailers that
are sending you junk e-mail (also known as spam).

The Internet header information is not displayed in the message header above the
actual message, but rather in the Internet Headers pane in the Message Options dialog
box (see Figure 4-9). While in the Message window, choose View | Options to open
the Message Options dialog box.

MOUS EXAM PRACTICE
_In this section, we covered opening and reading e-mail messages, the most basic of Outlook
tasks. Now try the various methods available for opening and viewing messages to see which
works best for you. In addition, try changing the formatting on some of your incoming
messages so you're ready if you ever need to edit a piece of e-mail you receive. It's also a good
idea to familiarize yourself with the way headers work on both Microsoft Exchange Server
mail and Internet mail. Practice hiding and displaying the message headers, and locating
the Internet header information on messages you receive over the Internet._

Responding to and Forwarding Messages

While many messages you receive may be informational only, there will probably be
a large percentage that require something more than simply reading and storing (or
deleting). When you run into one of these messages, you'll have a choice of actions to

take. The most common action taken is responding to the sender. If the message was sent to multiple recipients, including yourself, you may elect to respond not only to the sender, but to all your fellow recipients as well. In some cases you may not want to respond to the message, but rather to send it on to someone else to read. This is called forwarding. No matter which action you choose, the ability to do more than read and store e-mail makes it a powerful form of communication.

Before you jump into replying and forwarding messages, there is one thing you should be aware of that applies to all three features (Reply, Reply To All, and Forward). When you send the message, Outlook adds a banner to the original message indicating action taken (replied to or forwarded), and the date and time the action was taken.

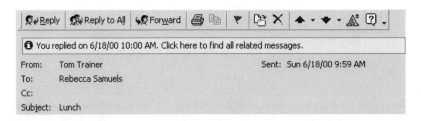

The same thing happens when you save the reply or forwarded message to the Drafts folder to finish it later, or when you delay the delivery of the message by setting Do Not Deliver Before option in the Message Options dialog box. This is all well and good, except for two potential problems. First, the banner in the original message remains even if you change your mind and decide not to send the reply or forward. Second, the date and time in the banner reflect the date and time the action was taken, not the date and time the message was actually sent. If you set the message to be sent some time in the future, this may cause confusion when, from your end, it appears your reply or forward was sent much sooner than the recipient received it.

Replying to E-mail Messages

Frequently, incoming e-mail either asks a direct question or by virtue of the contents deserves or perhaps begs a response. When you encounter such a message, the natural thing to do is respond. It's actually quite simple. All you have to do is click the Reply button on the message form Standard toolbar while the message is open.

Tip   *You can also select the message in the Inbox Information viewer and click the Reply button on the Inbox Standard toolbar, or right-click the message and select Reply from the shortcut menu that appears.*

This opens a new mail message form addressed to the sender and, by default, containing the contents of the original message, including the header information (see Figure 4-10).

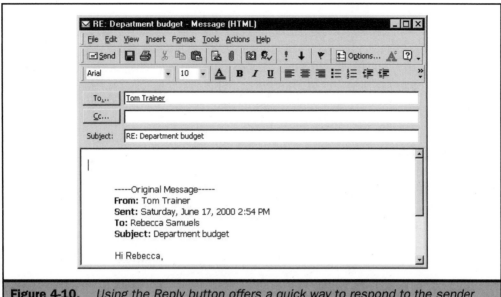

Figure 4-10.   *Using the Reply button offers a quick way to respond to the sender*

Although the entire text of the original message is, by default, included in a reply, it's not always necessary or desirable to leave it in the reply. By keeping the original text, you are increasing the size of your reply, which requires more bandwidth when sending it and more hard disk space when storing it. This is especially true as a message thread or conversation develops, in which the sender responds to your reply with a message that requires a response, which requires a response, which requires a response—you get the picture. By the third or fourth response, the message may be several pages long. Therefore, you should retain the original message or relevant parts of it only when their omission might lead the recipient to misunderstand your reply.

Tip   *You can change the default setting that causes Outlook to retain the original message in a reply. Choose Tools | Options and click the E-mail Options button on the Preferences tab to open the E-mail Options dialog box. Select the new setting from the When Replying To A Message drop-down list. See Chapter 8 for more information.*

As you can see in Figure 4-10, the Subject line is already filled in as well. But now the Subject line from the original message is preceded by RE, meaning "in reference to." You'll also note that the cursor is in the message body window, ready for you to type your response. Enter your reply, apply any formatting you want, add any desired attachments, and you're ready to send your reply back to the sender. The final step is to click the Send button and transmit the message.

Replying to All

When you receive a message with multiple recipients, you can respond to all the other recipients as well as the sender by using the Reply To All feature. It is identical to the Reply feature except that the new message created is automatically addressed to the sender and any recipients in the To and Cc fields in the original message. Anyone who was sent a blind copy (Bcc) of the original message does *not* receive a copy of the response when Reply To All is used.

Forwarding Messages to Others

Some messages contain information that you want or need to share with others who did not receive the message. While you could certainly cut and paste the information into a new message and send it to the person with whom you want to share the information, there's a much simpler way: forward the original message. The most direct method is to click the Forward button on the message form Standard toolbar while the message is open. As you can see in Figure 4-11, this opens a new message form that looks strikingly similar to a reply message form.

When you look closely, you'll see the differences include the fact that there are no recipients added, and the Subject line contains the Subject line from the original

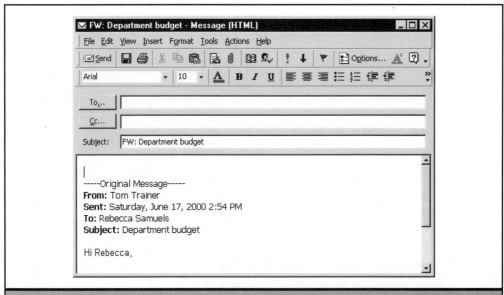

Figure 4-11.   *A forwarded message is indicated by the "FW:" in the Subject field*

message preceded by FW rather than RE. The FW, as you've probably already deduced, designates it as a forwarded message.

Now enter the recipient(s) to whom you want to pass this message, and add your own note (such as, "Thought you might find this interesting"). Apply any formatting you want, and click Send to transmit the forwarded message.

As is the case with both the Reply and the Reply To All features, you can forward a message without opening it. Select it and click the Forward button on the Inbox Standard toolbar, or right-click the message and select Forward from the shortcut menu.

Automating Message Replies and Forwarding

As easy as replying and forwarding is, Outlook provides a way for you to reply to and forward messages without ever lifting a finger. This little bit of digital wizardry is the domain of none other than the Outlook Rules Wizard. It enables you to create special rules that automatically create and send a predetermined response, or that forward an incoming message to others without clicking a single mouse button (except while you're creating the rules, of course).

Creating a reply or forwarding rule is easy with the Rules Wizard. Since the possibilities are endless, the following exercise walks you through creating a rule that forwards all messages from your former team members to the new team leader who has just taken over for you:

1. Choose Tools | Rules Wizard from the Menu bar to display the Rules Wizard dialog box. As you can see in Figure 4-12, the opening screen of the Rules Wizard displays any existing rules you may have.

2. Click New to move to the next screen and begin creating your rule.

3. Select Check Messages When They Arrive and click Next to move to the conditions screen.

4. Check From People Or Distribution List, then click the "people or distribution list" link in the Rule Description pane to open the Rule Address dialog box (see Figure 4-13).

5. Double-click the names of the people whose mail you want forwarded by this rule to add them to the Specify The Address Of The Sender list, and click OK to add them to the rule.

6. Click Next to move to the actions screen, and select Forward It To People Or Distribution List.

7. In the Rule Description pane, click the "people or distribution list" link to open the Rule Address dialog box again.

8. Select the name of the individual to whom you want the messages forwarded, and click OK to return to the Rules Wizard.

Figure 4-12. *The Rules Wizard performs magic when it comes to handling your e-mail messages*

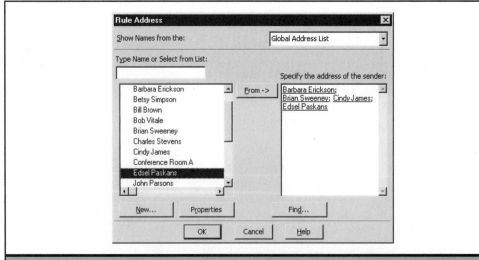

Figure 4-13. *The Rule Address dialog box provides access to all your address books*

9. Click Next to proceed to the exceptions screen, and select any appropriate exceptions to the rule.

10. Give the new rule a name and check the desired options, then click Finish to save the new rule and return to the opening Rules Wizard screen.

11. Click OK to close the Rules Wizard and return to the active Outlook window.

The next time mail arrives in your mailbox from any of the individuals you named in the new rule, it will be forwarded to the new team leader automatically. A banner is added to any messages forwarded by the rule indicating that the message was AutoForwarded.

There are a few things to be aware of when using automatic reply and forwarding rules. The first is that under certain circumstances the mail forwarding rule may not work. When this happens, it's probably one of two things (assuming the rule is valid). Either the message is marked as private, in which case it will not be forwarded in order to ensure the sender's privacy, or your Microsoft Exchange server version is 5.5 (or higher), which by default, does not allow Internet e-mail forwarding. If the problem is the latter, ask your network administrator to enable Internet e-mail forwarding.

The last thing to note is that mail forwarding rules are executed on the server, and as a result, do not place a copy of the forwarded message in your Sent Items folder. To add to the confusion, no banner is added to the original message indicating that a copy was forwarded to the new team leader. Unfortunately, you have to accept it on faith that Outlook is actually forwarding the messages. However, if you're from Missouri (the Show Me state) or just plain skeptical, you might want to check with the new recipient and see if forwarded messages from the indicated senders are making their way to his or her Inbox.

| Tip | *You can also use the Out of Office Assistant to automate replies and forwarding. For more information, see Chapter 19.* |

Using Voting Buttons

A handy feature available to Outlook C/W users on a Microsoft Exchange server is the ability to add voting buttons to an outgoing e-mail. A sender can pose a direct question in a message and provide voting buttons the recipient(s) can use to reply. Should you receive such a message, replying is almost too easy. As you can see in Figure 4-14, there's no need to type a response unless you want to.

Simply click the appropriate voting button, and a dialog box appears asking if you want to send the response immediately or edit the message first. Make your selection and click OK. If you choose to edit the message, a new message form appears with your response as the Subject line. Enter whatever text you want and click Send.

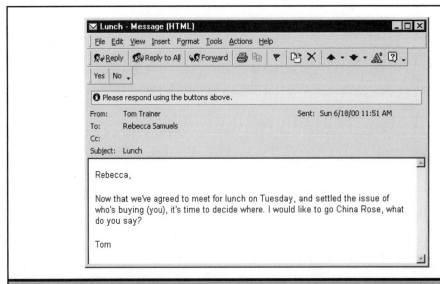

Figure 4-14.   *Outlook even alerts you to the fact that the message contains voting buttons*

MOUS EXAM PRACTICE

In this section, you learned the finer points of replying to and forwarding e-mail messages. Now you can practice the various methods described for replying and responding. You might want to send replies and forward non-sensitive messages to coworkers or friends who won't mind your practicing on them. Just to be on the safe side, add a note that lets them know what you're doing. Create some Rules Wizard rules that handle the tasks automatically, then follow up and see if what you think you're sending is what the recipients are actually receiving.

Handling Attachments

Ask any writer what his or her favorite e-mail feature is and chances are, the response you'll get is "file attachments." Thanks to the ability to send and receive fully formatted documents as e-mail attachments, deadlines are sometimes met with only seconds to spare. Sure, you can fax documents and have them arrive almost instantaneously. Ever tried faxing a 50-page chapter? Or looked at the phone bill after you've done it? Then there's overnight delivery. It's fast, but still costs an extra day, not to mention a rather substantial amount of money (especially when compared to the cost of e-mail attachments). When it comes to delivering most files, documents, spreadsheets, artwork, and so on, there's no comparison in time, work, and financial savings—e-mail beats the other methods hands down.

If you're thinking that receiving attachments is a breeze, since they arrive automatically with the messages to which they're attached, you're only partially right. To receive attachments, just sit back and wait for someone to send them. However, if you want to put those attachments to good use when they arrive, you'll need to learn to save them, open them, and in some cases, even put them to work.

Saving Attachments

Getting junk e-mail has, unfortunately, become all too common. Getting junk attachments, fortunately, is not at all common. Therefore, if you receive an attachment, chances are it's something you want. If it has more than a momentary value, you'll probably want to store it on your hard disk for future use. Saving an attachment you receive is easy if you follow these steps:

1. Open the e-mail message containing the attachment. You can also save an attachment from the Preview Pane, if the attachment appears in the Preview Pane.

2. Right-click the attachment and select Save As from the shortcut menu to open the Save Attachment dialog box, seen in Figure 4-15.

3. From the Save In drop-down list choose the folder in which to save the attachment.

Figure 4-15. *The Save Attachment dialog box lets you choose the folder in which to save the file*

Tip

You can change the default Save In folder to suit your needs. However, to do so you must edit the Windows registry. Warning! Editing the Windows registry should only be done by experienced Windows users, and a backup (export) of the registry should always be performed prior to any registry editing. After you perform your backup, locate the HKEY_CURRENT_USER\Software\Microsoft\Windows\CurrentVersion\Explorer\ User Shell Folders key and change the data in the Personal value to the path of the folder you want to designate as the new default Save In folder. The change won't take effect until you restart Windows.

4. Click Save to place a copy of the attachment in the selected folder, and return to Outlook.

5. Close the open message and you're all finished.

Now, whenever you need the attachment, simply return to the folder in which you stored it and retrieve it. If you have a number of attachments that you plan to save in different folders, you can open the Windows Explorer and drag attachments from messages to the desired folders. You can also drop attachments on the My Documents or Favorites shortcuts in the Other Shortcuts group.

Opening Attachments

If the program with which the attachment is associated is installed on your computer, you can open the attachment by double-clicking it. In other words, if you have Microsoft Word installed on your computer, you can open a Word document you receive as an attachment by double-clicking the file. As soon as you double-click an attachment, the associated program launches and opens the file. To open an attachment in the Preview Pane, you can either double-click the attachment or click the paperclip icon in the top right corner of the Preview Pane header and select the attachment from the list.

Note

Files or objects opened in the Preview Pane are read-only, which means they can be viewed, but they cannot be modified. If you want to edit an attachment, you must first open the message to which the object is attached, and then open the attachment.

You can also open attachments by right-clicking the attachment and selecting Open from the shortcut menu that appears. If Quick View appears on the menu as one of the choices, this means there is a file viewer available to display the file without launching the associated program. However, in order to edit the file you'll have to have the associated program installed.

Using Outlook Items Received as Attachments

One of the nice things about using Outlook is the fact that you can share all kinds of information with other Outlook users. The ability to add Outlook items such as contacts, appointments, tasks, and notes to e-mail messages makes exchanging data almost fun, and most certainly, a snap. When you receive an Outlook item as an attachment, all you have to do is drag it to the appropriate folder or Outlook Bar shortcut and drop it. The item becomes part of that folder.

For example, suppose a coworker sends you a contact record from her Contacts database. To add it to your Contacts database, simply drag it to the Contacts shortcut icon on the Outlook Bar or the Contacts folder in the Folder List and drop it. It's added to your Contacts database automatically.

You can also drag Outlook item attachments to folders of a different type (for example, a Contact record to the Calendar folder) to create a new item using the information contained in the attached item.

MOUS EXAM PRACTICE

In this section, you learned how to deal with attachments, an integral part of e-mail management. Now ask friends and coworkers to send you various types of attachments (keep them as small as possible to avoid taking up a lot of bandwidth and storage space) that you can practice on. Make sure you get a selection of different file types and Outlook items. Try your hand at saving them to the hard disk, opening them, viewing them, and even editing them. When you receive Outlook items, add some of them to the appropriate folder and use others to create new items using the item information.

Creating Address Book Entries from Received Mail

Adding a sender's or fellow recipient's e-mail address to your Contacts folder is not really a major chore, but why waste your time entering it manually when you can have Outlook do the work for you? Save your energy and time for something more productive.

To add an address from an e-mail message into your Contacts folder, open the message, right-click the address you want to enter, and select Add To Contacts. Immediately, a new Contact form opens with the user's name and e-mail address already entered. You can add other information now or at some time in the future. Click Save and Close to save the new Contact and return to the active Outlook window.

Printing Messages

When you receive a great compliment via e-mail, or one of the kids sends you a great poem or letter, you might want to print a hard copy you can carry around and show everyone.

All you have to do to print an e-mail message is open the message and click the Print button. Next thing you know, you've got a hard copy. If you're connected to more than one printer or if you want to change the printer properties, you can open the Print dialog box shown in Figure 4-16 by choosing File | Print from the message form Standard toolbar.

Figure 4-16. *The Print dialog box enables you to choose the printer and set print options*

Note *If you're printing an HTML message, the Print dialog box that appears is a little different from the one pictured in Figure 4-16.*

If you're connected to multiple printers, select the printer from the Printer Name drop-down list. Click the Properties button to modify the settings for the printer you select. What you see in this dialog box depends entirely on the make and model of the printer you select. The other options include the number of pages to print of a multiple-page document as well as the number of copies you want to print. In the Print dialog box displayed from Plain Text and Rich Text messages (see Figure 4-16), you can also modify the page setup and even define your own print styles.

Exam | MOUS Exam Objectives Explored in Chapter 4

Objective	Activity	Heading
OL2000.1.1	Read mail	"Opening and Reading E-mail"
OL2000.1.6	Use mail features (reply, forward)	"Responding to and Forwarding Messages"
OL2000.1.12	Work with attachments	"Handling Attachments"
OL2000.2.3	Set viewing options	"Configuring the Inbox"

The
Complete
Reference

Outlook 2000

Chapter 5

Tracking and Managing Mail

If the only service Outlook e-mail provided was the sending and receiving of messages and attachments, it would still be an exceptional communication tool. However, it doesn't stop there. In addition to sending and receiving mail, Outlook also offers a powerful set of e-mail management and tracking features, which is what this chapter is all about. Here you'll discover ways to store, view, and manipulate e-mail messages you send and receive. You'll even learn to automate e-mail handling by using the Rules Wizard.

Viewing E-mail

One of the things frequently taken for granted is the way information appears on the screen. When you open an Outlook mail folder, whether it's the Inbox, Outbox, or Sent Items folder, the message data appears in the Information viewer, giving you a quick glimpse of the folder contents. This is usually the first place you look when searching for a stray piece of e-mail. Using the Advanced Find feature is great if it's a complex search, but when you know the message you're searching for is there, and you know who sent it and approximately when it arrived, it's much easier to just take a quick peek in the folder.

Now, take a closer look at the Messages view, the default view of the Inbox, and see what makes it tick. The first thing to do is pick it apart and examine each of its elements. You'll soon see that each part, taken separately, doesn't amount to much, but put them all together and you've got a powerful tool for displaying and manipulating your Inbox information (see Figure 5-1).

Note	*All of the Inbox views, with the exception of the Message Timeline, incorporate the same basic elements.*

The Messages view is practically the same in all the mail folders. The only difference is that the Inbox folder includes From and Received information, whereas the other mail folders display To and Sent data. This, of course, makes sense since the Inbox holds incoming mail and the Outbox, Drafts, and Sent Items folders contain outgoing mail.

If you understand the various pieces of information that make up the Messages view, a single glance can tell you a lot about the messages in your Inbox:

■ **Importance**   The Importance column indicates whether the message is (according to the sender) of high, normal, or low importance. High and low importance are indicated by symbols (see Table 5-1), while normal importance is indicated by the lack of a symbol.

■ **Icon**   The Icon column indicates whether a message has been opened or not, what type of message it is, and any action that has been taken. See Table 5-1 for an explanation of the symbols used.

Figure 5-1. *The Messages view offers a wealth of information about the contents of your Inbox*

- ■ **Flag Status** A red flag in this column indicates the message has been flagged for follow-up either by the sender or by you. A gray flag in this column indicates the follow-up has been performed and marked completed.

- ■ **Attachment** If the message has one or more attachments, a paperclip icon appears in this column.

- ■ **From** Here you'll find the sender's name. This does not include the sender's e-mail address, but rather the display name on the mailbox or Internet mail account the sender uses.

- **Subject**   The message's Subject line text appears in this column.
- **Received**   This column includes the date and time the message was received. One thing to note about this information is that it's determined not by your computer, but rather by the Microsoft Exchange server. Since your mailbox is on the server, the date and time in the Received column reflect the date and time set on the Microsoft Exchange server. In other words, if the server is an hour faster than your computer, you'll appear to be receiving messages from the future.

As you can see, each of the columns provides a small piece of information. Together they present a comprehensive view of your Inbox contents. For an explanation of the symbols that appear in each column, see Table 5-1 and Table 5-2. These symbols are used in all Inbox views, including the Message Timeline view.

The symbols in Table 5-1 can be found in both the C/W and the IMO configurations of Outlook 2000. However, for those users on a Microsoft Exchange Server network, the additional symbols shown in Table 5-2 may appear as well.

This Symbol	In This Column	Means
!	Importance	The message has a high importance or priority (according to the sender).
↓	Importance	The message has a low importance or priority (according to the sender).
✉	Icon	The message has been read.
✉	Icon	The message is unread.
✉	Icon	The message has been forwarded.
✉	Icon	The message has been replied to.
✉	Icon	The message is unsent, saved, or both.
✉	Icon	The message is encrypted.

Table 5-1.   *Standard Symbols Used in Mail Folders*

This Symbol	In This Column	Means
	Icon	The message contains a digital signature.
	Icon	The message contains an invalid digital signature.
	Icon	The message is a Microsoft Mail 3.x form.
	Icon	The message is a meeting request.
	Icon	The message is a meeting request that has been accepted.
	Icon	The message is a meeting request that has been tentatively accepted.
	Icon	The message is a meeting request that has been declined.
	Icon	The message is a cancelled meeting notice.
	Icon	The message is a task request.
	Icon	The message is a task request that has been accepted.
	Icon	The message is a task request that has been declined.
	Flag Status	The message has been flagged for follow-up.
	Flag Status	The message is flagged as complete.
	Attachment	The message has an attachment.

Table 5-1. *Standard Symbols Used in Mail Folders* (continued)

This Symbol	In This Column	Means
	Icon	The message has been posted to a folder.
	Icon	An attempt to recall the message was made.
	Icon	The message was successfully recalled.
	Icon	The message recall failed.
	Icon	The message is a delivery receipt for a message successfully delivered.
	Icon	The message is a read receipt for a message that has been read.
	Icon	The message is a delivery receipt for a message that was not delivered.
	Icon	The message is a read receipt for a message that has not been read.
	Icon	The message is a Remote Mail header only.
	Icon	The Remote Mail header is marked for download of the actual message.
	Icon	The Remote Mail header is marked for copy and download of the actual message.
	Icon	The message is a conflict notification for an offline folder item.

Table 5-2.   *Microsoft Exchange Server Symbols Used in Mail Folders*

If you find the symbols confusing, you can change three of the four columns (Importance, Flag Status, and Attachment) that display symbols to display text instead. Right-click the desired column header and select Format Columns to open the Format Columns dialog box.

From the Format drop-down list, select Text With Popup List for the Importance or Flag Status column. The Attachment column has several choices for text. After you make your choice, click OK to save the change and return to the Inbox. Since the columns don't automatically resize themselves (at least not by default), you'll have to widen the column to see the text. Move the mouse pointer to the vertical line separating the column header from the next column until the mouse pointer turns into a crosshair with a pair of double-sided arrows pointing left and right.

Hold down the left mouse button and drag to the right to widen the column and display the text that now replaces the symbol.

 You can also use the Best Fit command to resize the column to accommodate either the column name or the longest field entry in the column, whichever is longer. Right-click the column header and select Best Fit from the shortcut menu.

If you change your mind and decide you'd rather have the symbol, return to the Format Columns dialog box and choose Bitmap With Popup List from the Format drop-down list. The column returns to its original width.

Sorting E-mail

 Before jumping into sorting, you should familiarize yourself with the concepts and terms used. The first thing to understand is that the Inbox, like the other Outlook folders, is primarily a database. A database is a storage container for information. It is composed of individual records, which in turn are composed of fields. Databases are all around you. Take a cookbook, for example. The cookbook (the database) is a collection of recipes (the records), which contain ingredients and steps (the fields).

The Inbox database contains messages, which are the records. Each message is comprised of fields such as From, To, Cc, Subject, Received, and so on. The fields displayed in the Messages view are Importance, Icon, Flag Status, Attachment, From, Subject, and Received. These fields are used to perform a sort. Sorting involves rearranging the order in which the records (messages in this case) appear based on the information contained in one or more fields. Understanding the following terms will make sorting a breeze:

- **Sort order**   The order in which the messages (records) are arranged in the Inbox. The sort order, which is determined by the field(s) selected for the sort, can either be ascending or descending.

- **Ascending**   Records are arranged from first to last as determined by the first character of the sort field. An ascending alphabetical listing is sorted from A to Z, with A appearing at the top of the list and Z appearing at the bottom. A numerical listing with an ascending sort order displays the lowest numbers at the top and the highest at the bottom. For example, if you use the From field to do an ascending sort, Athena appears at the top of the Message viewer, while Zeus appears at the bottom. If you use the Received field, and have messages ranging from May 1st to May 31st, May 1st appears at the top of the view, and May 31st at the bottom.

- **Descending**   This one's easy—it's the opposite of ascending. Z appears at the top of the list and A drops to last place.

| Note |

The hierarchy of internal data fields such as Importance, Icon, Flag Status, and Attachment is predetermined, and has nothing to do with alphabetical or numeric considerations.

By default, the Messages view displays your e-mail messages in the order of their Received date/time information. The default sort order is descending, which means the most recent messages appear at the top of the list. As handy as this may be, there will undoubtedly be times when you want to see the order reversed, or when you want to use a different sort criterion altogether, such as sender, subject, or message type. Fortunately, changing the sort order in Outlook is as easy as it is flexible.

To begin with, you can change the sort order or criterion with a single mouse click. In the default view, Messages, you can change the sort order from descending to ascending (oldest messages first) simply by clicking the header on the Received column. The recessed triangle (arrow) in the header changes from pointing downward (descending) to pointing upward (ascending).

In addition to changing the sort order, you can also change the sort criterion with a click of your mouse. Click any of the column headers to sort the Inbox by that particular piece of information. For example, if you want the messages sorted by sender, click the From column header. The Inbox is immediately sorted by sender in ascending order. The default sort order for all Inbox columns except Received is ascending. If you want to change the sort order to descending, click the header again, and the triangle now points in the opposite direction.

| From   / |

Ascending sort

| From   ▽ |

Descending sort

Tip   *The Importance, Icon, Flag Status, and Attachment column headers do not display the recessed triangle indicating sort order, which means you may have difficulty determining whether the order is ascending or descending. Right-click the column header and select Sort Ascending or Sort Descending to be sure you've got the sort order you want.*

What makes the sort feature even handier is the fact that you're not limited to sorting by a single field. You can sort by as many as four fields at one time. This means that if you have a lot of messages of varying types and importance from each of your senders, you can perform an ascending sort by Importance to ensure the high priority messages appear at the top of the Inbox. Then do an ascending subsort by From to see all high priority (from the Importance sort) messages by Angela first, followed by all high priority messages from Bill next, and so on. If you're so inclined, you can then do an additional descending subsort by Received to see all the high priority messages from Angela, starting with the most recent, followed by all the high priority messages from Bill, starting with the most recent, and so on.

When performing multiple sorts, Outlook applies additional subsorts to the existing sorts. The way you perform a sort using multiple fields is almost as easy as sorting by a single field. All you have to do to include a column in the sort is hold the SHIFT key down while clicking the column header. In the preceding example, you would start by right-clicking the Importance column header and selecting Sort Ascending. Next, hold down the SHIFT key and click the From column header. Still holding the SHIFT key down, click the Received column header. Your Inbox should now be sorted first by Importance, next by From, and finally by Received. As you've by now surmised, holding down the SHIFT key retains the existing sort criteria, and adds additional field(s) as subsort criteria.

Note   *To change the order (ascending or descending) of a secondary sort field, you can click the column header while holding the SHIFT key.*

In addition to using simple sorts, there is another Outlook feature called grouping. It allows you to add messages to specific groups for easier sorting and viewing. For more information on grouping and sorting, see Chapter 22.

One last thing to keep in mind: You can sort any mail folder, including Drafts, Outbox, Sent Items, or a custom folder you create to hold mail, using the techniques described here. As a matter of fact, these sorting methods work on any table view (a view with columns and rows) in Outlook.

MOUS EXAM PRACTICE

In this section, you learned about sorting, a helpful tool for organizing all your e-mail. Now spend a little time honing your sorting skills. First, practice sorting your Inbox and other mail folders. Start with a simple sort using the From field. That generally provides the clearest illustration of sorting. Next, change the sort order from ascending to descending or vice versa. Move on to the other fields and sort each of them to see what happens. Don't forget, sorting the fields with symbols can be confusing unless you right-click the column header and choose the sort order from the shortcut menu. Finally, try your hand at using multiple sort criteria.

Locating E-mail Messages

The most direct method for locating messages is to use the Outlook Find feature, which comes in two flavors, Find and Advanced Find. Find is a simple, one-criterion text search that is quick and dirty. However, it's not very robust.

To use the Find feature, click the Find button on the Standard toolbar. This opens the Find window just shown. Now all you have to do is enter the text you want to search for, indicate whether or not you want the search to include all text fields in the message, and click Find Now. The results of the search are displayed in the Information viewer below the Find window.

If your search was successful, you can close the Find window and go about your business. However, if the message(s) you were looking for did not appear, you can try again, or, if you're ready to bring out the big guns, you can use Advanced Find (see Figure 5-2).

While the Find feature automatically looks in the current folder, the Advanced Find dialog box gives you the option of searching item or file types no matter which folder they reside in. In addition, since the results may come from multiple folders, the found

Figure 5-2.   *Use Advanced Find when the Find feature just isn't enough*

messages are displayed in a separate window at the bottom of the Advanced Find dialog box (see Figure 5-2).

Note   *When adding search criteria to the Advanced Find dialog box, be advised that there is an implied AND between every condition you add. In other words, a search with more than one criterion finds only those messages that meet* **all** *the search criteria.*

To use the Advanced Find feature to locate messages, follow these steps:

1. Press CTRL-SHIFT-F, or right-click the Folder banner and choose Advanced Find, to display the Advanced Find dialog box.

Tip   *You can also right-click a shortcut in the Outlook Bar and choose Advanced Find from the shortcut menu or choose Tools | Advanced Find.*

2. Select Messages from the Look For drop-down list.

3. To change the folder in which the search is conducted or to include additional folders, click the Browse button to display the Select Folder(s) dialog box, seen in Figure 5-3.

4. Check each folder you want to include in the search.

5. Enter the search criteria in the remaining options on the Messages tab. Your choices include:

   ■ **Search for the word(s)** Type the words, characters, or phrases you want to search for. One nice thing about this field is that it retains previously entered data for use at a later time. Open the drop-down list to see a selection of previously used words or phrases.

   ■ **In** Indicate which text fields you want to include in the search for the designated text. Like the Search For The Word(s) field, the In field also retains previously entered search data that can be accessed from its drop-down list.

   ■ **From** If you want to find messages from specific senders, enter their display names or e-mail addresses here. You can also add senders by

Figure 5-3.   *You can perform the search on as many folders as you like*

clicking the From button to display the Select Names dialog box, which provides access to all your address books. However, be careful not to use any display names that contain additional text beyond the actual name. For example, (E-mail) is automatically added to the name of each individual in the Contacts list who has an e-mail address. Consequently, when the search is performed, Outlook looks for only those messages that contain the name *and* the appended text.

■ **Sent To**   This field works the same as the From field, including the caveat about using the Contacts list to select names. The only difference between the two is that the names entered here are searched for in the To, Cc or Bcc fields in outgoing messages.

■ **Where I am**   Indicate whether you're the only recipient, one of multiple recipients in the To field, or one of multiple recipients in the Cc field.

■ **Time**   Use this field to search on the basis of a date field, such as Received, Sent or Due. Select the date field from the first drop-down list, and the time frame from the second drop-down list.

6. Click the More Choices tab to view additional search options (see Figure 5-4).

Figure 5-4.   *The More Choices tab provides just that—more choices for narrowing your search*

COMMUNICATING WITH E-MAIL

7. Set the More Choices search criteria. Your options include:

- **Categories**   If you assign messages to categories, enter the category or categories to which the messages you're looking for are assigned. There is one thing to note about this field. If you perform a search that includes multiple categories, it will locate not only messages assigned to both, but also messages assigned to either. This is because Outlook sticks an implied OR between multiple selections in this field. Unfortunately, there's no way around it.

- **Only items that are**   You can choose to search for messages that have been read or messages that remain unread. Use the drop-down list to make your selection.

- **Only items with**   This option lets you include or exclude items that contain attachments.

- **Whose importance is**   If you know the Importance status of the message(s), indicate by making your selection from this drop-down list.

- **Match case**   If you've entered text in the Search For The Word(s) field on the Messages tab, you can use this option to search only for those instances of the word(s) that match the exact case of the text you entered. Check the option to enable it.

- **Size (kilobytes)**   This option can be helpful if you know that you received a rather large attachment with your message. Indicate an operator (equals, between, less than, or greater than) and the size.

8. Set the options on the Advanced tab. For more information on setting Advanced options, see Chapter 22.

9. Click Find Now to perform the search. As you can see in Figure 5-5, the results are displayed in a window appended to the Advanced Find dialog box.

Okay, now that you've found the messages you're looking for, what are you going to do with them? Fortunately, you've got quite a few options. You can open them, print them, even move, delete, or reply to them. Right-click one of the messages to display the shortcut menu with available commands.

Figure 5-5.   *Advanced Find displays header information for all messages meeting your search criteria*

COMMUNICATING
WITH E-MAIL

Note   *If you receive a task request, meeting request, or an e-mail message using voting buttons, you'll also find the related options on the shortcut menu. For example, the shortcut menu displayed when you right-click a task request includes Accept and Decline. A meeting request shortcut menu includes Accept, Tentative, and Decline. A voting button message might contain Yes, No, and Maybe, or whatever other choices the sender included. If you get a message from the System Administrator, the Reply and Reply To All commands are missing because these messages are automatically generated.*

In addition to the shortcut menu of commands, the menu bar in the Advanced Find dialog box provides a large selection of commands. While it's not as extensive as the commands available in the Inbox, there's still quite a bit you can accomplish using the Advanced Find menu bar. One last thing—if you want to start over, click the New Search button to clear the existing search criteria and start from scratch.

In this section, you learned how to use the Find and Advanced Find features. Now try your hand at searching for messages. Begin by performing a simple text search using the Find feature. Try locating messages with certain data in the various message text fields (Subject, To, Cc, the message body). When you're comfortable with the Find feature, move on to Advanced Find. Search for messages containing a single criterion. Try all the different options. If you don't have mail that meets different criteria, send yourself some. Add attachments, categories, importance levels, or whatever you need. After you find the messages you searched for, perform actions on them using the shortcut menu. Finally, try using some of the commands located on the Advanced Find menu bar.

Applying Filters

The Filter feature provides a means for displaying only selected messages in a folder, while hiding the rest. Filtering is basically an Advanced Find performed on a single folder. Messages that meet the filter (search) conditions appear. Those that fail to meet the conditions are hidden.

As you can see in the following illustration, the Filter dialog box is a stripped down version of the Advanced Find dialog box. Missing are the Look For and In options, as well as the Browse, Find Now, Stop, and New Search buttons, and the menu bar of commands.

To filter messages, follow these steps:

1. Right-click a blank spot on the Inbox Information viewer below the last message and select Filter to open the Filter dialog box, shown here. You can also open the Filter dialog box by right-clicking a column header, selecting Customize Current View and clicking the Filter button on the View Summary dialog box.

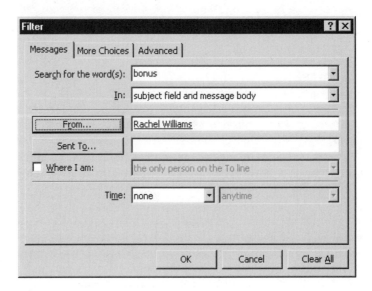

2. Enter the filter conditions in the Messages tab. See the earlier section entitled "Locating E-mail Messages" for a detailed explanation of each option.

Remember   *Don't add any names that have additional text appended to them, such as Contacts list entries that include (E-mail) or (Business Fax). If you do, Outlook will search for the appended text and, when it doesn't find it, exclude the messages even though they may be from the correct party.*

3. Set the filter conditions on the More Choices tab. Again, see the section "Locating E-mail Messages" for detailed explanations of these options.

4. Set the options on the Advanced tab to suit your needs. For details on Advanced options, see Chapter 22.

5. Click OK to filter out all messages that do not meet the criteria you established in the Filter dialog box.

When you return to the Inbox or other folder to which you've applied the filter, you'll notice the words (Filter Applied) on the right side of the Folder banner. This comes in handy when you have one of those days and open your Inbox only to find most of your messages missing. Before you panic, check the Folder banner and see if you forgot to remove your last filter.

If the filter doesn't work as anticipated, open the Filter dialog box and carefully examine the conditions you've set. Remember, if your filter contains multiple conditions, the message must meet all conditions or it is excluded. Another common problem encountered by everyone, including the experts, is the ever-popular typo. A single misspelling or a transposed number can ruin an otherwise perfect filter.

To remove a filter, reopen the Filter dialog box and click Clear All. Then click OK to return to the active Outlook folder. The filter is removed, all your records reappear, and the (Filter Applied) disappears from the Folder banner.

> **MOUS EXAM PRACTICE**
> *In this section, you learned to work with filters, a powerful tool for finding and viewing messages based on the particular criteria you define. Now practice applying all sorts of conditions to your messages to get a feel for exactly how conditions are met and applied. Try creating a filter with a single condition first. Then add a second condition, and then a third, and so on, until you understand how filtering works.*

Switching Views

The Inbox and other mail folders come with a selection of predesigned views. The Message view is the default view for all Outlook mail folders. However, you may find that one of the other views provides a more useful display of your folder contents. To switch between views, choose View | Current View to display the submenu of available views, as shown in Figure 5-6.

Actually, all but the last, Message Timeline, are variations on the original view, Messages. In most cases, the variation is the application of a filter or a grouping. Occasionally, additional fields are added, as in the case of the By Follow-Up Flag view.

The Message Timeline view, shown here, provides an actual timeline on which the individual messages are plotted according to the Received field.

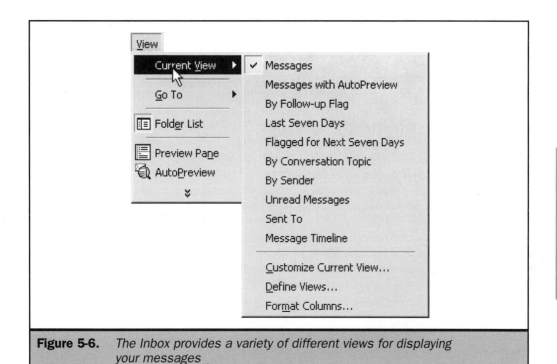

Figure 5-6.   *The Inbox provides a variety of different views for displaying your messages.*

Another way to change views is by displaying the Advanced toolbar. Right-click anywhere on the Standard toolbar and choose Advanced from the shortcut menu that appears. The Advanced toolbar includes a Current View drop-down list, which contains all the views available in the current folder. You can even add the Current View drop-down list to the Standard or other toolbar if you want. See Chapter 23 for details on adding commands to toolbars.

Following Message Threads or Conversations

If you spend any time on newsgroups you're probably familiar with message threads. They are a series of messages all spawned by a single message. Threads include the original message, responses to the original message, responses to the responses, and so on. Message threads, or conversations—as Microsoft likes to call them—are now a feature of Outlook.

Here's the way it works. Every original message contains a hidden field called Conversation, which holds a duplicate of the text entered in the Subject field. When you forward or reply to a message, the text in the Conversation field of the original message is automatically assigned to the Conversation field of the response or forward. The same Conversation field data is passed on to each subsequent reply or forward for as long as the responses/forwards continue. Since the information is contained in a separate Conversation field, you can change the Subject field and still retain the link to the conversation.

As handy as this feature is, there are a couple of things that can throw a monkey wrench into the works. The first is two original messages with identical Subject lines, and therefore, identical Conversation fields. In that case, all messages relating to either will show up in the same message thread or conversation. There's no way around it.

The second thing that can bollix up the works is mail responses or forwards from the Internet. You're fine as long as the responder doesn't change the Subject line. When Outlook receives a reply or forward from an Internet mail account, it strips RE or FW from the Subject line and enters the remaining text in the Conversation field. If there's no RE or FW it merely inserts the Subject line in the Conversation field.

Now that you understand what message threads are, the next step is to utilize them. Suppose you run into a complex problem and send out a message requesting help from several co-workers, who either respond or forward your note to someone else who might have an answer. By the time you're done, you may have a large number of responses, many of which could possibly contain helpful information. Rather than attempting to sort or apply filters, you can easily gather all the messages together by locating the conversation.

It's actually rather simple. Right-click any message and select Find All | Related Messages to open the Advanced Find dialog box with the search conditions automatically entered on the Advanced tab (see Figure 5-7). The search is conducted automatically, so there's no need for you to do anything except sit back and wait for the results.

You can also locate all messages in a conversation by selecting one message from the thread and then choosing Actions | Find All | Related Messages from the Menu bar to open the Advanced Find dialog box, and start the search.

Storing E-mail Messages

One reason for e-mail's vast popularity is that it provides an electronic "paper trail" of all your important communications. What's especially nice is that, unlike actual paper communications, you can store a vast quantity of e-mail information in a thimbleful of space. As your collection of important e-mail grows, it will lose its value if it's not readily available when you need it. Therefore, you should devise and execute a plan for storing your e-mail so you have ready access to it.

Note *If you're wondering why it's necessary to organize your e-mail at all since Outlook provides such powerful sorting, searching, and filtering tools, the answer is simple. If you can't remember the sender, subject, or other important piece of information that will enable you to find the message(s), those powerful tools will be about as useful as an electric blanket on a wilderness trek. The other thing to consider is efficiency. The larger the number of messages that have to be searched, the longer the search takes, and the greater the chance you'll also turn up messages you don't really want.*

Figure 5-7. *The Advanced Find searches for all messages with matching data in the Conversation field*

The storage system provided by Outlook is not unlike the typical filing cabinet storage system used for paper documents. It's just cleaner, quicker, completely searchable, and takes up no floor space at all. Outlook, as you already know, is a folder-based program. Everything in Outlook is stored in a folder. By default, the only folders that exist are Calendar, Contacts, Deleted Items, Drafts, Inbox, Journal, Notes, Outbox, Sent Items, and Tasks. Fortunately, you are by no means limited to just those ten folders. As a matter of fact, the number of folders you can have is theoretically unlimited. However, folders stored on the Microsoft Exchange server are limited by three factors: the version of Microsoft Exchange running on the server, the hard disk space available on the server, and any restrictions placed on mailbox folder size by the administrator. If you use Personal Folders to store information, you are limited by the amount of disk space on your computer.

To effectively store your important e-mail, you should create a system of Outlook folders that separates mail either by sender, subject, or some other criterion that suits your purpose. For example, you might create one folder called Vendors and another called Customers. You could then create a series of subfolders under Vendors for each vendor you buy from, and a series of subfolders under Customers for each customer you sell to. Regardless of the system you devise, the process for creating and managing the folders is the same.

Creating Mail Folders

Creating mail folders in Outlook is so easy that even your boss could do it. Here's all you have to do:

1. Press CTRL-SHIFT-E, or right-click the Folder banner, or a folder in the Folder List and select New Folder, to open the Create New Folder dialog box, shown in Figure 5-8.

2. Enter a name for the new folder. Make the name brief and descriptive so you don't have trouble recognizing it in the future. This may sound silly when you only have a few folders in your mailbox or Personal Folders, but as the number of folders grows so does the potential for confusion.

Figure 5-8. *Use the Create New Folder dialog box to indicate the name, content type, and location of the new folder*

3. Select Mail Items from the Folder Contains drop-down list. Since each folder is a separate database in Outlook, it can hold only one type of information.

4. In the Select Where To Place The Folder list, choose the folder to which you want to add the new folder. If you want to create a new folder at the same level as the existing folders, select Mailbox.

5. Click OK to create the new folder. The first time (and every time, unless you disable the feature), the Add Shortcut To Outlook Bar? dialog box appears.

6. Click Yes if you want a shortcut to the folder added to the Outlook Bar.

To stop Outlook from displaying this dialog box each time you create a new folder, check the Don't Prompt Me About This Again option.

 If you already have an existing mail folder that you've customized with permissions, rules, forms, and views, you can create a new folder that contains the same customizations by right-clicking the folder you want to copy and selecting Copy [folder name] from the shortcut menu. If you only want to copy certain customizations from the original folder, choose File | Folder | Copy Folder Design to open the Copy Design 7From dialog box.

 MOUS EXAM PRACTICE
In this section, you discovered how to create new storage folders for your e-mail. Now take some time to outline an e-mail storage plan. Then implement it by naming and creating the necessary folders in the appropriate locations. Customize at least one folder and use the Copy and Copy Folder Design commands to see exactly what gets carried over.

Moving and Copying Messages

 The next step in organizing your e-mail messages is to move the messages you want to keep into your new storage system. The two main commands you'll need to master for manipulating your messages are Move to Folder and Copy to Folder. You might also brush up on Cut, Copy, and Paste, as well as your drag and drop skills since you can also use them to move and copy messages.

The first thing to do is select the messages you want to cut or copy. To select a single message, click the message to highlight it. To select multiple adjacent messages, click the first message in the series, hold down the SHIFT key, and select the last message in the series. Outlook automatically selects everything in between. You can select multiple non-adjacent messages by selecting the first message, and then holding down the CTRL key while selecting additional messages.

To move messages with the Move To Folder command, highlight and press CTRL-SHIFT-V to open the Move Items dialog box.

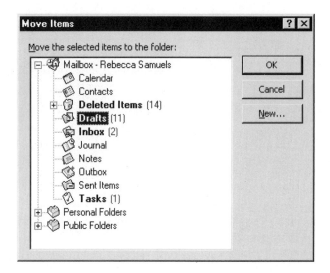

| Tip | *You can also right-click the highlighted message(s) and select Move to Folder from the shortcut menu that appears, or you can choose Edit | Move to Folder.* |

In the Move Items dialog box, select the folder to which you want to move the highlighted messages, and click OK to complete the move and return to the active Outlook window. If you don't see an appropriate folder to move the messages into, you can create a new folder on the fly. Click the New button to open the Create New Folder dialog box. Enter a name for the new folder, leave the folder type as Mail Items, and select the location for the new folder. Finally, click OK to create the new folder and return to the Move Items dialog box, where the new folder now appears in the list. If this is the first folder you've created, you'll be prompted to add a shortcut to the Outlook Bar for the new folder. Make your choice and proceed.

The Copy to Folder option works in a similar fashion. Highlight the messages to copy and choose Edit | Copy to Folder to display the Copy Items dialog box.

As you can see, the Copy to Folder dialog box appears identical to the Move to Folder dialog box except for its name. Choose the folder in which you want to place a copy of the selected messages and click OK to complete the copy.

Although Outlook has specific commands for moving and copying messages from one folder to another, many users find drag and drop is the quickest and easiest way to get the job done. Display the Folder List, open the folder from which you want to move messages, highlight the messages you want to move, drag them to the Folder List, and drop them on the folder you want to move them to. You can also use drag and drop to copy folders, however, you use the right mouse button to drag them to the new folder. When you release the right mouse button to drop the messages, choose Copy from the shortcut menu that appears.

Now, if you're an experienced word processor user, you'll be happy to know that you can use Cut, Copy, and Paste to move and copy messages as well. Highlight the messages you want to move, press CTRL-X to cut or CTRL-C to copy, move to the target folder, and press CTRL-V to paste the messages. You can also invoke the Cut, Copy, and Paste commands from the Edit menu if you prefer.

Deleting Messages

If storing messages is not in the plans, you may want to do a little housekeeping and get rid of all the unwanted messages hanging around taking up space. Remember, there's probably a size limit on your mailbox, imposed by your system administrator. Therefore, you should limit the amount of unnecessary e-mail you retain. Deleting messages is as simple as highlighting them and pressing the DELETE key. Of course, like most other tasks in Outlook, there are a number of different ways to delete messages. You can highlight the messages and:

- Press CTRL-D.
- Right-click and select DELETE from the shortcut menu.
- Click the Delete button on the Standard toolbar.
- Choose Edit | Delete from the Menu bar.
- Drag them to the Deleted Items folder.

Take your choice—they all accomplish the job of tossing your unwanted messages in the Deleted Items folder. However, before proceeding, there are a couple of things you should know about the Deleted Items folder. First of all, it's actually a way station for messages on their way into the electronic ether. The messages (or other Outlook items) are not really deleted, they're just transferred here to await your final decision. Should you change your mind about eliminating a message, you can open the Deleted Items folder and retrieve it. That's the good news.

Note   *The Deleted Items folder is like any other Outlook folder. You can set its properties, add subfolders to it, and do practically anything with it that you can do to other Outlook folders.*

The bad news is that, in effect, all you've done by deleting a message is move it from one Outlook folder to another. You haven't really cleaned up your mailbox at all. It's kind of like straightening up by throwing everything in the closet and slamming the door shut. So, if you're trying to reduce the size of your mailbox, you'll have to go one step further and empty the Deleted Items folder. Fortunately, this is a simple matter of right-clicking the Deleted Items folder or the Deleted Items shortcut on the Outlook Bar and selecting Empty "Deleted Items" Folder from the shortcut menu. You'll also find the same command on the Tools menu. To ensure you really want to delete the contents of the Deleted Items folder, Outlook asks you to confirm your decision.

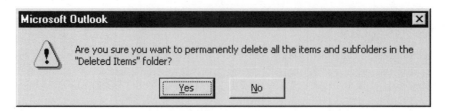

Outlook provides one additional safety net in case you're having a really bad day and empty your Deleted Items folder while dazed and confused. It's the Recover Deleted Items command. Highlight the Deleted Items folder and choose Tools | Recover Deleted Items to open the Recover Deleted Items From – Deleted Items dialog box, shown in Figure 5-9.

Since the Recover Deleted Items only works on items stored on a Microsoft Exchange server, the command is not available in the IMO configuration.

Select the items you want to recover and click the Recover Selected Messages button. Voila! Your messages are restored to your Deleted Items folder.

 If the Recover Deleted Items From – Deleted Items dialog box doesn't contain the messages you're looking for, the reason is probably that the time limit for retaining deleted items on the server has expired. Check with your system administrator about the length of time deleted items remain on the server, and if the missing messages can be recovered from a server backup.

The Recover Deleted Items From – Deleted Items dialog box has an additional feature that enables you to permanently delete sensitive messages so that they can

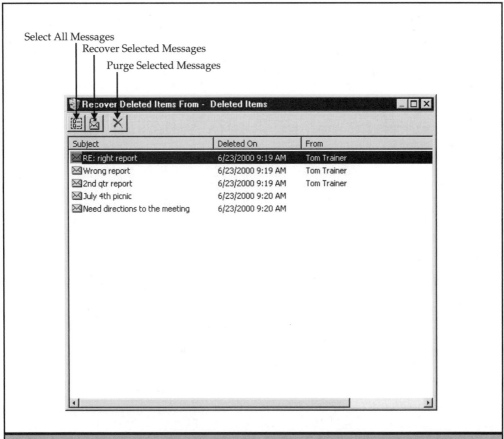

Figure 5-9. *The Recover Deleted Items From – Deleted Items dialog box gives you a second chance to save files you mistakenly deleted*

COMMUNICATING
WITH E-MAIL

never be recovered. It's called Purge. Select the message(s) you want to send into electronic oblivion and click the Purge Selected Messages button.

Modifying Incoming Message Options

Contrary to what many users think, message options are not only for outgoing messages. There are several ways you can organize your incoming messages by changing their options. This includes changing the Importance level, adding or removing flags, changing the expiration date, and assigning messages to contacts and categories.

Reprioritizing Messages

If you've received any mail marked with a high Importance level, you've probably realized that not everyone has the same priorities. What seems extremely important to one person may be of little or no consequence to another. Therefore, when you receive e-mail messages whose Importance setting is inappropriate according to your standards, you can change it.

All you have to do is right-click the message, select Options from the shortcut menu and choose a different Importance level from the Importance drop-down list. Then click Close to effect the change. Before returning you to the active window, Outlook asks if you want to save the changes. Click Yes to save the new Importance level. When you return to the active window, you'll see the Importance column now reflects the new Importance level.

Flagging Received E-mail for Future Action (or Inaction)

Follow-up flags serve the purpose of adding comments and reminders to a message, notifying the recipient of any additional action that should be taken concerning the message. There are any number of reasons for changing the flagged status of incoming messages. You may want to add a flag to remind yourself to follow up on the message, or you may want to change the comment or reminder time on a message with an existing flag. Of course, when you've completed the follow-up action, you'll want to either mark the flag as completed or perhaps remove the flag altogether.

To modify an existing flag, select the message and press CTRL-SHIFT-G, or open the message and click the Flag button on the Standard toolbar in the message form. This opens the Flag for Follow Up dialog box containing the flag information.

To change the comment, select a different flag from the Flag To drop-down list. To change the reminder manually, edit the Due By field or select a different date from the drop-down calendar available in the field. You can click the Clear Flag button to remove the flag or check the Completed option to mark the flag completed.

Note
If you use the drop-down calendar to reset the reminder date, remember to manually edit the time, since the calendar automatically inserts the default end of workday time set in the Calendar folder.

To add a flag to a flagless message, right-click the message and select Flag for Follow Up from the shortcut menu. The Flag for Follow Up dialog box appears. Select the desired comment from the Flag To drop-down list, and set the reminder in the Due By field. Then click OK to add the flag. When you return to the mail folder, you'll see a flag icon in the Flagged Status column.

To mark a flag completed, right-click the message and select Flag Complete from the shortcut menu. Using this command changes the comment in the message to indicate the date and time the flag was completed and changes the flag icon from red to gray.

To remove a flag altogether, right-click the message and select Clear Flag from the shortcut menu. The flag icon disappears from the mail folder and the comment line is removed from the message. There is no evidence remaining that the flag ever existed.

MOUS
MOUS EXAM PRACTICE
In this section, you saw how flagging messages provides an additional means of ensuring that they receive the proper attention in a timely fashion. Now practice flagging messages in your own Inbox. Start by adding flags to messages that arrive without one. After you add a flag, open the Flag for Follow Up dialog box and change both the comment and the reminder. Next, mark the flag as completed, and finally remove the flag altogether.

Assigning Messages to Contacts and Categories

 One of the handiest things about having your e-mail management and your personal information management handled by the same program is the ability to link your messages to other components. One way in which Outlook provides this service is by letting you assign e-mail messages (and other items) to individual contacts. In other words, if you get an e-mail message from a particular contact or that relates to a particular contact, you can assign the message to that contact. The message then appears in the Activities tab of the individual's contact form when you search for All Items or for E-mail Items.

What's nice about this is that you don't actually move the message from its original location, you merely link it to the contact. It can remain in its designated storage folder and still be accessible from the contact's record.

Using categories is another means of organizing your messages that transcends all methods of physically—electronically speaking—arranging your messages. By assigning messages to categories, you can create organizational collections of related messages regardless of which folders they reside in.

To assign an incoming message to a category, right-click the message and choose Categories from the shortcut menu. You can also select the message and choose Edit | Categories to open the Categories dialog box, as shown in Figure 5-10.

Check the category or categories to which you want to assign the message. Checking a category adds the category name to the Item(s) Belong To These Categories list. Click OK to make the assignment and return to the active Outlook window. You can also assign messages to categories by using the Categories field in the Message Options dialog box. Right-click the desired message and select Options from the shortcut menu to open the Message Options dialog box. Then click the Categories button to display the Categories dialog box.

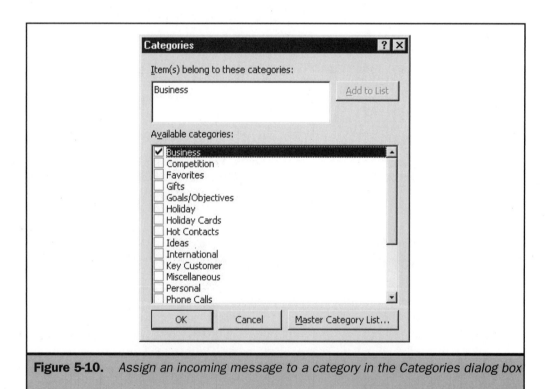

Figure 5-10.   *Assign an incoming message to a category in the Categories dialog box*

To view messages by category, right-click any of the column headers in the Information viewer and choose Customize Current View to display the View Summary dialog box.

View Summary	? X
┌─ Description ──────────────────────────────────
[Fields...]	Importance, Icon, Flag Status, Attachment, From, Subject, Received
[Group By...]	None
[Sort...]	Received (descending)
[Filter...]	Off
[Other Settings...]	Fonts and other Table View settings
[Automatic Formatting...]	User defined fonts on each message
[OK] [Cancel]	

Now click the Group By button to display the Group By dialog box. From the Group Items By drop-down list, select Categories, and click OK to return to the View Summary dialog box. Click OK to return to the mail folder, which should look something like Figure 5-11.

The easiest way to open the Group By dialog box is to right-click the Information viewer column header and select Group By Box from the shortcut menu. This displays the Group By Box directly above the column headers. It's just a wide, dark gray band the width of the Information viewer that holds field names when a group view is enabled. Double-click anywhere in the Group By Box and the Group By dialog box opens. To hide the Group By Box, right-click a column header and select Group By Box again.

If you're reading this tip and thinking that it's easier to right-click a blank spot in the Information viewer and select Group By from the shortcut menu, you're only partially right. First of all, if your Inbox is loaded you have to scroll to the bottom of the Information viewer. Second, if you don't keep your Outlook window maximized, you may not be able to find a blank spot at the bottom of the Information viewer. This method works every time, without having to scroll to the bottom of your Information viewer or look for a blank spot.

Figure 5-11.   *The Group By command organizes your e-mail messages by the categories to which they're assigned*

To view your messages, click the plus sign to the left of the group header to expand the group and display the messages. You can also expand and contract groups by double-clicking anywhere on the header (except the plus sign).

 The Group By feature only works in table and timeline views.

To remove the category groups, return to the Group By dialog box and select None from the Group Items By drop-down list. Then click OK to return to the active Outlook view.

Archiving E-mail

 One of the lessons most users have to learn the hard way is the value of backing up important information. It generally only takes one incident to bring home the fact that a tremendous amount of work can be saved by spending a few minutes making a backup copy of your data. In Outlook, backing up is called archiving, and it can be done automatically. Therefore, no Outlook user should ever be without an archive of important e-mail messages.

Archiving moves messages that meet the archive criteria into a personal folder (.pst) on your hard drive. The directory structure of your mailbox is retained as messages are archived. For example, if you archive a subfolder, the parent folder is created in the archive file to maintain the directory structure, even though the parent folder's contents are not archived.

Using AutoArchive

By default, certain Outlook folders are scheduled for regular AutoArchiving, as the automatic archiving process is called. Unfortunately, the mail folders are not among those set to AutoArchive by default. However, you can schedule AutoArchive to periodically back up your mail folders, and you can perform a manual archive whenever you want.

The first thing you may want to do is set the general AutoArchive options, which include the length of time between archives, whether you want to be prompted before AutoArchiving begins, and the name and location of the default archive file.

To change the basic AutoArchive options, follow these steps:

1. Choose Tools | Options and click the Other tab.

2. Click the AutoArchive button to display the AutoArchive dialog box.

3. Set the AutoArchive options to suit your needs. Your choices include:

■ **AutoArchive Every __ Days**   Check this option to enable AutoArchiving. Then select the desired numbers of days you want to pass between AutoArchive sessions.

■ **Prompt Before AutoArchive**   If you want Outlook to warn you before it performs an AutoArchive, check this option.

- **Delete Expired Items When AutoArchiving (E-Mail Folders Only)** Only mail items with expiration dates are affected by this option. During an AutoArchive, messages with expiration dates that have passed are moved to the Deleted Items folder if you check this option.

- **Default archive file** The location and name of the default archive (.pst) file are shown in this box. To change either one, click the Browse button to open the Find Personal Folders dialog box, where you can select a different archive file or create a new archive file. The first time you set the AutoArchive options, it's a good idea to change the default archive file to one with a unique name, especially if you share your computer with other Outlook users. The default file is named Archive.pst and will end up being used by everyone on the computer, which means multiple users' archive data will all be tossed into one archive file.

4. Click OK to close the AutoArchive dialog box and return to the Options dialog box.

5. Click OK to return to the active Outlook window.

Once you have the basic options taken care of, it's time to move on to setting the AutoArchive schedule for the Inbox. Start by right-clicking the Inbox shortcut in the Outlook Bar or the Inbox folder in the Folder List, and selecting Properties from the shortcut menu. Next, click the AutoArchive tab to view the AutoArchive options, shown in Figure 5-12.

Check the Clean Out Items Older Than option and enter the number of days, months, or years you want to use to determine the age limit of items retained in your Inbox. Select the action you want applied to those messages that meet the criteria:

- **Move Old Items To** Check this option to save archived items to the archive folder listed in the text box below the option. To change the archive folder, click Browse and select a different .pst file.

- **Permanently Delete Old Items** The operative word here is "permanently." Check this option only if you want to delete messages meeting the age criteria, never to see them again. They do not go to the Deleted Items folder, and they are not available for recovery using the Recover Deleted Items command.

When an AutoArchive is performed, any messages that meet the age requirement are moved from the Inbox to the archive file or permanently deleted depending on your selection. That's all there is to it. Now click OK to save the settings and return to the active Outlook window.

An AutoArchive will be performed the next time you start Outlook after the appropriate time period indicated in the AutoArchive dialog box has passed.

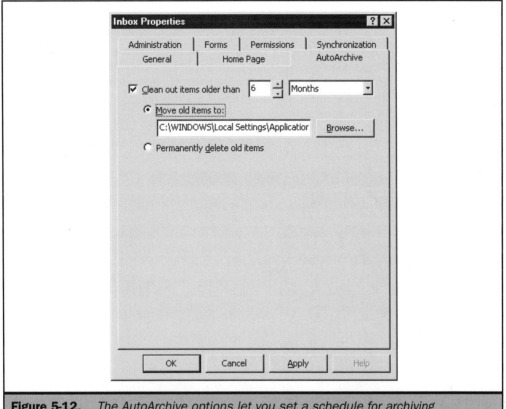

Figure 5-12.   *The AutoArchive options let you set a schedule for archiving automatically*

Note   *Outlook does not check to see if an AutoArchive is due unless you shut Outlook down and restart it every day. In other words, if you leave your computer on 24 hours a day (as many users do) with Outlook running, AutoArchiving will never take place. If you shut down your computer (or at least Outlook) every night and restart it the next day you'll have no problem.*

When Outlook performs an AutoArchive, it indicates the AutoArchive progress on the right side of the status bar at the bottom of the Outlook window. If you decide you want to stop the archive for any reason, click the down arrow to the right of the archive indicator and choose Cancel from the shortcut menu that appears.

Archiving Manually

As good as AutoArchive is, it can't handle every possible situation. Suppose you've just received a ton of important e-mail or created a new folder that contains valuable data, and your next AutoArchive session isn't scheduled for a few days. You could wait until the next AutoArchive and hope nothing happens to your data, or you could archive it manually. The smart money is on archiving it manually.

To perform a manual archive, follow these steps:

1. Choose File | Archive from the Menu bar to open the Archive dialog box.

2. Select the type of archive to perform by choosing one of the first two options:

   - **Archive all folders according to their AutoArchive settings**   Instead of waiting for the next scheduled AutoArchive, you can accelerate the schedule by selecting this option. Everything is done automatically using the existing AutoArchive settings for each folder.

   - **Archive this folder and all subfolders**   If you want to archive individual folders or folders not scheduled for AutoArchive or you want to change the age criteria, use this option.

3. If you selected the Archive All Folders According To Their AutoArchive Settings option, skip to step 5. Otherwise, select the folder(s) you want to include in this manual archive.

4. Set the remaining archive options:

- ■ **Archive items older than**   Enter a date or select one from the drop-down calendar to determine the items you want included in this archive.

- ■ **Include items with "Do Not AutoArchive" checked**   Check this option to archive items that are marked Do Not AutoArchive. To see if a message is marked Do Not AutoArchive, open the message and choose File | Properties from the message form menu bar.

- ■ **Archive file**   Select the archive file into which you want the selected folders archived. Click the Browse button to select a different archive file.

5. Click OK to start the archive.

As is the case with an AutoArchive, you can see the archive progress indicated in the Outlook window status bar. To cancel the archive, click the down arrow to the right of the archive indicator and choose Cancel from the shortcut menu that appears.

Troubleshooting Archive Problems

As simple and straightforward as archiving and AutoArchiving seem to be, there are a few problems that can turn an archiving session into a nightmare of confusion and frustration. When you perform an archive, whether it's an AutoArchive or a manual archive, and nothing seems to happen or not all the messages that should be archived are archived, don't panic. There's probably a simple solution.

The most common reason for messages not being archived is because they don't meet the criteria necessary for inclusion. Unfortunately, the criterion used by the Outlook archiving feature (manual or AutoArchive) to determine the age of messages is not, as you might think, the date of the message, whether it's the Received or Sent date. The date Outlook uses to determine the age of items is the Modified date, a hidden field that changes when you perform one of the following actions on the item:

- ■ Forward the item
- ■ Reply to the item
- ■ Reply to All
- ■ Edit and Save the item
- ■ Move or Copy the item

The last set of actions, Move and Copy, change the date of items in mailbox folders, but not in Personal Folders. If you move or copy items within Personal Folders or from mailbox folders to Personal Folders, the Modified date does not change. However, if you move or copy an item from a Personal Folder to a mailbox item, the Modified date does change.

To view the Modified date of messages, follow these steps:

1. Open the mail folder containing the messages you want to archive.

2. Right-click one of the column headers in the Information viewer and choose Field Chooser to display the Field Chooser.

3. From the drop-down list of field sets (Frequently-Used Fields appears by default), select All Mail Fields.

4. Scroll down the list of fields and locate Modified.

5. Drag the Modified field to the Information viewer header and drop it when a pair of red arrows appears above and below the header row. The arrows indicate the point at which the new field header will be inserted.

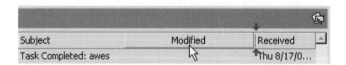

When you drop the field on the header row, a new header for the field appears at the insertion point indicated by the red arrows. Now the Modified date for messages in the folder appears in the column below the header. If your messages have not been archiving as you expected, this date is probably the reason.

Although the Modified date is the most likely culprit, there are a couple of other things that can cause an archive to malfunction. Of these two, the most likely is the simple fact that you've exceeded your mailbox limits. Creating an archive requires messages to be copied on the server first. If you're at or near your mailbox limit, there won't be enough room to make the necessary copies. Check with your administrator to see if this is the problem.

The last thing, which is rare, pertains only to Personal Folders. By default, a Personal Folders (.pst) file cannot contain more than 16,384 folders, each with a maximum of 16,384 items. If you exceed that number, archiving fails. To relieve the problem, open the Mail (Mail and Fax) applet in the Control Panel and select Personal Folders. Then click the Properties button to display the Personal Folder properties dialog box. Check the Allow Upgrade To Large Tables option to create a new .pst file that can hold the same 16,384 folders, but with as many as 65,536 items each. Just for the record, there's also a two gigabyte limit on the size of a .pst file.

To enable Allow Upgrade To Large Tables in an IMO configuration, right-click the Outlook Today icon in the Outlook Bar, and choose Properties. In the Personal Folders Properties dialog box click the Advanced button to display the Personal Folders dialog box. Then check the Allow Upgrade To Large Tables option.

Personal Folders (.pst) files that have been upgraded to large tables may or may not be accessible to older versions of Outlook.

Retrieving Archived Messages

Now that you've got your messages safely tucked away in an archive file, there remains one last thing to consider: how to access them should the need arise. The answer is relatively simple, in spite of the fact that you have a couple of options. You can either add the archive (.pst) file to your profile as a Personal Folders service, or you can import the messages directly into your existing folders.

To add the archive file to your profile as an information service, choose Tools | Services to display the Services dialog box for your profile. Click Add to open the Add Service To Profile dialog box.

This option is available in the C/W configuration, since the IMO configuration does not use profiles. In an IMO configuration, simply open the archive.pst file by choosing File | Open | Personal Folders File (.pst) and locating the archive file.

Select Personal Folders from the list of available information services, and click OK to display the Create/Open Personal Folders File.

Locate the archive file (C:\WINDOWS\Local Settings\Application Data\ Microsoft\Outlook\Archive.pst, by default) and click Open. The Personal Folders dialog box opens.

Here you can change the display name and add or change your password for the Personal Folders, and even compress your Personal Folders to save space. To set or change a password, click Change Password to open the Change Password dialog box. If you're changing an existing password, enter it in the Old password field, otherwise leave it blank. Enter the new password twice (New and Verify fields) to ensure you don't make a typo. If you only want the password activated when you or someone logs on as a different user check Save This Password In Your Password List. Click OK to close the dialog box, and save your new password.

As you delete items from your folders the items themselves are removed, but the space they took up remains. Compacting removes that empty space. It's a little like pushing your bookends together after several books have been removed. To compress your Personal Folders click Compact Now. See the previous section, entitled "Troubleshooting Archive Problems," for an explanation of the Allow Upgrade To Large Tables option.

After you set the desired options click OK to save the settings and return to your Profile Properties dialog box. The new information service appears in the Properties dialog box, identified with the name entered in the Name field of the Personal Folders dialog box. Click OK to return to the active Outlook window. To view or use the new folders (Archive Folders if you left the default name in place) open the Folder List.

Importing the archived data enables you to return it to the folder, so to speak, rather than open it in a separate set of folders. To import messages from your archive file, use the Import and Export Wizard:

1. Choose File | Import From to start the Import and Export Wizard.

2. Select Import From Another Program Or File, and click Next.

3. Scroll down the list of file types and select Personal Folder File (.pst). Then click Next to display the File To Import options in the Import Personal Folders dialog box.

COMMUNICATING WITH E-MAIL

4. Click the Browse button to display the Open Personal Folders dialog box, from which you can locate the archive file.

5. Set the remaining options, which include:

■ **Replace duplicates with items imported** If the imported data includes items identical to those already contained in the folder into which you're importing the data, the existing items will be replaced with ones being imported.

■ **Allow duplicates to be created** Select this option to create a duplicate item rather than replace an existing item with an identical imported item.

■ **Do not import duplicates** This option prevents duplicate items from being imported at all.

6. Click Next to display options for the source folder(s) and the target folder(s).

7. Select the top level folder (Archive Folders in this illustration) to import items from all folders, or select a single folder to limit the import to that folder.

8. Set the remaining options:

- **Include subfolders**   Check this option to import the contents of any subfolders of the folder selected in step 7.

- **Import items into the current folder**   Enable this option to use the folder you were in when you launched the Import and Export Wizard as the target folder for imported items.

- **Import items into the same folder in**   Choose this option and make a selection from the drop-down list to import the items into a mailbox or set of personal or public folders.

- **Filter**   To apply filtering conditions to the imported items, click this button, which opens the Filter dialog box. For more information on using filters, see the section entitled "Applying Filters," earlier in this chapter.

9. Click Finish to start the import.

After the import finishes, the imported items should appear in the appropriate folder(s). The import process does not move archived items, but rather places copies of the archived items into the target folders. Therefore, the archived file remains unchanged by the import process.

MOUS EXAM PRACTICE

In this section, you learned about archiving, one of the most important tasks you can perform in Outlook. Now begin your practice by setting the general AutoArchive options found on the Other tab of the Options dialog box. Next, open the properties dialog boxes for each of your mail folders and set the AutoArchive options for each folder. Then try your hand at performing a manual archive. After you feel comfortable getting your important data into an archive file, practice getting it back out. Try adding your archive file to your profile as an information service. Next, use the Import and Export Wizard to retrieve archived items into your existing folders. As you're working with the archive feature, whether automatic or manual, remember that Outlook uses the hidden Modified date field to determine which messages meet the age criteria.

Printing E-mail Messages

No matter how much you love electronic communication and storage technology, there are bound to be times when nothing short of a printed copy (hard copy) of your messages will do. Some messages are important enough to save a copy in every medium available to you, including hard copy. Perhaps you're on your way to a meeting and will need a copy to reference during the meeting. There are any number of reasons for printing messages you receive in Outlook. Fortunately, the process is simple, as long as you're connected to a printer.

Printing Basics

To make a quick printed copy of a message, select the message in the Inbox (or other mail folder) Information viewer and click the Print button located on the Standard toolbar. Outlook immediately sends the message to the installed printer designated as the default printer.

Tip *Outlook 2000 contains a printing bug that rears its ugly little head sporadically. When printing HTML messages from the Information viewer, Outlook always goes through the motions of printing, but doesn't always print the message. To ensure HTML messages print every time, open each message before printing it.*

If you want to print multiple messages at the same time, highlight the messages you want to print in the Information viewer and click the Print button.

Unless you change the default print options, multiple messages print continuously, without a page break between messages. If you want each message on its own page, you must enable the Start Each Item On A New Page option in the Print dialog box. Be advised that if your default mail format is HTML you cannot print multiple messages on the same page. It's the result of a bug that automatically checks, and then disables, the option when you have multiple messages selected. When you only have one message selected, the option reappears. Of course, with one message selected, the option is meaningless.

If you want more than just a quick hard copy of your messages, or if you want a report that lists your messages and includes basic header information, you may want to customize the Outlook print options.

Tip *If you want a hard copy of an e-mail message, but want to keep the sender (or recipients) confidential, you can prevent some or all of the header information from appearing on the printout. Open the message and choose Tool | Forms | Design This Form to open the message in the Design mode. Then right-click the header field you want to hide in the printout and choose Properties from the shortcut menu. Click the Validation tab and remove the checkmark from the Include This Field For Printing And Save As option. Click OK to save the change, then press ALT-F4 to close the message form. Answer Yes when asked if you want to save changes. The next time you print the message, the header information you deselected does not appear on the printout.*

Setting Print Options

 Like most other Outlook features, printing offers a number of customization options, enabling you to control the way Outlook prints your messages and reports. You can determine how many copies to print, which pages of a multipage message to print, whether you want each message printed on a separate page, and more.

To set the Outlook print options, follow these steps:

1. Choose File | Print to open the Print dialog box, seen in Figure 5-13. You can also right-click a message in the Information viewer and select Print from the shortcut menu.

Tip *Another Outlook printing bug disables most of the printing options when you select a single HTML message from the Information viewer and open the Print dialog box (the problem does not appear if you select multiple messages). To regain the lost print options, open the message first, then choose File | Print from the message form menu bar. This opens the print dialog box used by Internet Explorer, which contains most of the same print options.*

Figure 5-13.   *The Print dialog box is your print options control center*

2. Set the Printer options, which include:

   ■ **Name**   From the Name drop-down list, select the printer you want to use.

   ■ **Properties**   Click this button to display the properties dialog box for the selected printer. What you see here depends entirely on the printer you select in the Name drop-down list.

   ■ **Print to file**   If you want to create a print file rather than a hard copy, check this option. The message is then sent to a file, which you can later use to print a hard copy.

3. Choose the print style and set the Print Style options:

   ■ **Table Style**   Select this style to print your message information as it appears in the Information viewer.

   ■ **Memo Style**   This is the default style, which prints both the header information and contents of each message selected.

- **Page Setup** Click Page Setup to display the Page Setup dialog box for the selected print style. Here you can modify the font used, as well as the type and size of paper. You can also set margins and orientation, and even add headers and footers to the style.

- **Define Styles** If you want to create your own custom style, click this button and select the style you want to use as the foundation for the new style. You can then customize all the Page Setup properties for the new style.

4. Configure the Print options:

- **Start each item on a new page** If you select multiple items for printing, check this option to ensure each message prints on a separate page. If this option is not checked, multiple messages print continuously, squeezing as many messages as will fit on each page.

- **Print attached files with item(s)** If the message you're printing has an attachment that is printable, select this option to print it at the same time the message prints. If the attachment is an Outlook item, it prints on a separate page. However, for other files, you must have a program installed that can open the attachment for printing. Depending on the document type, you may see the Opening Mail Attachment dialog box, which asks if you want to open the message or save it to disk. If you know the source of the file and want to print it, choose to open the message. If you have a program installed that is associated with this file type, it will print; otherwise, Outlook informs you that there is no program associated with it and it cannot print the attachment.

5. Set the Copies options next:

- **Number of pages** If the message is a multipage message, select the pages you want to print. Your choices include All, Odd, and Even.

- **Number of copies** Indicate the number of copies of the selected message(s) you want to print.

- **Collate copies** This feature comes in handy when printing multiple copies of multipage messages. It prints out a full copy of the message before starting on copy two. Without this option selected, all copies of page one are printed, followed by all copies of page two, and so on. You then have to collate (put together) the messages when you're finished printing. The only reason not to select this option is that it can be rather time-consuming if you're printing large messages, large quantities, or both. Normally, a print job is sent to the printer once, and multiple copies are printed from the same information. However, with Collate Copies enabled, the print job is resent each time a new copy is started.

6. Click OK to start the print job.

COMMUNICATING
WITH E-MAIL

If you want to see what the printout will look like before actually printing it, click the Preview button. This gives you a fair representation of how the printed document will appear.

MOUS EXAM PRACTICE
This section on printing actually covers two MOUS objectives: printing mail and setting print options. Start your practice by printing a single message from the Inbox. Then open the message and print it. Now, in the Information viewer, hold down the CTRL key and select a number of different messages to print. Next, set the print options. Select a couple of messages in the Inbox and open the Print dialog box. Print the messages continuously, and then set the appropriate option to print each message separately. Then try printing two copies of a message. You might also print the Information viewer contents using the Table Style. If you have any messages with attachments, try printing them and note what happens to the different attachment types.

MOUS Exam Objectives Explored in Chapter 5

Objective	Activity	Heading
OL2000.1.4	Print mail	"Printing E-mail Messages"
OL2000.1.8	Flag mail messages	"Flagging Received E-mail for Future Action (or Inaction)"
OL2000.1.10	Find messages	"Locating E-mail Messages"
OL2000.1.11	Configure basic mail print options	"Setting Print Options"
OL2000.2.1	Create folders	"Creating Mail Folders"
OL2000.2.2	Sort mail	"Sorting E-mail"
OL2000.2.4	Archive mail messages	"Archiving E-mail"
OL2000.2.5	Filter a view	"Applying Filters"
OL2000.4.2	Move items between folders	"Moving and Copying Messages"
OL2000.4.6	Sort information using categories	"Assigning Messages to Contacts and Categories"

The Complete Reference

Chapter 6

Setting E-mail Options

f there's one thing Outlook has plenty of, it's options. The e-mail client, being one of the most important components of Outlook, has more than its share. The e-mail options include everything from setting the default message format to selecting the punctuation character used for separating addresses in outgoing messages. By judiciously enabling and disabling the desired options, you can ensure that Outlook e-mail functions precisely the way you want it to.

Setting E-mail Options

The first and primary set of options is aptly named E-mail Options. These settings let you decide how Outlook handles messages as well as replies and forwards. To access the E-mail Options, choose Tools | Options from the Menu bar, then click the E-mail Options button on the Preferences tab to open the E-mail Options dialog box shown in Figure 6-1.

As you can see, the first set of options is the Message Handling group, which includes the following:

- **After moving or deleting an open item**   From this drop-down list, select the action you want Outlook to take after you move or delete an open message. You can have Outlook open either the next or the previous message, or simply close the Message window and return to the Inbox Information viewer where you can select your own message to open.

- **Close original message on reply or forward**   Unless you check this option, the original message remains open, even after you click Reply or Forward. Once you respond to a message in such a manner you can have Outlook close the original message by checking this option.

- **Save copies of messages in Sent Items folder**   If you want to maintain a record of e-mail you send to others, this option is a must! When you enable this option, a copy of every message you send is automatically saved in the Sent Items folder.

- **Display a notification message when new mail arrives**   Turned off by default, this option when enabled results in a small notification message displaying each time a new message arrives in your Inbox. This includes messages that are moved to other folders by any rules you create, since all messages are deposited in the Inbox before rules are applied. However, it's interesting to note that you do not receive a notification if you happen to be in the folder to which a message is sent by a rule when the message arrives. So keep your eyes open.

- **Automatically save unsent messages**   If you get a lot of phone calls or other interruptions, you'll probably want to enable this option. Every three minutes, it saves a copy of any open messages you're working on to the Drafts folder. In the event that your system crashes or you close and save the unfinished message, you can return to the Drafts folder and pick up where you left off.

Figure 6-1.   *Customizing the Outlook e-mail client is a breeze with this extensive set of options*

- ■ **Advanced E-mail Options**   Click this button to display the Advanced E-mail Options dialog box, described in detail later in the section entitled "Configuring Advanced E-mail Settings."

- ■ **Tracking Options**   This button opens the Tracking Options dialog box, which is covered later in the section entitled "Selecting E-mail Tracking Options."

The next set of options available in the E-mail Options dialog box is the On Replies And Forwards options. These options give you the opportunity to determine how the contents of the original message are handled, as well as any comments you add to the reply or forward. Frequently when replying to a message, you want to include all or part of the original message to ensure there's no confusion about your reply. When forwarding a message, there's no doubt about including the original message, but Outlook lets you decide how you want the original message included.

Unfortunately, Outlook does not provide a simple way to include only part of the original message in your reply. Therefore, you have two choices. You can leave the original message out of your reply and copy and paste those parts of the original message you want included, or you can include the original message and use the Mark My Comments With option. You can then insert your comments in the original message and delete those parts that don't require responses.

Note *The small display boxes to the right of the first two options provide a crude preview of the way your reply or forward will look with the options you select.*

The options for replies and forwards include:

- **When replying to a message** From this drop-down list, choose the manner in which you want the original message handled when replying. You can choose to leave it out of your reply, include it as an attachment, include the text, include but indent the text, or include the text and precede each line with a special character separating it from your comment. One minor fly in the ointment: when replying to a Plain Text formatted message, the Include And Indent Original Message Text option fails to indent the original text.

- **When forwarding a message** Your options for forwarding a message are identical to those for replying with one exception. There is no option to *not* include the original message, which makes sense since the object of forwarding is to pass the original message on to someone else.

- **Prefix each line with** If you elect to prefix the lines of the original message when including it with a reply or forward, this option becomes available. Enter the character(s) you want to use to set the original message apart from your reply or note. Although the character you enter here appears when replying to or forwarding a Plain Text or Rich Text message, it does not work with an HTML message. Regardless of the character you enter here, the original HTML message is offset by a blue vertical line running down its left margin. One more thing: if you're using Microsoft Word as your e-mail editor, this option is grayed out. If you select Prefix Each Line Of The Original Message in either of the two previous options, Outlook automatically changes it to Include And Indent Original Message.

- **Mark my comments with** If you want to leave the original message intact, and insert comments where needed, use this option to insert your name, initials, or some other appropriate text, in brackets, preceding your comments. This option does not work when replying to Plain Text messages. In addition, this option is unavailable if you use Microsoft Word as your e-mail editor.

The IMO E-mail Options dialog box contains an additional option called Automatically Put People I Reply To In. With this option enabled, Outlook adds the recipient(s) of your reply to a contacts folder specified in the text box that appears below.

Any changes you make in the E-mail Options dialog box take effect as soon as you click OK twice (once to close the E-mail Options dialog box, and again to close the Options dialog box), and return to the active Outlook window.

Configuring Advanced E-mail Settings

While the basic e-mail options cover basic message handling, and reply and forward handling, the Advanced E-mail Options dialog box deals with saving and sending messages, as well as enabling e-mail notification. Here you'll discover options to change the time between AutoSaves of unsent messages, to set the default sensitivity and importance of outgoing messages, and more.

To change the advanced settings, follow these steps:

1. Choose Tools | Options to open the Options dialog box.

2. Click the E-mail Options to display the E-mail Options dialog box.

3. Click the Advanced E-mail Options button to open the Advanced E-mail Options dialog box.

4. Set the Save Messages options, which include:

- **Save unsent items in** From this drop-down list, select the mail folder into which you want unsent items saved. Your choices are limited to the four standard mail folders: Drafts, Inbox, Sent Items (incorrectly listed as Sent Mail), and Outbox. Unless you have a good reason for changing this option, it's best left at Drafts. Storing unsent messages anywhere else will be confusing at best.

- **AutoSave unsent every __ minutes** Check this option to automatically save unsent messages to the folder indicated in the previous option. Set the number of minutes between saves. The maximum time between saves is 99 minutes. If you type a long message without stopping, the AutoSave feature does not kick in until about 15 to 20 seconds after you stop typing, regardless of the number of minutes you set. However, if you're using Microsoft Word as your default e-mail editor, the Word AutoRecover feature is used to save the message in the specified folder. Unlike the Outlook AutoSave, the Microsoft Word AutoRecover feature works regardless of any detected keyboard activity. One more thing: when you use Microsoft Word, the Word AutoRecover settings for time are used. Therefore, if you have Outlook AutoSave set for every three minutes and Microsoft Word AutoRecover for every ten minutes, it will be ten minutes between AutoSaves.

■ **In folders other than the Inbox, save replies with original message**   If you save and reply to messages in a folder other than the Inbox, you can check this option to have copies of replies or forwards saved in the same folder as the original message. When the option is disabled, replies and forwards are saved (along with other sent mail) in the Sent Items folder regardless of the location of the original message. This option works in conjunction with two other options: the Save Copies Of Messages In Sent Items Folder option in E-mail Options, and Save Forwarded Messages in Advanced E-mail Options.

■ **Save forwarded messages**   If you want copies of forwards saved in your Sent Items folder or other designated folder (see previous option), check this option.

5. Next, set the arrival notification options.

■ **Play a sound**   With this option checked, Outlook plays the Windows New Mail Notification sound every time a new message arrives in your Inbox. To change the sound, open the Sounds applet in the Windows Control Panel (Start | Settings | Control Panel | Sounds) and select the Windows New Mail Notification event. Then click the Browse button to select another sound file with which to replace it.

■ **Briefly change the mouse cursor**   Check this option and your mouse pointer briefly changes to a mail symbol each time a new piece of e-mail arrives.

6. Set the When Sending A Message options.

■ **Set importance**   Make your selection from the drop-down list to set the default importance level for outgoing messages. All messages you send, including replies, are sent with the importance level you set here. Forwards are not affected by this option, and retain their default importance level of Normal. Of course, you can still change the importance level of individual messages as you see fit, regardless of the setting in this option.

■ **Set sensitivity**   Similar to Set Importance, this option enables you to set the default sensitivity level for outgoing messages. However, this option only applies to new outgoing messages and not to replies or forwards.

■ **Allow comma as address separator**   By default, Outlook uses a semicolon as the separator between addresses in a message with multiple recipients in the To, Cc, or Bcc fields. With this option checked, you can use either a semicolon or a comma as the separator when you enter addresses manually.

■ **Automatic name checking**   If you enter addresses manually, it's a good idea to leave this option enabled. It double-checks the address you enter to ensure it is either in one of your address books or is a valid Internet address. If the address is valid, it's underlined. However, when it comes to Internet addresses, Outlook is only interested in the format. In other words, any Internet address that conforms to the Internet address format (username@domainname) is considered valid, regardless of whether or not the address appears in your address books. If multiple addresses are found, the address you entered is underlined with a red wavy line. Right-click to view the other available addresses. If multiple addresses are found, but one has previously been used, the name is underlined with a green, broken line to remind you there are other addresses. If you type a partial name or address, and only one matching entry is found, Outlook automatically enters the matching entry in the address field as soon as you move to another field.

■ **Delete meeting request from Inbox when responding**   If you want Outlook to do a little housecleaning on its own, check this option. When it's enabled, any meeting request to which you respond is automatically removed from your Inbox.

7. Click OK to save the new settings and return to the E-mail Options tab. Then click OK again to return to the Options tab, and finally click OK a third time to return to the active Outlook window.

The new settings take effect immediately.

Selecting E-mail Tracking Options

E-mail tracking options provide you with a means of controlling the way in which Outlook handles requests, read receipts, and voting responses. You can determine when and how requests and responses are processed, how to handle Internet e-mail requests for read receipts, and more.

For tracking options to work as expected, you must be exchanging e-mail with Outlook users who are on a Microsoft Exchange Server-compatible mail system. Delivery and read receipts returned as Plain Text messages are not recognized by Outlook as true receipts and as a result are not tracked.

Follow these instructions to set Outlook tracking options:

1. Choose Tools | Options and click the E-mail Options button to display the E-mail Options dialog box.

2. Click the Tracking Options button to open the Tracking Options dialog box seen in Figure 6-2.

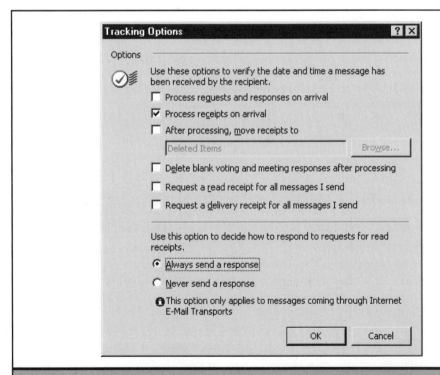

Figure 6-2. *The Tracking Options dialog box contains a multitude of options for automating the processing of requests, responses, and receipts*

Note   *Processing responses and receipts can be performed manually or automatically. When a response or receipt notification is opened or deleted, it is manually logged. When you set automatic processing options, the responses and receipt notifications are logged automatically, regardless of whether or not you open or delete the notifications. However, for automatic logging to occur, certain conditions must be met. The receipt must remain in the Inbox folder, the original message you sent with the request must remain in the Sent Items folder, and a period of approximately one minute must pass with no mouse or keyboard activity.*

3. Set the desired options from the following:

- **Process requests and responses on arrival**   This option automatically logs voting button as well as meeting and task request responses. For voting button responses, you can see the results on the tracking tab of the original message you sent. Task request responses are indicated on the information bar of the original sent message. Meeting request responses are logged in the meeting request form itself, not in the e-mail message sent.

- **Process receipts on arrival**   This option automates the processing of incoming receipts. If you receive a delivery or read receipt notification from a message you've sent that included requests for either, the receipt(s) will be logged on the Tracking tab of the sent message even if you don't open the receipt notification. If this option is disabled, the receipts are not logged until you manually process them (open or delete them). By the way, the help files tell you this option automatically deletes delivery and receipt notifications. Unfortunately, the help files are wrong.

- **After processing, move receipts to**   Use this option to move notification receipts to another folder after they've been processed, either manually or automatically. Of course, the target folder must be a mail folder.

- **Delete blank voting and meeting responses after processing**   Voting button and meeting request responses in which the recipient only selects the desired button, and does *not* edit the response are deleted automatically after the response has been processed. Task responses, which are not affected by this option, are always deleted after they are processed.

- **Request a read receipt for all messages I send**   Select this option to automatically include a request for a read receipt on all your outgoing messages, including meeting and task requests. You can override this setting on individual messages by changing the option in the message Options (regular e-mail) or Properties (task and meeting requests) dialog box.

- **Request a delivery receipt for all messages I send**   If you want to make sure all your outgoing messages make it to their destinations, check this option. All outgoing messages, including task and meeting requests, are automatically sent with a delivery receipt requested. You can also override this setting for individual messages. (C/W configuration only.)

- **Always send a response** If you have an Internet account added to your profile, you will also see this and the next option. You can use these options to decide how to handle read and delivery receipt requests from Internet e-mail senders. Check Always Send A Response if you want Outlook to automatically generate and send the appropriate notification in response to a request.

- **Never send a response** With this option checked, Outlook always ignores requests for receipts from Internet mail messages.

 If you've installed Outlook with the IMO configuration, you'll find an additional option, Ask Me Before Sending A Response. Check this option to instruct Outlook to prompt you for approval before sending a response.

4. Click OK until you return to the active Outlook window.

As soon as you return to Outlook, the new options take effect. Some options are retroactive, while others only work on new responses or receipts. The processing options (the first two) only work on new items. The move option (third) works on existing items that meet the conditions.

Changing the Default Message Format

Outlook gives you three options for the default format for outgoing messages to ensure that any recipient can receive and read your message, there is Plain Text. For fancier-looking e-mail, you can use HTML or Rich Text formats, both of which permit font and paragraph formatting. However, when selecting either of the last two formats you run the risk of a recipient receiving a message that appears differently from what you sent. They may not be able to read the message at all. When exchanging e-mail with other Outlook users, you can use any of the formats without worry. However, when exchanging e-mail with users who employ a different e-mail client, it's always a good idea to try a sample message to be sure their software is compatible with Outlook when it comes to message formatting in anything other than Plain Text.

To change the default message format, choose Tools | Options to open the Options dialog box. Then click the Mail Format tab to set formatting, signature, and stationery options for outgoing messages, as shown in Figure 6-3. See Chapter 19 for more on signatures and stationery.

 The Mail Format tab in the IMO configuration does not contain the Send Pictures From The Internet option.

From the Send In This Message Format drop-down list choose the default format for outgoing messages. You can always change the message format for individual messages before sending them.

Figure 6-3. *The options on the Mail Format tab of the Options dialog box will determine how your messages look*

In addition to setting the default format for messages, you can also elect to use Microsoft Word as your default e-mail editor by selecting Use Microsoft Word To Edit E-Mail Messages.

There's a final message format option you can set if you select HTML as your default message format. It's the Send Pictures From The Internet option, which is grayed out when you select any format other than HTML as the default message format. By checking this option, you can embed images in your e-mail messages rather than simply include pointers to the images.

Setting International Options

For those users of non-English versions of Outlook, there are some options that may be of interest. To access the international options, choose Tools | Options and click the Mail Format tab. Then click the International Options button to display the International Options dialog box.

The International Options include the following:

- **Use English for message flags** When this option is checked, Outlook uses the English version for message flags regardless of what your default language is.

- **Use English for message headers on replies and forwards** This option is similar to the previous option in that it utilizes the English version for message header information such as To, From, Sent, and Subject, regardless of your default language.

- **Use this encoding for outgoing messages** From the drop-down list, select the default language to use for outgoing messages. You must, of course, have the selected language installed to use this option.

- **Use this encoding for unmarked received messages** Messages that arrive without a specified language automatically use the language selected here. Like the previous option, you must have the selected language installed for this to work.

If you receive any volume of e-mail in languages other than your default language, you should not use the Preview Pane for reviewing incoming messages. When you respond to messages viewed in the Preview Pane, your default language is used in the reply rather than the language specified in the original message. By opening the message before replying, the language in the original message is used in the response rather than your default outgoing language.

Setting Internet E-mail Options

If you have an Internet e-mail account added to your profile, you'll see an Internet E-mail tab on your Options dialog box (see Figure 6-4).

To access the Internet E-mail options you must have an Internet e-mail account added to your profile as an information service. For details on adding information services to your profile, see Chapter 2. To access the Internet E-mail options, choose Tools | Options, and click the Internet E-mail tab on the Options dialog box.

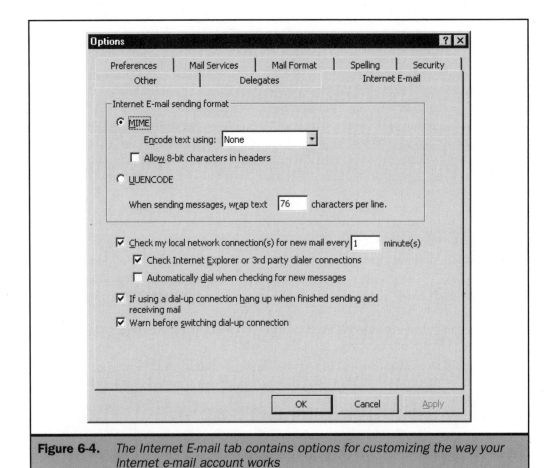

Figure 6-4.   *The Internet E-mail tab contains options for customizing the way your Internet e-mail account works*

You'll find the following options on the Internet E-mail tab:

- **MIME**   By default, Outlook and most Internet e-mail programs use the Multipurpose Internet Mail Extensions (MIME) format to encode e-mail messages and attachments. Unless the majority of your Internet e-mail is exchanged with UNIX or other non-MIME-compatible e-mail systems, you should leave MIME as the default. The additional MIME options let you select bit and binary encoding formats (Encode Text Using) and allow the use of other character sets in message headers without encoding (Allow 8-bit Characters In Headers).

- **UUENCODE**   Select this format when exchanging e-mail with UNIX e-mail clients or other non-MIME-compatible e-mail programs.

■ **When sending messages, wrap text __ characters per line**   Set the number of characters allowed on each line of a message before automatic wrapping takes place. The default setting of 76 is appropriate for most popular e-mail programs. If you decide to change this number, keep in mind that some older e-mail programs can't properly display messages with line lengths over 80 characters.

■ **Check my local network connection(s) for new mail every __ minute(s)**   You can enable this option to have Outlook automatically check your Internet e-mail account(s) at the designated interval. If you're connected to the Internet via a local area network (LAN), leave the suboptions unchecked. To have Outlook use your Internet Explorer or other third-party connection, enable the Check Internet Explorer Or 3rd Party Dialer Connections option. To use an existing dial-up networking connection, enable the Automatically Dial When Checking For New Messages option. If this option is cleared, you must use the Send And Receive command on the Tools menu to check your e-mail.

■ **If using a dial-up connection hang up when finished sending and receiving mail**   If you're using a dial-up networking connection, check this option to have Outlook disconnect automatically after you finish sending and receiving.

■ **Warn before switching dial-up connection**   If you have multiple dial-up networking connections, enabling this option causes Outlook to display a message offering you the opportunity to try a different connection when the currently selected connection isn't working.

After you finish setting your Internet E-mail options, click OK to save the new settings and return to the active Outlook window.

The Complete Reference

Outlook 2000

Chapter 7

Working with Address Books and Directory Services

ince the Outlook e-mail component is one of the most important elements of the program, the ability to store and locate e-mail addresses easily is critical. Fortunately, Outlook provides the means to do both. By using directory services to locate e-mail addresses from all around the globe, and employing the Address Book to store and retrieve them, you can make light work of managing your e-mail addresses. This chapter takes you on a tour of the Address Book, walks you through installing and using address books, and helps you understand and work with directory services.

The IMO Address Book is much more limited than the C/W Address Book discussed in this chapter. The IMO Address Book contains contacts data from the Contacts folder only. As a result, much of the information contained in this chapter will be relevant only for users with a C/W configuration.

Understanding the Address Book

The Corporate or Workgroup (C/W) Address Book is actually not a single address book, but rather a collection of all your installed address books. The Address Book provides an interface that enables you to access any of your address books from within the same dialog box. Depending on your Outlook configuration and the information services installed, you may have one or more of the following address books:

- **Global Address List (GAL)**   This is the primary address list for your organization's e-mail system. Maintained by the system administrator, the Global Address List contains all company user, group, and distribution list e-mail addresses. To ensure its integrity, only the system administrator can add, delete, or modify entries in the Global Address List. This address book is always stored on the Microsoft Exchange server.

- **Outlook Address Book**   This is an address book automatically generated from data in your Contacts folder. The Outlook Address Book is directly linked to your Contacts folder. This means that changes made to individual contacts in the Contacts folder are automatically reflected in the Outlook Address Book. Since the information in the Outlook Address Book is taken directly from the Contacts folder, attempting to edit an Outlook Address Book entry opens the corresponding contact form in the Contacts folder. Depending on the Contacts folder used to create the Outlook Address Book, this address book can be stored either on the Microsoft Exchange server or on your local hard disk.

- **Personal Address Book**   For those e-mail addresses you want to keep private and store on your own computer, you can use the Personal Address Book (PAB). This address book is not connected to either the Global Address List or the Outlook Address Book.

Address books are considered information services and are added to individual profiles. The type of address books added to your profile depends on your Outlook configuration. C/W configurations connected to a Microsoft Exchange Server network have the Global Address List and the Outlook Address Book added by default. IMO configurations, on the other hand, only have the Outlook Address Book installed.

Installing Address Books

If the address book you want to use is not available in your profile, you can add it as an information service. Of course, you cannot use a Global Address List unless you're on a company-wide mail system and have installed the Outlook C/W configuration.

To add an address book to your profile, follow these steps:

1. Choose Tools | Services to open the Services dialog box for your profile.

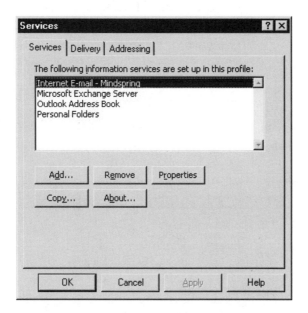

2. Click Add to open the Add Service to Profile dialog box.

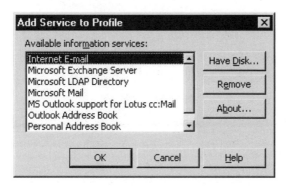

3. Select the type of address book to add. Your list of available services may differ from the list illustrated here.

You can only add one instance of the Outlook Address Book. Attempting to add a second instance results in an error message informing you the service is already installed. If by chance the Outlook Address Book is not one of the choices on the list, you may have a bad or missing Contab32.dll or Mapisvc.inf file, both of which are located on the original Outlook 2000 or Office 2000 CDs.

4. Click OK to add the service. If you're adding the Outlook Address Book, skip to step 7. If you're adding a Personal Address Book, the Personal Address Book dialog box shown in Figure 7-1 opens.

5. Complete the necessary information for the Personal Address Book:

   ■ **Name** Since you can have multiple Personal Address Books, you may want to give each one a unique name (Friends, Family, and so on). If you use a distinctive name, it will appear on the list in parentheses next to Personal Address Book—for example, Personal Address Book (Family).

   ■ **Path** If you want to store your Personal Address Book in a different location than the one selected by default, enter the new path here. If you're not sure of the location you want to use, click the Browse button to display the User Personal Address Book dialog box. You can then select an existing Personal Address Book or specify a location for a new Personal Address Book.

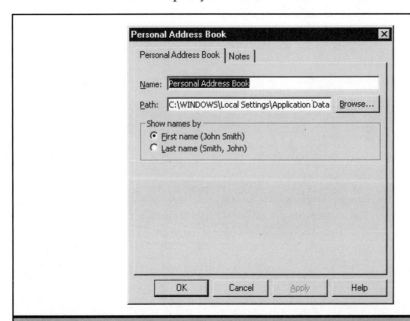

Figure 7-1. *Use the Personal Address Book dialog box to specify the name and path of the new address book*

- **Show names by**   Set this option to determine the default sort order for names listed in the new Personal Address Book.

- **Notes**   Click the Notes tab and enter a description or any miscellaneous information related to the new Personal Address Book in the Notes text box.

6. Click OK to save the settings and return to the Services dialog box.

> **Note**   *No matter which address book you add, a notification message displays informing you that the new service will not become available for use until you exit and log off, and then restart Outlook.*

7. Repeat the process as needed.

8. Click OK to return to the active Outlook window.

9. Choose File | Exit and Log Off to close Outlook.

10. Restart Outlook using the same profile to which you added the new address book(s).

As soon as you restart Outlook, the new address books are available for use. By default, Outlook uses your Contacts folder as the Outlook Address Book. If you have folders in addition to the Contacts folder, that contain contact items, you can designate them as Outlook Address Books by opening the Folder Properties dialog box (right-click the desired contact folder in the Folder List and select Properties), and checking the Show This Folder As An E-Mail Address Book option on the Outlook Address Book tab.

> **Note**   *If the Show This Folder As An E-Mail Address Book option on the Outlook Address Book tab is grayed out, it means one of three things: the Outlook Address Book service is not added to the current profile; you've added the service but forgotten to exit and log off and then restart Outlook; or your profile is damaged and doesn't recognize the Outlook Address Book service.*

Using the Address Book

Although there are numerous Outlook components that access the Address Book information, there is only one Address Book dialog box that gives you access to all the Address Book features. Therefore, the first order of business is to open the Address Book. From any folder, click the Address Book button on the Standard toolbar, press CTRL-SHIFT-B, or choose Tools | Address Book from the Menu bar to open the Address Book dialog box (see Figure 7-2).

As you can see in Figure 7-2, the Address Book dialog box displays names from the default address list upon opening. On a Microsoft Exchange Server mail system, the default address list is usually the Global Address List. See "Setting Address Book Options," later in this chapter, for details on changing the default address book. Regardless of which address book you designate as the default address list, you can

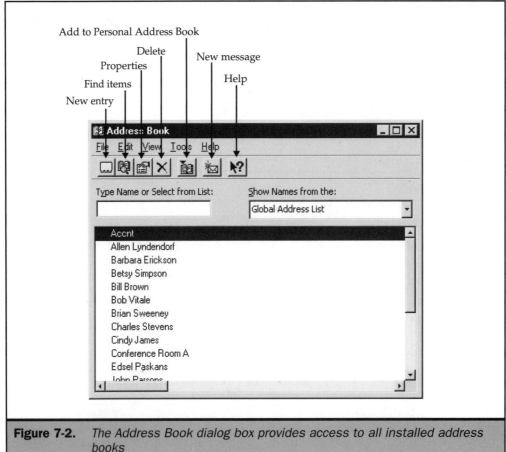

Add to Personal Address Book

Delete

Properties   New message

Find items   Help

New entry

Figure 7-2.   *The Address Book dialog box provides access to all installed address books*

access all the installed address books from the Address Book dialog box by making the appropriate selection from the Show Names From The drop-down list.

Addressing E-mail

Addressing e-mail from within the Address Book is simple and straightforward. Select the address book of your choice and highlight the names you want to include in the To field of a new e-mail message. Then click the New Message button on the toolbar to create a new mail message with the selected names entered as recipients in the To field. If you want to include recipients in other fields or from other address lists click the To, Cc, or Bcc button to display the Select Names dialog box. Then select the desired address book from the Show Names From The drop-down list. Now select the names and click the appropriate button.

Adding, Modifying, and Deleting Address Book Entries

Any address book is only as good as the information it contains. Therefore, you'll want to make sure you keep yours up to date by adding new entries as needed, modifying existing entries that change, and deleting old entries you no longer need.

To add a new entry to the address book, follow these steps:

1. Click the Address Book button on the Standard toolbar to open the Address Book. You can also press CTRL-SHIFT-B, or choose Tools | Address Book from the Menu bar to open the Address Book.

2. Click the New Entry button or choose File | New Entry from the Menu bar to open the New Entry dialog box.

3. Choose where to include the new entry by selecting one of the Put This Entry options:

   ■ **In the __**   From the drop-down list, select the address book in which you want to place the new entry. The address book designated as the default address book to keep personal addresses in is displayed. You'll notice that the only address books in which you can create new entries are any Personal Address Books you've added and any contacts folders you've designated to be used as address books. The latter appear under the Outlook Address Book item.

   ■ **In this message only**   This option is only available if you open the Address Book from within an e-mail message form and create a new entry. Of course, when you open the Address Book from within an e-mail message, it appears as the Select Names dialog box.

COMMUNICATING WITH E-MAIL

4. Choose the type of entry you want to create. Your choices depend on the type of address book you select in the Put Entry In option:

- **Contacts** When you select Contacts or any other contacts folder designated as an address book, you can create a new contact or a new distribution list. In each case, the corresponding Outlook form opens, enabling you to create the desired item on the fly.

- **Personal Address Book** If you select a Personal Address Book, you're presented with a selection of different mail system address types. Select the appropriate mail system type for the new entry.

5. Fill in the necessary information. The form you see depends entirely on the entry type you select.

6. After you've entered the appropriate information, click OK to save the new entry.

The new entry now appears in the designated address book. To use it, simply select the appropriate address book from the Show Names From The drop-down list, and click the New Message button on the Address Book toolbar.

If you find that you need to make a change to an entry, choose the address book in which it resides, and double-click the name to open its form. Make the necessary changes and click OK to return to the Address Book.

Deleting an Address Book entry is even easier. Select the address book containing the entry, highlight the entry, and press the DELETE key or click the Delete button on the Address Book toolbar. Since entries you delete cannot be recovered, Outlook asks if you're sure you want to delete the entry. If you're sure, click Yes, otherwise click No. You can also right-click an entry and select Delete from the shortcut menu that appears.

In addition to the New Entry command, there are a couple of other ways to add information to the Address Book. Since only the administrator can add Global Address List entries, these methods only work for the Outlook Address Book and the Personal Address Book:

- **From an e-mail message** Open the e-mail message and right-click the name in the message header. Then choose Add to Personal Address Book or Add to Contacts. If you don't see Add to Personal Address Book, it's probably because you've selected an Outlook Address Book contacts folder as the folder in which to store personal addresses. When you select an Outlook Address Book contacts folder, you only have the choice of saving as a contact. When you select a Personal Address Book, your choices include both. You can change this setting by choosing Tools | Services, and clicking the Addressing tab. From the Keep Personal Addresses In drop-down list, select the Personal Address Book you want to use.

■ **Add an existing entry to the Personal Address Book**   Before jumping into the mechanics of this method there is one thing you must understand. For this method, Outlook redefines the term Personal Address Book. Here, Personal Address Book refers to the address book selected in the Keep Personal Addresses In option on the Addressing tab of the Services dialog box. Therefore, if you have an Outlook Address Book contact folder selected in this option, adding an entry to the Personal Address Book, means creating a new contact. If, on the other hand, you have a "real" Personal Address Book selected in the Keep Personal Addresses In option, adding an address to the Personal Address Book means just that. To add an existing address list entry to the [newly defined] Personal Address Book, right-click the entry and select Add to Personal Address Book from the shortcut menu. One more thing to note, you can add entries from the Global Address List or from any address book except the one that appears in the Keep Personal Addresses In option.

Note *When you add an entry from the Global Address List to the Personal Address Book, the display name may change due to the fact that the Personal Address Book uses the first name and last name fields to create the display name. If the display name in the Global Address List is not a combination of the two, the display names will not match up.*

If your designated Personal Address Book is a real Personal Address Book and not a contacts folder, the Add to Personal Address Book command disappears from the shortcut menu, and is grayed out on the File menu. Since the source and target address books are the same, it's like trying to lift yourself by your own bootstraps. No matter how hard you try, it won't work.

Note *When an Outlook Address Book contacts folder is the designated Personal Address Book, and you attempt to save a Global Address List entry to your Personal Address Book, you cannot use the Save And New command on the new contact form to save the new entry. You receive an error message informing you that a dialog box is open and you must close it. This is a bug. Simply use the Save And Close command instead.*

Sorting the Address Book

Sorting your Address Book will enable you to find addresses quickly. The sort order of the Global Address List, like everything else about the Global Address List, is determined by the administrator and cannot be changed by users. However, the Outlook Address Book and the Personal Address Book can be sorted according to your preferences. To sort both (assuming you have a Personal Address Book added to your profile), requires two similar, but separate procedures.

To change the sort order of an Outlook Address Book, choose Tools | Services to open the Services dialog box. Double-click Outlook Address Book to display the Microsoft Outlook Address Book.

By default, the sort order is first name, last name. To reverse it, select File As (Smith, John) in the Show Names By options. Click Close when you're finished. In order for the change to take effect, you must exit and log off Outlook and then restart it.

Changing the sort order of a Personal Address Book is similar. Start by opening the Services dialog box (Tools | Services). Then double-click the Personal Address Book for which you want to modify the sort order. This opens the Personal Address Book dialog box.

Like the Outlook Address Book, the Personal Address Book default sort order is first name, last name. Make your selection in the Show Names By options to change the setting.

If you change the sort order of a Personal Address Book and the Address Book listing remains the same, it may be the result of having both the first and last names entered in the First Name field. This is a common problem with names entered manually in the Personal Address Book. When you create a new entry and place both first and last names in the Display Name field, they are both automatically entered in the First Name field. Since the sort is based on first and last names, it will not work without data in both fields. If both names are in the First Name field, the sort order remains the same no matter what your sort order selection. To remedy the situation, edit the entry so the first and last names are in the appropriate fields.

Searching the Address Book

There are two methods for searching the Address Book after you open it by clicking the Address Book button on the Standard toolbar. For a simple search, start typing the name you're searching for in the Type Name or Select From List search box. For a more sophisticated search, use the Find feature.

To use the Find feature, click the Find Items button on the toolbar or press CTRL-SHIFT-F to open the Find dialog box. Depending on the address book selected in the Show Names From The drop-down list, you'll see either the Find dialog box shown in Figure 7-3 or the one shown in Figure 7-4.

Enter the search criteria in the appropriate field(s) and click OK to search the selected address book. The Find feature filters out all address book entries that do not meet the search criteria and displays only those entries that do match the criteria.

Importing Address Books

Whether you want to use an existing address book that belongs to another Outlook user or you want to use an address book from your old e-mail software, you'll appreciate the ability to import address books into Outlook. The Outlook import feature enables you to convert address book information from a variety of programs, including Outlook, Outlook Express, ACT!, ECCO, Eudora, and more.

Importing an Outlook Personal Address Book

Outlook has a powerful import feature, which enables you to import Outlook Personal Address Books as well as information from other programs. How the importing of a Personal Address Book works depends on the services in your profile. If you've already installed a Personal Address Book as an information service, the import works differently than if you have no Personal Address Book installed.

With the service already added to your profile, you can only import your existing Personal Address Book into a contacts folder. If you haven't installed Personal Address Book as an information service, you can import any Outlook Personal Address Book from any source into a contacts folder.

COMMUNICATING WITH E-MAIL

Figure 7-3. *The Find dialog box displayed when searching the Global Address List*

Figure 7-4. *The Find dialog box used when searching the Outlook Address Book or the Personal Address Book*

To import a Personal Address Book, follow these steps:

1. Choose File | Import And Export to launch the Import and Export Wizard.

2. Select Import From Another Program Or File and click Next to display the Import A File screen.

Tip *You can double-click your selection in most of the Import and Export Wizard screens to make your selection and move to the next screen without having to click the Next button.*

COMMUNICATING WITH E-MAIL

3. Scroll down, select Personal Address Book, and click Next. If you have a Personal Address Book information service added to your profile, you'll see the dialog box shown in Figure 7-5; otherwise you'll see the dialog box shown in Figure 7-6.

4. Select the destination folder if you see the dialog box shown in Figure 7-5. Enter the path and name of the Personal Address Book file to import if you see the dialog box shown in Figure 7-6.

5. Click Next to display the summary screen, which indicates the action to be performed and gives you a chance to map custom fields and change the target folder.

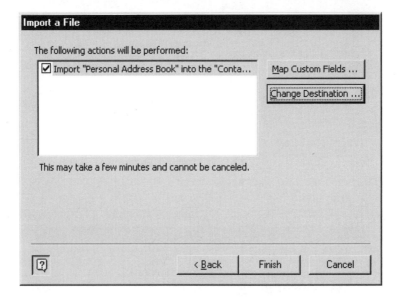

The Map Custom Fields button enables you to indicate which fields in the destination folder will hold information from custom fields you created in the Personal Address Book you're importing.

Note

6. Click Finish to complete the import.

When you open the Contacts folder into which you imported the Personal Address Book, you'll now see a contact record for each individual in the original Personal Address Book.

Note

If you import a Personal Address Book that contains a Personal Distribution List, you may end up with duplicate contacts. This is due to the fact that a separate contact is created for each entry in the Personal Distribution List. If the Personal Address Book also contains a separate listing for the individuals included in the Personal Distribution List, duplicate records result. You'll have to weed them out manually.

Figure 7-5.   *If this dialog box appears, you already have a Personal Address Book
information service added to your profile*

Figure 7-6.   *You'll see this dialog box only if you don't already have a Personal
Address Book information service added to your profile*

Although the import feature is limited to importing Personal Address Books, there is a way to import your Global Address List into a contacts folder. You must have a Personal Address Book information service added to your profile to perform this operation. See Chapter 2 for details on adding information services.

Start by opening the Address Book and selecting the Global Address List. Highlight all the names you want to add to the contacts folder, right-click one of the highlighted names, and select Add To Personal Address Book from the shortcut menu. Now follow the previous steps in this section on importing a Personal Address Book to a contacts folder.

Importing from Other Files

Importing e-mail and contact information from other files and programs is similar to importing Outlook Personal Address Books. Choose File | Import And Export from the Menu bar to launch the Import and Export Wizard. Select Import From Another Program Or File to import address information from contact managers such as ACT! and ECCO, or choose Import Internet Mail And Addresses to import address information from other e-mail software such as Eudora and Netscape Mail.

Note *To import files from contact managers and text-delimited files, you must first install a special import/export engine for the file type. If it's not installed and you select a file type other than .mmf, .pab, or .pst, an error message appears asking if you want to install the import/export engine. You'll need your Outlook 2000 or Office 2000 CD to complete the install.*

If you select Import From Another Program Or File and the import/export engine is installed, the Import A File dialog box appears.

If your program is not listed on the Import A File screen, try exporting the address information from your program to a delimited (separated) text file, and then import the resulting text file into Outlook using the appropriate Comma Separated Values or Tab Separated Values file type.

Selecting Import Internet Mail And Addresses, which requires no additional import/export engine, opens the Outlook Import Tool dialog box.

Whichever option you choose, follow the instructions on each screen to finish importing the address information into Outlook.

Outlook will not directly import address information from Netscape 4.5x and higher. The solution is a little complicated, but works nevertheless. Export the address information as LDIF. Next, import the information into Outlook Express. That's right, Outlook Express, not Outlook. Finally, import the Outlook Express data into Outlook using the Import Internet Mail And Addresses action.

When you import Outlook Express address information into Outlook, Digital IDs are left behind. You'll have to export them manually and import each one into the appropriate Outlook contact record.

Sharing the Personal Address Book

If you want to share your Personal Address Book with another Outlook user on the same computer, or if you have multiple profiles on the same computer, there's a simple way to copy the Personal Address Book from one profile to the next. However, there are two things to keep in mind. One, this only works on profiles that do not yet have a Personal Address Book added. If the target profile already has a Personal Address Book installed, you receive an error message informing you that the service has already been added and another instance cannot be installed. Two, both profiles will be using the same Personal Address Book. This means changes made in one profile will be reflected in the Personal Address Book of the other profile.

To copy your Personal Address Book to another profile, follow these steps:

1. Choose Tools | Services from the Menu bar to open the Services dialog box.

2. Select Personal Address Book and click Copy to open the Copy Information Service dialog box.

3. Select the profile to which you want to copy the Personal Address Book.

4. Click OK to add the Personal Address Book to the selected profile and return to the Services dialog box.

5. Click OK to close the Services dialog box and return to the active Outlook window.

The next time the profile is used, the copied Personal Address Book will be available, containing all the address information from the original.

If you want to make a separate copy of the Personal Address Book rather than share the existing copy, you can locate the .pab file (check the properties for the Personal Address Book in the Services dialog box to see the path and name) using Windows Explorer or My Computer and make a copy. Give it a unique name, return to the profile to which you want it added, and assign it to the Personal Address Book information service (Choose Tools | Services, double-click Personal Address Book, click the Browse button, and locate the newly made copy).

Making the Address Book Work Your Way

While less complex than some Outlook components, the Address Book still has its share of customizing options. To get the most out of your Address Book, you might want to spend a little time whipping it into shape.

Setting Address Book Options

The Address Book options enable you to designate the default address list, the location for storing personal addresses, and the order of address books used for name checking. To set the address book options, choose Tools | Options from the Address Book menu bar to display the Addressing dialog box shown in Figure 7-7.

From the Show This Address List First drop-down list, choose the address book you want automatically displayed each time the Address Book or a Select Names dialog box opens. All your installed address books appear on the drop-down list.

Use the Keep Personal Addresses In drop-down list to designate the Personal Address Book or contacts folder to use for personal addresses. Your selection here

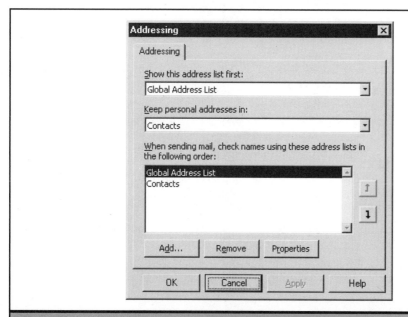

Figure 7-7. *The Addressing dialog box is where to determine how your address lists will be used*

determines which address book Outlook uses to store addresses when you employ the Add to Personal Address Book command. The drop-down list includes Personal Address Book (if you have Personal Address Book added to your profile) and all contacts folders whose properties are set to show as an e-mail address book.

The final option lets you decide which address books are used and the order in which they're used to perform name checking. You can add, remove, and reorder the address books used. Click the Add button to include an installed address book not listed. To keep an address book from being used in name checking, highlight it and click Remove. This does not affect the address book itself. It simply removes it from the name checking list. Finally, you can change the order in which the address books are used in name checking by selecting an address book in the list and clicking the up or down arrow button to change its position.

As you may have noted, the Addressing dialog box is identical to the Addressing tab of the Services dialog box. Therefore, you can also change these options by choosing Tools | Services from the Outlook Menu bar and clicking the Addressing tab.

Modifying the Appearance of the Address Book

The way the Address Book looks is almost etched in stone. However, with a little tinkering you can make at least one change to its appearance. By making a change to the Windows registry, you can adjust the width of the Address Book columns.

 Making changes to the Windows registry can have unexpected results and could even cause your system to malfunction, requiring a reinstallation of the operating system. Only experienced users should attempt to modify the Windows registry. Always make a backup of your registry before making any changes.

Open the registry and make a backup copy before proceeding. Next, locate the HKEY_CURRENT_USER\Software\Microsoft\Exchange\Client\Options key. Add a new DWORD Value, and name it **AddressBookColWidth**. Double-click AddressBookColWidth and enter a number between 0 and 1025 in the Value data field (try 50 to start). Leaving the registry open, return to Outlook and open the Address Book. If the column width looks good, you're all set. If not, return to the registry, change the Value data, and return to Outlook. Close the Address Book and reopen it to see the effect of the new Value data. Repeat the process until you have the desired column width. Close the registry when you're finished.

Working with Distribution Lists

Distribution lists are handy devices for speeding up addressing of e-mail by creating groups of frequently used recipients. For example, suppose you're a project leader and it's your job to keep all team members informed of progress and changes involving the project. You could, of course, create an e-mail message, open the Select Names dialog box and add each team member to the recipients list. However, why bother, when all you have to do is create a distribution list containing the names of all team members? The next time you send a message to the team, you only have to select the distribution list from the Address Book, and the e-mail is automatically addressed to everyone on the team. Distribution lists can be used for e-mail messages, task requests, meeting requests, and can even be included in other distribution lists.

Creating Distribution Lists

Building a distribution list is a snap. You can create one from existing entries in your Address Book, you can enter new addresses on the fly, or you can use a combination of both.

Follow these steps and see how easy it is for yourself:

1. Press CTRL-SHIFT-L or choose File | New | Distribution List to open a blank Distribution List form.

<table>
<tr><td>**Note**</td><td>*If you happen to be typing an e-mail message when you decide to create a new distribution list, use the menu method. Pressing CTRL-SHIFT-L in the body of a message will not open a new distribution list form. Instead, it will either do nothing (Plain Text message) or insert a bullet in the text (Rich Text or HTML message). Although this is a bug, you can use it as a shortcut key to add bullets to your messages. In the unlikely event that Microsoft fixes the bug, you'll be out of luck.*</td></tr>
</table>

COMMUNICATING WITH E-MAIL

2. Enter a brief and descriptive name for the new distribution list.

3. Click the Select Members button to display the Select Members dialog box.

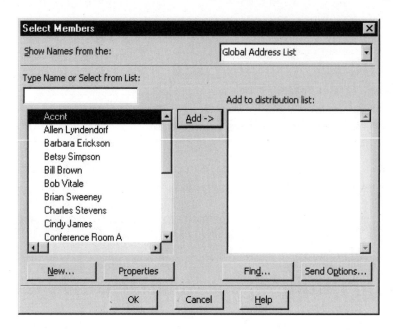

4. Select the desired address book from the Show Names From The drop-down list to display its entries.

5. Select the names you want to include in the new distribution list and click Add.

Note *If you're creating a distribution list in a Microsoft Exchange Server personal mailbox or public folder, the number of entries you can include is limited to 165 contacts or 141 address book items.*

6. If necessary, repeat the process for each address book installed.

7. Click OK to close the Select Members dialog box and return to the distribution list form.

8. If you want to add any names not found in your address book, click Add New to display the Add New Member dialog box.

9. Fill in the appropriate information and click OK to add the entry to the new distribution list form.

10. Use the Notes tab to record notes or miscellaneous information (project date, purpose, team member responsibilities, and so on) about the new distribution list.

11. To assign the new distribution list to a category, click the Categories button on the Members tab and select the appropriate category.

12. If you want to mark the new list as private, check the Private box in the bottom-right corner.

13. Click Save and Close to add the distribution list to the Contacts folder.

The new distribution list appears in the Contacts address book and in the Contacts folder. To add or remove names from a distribution list, open the Contacts folder and double-click the list. Select names and click Remove to eliminate them from the list. Add new names by clicking Select Members or Add New. When you make changes to an original contact or Personal Address Book entry, the change is not reflected in the distribution list until you click the Update button. So if you add a contact whose e-mail address later changes, changing the e-mail address in the contact form will not change the contact's e-mail address in the distribution list until you open the list and click the Update button.

Using Distribution Lists

Using a distribution list is no different than using a single e-mail address. Only the results are different. To address an e-mail using a distribution list, create the e-mail, click the To, Cc, or Bcc button, select Contacts from the Show Names From The drop-down list, and add the distribution list of your choice.

Distribution lists are great for meeting and task requests as well. If you already have a distribution list in place to exchange information with team members, calling a meeting or assigning a task is a snap. For a task request, it's simply a matter of opening a new task request form and entering the distribution list name in the To field. The task request is then sent to the individuals on the distribution list.

Outlook cannot track tasks sent to multiple recipients. Therefore, your copy of the task will not be updated as the recipients make changes to the original task.

To use a distribution list in a meeting request, press CTRL-SHIFT-Q to open a new meeting request form. Type the distribution list name in the To field or click the To button, open the Contacts address book, and select the desired distribution list. When you open the Attendee Availability tab, you'll see that the distribution list appears as a required attendee. You can expand the list to add the individual names to the attendees list by clicking the plus sign (+) to the left of the distribution list.

You can also open a new Meeting Request form by clicking the down arrow on the New button and selecting Meeting Request, or by choosing File | New | Meeting Request.

It's a good idea to expand the list for two reasons. First, if you don't expand it, any recipients who respond will be listed as Optional rather than required, since Outlook checks the names against the attendees list. If it finds only an unexpanded distribution list, it assumes the respondent(s) to be optional. The second reason for expanding the list is to ensure that all recipients receive the correct updates. If a meeting request is sent to an unexpanded distribution list which is later expanded and changed, attendees may receive the wrong update messages.

After you expand a distribution list on the attendees list, you cannot contract it again. It's like letting the genie out of the bottle—it's easy to let him out, but impossible to get him back in.

Viewing Distribution Lists

By default, the only way to view distribution lists is by scrolling through your Address Book or picking through the Contacts folder. This is fine if you only use a handful of distribution lists. However, if you create and use a large number of distribution lists, you may want to consider creating a custom view to display all your distribution lists at a glance.

Here's how:

1. Open the Contacts folder.
2. Choose View | Current View | Define Views to open the Define Views For "Contacts" dialog box.

3. Click New to open the Create A New View dialog box.

4. Enter **Distribution List** in the Name Of New View field.

5. Select Table from the Type Of View list, and click OK to display the View Summary dialog box.

6. Click the Filter button and select the Advanced tab to display the advanced filter options.

7. Click the Field button and choose All Distribution List Fields | Message Class from the menu that appears.

8. From the Condition drop-down list, select Is (Exactly).

9. Enter **IPM.DistList** in the Value field and click Add To List.

10. Click OK to close the Filter dialog box, and click again to close the View Summary dialog box.

11. Click Close to finish creating the new view and return to the Contacts folder.

12. Choose View | Current View | Distribution List to display all your distribution lists.

If you prefer a card view to a table view, you can select Card as the type of view in the Create A New View dialog box. Each distribution list will appear as an address card.

Understanding Directory Services

Outlook 2000, like its predecessor Outlook 98, supports Lightweight Directory Access Protocol (LDAP) directory services. LDAP provides access to online databases of searchable information. In this context, directories are databases of information that are used primarily for data lookup and are usually updated at regular intervals. At their most basic level, directory services could be compared with the hard copy telephone books that everyone has at home. They contain named entries, which in turn consist of a series of attributes of varying types and values. Using the phone book example, the individual's name is the named entry, "phone number" is an attribute type, and the actual digits that make up the number are the attribute's value.

LDAP services are mainly used in Outlook to perform lookups and name checking on large Internet directories.

Adding LDAP Directory Services

The Lightweight Directory Access Protocol should be installed when you install Outlook. However, individual LDAP directories are not. Therefore, before you begin using LDAP services, you must first add each LDAP directory service you want to use to your profile.

 If the Lightweight Directory Access Protocol is not installed, you'll need your Outlook or Office 2000 CDs to install it. You'll be asked to insert the appropriate CD if necessary.

The following steps will walk you through the process:

1. Choose Tools | Services to open the Services dialog box.
2. Click the Add button to display the Add Service To Profile dialog box.

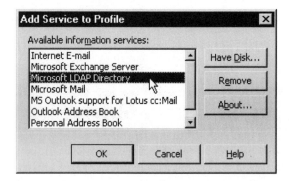

3. Select Microsoft LDAP Directory and click OK to display the LDAP Directory Service dialog box.

4. Set the options on the General tab.

- **Directory Service Account**   Enter the name of the directory service you're adding.

- **Server Hostname**   Enter the name of the server on which the LDAP directory is running. You can enter the hostname or the IP address of the LDAP server.

- **Server Port Number**   By default, the port number is 389. If you access the Internet through a local area network (LAN), you may need to use a different port number. Check with your system administrator.

- **Server Search Timeout**   Set the amount of time you want Outlook to search for the directory service before giving up. It's best to leave this setting at 60 seconds unless you are encountering regular timeout problems.

- **User Name**   Most Internet directories do not require a user name and password. However, if you're using one that does, enter it here. Enter your Distinguished Name (DN) here. A Distinguished Name is a collection of information that uniquely identifies you throughout the world. It's similar to the way your full name and physical address (Jane Doe, 123 Appleview Drive, Philadelphia, PA 19118, USA) uniquely identifies you. The format of the distinguished name (dn) is common name (cn), organization (o), country (c)—for example, cn=Jane Doe, o=McGraw-Hill, c=US. If the directory service requires a user name, check with your administrator for the precise distinguished name to use.

■ **Password**   If no user name is required, you can leave this field blank. If a user name is required, check with your administrator to find out if a password is required as well.

■ **Search Base**   This field lets you narrow your search by indicating the topmost level of the directory to include in the search. LDAP directories are hierarchical in nature, starting with country at the top, organization next, and distinguished names next. Therefore, if you want to restrict the search to Microsoft employees in the United States enter o=Microsoft, c=US.

5. Click OK to save the new LDAP service and return to the Services dialog box.

6. Click OK to return to the active Outlook window.

7. Choose Exit and Log Off to close Outlook.

8. Restart Outlook.

After you restart Outlook, the new LDAP directory service will be available for use. Keep in mind that you're not limited to only one LDAP directory service. You can install as many as you wish.

Using Directory Services

Using an LDAP directory service is almost as easy as using any other Outlook address book. To search an Internet LDAP directory, make sure you have an open connection to the Internet established. Then press CTRL-SHIFT-B or click the Address Book button on the Standard toolbar to open the Address Book. Select the desired LDAP directory and press CTRL-SHIFT-F or click the Find Items toolbar button to display the Find dialog box.

Enter the name or text string you want to search for and click OK to perform
the search. If matching entries are found, they appear in the Address Book
display window.

The Complete Reference

Part III

Working with Contacts

The Complete Reference

Chapter 8

Understanding and Using Contacts

If you've ever used an address book, collected business cards, or written a phone number on a cocktail napkin, you've already performed basic contact management chores. Outlook takes each of those methods of managing contacts to new heights by simplifying and automating the storing, organizing, retrieving, and utilizing of contact information. In this chapter, you'll learn to enter contact information in the Outlook Contacts folder, organize and display it in a variety of ways, and even use it to create e-mail messages and appointments automatically.

Adding Contacts

As you'll no doubt agree, there's not much point in having a Contacts folder without contacts. Therefore, the first order of business is to enter your contact information into the Outlook Contacts folder. You actually have a couple of ways to accomplish that task. You can either enter the information manually or import it from another address book, a contact manager, or a delimited text file.

Adding Contacts Manually

Even if you have an existing address book or file to import into Outlook, you'll eventually have to enter some contact information manually. The process is as simple and quick as you want or need it to be. You begin by opening a new contact form and adding at least a name. After that, it's up to you just how much information you include. Of course, since the purpose of maintaining contact information is to be able to get in touch with the individuals you're keeping track of, it only makes sense to add a phone number, mailing address, or some other tidbit of actual contact data.

To add a contact to your Contacts folder, follow these steps:

1. Press CTRL-SHIFT-C to open a new contact form (see Figure 8-1). There are a number of ways to open a blank contact form. From any Outlook folder, you can press CTRL-SHIFT-C, choose File | New | Contact from the Menu bar, or click the down arrow on the New button and choose Contact. From within the Contacts folder, you can press CTRL-N, click the New button, or right-click a blank spot in the Information viewer and select New Contact.

   As you can see in Figure 8-1, the contact form contains five tabs, each of which contains different information relating to the contact:

   - **General** The General tab contains fields for basic contact information such as name, address, phone number, and so on.

   - **Details** The Details tab provides fields for maintaining additional contact information such as birthday, spouse's name, and more.

   - **Activities** Here you'll find all Outlook items linked to the contact. E-mail messages, other contacts, journal entries, notes, and tasks that are connected to the contact are listed here.

Figure 8-1. *Use the contact form to enter as little or as much contact information as you wish*

- **Certificates**   The Certificates tab displays any digital certificates you use to encrypt mail sent to this contact.

- **All Fields**   Use this tab to display fields and their contents as related to the selected contact.

2. Enter the desired information on the General tab. Although filling out the form is mostly common sense, there are a couple of things to be aware of:

- **Full Name**   You can enter the contact's complete name in the Full Name field and Outlook will separate it into first and last. If there is any question about the way Outlook parses the name, click the Full Name button to display the Check Full Name dialog box. Here you can adjust the name so it's recorded properly.

- **File as**   By default Outlook assumes you want to file contact names by last name first, then by first name. However, you can change the order by making the appropriate selection from the drop-down list. Since this is merely a matter of preference, make the choice you feel the most comfortable with. However, no matter what your choice is, maintain it for all contacts to avoid confusion when sorting and searching.

- **Address**   This field is similar to the Full Name field in that you can enter the address and Outlook automatically separates it into the various components. Click the Address button to verify that Outlook has done so correctly.

- **Phone numbers**   Outlook provides multiple fields for most phone numbers. Click the down arrow button to select a different phone number field.

- **E-mail**   As with the phone number fields, Outlook provides multiple e-mail fields that can be selected by using the drop-down menu that appears when you click the down arrow. You can also add an e-mail address from the Address Book by clicking the Address Book button to open the Select Name dialog box.

- **Contacts**   You can link the current contact with other contacts to create contact groups. This is a great way to organize contacts from the same company or co-workers on the same project.

- **Categories**   By assigning contacts to categories, you can break your contacts down into broad, related groups such as business contacts and personal contacts.

- **Private**   You can mark individual contacts Private to prevent them from being visible to others with whom you share your Contacts folder.

3. Enter additional infsormation about the contact on the Details tab (see Figure 8-2).

   As with the General tab, there are a couple of fields you might want to pay extra attention to:

- **Directory server**   If you have NetMeeting installed and use a particular Internet Locator Service (ILS) server for conducting online meetings, enter the server name or IP address here.

- **E-mail alias**   This is generally the contact's e-mail address.

- **Internet Free-Busy Address**   Outlook enables you to share your free/busy information with others by publishing it to a Web site, FTP site, or network server. Use this field to enter the location of the file in which your free/busy information is stored. This can be a URL (http://...), an FTP site (ftp://...), or a network server (file://...).

4. If you want to use digital certificates to encrypt e-mail you send to this contact, click the Certificates tab and use the Import button to locate and import the desired certificate.

5. Click Save And Close to save the new contact and return to the active Outlook window.

Figure 8-2.   *Add a personal touch by tracking important information such as birthdays and anniversaries*

The new contact is immediately added to your Contacts folder. If you open the Contacts folder to the default view, Address Cards, you'll find a new address card for the contact you just created.

Automating Contact Entry

Outlook is a productivity tool, so it should come as no surprise that it gives you the opportunity to create new contacts with a minimum expenditure of time and effort. Since Outlook can't read your mind (at least not yet), you will, of course, have to supply some of the contact data. However, Outlook lets you take advantage of its storage and retrieval features to create new contacts by using existing contacts to provide some of the information.

Using the New Contact From Same Company Command

If you want to create a new contact based on an existing contact, you can simplify matters by selecting the original contact and choosing Actions | New Contact From

Same Company from the menu bar. This opens a new contact form with the company, address, business phone, and business fax already entered. Outlook copies the data for these fields from the original contact and enters it automatically in the new form. Fill out the remaining information and click Save And Close to save the new contact. You can also use the New Contact From Same Company command from within an open contact by selecting Action | New Contact From Same Company from the menu of the contact form.

Adding Multiple Contacts with Save And New

When you're creating more than one contact in a single session, you might want to use the Save And New command found on the File menu. This command enables you to save the contact you're working on and open a blank contact form, all in one fell swoop. Open a new contact form, enter the appropriate information and choose File | Save And New to save the contact and open a blank contact form.

Even handier than Save And New is a command that not only saves the existing contact, but also opens a new contact form and fills in some of the contact information using the most recently saved contact as the source. This command, Save And New In Company, is not available on any of the standard contact form toolbars or menus. However, you can easily add it to any toolbar or menu on the contact form.

Here's how to add it to the contact form Standard toolbar:

1. Open a new contact form.

2. Double-click a blank spot to the right of the Standard toolbar in the form to open the Customize dialog box.

3. Click the Commands tab to view the available commands.

4. Select File in the Categories list and locate Save And New In Company in the Commands list.

5. Drag the Save And New In Company command to the contact form Standard toolbar and drop it between the Save And Close button and the Save And New button. You can drop the command as soon as your mouse pointer turns into a vertical I bar.

6. Right-click the new button and select Begin A Group to insert a vertical separator between the Save And Close button and the Save And New In Company button.

7. Click Close to exit the Customize dialog box and return to the contact form, where you'll now see the Save And New In Company button on the toolbar.

The next time you want to create multiple contacts from the same organization, create the first contact and fill in all the appropriate information. When you're finished, click Save And New In Company to save the contact. Outlook immediately opens a new contact form containing the following information from the saved contact:

- Company
- Business phone
- Business fax
- Address

You'll also notice that the File As field is filled in using the company name. However, since this is generally used for the contact name, it will change unless you're recording a contact with no name.

For more information on customizing toolbars and menus, see Chapter 23.

Using Copy to Create Similar Records

Another method you can use to speed up contact entry is the Copy command. It makes an exact copy of the selected contact. To use the Copy command, open the Contacts folder, select the contact you want to duplicate, and press CTRL-C. Now press CTRL-V to paste a copy of the selected contact in the Contacts folder.

You can also make a copy of a contact by holding down the CTRL key, then dragging the contact you want to copy and dropping it on the Contacts shortcut on the Outlook Bar or the Contacts folder in the Folder List.

Open the copy, change the name and other appropriate information, and save the new contact. Make sure you change all pertinent information such as linked contacts, birthdays, and so on.

Although Outlook 2000 duplicate checking is turned on by default, it does not warn you when you create or save a duplicate created using the Copy command. Therefore any copy you create and fail to change will remain in your Contacts folder as a duplicate until you weed it out manually.

Adding Contacts from Other Outlook Components

In addition to the straightforward methods of creating a contact by opening a new contact form and entering or modifying the contact data, you can also create new contacts from existing Outlook items such as e-mail messages and appointments.

Creating a Contact from an E-mail Message

One of the most common ways to create a contact from an Outlook item is to use an incoming e-mail message. Since the message already contains the sender's display name and e-mail address, it gives you a head start on entering the contact data.

To create a contact from an e-mail message, follow these steps:

1. Click the Inbox icon to open the Inbox.

2. Double-click the incoming message you want to use to create a new contact.

3. Right-click a display name or e-mail address in the From, To, or Cc field in the header and choose Add To Contacts. A new contact form opens with the display name entered in the Full Name field and the e-mail address in the E-mail field.

If you want to add multiple contacts from the same e-mail message, you'll have to do it one at a time since you cannot select multiple display names or addresses.

4. Fill in the remaining contact information as desired, and click Save And Close.

That's all there is to it. The contact is immediately added to your Contacts folder.

Creating Contacts from Other Outlook Items

Another handy but often-overlooked method of creating contacts is the use of drag and drop. You can drag other Outlook items such as notes, tasks, and e-mail messages to the Contacts folder icon and drop them to create new contacts. You can drop the items on the Contacts shortcut on the Outlook Bar or on the Contacts folder in the Folder List. When you drop the item, a new contact form containing information from the dropped item opens. The information that appears depends on the item type you drop.

- **E-mail messages** The sender's display name and e-mail address are entered automatically in the new contact form. In addition, the message header, contents, importance, and categories are included in the Notes field of the contact form.

- **Appointments and meetings** The name and e-mail address of the originator of the appointment or meeting are entered in the new contact form. The appointment or meeting contents are included in the Notes field of the new contact form.

- **Tasks** Regular tasks as well as incoming task requests generate a new contact using the display name and e-mail of the originator of the task (you) or the task request (the sender). Tasks you assign to others generate contacts using the task request recipient. If a task request contains multiple recipients, only the first recipient is used. The content of the task or task request is included in the contact form Notes field.

- **Notes and journal entries** The contents of the note or journal entry are included in the contact form Notes field.

- **Files** If you drag a computer file to the Contacts icon, a new contact form opens and a shortcut to the file is added to the Notes field of the form.

You can also right-drag (hold down your right mouse button instead of your left, and drag the item) Outlook items to the Contacts icon and drop them with somewhat different results. As soon as you drop the item, a shortcut menu appears providing you with several choices.

Copy Here as Contact with Text
Copy Here as Contact with Shortcut
Copy Here as Contact with Attachment
Move Here as Contact with Attachment

Cancel

- **Copy Here as Contact with Text** Copies the item following the earlier rules and adds the item contents as text in the contact form Notes field. This is the default command for a regular drag and drop action.

WORKING WITH CONTACTS

- **Copy Here as Contact with Shortcut**   Enters name and e-mail address information following the earlier rules and adds a shortcut to the item in the contact form Notes field.

- **Copy Here as Contact with Attachment**   Enters name and e-mail address information following the earlier rules and inserts the item as an attachment in the contact form Notes field.

- **Move Here as Contact with Attachment**   Enters name and e-mail address information following the earlier rules, adds the item to the new contact as an attachment, and deletes the original item.

When you use the Move Here As Contact With Attachment option and change your mind before saving the new contact, the original item is deleted anyway. Fortunately, Outlook stores it in the Deleted Items folder so you can retrieve it if need be.

Creating Contacts from E-mail Attachments

In addition to creating contacts from e-mail messages, you can also create contacts from contacts or vCards sent as e-mail attachments. Another Outlook user can attach a single contact from his or her Contacts folder to an e-mail message and send it to you to incorporate into your Contacts folder. You can also receive contact information from non-Outlook users in the form of vCard attachments to e-mail. vCard is a file format that enables users of compatible contact managers to exchange electronic business cards.

When you receive an Outlook contact as an attachment, all you have to do is drag the attachment to your Contacts folder and drop it. You can use the Contacts shortcut on the Outlook Bar or the Contacts folder in the Folder List. In theory, you can open the contact and click Save And Close to add the new contact to your Contacts folder. However, there appears to be a bug in Outlook 2000 that prevents this method from working.

You can add a vCard attachment to your Contacts folder in the same manner. Drag it to the Contacts shortcut on the Outlook Bar or the Contacts folder in the Folder List and drop it. A new contact form opens with the information from the vCard already entered. Click Save And Close to save the new contact.

Receiving Contacts in E-mail

Since e-mail provides a quick and easy method of sharing all types of information, it only makes sense that you can exchange contact information with others via e-mail. The two most common forms of contact information you're likely to receive are Outlook contact records from other Outlook users and vCards from both Outlook and non-Outlook users.

Both Outlook contact records and vCards are sent as e-mail attachments. When you receive either one, the easiest way to add the information to your Contacts folder is to drag the attachment(s) to the Contacts shortcut on the Outlook Bar or the contact folder in the Folder List. Dropping a contact item on the shortcut adds the contact to your folder with no muss or fuss. The only time you'll have to do anything is if you already have a contact by the same name or with the same e-mail address in your Contacts folder.

When you drag a vCard to the Contacts shortcut or to the Contacts folder, a new contact form opens with all the information in the vCard entered in the appropriate field(s). Modify the information as needed and click Save And Close.

Importing Contacts from Other Sources

In addition to using Outlook contacts from other users and vCards from vCard-compatible contact managers, you can also utilize contact information from a wide range of compatible and incompatible sources, including contact managers, databases, and spreadsheets. You can accomplish this by importing the data from the original source into Outlook, which has converters for the following popular contact managers, databases, and spreadsheets, among others:

- ACT! 2.0, 3.x, 4.0
- dBase
- ECCO 2.0, 3.0, 4.0
- Lotus Organizer 1.0, 1.1, 2.1
- Lotus Organizer 97
- Microsoft Access
- Microsoft Excel
- Microsoft FoxPro
- Schedule Plus
- Sidekick 95
- Sidekick for Windows 2.0

If you don't find your program on the list don't panic, there's still hope. In addition to importing specific file formats, Outlook also imports delimited text files. Delimited text files are ones in which information contained in individual fields is separated (delimited) by a special character, and individual records (groups of related fields) are separated by a hard return or other special character. This enables other programs to recognize both fields and records, and therefore to import the information with a minimum amount of fuss. Any contact manager, database, or spreadsheet program worth its salt can export information to a delimited text file.

To import contact data, begin by launching the Import and Export Wizard. Choose File | Import And Export from the Menu bar.

After the Import and Export Wizard opens, select Import From Another Program Or File and click Next. This opens the Import A File screen. Select the file format of the information you want to import and click Next.

Depending on the format you choose, you may have to insert your Outlook or Office CD. Not all converters are added when you install Outlook. If the converter you want to use isn't installed, insert your CD and follow the onscreen instructions.

From this point forward, the file type selected dictates the remaining screens. Follow the instructions, entering information and setting options as needed. One thing you should be aware of is the mapping of custom fields. This is especially helpful if you're importing a non-contact manager file, such as a database, spreadsheet, or delimited text file. The manner in which you name your fields (Name, Address, Phone, and so on), may be confusing to Outlook, and it may require that you specify which imported fields match up with which Outlook fields. This is called field mapping.

As you can see in Figure 8-3, the Map Custom Fields dialog box presents you with a list of fields from the file you're importing, on the left, and a list of Outlook fields on the right.

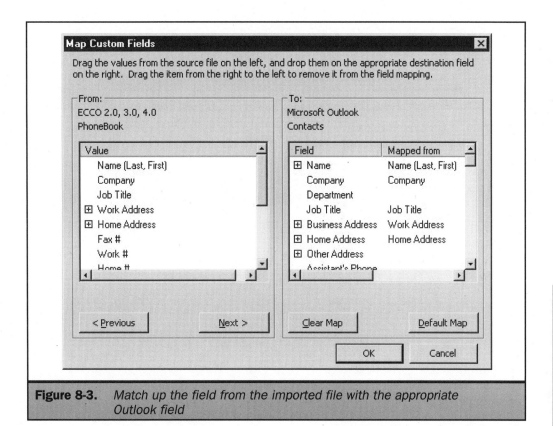

Figure 8-3.   *Match up the field from the imported file with the appropriate Outlook field*

To match (map) the fields, drag them from the list on the left to the corresponding fields on the right. This enables Outlook to enter the correct contact data in the new contacts records that are created when you complete the import process.

For more information on importing data into Outlook, see Chapter 20.

Dealing with Duplicate Contact Records

If you maintain a large Contacts database, you'll find that duplicate records are a fact of life. Whether your memory is slipping and you forget someone's already in your Contacts folder or you receive contacts as attachments from others, you're bound to end up with duplicate contacts. Fortunately, Outlook 2000 incorporates automatic duplicate checking, which keeps an eye out for contacts with identical names or e-mail addresses. When you attempt to add a duplicate record, Outlook warns you and offers a couple of options.

If you want to proceed, you can either add the duplicate and have two records containing the same name or same e-mail address, or you can elect to have the existing record updated using the new record you're adding. If you update the contact, a copy of the original contact is placed in the Deleted Items file where you can later retrieve it if necessary.

When you elect to update the existing contact, all information from the new contact is copied to the existing contact and replaces the original information. There are some exceptions. Categories, text in the Notes field, and attachments are not copied. You'll have to manually copy these yourself. Certificates as well as links on the Activities tab are copied, but do not replace the original data. They are added to any existing certificates or links.

Remember, using the Copy and Paste or Cut and Paste commands to create new contacts from existing contacts does not trigger duplicate detection by Outlook.

What do you do if, accidentally or intentionally, you create duplicate records? Obviously, you cull the unwanted duplicates out. However, there's one small problem. How do you decide which one to keep and which to delete? While there's no perfect solution other than opening each record and comparing it field for field, there are a couple of indicators you may find helpful in weeding out duplicates.

The best way to spot duplicates is to change the Contacts folder view to a table view such as the Phone List view. Then click the Full Name header to sort the list by name. This will enable you to readily see those contacts with duplicate names.

Now, how do you decide which of the duplicates to keep? While you could open each duplicate and see which one has the most current information, there's an easier way—add the Modified field to the view. The Modified field contains the date the record was created or last changed. To add the Modified field, right-click any column header and select Field Chooser to open the Field Chooser dialog box seen in Figure 8-4.

From the field type drop-down list, choose All Contact Fields. Scroll down and locate the Modified field. Drag it to the Information viewer and drop it between the Full Name header and the Company header. Expand the column width so you can see the date and time the contact records were last modified. Next, return to the Field Chooser and locate the Size field. Drag it to the Information viewer and drop it between the Modified header and the Company header. This field indicates the size of the record. Now you can compare duplicates to see which is the most recent and which contains the most data. This should help make the decision.

MOUS

MOUS EXAM PRACTICE

In this section, you learned about creating contacts using different sources. Now you can practice the various techniques. Begin by opening a new contact form and filling out the information. Try using each of the different methods available for opening blank contact forms. Use the Save And New command, and take advantage of the Copy and Paste commands as well. Next, create contacts from incoming e-mail messages. Finally, try your hand at dragging and dropping to create contacts from other Outlook items.

WORKING WITH CONTACTS

Figure 8-4. *Adding fields to a view is easy with the Field Chooser*

Modifying and Deleting Contacts

Adding contacts to your Contacts folder is only half the battle. As with most things in life, your contacts' information is bound to change from time to time, and in some cases, become totally obsolete. When that happens, you'll need to change those records that need modifying and delete those records that no longer serve a useful purpose.

Editing Existing Contacts

Modifying existing contacts is actually pretty straightforward. It's a simple matter of double-clicking the contact record to open it, making the necessary changes, and then saving the record to retain the changes. If you're fortunate enough to have a co-worker who is maintaining the same contact information and who has updated records for some of your contacts, it's even easier. In that case, you can ask your co-worker to send you the updated contacts, which you can then add to your Contacts folder. When asked if you want to update existing contacts, answer yes, and the latest information replaces the old, outdated information.

If you find yourself in a situation in which the same information has changed in a number of contacts, such as the company name or address, you can make the changes without opening and closing each contact record by using a table view.

Open the Contacts folder and choose View | Current View | Phone List to display your contacts in the Phone List view. Sort the list by the field you want to modify by clicking the field header (see Figure 8-5).

If the field doesn't appear in the list, right-click one of the field headers and select Field Chooser from the shortcut menu. From the Field Chooser, drag the field you want to modify and drop it between the Full Name header and the Company header. Repeat for all the fields you want to change. If the field doesn't appear in the Frequently-Used Fields group, use the drop-down list to select All Contact Fields.

Move to the first record you want to change and click the field you want to edit. This places the cursor at the end of the field entry. Replace or modify the information as needed, then press ENTER to save the change. Highlight the new information and press CTRL-C to copy it. Move to the next record, highlight the old field entry and press CTRL-V to replace it with the new (copied) information. Press ENTER to save the record. Repeat the process for each record you want to change.

Figure 8-5. *Line up all the records by the field you want to change*

In addition to changing the contents of a contact record, you can also change a couple of its basic properties. Open the contact record and choose File | Properties to display the contact's Properties dialog box (see Figure 8-6).

As you can see, the Properties dialog box tells you a lot about the contact record. It indicates the record's location, its size, when it was sent, received, and last modified, and it offers you the opportunity to change two contact record options: Importance, and whether or not to AutoArchive the item. To change the Importance level, make a new selection from the Importance drop-down list. If you want the Outlook AutoArchive feature to skip this record when performing a scheduled AutoArchive operation, check the Do Not AutoArchive This Item checkbox. Click OK when you're finished.

Figure 8-6. *The contact's Properties dialog box provides a wealth of information about the contact record*

By default, the remaining options are determined by other Outlook settings and are therefore read-only options. In other words, you can't change them. However, there's a way to circumvent the read-only restriction. Choose Edit | Revise Contents from the contact form menu bar before opening the contact's Properties dialog box.

Eliminating Unwanted Contacts

When business associates change jobs and friends lose touch, you may find yourself with contact records that are no longer of any use to you. In that case, you'll want to do a little housecleaning and get rid of the unwanted contacts. Not only do they unnecessarily clutter up your Contacts folder, but they also take up valuable hard disk space, and slow down your search and sort operations.

If you find yourself with unwanted contacts, the solution is simple: delete them. How you delete them is up to you, and you have a number of methods from which to choose. You can delete them individually, or you can delete them en masse.

To eliminate a single contact record, open the Contacts folder, select the record, and press DELETE or click the Delete button on the Standard toolbar. You can also press CTRL-D or right-click the contact and select Delete from the shortcut menu. In addition, you can select the record and choose Edit | Delete from the Menu bar.

In either an Address Cards view or a table view, you can select multiple contacts by holding down the CTRL key and clicking the contacts you want to select. Then use any of the available methods to delete all the selected contacts in one operation. You can also select a series of sequential contacts by clicking the first contact, holding down the SHIFT key, and clicking the last contact in the series. The first, last, and all contacts between are selected.

MOUS EXAM PRACTICE

In this section, you began to familiarize yourself with the techniques necessary to edit and delete contacts. Now practice by creating a few "dummy" contacts you can modify and delete without fear of losing important information. Then make some simple changes to a single contact. Next, open a table view and try editing a series of contacts. When you've got the hang of modifying contacts, delete the "dummy" contacts using the methods described earlier.

Working with Contacts

Creating contacts is just the beginning. In order to use your Contacts database effectively, you should also take advantage of some of the more advanced contact features available in Outlook, such as adding attachments, flagging contacts for follow-up, linking items and files to contacts, and more.

Attaching Items to a Contact Record

Attaching items to a contact record is very similar to the procedure used for attaching items to e-mail messages. Open the contact record and choose Insert from the Menu bar to view the menu of items you can insert in a contact.

Tip *If you want to insert an object and the choice is grayed out on the menu, close the menu and return to the contact form. Place the cursor in the Notes field of the contact form and open the Insert menu again. Now all three choices, including Object, are available.*

Select the type of item to insert and follow the onscreen instructions. Your choices include:

- **File** If you want to attach a computer file, this is the selection to use. It displays the Insert File dialog box, which enables you to locate and select the desired file from anywhere on your computer system.

- **Item**   To attach an Outlook item, choose Item. This opens the Insert Item dialog box, which provides you with a tree-like view of your folders, from which you can choose one or more items to attach.

- **Object**   You can embed a data object, such as a picture or spreadsheet, into the contact record. Choosing this command opens the Insert Object dialog box from which you can select the object to attach.

Tip   *If you want to attach a file, you can click the Insert File button on the contact form Standard toolbar.*

The attachments are inserted into the Notes field of the contact form (see Figure 8-7). File and item attachments are represented by their respective icons. In Figure 8-7, the 1Qtr Summary.doc file is a Microsoft Word document; Modem Settings is an Outlook note. Objects are embedded in their entirety—you see the entire object, not merely a representation, as in the case of the embedded spreadsheet in Figure 8-7.

To open a file or item attachment, double-click the icon. In the case of a file attachment, the program associated with the file launches and opens the file. This,

Figure 8-7.   *Use attachments to keep information related to the contact at your fingertips*

of course, means you must have either the associated program or a file viewer that supports the file format installed on your computer.

You can modify an embedded object by double-clicking it and making changes directly to the object. If, instead of embedding the object you chose to link the object, double-clicking it opens the associated program. From there you can make any necessary changes. As with a file attachment, you must have the associated program installed on your computer to modify a linked object.

Flagging Contacts

Flagging is not merely reserved for e-mail messages. Any time you want to remind yourself—or someone else to whom you send or forward a contact—to follow up on a contact, you can set a follow-up flag to ensure you don't forget. For example, suppose you know the contact is moving to a new office and will have a different address and phone number in two weeks. Rather than make the change now and create confusion if you need to get in touch before the two weeks is up, why not flag the contact for follow-up on the date the change becomes effective?

To flag a contact, open the contact and click the Flag for Follow Up button on the contact form Standard toolbar to open the Flag for Follow Up dialog box.

Flag for Follow Up	? X

Flagging marks an item to remind you that it needs to be followed up. After it has been followed up, you can mark it complete.

Flag to: `Follow up` ▾ `Clear Flag`

Due by: `Thu 7/27/00 7:00 PM` ▾

☐ Completed

`OK` `Cancel`

From the Flag To drop-down list, select the type of flag. If you want to set a reminder for the flag, enter a date and time in the Due By field or select a date from the drop-down calendar that appears when you click the down arrow at the end of the field. By default, Outlook uses the end of workday time as the reminder time. You can change it by placing your cursor in the Due By field and editing it manually. Click OK to save the flag and return to the contact. An information bar appears at the top of the General tab indicating the flag type and reminder date and time.

When viewing flagged contacts in an Address Cards view, the first line of the card indicates the flag type. In a table view, a red flag appears in the flag column indicating the contact has been flagged.

Linking Activities to a Contact Record

As handy as attachments are, they have one drawback: they increase the size of the contact record to which they're attached. Since the attached file, item, or object is actually stored in the contact record, the size of the record is increased by the size of the attachment. This can be a problem depending on the number of contacts and attachments, as well as any size limitations imposed by the administrator on your mailbox space on the server.

Fortunately, there's a way to have your cake and eat it too! Rather than attach the items, you can create a link from the contact record to the item. This enables you to keep the item immediately accessible without having to store the item and utilize valuable hard disk space. As always, Outlook provides a couple of different ways for you to achieve your goal. The first is the Link command. The second method is through the use of hyperlinks.

Using the Link Command

For linking most items and files you'll find the Link command to be the quickest and easiest method to use. It provides a dialog box from which you select the item or file and does not require you to know the names of items or the proper syntax to use when creating the link. To see just how easy it is, try the following steps to link an item to a contact:

1. Open the contact in which you want to create the links.

2. Choose Actions | Link | Items to display the Link Items To Contact dialog box.

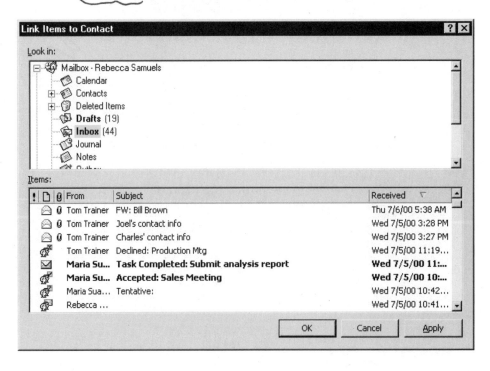

3. From the Look In list, select the folder containing the item(s) you want to link.

4. Select the Item(s) from the Items list.

5. Click OK to create the link and return to the contact.

Linking files is a little different. Rather than creating a direct link to the file, Outlook creates a journal entry that includes a shortcut to the file.

Begin by choosing Actions | Link | Files to open the Choose A File dialog box. Next, locate and double-click the desired file to open the Journal Entry dialog box.

Make any necessary changes to the journal entry and click Save And Close.

When you return to the contact record, nothing appears to have changed. To see the new links, click the Activities tab. At first glance, nothing may appear. This is because Outlook has to search for the linked activities. If there is a delay, you'll notice the blue magnifying glass to the left of the Stop button going around and around. This indicates the search is in progress. When the search is complete, the magnifying glass stops and the linked activities are listed.

By default, Outlook displays all linked items. However, you can narrow the search by selecting a different activities view from the Show drop-down list. To view a linked item in the Activities tab, double-click it. If it's an Outlook item, it opens immediately. If it's a file, it opens in the program associated with the file type.

When you delete an item from the Activities tab, you are actually deleting the listed item, not merely the link to the item. In the case of a linked file, you're deleting the journal entry containing the file shortcut. Fortunately, anything you delete from the Activities tab is immediately sent to the Deleted Items folder, from which you can retrieve it if necessary.

You can't use the Link command to link objects to a contact form. However, you can elect to link an object when inserting it as an attachment. Although it saves some (not all) disk space, it does not add the linked object to the Activities tab. Your best bet is to link the object as a file, using the Actions | Link | File command.

Using Hyperlinks

While the Link command is quick and easy, it is also limited. The only things you can link to a contact with it are files and Outlook items. Hyperlinks expand the types of things you can link to include Outlook folders, personal and public folders, items, files, Web sites, and FTP sites. To create a hyperlink, you must know the name and location of the folder or item you want to link to. You must also know the proper syntax to use.

Start by opening the contact in which you want to create the link. Then move your cursor to the Notes field. Type the link using the syntax in Table 8-1.

If the text string you're entering for the link contains no spaces, you can leave the less than (<) and greater than (>) signs off the beginning and end, respectively, of the link.

One last thing to be aware of: links cannot contain items that include the following four characters in the item name: \ / " >. Outlook also has a bit of trouble when using hyperlinks to link to messages that have been replied to or forwarded. If you leave the RE: or FW: off and use the rest of the subject as the item name, Outlook finds the first message containing the specified text in the subject field.

Calling Contacts

Next to e-mail, the phone is probably your most frequently used means of communicating with business associates, friends, and co-workers. Since the Contacts folder is the logical place to store the phone numbers for those folks with whom you stay in touch via telephone, it's also the logical place from which to initiate phone calls. Fortunately, nothing could be simpler.

Obviously, the first thing to do is look up the contact. The next step depends on whether or not you have a modem hooked up to your phone line. If you have a modem, you may be able to let Outlook do the dialing for you. However, if you're in a corporate environment, chances are, even with a modem hookup, you're not going to be able to take advantage of the AutoDial feature. Most modem hookups in a corporate environment are separate from the company phone system, and therefore, not able to work or play together.

To Open This	Use This Syntax	Example
An Outlook folder on the server	\<Outlook:Foldername\>	\<Outlook:Inbox\>
A personal or private folder	\<Outlook://Foldername\>	\<Outlook://Personal Folders/Customers\>
An Outlook item	\<Outlook:Foldername/~Itemname\>	\<Outlook:Contacts/~Bob Smith\>
An Outlook item in a subfolder	\<Outlook:Foldername/Subfoldername/~Itemname\>	\<Outlook:Contacts/Vendors/~Pete Brannigan\>
An item in a public folder	\<Outlook://Public Folders/Foldername/~Itemname\>	\<Outlook://Public Folders/Authors/~Stephen King\>
A file in a public folder	\<Outlook://Public Folders/Foldername/filename.ext\>	\<Outlook://Public Folders/Reports/1QtrSales.doc\>
A folder on your computer	\<file://computername/driveletter/foldername\>	\<file://Florida/c/My Documents\>
A file on your computer	\<file://computername/driveletter/foldername/filename.ext\>	\<file://Florida/c/My Documents/1QtrSales.xls\>
A Web site	\<http://www.domain name\>	\<http://www.ezwidgets.com\>
An FTP site	\<ftp://domain name\>	\<ftp://ezwidgets.com\>

Table 8-1.   *Syntax Used When Creating Outlook Hyperlinks*

WORKING WITH CONTACTS

However, if you have a phone line that's attached to both your modem and your phone, you can take advantage of the AutoDial feature. Open the contact you want to call and click the AutoDialer button to open the New Call dialog box.

If you haven't already set up your dialing properties, click the Dialing Properties button and do so now. The required information is pretty much common sense. When you're finished setting up the dialing properties, click Close to return to the New Call dialog box. You're now ready to let Outlook do the dialing for you. If you want to track the call with a journal entry, check the Create New Journal Entry When Starting New Call option. Click Start Call to place the call. Outlook dials the selected number and displays the Call Status dialog box.

When the party answers, click Talk. If no one answers, click Hang Up to end the call. When you're through with the call, hang up and click End Call. That's all there is to it.

Mapping a Contact Address

A new and potentially handy feature of Outlook 2000 is the ability to display a map showing the contact's address. To use this feature, you must have an Internet connection. First, establish your connection to the Internet. Then open the contact whose address you want to map. Click the Display Map Of Address button on the contact form Standard toolbar. This launches your Web browser and takes you to the Expedia.com Web site (see Figure 8-8).

The initial view is an overview of the area. To see more detail, click the magnifying glass with the plus (+) sign or select a wider line in the Zoom Level box in the lower-right corner, above the Print button. You can use the Map Mover arrows to pan the map. You can even get driving directions to the location by clicking the Get Driving Directions To This Location link. When you're finished, return to Outlook and close the contact.

If you're planning to visit the client, you might want to click the Get Driving Directions To This Location link and copy the directions into the Notes field of the contact form.

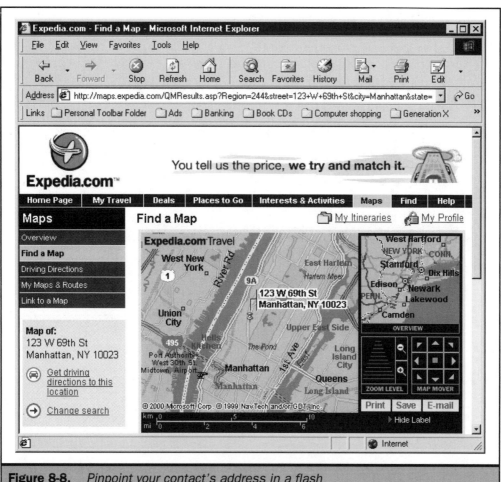

Figure 8-8.   *Pinpoint your contact's address in a flash*

Printing Contact Information

As convenient as an electronic address book is, there are times when nothing short of a hard copy will do. It's a little difficult standing at an airport phone cubicle and trying to fire up your laptop just to get a phone number. Or suppose you're in a meeting and you need a phone number to get some quick information from a colleague or business associate. Again, using a laptop is not only cumbersome, but also unnecessary. When the need arises, having a printed copy of your contacts can be a lifesaver.

To make life even easier, Outlook accommodates a variety of paper sizes and different address book types, such as Day-Timers, Day Runners, and Franklin Day Planners, as well as customized formats.

To print your contact information, follow these steps:

1. Open the Contacts folder and click the Print button to display the Print dialog box shown in Figure 8-9.

2. From the Name drop-down list, select the printer you want to use.

3. Click the Properties button to set options for the selected printer. The options that appear depend entirely on the printer you've selected. Each printer has its own unique set of options.

Figure 8-9.   *The Print dialog box lets you decide how and what to print*

4. Choose a style for the hard copy from the Print Style list. Your options depend on the current view selected in the Contacts folder. If the current view is an Address Cards view, your choices include:

- ■ **Card Style**   Each contact appears on the printout displaying the same information and in the same format as it appears in the Address Cards view. The page setup calls for printing on a full 8.5 × 11-inch sheet of paper.

- ■ **Small Booklet Style**   This is the Card Style with a page setup calling for an 8.5 × 11-inch sheet using the 1/8 sheet booklet size setting. In other words, dividing the full page into eight smaller pages, which can later be folded to form a small booklet.

- ■ **Medium Booklet Style**   The Medium Booklet Style is also the Card Style with a different page setup. It uses an 8.5 × 11-inch sheet and divides it into four sections employing the 1/4 sheet booklet size setting.

- ■ **Memo Style**   Use the Memo Style when you want to print more complete information for each contact. In addition to the fields from the General tab of the contact record, a number of fields from the Details tab are included. You can even include notes and attachments.

- ■ **Phone Directory Style**   This is a great style to use when you want a phone list that is broken down alphabetically. Each contact is listed with all available phone numbers.

Note   *When you use any of the address card print styles, distribution lists are not distinguished from regular contacts in any way. However, when you use the Table Style, distribution lists appear in bold in the printout and each distribution list name is preceded by the distribution list icon.*

5. Click Page Setup to open the Page Setup dialog box and change the settings for the selected style. The Page Setup dialog box may appear different from the one in Figure 8-10 depending on the print style selected.

6. Change the Format options to suit your needs. Different print styles offer a different range of options. Figure 8-10 shows the Format options for the Card Style, as well as the Small and Medium Booklet Styles. The other print styles have more limited Format options.

- ■ **Preview**   Keep an eye on this small display area. It provides a rough estimation of the appearance of your printout, depending on the options you choose.

WORKING WITH CONTACTS

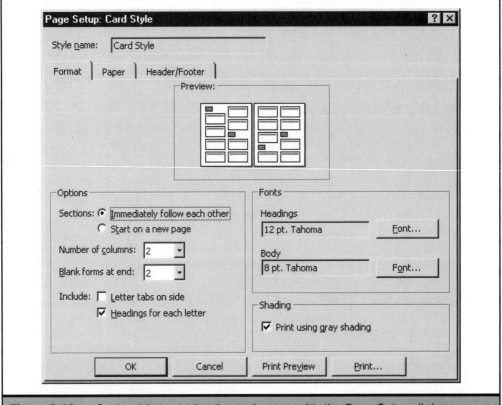

Figure 8-10.   *Customizing your hard copy is easy with the Page Setup dialog box options*

- **Sections**   Your selection here determines whether each alphabetical section (A, B, C, and so on) begins where the last section leaves off, or if it starts on a new page regardless of where the last section ends. Choose Immediately Follow Each Other for a continuous printout with each section starting where the last one ends. Choose Start On A New Page to start each section on its own page.

- **Number of columns**   Select the number of columns you want to appear on each page of the printout.

- **Blank forms at end**   This option enables you to designate the number of blank address book forms you want added to the printout. The pages are not actually blank, but contain field names and lines to enable you to easily enter contact information. In theory it sounds good. However, it rarely gets used and is generally nothing more than a waste of paper. Therefore, you should set it to zero unless you find you actually use the "blank" pages.

■ **Include**   If you have a large number of contacts to print, adding headings and letter tabs can prove helpful when searching for specific contacts. Check Letter Tabs On Side to include a vertical letter bar similar to the one that appears on address card views. The letters represented on each page appear in black. To add a letter heading to the beginning of each alphabetical section, check Headings For Each Letter.

■ **Fonts**   You can change the fonts used to print both headings and the body of the printout. Click the appropriate Font button and select the font, the font style, font size, and language.

■ **Shading**   While it may seem like a minor option, this can make all the difference in the appearance of your printout. With Shading checked, each contact name is offset in a shaded box, enabling you to quickly discern names at a glance. It also adds shading to letter tabs if you include them.

7. Click the Paper tab and adjust the settings as needed. Here's what you'll find:

■ **Type**   This selection indicates the actual type of paper you're using. It includes most standard paper types as well as a number of address book papers from Avery and one from FiloFax. In addition, you can specify a custom paper if your paper type doesn't appear on the list.

■ **Dimensions**   The width and height of the paper type selected are displayed here. If you're using a standard paper type, leave these dimensions as they are. If you select a custom paper, enter your own dimensions.

■ **Paper Source**   Let Outlook know where to find the paper by making your selection from the Paper Source drop-down list. Unless your printer has multiple trays or unless you plan to feed the paper manually, you can leave this at the default setting.

■ **Margins**   Indicate the distance from the top, left side, right side, and bottom of the page you want the printing to appear. Inches are automatically assumed, therefore, you can just enter the distance and Outlook will add inch marks (").

■ **Size**   At first glance you might think that paper type and page size are the same. Be assured, they are not. The paper type indicates the exact size of the sheet used for printing. The page size refers to the page layout that gets printed on each sheet. For example, a small booklet may have as many as eight pages printed on a single sheet.

■ **Orientation**   Select Portrait to print the page vertically, or Landscape to print the page horizontally. The height and width of the page automatically adjust to the selected orientation. The preview box to the left of the orientation choices displays a rough estimation of the way the sheet will print depending on the options you've selected.

8. Click the Header/Footer tab to add headers and/or footers to the printout. Header information appears at the top of each page, while footer information appears at the bottom of each page. Text or data entered in the left text box appears on the left side of the page, text entered in the middle text box appears in the middle of the page, and so on. You can use the Header/Footer toolbar to add such things as page number, total number of pages, and more.

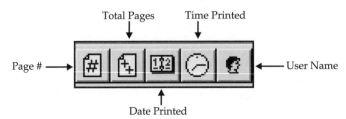

9. Click OK to save your settings and return to the Print dialog box.

10. Select the range of items you want to print. Your choices include All Items and Only Selected Items. If you highlighted certain contacts prior to opening the Print dialog box, choosing Only Selected Items prints only those items, otherwise choose All Items to print all contacts in the current view.

Tip *If you want to print a selection of contacts without selecting each one individually, apply a filter to the view before clicking the Print button. When you go to print, choose All Items to print everything in the filtered view.*

11. Set the Copies options, which include the following:

- **Number of pages** You can elect to print all pages, odd numbered, or even numbered pages. This is especially handy if you want to use both sides of the paper. Print only the even numbered pages, then reinsert the printed copies in the printer and print the odd numbered pages. Of course, you'll have to be careful to reinsert them in the correct order and facing the right direction or you'll end up with a mess. Try printing a couple of test pages before printing your entire Contacts folder.

- **Number of copies** The name pretty much says it all.

- **Collate copies** This potentially handy option automates the collating of multiple copies of multipage printouts. Normally, Outlook sends the print data for each page to the printer, which then prints the specified number of copies before moving on to the next page. Therefore, if you print ten copies of a five-page contact list, you'll end up with ten copies of page one, followed by ten copies of page two, and so on. You then have to separate them and put each five-page copy together manually. If you select Collate Copies, Outlook instructs the printer to print a single copy of each of the five pages, and then start over until all ten copies are complete.

While the Collate Copies option sounds great, it can be time consuming since Outlook is forced to keep resending the same page information to the printer each time it starts a new copy. In the earlier example, with collating turned off, Outlook would send the page information only five times. However, with collating turned on it is forced to send the page information 50 times. Depending on the size of the print job and how quickly your printer assimilates the data, this could result in an extremely lengthy print process. If you have a large print job, do a small test run before letting Outlook collate the whole thing.

12. Click OK to print the contact information.

If you want to see what your printout is going to look like before printing it, click the Print Preview button in the Print dialog box.

Creating Other Items from Contacts

Earlier in this chapter, you discovered how to create contacts from other Outlook items. Now, taking advantage of the close integration of the various Outlook components, you're going to learn how to generate an assortment of Outlook items from contacts.

E-mailing Contacts

If you've got e-mail and you've got contacts, it's only natural that the two should converge. Clearly, one of the most common ways of communicating with a contact is by e-mail. And what better way to share contact information than via e-mail?

Sending E-mail to Contacts

If you're working in the Contacts folder and decide to send e-mail to a contact, there's no need to head back to the Inbox to do it. Simply right-click the contact you want to e-mail and select New Message To Contact from the shortcut menu that appears. Next thing you know, a new mail message form opens addressed to the selected contact. If you're so inclined, you can even select multiple contacts. Then choose Actions | New Message To Contact to open a new mail message addressed to all the selected contacts.

Another method you can use to create an e-mail message from a contact is the drag and drop method. Drag the contact to whom you want the message addressed and drop it on any mail folder (Inbox, Outbox, Drafts, Sent Items) shortcut in the Outlook Bar or the desired mail folder in the Folder List. A new message form addressed to the contact(s) opens immediately.

Sending Contact Information via E-mail

 In addition to sending e-mail to contacts, you can also send contacts to e-mail recipients. It's a great way to share contact information with co-workers, business associates, and friends. For sharing with other Outlook users, you can simply attach Outlook contacts to your e-mail message. To send contact information to non-Outlook users, you can attach contact information in the form of vCards (electronic business cards). Either way, the recipients can access and use the contact information.

To send Outlook contacts to other Outlook users, follow these steps:

1. Open the Contacts folder.
2. Select the contact(s) to send and press CTRL-F or choose Actions | Forward to open a new mail message form. Outlook attaches the contact(s) to the message. If you select a single contact, the subject line includes the contact name preceded by FW:, indicating a forward. If you select multiple contacts, the subject line is blank, and all the shortcuts appear in the message body.

You can also right-click the selected contact(s) and choose Forward Items. However, if you select a distribution list, the Forward command is not available on the shortcut menu. You'll have to press CTRL-F or choose Actions | Forward from the Menu bar.

3. Add the desired recipients to the To, Cc, and Bcc fields.
4. Type your message in the message body.
5. Click Send to transmit the message and its attached contact item.

If you're a drag and drop fan, you can right-drag a contact and drop it on a mail folder shortcut on the Outlook Bar or in the Folder List. From the shortcut menu that appears, select Copy Here As Message With Attachment. This opens a new mail message form with the contact name as the subject line and the contact item inserted as an attachment. If you select multiple contacts, the subject line is left blank and the contacts are inserted as attachments.

  Using the Move Here As Message With Attachment produces the same results with one difference: the contact is removed from the Contacts folder.

To share information with non-Outlook users, you can send contact information in the vCard format. Most popular contact managers and personal information managers (PIMs) support the vCard format. To send a contact as a vCard, select the contact(s) you want to send and choose Actions | Forward As vCard. This opens a new mail message form with the contact(s) included as attachment(s).

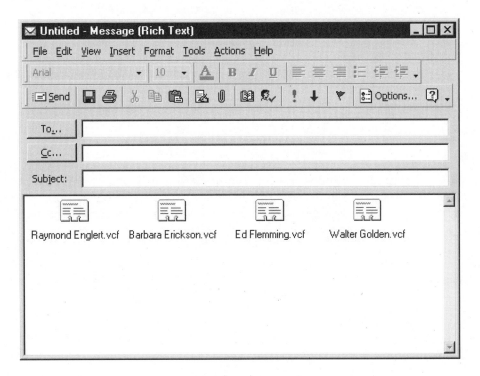

WORKING WITH CONTACTS

If you forward a single vCard, the subject line includes FW: followed by the contact name, otherwise the subject line is blank.

  You cannot forward distribution lists as vCards. If you select a distribution list or multiple contacts, one or more of which is a distribution list, the Forward As vCard command is unavailable.

You can also create vCards from contacts, and store them on your computer for later use. This is especially helpful if you want to create a vCard of your own contact information to attach to an e-mail signature.

To create a vCard from a contact, open the contact and choose File | Export To vCard file to display the VCARD File dialog box, which automatically opens to the Signature folder. You can save the vCard file as is by clicking Save, or you can change the name and location before clicking Save. A new file using the contact name and the .vcf extension is created in the designated folder.

MOUS

MOUS EXAM PRACTICE
In this section, you saw how combining the power of contact management with the ease of e-mail provides an effective tool for sharing information with others. Now try your hand at the various methods discussed here. Start by creating a couple of dummy contacts. Then attach them to e-mail messages using both the Forward command and the right-drag (click and hold your right mouse button when dragging) method. Next, attach the same dummy contacts to e-mail messages as vCards. Create a contact record containing your own contact information and then create a vCard for later use by using the Export To vCard file command.

Creating Tasks, Meeting Requests, Notes, Journal Entries, and Appointments

Creating tasks, meeting requests, and appointments from contacts is as easy as selecting the contacts and choosing the appropriate command from the Actions menu. If you're using a single contact to create these items, you can right-click the contact and select the appropriate command from the shortcut menu.

The Advanced toolbar contains buttons for the New Meeting Request To Contact and the New Task For Contact commands. Right-click the Standard toolbar and select Advanced from the shortcut menu.

The available commands are:

- **New Appointment with Contact**   Opens a new appointment form with the selected contact(s) entered in the Contacts field.

- **New Meeting Request to Contact**   Opens a new meeting request form addressed to the selected contact(s), and including the selected contact(s) in the Contacts field.

- **New Task for Contact**   Opens a new task form and enters the selected contact(s) in the Contacts field. If you click the Assign Task button, the task form is converted to a task request addressed to the selected contact(s).

■ **New Journal Entry for Contact**   Opens a new journal entry form with the contact name as the subject, and with the contact in the Contact field. If you select multiple contacts, only the first contact is used in creating the journal entry.

You can also create these Outlook items by dragging contacts to the appropriate Outlook Bar shortcut or Folder List folder. Dragging and dropping a contact on the Calendar shortcut or folder creates a new meeting request addressed to the contact. However, if you right-drag (click the right mouse button and hold while dragging) the contact to the Calendar shortcut or folder, you can choose to create a new appointment or a new meeting request.

Dragging a contact to the Tasks shortcut or folder produces similar results. A simple drag and drop operation results in a new task request addressed to the contact. Right-dragging the contact, however, displays a shortcut menu that offers you the opportunity to create a task request or a task.

Dragging a contact to the Journal shortcut or folder creates a new journal entry with the contact as the subject, in the Contacts field, and added to the Notes field as a shortcut. Right-dragging provides the additional choice of adding the contact as an attachment. Dragging or right-dragging multiple contacts leaves the Subject and Contacts fields blank, but includes the selected contacts as shortcuts or attachments, depending on your method and choice.

To create an Outlook note from a contact, you have but one choice: drag the contact to the Notes shortcut or folder and drop it. If you right-drag the contact, the shortcut menu offers a single choice for creating a note: Copy Here As Note With Text. It produces exactly the same results as a simple drag and drop. If you try to drag multiple items, only one note is created, using the first contact item.

Writing Letters to Contacts

If you have Microsoft Word 97 or later installed on your computer, you can even use your contacts to automate the process of letter writing. Select the contact to whom you want to write a letter and choose Actions | New Letter To Contact from the Menu bar. This opens Microsoft Word and launches the Letter Wizard, which walks you through the steps of creating the letter (see Figure 8-11).

Set the appropriate options on the Letter Format tab and click Next to view the Recipient Info tab. Here you'll find that the name, company, and address information from the selected contact has already been entered. Make any necessary changes and click Next to move to the Other Elements tab. Set the additional options found here and click Next to display the Sender Info tab. Enter your name, return address, and closing information. Click Finish to create the new letter to the selected contact.

Note   *If you have Automatic Journaling turned on for the selected contact and for Microsoft Word, a journal entry is created for the letter. However, the entry is not associated with the contact to whom the letter is written. Consequently, it does not appear in the Activities tab of the contact's form. If you want the letter associated with the contact, you have to open the journal entry and enter the contact's name in the Contact field.*

WORKING WITH CONTACTS

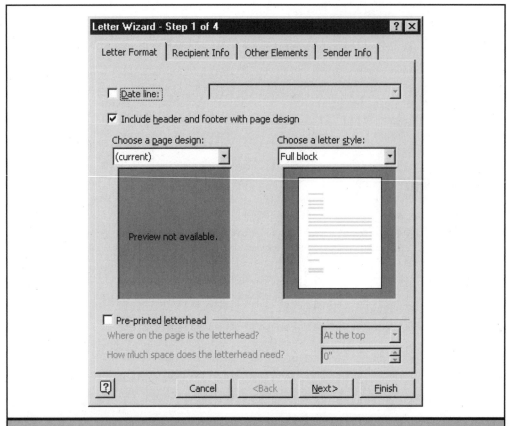

Figure 8-11. *Creating a letter is a walk in the park when you use the Letter Wizard*

MOUS Exam Objectives Explored in Chapter 8

Objective	Activity	Heading
OL2000.5.1	Create contacts	"Adding Contacts"
OL2000.5.1	Edit and delete contacts	"Modifying and Deleting Contacts"
OL2000.5.2	Send contact information via e-mail	"Sending Contact Information via E-mail"
OL2000.5.5	Link activities to contacts	"Linking Activities to a Contact Record"

The
Complete
Reference

Outlook
2000

Chapter 9

Managing Contacts

Using contact information effectively requires the ability to view, locate, sort, and organize contacts quickly. Outlook provides all the tools you need to make sure your contact information is readily available when you need it. All you have to do is learn to put each of these tools to work for you. In this chapter, you'll learn to switch between the various standard views, as well as use and create your own custom views. In addition, you'll discover a number of different methods for finding contacts as well as sorting and organizing contacts.

Viewing Contacts

Whether you want to merely inspect the contents of your Contacts folder or search for a particular piece of data, Outlook offers a variety of ways to view your contact information. The Contacts folder offers two types of views: address card views and table views. The address card views, of which there are two by default, display primary contact information in a manner similar to what you might find on a Rolodex card display (see Figure 9-1). Table views, on the other hand provide a column and row

Figure 9-1.   *The Address Cards view provides a quick view of basic information for each contact*

listing of contact information, in which the rows represent individual contacts and the columns contain specific pieces of information about the contact (see Figure 9-2).

The Address Cards view displays a limited number of fields in each "card." Therefore, contacts with information in none, or only some of those fields appear smaller and less complete.

Changing Views

To facilitate viewing your contact information, Outlook offers a number of standard views you can use. As noted earlier, they come in two flavors: address card views and table views. Switching between views is simple. Open the Contacts folder and choose View | Current View to display a submenu of available views.

The Advanced toolbar contains a Current View drop-down list that makes switching views a lot easier. Right-click anywhere on the Standard toolbar and select Advanced from the shortcut menu to display the Advanced toolbar.

Figure 9-2.   *The Phone List view is a frequently used table view that offers a simple listing of contacts and their phone numbers*

The address card views include:

■ **Address Cards**   This view provides a separate card for each contact and displays the mailing address, all four primary phone numbers, and all e-mail addresses for the contact.

■ **Detailed Address Cards**   As the name implies, this view is the same as the Address Cards view with more data. The additional information displayed includes full name, company, job title, home address, alternate phone numbers, Web page, categories to which the contact is assigned, and any notes you've entered.

The table views available in the Contacts folder include:

■ **Phone List**   Here you'll find each contact listed along with the company name, the File As designation, the four primary phone numbers (business phone, business fax, home phone, and mobile phone), the AutoJournal setting, and categories to which the contact is assigned.

■ **By Category**   Contacts are grouped by categories and display full name, company, File As, categories, business phone, business fax, home phone, and mobile phone information.

■ **By Company**   This view groups contacts by company and displays full name, job title, company, File As, department, business phone, business fax, home phone, mobile phone, and categories information.

■ **By Location**   Contacts in this view are grouped by the Country/Region field and display full name, company, File As, state, country/region, business phone, business fax, home phone, mobile phone, and categories information.

■ **By Follow-up Flag**   This view groups contacts by follow-up flag and displays icon, attachments, follow-up flag, full name, company, File As, business phone, business fax, home phone, mobile phone, and categories information.

One thing to note about both types of views is that, by default, you can edit most of the information in the view without opening the contact record. However, certain fields, such as Icon, Attachments, and Notes, cannot be edited unless you open the contact record.

Tip   *If you want to ensure that you or someone else doesn't accidentally change the contents of a field while in a contacts view, you can disable in-cell editing. Choose View | Current View | Customize Current View and click Other Settings in the View Summary dialog box. Click the Other Settings button and remove the checkmark in the Allow In-Cell Editing option.*

Customizing Contact Views

Contact views, like other Outlook views, are highly customizable. You can add and remove fields, change fonts, column widths, in-cell editing, and more. To customize the currently displayed view, choose View | Current View | Customize Current View to open the View Summary dialog box.

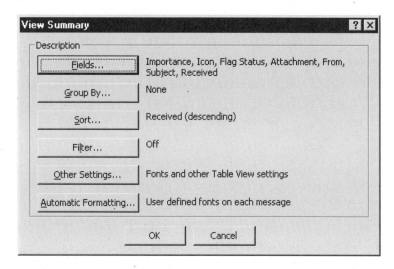

Click the appropriate button to customize the view settings. For details on customizing Outlook views, see Chapter 22.

Sorting Contacts

Without the ability to sort your information, the contact views would lose a great deal of their usefulness. Seeing your information may be nice, but manipulating it to suit your needs is where the real value lies. Fortunately, Outlook provides a variety of ways in which you can manipulate your contact information. Sorting, as you're probably aware, is the arranging of information in a specific order based on criteria you select. For example, if you want a listing of all contacts arranged by their location, you would perform a sort using the Country/Region field as the sort criterion. If you wanted to sort on multiple fields, you might set a secondary sort for State, and a third for Last Name.

The other important aspect of sorting to understand is whether the sort is ascending or descending. Ascending sorts are arranged from bottom to top, and descending sorts are just the opposite—from top to bottom. Using the earlier example of a sort based on Country/Region, Albania would appear before Zimbabwe in an ascending sort, and after Zimbabwe in a descending sort.

Using a Quick Sort in Table Views

To make life easier, Outlook affords you the opportunity to perform a quick sort within a view simply by clicking the column header of the field you want to use for the sort. In other words, if you're in the Phone List view and you want to sort the list by company, click the Company header. Like magic, the Phone List rearranges itself and displays contacts by company. The first time you click a header, the sort is ascending. Click the header a second time and the order is descending. Each time you click the header the sort order is reversed.

Tip *You can also right-click a field header and select Sort Ascending or Sort Descending from the shortcut menu.*

In the event that you want to sort a view by more than a single field, you can do so with the use of the SHIFT key. Set the sort order for the first field, then hold down the SHIFT key and click the header of the field you want to use for the secondary sort. If need be, while still holding down the SHIFT key, click the header a second time to change the order (ascending or descending). You can continue to hold the SHIFT key and select up to four fields for the sort order. If you try to exceed four sort fields, Outlook informs you that you're attempting to use too many sort levels.

Note *If you change your mind about including a field in a multifield sort, you'll have to start over. There's no way to remove a field from the sort except to release the SHIFT key and click the first field in the new sort. Of course, you can always return to the Sort dialog box and click Clear All, but that still removes the sort from all fields, not just the one you want to delete.*

An example of a multilevel sort would be the Phone List view sorted first by Company, then by Last Name, and finally by First Name. Assuming the sort order for each field is ascending, all contacts from company A would appear first, followed by all contacts from company B, and so on. Within each company group, contacts whose last names start with A would appear first, followed by contacts with last names starting with B, and continuing until the end of the alphabet is reached. In the event that two or more contacts within any company have the same last name, the one whose first name begins with A appears first, followed by the one whose first name begins with B, and so on.

A salesperson who travels a regular route might add a Zip Code field to the Phone List and then sort the view first by Zip Code, then by Company, and finally by Last Name. When it comes time to make the rounds, it would be easy to set up appointments in a logical fashion based on the route traveled.

Using the Sort Dialog Box

To sort card views or table views using fields that don't appear in the view, you can use the Sort dialog box. It enables you to select any field available in the contact form and use it to perform a sort, regardless of whether the field appears in the view you want to sort.

To use the Sort dialog box, follow these steps:

1. Open the Contacts folder.

2. Open the view you want to sort.

3. Choose View | Current View | Customize Current View to display the View Summary dialog box.

Tip *You can also right-click a blank spot in the view and select Sort from the shortcut menu to display the Sort dialog box. In a table view, you can right-click any column header and select Customize Current View to display the View Summary dialog box.*

4. Click the Sort button to open the Sort dialog box.

5. From the Select Available Fields From drop-down list choose All Contact Fields. This ensures that all the fields used in the contact form are available for use as sort criteria.

6. Select the field to use as the primary sort field from the Sort Items By drop-down list.

7. Select the Ascending or Descending option, as appropriate.

8. If you want to perform a multilevel sort, repeat the field and sort order selections using the three Then By options as needed.

9. Click OK to close the Sort dialog box.

WORKING WITH CONTACTS

Note   *If any of the fields you've selected do not appear in the view by default, Outlook asks if you want them added when the view is sorted. Click Yes to add the field to the view or No to sort by the field without adding it to the view. If you elect to add the field, it appears as the very last column. Also, the field remains in the view until you remove it.*

10. Click OK to perform the sort and close the View Summary dialog box.

Although you can sort on most contact fields, there are a few that cannot be used. These include Categories, Notes, Children, and Send Plain Text Only. If you add any of these fields to a customized view, and attempt to sort using one of them, you receive a curt message informing you that "You cannot sort by this field."

MOUS   *MOUS EXAM PRACTICE*
In this section, you learned to sort contact records. Begin your practice now by applying a quick sort using a single field. Start with a table view and click the field header to sort the view by that field. Note the type of sort that's applied. Is it ascending or descending? Now reverse the sort by clicking the header again. Right-click a header and use one of the sort commands. Next, try sorting using multiple fields by holding down the SHIFT *key and clicking each header. Finally, switch to an address card view, right-click a blank spot in the Information viewer, and select Sort to display the Sort dialog box. Choose a single field and sort order first, then try multiple fields.*

Applying Filters to Contacts

In addition to sorting your contact views, you can also modify them by filtering out certain records and displaying only those that meet the criteria you determine. Filters enable you to temporarily hide those contacts that do not meet your criteria. To apply a filter to your contacts, open the Contacts folder and select the view of your choice. Right-click a column header in the Information viewer and select Customize Current View to display the View Summary dialog box. Now click Filter to display the Filter dialog box.

Tip   *You can directly access the Filter dialog box by right-clicking a blank spot on the Information viewer and selecting Filter from the shortcut menu.*

Use the Contacts tab to apply a simple filter based on keywords found in a particular field, an e-mail address, or the time a contact was created or modified. Enter the keyword(s) in the Search For The Word(s) field and select the field type in which to search for the keyword(s). You can type an e-mail address directly into the E-mail field, or click the E-mail button and select an existing e-mail address from one of your address books. To filter contacts based on their creation or modification dates, make the appropriate selection from the Time drop-down lists. The first list lets you determine whether to use the Created or Modified date. From the second Time drop-down list, select the timeframe to use. Click OK to save the filter settings and return to the View Summary dialog box. Click OK again to apply the filter and return to the Contacts folder.

In a Microsoft Exchange Server environment, the Created and Modified dates are determined by the Microsoft Exchange server's clock, not your desktop's clock. However, the Outlook Filter feature uses your desktop's clock when searching for date criteria. In other words, if your desktop clock indicates today's date is the 15th of the month, but the Microsoft Exchange server's clock says it's the 14th, all contacts you modify today will bear a Modified date of the 14th. However, when you apply a filter using Today as the Modified date, Outlook searches for contacts bearing a Modified date of the 15th.

If you want to apply a more sophisticated filter, return to the Filter dialog box and click the More Choices tab. Here you'll find additional criteria on which to base the filter.

The More Choices tab offers the following filter criteria:

■ **Categories** Enter the category or click the Categories button and choose the category from the dialog box that appears. To use multiple categories, separate each one with a comma. However, be aware that there is an implied OR between each category you enter. Therefore, a filter that includes both Business and Competition in the Categories field will search for any contacts that are assigned to either the Business category or the Competition category, or both. Fortunately, there's a way to get around this problem using the Advanced tab. Take the earlier example of Business and Competition categories. Enter filter criteria that says "Categories contains Business and Competition."

- **Only items that are** Since the only choices here are Read and Unread, this option is of little use in filtering contacts.

- **Only items with** If you want to filter out contacts on the basis of attachments (with or without), check this option and make the appropriate selection from the drop-down list.

- **Whose importance is** In spite of the fact that you can actually set the Importance level for a contact in the contact Properties dialog box, this option is grayed out. The apparent reason is that Importance is not a standard contact field.

- **Match case** Check this option to force Outlook to search for the exact combination of upper- and lowercase letters entered in the Search For The Word(s) option on the Contacts tab.

- **Size (kilobytes)** Select the appropriate conditional operator from the drop-down list and enter the value in kilobytes.

The third and final tab in the Filter dialog box is the Advanced tab, which enables you to add sophisticated filtering criteria based on multiple fields.

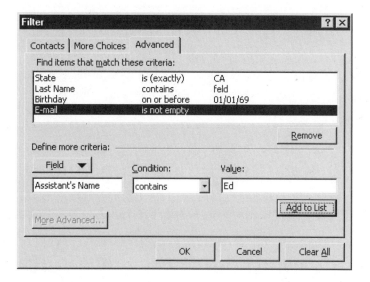

In addition, it offers the full range of contact fields to choose from. To create an advanced filter, click the Field button and move your mouse pointer to All Contact Fields. A large menu containing all the contact fields appears. Select the field you want to use for the first set of conditions. From the Condition drop-down list, select the appropriate conditional operator. In the Value field, enter the data corresponding to the field on which the condition is based. In other words, if you select a name or other text field, the information you enter should be text. If you select a date field, such as Birthday, the information should be in a date format (mm/dd/yy).

You can use And between multiple values to search for only those records containing all values entered. You can also use Or between values to search for any of the values entered.

When you've entered all necessary information, click the Add To List button to add the new condition to the Find Items That Match These Criteria list. Repeat the process for each filter condition you want to use. Then click OK to apply the filter. All records matching the filter criteria you entered appear, while the remaining records are temporarily hidden.

When you're finished using the filtered view, it's always a good idea to remove the filter. Opening your Contacts folder at some later date only to find that half your contacts seem to have disappeared can be rather disconcerting. Fortunately, Outlook provides a reminder by adding (Filter Applied) to the Folder banner. Whenever you decide to remove the filter, it's quite simple. Open the Filter dialog box and click Clear All.

Finding Contacts

Being able to locate contact information when you need it is one of the primary benefits to using the Outlook Contacts folder. While you can certainly apply a filter when necessary, there are much simpler ways to find individual contacts or groups of related contacts. As with most tasks, Outlook provides a variety of ways to locate contact data:

- **Keyboard**   Search by the first letter(s) of a contact name.
- **Letter tabs**   Use this feature for an alphanumeric search.
- **Find A Contact**   This feature provides a simple search for contacts.
- **Find**   For a more sophisticated search, use the Find button located on the Standard toolbar or choose Tools | Find. This displays the Find Items In Contacts pane, which enables you to search for any text string in the Name, Company, Addresses, and Category fields.
- **Advanced Find**   The Advanced Find feature provides the ability to extend your search to every field and to use multiple search criteria. It will help you achieve the equivalent of finding a needle in a haystack.

Using the Keyboard

If you open an address card view in the Contacts folder and type the first letter or first few letters of a contact name, Outlook takes you to the first contact whose name begins with the letter(s). If you enter multiple letters, they must be quickly typed in succession for the procedure to work properly. Pausing too long between letters causes Outlook to consider them separate searches, and results in locating the contact whose File As name begins with the second letter typed.

Using the Letter Tabs

Both the Address Cards view and the Detailed Address Cards view contain letter tabs that run down the right side of the Information viewer (see Figure 9-3).

 Since the letter tabs are only useful for an alphanumeric search, sorting an address card view by a non-text field, such as Anniversary or Birthday, causes the letter tabs to disappear. When you resort the view using a text field, the letter tabs reappear.

Figure 9-3.   *The letter tabs provide one-click navigating through the Contacts folder*

The vertical bar contains buttons with letters of the alphabet (and one button with numbers). Click a button to view contacts beginning with the letter(s) appearing on the button.

Right-clicking anywhere on a letter tab displays the same shortcut menu that appears when you right-click a blank spot on the Information viewer.

Using Find A Contact

Use this option, located on the Standard toolbar, to conduct a simple search for contact information.

Find A Contact

Enter a contact name in the Find A Contact text box or select a previously used name from the drop-down list. Then press ENTER to locate the contact record. Outlook begins by searching both First Name and Last Name fields in the Contacts folder and its subfolders, and then moves on to other address books. It displays the first contact or addressee it encounters. If multiple matches are found, the Choose Contact dialog box appears.

If you encounter a problem searching on a last name, it may be the result of a contact whose entire name is entered in the First Name field of the Contact form. This frequently happens when Personal Address Book entries are imported into the Contacts folders. Find A Contact will not locate a last name when it is part of the First Name field. Find the contact by searching on the first name, and edit the record to reflect the correct entries in the First Name and Last Name fields.

One handy feature of the Find A Contact option is that it retains previous entries you've searched for. Therefore, you can repeat a search at a later time simply by selecting one of your past searches from the drop-down list.

Note

If Outlook hangs and you receive an application error or page fault error while using the Find A Contact feature, it may be the result of a corrupt QuickFindMRU registry key. To resolve the problem, close all programs, open the Windows registry and delete the HKEY_CURRENT_USER\Software\Microsoft\Office\ 9.0\Outlook\Contact\QuickFindMRU *key. Restart Windows and a new QuickFindMRU key will be regenerated automatically when you open Outlook.* Warning! *Only experienced users should modify the Windows registry. Always back up your registry before making any changes.*

The drop-down list retains the last 12 names you've used as the search criterion. Once you hit 12, the last item on the list is removed to make room for your latest search name.

Using the Find Feature

If the Find A Contact feature is too limited for your needs, try the Find feature, which enables you to search on more than just the First Name and Last Name fields. Click the Find button on the Standard toolbar to display the Find pane in the Information viewer, as shown in Figure 9-4.

Enter the keyword(s) for which you want to search and click Find Now. If you want to search on more than one keyword, separate them with commas. Without the Search All Text In The Contact option checked, only the Name, Company, Addresses, and Category fields are searched. Any contacts containing the keyword(s) are displayed in the Information viewer. To expand the search, check the Search All Text In The Contact option. Unfortunately, the option is misleading and does not include all text fields in the contact record. The only additional fields searched are the E-mail fields and the Notes field.

Tip

One handy feature of the Find option is that, unlike the Find A Contact and Advanced Find features, it restricts its search to the contact items in the current view. Therefore, you can apply a filter to the view and use Find to search only those items displayed after the filter is applied. Both Find A Contact and Advanced Find ignore the filter and search the entire Contacts folder.

If the search is unsuccessful, you can click the Clear Search link and try a new search, or you can click the Go To Advanced Find link to open the Advanced Find dialog box, seen in Figure 9-5.

The Advanced Find feature is almost identical to the Filter feature discussed earlier in this chapter. The only difference is in the ability to select the type of item to search

WORKING WITH CONTACTS

Figure 9-4.   *The Find pane provides additional search capabilities*

for and the folder in which to conduct the search. Also, the results are displayed in a pane at the bottom of the Advanced Find dialog box. For details on using the Advanced Find feature, see the earlier section entitled "Applying Filters to Contacts."

Organizing Contacts

Keeping your contacts organized ensures the most efficient use of your time by providing ready access to data when you need it. Outlook offers a variety of ways to impose order on your contact information. You can utilize the flexible folder system upon which Outlook is based to create a hierarchy of contacts folders and maintain separate contacts databases. If you have an extremely large database of customers, vendors, and employees, you might create a subfolder for each, thereby eliminating the need to sift through the entire database when searching for any one of the three. If you have a small to medium sized database of contacts that includes customers, vendors, and employees, you can keep them all in the same folder, but assign them to different categories. This enables you to filter out one group or the other when the need arises.

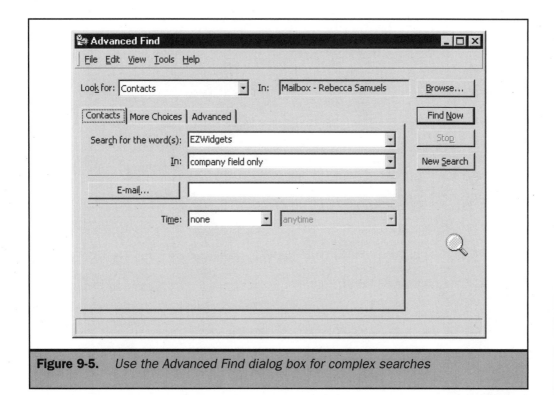

Figure 9-5. *Use the Advanced Find dialog box for complex searches*

You can even use custom formatting to make sure specific contacts or groups of contacts stand out when you view the Contacts folder.

Using the Organize Feature

The Outlook Organize feature offers one-stop shopping for tools to whip your Contacts folder into shape. It lets you utilize folders, categories, and views to organize your contact information. Open your Contacts folder and click the Organize button on the Standard toolbar to display the Organize pane, shown in Figure 9-6.

Assigning Contacts to Categories

By default, the Organize pane opens to the Using Categories options (shown in Figure 9-6). To assign one or more contacts to a category, select the contacts in the Information viewer (to select multiple contacts hold the CTRL key down and click the desired contacts). Then choose the category from the Add Contacts Selected Below To drop-down list, and click the Add button. All the selected contacts are assigned to the designated category. If you open any of the contacts, you'll see the category assignment in the Categories field of the contact form.

Figure 9-6.   The Organize pane gives you quick access to folders, categories, and views

Note   *There's no way to assign contacts to more than one category at a time using the Organize feature. However, the selection of contacts remains intact until you change it. Therefore, you can repeat the assignment process for as many categories as you want without having to reselect the same group of contacts each time.*

You can even create a new category if the existing categories don't meet your needs. Simply type the category name in the Create A New Category Called field and click the Create button. The new category is created and added to the Add Contacts Selected Below To drop-down list. You can assign contacts to the new categories as you would assign them to any category.

Using Folders

Another feature of the Organize pane is the Using Folders feature. It enables you to move contacts from one folder to another and even create new folders on the fly. Click the Using Folders link in the Organize pane to display the folders options.

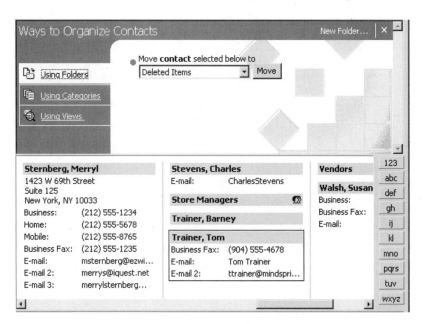

In the current view, select the contact(s) you want to move to another folder. From the Move Contact Selected Below To drop-down list, choose the folder into which you want to move the selected contact(s). Remember, you can only move contact items to a folder designated to hold contact items. Select Other Folder to move the contact(s) to personal folders, public folders, or other mailbox folders. Click the Move button to complete the move.

Moving contact items to a non-contact folder creates items of the type the folder holds, using the information from the contact records you're attempting to move. You can take advantage of this to create e-mail messages addressed to selected contacts, as well as appointments, tasks, or notes for the selected contacts by moving them to the appropriate folder.

If you want to create a new contacts folder, click the New Folder button located in the upper-right corner of the Organize pane to open the Create New Folder dialog box (see Figure 9-7).

Enter a name for the new folder, select the existing folder to which you want the new folder added as a subfolder, and click OK to create the new folder. It immediately appears in the Move Contact Selected Below To drop-down list. Click the Move button to send the selected contacts to the new folder.

Figure 9-7.   *Use the New Folder button to create new folders on the fly*

Using Views

The third feature found in the Organize pane is one that enables you to change and customize views. Click the Using Views link to display the views options.

The current view is highlighted in the Change Your View list. To change the view, scroll down the list and select the desired view. The Information viewer immediately reflects your choice. To modify the view, click Customize Current View in the top-right corner of the Organize pane. This displays the View Summary dialog box, from which you can add and remove fields, apply sort and filter conditions, and more. See Chapter 22 for more information on customizing views.

When you're finished using the Organize pane, you can close it by clicking the Organize button on the Standard toolbar or the small X located in the top-right corner of the Organize pane.

Using the Move To Folder Command

The Organize pane, while useful, also takes up quite a bit of the Information viewer space. Therefore, if your goal is to move contacts, you may prefer to use the Move To Folder command. Select the contact(s) you want to move, right-click any of the selected items or click the Move To Folder button on the Standard toolbar, and select Move To Folder to display the Move Items dialog box.

Select the folder to which you want the items moved and click OK to effect the move. That's all there is to it. You can even create a new folder by clicking the New button and providing a name and location for the new folder.

In addition to using the Move To Folder command, you can also drag selected contacts to the target folder in the Folder List or to an Outlook Bar shortcut icon.

Using Categories to Organize Contacts

Categories provide a simple and effective way to create groups of related contacts without having to physically segregate them. While extremely large contact databases may see a significant reduction in search times by separating related groups of contacts and placing them in separate folders, the benefit for small databases will be negligible. As a matter of fact, separating small databases into a series of folders will probably cost more time spent in hopping from folder to folder when searching for information. The easiest and most efficient way to create groups of related contacts in a small to medium sized contacts database is with the use of categories.

Using the Categories Command

The quickest and easiest way to assign a contact to a category is by using the Category button on the contact form during the creation or modification of the contact. Located at the bottom of the contact form, the Categories button, when clicked, displays a list of all existing categories (see Figure 9-8).

You can assign the contact to as many categories as you want by checking each category. To create a new category, enter a name for the category in the Item(s) Belong To These Categories list and click the Add To List button.

You can also assign multiple contacts to one or more categories at the same time by using the Categories command:

1. Open the Contacts folder.

2. Select the contacts you want to assign to one or more categories.

3. Choose Edit | Categories from the Menu bar to open the Categories dialog box.

Figure 9-8.   *Check all the categories to which you want the selected contact assigned*

If any of the selected contacts are already assigned to categories, those categories appear with a checkmark in a gray box.

4. Check the category or categories to which you want to assign the selected contacts.

 You can use categories that are already assigned (checkmark in a gray box) to some of the selected contacts by removing the checkmark and adding it again. This does not add a second assignment to the contacts already assigned, merely a single assignment to those selected contacts not previously assigned.

5. Click OK to make the category assignments and return to the Contacts folder.

To remove category assignments, follow the preceding steps and remove the checkmarks in gray boxes from the categories whose assignments you want eliminated.

You can also add a new category while making the assignments. Enter a name for the new category in the Items Belong To These Categories box and click the Add To List button.

Using the Outlook Organize Feature

As discussed in an earlier section, you can use the Organize feature to assign contacts to categories. Click the Organize button to display the Organize pane, which opens, by default, with the Using Categories options visible. In the Information viewer, select the contact(s) you want to assign to a category. From the Add Contacts Selected Below To drop-down list, choose the category to which you want the contact(s) assigned, and click Add. To create a new category, enter a name in the Create A New Category Called field and click Create.

Using the By Category View

Realizing the importance of using categories to organize contacts, the Outlook programmers thoughtfully provided a standard view for displaying contacts by category assignments. The view, called By Category, creates a contact group for each category used. Choose View | Current View | By Category to switch to the view. As you can see in Figure 9-9, the groups are arranged alphabetically by category name.

Contacts assigned to multiple categories appear in all category groups to which they're assigned. To display the contacts in a category group, click the plus (+) sign to the left of the category name. To hide the contacts, click the minus (-) sign.

 MOUS EXAM PRACTICE
In this section, you saw how categorizing your contacts can make searching and sorting your Contacts folder a lot easier. Start by opening an existing contact and using the Category button to assign the contact to a category. Next, select multiple contacts in the Contacts folder and use the Categories command to assign them to one or more categories. Add a couple of new categories, and use the Organize feature to categorize some of your contacts. After you've assigned your contacts to categories, see how they appear when you display them in the By Category view.

Figure 9-9.   *The By Category view lets you organize your contacts according to their category assignments*

Using Custom Colors to Classify Contacts

There's a handy new feature in Outlook 2000 called Automatic Formatting that enables you to classify contacts by using custom colors and fonts. While it doesn't create groups of contacts, it does enable you to visually identify contacts of different types without having to resort to additional actions such as sorting and filtering. As a matter of fact, if you've added any distribution lists to your Contacts folder you've already seen the results of Automatic Formatting. All distribution list items are automatically bolded, as a result of a default rule created using Automatic Formatting.

To create your own Automatic Formatting rules, follow these steps:

1. Open the Contacts folder.

2. Choose View | Current View | Customize Current View to display the View Summary dialog box.

3. Click the Automatic Formatting button to open the Automatic Formatting dialog box.

4. Click the Add button to create a new rule.

5. Enter a name for the rule in the Name field.

6. Click the Font button and select the font, font style, font size, and font color from the font dialog box that appears. Click OK to return to the Automatic Formatting dialog box.

Be sure not to duplicate the formatting used in an existing rule or you won't be able to tell the items apart by visual cues. You can check existing rules by highlighting the rule and examining the contents of the Font field.

7. Click the Condition button to display the Filter dialog box. This is the identical Filter dialog box used to create filters. See the section in this chapter entitled "Applying Filters to Contacts" for details on using the Filter dialog box.

8. After you set the condition(s) for the new rule, click OK to return to the Automatic Formatting dialog box. An example would be creating a rule called Department Heads based on filter condition that states the Job Title field contains the words Department Head.

9. Click OK to save the new rule and return to the View Summary dialog box.

10. Click OK to return to the Contacts folder and apply the new formatting.

You can disable a rule without deleting it by opening the Automatic Formatting dialog box and removing the checkmark next to the rule. Should you decide to remove a rule altogether, you can do so by selecting the rule and clicking the Delete button.

Setting Contact Options

Although Outlook can hardly be considered stingy when it comes to options, the Contacts folder is somewhat limited in customizable features. There are two sets of options you can customize for the Contacts folder: the Contact Options found on the Preferences tab of the Options dialog box, and the options located in the Contacts Properties dialog box.

Contact Options

The Contact Options enable you to set the default order for the Full Name and File As fields found in the contact form and to select the contacts for which AutoJournaling is turned on. To set these options, choose Tools | Options to open the Options dialog box with the Preferences tab displayed. Click the Contact Options button to display the Contact Options dialog box.

From the Default "Full Name" Order drop-down list, select the order in which you want the name information displayed in the Full Name field of each contact record. Move to the next option and select the information and order of appearance for the File As field. You can elect to use the contact name, the company name, or both. Click OK when you're done and return to the Options dialog box.

If you would like to set AutoJournaling options for your contacts, click the Journal Options button to display the Journal Options dialog box.

From the Automatically Record These Items list, select the Outlook items you want automatically recorded in the journal. Then move to the For These Contacts list and choose for which contact you want the selected Outlook items recorded. If you want to include items from other Microsoft Office applications, make the appropriate selection(s) in the Also Record Files From list. Only compatible, installed programs appear on this list. Click OK to return to the Options dialog box.

Setting Contacts Folder Properties

The Contacts folder, like all Outlook folders, has a variety of properties that can be set to change the way it behaves and appears. These properties include everything from the form used to post items to the folder to designating a home page for the folder. To access the Contacts Properties dialog box, right-click the Contacts shortcut on the Outlook Bar (or the Contacts folder in the Folder List) and select Properties (see Figure 9-10).

The Folder List must be locked into place before right-clicking works. If you click the folder name to display the Folder List, and then try right-clicking, you'll find that nothing happens. Click the yellow pushpin in the top-right corner of the Folder List to keep it open.

In the IMO configuration only the first four tabs appear. The options are identical on those four tabs regardless of which configuration you have installed.

As you can see, the Contacts Properties dialog box contains eight tabs, which in turn contain a variety of options that affect the way the folder looks and works.

Figure 9-10. *Folders get their fair share of customization options*

Here's a quick rundown of what each tab contains:

- **General**   The General tab contains the name, description, and default form used for the folder. In addition, you can view the folder size, including the size of any subfolders.

- **Home Page**   This tab contains options enabling you to assign a home page to the folder, and make it the default view when the folder is opened. Whether a Web page, URL, or document, the item designated as the home page appears when you choose View | Show Folder Home Page. If you don't enter a URL or path in the Address field, the Show Folder Home Page doesn't appear on the View menu at all. To have Outlook display the designated home page as the default view every time you open the folder, check the Show Home Page By Default For This Folder option.

- **Outlook Address Book**   Use this tab to set options to display the contents of the folder as an Outlook Address Book, and add it to the Show Names From The drop-down list in the Address Book.

- **Activities**   Use this tab to designate those Outlook items associated with a contact that you want to keep track of for each contact in the folder.

- **Administration**   Here you'll find options for administering the folder. However, these options are available only to users with administrator rights. The only folders for which Outlook users generally have administrator rights, and therefore access to Administration options, are public folders they've created.

- **Forms**   This tab provides options to determine which forms can be used to post information to the folder.

- **Permissions**   Use this form to give others access to the folder by granting permissions. The Permission tab options are available only to the folder owner. Other users can see the tab if they have access to the folder, but they cannot change the permissions.

- **Synchronization**   This tab contains options for enabling offline use of the folder and setting filters to determine how the folder is synchronized.

 Unless you have the Exchange Extensions and Exchange Extensions Property Pages add-ins installed you may not see all eight tabs in a C/W configuration. To install the add-ins choose Tools | Options | Other | Add-In Manager and check both add-ins.

Of these Contacts Properties dialog box tabs, only the Outlook Address Book and Activities tabs are unique to the Contacts folder. The remaining tabs are common to various other Outlook folders, and are covered in detail in Chapter 18.

Setting Outlook Address Book Tab Options

The Outlook Address Book tab enables you to designate a contact folder as an Outlook Address Book, and give the address book a unique name distinct from the folder name (see Figure 9-11). This means the folder appears as a selection in all address book lists in Outlook (Address Book, Select Names dialog box, and so on). The Outlook Address Book tab itself is simple and straightforward, containing only two options.

To use the folder as an Outlook Address Book, check the Show This Folder As An E-Mail Address Book option. By default, the folder name is automatically inserted as the name for the Outlook Address Book. You can change it by entering the name of your choice in the Name Of The Address Book option.

If you don't want to use the folder as an Outlook Address Book, remove the checkmark. When you're through, click OK to save the settings and return to the active Outlook window. If you want to make further changes, click Apply to activate the changes and keep the dialog box open.

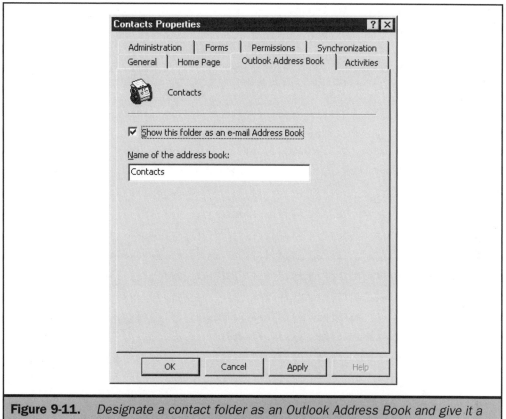

Figure 9-11.   *Designate a contact folder as an Outlook Address Book and give it a unique name*

Using the Activities Tab Options

The Activities tab of the contact folder Properties dialog box (see Figure 9-12) displays the existing folder groups, which are selections of one or more Outlook folders from which activities linked to contacts in the folder are displayed. Folder groups are used to create custom views in the Activities tab of the contact record form. When you open a contact record, click the Activities tab, and display the contents of the Show drop-down list, you are looking at all the existing folder groups found in the Activities tab of the contact folder Properties dialog box.

The Folder Groups pane displays the existing folder groups and indicates which folders are included in each group. The options below the display pane enable you to modify existing folder groups, add new ones, and set the default view for the Activities tab of the contact record form. Your options include the following.

- **Copy**   Click this button to create a copy of an existing folder group. This is useful if you want to use the existing folder group as the basis for a new folder group. Make the desired changes and give the group a new name.

- **Modify**   To change an existing folder group, select the group and click Modify. The View Title and Folders dialog box opens. You can then add or remove individual folders from the group, and change the folder group name.

- **Reset/Delete**   The name of this button changes depending on the type of folder group selected. When a default folder group (Journal, Upcoming Tasks/Appointments, Contacts, Notes, E-mail, and All Items) is selected, the button name is Reset. Clicking the Reset button removes any changes made to the selected folder and returns it to its original state. When you select a non-default folder group, the button name changes to Delete, and as you might surmise, deletes the selected folder group.

Figure 9-12.   *View existing folder groups using the Activities tab of the Contacts Properties dialog box*

- **New**   Use this button to create a new folder group.
- **Default activities view**   Select the folder group you want to set as the default view for the Activities tab of the contact record form. The folder group you select here appears in the Show field of the contact form Activities tab, and the related activities are displayed.

While the Reset/Delete button performs its action directly, the Copy, Modify, and New buttons open the View Title And Folders dialog box, from which you can make your own selections, as shown in Figure 9-13.

The tree-like display of folders is the same no matter which button you click. The only differences are the text displayed in the Name field, and the folders checked in the display window. Using the View Titles And Folders dialog box is easy. Check the folders you want included in the folder group, indicate whether to search subfolders (this option appears even if no subfolders exist, but will apply in the event you later create subfolders), modify the name if necessary, and click OK to save the folder group.

WORKING WITH CONTACTS

Figure 9-13.   *Clicking the Copy, Modify, or New buttons on the Folder Groups pane brings up the View Title And Folders dialog box*

There are a couple of things you should know about folder groups to make using them a little easier:

- You can change the folders included in a default folder group, but you cannot delete or rename the group.

- Different folder groups display different fields in the Activities tab of the contact record form. A folder group created with the New button retains the display format of the All Items folder group. A new folder group created using the Copy button retains the display format of the original folder group.

- Each time you restart Outlook, folder groups containing public folders do not automatically restore activities links. If you try to use such a folder group, it may appear that the activities have disappeared. To resolve this, simply open the public folder containing the linked items. This happens by design to prevent a prolonged Outlook startup while the links are being recreated.

After you finish modifying and creating folder groups, click the OK button to save your changes and return to the active Outlook window.

Exam | MOUS Exam Objectives Explored in Chapter 9

Objective	Activity	Heading
OL2000.4.4	Modify the Master Category List	"Using a Categories Command"
OL2000.4.5	Assign Items to a Category	"Assigning Contacts to Categories"
OL2000.5.3	Organize contacts by category	"Using Categories to Organize Contacts"
OL2000.5.6	Sort contacts using fields	"Sorting Contacts"

The Complete Reference

Outlook 2000

Part IV

Managing Time and Details

The Complete Reference

Outlook 2000

Chapter 10

Working with the Calendar

The Outlook Calendar is a powerful scheduling tool. When used effectively and consistently, it can create order out of chaos. As a matter of fact, you may become so efficient that instead of needing more hours in the day, you'll find yourself heading home early. However, to get to that point, you must develop the necessary skills to master the Calendar. That's what this chapter is all about: helping you become proficient in Calendar basics. You'll learn to get around the Calendar folder, switch and customize Calendar views, and more.

Navigating the Calendar Window

The first thing to do in any software component, including the Outlook Calendar, is to familiarize yourself with the working environment or user interface. You've got to learn what each of the elements on the screen is, what it does, and how it operates. It's like checking out a new power tool and figuring out where all the buttons and switches are and what they do.

Touring the Calendar Window Components

The best place to start learning about what makes the Calendar tick is with the default view, Day/Week/Month. As you can see in Figure 10-1, the Day/Week/Month window consists of three distinct elements: the Appointment area, the Date Navigator, and the TaskPad.

These three primary elements provide you with everything you need to regain control of your schedule and your time.

- **Appointment area** This is where you record your appointments, meetings, and events. The Appointment area, like any good appointment book, provides time blocks into which you can insert your appointment information. Unlike a typical appointment book, the Outlook Calendar Appointment area is flexible enough to handle even the most unpredictable schedule.

- **Date Navigator** This pair of mini-calendars offers a view of the current month and the next month. In addition to providing you with a handy view of two months' worth of dates, the Date Navigator also lets you switch dates quickly, change appointment dates, and even display multiple days in the Appointment area.

- **TaskPad** The TaskPad is a mini-version of the Tasks folder. It lets you create tasks and to-do lists on the fly without having to leave the Calendar folder. Items entered in the TaskPad become part of the Tasks folder, and items entered in the Tasks folder are added to the TaskPad. Changes in one are reflected in the other.

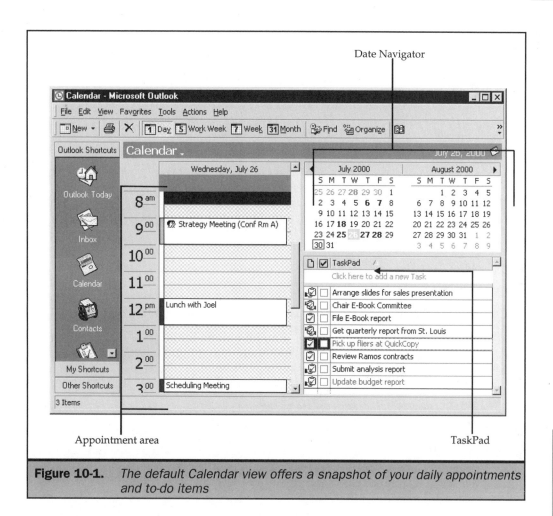

Figure 10-1.   *The default Calendar view offers a snapshot of your daily appointments and to-do items*

MANAGING TIME
& DETAILS

Using Shortcut Keys to Get Around

If you're into shortcuts, hate your mouse, or just like to have alternative ways to do things, you may be interested in the shortcut keys available for navigating the Day/Week/Month view. See Table 10-1 for a listing.

Using a two-key shortcut requires holding the first key down while pressing the second key. If the shortcut includes three keys, hold the first two down and press the third.

Switching Dates

By far the easiest way to switch to dates in the recent past or immediate future is by using the Date Navigator. Click a date on one of the visible Date Navigator calendars

Press	To Go To
LEFT ARROW	Previous day
RIGHT ARROW	Next day
TAB	Next appointment
SHIFT-TAB	Previous appointment
ALT-HOME	First day of the current week
ALT-END	Last day of the current week
ALT-UP ARROW	Same day of the previous week
ALT-DOWN ARROW	Same day of the next week
ALT-PAGE UP	First day of the month
ALT-PAGE DOWN	Last day of the month
CTRL-TAB or F6	Move between Appointment area, TaskPad, and Folder List (when open)

Table 10-1.   *Shortcut Keys for Navigating the Day/Week/Month View*

to display the desired day in the Appointment area. To switch to another month, use the arrows on either side of the Date Navigator calendars. The left arrow moves you back one month at a time, and the right arrow moves you forward one month at a time. You can also click (and hold) the month name and year to display a pop-up list of the previous three months and the next three months.

If you want to switch a date in the distant past or future, it's easier to use the Go To Date command. Right-click a blank slot in the Appointment area and select Go To Date. You can also choose View | Go To Date. Both methods open the Go To Date dialog box.

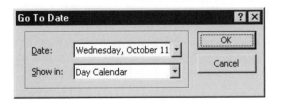

The dialog box opens with the currently selected date in the Date field. Enter the date you want to switch to. You can use one of the following methods to enter the date:

- **Type the date**   Type the date you want to move to. Use the date format designated in the Regional Settings applet of the Control Panel.

- **Use the Date pop-up calendar**   Click the down arrow at the right end of the Date field to display the pop-up calendar. Select the date from the calendar. The pop-up calendar works the same as the Date Navigator calendars. The right and left arrows move you forward and back through subsequent months, and clicking the month name and year displays the previous and next three months in a pop-up list. You can also click the Today button to return to the date indicated by the clock on your local computer as today.

- **Use plain English**   If you don't want to mess around with dates and calendars, you can also use plain English. If you want to go to next Tuesday, just say so. Type **next Tuesday** and Outlook understands, taking you to the first upcoming date that falls on a Tuesday. The variety of words, phrases, and abbreviations you can use is extensive. Try things like **a week from next Wednesday** or **30 days from the 1st of next month**. You can abbreviate the names of months and days (such as Feb, Jan, Tues, Wed, and so on). You can even use holiday names such as **Christmas 2001** for December 25, 2001, or **Independence Day 2003** for July 4, 2003.

From the Show In drop-down list, choose the calendar in which to display the selected date. Your choices include the Day Calendar, Week Calendar, Month Calendar, and Work Week Calendar. Click OK to display the selected date in the appropriate calendar view.

MOUS EXAM PRACTICE
Begin by familiarizing yourself with the Calendar's basic components: the Appointment area, the Date Navigator, and the TaskPad. Next, try moving around the Day/Week/ Month view using keyboard shortcuts. Finally, try your hand at switching dates in the Day/Week/Month view using both the Date Navigator and the Go To Date command.

Exploring Calendar Views

Outlook provides a number of different views for displaying your Calendar information. The default view, Day/Week/Month, offers an ideal environment for managing your daily schedule and to-do items. However, when you need a quick look at everything that's on your plate, you may want to take advantage of one of the available table views.

Switching Views

The Calendar folder comes with seven different standard views—ten if you count the three variations on the Day/Week/Month view. Here's a quick look at those standard views and what they do:

- **Day/Week/Month**   The default view, which contains the Appointment area, the Date Navigator, and the TaskPad.

- **Day/Week/Month View with AutoPreview**   True to its name, this view turns on the AutoPreview in the Day/Week/Month view. Notes from Calendar items appearing in the Appointment area are displayed when you use this view.

- **Active Appointments**   Use this view to display Calendar items that have not yet occurred. All appointments in the past are excluded from this view.

- **Events**   If you've scheduled any events (appointments or activities that last more than 24 hours), you can use this view to display them all at once.

- **Annual Events**   This view is handy for separating out those events that occur only once a year, such as birthdays and anniversaries.

- **Recurring Appointments**   You know what these are: the boss's Monday morning pep talks, the monthly visits to see your parole officer, your weekly excursions to the canine therapist because your dog thinks he's a cat, and so on. The Recurring Appointments view excludes all Calendar items except those that are recurring items.

- **By Category**   If you assign Calendar items to categories, you can use this view to display all items grouped by category.

To switch between standard Calendar folder views, choose View | Current View to display the submenu of available views. You can also display the Advanced toolbar, which contains a Current View drop-down list from which you can select the view to use. Right-click anywhere on the Standard toolbar and select Advanced from the shortcut menu to display the Advanced toolbar.

The Day/Week/Month view has its own selection of subviews, each of which is accessible from the Standard toolbar. These views include:

- **Day**   This is the default view in which a single day's worth of appointments appear in the Appointment area.

- **Work Week**   When you select this view, the Appointment area displays the days designated as your work week in the Calendar options.

- **Week**   The Week view changes the Appointment area to display the current week as a group of seven boxes, one for each day of the week. The appointments for each day appear in the box.

- **Month**   The Month view is similar to the Week view in that each day of the month is displayed as a separate box. However, by default, the Month view takes up the entire Information viewer, hiding the Date Navigator and TaskPad.

Tip   *You can display the Date Navigator and TaskPad in the Month view by dragging the right border of the Information viewer to the left. The border moves left in increments large enough to display one or more Date Navigator calendars. Since Outlook fails to remember this setting, you'll have to resize the Month view each time you switch to another view and back to the Month view.*

Switching between the Day/Week/Month variations is a snap since there's a button for each on the Standard toolbar. Click the appropriate button to display the view. If you happen to be a shortcut lover, there's even better news. Outlook provides a number of keyboard shortcuts that enable you to both switch between and modify the Day/Week/Month views. See Table 10-2 for a list of available shortcuts.

Note   *Although you can use the number pad for the minus sign in the shortcuts in Table 10-2, you cannot use it to enter numbers. The shortcuts only work if you use the row of number keys above the letters on the keyboard.*

Press	To Display
ALT-1	Day view
ALT-5	Work Week view (regardless of the number of days in your Work Week)
ALT-- (ALT + minus sign)	Week view
ALT-= (ALT + equals sign)	Month view
ALT-2 through ALT-4	Day view displaying 2 to 4 days (ALT-2 displays 2 days, ALT-3, 3 days, and so on)
ALT-6 through ALT-0	Day view displaying 6 to 10 days

Table 10-2.   *Shortcut Keys for Switching Between Day/Week/Month Views*

MANAGING TIME
& DETAILS

Using the Date Navigator

The Date Navigator is a handy device that not only lets you switch between dates quickly with a mouse click or two, but also provides an easy means of customizing the information displayed in the Appointment area. The Date Navigator is the pair (by default) of mini-calendars that appears in the top-right corner of the Calendar window.

To switch dates using the Date Navigator, simply click the desired date or click the month name and year to display a pop-up menu containing the currently selected month, the three previous months, and the next three months. Select the month you want to view and then select the date.

While it's a great time-saver for switching dates, the real value of the Date Navigator is in its ability to customize the Appointment area of the Day view. You can display multiple dates in the Appointment area by highlighting the desired dates in the Date Navigator using one of the following methods:

- **Select consecutive days**   You can select any number of days in a given week by dragging your mouse pointer over the desired days. However, once you pass either end of the week, the entire week and the next (or previous) week are selected. To select multiple consecutive days spanning, but not including, two weeks, hold the SHIFT key down while dragging your mouse pointer.

- **Select nonconsecutive days**   You can select up to 14 nonconsecutive days by holding down the CTRL key and selecting each date. However, regardless of the order in which you select them, they are displayed in ascending date order in the Appointment area.

- **Select weeks**   To select a week at a time, move the mouse pointer to the left of the week row and click as soon as the pointer shifts from left to right. You can display up to six weeks' worth of dates in the Appointment area using this method.

- **Select months**   If you want to display an entire month's worth of dates in the Appointment area, click anywhere on the top row displaying the letters representing the days of the week. This is a great way to display the Month view without hiding the Date Navigator and the TaskPad.

You can also use the Date Navigator to change the week displayed in the Work Week view. Click the Work Week button on the Standard toolbar. Then click a date in the Date Navigator, and the work week in which the date falls displays in the Work Week view. However, if you use a nonstandard work week (such as Tuesday through Saturday), clicking some dates may display the next or previous work week instead.

If you find the Date Navigator in need of a little sprucing up, you can change its font by opening the Other tab on the Options dialog box (Tools | Options) and clicking the Advanced Options buttons. There you'll find the Date Navigator Font button, which enables you to select a different font, including size, style, and color.

Working with Calendar Views

Each of the Calendar views offers a different look at your scheduling information. Managing your schedule effectively often requires using different views to accomplish different scheduling tasks.

Using the Day View

The Day view, which is the default Day/Week/Month view, displays a single day in the Appointment area. As you can see in Figure 10-2, each appointment appears in the appropriate time slot.

If the Day view is not visible, you can display it by clicking the Day button on the Standard toolbar or pressing the shortcut key ALT-1. Once you have the Day view open, you can change the dates using either the Date Navigator or the Go To Date command, both of which are discussed earlier in this chapter. Using the Date Navigator, you can even display multiple dates in the Appointment area of the Day view.

To utilize the Day view effectively, there are a couple of things you should know:

- The Appointment area scroll bar enables you to move through the time slots for the selected day.

- Double-clicking an appointment opens the appointment form.

- Right-clicking an appointment displays a shortcut menu with commands that affect the selected appointment.

- Right-clicking the date header or a blank spot in the Appointment area displays a shortcut menu with general Calendar folder commands.

- Double-clicking the date header opens a blank Event form using the current date for the Start and End times.

- Double-clicking an open time slot in the Appointment area opens a blank appointment form using the current date and the selected time slot as the date and time for the appointment.

Figure 10-2.   *The Day view provides a quick look at a single day's worth of appointments*

■ Double-clicking the time bar (the vertical bar containing the time of day) opens a blank appointment form using the current date and selected time as the date and time for the appointment.

■ Right-clicking the time bar displays a shortcut menu containing commands for creating new calendar items and for customizing the time bar.

■ A small yellow box with an up or down arrow appears at the top and/or bottom of the time bar when additional appointments are scheduled but not visible.

Using the Work Week View

The Work Week view, which opens when you click the Work Week button or when you use the shortcut key ALT-5, is the Day view with multiple dates displayed. The dates displayed are those days of the current week that are designated as the days of your work week. By default, the work week days include Monday through Friday (see Figure 10-3).

Figure 10-3.   *Use the Work Week view for a quick glance at your appointments for the current work week*

Since the Work Week view is a variation of the Day view, all commands and features used in the Day view also apply to the Work Week view. See the previous section on the Day view for details.

Using the Week View

The Week view, shown in Figure 10-4, displays the days of the current week in the Appointment area. As you can see, the time bar and time slots are replaced by date boxes that hold information about scheduled items.

To open the Week view, click the Week button on the Standard toolbar or use the ALT-- (ALT + the minus key) shortcut. The Week view provides a number of options for getting things done quickly:

- Use the scroll bar to move through the weeks of the year. Although the scroll bar appears to have a limit of one year if you drag it from top to bottom, you can continue to scroll in either direction by clicking the arrow buttons at either end of the scroll bar.

- Double-click an appointment to open the appointment form.

MANAGING TIME
& DETAILS

Figure 10-4.   *The Week view provides a compact view of your weekly calendar*

- Right-click an appointment to display a shortcut menu containing commands that affect the appointment.

- Right-click the date or a blank spot on the Appointment area to display a shortcut menu of general Calendar folder commands.

- Double-click the date or a blank spot to open a new event form scheduled for the date selected. Since time slots are not available in the Week view, you cannot use a double-click to open a new appointment form. However, you can right-click the date and select New Appointment to open a blank appointment form for the selected date.

- To create an event spanning several days, highlight multiple dates by dragging your mouse pointer over them. Then right-click any of the selected dates and choose one of the commands for creating a new appointment, event, or meeting request.

- A small yellow box with an up or down arrow appears at the top and/or bottom of the time bar when additional appointments are scheduled but not visible. To view the additional appointments, click the yellow box to open the Day view.

- To change the date of a scheduled item, drag it to the appropriate date box.

Using the Month View

The last variation of the Day/Week/Month view is, appropriately, the Month view, which displays an entire month's worth of dates in the Information viewer. As Figure 10-5 shows, the Month view hides the Date Navigator and TaskPad to make room for the large number of days it must display.

If you prefer to restrict the Month view to the Appointment area and keep the Date Navigator and TaskPad onscreen, you can drag the right border of the Information viewer to the left until both components reappear.

Displaying the Month view is as easy as clicking the Month button on the Standard toolbar or using the ALT-= (ALT + the equals sign) shortcut key.

There's another way to display the Month view that automatically confines it to the Appointment area without having to drag the Information viewer border. Move to the Date Navigator and click anywhere in the row of letters representing the days of the week. This immediately opens the Month view in the Appointment area only, leaving the Date Navigator and TaskPad as they are.

Figure 10-5. *Use the Month view to see how your schedule for the entire month is shaping up*

Since the Month view is an expanded version of the Week view, it functions in the same manner. For details on manipulating the Month view, see the previous section on the Week view.

Note *Depending on the size of your Outlook window, the start times of appointments may or may not display in the Month view.*

Using Table Views

The Calendar folder table views display your Calendar information using the column and row format. You can switch to the table views by choosing View | Current View and selecting one of the table views from the submenu that appears. You can also use the Current View drop-down list found on the Advanced toolbar. To display the Advanced toolbar, right-click anywhere on the Standard toolbar and select Advanced from the shortcut menu.

For more information on using and customizing table views, see Chapter 22.

Using AutoPreview and the Preview Pane

As with most Outlook folders, the AutoPreview and Preview Pane features are offered in the Calendar folder. The AutoPreview feature is only available in table views and a special Day/Week/Month view, appropriately named the Day/Week/Month View With AutoPreview. As you can see in Figure 10-6, with AutoPreview enabled, the first couple of lines of notes from the appointment, event, or meeting form are displayed.

To enable AutoPreview, switch to a table view and choose View | AutoPreview. Return to the View menu and click AutoPreview a second time to turn AutoPreview off.

The Preview Pane available in both table and Day/Week/Month views splits the Information viewer into two panes. The Preview Pane appears on the bottom and contains a header with subject, location, and date information pertaining to the selected Calendar item. The body contains any notes included in the item.

Choose View | Preview Pane to activate the Preview Pane. To hide the Preview Pane, right-click the Preview Pane header and select Preview Pane. You can also return to the View menu and click Preview Pane to turn the Preview Pane off.

For information about customizing the Preview Pane, see Chapter 22.

Figure 10-6.   *AutoPreview gives you a peek at the appointment details*

Customizing the Calendar

As powerful and easy to use as the Calendar is, you may want to do some fine tuning to make it work just the way you like. Fortunately, Outlook provides a number of features and options you can use to customize the Calendar folder.

Setting Basic Calendar Options

The first thing you'll want to do is check the Calendar options to ensure the default settings are optimized for your needs. To access the options, choose Tools | Options to display the Options dialog box, shown in Figure 10-7.

Figure 10-7.   *Check your Calendar settings in the Options dialog box*

The first Calendar option appears on the Preferences tab in the Calendar section. It enables you to set the reminder default. Place a checkmark in the Default Reminder box to include a reminder in each new appointment, event, or meeting request form. Use the drop-down list to designate how long prior to the appointment you want the reminder activated.

Click the Calendar Options button to display the Calendar Options dialog box.

The Calendar Options dialog box contains a variety of options for customizing your work week, changing the Date Navigator appearance, and more. Your options include the following:

- **Calendar work week** Begin setting the work week by checking the days that comprise your work week. Since most jobs are Monday through Friday, those days are selected by default. Next, use the First Day Of Week drop-down list to designate the starting day for your week. This day determines the order that days appear in the Week view, Month view, and Date Navigator. From the First Week Of Year drop-down list, select the start date for your year. Next, enter the start time for your day. This is the first time slot that appears in the Day view. The default is 8:00 AM, however, if you work the third shift and start at eleven at night, enter 11:00 PM. Finally, enter the time your workday normally ends. See the notes following this list for additional information about setting Work Week options.

■ **Show week numbers in the Date Navigator**   Check this option to display a week number next to each week in the Date Navigator. The numbers range from 1 to 52, indicating the position of the week in the currently selected year.

■ **Use Microsoft Schedule+ as my primary calendar**   This option is only available if Schedule+ was running on your computer before Outlook was installed. It is used mainly in mixed environments (some Outlook users and some Schedule+ users) to make sure everyone can view shared calendar information. See your administrator for more information.

■ **Always use local calendar**   This handy option lets you improve Calendar performance while reducing the workload on the Microsoft Exchange server by using a calendar on your local machine. To ensure that the calendar information is up to date, Outlook performs regular background synchronization between the Microsoft Exchange server calendar and an offline folder file (.ost) on your local computer. The synchronization starts within ten seconds of making a change to your calendar.

■ **Send meeting requests using iCalendar by default**   If you send a lot of meeting requests to non-Outlook users (they must have iCalendar-compliant software) or Outlook users using Internet mail, you may want to check this option. It sends each meeting request in iCalendar format.

■ **Background color**   The color you select from this drop-down list appears as the background for the Appointment area in both the Day and Work Week views.

The remaining buttons on the Calendar Options dialog box provide extensive options for customizing different Calendar features. Therefore, each one is covered in the sections that follow.

Before moving on, there are a couple of things you should be aware of when setting your Work Week options.

■ You cannot set working hours that span midnight. For example, if you work the third shift, your workday may start at 11:00 PM and end at 7:30 AM the next morning. Setting those times as the Start and End times results in an error message informing you that "The end date you entered occurs before the start date." Unfortunately, this is a bug and there's no way around it.

■ Setting Sunday as the First Day Of Week displays Monday, not Sunday, as the first day in the Week view and the Month view. This is due to the fact that Outlook considers Saturday and Sunday a single entity, which it displays at the end of the week. If you change the First Day Of Week option to Saturday, the Sat/Sun block appears as the first day in both the Week and Month views.

Modifying and Adding Time Zones

If you travel a lot, or if you regularly do business with contacts in another time zone, you'll find the Time Zone options come in quite handy. When you're on the road, you can change the Calendar folder time zone to match the time zone in which you're traveling. If you do business with individuals in a different time zone, you can even add their time zone to your Day/Week/Month view to make scheduling decisions based on both time zones.

Choose Tools | Options to open the Options dialog box. Then click the Calendar Options button to display the Calendar Options dialog box. Finally, click the Time Zone button to open the Time Zone dialog box.

 You can also access the Time Zone options by right-clicking the time bar in the Day or Work Week view and selecting Change Time Zone.

Set the Time Zone options to suit your needs.

- **Label**   Use this field to give the default time zone a name. The name appears at the top of the time bar in the Day and Work Week views.

- **Time zone**   Set or change the default time zone used in the Calendar and other Outlook folders. Be advised, however, that this also resets the Windows Regional Settings time zone, which controls the clock on your local computer. Changing this time zone affects all other applications that use the clock.

- **Adjust for daylight saving time** Check this option if you want the time adjusted for daylight saving time. Again, this option resets the Regional Settings applet option and affects all Windows applications.

- **Current time** This field, which is for informational purposes only, displays the current time for the selected time zone. It cannot be edited from within Outlook. Double-click the time display in the Windows taskbar system tray to reset the system time.

- **Show an additional time zone** Check this option to display a second time zone in the Day and Work Week views. Checking the option enables additional Label, Time Zone, and daylight saving fields. Enter a name, select a time zone, and set the daylight saving option for the second time zone. This time zone is for convenience and does not affect Outlook or any other Windows applications *unless* you use the Swap Time Zones button.

- **Swap Time Zones** If you've added a second time zone, click this button to reverse the order in which the time zones appear and the way they are used. Switching time zones changes the Windows clock settings and therefore affects all Outlook folders and any Windows applications that use the clock. This option is especially handy if you divide your time between two time zones. It continues to work even if you choose not to display the second time zone.

With a secondary time zone selected, the time bar in the Day and Work Week views displays hours for both time zones. The secondary time zone hours appear to the left of the default time zone hours.

Tip
If the Time Zone options aren't enough to take care of your needs, you can always make adjustments using the Regional Settings applet in the Windows Control Panel. However, it's important to remember that the settings here affect all Windows applications, including Outlook. In addition to changing the default time zone and daylight saving settings, you can also change the time format, date style, and date separator. To modify these settings choose Start | Settings | Control Panel from the Windows taskbar to open the Control Panel dialog box. Then double-click the Regional Settings applet to display the Regional Settings Properties dialog box.

Adding Holidays

Having your Outlook Calendar display upcoming holidays can be a great help. However, since holidays are not automatically included with the typical Outlook installation, you'll have to add them yourself if you want them to appear on your Calendar. Fortunately, this is easy enough for even the most inexperienced user to accomplish with little effort.

Follow these steps to add holidays to the Outlook Calendar:

1. Choose Tools | Options to open the Options dialog box.

2. Click Calendar Options on the Preferences tab to display the Calendar Options dialog box.

3. Click the Add Holidays button to show the Add Holidays To Calendar dialog box.

4. Select the regional holidays you want to include on the Calendar. You can select multiple sets of holidays if you want. This is great if you have a mix of ethnic contacts whose holidays you want to remember.

5. Click OK to add the holidays and return to the Calendar Options dialog box.

6. Click OK to close the Calendar Options dialog box, and again to close the Options dialog box.

 Although you can add multiple Calendar subfolders to the original Calendar folder, you cannot add holidays to any Calendar folder except the original. Attempting to add holidays to a subfolder results in the holidays being added to the main Calendar folder. If the Calendar folder already contains the holiday set selected, duplicate holidays will appear. This is by design.

The next time you open your Calendar, the holidays you've added will appear in the appropriate date slot as all day events.

Setting Resource Scheduling Options

This set of options is generally used for automating the scheduling of resources such as conference rooms, equipment, and so on. Therefore, you should not change the settings unless you are the administrator of such resources and the delegate of the resource mailbox. For details on scheduling resources and setting Resource Scheduling options, see Chapter 12.

MOUS EXAM PRACTICE

Customizing the Calendar folder primarily involves setting options. Setting options does not, in itself, require much practice. However, understanding the consequences of your actions may. Therefore you should try setting the different options and observe the effect your changes have on the Outlook Calendar.

Understanding Free/Busy Time

When you schedule an item in your Calendar, Outlook marks the block of time for which the item is scheduled with a free/busy designation. You can see the free/busy times when you click the Attendees tab of a meeting request. The time designations are described in Table 10-3.

By default, free/busy time is stored in your mailbox on the server. However, if you work offline, or interact with people who are not connected to your Microsoft Exchange server, you can provide access to your free/busy time by publishing it in a separate file (.vfb) to another site. You can publish free/busy time to a Web site, intranet, FTP site, or another computer on the network.

Note

Outlook searches for free/busy information in one of three places. It first checks the location specified in the Global Address List entry, then in the contact record Internet Free-Busy Address field, and finally, in the Publish At This Address field in Free/Busy options.

Free/Busy Designation	Indicates	Color Used in Free/Busy Table
Free	Time slot is available for scheduling	White or clear
Busy	Time slot is already spoken for	Blue
Out of office	User will be unavailable	Purple
Tentative	User has tentatively filled this time slot (but may be open to a better offer)	Light blue
Unknown	The user's free/busy information is unavailable	Diagonal lines

Table 10-3. *Free/Busy Time Designations*

Whether you use the Microsoft Exchange server to store your free/busy information or a separate .vfb file at another location, or both, you can use the Free/Busy Options dialog box to configure the way Outlook manages your free/busy information. Follow these steps to set the Free/Busy options:

1. Choose Tools | Options to open the Options dialog box.

2. Click the Calendar Options button to display the Calendar Options dialog box.

3. Click the Free/Busy Options button to open the Free/Busy Options dialog box.

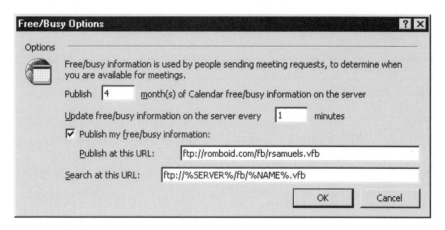

4. Set the Free/Busy Options. Your choices include:

■ **Publish ___ month(s) of Calendar free/busy information on the server**
Indicate the number of months' worth of free/busy time to publish on the server.

■ **Update free/busy information on the server every ___ minutes** As you schedule and accept appointments and meetings your free/busy time changes. Use this option to determine how often you want your free/busy time updated on the Microsoft Exchange server. Since frequent updating may cause a strain on the server, you should check with your administrator before reducing the time between automatic updates.

■ **Publish my free/busy information** If you want to publish your free/busy time to a location other than the Microsoft Exchange server, check this option.

■ **Publish at this URL** If you don't indicate the URL (location and name) of the .vfb file in which your free/busy information is stored, you cannot publish it. It's a good idea to make sure all users employ the same folder name, such as fb, when storing their free/busy time, no matter which location they choose. The folder must be shared if it's on a local computer or server on the network. In addition, correct syntax is critical for proper publishing.

■ **Search at this URL** This option lets Outlook know where to look for other users' free/busy information if it doesn't find it on the Microsoft Exchange server. Enter the server on which the free/busy (.vfb) file is stored. You can use %SERVER% and %NAME% parameters when entering the URL. For example, if you use an FTP site you might enter **ftp://%SERVER%/fb/%NAME%.vfb**. Outlook substitutes the server and user's name when searching. When sending meeting requests via Internet e-mail, Outlook uses the SMPT address to search for the free/busy file. Outlook replaces %SERVER% with the e-mail address server information (everything after the @ sign), and replaces %NAME% with the e-mail address name (everything before the @ sign).

Note *Publishing your free/busy time requires the Web Publishing Wizard. Therefore, if it was not installed during the Windows installation you will be asked to install it before you're allowed to publish your free/busy information.*

5. Click OK three times to close the dialog boxes and return to the active Outlook window.

Tip *If you plan to use an FTP site, make sure it allows anonymous logins and make sure the permissions for the fb folder allow users to read and write to the folder.*

The Microsoft Exchange server will now update your free/busy information on the server in accordance with the settings in the first two options.

Note *Outlook applies the Free/Busy options on a per user, not per profile basis. Therefore, changing the options in one profile changes them for all profiles created by the user currently logged on.*

If you checked the Publish My Free/Busy Information option and filled in the appropriate target URL, you can manually publish your information as long as you're connected to the server via a LAN or the Internet. To publish your free/busy information, choose Tools | Send/Receive | Free/Busy Information.

Tip *If you rely on published free/busy information, you should empty your Internet Explorer cache on a regular basis since Outlook uses Internet Explorer to retrieve free/busy information. If you're lax in this minor housekeeping chore, you may end up viewing old, cached free/busy data. To clear the cache, open the Internet Options dialog box (from Internet Explorer or the Control Panel) and click Delete Files. Check Delete All Offline Content and click OK. Click OK again to close the Internet Options dialog box.*

Integrating Calendar with Other Outlook Components

The integration of its various components is one of Outlook's most attractive features. In addition to the integration found in the other components, the Calendar folder has the added advantage of having a direct pipeline to the Tasks folder. It's called the TaskPad, and it enables you to add, remove, edit, and view tasks without leaving the Calendar folder.

Creating To-Do Lists with TaskPad

The TaskPad is a handy device that appears in the Calendar folder default view. As you can see here, the TaskPad resembles a small lined pad used for jotting down to-do list items.

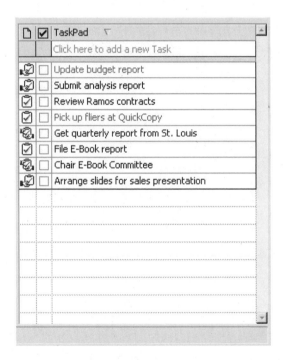

The first thing to understand about the TaskPad is that it is an extension of the Tasks folder. Items added to or changes made in the TaskPad appear in the Tasks folder and vice versa. The major functional difference between the two is in the available views. The TaskPad views are fewer and more limited than the Tasks folder views. In addition, any changes made to a view in one do not affect the view of the same name in the other.

Using the TaskPad is as simple or complex as you need it to be. For adding quick to-do items, just click the Click Here To Add A New Task field and start typing. Press the ENTER key when you're finished. If you want to add a task with dates, times, reminders, or details, double-click the Click Here To Add A New Task field or a blank line in the TaskPad to open a new task form (see Figure 10-8).

Enter the appropriate information in the new task form and click Save And Close to add the task to the TaskPad and the Tasks folder. For detailed information on creating tasks, see Chapter 13.

To edit a TaskPad item subject, click the item and make the change. To edit an item's details, double-click the item to open the form and make the necessary change(s).

Figure 10-8. *The TaskPad isn't just for to-do items*

Viewing TaskPad Items

Although not as versatile as the Tasks folder, the TaskPad is no slouch when it comes to views. It comes with six standard views and an option to show or hide items without due dates. You can even customize TaskPad views. The one thing you can't do is create new views for the TaskPad. If you don't like the standard views, you'll have to switch over to the Tasks folder and create your custom view there.

To change views in the TaskPad, choose View | TaskPad View to display a submenu of available views. You can also right-click the Click Here To Add A New Task field or a blank spot on the TaskPad and select TaskPad View from the shortcut menu. The available TaskPad views include:

- **All Tasks**   This one's pretty straightforward—it includes all tasks. One thing to note: this view ignores the Include Tasks With No Due Date option, showing tasks regardless of whether they have due dates.

- **Today's Tasks**   Use this view to see all tasks with no start date or with a start date equal or prior to today's date.

- **Active Tasks for Selected Days**   This view works in conjunction with the Date Navigator. It displays tasks with no due dates or with due dates that fall on or after the date(s) selected.

- **Task for Next Seven Days**   This view utilizes the start date, showing only those tasks with no start date or with start dates within seven days of today's date.

- **Overdue Tasks**   Any task whose due date has passed is included in this view.

- **Tasks Completed on Selected Days**   Use this view with the Date Navigator to display only those dates marked complete on selected dates.

- **Include Tasks with No Due Date**   This option, which instructs Outlook to display tasks without due dates in all reports, is enabled by default. Click it to disable it.

You can customize the TaskPad views, just as you can customize all Outlook views. However, the amount of space allocated for the TaskPad severely limits the usefulness of customizing TaskPad views. You're probably better off moving to the Tasks folder if you want to see customized views of your task and to-do items. See Chapter 22 for details on customizing Outlook views.

In addition to customized views, the TaskPad also offers the AutoPreview feature. To turn it on, right-click the Click Here To Add A New Task field or a blank spot on the TaskPad and select AutoPreview.

Note   *The TaskPad also contains a Show Preview Pane option in the Other Settings dialog box. Unfortunately, it doesn't work. This is a bug for which there was no workaround at the time of this writing.*

Sorting and Filtering TaskPad Items

Sorting and filtering the TaskPad is identical to sorting and filtering any other table view. Click a field header to sort by that field. Click the field header a second time to reverse the sort order. To sort by multiple fields, hold down the SHIFT key and click the desired field headers. You can also right-click any of the field headers and select Sort Ascending or Sort Descending from the shortcut menu. For more sophisticated sorts, you can open the View Summary dialog box by right-clicking a field header and selecting Customize Current View. Click the Sort button and create your custom sort in the Sort dialog box.

Tip	*You can rearrange your TaskPad items manually by dragging them up and down the list. However, once the list has been sorted or grouped, dragging no longer works. To remove Sort or Group By attributes, right-click the TaskPad banner, select Customize Current View, and open the appropriate dialog box (Sort or Group By) and click Clear All.*

Applying filters to the TaskPad is accomplished using the View Summary dialog box. Click the Filter button to open the Filter dialog box. Enter your filter criteria and click OK to apply the filter. See Chapter 22 for more information on sorting and filtering Outlook views.

Using Drag and Drop to Create Outlook Items in the Calendar

Outlook offers tight integration between all components. The Calendar folder, with its embedded TaskPad, offers even tighter integration than the other primary Outlook folders. The ability to create tasks and to-do items from within the Calendar folder is only part of the story. It also offers the ability to create other Outlook items from both Calendar items and task/to-do items.

The most direct method for creating new Outlook items is to use drag and drop. For example, in the Day/Week/Month view, you can drag a to-do item to the Appointment area or the Date Navigator and create a new appointment item scheduled for the selected date, and include the to-do item information in the notes field.

Note	*No matter where you drop the to-do item, the default time set for the new appointment is the time designated as the start of your workday. This is true even if you drop the to-do item on a specific time slot in the Day view or the Work Week view.*

You can also create a task item by dragging an appointment from the Appointment area and dropping it on the TaskPad. This opens a new task form that includes the appointment subject, date, and details.

Using either appointments or tasks, you can employ the drag and drop method to create other Outlook items as well. Simply drag the appointment or task, and drop it on the appropriate shortcut on the Outlook Bar or on a folder in the Folder List. If you want to include the appointment or task as an attachment, right-drag it and make the appropriate selection from the shortcut menu that appears when you drop the item.

MOUS EXAM PRACTICE

You can manage schedules and tasks, as well as create other Outlook items, from within the Calendar folder. Begin your practice by putting the TaskPad to use. Create simple to-do items first, then create full-fledged tasks with due dates, reminders, and details. Use TaskPad views to display task and to-do item information. Then move on to creating other Outlook items using both calendar and task items. Use the standard drag and drop method to create new items using the information from the original items. Then try right-dragging calendar and task items to create new items.

Using iCalendar and vCalendar

Outlook supports both iCalendar and vCalendar, the two leading file formats used for exchanging calendaring and scheduling data across a variety of platforms and software applications. Both formats are transportable over the Internet. Outlook users can take advantage of either format for exchanging calendar and free/busy information with other Outlook users and non-Outlook users.

Outlook provides a number of ways you can exchange calendar information using one format or the other:

- **Forward as iCalendar** Select the Calendar item(s) to forward and choose Actions | Forward As iCalendar to create a new e-mail message with the item(s) inserted as attachments. You can perform the same action from within an open Calendar item form.

- **Send as iCalendar** This command is available only from within an open meeting request form. Create a new meeting request and choose Tools | Send As iCalendar to enable the iCalendar format. Then click Send to dispatch the meeting request. You can also use the command if you make changes to an existing meeting request and want to send updates. In that case, enable Send As iCalendar and click Save And Close.

- **Save as iCalendar or vCalendar** To save a Calendar item as an iCalendar or vCalendar file that you can later attach to an e-mail, select the Calendar item and choose File | Save As to open the Save As dialog box. From the Save In drop-down list, choose a location in which to store the file. Select the appropriate file type from the Save As Type drop-down list, change the filename if necessary, and click Save.

- **Open an iCalendar or vCalendar attachment**   If you receive an iCalendar or vCalendar attachment in e-mail, double-click the attachment to open the item in Outlook. Click Save And Close to add it to your Calendar.

- **Import an iCalendar or vCalendar file**   You can also use the Import and Export Wizard to import an iCalendar or vCalendar file you receive on disk. See Chapter 20 for more information on importing and exporting.

If you forward an iCalendar item via Internet e-mail to individuals who use an e-mail client other than Outlook, they may not receive the iCalendar item as an iCalendar attachment. If you encounter this problem, it's most likely due to an incorrect Content Type association in Windows. This is the result of a bug in the Outlook 2000 installation procedure. To fix the problem, do the following:

1. Open Windows Explorer or My Computer and choose View | Folder Options to display the Folder Options dialog box.

2. Click the File Types tab to display the options for managing file type associations.

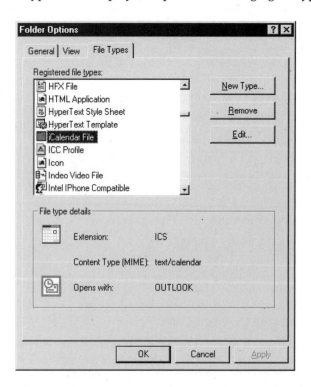

3. Scroll down the Registered File Types list and select iCalendar File. Click Edit to display the Edit File Type dialog box.

4. In the Content Type (MIME) field, type **text/calendar**.

5. Click OK twice to close the dialog boxes and save the changes.

The next time you send or forward iCalendar data via the Internet, all your recipients should receive the iCalendar attachment regardless of the e-mail client they're using.

Publishing Your Calendar as a Web Page

The capability to publish your Calendar as a Web page lets you share your Calendar information across platforms and around the globe. You can publish your Calendar as an HTML document on a local computer, an intranet, or a server on the Internet. Anyone with a browser and access to the host computer can view your Calendar information.

There are a couple of requirements for publishing a calendar as a Web page. First, the Windows Web Publishing Wizard must be installed. Second, the Office Server Extensions Support and Office Web Components must also be installed. If any of these items are not installed on your computer, you'll be asked to insert the appropriate disk and install them before continuing. You'll also need access to the target computer either through a LAN or Internet connection.

The actual publication of your Calendar is relatively simple. From the Calendar folder, choose File | Save as Web Page to display the Save As Web Page dialog box.

By default, Outlook assumes you want to publish the current and next months' Calendar information. To modify the range of information, change the Start Date and End Date by entering the desired dates. You can also select the desired dates from the pop-up calendar available in each field. If you want the Notes information for each Calendar item published as well, check the Include Appointment Details option. You can spruce up the published calendar by including a graphic to be used as the background. Check the Use Background Graphic option, and enter the path and name of the image file to use.

The next step is to give the published calendar a title and indicate the location and filename to which you want it saved. In the Calendar Title field, enter a name to appear as the title in the published document. Enter the path and filename for the published calendar in the File Name field. Use the appropriate protocol (file:// for a file on a network server, http:// for the Internet, ftp:// for an FTP site). If you want to save the calendar to your computer or another computer on the network, click the Browse button, select the location, and enter a filename. Select the final option, Open Saved Web Page In Browser, if you want to immediately open the saved calendar using your default browser. It's a good idea to leave this checked so you can verify that the calendar has been properly published.

Note   *A bug in Outlook 2000 results in the creation of an extra folder bearing the same name as the file regardless of where you publish the calendar. In other words, if you enter **ftp://ezwidgets.com/cal/rsamuels.htm** in the File Name field, the published document (rsamuels.htm) ends up in ftp://ezwidgets.com/cal/rsamuels/.*

Now you're ready to begin publishing. If you're publishing via a LAN or Internet connection, make sure the connection is established. Click the Save button. What happens next depends on the location to which you're publishing. If you selected a local or network computer as the target, the calendar is published immediately and opens in your browser (if you checked the Open Saved Web Page In Browser option). That's all there is to it.

If, however, you elected to publish the calendar to a server by entering the path and filename using one of the protocols discussed earlier, the Web Publishing Wizard opens (shown in Figure 10-9).

Click Next to start the process. Enter a descriptive name for the Web server to which you plan to publish the calendar. This name is for your reference only. If you want to specify your connection method, click the Advanced button and make the appropriate selection from the drop-down list. Unless you're an experienced user, you should leave the default setting, Automatically Select Connection Method.

Click Next to open the Specify The FTP Server And Subfolder page.

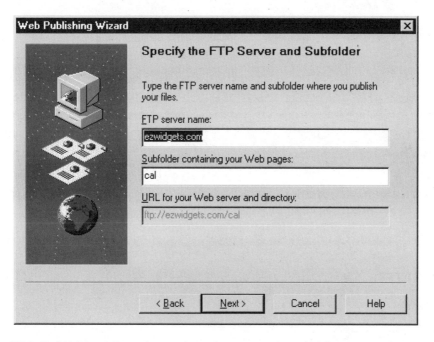

The Web Publishing Wizard uses the information from the File Name field in the Save As Web Page dialog box to automatically fill in this page. If the information is incorrect, change it; otherwise, click Next to proceed to the summary page. Click Finish to publish your calendar to the designated site.

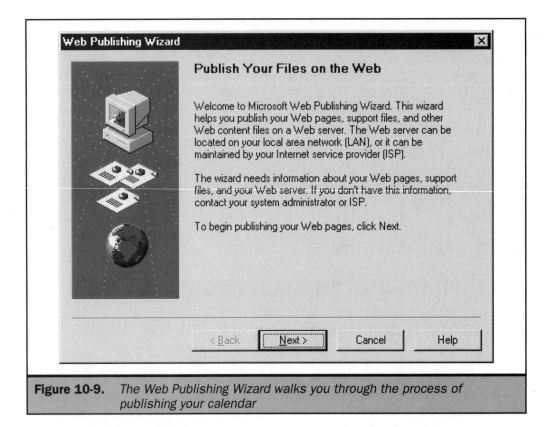

Figure 10-9. *The Web Publishing Wizard walks you through the process of publishing your calendar*

Before allowing you to complete the publishing process, Outlook displays the Enter Network Password dialog box.

If the site you're publishing to requires a user name and password, enter it here and click OK to finish publishing.

If you're publishing to an FTP or Web site and are familiar with FTP software, you can bypass the Web Publishing Wizard by publishing the calendar to your local drive and then uploading it to the site using FTP software. The only thing to be careful about is making sure all filenames are in lowercase when uploading to a UNIX server. UNIX is not fond of uppercase or mixed-case filenames. As a result, the calendar may not display properly unless all filenames are in lowercase.

MOUS

MOUS EXAM PRACTICE
Publishing your calendar as a Web page is a fast and easy way to share your calendar across platforms. Start by publishing your calendar to your local hard drive. Change the options for the amount and detail of information to publish and see the difference. When you've got the hang of publishing basics, try your hand at publishing to an Internet server. Ask your administrator if the company has an FTP site you can use. If not, check with a friend who may have one.

Archiving the Calendar Folder

As your Calendar information grows, you'll find that doing a little housekeeping on a regular basis helps keep your Calendar uncluttered, and makes your Microsoft Exchange Server administrator happy by reducing the load on the server. However, you may not be prepared to permanently delete old, expired Calendar items that often prove useful when trying to piece together events from the past. Fortunately, Outlook offers a compromise: move the obsolete information to an archive file for storage and easy retrieval at a later date.

You can perform archiving operations automatically, using the AutoArchive feature, or manually by using the Archive command. The Calendar folder is one of the primary folders for which AutoArchiving is turned on by default. Whichever method you use, archiving the Calendar folder is the same as archiving other Outlook folders. For more information on archiving automatically and manually, see Chapter 18.

Although the process is the same no matter which Outlook folder you archive, there are a couple of things you should be aware of when archiving the Calendar folder:

- Past occurrences of recurring appointments are not archived if any future occurrences are still due. Outlook needs all occurrences in the series to keep track of future occurrences.

- If you archive an item after "snoozing" its reminder, the reminder is still active. Therefore, the reminder will reappear at the scheduled time, but you will not be able to open the item unless you retrieve it from the archive file.

Using the Calendar Folder Print Features

Although you'll probably spend the majority of your time working on the electronic version of your Calendar, there are times when a hard copy comes in handy. When you find you need one to take on the road, or you want a printout for a colleague, Outlook provides a number of options for printing your Calendar information.

Printing the Calendar

You can print from the Day/Week/Month view and any of the table views. However, depending on where you are when you decide to print your Calendar, you'll find you have significantly different choices.

Printing from the Day/Week/Month View

If you're in the Day/Week/Month view and decide to print your Calendar, you have a wide variety of styles to choose from. No matter which Day/Week/Month view you're in (Day, Work Week, Week, Month), the choices remain the same.

To print your Calendar from the Day/Week/Month view, follow these steps:

1. Click the Print button on the Standard toolbar or press CTRL-P to open the Print dialog box, shown in Figure 10-10.

2. Select the printer to use from the Name drop-down list. The Properties button displays options that are unique to the specific printer you select. See the printer manual for information on setting printer properties.

3. Choose a style from the Print Style list. Your choices include:

   ■ **Daily Style**   Use the Daily Style to print a single day's worth of appointments per page. The date and Date Navigator calendars for the current and next month appear at the top of each page. In addition, the TaskPad and a blank notes area are included. The notes area in the lower-right corner is for you to jot your own notes, not for notes from Calendar items. A separate page is printed for each date in the print range.

   ■ **Weekly Style**   The Weekly Style prints the Week view on a single page, which is headed by the date and the Date Navigator calendars for the current and next month. Each week in the print range prints on a separate page. Neither the TaskPad nor the notes area is included in the Weekly Style by default.

   ■ **Monthly Style**   If you've been paying attention, you'll have already figured out that the Monthly style prints the Month view for the date(s) in the Print Range field. As with the other styles, the date and Date Navigator calendars for the current and next month appear at the top of each page. Each month prints on a separate page. Once again, the TaskPad and notes area do not appear in this style by default.

Figure 10-10.   *Set the Print options to suit your needs*

- **Tri-fold Style**   This style is handy for creating three-fold booklets from your Calendar. By default, the left pane contains the daily calendar, the middle pane contains the TaskPad, and the right pane contains the weekly calendar. Sorry, no Date Navigator calendars in this one.

- **Calendar Details Style**   If you just need a quick listing of your Calendar items by date and time, this is the style for you. Dates are separated by date headers, and Calendar items are listed by appointment times. Detail information is included for each Calendar item.

- **Memo Style**   The Memo Style prints the selected Calendar item and all its details. The Print Range field disappears and only the one selected appointment prints.

Note   *The Memo Style options include Start Each Item On A New Page and Print Attached Files With Item(s). Their names clearly describe their functions.*

4. If you selected any style *except* Memo Style, set the range of dates you want to include by entering a start date and an end date. You can enter the dates manually or by selecting them from the pop-up calendar available in each field.

Note

If the start date is in the first week of the current month and the week contains days from the previous month, the Date Navigator calendars at the top of each printed page will be the current month and previous month. Otherwise, they will be the current month and the next month.

5. If you want to print the appointment without any specific information other than the date and time, check the Hide Details Of Private Appointments option. The item appears on the printout as Private Appointment.

6. From the Number Of Pages drop-down list, select the pages you want to print. To print on both sides of the paper without having a duplex printer, first print the even pages, then reinsert the paper in the printer and print the odd pages.

7. Enter the number of copies you want to print.

8. Check the Collate Copies option if you're printing multiple copies of multipage calendars, and you want each copy assembled individually. In other words, a single copy of each page is printed until one complete copy of the calendar is finished. This process is repeated until all copies of the calendar are printed. Without the Collate Copies option selected, all copies of page 1 are printed, followed by all copies of page 2, and so on. You then have to assemble each copy yourself.

Tip

Although it sounds like a great time saver, Collate Copies can actually take longer depending on the size of the job and your printer. Without automatic collating enabled, the data for each page is sent to the printer only once, and multiple copies of that page are printed. When the Collate Copies option is enabled, the data must be resent to the printer for every page printed. Therefore, with Collate Copies checked, printing 20 copies of a 5-page calendar requires that data for 100 pages be sent to, and assimilated by, the printer. Whereas, with Collate Copies disabled, only 5 pages of data are transmitted to and processed by the printer.

9. Click OK to print your Calendar.

You can also click the Preview button to see what the printout will look like before actually committing yourself to the print job.

Printing from a Table View

Since table views are less complex than Day/Week/Month views, the choices and options for printing from table views are rather more limited. However, the process

Figure 10-11. *Printing from table views offers a limited selection of styles and options*

is the same. With a Calendar table view open, click the Print button or press CTRL-P to open the Print dialog box, seen in Figure 10-11.

From the Name drop-down list, select the printer to use. Set the properties for your printer by clicking the Properties button. Consult your printer manual for information on setting printer properties. Next, move to the Print Styles list and choose the style for this printout. The standard styles include:

- **Table Style**   This is a straightforward recreation of the table view on your screen in hard copy.

- **Memo Style**   Use the Memo Style to print selected Calendar items with all their detail information.

If you're using the Table Style, check the appropriate option to determine whether to print all items (All Rows) or only selected items (Only Selected Rows). Next, select the pages to print. To print using both sides of the paper without a duplex printer, choose Odd, then reinsert the paper upside down and print again, choosing Even. Finally, select the number of copies to print and decide whether you want Outlook to collate the copies for you or if you want to do it yourself.

For the Memo Style, your options include Start Each Item On A New Page and Print Attached Files With Item(s), plus the standard Number Of Pages, Number Of Copies, and Collate Copies options.

Due to an Outlook 2000 bug, when your default Mail Format is set to HTML, the Start Each Item On A New Page option is only available if you select a single item, in which case it's unnecessary. If you select multiple items, the option is grayed out, and each item prints on a separate page by default.

To print the job, click the OK button. If you want to see what the finished job will look like, click the Preview button.

MOUS EXAM PRACTICE
In this section, you learned to select printers and print styles, set print options, and print a hard copy of your Calendar. Rather than wasting paper, ink, and your administrator's patience, practice printing by selecting various print styles and option settings and using the Preview button to see how your selections will look. Try printing (previewing really) from different Calendar views and see how they affect your print options.

Customizing Print Styles

In addition to setting general print options for each style, you can also modify their Page Setup options. Outlook provides three sets of Page Setup options for each print style.

Formatting Options

The formatting options, found on the Format tab of the Page Setup dialog box, enable you to modify the basic design of each printed page. To set the Page Setup formatting options, choose File | Page Setup to display a submenu of print styles. Select a print style to display the associated Page Setup dialog box (see Figure 10-12).

By default, the Page Setup dialog box opens to the Format tab, which contains three groups of settings:

- **Options** The Options settings vary from print style to print style. They generally consist of options for including such things as the TaskPad, a notes area (not to be confused with a Calendar item Notes field), page layout information, and a print range. All styles with the exception of the Memo Style, which has no Options settings, include some or all of these Options settings.

- **Fonts** In all print styles except the Memo Style, you can use the Font options to change the font used in the date headings that appear at the top of the report and the Calendar item listings. Click the appropriate font button to display the Font dialog box, in which you can select a different font, font style,

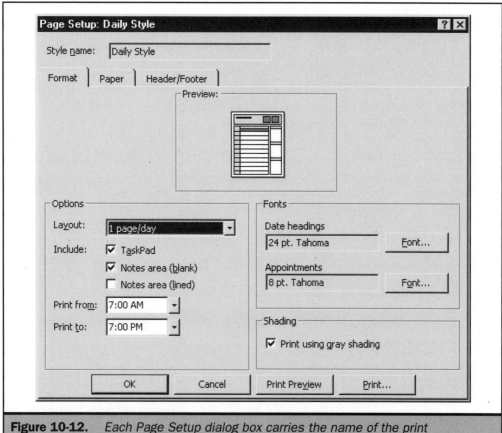

Figure 10-12.   *Each Page Setup dialog box carries the name of the print style selected*

and/or font size. The Memo Style also has font options. However, they affect the title (the calendar owner's name) and the field names (Subject, Locations, and so on).

■ **Shading**   Most of the styles use gray shading to offset title and date headers. You can elect to add or remove the shading using the Print Using Gray Shading option.

Note   *When you turn on gray shading and use the Print Preview button to see what the final printout will look like, it appears that the gray shading option isn't working. This is a bug. In spite of the fact that you can't see it, the printout will contain the gray shading. For a rough idea of where gray shading is used, check the small Preview pane above the options on the Format tab. It always displays the page with shading enabled.*

Paper Options

The Paper tab of the Page Setup dialog box, shown in Figure 10-13, contains options for designating the type, size, and source of the paper you're going to use, and more. The Paper options are identical for all print styles:

- **Paper**   The paper options let you select from a list of standard paper types and sizes. You can even select a custom size and indicate the dimensions manually. If your printer has multiple paper trays, or if you plan to feed the paper manually, you can designate the source for the paper as well.

- **Page**   The Page options determine how the individual page layouts designed on the Format tab are arranged on the individual sheets of paper of the type and size selected in the Paper options. You can select standard page sizes, for which the dimensions are set, or you can designate a custom size and enter the dimensions yourself. Use this option to squeeze more data on a single sheet of paper or to create small booklets.

- **Margins**   The margins are the spaces between the edge of the paper and the beginning of the print. Adjust them according to your needs. Since most printers

Figure 10-13.   *Use the Paper tab to select your paper and finalize the page layout design*

need a minimum amount of margin space to grip the paper as it passes through the printer, you probably won't be able to set the left or right margins too close to zero. If the margins are too small, Windows will alert you to the fact.

- **Orientation**   Although orientation is normally a simple and straightforward decision between Portrait and Landscape, the introduction of Page options complicates it a little. The definitions of Portrait and Landscape don't change, just the way they're applied. Portrait prints the page vertically and Landscape prints the page horizontally. In most print jobs, the paper and the page are one and the same. In the Outlook Calendar, however, that's not always the case. Therefore, check the preview display in the Orientation section to verify that your choice is the correct one.

Header/Footer Options

The final set of Page Setup options can be found on the Header/Footer tab of the Page Setup dialog box (see Figure 10-14).

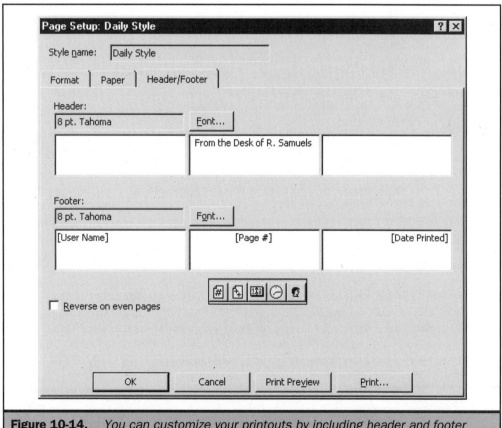

Figure 10-14.   *You can customize your printouts by including header and footer information*

As you can see in Figure 10-14, the options consist mainly of text boxes in which you can enter any information you want to add to the top or bottom of each printed page. The Header/Footer options are pretty straightforward. They contain a text box for the left, middle, and right portion of the page for headers, which appear at the top of the page, and for footers, which appear at the bottom of the page.

You can enter the text you want to display or you can use the Header/Footer toolbar located beneath the middle pane of the Footer option.

To use the toolbar, place the cursor in the desired box and click the appropriate button on the toolbar.

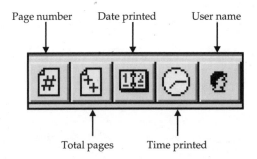

If you so desire, you can even include multiple items in a header or footer section. For example, you might want the Date Printed and the Time Printed to appear one after the other in the top-right corner of the page. Place your cursor in the right Header text box and click the Date Printed button. Then press the SPACEBAR to add a space, and click the Time Printed button.

The last option on the Header/Footer tab lets you reverse the position of the right and left panes of both the headers and footers. This comes in handy when you're printing booklets and you want certain information to always appear either on the outside or inside edge of the page. To reverse the left and right pane positions, check the Reverse On Even Pages option.

MOUS   *MOUS EXAM PRACTICE*
Configuring Page Setup options gives you complete control over your Calendar printouts. There are a lot of options to set, so you may want to spend some time trying them out and observing the results. As with the other print options, the best way to practice is to make changes and use the Print Preview button. Begin by opening, examining, and changing the Format options for each of the print styles. Then select the Paper tab and utilize the Page options to see which layouts work for you. Finally, move to the Header/Footer tab and enter some text information, then use the toolbar to add additional system information.

Exam | MOUS Exam Objectives Explored in Chapter 10

Objective	Activity	Heading
OL2000.3.1	Navigating within the Calendar	"Navigating the Calendar Window"
OL2000.3.4	Print in Calendar	"Printing the Calendar"
OL2000.3.6	Configure Calendar print options	"Printing the Calendar" "Customizing Print Styles"
OL2000.3.7	Customize the Calendar view	"Customizing the Calendar"
OL2000.3.12	Save a team or personal calendar as a Web page	"Publishing Your Calendar as a Web Page
OL2000.3.14	Integrate Calendar with other Outlook components	"Integrating Calendar with Other Outlook Components"

Chapter 11

Scheduling Appointments and Events

If there's one Outlook component that can increase your productivity and help you organize your time effectively, it's the Calendar. Not only does it let you keep track of your appointments and events (appointments that last 24 hours or more), it also provides reminders to ensure you don't forget your appointments. In addition, you can insert attachments, link contacts to appointments, and even create recurring appointments and events. In this chapter, you'll learn to add, modify, customize, and delete appointments and events.

Calendar Item Basics

Before jumping into the details of scheduling and tracking, there are some basics you should learn that apply to all Calendar items, including appointments, events, and meetings. These basic features include:

- **Locations** For each scheduled item, you can include the site at which the activity takes place. Although there are no default locations, each time you enter a new location it becomes part of the Location drop-down list.

- **Reminders** To ensure you don't forget a scheduled item, you can have Outlook tap you on the shoulder and alert you when it's due. Just set a reminder.

- **Attachments** You can keep track of files, documents, and Outlook items that are related to a scheduled item by inserting them in the scheduled item as attachments.

- **Editing and deleting techniques** Opening, closing, modifying, and deleting Calendar items are the same no matter which type of Calendar item you're working with.

A good understanding of these features will make your scheduling chores a lot easier.

Designating Locations

A location is exactly what the name implies: a place where the scheduled appointment, event, or meeting occurs. The Appointment tab of the new Calendar item form contains a Location field into which you can enter the appropriate location for the item. The nice thing about the Location field is that it retains the last ten locations you entered, in a drop-down list. The next time you create a new scheduled item, you can select the location from the list. However, after the tenth location, each new entry you make replaces the oldest location on the list.

While there's no way to selectively edit the Location drop-down list, you can delete the entire list and start over. This comes in handy if you move to a new location in which none of the old Location descriptions apply. Be advised, however, that this procedure involves editing the Windows registry, which should be done by experienced users only. Be sure to make a backup of your registry before making any changes. To erase the contents of the Location drop-down list, find the `HKEY_CURRENT_USER\Software\Microsoft\Office\9.0\Outlook\Preferences` key and delete the LocationMRU value. Close the registry and return to Outlook. You'll see that the Location drop-down list is now blank. The next time you make an entry in the list, the LocationMRU value is recreated in the registry.

Staying on Schedule with Reminders

When it comes to getting your Calendar organized, scheduling appointments, events, and meetings is only half the battle. The most important part of getting organized is remembering to attend all your scheduled activities. Fortunately, Outlook provides not only the precise tools you need to get organized, but also handy little devices called reminders that make sure you stay on schedule. Reminders are notices that alert you with both visual and aural cues when scheduled items are due. Using reminders is quick and easy once you understand the way they work.

Setting Reminders

When you create any scheduled item, whether it's an appointment, event, or meeting request, you fill out the Appointment tab of the Calendar item form. Although there are some minor differences between the Appointment tabs of the three different Calendar item types, each one contains identical Reminder features (see Figure 11-1).

The first thing you have to do is place a checkmark in the Reminder box to turn the reminder on. Next, select the amount of time prior to the scheduled item you want the reminder to go off. For this you have two choices. You can either select a predefined time from the Reminder drop-down list or you can enter the time manually. To enter times manually, you must include the number and the time unit. For example, you can type in **13 minutes**, **3 hours**, or **2 days**. You cannot, however, enter a combination of time units. So if you want a reminder that goes off 1 day, 3 hours, and 15 minutes before a scheduled item, you'll have to convert everything to a single time unit such as 1635 minutes or 27.25 hours.

*You can use **m** for minutes, **h** for hours, or **d** for days rather than type the entire word. Outlook will finish it for you.*

Check here to enable the reminder.

Enter or select the reminder time.

Change the reminder sound.

Figure 11-1. *The Appointment tab of all Calendar item forms contains the same Reminder features*

The next reminder option you can set changes the sound produced when the reminder activates. Click the sound button located next to the Reminder time drop-down list to display the Reminder Sound dialog box.

If you want to prevent a sound from playing when a reminder displays, remove the check from the Play This Sound option. To change the sound played, click Browse to display the Reminder Sound File dialog box, from which you can choose any sound file located on your local or network drives. When you're finished changing the options in the Reminder Sound dialog box, click OK to save the changes and return to the Appointment tab of the form.

Using Reminders

After you set reminders, you can forget about your appointment or other scheduled item until it's time for the reminder to go off. As long as you set the reminder properly, and your system clock is set with the correct date and time, the reminder will pop up at the designated time to let you know the appointment is due.

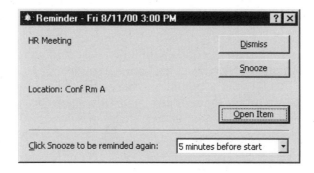

When a reminder appears, you have several ways to deal with it. You can toss it away, reset it to go off at a later time, or open the item to which it refers. To eliminate the reminder altogether, click the Dismiss button. This deletes the reminder and leaves you on your own to remember the scheduled item. If you want Outlook to remind you again as the appointment gets closer, select a time from the Click Snooze To Be Reminded Again drop-down list and click the Snooze button. This works like the snooze button on your alarm clock, only here you have the option to select the amount of time before the reminder reappears. Unfortunately, you can't enter the time manually. You must make a selection from the drop-down list.

If you want to view or edit the scheduled item before doing anything with the reminder, click the Open Item button to display the item itself. When you close the item, the reminder is still displayed and awaiting your command. Either Dismiss it or Snooze it.

Setting Reminder Options

The changes you make to reminder options in individual Calendar items affect only the forms in which you make the changes. In the event that you want to turn off reminders or change the sound file used for all reminders, you can change the reminder default settings.

Choose Tools | Options to display the Options dialog box. Click the Other tab and click Advanced Options to open the Advanced Options dialog box. Now click the Reminder Options button to display the Reminder Options dialog box.

As you can see, the options are the same as those you can set on an individual Calendar item form. However, the settings in the Reminder Options dialog box apply to all new forms created. To turn reminders off for all new forms, clear the checkmark from Display The Reminder. If you want to eliminate sounds for all new forms, remove the checkmark from Play Reminder Sound. To change the default sound file, click Browse and select the sound file to use. When you're finished, click OK three times to save the new settings and return to the active Outlook window.

MOUS EXAM PRACTICE

This section covered setting and using Outlook reminders. Rather than take a chance that you've incorrectly set a reminder for an important appointment, create some practice appointments and set reminders for them. Try entering reminder times by using the drop-down list and by typing the times manually. When the reminders activate, discard some using the Dismiss button, and reset others using the Snooze button. Finally, set the reminder options in the Reminder Options dialog box to see how your changes affect new Calendar items.

Including Attachments

Attachments are not only useful for transmitting information with e-mail messages, but also for keeping track of information related to scheduled items. Inserting attachments in scheduled items lets you include files, documents, and Outlook items associated with the scheduled item. For example, you might want to include all the contact records for attendees of a meeting, or budget reports in Excel or Word for an appointment with the budget director.

Including attachments with Calendar items is very much the same as inserting attachments in e-mail messages or other Outlook items. Begin by opening the scheduled item into which you want to insert the attachment. Then select the type of attachment you want to add from the Insert menu.

If you want to include an object such as a graph, worksheet, or image, click the Notes field first. Otherwise, the Object command is grayed out (unavailable).

Depending on the type of attachment you select, an appropriate dialog box appears. The following types of attachments can be inserted in a scheduled item:

- **File**   Select File to include a computer file in the scheduled item. The Insert File dialog box opens, from which you can select any file on your available local or network drives.

- **Item**   Use this command to insert an Outlook item as an attachment. The Insert Item dialog box appears, providing you with a view of all your Outlook folders and their contents.

- **Object**   This command adds an actual object (as opposed to a file) as an attachment. For example, if you include an Excel worksheet using the Object command, the entire worksheet appears in the Notes field of the scheduled item, not just an icon representing the worksheet file. When you select Object, the Insert Object dialog box displays. Here you can create a new object from scratch or use an existing file to create the object.

 If you want to include a file as an attachment, you can avoid the extra step required when using the Insert menu by clicking the Insert File button (shown to the left) to open the Insert File dialog box.

 You can insert files and Outlook items using the drag and drop method. Tile Outlook and the scheduled item side by side. Open the Outlook folder of your choice (including My Computer) and drag items (or files) into the Notes field of the scheduled item. You can include objects by using the Copy and Paste commands.

Unfortunately, attachments do not travel well in Calendar items sent via e-mail in the iCalendar format. Therefore, if you plan to send Calendar items with attachments to others through your local e-mail system or through Internet e-mail, do not use the Forward As iCalendar command on the Actions menu. If you have an Internet e-mail service added to your profile, you might also want to make sure the Send Meeting Requests Using iCalendar By Default option found in the Calendar Options dialog box (Tools | Options | Calendar Options) is disabled. By the way, you'll get a warning even if the option doesn't exist (no Internet e-mail service installed) or if it's disabled. In either of those cases, you can safely ignore it and your attachment will get through just fine.

Modifying and Deleting Calendar Items

Although there are a number of differences between appointments, events, and meetings, the methods used to edit and delete all three are the same. To edit a scheduled item, simply open the item and make the necessary change(s). You can open an item by double-clicking it in any view, or by selecting it and pressing the ENTER key or CTRL-O. You can also right-click the item in any view and select Open from the shortcut menu. If you select multiple items, they will open using any of these techniques. Regardless of how you open the item, make sure you click Save And Close to save any changes you make while it's open.

You can select multiple items in a table view by moving the mouse pointer to the left edge of the table. When the cursor turns into a right-pointing arrow, hold down the left mouse button and drag up or down to select adjacent items.

Deleting scheduled items is even easier. Select the item(s) you want to remove and press the DELETE key or CTRL-D. You can also use the Delete button found on the Standard toolbar, or you can right-click selected items and choose Delete from the shortcut menu. All scheduled items you delete are placed in the Deleted Items folder from which they can be recovered until the folder is emptied.

*Recover Deleted Items, which allows you to recover deleted items even after the Deleted Items folder has been emptied, is not available for the Calendar folder. However, you can turn it on by making a change to the Windows registry. Caution! Only experienced users should edit the Windows registry. All users should back up the registry before making any changes. To enable Recover Deleted Items for all Outlook folders, add the DWORD value **DumpsterAlwaysOn=1** to the HKEY_LOCAL_MACHINE\ SOFTWARE\Microsoft\Exchange\Client\Options key.*

If you're running out of storage space on the server and want to minimize the amount of stuff that collects in the Deleted Items folder, you can bypass the folder altogether by holding down the SHIFT key when you delete Calendar items. However, unless you've turned on Recover Deleted Items for all folders by making a change in the Windows registry, the item is permanently deleted and cannot be recovered.

Adding Appointments and Events

Appointments and events are similar creatures with some small differences. Both are scheduled items that do not include any outside attendees or resources. That's not to say you can't add an appointment or event for which you plan to meet with other people. It simply means that no invitations, either for people or resources, will be dispatched when you create the scheduled item. The main difference between an appointment and an event is the duration of the activity. Events are appointments that last a full day (24 hours) or more. Conventions, business trips, vacations, and marathon negotiating sessions are examples of activities that would likely fall into the category of events.

Although appointments and events do not include inviting outside attendees and resources, they can be converted to Calendar items that do. An appointment to which attendees and resources are invited is a meeting. Events to which you invite people and resources are called invited events. Both are covered in the section entitled "Scheduling Events" later in this chapter.

Adding Appointments

You can create an appointment from anywhere within Outlook. If you happen to be in the Calendar folder, press CTRL-N or click the New button to open a new appointment form (see Figure 11-2). You can also double-click a blank time slot in the Day view or a blank spot in any other view in the Calendar folder.

If you're in an Outlook folder other than the Calendar folder, press CTRL-SHIFT-A to open a new Appointment form.

In the Subject field of the open form, enter a brief description of the appointment. This is the data that shows in all the Calendar views, so make it clear and concise. If the appointment is going to take place in a special location, enter it in the Location field. If it's a location you've used before, select it from the Location drop-down list

Figure 11-2.   *Use the Appointment form to schedule an activity that does not require Outlook to send invitations or notices to people or resources*

MANAGING TIME & DETAILS

(see the "Designating Locations" section earlier in this chapter for more on locations). Since this is a regular appointment, ignore the This Is An Online Meeting Using option. If this activity is going to last 24 hours or more, check the All Day Event option to convert the form to an event form.

Select the date and time the appointment begins from the Start Time drop-down lists. You can also enter the dates and times manually if you prefer. When entering dates manually, you can use plain English phrases such as **next Tuesday** or **a week from Friday**. Although you don't have quite as much latitude when entering times, you can eliminate the colons and the AM or PM. For example, if you want to set the start time to 3:12 in the afternoon, you can enter 312p, which Outlook immediately converts to 3:12 PM. If you're using an event form, the time fields do not exist.

Tip   *You can also cycle through the start and end times by placing the cursor in either field and using the UP and DOWN ARROW keys. Pressing the DOWN ARROW key decreases the time by the designated interval (30 minutes by default), while pressing the UP ARROW key increases it by the same amount.*

By default, Outlook assumes you want each appointment to last 30 minutes. Therefore, the date and time in the End Time fields are adjusted to be 30 minutes (or the current default time interval) after the Start Time. You can manually change the end time, which leaves the Start Time as is.

Tip   *To change the default appointment duration, open the Day or Work Week view and right-click the time bar. From the shortcut menu, select the time interval to use. This not only changes the time slots in the view, but also the default time interval used in all appointment, event, and meeting forms.*

If you want Outlook to remind you about the appointment, check the Reminder option and set the time and sound options. See the section entitled "Staying on Schedule with Reminders" earlier in this chapter for more information on setting and using reminders. To the right of the Reminder options, you'll find the Show Time As option. Use this option to designate the manner in which the time slot for this appointment is displayed when others view your free/busy information. Make the appropriate selection from the drop-down list.

Use the Notes field (the large text box below the Reminder options) to enter any pertinent information relating to the appointment. It's great for jotting down notes and ideas that occur to you prior to the meeting. When the meeting comes due, you can print the item, including all notes and even the attachments. When you attend the meeting, you'll have your agenda and necessary materials at your fingertips with little or no last-minute effort.

If the appointment is with, or concerns, one or more individuals in your Contacts folder, you can link those contacts to the appointment by clicking the Contacts button to display the Select Contacts dialog box. Choose the appropriate Contacts folder and select all the contacts associated with the appointment. Click OK to close the dialog box and return to the appointment form. If you're using categories to track Calendar items, click the Categories button and select the categories to which you want the item assigned. The final option on the appointment form is the Private option. Check this option if you want the appointment hidden from others with whom you share your Calendar folder.

The Attendee Availability tab is only for meetings and invited events, so you can ignore it when scheduling an appointment. When you're through, click Save And Close to save the new appointment or event.

MOUS EXAM PRACTICE
In this section, you learned to create appointments. Start your practice by opening an appointment form from within the Calendar folder. Enter the appropriate information and save the new appointment. Don't forget to utilize English phrases when entering dates, and shortcuts when entering times.

Scheduling Events

Events, as mentioned earlier, are appointments that last for 24 hours or more. This means you can create events that span a single day or multiple days. As you can see in Figure 11-3, the event form is comparable to the appointment form with some small differences:

- The form title bar says Event rather than Appointment.
- The All Day Event option, which is unchecked for an appointment, is checked for an event.
- The times of day for the Start Time and End Time fields are hidden in the event form.
- The Show Time As option, which is set to Busy for an appointment, is set to Free by default for an event.

As you can see in Table 11-1, Outlook offers a variety of ways to create an event. The procedure for filling out an event form is almost identical to that used in completing an appointment form. Therefore, you should refer to the previous section "Adding Appointments" for details and tips on filling in the event form fields. The only differences are in checking the All Day Event option, and not setting any start and end times (dates, yes; times, no). Although the default value for Show Time As is different, setting the option is the same in either form.

MOUS EXAM PRACTICE
This section covered the methods used for creating events. Start by opening an appointment form and use it to create an event. Then use one of the methods described earlier in this section to open an event form. Finally, use the Work Week, Week, or Month view to create multiday events.

MANAGING TIME
& DETAILS

Figure 11-3. *The event form is almost identical to the appointment form*

To Create an Event From	Do This
Any Outlook folder	Press CTRL-SHIFT-A
Calendar folder	Press CTRL-N or click the New button
Calendar folder	Choose Actions	New All Day Event
Day/Week/Month view	Double-click the date header
Week or Month view	Double-click a blank spot in a date box
Work Week, Week, or Month view	Select multiple dates and press CTRL-N or click the New button on the Standard toolbar
An appointment form	Check the All Day Event option

Table 11-1. *Methods for Creating an Event*

Creating Recurring Calendar Items

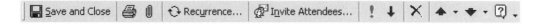

If you have appointments, events, or meetings that occur at regular intervals, you can save yourself a lot of time and work by creating a single recurring item rather than individual items for each occurrence. For example, if you have an employee meeting every Monday morning, a lunch date every Tuesday, a sales meeting the last Thursday of each month, or even a weekend retreat every quarter, you've got ideal candidates for recurring Calendar items.

Begin by creating a regular appointment, event, or meeting. Then, with the item form open, click the Recurrence button on the Standard toolbar in the form.

The Appointment Recurrence dialog box seen in Figure 11-4 opens, providing you with the necessary options for establishing a recurrence pattern for the item.

As you can see in Figure 11-4, the Appointment Recurrence dialog box uses information from the Appointment tab of the Calendar item form to make certain assumptions about the recurring item. The Start, End, and Duration fields are filled using information from the Start Time and End Time fields in the form. You can change any of the three fields by making selections from the drop-down lists or

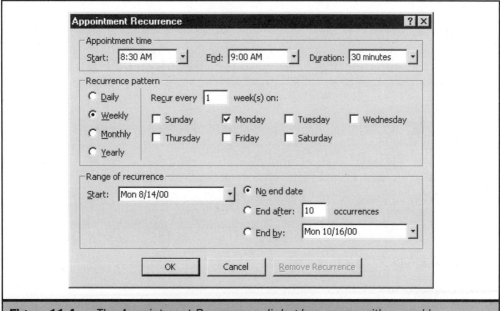

Figure 11-4.   *The Appointment Recurrence dialog box opens with a weekly recurrence pattern by default*

MANAGING TIME & DETAILS

entering your own data. As you modify data in one field, the other field affected by the change is recalculated automatically. For example, if you change the Start time, the End time adjusts itself to accommodate the information in the Duration field. Changing the End time results in the Duration field being updated to reflect the difference between the Start and End times. If you decide to change the Duration data, the End time is adjusted to ensure the appropriate difference between Start and End times.

Outlook assumes the recurrence for all items is going to be weekly, starting on the Start date, and recurring every week on the same day of the week, using the Start day. You have a multitude of options here. As a matter of fact, by combining the three different sets of options, the possibilities are limitless. Start by selecting the type of recurrence. Your choices include Daily, Weekly, Monthly, and Yearly. Depending on the recurrence type you select, the dialog box changes to accommodate the related options.

Figure 11-4 shows the default recurrence type, Weekly. The Weekly type lets you indicate the number of weeks between recurrences, and the day or days on which you want the item to recur. For your Monday morning pep talk to your employees, you could leave the settings as they are. However, for a production meeting that occurs on Tuesday and Friday of every other week you would change the Recur Every __ Week(s) On option to 2, and check off Tuesday and Friday.

For a Daily recurrence pattern, your choices are more limited (see Figure 11-5). You can select the number of days between recurrences by adjusting the Every __ Day(s) option. If the item occurs every Monday through Friday, select Every Weekday.

The next recurrence type is Monthly, the options for which are shown in Figure 11-6.

There are two options for items recurring monthly. You can set the items to repeat based on the date of the month or on the day of the week. The first set of options is for using the date of the month. In the example shown in Figure 11-6, the item is scheduled for August 14, 2000. Therefore, Outlook assumes you want to repeat the item on the 14th of each month. With this option selected, you can change the date and the number of months between recurrences.

However, August 14, 2000, is also the second Monday in the month. Therefore, you can elect to have the item repeat every second Monday of each month, regardless of the date on which it falls. Use this option for your monthly sales meeting, for example. With the option enabled, you can select the week of the month (first, second, third, fourth, or last), the day of the week, and the number of months between recurrences. The day of the week drop-down list offers a variety of choices in addition to the specific days of the week. Other choices include day, weekday, and weekend day.

The final recurrence type, Yearly, offers options similar to those found in the Monthly type. As you can see in Figure 11-7, the first option lets you select the month and date for the annual occurrence. Using the second option, you can elect to have the item repeat on a specific day of the month each year.

As far as Outlook is concerned, the recurring item is going to last forever, unless you indicate otherwise in the Range Of Recurrence options. The Start date is the date from the Start Time field in the original item. You can change it by entering another

Figure 11-5. *Set intervals between daily occurrences or choose weekdays only*

Figure 11-6. *You can set monthly recurrences by date or by day*

Figure 11-7.   *Use the Yearly recurrence pattern for birthdays, anniversaries, and other annually recurring events*

date in the future or by selecting a future date from the pop-up calendar. As with other Outlook date fields, you can use plain English when entering the Start date.

The options for ending the recurring item include the following:

- **No end date**   If you want the recurring item to repeat for an indefinite time, select this option. The recurring item will continue to repeat using the current settings until you change the option or delete it.

- **End after __ occurrences**   If the recurring item has a limited number of recurrences, such as a class or seminar, use this option. Indicate the number of times you want the item to repeat. Changes you make here are reflected in the End By date as well.

- **End by**   If the recurring item has a specific end date, enter it here. You'll notice that changing the End By date also changes the End After __ Occurrences number to reflect the number of occurrences between the Start date and the End By date.

After setting the Appointment Recurrence options, click OK to return to the Calendar item form. If any occurrences of the item conflict with existing scheduled items, a banner appears informing you of the fact (see Figure 11-8). Unfortunately, Outlook doesn't provide you with details other than the number of conflicts, so you'll have to track the conflict(s) down yourself.

Figure 11-8. *The Start Time and End Time fields in a recurring item form are replaced with the recurrence pattern information*

While the basics are the same for regular Calendar items and recurring Calendar items, there are differences when it comes to editing and deleting them. Recurring items are not single items—they are a series of identical single items. Therefore, when it comes to editing and deleting, you have to tell Outlook whether it's the series or an individual item you're changing or deleting.

To edit a recurring item, use the method you normally use to edit any other Calendar item (double-click the item, select the item and press ENTER, and so on). Before the item opens, the Open Recurring Item dialog box appears.

MANAGING TIME & DETAILS

Indicate whether it's the individual occurrence or the entire series you want to open. If you select Open This Occurrence, a regular form opens for the item. You can then make the necessary changes and click Save And Close to apply them. Use this method to reschedule occurrences that conflict with other scheduled items. If, however, you want to change every instance of the recurring item, select Open The Series. This opens the recurring item form in which you can change everything except the start and end dates and times, and recurrence patterns. Use this method if your Monday morning pep talk is being changed to a Tuesday morning pep talk.

Deleting a recurring item offers basically the same options. The Confirm Delete dialog box appears, offering you a choice between deleting the selected instance of the recurring item or the entire series.

Caution   *Viewing a recurring item in Outlook Today opens the entire series. Therefore, if you decide to delete the item, you are actually deleting the entire series, not just a single instance. Unfortunately, Outlook doesn't bother to ask if you want to confirm the deletion, it just does it. On the plus side, however, Outlook does drop the deleted recurring item into the Deleted Items folder. To recover the recurring item, move it back to the Calendar folder.*

MOUS   *MOUS EXAM PRACTICE*
Now that you've learned how to create, edit, and delete recurring Calendar items, start your practice by taking an existing appointment and making it a recurring appointment. Next, create a recurring appointment from scratch. Try each of the different recurrence types and set the options accordingly. After you create some recurring items, open them and change both individual occurrences and the entire series. When you're through, use both methods to delete the recurring items you created for the practice session.

Exam

MOUS Exam Objectives Explored in Chapter 11

Objective	Activity	Heading
OL2000.3.2	Schedule appointments and events	"Adding Appointments" "Scheduling Events"
OL2000.3.3	Set reminders	"Staying on Schedule with Reminders"
OL2000.3.5	Schedule multiday events	"Scheduling Events"
OL2000.3.8	Schedule recurring appointments	"Creating Recurring Calendar Items"

MANAGING TIME
& DETAILS

The
Complete
Reference

Chapter 12

Scheduling Meetings and Invited Events

eetings and invited events are two Calendar items that involve other people and resources. You're probably all too familiar with meetings, so there's no need to explain what they are. Invited event, on the other hand, is a term not frequently encountered beyond Outlook. Events, as we discuss in Chapter 11, are activities that last 24 hours or longer. An invited event is simply an event to which you formally invite people and/or resources. A weekend retreat, a two-day seminar, or a trade show you want others to attend all fall into the category of invited events. Resources are things such as conference rooms, audio/video equipment, and other similar items that may be required for meetings.

Using the Meeting Planner

The Meeting Planner, also known as the Plan A Meeting dialog box, provides you with all the tools you need to plan and organize a meeting of any size. Using the Meeting Planner enables you to quickly and easily determine the best time for yourself, the proposed meeting attendees, and the resources you require. Planning a large meeting without the Meeting Planner often results in endless "No, that's not good for me. How about....?" conversations or e-mail messages with each attendee. Think about doing that with five, ten, or fifty attendees! Using the Meeting Planner eliminates the need to have even a single discussion about attendees' schedules. You can access the Meeting Planner (shown in Figure 12-1) by choosing Actions | Plan A Meeting from the Calendar folder Standard toolbar.

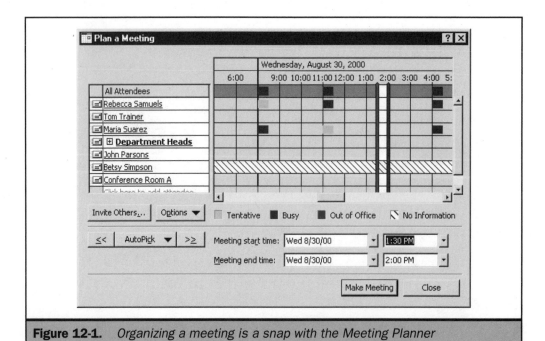

Figure 12-1. *Organizing a meeting is a snap with the Meeting Planner*

Adding and Removing Attendees

Begin by adding the desired participants to the All Attendees list. You can either type the attendees' names (separated by semicolons) or click the Invite Others button to display the Select Attendees And Resources dialog box, shown in Figure 12-2.

Using the Select Attendees And Resources dialog box is much the same as adding recipients to e-mail messages. The process is the same: select the address book, then choose the attendee or resource from the listing on the left, and click the appropriate button to add it to the "invited" list on the right. The difference is in the buttons, which include:

- **Required**   Use this button to select attendees whose presence is required at the meeting. The meeting request lists required and optional attendees separately. In addition, if no other item is scheduled, Outlook automatically marks the time slot on required attendees' calendars as Tentative until they respond. Their free/busy time is updated accordingly when they respond to the meeting request.

- **Optional**   For attendees whose presence at the meeting is not critical, use the Optional button. These attendees will be listed on the meeting request as Optional, and the meeting is added to their calendars with the free/busy time marked as Tentative.

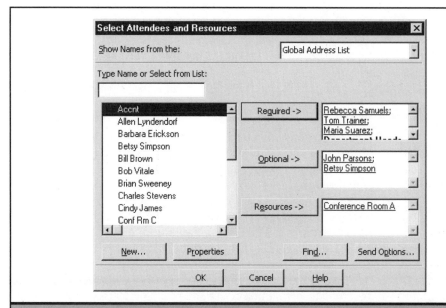

Figure 12-2.   *You can invite attendees and resources from any of your address books*

MANAGING TIME & DETAILS

■ **Resources** Use this button to include conference rooms, equipment, furniture and other items that have been set up as resources. In order for a resource to be available for a meeting request, it must have its own mailbox on the server and appear on the Global Address List.

Outlook permits you to select distribution lists as attendees. However, regardless of which designation (Required or Optional) you give them, the individual members of the list appear as optional attendees when they accept your invitation. That's because Outlook compares the meeting request responses with the All Attendees list and assumes anyone not specifically listed is an optional attendee. Unless you expand the distribution list on the All Attendees list, only the distribution list name appears. To make sure all distribution list members are treated as required attendees, expand the distribution list before sending the invitations. Expanding the distribution list before sending invitations also ensures that updates to the meeting reach the correct attendees.

Note *Attendees who are part of the distribution list and who are already on the All Attendees list will be added a second time. To avoid confusion, make sure you eliminate duplicates before sending invitations.*

After you select the attendees and resources, click OK to add them to the All Attendees list. If you decide you want to eliminate an attendee or resource from the list, you have a couple of options. You can highlight the name in the All Attendees list and press the DELETE key, or you can right-click the name and select Clear from the shortcut menu. You can also delete attendees from the Select Attendees And Resources dialog box by highlighting the name and pressing the DELETE key.

Tip *If you find yourself with a blank listing in the All Attendees list that you can't seem to eliminate, it's probably due to a space you mistakenly entered in the line. Place your cursor on the line and press the BACKSPACE key. When you move to another line or option, the blank listing disappears.*

One thing to be aware of when entering a large number of attendees is that the All Attendees list can hold more names than it displays. As you add more names, it may appear that earlier names have disappeared from the list. This usually happens when you use the TAB key to scroll through the list. Don't worry, the attendees are still there. You can see them by enlarging the Meeting Planner window.

Next, check the availability of attendees and resources to make sure there are no conflicts. The Meeting Planner displays the free/busy time for all invited attendees. Of course, free/busy information is available only for those attendees who are either on the Microsoft Exchange Server network or who publish their free/busy time to a server for which you've designated the appropriate search path in your Free/Busy Options (see Chapter 10 for more information on free/busy data).

To make sure you have the latest available free/busy information, you may want to click the Options button and select Update Free/Busy from the menu that appears.

If there's a conflict with anyone's (or anything's) schedule, you can use the AutoPick button to locate a time at which everyone is available according to their published free/busy data. The AutoPick feature searches for the first time slot for which all or some of the attendees and resources are free. When you click the AutoPick button, a drop-down menu appears offering several choices. You can elect to find a time slot in which all attendees and resources are available, all attendees and a single resource, all required attendees, or all required attendees and a resource.

The AutoPick feature treats those schedules for which no free/busy time is available as if the time were marked Free.

The Meeting Planner uses the currently selected date and time for the meeting. If you want to change either, edit the Meeting Start Time and Meeting End Time fields.

MOUS EXAM PRACTICE
Since this section deals with adding and deleting attendees and resources, you should begin your practice by entering some names in the All Attendees list. Then use the Invite Others button to display the Select Attendees And Resources dialog box. Add some required attendees, some optional, and at least one resource. While you're in the dialog box, remove some of the attendees after you add them. After you close the Select Attendees And Resources dialog box, try removing a couple of attendees directly from the All Attendees list.

Working with the All Attendees List

The Meeting Planner also offers a few other options for manipulating the All Attendees list. If you want to leave an attendee or resource on the list without sending an invitation, click the envelope icon to the left of the name and select Don't Send Meeting To This Attendee. You can also display a shortcut menu of commands that apply to the attendees by right-clicking an attendee name. The available commands include some or all of the following:

- **Properties**   This command displays the properties dialog box or contact record for the attendee, depending on the Select Attendees And Resources dialog box source from which the attendee was selected. For example, an attendee who is listed in both the Global Address List and the Outlook Address Book will display the properties dialog box if added to the meeting request form from the Global Address List, and the contact record if added from the Outlook Address Book.

MANAGING TIME
& DETAILS

- **Send Options** Unfortunately, this command will probably net you nothing more than an error message indicating that the command "is not valid for this recipient." The Outlook address books do not currently provide these send options.

- **Add to Contacts** Use this command, which is unavailable for attendees added to the list from the Contacts folder, to create a record in the Contacts folder for the selected attendee. However, if you add an attendee from the Global Address List who also has a contact record, the option is available in spite of the fact that a contact record already exists. If you attempt to add the attendee, Outlook warns you (when you save the new contact record) that you're about to create a duplicate contact record.

- **Look up Contact** Use this command to search for the attendee in the Contacts folder. This command is available only for those attendees not selected from the Contacts folder to begin with. Since clicking the Properties command for an attendee selected from the Contacts folder displays the contact record, there's no reason to have to go searching for the record.

- **Open Attendee's Calendar** If the attendee has a mailbox on the server, *and* you have the proper permissions, you can view his, her, or its (a resource) calendar for the meeting date by using this command.

- **Editing Options** The remaining commands are common text editing options that work as anticipated.

Tip

Double-clicking an attendee name in the All Attendees list opens the attendee's properties dialog box or contact record (depending on the source from which the attendee was selected).

This ends the Meeting Planner phase of scheduling a meeting. The next stage involves using the meeting request form to send the invitations.

MOUS

MOUS EXAM PRACTICE
In this section, you learned to use the Meeting Planner to take the hassle out of scheduling meetings. For this practice session, open the Meeting Planner and add attendees and resources from all your address books. If you have distribution lists, add one of those also. Check the schedules for those attendees whose free/busy time is available. Schedule the meeting for a time when others have conflicting appointments. Then use the AutoPick feature to find a time slot when everyone is free. Next, use the options and commands associated with the All Attendees list to view attendees' properties and calendars.

Using the Meeting Request Form

When all the attendees and resources have been added and the schedule is set, it's time to get the ball rolling and send out the invitations. Click the Make Meeting button to create a meeting request (see Figure 12-3) utilizing the information you've entered into the Meeting Planner.

Tip *If you'd prefer to bypass the Meeting Planner, you can start with a meeting request form by choosing Actions | New Meeting Request. From any other folder, press CTRL-SHIFT-Q.*

Enter a brief description of the meeting purpose in the Subject field. This is also your opportunity to turn the meeting into an invited event. Check the All Day Event option to remove the time fields and change the form title to Invited Event.

Figure 12-3.   *The meeting request form sends an invitation to all the attendees and resources*

In the Notes field, add your comments or any additional information or attachments pertinent to the meeting. If there are any individuals in your Contacts folder who are associated with the meeting, you may want to link them to the meeting request by clicking the Contacts button and selecting them from the Select Contacts dialog box. If you use categories to organize your folders, click the Categories button to assign the meeting request to one or more categories.

To make changes to the attendees or review their schedules, click the Attendee Availability tab, which as you can see in Figure 12-4 is a near replica of the Meeting Planner attached to the meeting request form.

If some of your attendees seem to have disappeared from the All Attendees list, maximize and restore the meeting request form to force a redraw. The lost attendees should reappear.

Making changes here is the same as making changes on the Meeting Planner. What's different is the ability to check the status of attendees and resources by clicking the Show Attendee Status option above the All Attendees list. This displays the attendee status window, shown in Figure 12-5.

Figure 12-4.   *The only thing missing from the Attendee Availability tab is the Make Meeting button*

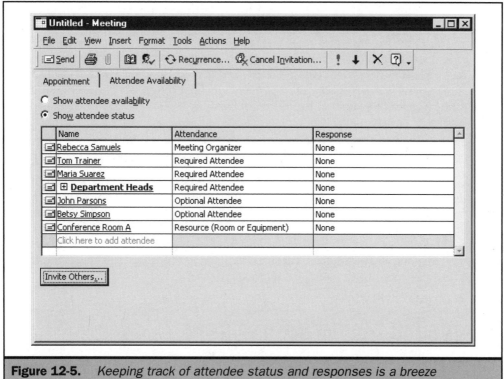

Figure 12-5. *Keeping track of attendee status and responses is a breeze*

If you're having second thoughts about the Required/Optional status of a particular attendee, you can change it by clicking the Attendance field and selecting a different status from the drop-down list that appears. You can also add or change an attendee's Response information by clicking the Response field and making the appropriate selection from the drop-down list. This is useful if the individual responds by phone or some means other than e-mail, which Outlook tracks automatically.

Tip *If you've gotten verbal commitments from all your attendees, or you're the boss and no one dares to refuse your meeting requests, you can eliminate all responses by choosing Actions | Request Responses from the meeting request form Standard toolbar. Removing the checkmark suppresses both automatic and manual responses from attendees. However, since it does the same with resources, you will not be notified of any problems that render the resource unavailable.*

When you're ready to send the invitations, click the Send button on the form's Standard toolbar. All you have to do now is sit back and wait for the responses to start rolling in. One more thing: the first time you book resources that are available and for which you have the appropriate permissions, a Resources Booked dialog box appears informing you that the resources were successfully booked. If, on the other hand, the resource is unavailable or you don't have proper permissions, a dialog box appears notifying you that your request was declined, and the reason why. There are actually a number of reasons why resource requests may be turned down. See the section titled "Scheduling Meeting Resources" for more information.

Converting Existing Appointments and Events

As you're no doubt aware, all Calendar item forms contain an Attendee Availability tab. In addition, appointments and events contain an Invite Attendees button (located on the form's Standard toolbar). You can use the Invite Attendees button to convert the appointment into a meeting request. Then use the Attendee Availability tab to add attendees and resources, check schedules, and track responses. See the section titled "Using the Meeting Request Form" earlier in this chapter for more information on using meeting request forms and the Attendee Availability tab.

Scheduling Meeting Resources

 The ability to treat meeting resources like meeting participants makes scheduling meeting and invited events even easier. No more telephone tag with the resource administrator, trying to determine if and when the resource is available. A simple meeting request and an almost instantaneous response let you know whether the resource is available and if you can reserve it. However, as with other meeting invitees, there are some requirements that must be met before resources can be scheduled. A resource account must be established and options set.

Setting Up a Resource Account

To take advantage of resource booking, you must first set up an account for each resource you want to make available for scheduling. This requires a mailbox on the Microsoft Exchange server for each resource. Ask your system administrator to add the mailbox if one doesn't already exist. Generally, the resource mailbox will be assigned to one owner, who then controls the manner in which the resource behaves. There may be a resource coordinator or other individual in your organization who handles all resources, or the responsibility may fall to someone on the administrative staff. Whoever that person is, he or she alone will have the ability to determine how the resource account is configured.

The first thing the owner must decide is who will be permitted to book the resource. For example, a small conference room on the second floor will probably have different permission settings from the big, luxurious conference room on the top floor, used by the big brass. By setting the permissions and other resource options, you can regulate and automate much of the resource scheduling process. For the resource owner, this eliminates a lot of hassle checking each reservation to ensure there are no problems with improper bookings or conflicting schedules.

After the resource mailbox is set up on the Microsoft Exchange server, you (the owner) must create a profile for the resource. See Chapter 2 for detailed information on adding and removing profiles. It's only after the profile has been created that you can configure the resource account.

If Outlook is open, close it. Log back on to Outlook using the resource profile. Once you're logged on as the resource, all options you set apply to the resource account. Choose Tools | Options to open the Options dialog box, and click the Calendar Options button on the Preferences tab to display the Calendar Options dialog box. Now click the Resource Scheduling button to open the Resource Scheduling dialog box.

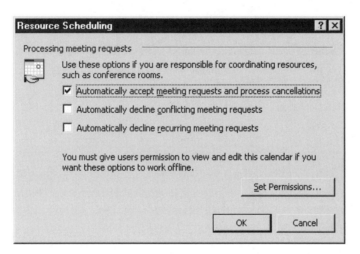

As you can see, the Resource Scheduling dialog box contains three options and a Set Permissions button. These four items provide the tools for you to control the resource and automate its response to meeting requests:

- **Automatically accept meeting requests and process cancellations** Check this option to enable automatic scheduling and responding on behalf of the resource. Any meeting requests and cancellations that do not conflict with any other resource settings will be accepted and processed automatically. In addition, turning this option on makes the next two options available.

- **Automatically decline conflicting meeting requests** Along with its own profile, the resource now also has its own calendar. As meeting requests arrive, the resource account checks its calendar against the incoming requests. Check this option to have the resource automatically decline any requests that conflict with its schedule.

- **Automatically decline recurring meeting requests** To ensure the resource does not get tied up for extended periods of time without your direct knowledge, you can check this option to prevent anyone from booking the resource on a recurring basis.

- **Set Permissions** The Set Permissions button provides quick access to the Calendar Properties dialog box. Using the options on the Permissions tab, you can control which users are allowed to reserve the resource.

If you want everyone in the organization to have the ability to book the resource, you can bypass the Set Permissions button and head right for the OK button. The first time you set the Resource Scheduling options and click OK to save them, Outlook displays the Set Permissions For Offline Use dialog box.

As you can see, the Set Standard Resource Permissions For All Users option is checked. This automatically sets the default permissions for the Calendar folder to Author, which means everyone on the Microsoft Exchange Server network can book the resource. To accept these permissions settings, click OK.

Setting Resource Permissions

Until you set the Calendar folder permissions, either through the Set Permissions For Offline Use dialog box or through the Permissions tab of the Calendar Properties dialog box, no one can book the resource except you (the owner). You can set or change permissions using the Permissions tab of the Calendar Properties dialog box, shown in Figure 12-6.

To schedule a resource, the user must have permissions to both read and create items.

Figure 12-6. *Use the Permissions tab to control who has access to the resource*

For detailed information on setting permissions for both resources and folders, see Chapter 18.

Managing Resources

Although setting up a resource account requires creating a profile and logging on as the resource, managing it is a lot easier. While you can log on using the resource profile each time, there's a way to manage the resource from within your own profile. However, to do this the resource mailbox must be assigned to your user account on the server.

The first thing to do is add the resource mailbox to your Microsoft Exchange Server service in the Services dialog box. Choose Tools | Services to display the Services dialog box. Then double-click Microsoft Exchange Server to open the Microsoft Exchange Server dialog box. Next, click the Advanced tab to display the Advanced options. Finally, click the Add button to open the Add Mailbox dialog box.

Enter the mailbox name in the Add Mailbox field. While you don't have to enter the entire name, what you do enter must be accurate since Outlook attempts to resolve the name based on the text you type.

If you don't know the exact name of the resource mailbox, Cancel out of all the dialog boxes and open your Address Book. In the Global Address List, right-click the resource listing and click Properties. Use either the Display name or the Alias, both of which appear on the General tab of the properties dialog box.

Click OK to add the mailbox. If the name resolves correctly, the mailbox is added and you return to the Microsoft Exchange Server dialog box. If the name doesn't resolve, Outlook tells you to try again. If Outlook finds multiple names containing the text you entered, the Check Name dialog box appears with all possible candidates. Select the correct one. Click OK until you return to the active Outlook window. You'll find that the resource mailbox has been added to your Folder List as another set of folders.

By right-clicking the Calendar folder in the resource mailbox folders, you can access the folder's Permissions tab and set and modify permissions for all users. In addition, you have complete access to all the resource mailbox folders including the Inbox and Sent Items folders. Here you'll find messages sent to the resource, and automatic responses sent from the resource to users who made requests.

If you don't like cluttering your Folder List with an additional set of folders, you can also access the resource mailbox folders by choosing File | Other User's Folder to display the Open Other User's Folder dialog box.

Click the Name button to display the Select Name dialog box. Choose the Global Address List and select the resource from the listing. Click OK to return to the Open Other User's Folder dialog box. Now select the desired folder from the Folder drop-down list. To set permissions for booking the resource, select the Calendar folder. Click OK to open the resource Calendar folder in a separate window (see Figure 12-7).

You can now view the Calendar, and add, remove, and modify Calendar items. You can also change permissions for the resource. In the resource folder window, choose File | Folder | Properties for [folder name] to open the resource folder properties dialog box. Click the Permissions tab and set user permissions following the methods outlined in the earlier section "Setting Resource Permissions." When you're finished with the folder, press ALT-F4 to close it.

MOUS EXAM PRACTICE

In this section, you learned to establish resource accounts, set user permissions, and manage resources. Depending on your needs you may or may not be able to get the administrator to set up the mailboxes needed to create resource accounts. Create a user profile for the resource, then log on to Outlook using the resource profile. Next, set permissions for different users and follow up with them to see the differences in their experiences depending on the permissions they've been assigned. Finally, add the resource mailbox to your Microsoft Exchange Server service in Outlook, and manage it by logging on with your own profile.

Figure 12-7. *The resource Calendar folder opens in its own window*

Changing a Scheduled Meeting

Editing a scheduled meeting or invited event is simply a matter of opening the meeting or invited event form and making and saving the appropriate changes. Start by opening the Calendar folder and locating the item you want to change. When you find the item, double-click it to open it. Make the necessary changes and click Save and Close. If you make changes to the dates, times, or location, Outlook kindly offers to send all attendees an e-mail notifying them of the changes. If you click Yes, Outlook e-mails each attendee an updated version of the meeting request. If you add or delete attendees, Outlook displays the Send Update To Attendees dialog box.

Here you can elect to send updates to all attendees, only those who have been added or removed, or to no attendees at all. Make your selection and click OK to continue.

If you decide to cancel a meeting, the process is equally simple. Locate the meeting on your Calendar and open it. Choose Actions | Cancel Meeting from the meeting form's menu bar. A Microsoft Outlook dialog box appears, asking if you want to delete the meeting and send cancellation notices to all attendees, or just delete the meeting without notifying anyone. Make your selection and click OK.

If you elected to cancel the meeting without sending notification, the meeting is removed from your Calendar and dumped into the Deleted Items folder. If, however, you choose to send notifications, you're returned to the meeting form where the information banner indicates that the meeting has been canceled. Click Send to cancel the meeting and send the cancellation notices to attendees.

Note   *Unlike meeting requests, which automatically add the meeting to the attendees' calendars, cancellations only send an e-mail notifying the attendee of the cancellation. However, the e-mail contains a Remove From Calendar button that makes deleting the meeting effortless.*

When you send cancellation notices, the meeting remains on your Calendar with the free/busy time marked as Free. If you want to remove the canceled meeting, select it and press the DELETE key.

Tracking Meeting Request Responses

As you receive responses to your meeting requests or invited event requests, you don't have to do anything to process them. Outlook automatically records both positive and negative responses, as well as the lack of a response. When you open the original meeting request, the information banner gives you a brief rundown of the responses received thus far. To see how each attendee responded, open the Attendee Availability tab and select Show Attendee Status. This may be all the tracking you require. However, if you arrange a large number of meetings, you will probably want something a little more comprehensive.

At first glance, creating a meeting response folder and then using the Rules Wizard to automatically move responses into it sounds like a great idea. Unfortunately, Outlook can only process meeting request responses from within the Inbox. If you create a rule to move them to a new folder, the move takes place almost instantaneously, which means the responses don't remain in the Inbox long enough for Outlook to process them. If you open the message in the new folder, Outlook can't find the meeting and again fails in its attempt to process the response.

A better idea is to create a custom Inbox view that groups messages by the Message Class field. Use the following steps to create your own custom view:

1. Open the Inbox folder and choose View | Current View | Define Views to open the Define Views For "Inbox" dialog box, shown here.

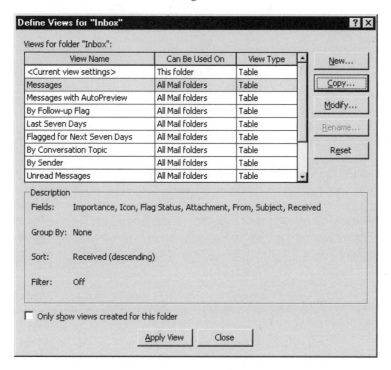

2. Select Messages in the Views For Folder "Inbox" list and click the Copy button to open the Copy View dialog box.

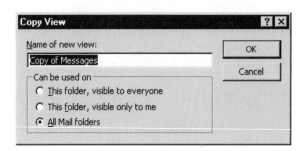

3. Enter a name for the new view. Use something like "Response Tracking."

4. Leave the All Mail Folders option selected and click OK to open the View Summary dialog box.

5. Click Fields to display the Show Fields button. From the Select Available Fields From drop-down list, select All Mail Fields.

6. Scroll down the Available Fields list and double-click Message Class. This adds the Message Class fields to the pane on the right.

7. Click OK to return to the View Summary dialog box.

8. Click Group By to open the Group By dialog box.

9. From the Select Available Fields From drop-down list, select All Mail Fields.

10. From the Group Items By drop-down list, select Message Class, then click OK to return to the View Summary dialog box.

11. Click OK to return to the Define Views For "Inbox" dialog box.

12. Click Apply View to return to the Inbox, which now displays your new view (see Figure 12-8).

As you can see in Figure 12-8, the new view does more than just separate out meeting responses. It also shows regular messages, meeting requests you've received, and other different types of messages. Therefore, you can also use it to track other things, such as incoming meeting or task requests. The next time you display your list of Current Views, you'll see the new view has been added to the bottom of the list.

Figure 12-8. *It's easy to track meeting responses with a custom view*

Replying to Meeting Requests You Receive

When you're on the receiving end of a meeting request, your options for handling the request are somewhat limited. You can open the request and respond to it, or you can ignore it. The latter method, which tends to make your boss and co-workers unnecessarily cranky, is not recommended unless you're seriously thinking about a career change. Therefore, the first method is probably your best bet.

Note   *There is a third alternative for dealing with meeting requests, but it's not recommended. You can use the Resource Scheduling Options, found in the Calendar Options dialog box (and discussed in the section titled "Setting Up a Resource Account" earlier in this chapter) to automate the process. These options apply to any mailbox, regardless of whether the mailbox owner is a person, place, or thing. However, no reminders are set, and you receive no notification when requests are accepted or declined automatically. As a result, you'll have no control over your schedule and may be totally ignorant of meetings you've agreed to attend.*

To reply directly to a meeting response, open it and click the appropriate response button. As you can see in Figure 12-9, the meeting request form contains three response buttons and a Calendar button.

The response buttons are straightforward. You can answer yes (Accept), no (Decline), or maybe (Tentative). If you want to check your schedule before replying, click the Calendar button to display your Calendar for the proposed meeting date. When you click one of the response buttons, a Microsoft Outlook dialog box appears asking if you want to send the response immediately, edit the response first, or simply not send a response at all. Make your selection and click OK.

Note   *After you send a response, the meeting request may disappear from your Inbox. If this occurs it's because the Delete Meeting Request From Inbox When Responding option in the Advanced E-mail Options is turned on (the default). To turn it off, choose Tools | Options, click the E-mail Options button on the Preferences tab, and then click the Advanced E-mail Options button. Remove the checkmark from the Delete Meeting Request From Inbox When Responding option.*

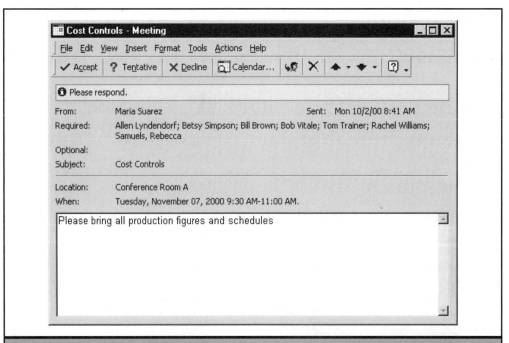

Figure 12-9.   *Use the meeting response buttons to notify the meeting originator of your intentions*

If you decline, the meeting is eliminated from your Calendar and moved to the Deleted Items folder. If you reply with Accept or Tentative, the response is recorded in the meeting form, which you can view by opening your Calendar to the scheduled date and double-clicking the scheduled meeting.

Exam | MOUS Exam Objectives Explored in Chapter 12

Objective	Activity	Heading
OL2000.3.10	Add and remove attendees	"Adding and Removing Attendees"
OL2000.3.11	Plan meetings involving others	"Using the Meeting Planner"
OL2000.3.13	Book office resources directly (for example, conference rooms and AV equipment)	"Scheduling Meeting Resources"

The Complete Reference

Chapter 13

Managing Tasks

In case you're thinking the reason the last three chapters focused on the Calendar and scheduling was to make sure you don't miss your appointments and meetings, you're only partially right. The most important reason for getting your schedule organized is to make sure you can find the time to do all the tasks on your seemingly endless to-do list. Fortunately, Outlook makes keeping track of your tasks easy, and even helps you find more time by enabling you to assign some of your tasks to others. In this chapter, you'll discover how to create, organize, track, and delegate tasks. By the time you're through you may even find time to add a round of golf to your list of to-do items.

Creating Tasks

Keeping track of your tasks starts with adding them to the task list. Not surprisingly, the way to get something on the task list is to create a task. Creating tasks, like creating most other Outlook items, involves opening the appropriate form (the task form in this case) and entering all pertinent information about the item (task).

Begin by pressing CTRL-SHIFT-K to open a new task form (see Figure 13-1).

The first field to fill out is the Subject field. Since this becomes the name of the task, enter something brief and descriptive. There's nothing worse than trying to find a particular task that's buried in a sea of cryptic names. The Due Date and Start Date

Figure 13-1.   *You can use the task form to enter a lot of information about the task at hand*

fields are next. They're self-explanatory and easy to fill in using either plain English commands (next Tuesday, a week from Friday, 27 days from Independence Day, and so on) or the pop-up calendar that appears when you click the drop-down arrow in each field.

Note   *You can enter a due date without entering a start date. However, you cannot enter a start date without a due date. If you enter a start date without a due date, Outlook automatically enters the same date in the Due Date field.*

Depending on the due date you enter, a yellow information bar may or may not appear above the Subject field. If the task is due in 14 days or less (or if it's *overdue* by 14 days or less) from today's date, the yellow bar appears and indicates the number of days in which the task is due (or overdue). If the due date is 15 days or more from today's date (in either direction), no information bar appears.

The Status field provides a drop-down list from which you can select several different status indicators. Select the one that suits your level of progress at this stage. To make life a little easier for you, this field automatically adjusts the % Complete field (and vice versa) depending on your selection. If you select Not Started, the % Complete field is set to 0%; if you select Completed, the % Complete field changes to 100%.

Use the Priority drop-down list to indicate just how important this task is. If the task is going to be completed in stages, you can indicate how much progress you've made by entering a percentage in the % Complete field, indicating how much of the job is done. As noted earlier, the % Complete field is associated with the Status field. Entering 0 here causes the Status field to be set as Not Started. When you enter 100 in the % Complete field, the Status field changes to Completed.

The next step is to adjust the reminder to ensure you're notified when the due date arrives. The reminder is automatically set for the default Reminder time of the Due Date day. To change the reminder date, enter a new date or select one from the pop-up calendar. Do the same for the time. If you want to change the sound associated with the reminder, or disable it, click the sound button and make the desired change.

Note   *You'll find the Reminder time option on the Preferences tab of the Options dialog box. Choose Tools | Options from the Outlook Menu bar (not the task form Menu bar) to display the Options dialog box.*

As you can see in Figure 13-1, the name of the task's owner also appears. However, since it reflects the original creator, or the person to whom the task has been assigned, it cannot be edited. This is true, even in a table view, where it appears you can edit it. If you create a custom view and add the Owner field, it appears, at first glance, that Outlook will allow you to edit the data. However, as soon as you try to save your change, a dialog box appears, informing you that you must be in a public folder to change this field, and as a result, your change will not be saved.

The next field available for your use is the notes field. It's handy for jotting notes about the task, associated things that need doing, phone numbers and addresses needed to complete the task, and anything else you can think of.

The remaining fields, Contacts, Categories, and Private, are located along the bottom of the form. Use the Contacts field to link the task to individuals in your Contacts folder. Either enter the contact's name or click the Contacts button and choose the contact(s) from the Select Contacts dialog box that appears. Assigning tasks to categories is a great way to organize them. Click the Categories button and check one or more categories to which you want the task assigned. Finally, check the Private option to prevent others who have access to your Tasks folder from seeing the task. This is excellent if you share folders with a co-worker whose birthday is coming up, for example. It would be a shame if he or she spotted a task to pick up a birthday present or organize a surprise lunch.

After you enter all the pertinent data about the task, click Save And Close to save the task and return to the active Outlook window.

Adding Attachments to Tasks

If you have other Outlook items that are related to the task, such as e-mail messages, appointments, or notes, you can insert them in the task form as attachments. You can also add files, documents, and objects to a task. The method used in the task form is the same as that used in e-mail messages and other Outlook items.

Open the task in which you want to include an attachment. Choose Insert from the Menu bar and select the attachment type from the Insert menu that appears. Your choices include File, Item, and Object.

Objects can only be added directly to the notes field. Therefore, unless the cursor is in the notes field, the Object command is unavailable on the Insert menu. Click anywhere in the notes field to position the cursor. Since the object will be inserted wherever the cursor appears, it's a good idea to place the cursor where you want the object to rest.

After you select one of the Insert commands, the associated dialog box appears. Make the appropriate selections and entries necessary to add the desired attachment. You can also drag other Outlook items and drop them in the task notes field to insert them as attachments.

Filling in Task Details

The Details tab, shown in Figure 13-2, provides another set of fields you can use for entering additional information about the task.

The information you can track using the Details tab includes the following:

■ **Date completed**   Once the task is completed, enter the completion date here. As with other Outlook date fields, you can enter the date in date format, with

Figure 13-2.   *The Details tab offers some simple project management tracking fields*

English words and phrases, or by displaying and using the pop-up calendar.
Entering a date in this field automatically updates two fields on the Task tab:
Status and % Complete. The Status field is changed to Completed and the %
Complete field to 100%. Conversely, marking those fields as Completed and
100% automatically enters the current date in the Date Completed field.

■ **Total work**   Use this field to enter the estimated number of minutes, days,
weeks, months, or years you expect this task to take. You can enter time using
abbreviations such as 2m for 2 minutes, 2h for 2 hours, or 2w for 2 weeks.
However, you must use only numerals to indicate numbers, and you are limited
to a single time unit. One other thing to be aware of: Outlook recalculates time
based on the length of your working day. For example, with the default workday
set to 8 hours, Outlook changes 12h to 1.5 days. Using that same algorithm,
3000m becomes 6.25 days, and 80h becomes 2 weeks.

■ **Actual work**   This is where you enter the time it really took you to complete
the task, not the fanciful number you entered in the previous field. It too
calculates using the same algorithm.

MANAGING TIME
& DETAILS

- **Companies** Enter the names of any organizations associated with the task. If there are none, feel free to improvise and use it to hold other data you may want to record. You can enter up to 255 characters.

- **Mileage** If you do any traveling to accomplish the task, enter the mileage you rack up here.

- **Billing information** If the task is a billable activity and you're using the Details tab to track billing information, use this field to enter rates, policies, and other billing-related information.

If you were paying attention when you glanced at Figure 13-2, you probably noticed there are a couple more items on the Details tab. They are the Update List field, and the Create Unassigned Copy button. These features are only available for a task that has been assigned to another user. Until then, they remain grayed out. For an explanation of what they do, see the next section, "Assigning Tasks."

MOUS EXAM PRACTICE

This section focused on creating tasks in your task folder. To hone your task management skills, practice creating tasks by opening and completing task forms. Next, try your hand at assigning some of your fictitious tasks to co-workers. Of course, check with them before doing so, and let them know you're just practicing. Ask them to respond in a variety of ways. Add attachments to some tasks and fill in the Details tabs on others

Assigning Tasks

If you're in a position to delegate tasks to others, or have the good fortune to work with colleagues willing to share the workload, you may find it necessary or desirable to assign some of your tasks to others on occasion. When the time comes, you can create a task request to assign a brand new task or you can transform an existing task into a task request. The resulting task request form, seen in Figure 13-3, is identical regardless of which method you use.

Creating a New Task Request

To create a task request, press CTRL-SHIFT-U from any folder, or choose Actions | New Task Request from within the Tasks folder. You can also click the New button from within the Tasks folder or from any folder, click the New down arrow and choose New Request from the menu. When the form opens (see Figure 13-3), use the To field to enter the name of the individual to whom you want to assign the task.

Figure 13-3.   *The task request form is a task form with additional options*

Tip   *You can also create a preaddressed task request form by right-dragging (place the mouse pointer over the desired item, then press and hold the right mouse button while dragging) a contact from the Contacts folder and dropping it on the Tasks icon on the Outlook Bar. From the shortcut menu that appears, select Address New Task.*

You can type the name or click the To button and select the name from the Select Task Recipient dialog box that appears.

Note   *You can assign a single task to multiple users or even to distribution lists. However, the original owner will not receive updates even if the update option is checked on the task request form. Nor will the original owner receive any status reports—unless the task is reassigned by one of the original assignees and accepted by the new assignee. At that point, the original owner receives status reports, and each assignee who reassigned the task receives updates and status reports.*

The next step is to fill in the task request form using the steps outlined in the earlier section on creating tasks. Although the task request form is almost identical to the task form, there are a couple of new options.

■ **Keep an updated copy of this task on my task list**   This option retains a copy of the assigned task on your task list. In addition, any changes made to the task by its new owner generate an e-mail, including update information, that is sent to you automatically. However, if you assign the task to multiple recipients, including a distribution list, the task will still be included on your task list, but it will not be updated.

■ **Send me a status report when this task is complete**   When the new owner(s) mark the task as complete, a special status report e-mail message is automatically generated and sent to you. Unlike the previous option, this option works even with multiple assignees.

Note	*Assigning a task with a reminder causes the reminder to be removed so the new owner can set his or her own reminder. In the event the task is declined and you elect to handle the task yourself, you'll have to set a new reminder.*

When all the information is complete, click Send to transmit the request. Now, before you sit back, put your feet on the desk, and start to relax, keep one thing in mind: the recipient(s) may decline your gracious offer, in which case the task drops back into your lap.

Assigning an Existing Task

If you have an existing task you would like to assign to a co-worker, there's no need to reinvent the wheel by creating a new task request form. All you have to do is convert the existing task to a task request form. It's as easy as opening the task and clicking the Assign Task button on the form's Standard toolbar. The task immediately turns into a task request form, sporting a To field and the two options for keeping a copy of the task on your list and sending a status report. See the earlier section on creating a new task request form for details on using the To field and the new options.

Reassigning Tasks

Not only can you assign tasks, you can also reassign them. Assuming that you're not at the bottom of the food chain in your organization, you can take a task assigned to you and reassign it to someone else. There are two ways to accomplish this: accept the task and reassign it, or simply pass the task along by reassigning it upon receipt.

To use the accept and reassign method, open the task request and click Accept to add the task to your task list.

You can accept (or decline) a task request without opening it by right-clicking the request in the Inbox and selecting Accept (or Decline) from the shortcut menu.

Next, open the task and convert it to a new task request by clicking the Assign Task button. When you accept the task, a Task Accepted message is sent to the previous owner. As soon as you assign the task, a Task Update message is sent to all previous owners. Depending on where you are in the chain of assignments, the ownership of the task may appear differently.

You can assign a task that appears on your task list (not to be confused with a task request in your Inbox) without opening it, by right-clicking the task and selecting Assign Task from the shortcut menu.

To reassign a task without accepting it, simply open the task request and click the Assign Task button to create a new task request. Enter the new assignee's name and click Send. When the new task request is sent, Task Update messages are also sent to all previous assignors or owners.

Creating Unassigned Copies of an Assigned Task

When tasks are assigned and reassigned, there's one additional feature available to everyone *except* the current task owner. It's the ability to create an unassigned copy of the task. You can use the Create Unassigned Copy button found on the Details tab of the task form in your task list (see Figure 13-4).

Clicking the Create Unassigned Copy button converts the existing copy (if you're not the current owner you only have a copy of the task) of the task into a full-fledged task of which you're the proud new owner. This feature comes in handy if the user to whom you assigned the task is unable to make any progress and you want to reassign it to someone else. You cannot assign the copy of the task retained in your task list since it is an assigned copy. Converting it to an unassigned copy gives you all the rights of an original owner.

The warning that appears when you click the Create Unassigned Copy button is somewhat misleading. It informs you that converting your copy of the task to an unassigned copy will result in you no longer receiving updates. That's not true. You will receive update notices. What is true, however, is that since the assigned task copy no longer exists, the updates cannot be processed. Therefore, you will continue to remain in the loop, but no longer have a task on your task list reflecting changes made by the current owner. In addition to update notices, you will also continue to receive all status reports sent by the current owner.

MANAGING TIME
& DETAILS

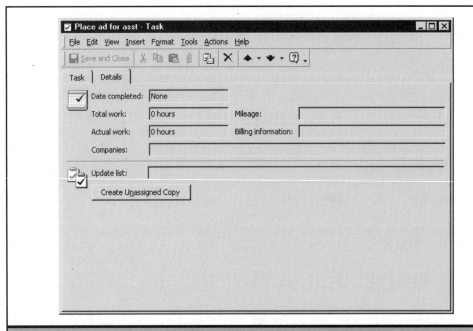

Figure 13-4. *Converting a copy of an assigned task is easy when you use the Create Unassigned Copy feature*

No one else in the chain of assignment is affected by the creation of an unassigned task. All other previous owners/assignors retain their copies of the original task and continue to receive updates, which can be processed.

MOUS EXAM PRACTICE
This section covered all aspects of assigning tasks. Since all task assignments use a task request form, practice by creating a task request form from scratch. Next, try assigning an existing task by using the Assign Task button to convert the task to a task request form. Ask some of your co-workers to assist in reassigning tasks. Have someone send you a couple of tasks and reassign them using the methods described in this section. Finally, create an unassigned copy of an assigned task you retained on your task list.

Modifying and Updating Tasks

You can edit any task you own. You cannot modify tasks you've assigned to others, even if you retained a copy on your task list by checking the Keep An Updated Copy

Of This Task On My Task List option on the task request form. Only the new owner of that task can edit it.

To make changes to a task, switch to the Tasks folder and double-click the task to open it. You can also right-click the task and select Open from the shortcut menu.

Make the necessary changes and click Save And Close to save your changes. If you're the original owner of the task, nothing further occurs. If, however, you inherited the task from someone else, all users appearing in the Update List on the Details tab of the task form will receive a Task Update message indicating the changes you've made.

Note   *Task Update messages are also sent to members of the task's Update List each time the task is assigned or reassigned. Unfortunately, these update notices, unlike those generated by editing a task, do not indicate the specific action (assigning the task) taken.*

When a task is marked done by changing its Status to Completed or its % Complete to 100%, the task is literally crossed off your task list. It still appears on the list but has a horizontal line drawn through it. If it happens to be an assigned task, all previous owners who elected to receive updates are automatically sent a Task Update message and a Task Completed status report. As soon as the Task Update message is processed, the task is also crossed off each of their task lists also.

Deleting Tasks

Deleting a task is quite easy. Open the Tasks folder, highlight the offending task, and use one of the following methods to eliminate it:

- Click the Delete button on the Standard toolbar
- Press CTRL-D
- Press the DELETE key
- Choose Edit | Delete from the Menu bar
- Right-click the task and select Delete from the shortcut menu

When you delete a task you own, it disappears from your task list, never to be seen or heard from again unless you resurrect it from the Deleted Items folder.

If you delete a task you assigned to someone else (and chose to retain an updated copy), you remove it from your Tasks folder. However, contrary to what the Help file states, you will continue to receive updates and status reports (assuming you requested both when you assigned the task). The information bar of Task Update messages informs you that the task was not found on your task list. Obviously a nonexistent task can't be updated, but you will at least continue to be kept apprised of its progress.

Creating Tasks from Other Outlook Folders

The beauty of Outlook is the tight integration of its various components. This is especially true of the Tasks folder. In addition to the usual ability to create folder items from other types of Outlook items, the Tasks folder also provides almost seamless integration with the TaskPad found in the Calendar folder.

Using the Calendar TaskPad

As you can see in Figure 13-5, the TaskPad, which is located in the Calendar folder, is a mini-version of the task list. In addition, it remains in constant communication with its parent, the Tasks folder. This means that changes made in one are immediately reflected in the other.

For detailed instructions on using the TaskPad, see Chapter 10.

Using Drag and Drop to Create Tasks

By now you should be an old hand at using drag and drop to create one type of Outlook item from another. If you're not, this may be the time to learn, and take advantage of the technique, which is quick and easy. Using drag and drop enables you

Figure 13-5. *You can add tasks to your Tasks folder without leaving the Calendar folder*

to create a task from an appointment, note, e-mail message, or any other Outlook item with a couple of mouse clicks. Outlook uses the original item to complete fields in the new task. The resulting task will of course vary, depending on the type of original item and its contents.

Begin by opening the folder containing the original item you want to use as the basis for the new task. Next, locate the item and drag it to the Outlook Bar and drop it on the Tasks shortcut. You can also drag it to the Folder List and drop it on the Tasks folder. Either way, a new task form opens with the appropriate information from the original item already entered in the new task form. Make any necessary changes and click Save And Close to add the new task to your task list.

You can also use right-dragging to create a task from another Outlook item. This time when you drop the item on the Outlook Bar icon, a shortcut menu appears, offering you several choices. They include:

- **Copy Here as Task with Text**   This command creates a new task and uses the original information to fill in the Subject field and Date field (if the original item has a date field). It also includes all basic information from the original item in the task's note field.

- **Copy Here as Task with Shortcut**   This command is the same as the previous command except the basic information from the original item is not entered in the task's note field. Instead, a shortcut to the original item appears in the note field.

- **Copy Here as Task with Attachment**   The only difference between this command and the Copy Here As Task With Shortcut command is that the shortcut in the task's note field is replaced with the original item as an attachment.

- **Move Here as Task with Attachment**   If you want to eliminate the original item from its folder, you can use this command, which is identical to the Copy Here As Task With Attachment, except that the original item is deleted from its folder.

If you right-drag a contact to the Outlook Bar Tasks icon or the Tasks folder in the Folder List, you'll find an additional command, Address New Task, on the shortcut menu that appears. Its action is a little different from the rest of the commands. Rather than creating a new task, this command creates a new task request form, addressed to the contact.

MOUS EXAM PRACTICE

This section showed you how to create tasks by using the TaskPad in the Calendar folder and by employing the drag and drop method. Open the Calendar view and create simple to-do list items first, then create detailed tasks using the TaskPad. Next, try creating tasks by dragging different Outlook items and dropping them on either the Tasks icon in the Outlook Bar or on the Tasks folder in the Folder List. Try right-dragging to accomplish the same thing.

Creating Recurring Tasks

Recurring tasks are those delightful jobs that just won't go away. Until you can find some way to eliminate or delegate them, you might as well make life easy and create a single recurring task, rather than individual tasks for each occurrence.

The first thing to do is open a task form and create the task as you would any other task (see the "Creating Tasks" section earlier in this chapter). After you enter all the pertinent information about the task, click the Recurrence button on the Standard toolbar of the task form. This opens the Task Recurrence dialog box, shown in Figure 13-6.

By default, the recurrence pattern selected is Weekly. As you can see in Figure 13-6, the Weekly pattern enables you to set several options that affect the frequency and duration of the recurrence. The Task Recurrence dialog box offers several options that enable you to customize recurring tasks. The first three sets of options included in the following list are all incorporated into the Task Recurrence dialog box under the heading Recurrence Pattern:

- **Recurrence type**   Your choices for the recurrence type are Daily, Weekly, Monthly, and Yearly, all of which are self-explanatory.

- **Recurrence interval**   This option, which varies according to the recurrence type you select, lets you set the frequency and specific date or day on which the task recurs.

- **Regenerate new task**   The Regenerate New Task option appears on all Task Recurrence dialog boxes, regardless of which recurrence type you choose. Since tasks, unlike appointments and meetings, do not disappear if you ignore them, you may want to utilize this option to make sure new instances are scheduled only when the last instance has been completed. As soon as you mark the task completed, it's crossed off your task list and a new identical task is added, with the due date set according to the other recurrence options you set.

- **Range of recurrence**   Regardless of which recurrence type you choose, the Range Of Recurrence options are the same. The only thing that alters them is selecting the Regenerate New Task option. It disables the End By option and grays it out. The Range Of Recurrence options let you designate when the recurring task starts and when it stops. These options are self-explanatory as well.

If you want more information on these options, see Chapter 11, which describes in greater detail recurring appointment options, many of which are identical to recurring task options.

Editing Recurring Tasks

You can edit a recurring task just as you would edit a non-recurring task. If you change anything but the start and end dates, clicking Save And Close saves the changes and applies them to all future occurrences. However, changing the start date or end date

Figure 13-6.   *Your recurrence options are almost limitless*

causes Outlook to warn you that you're about to change the date for the current instance of the recurring task. If you click OK, a new non-recurring task is added to your task list and the next regularly recurring task is also added. For example, if you have a weekly task that starts every Tuesday and you change the start date to Wednesday, Outlook creates (with your OK) a one-time task for this Wednesday and a recurring task starting next Tuesday.

Although the Help file fails to mention it, changing the due date in either a daily or yearly recurring task does not trigger the creation of a separate task. However, changing the start date in either does prompt Outlook to warn you that you're about to change the date of the current occurrence.

If the task becomes obsolete before it expires as a result of the Range Of Recurrence options you set in the Task Recurrence dialog box, you can remove it with a minimum amount of fuss. Select the task and press the DELETE key or right-click the task and choose Delete from the shortcut menu. A dialog box appears, asking if you want to delete the upcoming occurrence of the task or the entire series. If you just want to remove the current instance of the task select Delete This One. If you want to remove the recurring task permanently select Delete All.

Assigning Recurring Tasks

You can assign recurring tasks the same way you assign non-recurring tasks. However, since there is no command to create a recurring task request form, you must first create a recurring task, or receive a task request for a recurring task, and then assign it. Clicking the Assign Task button turns a recurring task into a [recurring] task request form. The assignment process is the same for recurring tasks and non-recurring tasks alike. There's only one difference. In the [recurring] task request form, the Keep An Updated Copy Of This Task On My Task List option is grayed out and completely unavailable. There are no exceptions with a recurring task. No one gets a task update no matter what actions are taken. However, the status report option remains functional, and when checked, previous owners receive all status reports sent by the current owner.

Working with Recurring Tasks

Since recurring tasks are series of tasks rather than individual tasks, there are some differences you should be aware of when working with recurring tasks. The first thing to remember is that certain actions taken on a recurring task can be applied to either the current task in the series or the entire series. For example, editing start dates and end dates can affect only the current instance or the entire series depending on how you effect the change. To change only the current instance, open the task, make the change, and click Save And Close. When warned that you are about to change this instance, click OK. A new, non-recurring task is created.

To change the start date or due date for the entire series, open the task and click the Recurrence button to open the Task Recurrence dialog box. Change the entry in the Start field to the new date on which you want the first occurrence to begin. The start date is dependent on the recurrence pattern. Therefore, if you enter a start date that is incompatible with the selected recurrence pattern, Outlook changes the date to agree with the recurrence pattern. For example, if your recurrence pattern is set for weekly and every Thursday, entering Monday's date as the start date will not work, since the task must start on a Thursday. Therefore, Outlook changes the start date to the date of the upcoming Thursday.

To change the due date, you must change the recurrence pattern. Using the example of a weekly recurrence due every Thursday, changing the day to Friday changes the due date from Thursday's date to Friday's date.

Outlook also offers a feature called Skip Occurrence, which applies only to recurring tasks. As you might guess, the Skip Occurrence command (Action | Skip Occurrence) allows you to eliminate the current instance of the recurring task, while leaving the series intact and unchanged. Unlike marking a recurring task Complete, which leaves a crossed-out copy of the task on your task list, using the Skip Occurrence command zaps the current instance, removing it from your task list permanently.

Since the function of the Skip Occurrence command is to eliminate the current instance of the task and make the next occurrence in line with the current task, it cannot work if the Regenerate New Task option is selected in the Task Recurrence dialog box. The Regenerate New Task option determines the date of the next occurrence based on the date on which you mark the current instance Complete. Therefore, Skip Occurrence has no means by which to determine what the next occurrence may be and "skip" to it. As a result, the Skip Occurrence option is grayed out and unavailable for a recurring task on which the Regenerate New Task option is enabled.

Responding to Task Assignments

MOUS

Unless you're the CEO of the company, you're bound to receive a task request now and again. When you do, you'll want to be prepared to respond. Knowing the consequences of your actions will help you make an informed decision. To begin with you have five choices for dealing with a task request:

- **Accept the task** Accepting a task request changes your role from temporary owner to owner.
- **Decline the task** When you decline a task, your temporary ownership ends and the task reverts to the individual who sent you the task request.
- **Assign the task** You can pass the buck by assigning the task to someone else, thereby transferring temporary ownership.
- **Delete the task request** While this may sound irresponsible, there are some good reasons for deleting a task request.
- **Ignore the task request** This action (inaction?), on the other hand, is not recommended. Not only is it impolite, but it also tends to make the sender cranky.

When you receive a task request and open it, you'll find that the Standard toolbar contains buttons to accommodate four of the five actions you can take to respond to the task request.

Accept the task
Decline the task
Assign the task
Delete the task request

Accepting a Task

If you decide to assume ownership of the task, all you have to do is click the Accept button. This adds the task to your task list and sends a Task Accepted e-mail message to the individual who assigned the task to you. However, before the message is sent Outlook gives you the opportunity to edit the response to the previous owner.

If you elect to edit the response, you can change any field in the task form except the To field. This comes in handy if you are willing to take the task, but must change the start or due date. You may also need to edit the response if you have already started the task and want to let the previous owner know how much has been done thus far. You can add a message in the notes field explaining the reasons for the change(s). If you choose not to edit the Task Accepted response, the message is sent immediately.

If, after clicking Accept and choosing to edit the response, you change your mind about accepting the task, you can still back out. At first glance it appears that you're stuck since there's no Cancel button. However, clicking the close button (the X in the top right corner of the form) or pressing ALT-F4 gives you the opportunity to close the form without saving the changes. This drops the task request right back in your Inbox without retaining the changes or sending any responses.

If the sender was not the original owner, a Task Update message will also be dispatched to all previous owners who elected to keep an updated copy of the task in their Tasks folder.

Task Update messages will not be generated if you were one of multiple assignees to whom the task was sent or if the task is a recurring task. See earlier sections in this chapter on assigning tasks and recurring tasks for more information.

Declining a Task

When you are unable or unwilling to accept a task request, you can click the Decline button. Like accepting a task, declining a task prompts Outlook to ask if you want to edit the response before sending it. However, in this case the only fields you can change are the Note, Contacts, Categories, and Private fields. You'll probably want to use the note field to let the sender know why you can't accept the task or perhaps the conditions under which you could accept the task. For example, if you're going to be out of town when the task is due, you might suggest you'd be willing to take it on if the task could be postponed.

MANAGING TIME
& DETAILS

> **Tip**
>
> *If you're declining the task, there's really no reason to change the Contacts and Categories fields. However, the Private field is another matter. By marking the Task Declined response Private, you prevent other users listed as alternate recipients on the previous owner's mailbox from receiving copies of your Task Declined response. Alternate recipients, who are generally assistants or co-workers sharing responsibilities for projects, can be assigned to a mailbox on the Exchange server by the administrator. By the way, you'll know if any alternates exist if you receive an "Undeliverable" message from the system administrator. Don't worry about the fact that the "Undeliverable" message states that the response could not be delivered to the sender. The reason the sender is listed instead of the alternates, who are the real undeliverables, is that the mailbox is in the sender's name and Exchange is protecting the identity of the alternates.*

Declining a task removes it from your task list (as soon as you receive a task request Outlook automatically adds it to your task list) and reverts permanent ownership to the sender, even if the sender was merely a temporary owner passing the task request along. In addition, any previous owners receive a Task Update message. However, this is the last update notice they'll receive. When a task is declined, the Update List on the Details tab of the task form is reset, cutting all previous owners out of the loop concerning any future actions taken on the task.

Reassigning a Task

If you don't want to accept or decline the task, you can always pass it along to some other unsuspecting soul. To do this, open the task request and click the Assign Task button. The task request e-mail message immediately becomes a task request form. Enter the address of the new assignee in the To field and click Send. This immediately sends a task request to the addressee, and a Task Update message to all previous owners. The Task Update messages do not indicate that the task has been reassigned, merely that you've taken some action on the task request.

> **Note**
>
> *As good as Outlook is, it cannot track tasks sent to multiple users or distribution lists. Therefore, if you assign the task to multiple users or a distribution list you receive a warning that the task will no longer be updated on previous owners' task lists.*

Reassigning a task, of course, has risks. Since the original assignor expects you to handle the task, you'll have to rely on your assignee to complete the job properly. If he or she fails to deliver, you're the one who will have to answer for that failure. Another thing to keep in mind is that if your assignee declines the task, you (regardless of whether you are the original owner or an assignee) become the permanent owner of the task.

Deleting a Task Request

At first blush, the thought of deleting a task request seems rude at best, and suicidal (career-wise) at worst. However, you may be perfectly justified if you already know the task is obsolete, and it just made its way to you. Or you may have gotten it by mistake. If you're the CEO and you receive a task request from the new kid in the mail room, it's probably safe to delete it without worrying too much.

Deleting a task request is easy. Click the Delete button on the Standard toolbar of the task request. A dialog box with several options appears.

The dialog box, which is aptly named Delete Incomplete Task, contains three options:

- **Decline and delete**   Use this option to remove the task from your task list and decline the request in one fell swoop.

- **Mark complete and delete**   If you've already done the task, you can remove it from your task list and notify the sender that it's done by using this option. Depending on the options selected in the original task request, this may generate both a Task Update message and a status report (completed).

- **Delete**   This is the last-resort option that simply deletes the task from your task list without notifying the sender or anyone else in the loop.

As soon as you click OK, the task is deleted from your calendar and any updates or reports generated by your selection are sent.

Ignoring a Task Request

While this is not really an option, there's nothing to prevent you from not acting on the task request. This can even happen unintentionally if you decide to close it and give it some thought before deciding what to do. Whatever the reason, the results are the same. The task is added to your task list and remains there until you take action on it. The sender receives no notification, and you are presumed to be the owner. In the event the task due date passes, the task is marked overdue on your task list. Once again, neither you nor any previous owners receive any notification.

Tip

While you're deciding what to do about the task, you might want to send all previous owners a status report letting them know that you're not ignoring them, merely giving the matter consideration. Open the task request, which should still be in your Inbox, or the actual task on your tasks list, and choose Actions | Send Status Report. This creates an e-mail message, addressed to everyone on the Update List, containing the basic information from the task request. Add a message explaining the reason for the delay and click Send.

MOUS

MOUS EXAM PRACTICE

To make sure you understand the implication and results of each of the ways you can deal with a task request, ask your co-workers to send you a bunch of task requests (fictitious, of course), to which you can respond. Use a different response for each. Edit some responses and just send others. Ask your co-workers to report back on the results of your responses.

Viewing and Tracking Tasks

If you have a lot on your plate and you depend on Outlook to manage your tasks, you'll find there are a number of ways to keep track of what you've accomplished, what's still ahead, and how tasks you've delegated are progressing. You can achieve this by using the viewing and tracking features available in Outlook. The Tasks folder, like other Outlook folders, provides a variety of views for organizing and manipulating task information. In addition, updating and tracking delegated (assigned) tasks is simple with the automatic updating and notification system built into the Tasks folder.

Using Tasks Views

The Tasks folder offers ten standard views that let you arrange and rearrange your task information so you can find what you need when you need it. The Tasks folder views consist of nine table views and one timeline view. They include everything from a simple task list to a couple of views used specifically for tracking assigned tasks. Of course, as with other folder views, you can customize the existing views and create your own as the need arises.

By default, the Tasks folder opens with the Simple List view. True to its name, the Simple List view contains only four fields (columns): Icon, Complete, Subject, and Due Date (see Figure 13-7).

To switch views, choose View | Current View to display a menu of available views. Select a view from the list or choose Customize Current view to make changes to the view presently on display. Since the views in the Tasks folder are consistent with other folder views there's no need to go into detail on the basics. For information on using Outlook views, see Chapter 22. The remainder of this chapter focuses on special features and troubleshooting for the Tasks folder views.

The best place to start is with a couple of useful features found only in the Tasks folder, which work hand in hand with each other. The first is the ability to manually

Figure 13-7. *The Simple List view provides a quick overview of your tasks*

rearrange the task items in table views by dragging them up and down the list. The second feature, called Save Task Order, enables you to save a manually arranged sort order as the default sort order for all views in the Tasks folder. There is one catch, however. Both features require that you first remove any Group By and Filter options that may be currently applied to the view. The manual sort feature requires that all Sort options be removed as well.

Sorting Tasks Folder Views Manually

As the previous section mentions, the first thing you must do to sort any task view (of the table type) manually is remove all Group By, Sort, and Filter options. Right-click any field header in the current view and select Customize Current View from the shortcut menu to open the View Summary dialog box.

If options are set for Group By, Sort, or Filter, click the corresponding button to open the associated dialog box. Then click the Clear All button to remove any settings, and click OK to return to the View Summary dialog box. When all three are cleared, click OK to return to the Tasks folder. Now you're set to start rearranging the view manually by dragging and dropping tasks. As soon as you move a task above or below the adjacent tasks, a red line with a pair of inward-pointing arrows appears between tasks. This indicates where the task will land if you choose to drop it.

You can also right-drag the task and have the choice of moving it or copying it when you reach your destination. As soon as you drop the task, a shortcut menu appears, offering you both options as well as Cancel.

Drop the task to relocate it. Continue the process until the list is sorted exactly the way you want it. When you've got it arranged to your satisfaction, it's time to take advantage of the second feature, Save Task Order.

Using the Save Task Order Command

Unless all Group By and Filter settings are disabled, the Save Task Order command is grayed out on the Action menu. When used in conjunction with a manual sort, this is no problem, since manual sorting requires Group By, Filter, and Sort options all to be turned off. However, if you want to use a sort on one or more fields rather than a manual sort, just make sure the Group By and Filter options have been removed. To check, right-click a column header in the task view and choose Customize Current View to display the View Summary dialog box. If Group By or Filter is enabled, click its button to open the associated dialog box and click Clear All. Click OK twice to return to the Tasks folder

When you have the task view in the order you want, choose Actions | Save Task Order from the Menu bar. From this point forward, all views will utilize the sort order applied when you used the Save Task Order command as the default sort order. However, any Group By, Sort, or Filter options applied will take precedence. Therefore, to return to the default sort order, you must clear those options.

Troubleshooting Tasks Folder Views

While using views in the Tasks folder you may encounter some problems not found in most other Outlook folders. The standard Tasks folder views are all table views with the exception of one timeline view. The problems you may experience are, for the most part, found in the table views.

Sorting Problems   If you create custom views by modifying existing views or by creating your own from scratch, you'll find you cannot sort by certain fields, including Company, Categories, Contact (as opposed to Contacts), Notes, or Read. There appears to be no clear reasoning behind these exclusions. In any event, attempting to sort by one of these fields results in an error message informing you that "You cannot sort by this field."

The way to work around this problem is to use the Group By feature instead of the Sort feature. Right-click a field header and select Customize Current View to display the View Summary dialog box. Click the Group By button to display the Group By dialog box.

From the Group Items By drop-down list, select the non-sorting field of your choice. If you want to display the field in the current view, check the Show Field In View option.

You cannot use more than one non-sorting field in the Group By dialog box. Outlook permits you to select more than one, but as soon as you click the OK button you will see an error message informing you that you cannot use the non-sorting fields at the same time.

Select either Ascending or Descending for the order and click OK twice to return to the active view. The view will now be grouped by the field chosen, enabling you to view your tasks in the order you desire.

Locating the Missing Private Field   Another problem you may encounter when customizing Tasks folder views is how to include the Private field in the view. While the Private field appears on both the task form and the task request form, the one place it does not appear is on the list of available Task fields you can use for customizing a Tasks folder view. Fortunately, there's a simple workaround for this problem. In either the Field Chooser or the Show Fields dialog box, select the Private field from the All Contact Fields list. The Private field doesn't appear in the All Task Fields list. However, both the Tasks folder and the Contacts folder use the same field for storing the Private status of records. You can access the Field Chooser by right-clicking a column header and selecting Field Chooser from the shortcut menu.

Printing a Timeline View   One thing the Tasks folder has in common with the Journal folder is the inability to print the timeline view. Actually, any folder containing a timeline view will exhibit the same behavior. The reason for this lack of printing support is easy to understand since it would require printing a banner. However, there is a way to improvise and get a printout of the information in the timeline. Export the data to an Excel file, and use the Excel Chart Wizard to create a Gantt chart, which you can print.

MOUS EXAM PRACTICE
This section covered some basic features and some not-so-basic features of the Tasks folder views. Switch between the different views to see what each view consists of. Then try sorting a table view manually. Once you've got the table view sorted manually, set the new sort order as the default, using the Save Task Order command.

Organizing Tasks

Since the Tasks folder provides the same basic sorting, filtering, and grouping features as the other Outlook folders, there's no need to cover them in depth here. You'll find detailed information on all three features in Chapter 22.

There are, however, a couple of differences of which you should be aware. The opening tab of the Filter dialog box is always named for the folder from which it's invoked. Therefore, when setting filter conditions for a Tasks folder view, the opening tab is called Tasks.

In addition, some of the options on the Tasks tab are unique to the Tasks folder. As you can see, the Status field, which appears in no other folder, appears as a filter criterion. Since task requests and notices are sent via e-mail, the Tasks tab also contains From and Sent To fields. The remaining filter criteria are standard for all Outlook folders.

Another difference you'll find is in the Tasks folder Group By feature. Here you'll find that certain fields cannot be used together in building a grouping. When you attempt to use more than one non-sorting field to create a grouping, Outlook balks and lets you know in no uncertain terms you can't do it. See the "Troubleshooting Tasks Folder Views" section earlier in this chapter for more information on this problem.

Keeping Track of Tasks with Categories

Although Outlook makes no claim to being a project management tool, you can perform rudimentary project management tasks by taking advantage of several Tasks folder features, including Categories, Group By, and the Task Timeline view.

Using the Tasks folder for simple project management starts with assigning tasks to categories. For each task that has multiple components you'll want to create a new category with a unique name—most likely the name of the primary task. For example, if you're in charge of organizing the next annual managers meeting, you'll have a number of subtasks that must be undertaken to achieve your goal. Therefore, you might create a new category called Managers Meeting 2001, to which all related tasks, such as reserving rooms, booking flights, renting cars, and so on, are assigned.

While you can create a category from any folder using the same steps, the following instructions assume you are in the Tasks folder. To create a new category, choose Edit | Categories to open the Categories dialog box, as shown in Figure 13-8.

In the Item(s) Belong To These Categories text box, type the name of the new category you want to create. Next, click the Add To List button to add the new category to the Available Categories list. The new category is added to the list and is automatically checked. The checkmark indicates that the currently selected task will be assigned to the category. Therefore, unless you selected a related task before creating the category, you'll want to remove the checkmark to ensure only tasks related to the primary task are assigned. Click OK to save the new category and return to the active view.

The next step is to assign all related tasks to the category. Open (or create) each related task and move to the bottom of the task (or task request) form. Click the Categories button and check the new category. Click OK to assign the task to the new category and return to the task form. Change or add any other necessary information and close the task form. Repeat the process for each related task. You can assign a task to more than one category.

You now have an easy method for sorting, grouping, and filtering all related tasks. Now you can create custom views grouped by category. To create a custom timeline view grouped by category, choose View | Current View | Define Views to open the Define Views For "Tasks" dialog box seen in Figure 13-9.

Figure 13-8.   *The Categories dialog box makes creating, using, and modifying categories a breeze*

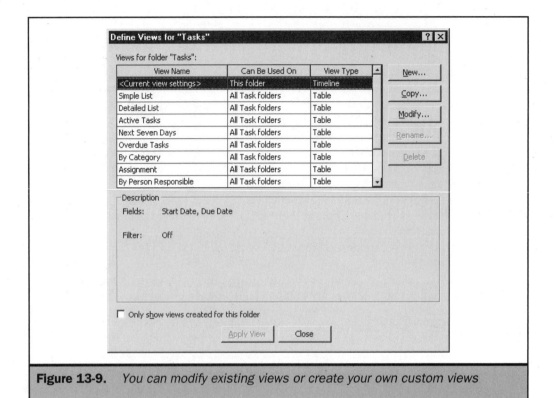

Figure 13-9. *You can modify existing views or create your own custom views*

Click New to display the Create A New View dialog box shown in Figure 13-10.
Enter a name for the new view. Then select Timeline from the Type Of View list.
Click OK to save the settings and display the View Settings For the [view name] dialog
box. Click the Group By button to display the Group By dialog box. From the Group
Items By drop-down list, select Categories. Click OK twice to save the Group By
settings and return to the Define Views For "Tasks" dialog box. Click Apply View to
return to the Tasks folder, where the new view is displayed (see Figure 13-11).

Another thing you might want to do is create a task item for the primary item and
attach each of the individual projects to it. In the example used for this section, you
would create a task called Meeting Manager and set the due date for the last date on
which everything had to be completed. Minimize all windows except Outlook and the
Meeting Manager task. Right-click a blank spot on the Windows task bar and select
Tile Windows Vertically. This places the Outlook window and the task form side by
side. Next, drag the related tasks from the Tasks folder and drop them in the Notes
field of the Meeting Manager task. Now, any time you open the Meeting Manager task
you can also open any of the related tasks by double-clicking the appropriate icon in
the notes field.

Figure 13-10. *View basics are pretty straightforward*

Figure 13-11. *The new view gives you a good overview of your projects*

As you discovered in this section, you can perform simple project management tasks by assigning your Outlook tasks to categories. Begin by creating several new categories. Then create a series of related tasks and assign each one to a category. Next, create a new timeline view grouped by categories. You might also create a table view grouped by categories.

Understanding Task Request Responses

Whether you're the original owner of a task request or the fourth assignee/owner in a chain of reassignments, tracking the progress and whereabouts of the task can be somewhat confusing—unless you understand the task request notification process.

There are two types of notifications:

- **Task responses**   Responses, which include Task Accepted messages and Task Declined messages, are direct replies to the last sender of the task request from the new assignee, indicating either an agreement or a refusal to accept ownership of the task.

- **Task updates**   Task Update messages are sent to all users whose names appear on the Update List of the task Details tab. Updates are sent when a task is reassigned or when the task owner makes a change to the task, such as changing the date(s) or modifying the status of the task. Updates are also sent to all previous assignors, except the last assignor (who gets a Task Response), when a task request is accepted or declined.

Updates generated by changes to a task that has been accepted are straightforward, reflecting the owner and the changes made. So far, so good. However, the confusing part comes when updates are generated by assignments and reassignments. The contents of these task updates are different depending on who sends them and who receives them. It's the task ownership that's in question. For example, if Joe assigns the task to Mary, who assigns it to Bill, who in turn assigns it to Ted, the updates will appear as follows: Joe's updates will indicate Mary is the owner, Mary's updates will indicate Bill is the owner, and Bill's update will indicate Ted is the owner. You can see how confusing this can get.

Note   *Reassigning tasks is a little like playing musical chairs. If someone declines the task, ownership reverts back to the last assignor. At this point, the assignor becomes the de facto owner of the task, and the Update List on the Details tab of the task is automatically cleared. All previous assignors disappear from the Update List and the current owner is now stuck with only two choices: add the task to his or her Tasks folder, or assign it to someone else. Declining the request from the previous assignor is no longer an option.*

Another thing to be aware of concerning task requests and updates is the manner in which they're processed. When a task request or update is opened and acted upon (regardless of the action taken), the task is modified accordingly in the Tasks folder, and the Task Request message or Task Update message is permanently deleted from the Inbox. It does not even stop at the Deleted Items folder—it just disappears. By default, Outlook tracking options are set to process task updates automatically. Therefore, a task update you receive will be processed and deleted within a very short period of time (depending on server traffic) if you don't spot it and open it first. This means you may not even be aware that an update has occurred. Since the task itself is updated with the same information included in the update message, this is not really a problem. However, it means the only way you may be aware of a change in the task is if you open the task and check.

Tip *If you want to be able to access those deleted updates and requests (and any other permanently deleted Outlook items) you can do so by adding a new DWORD value to an existing key in the Windows registry.* Warning! *Editing the registry can have unexpected results and should only be done by experienced users. Always make a backup of your registry before making any changes. Add the DWORD value **DumpsterAlwaysOn** to the* HKEY_LOCAL_MACHINE\Software\Microsoft\Exchange\Client\Options *key, and set its Value data to 1. Log off of Outlook and back on. Now, no matter what folder you're in, the Recover Deleted Items command appears on the Tools menu. See Chapter 5 for information on using the Recover Deleted Items command.*

To disable this automatic processing of task updates, choose Tools | Options from the Menu bar. On the Preferences tab of the Options dialog box, click the E-mail Options button to display the E-mail Options dialog box. Then click the Tracking Options button to open the Tracking Options dialog box. Remove the checkmark next to the Process Requests And Responses On Arrival option. Be advised, however, that this option also controls the automatic processing of meeting requests (not task requests), therefore you will be turning that feature off as well.

Setting Task Options

The Tasks folder has several options you can set to customize the way the folder looks and operates. To modify the default Tasks folder options, choose Tools | Options from the Menu bar to display the Options dialog box, shown in Figure 13-12.

As you can see in Figure 13-12, the Preferences tab of the Options dialog box contains a section entitled Tasks, which includes a Reminder Time drop-down list and a Task Options button. From the Reminder Time drop-down list, select the default time for all new tasks. Click the Task Options button to display the Task Options dialog box.

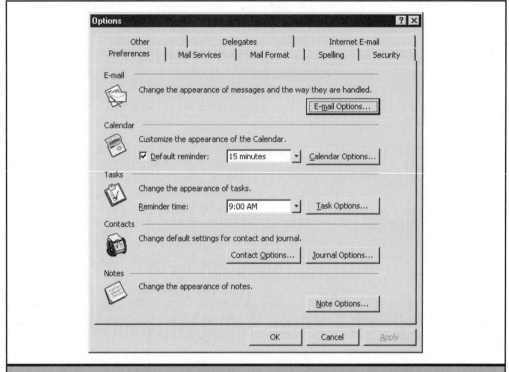

Figure 13-12.   *The Options dialog box is your headquarters for modifying most default settings*

Here you can designate the text color for displaying overdue and completed tasks in Tasks folder views. From each drop-down list, select the desired color. Then click OK to save the change(s) and return to the Preferences tab.

The next set of task options is buried a little deeper. Click the Other tab and then click the Advanced Options button to open the Advanced Options dialog box (see Figure 13-13).

In the Appearance Options section, you'll find two task-related options for setting working hours. In the Task Working Hours Per Day field, enter the number of hours you consider a workday. Although many people work more than eight hours a day, eight is still considered a standard workday and is therefore the default setting. The same goes for the next option, Task Working Hours Per Week. This is the number of hours your work week generally consists of. Both of these fields are used by Outlook when calculating the Total Work and Actual Work fields found on the Details tab of the task form. For example, if you leave the default settings for Task Working Hours

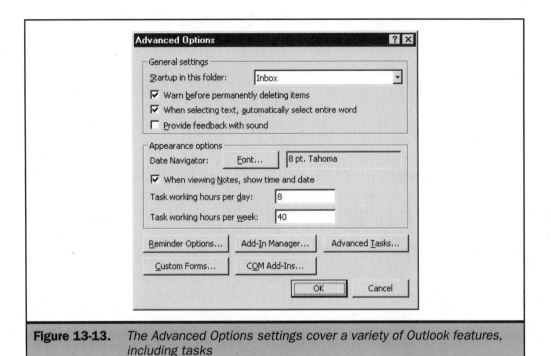

Figure 13-13.   *The Advanced Options settings cover a variety of Outlook features, including tasks*

Per Day at 8, and enter 4 hours in the Total Work field in the task form, Outlook converts it to 0.5 days.

Tip   *If you happen to be the type who always has to look under the hood and tinker, you can use the Windows registry to change both workday and work week lengths.* Warning! *Modifying the registry should only be done by experienced users, and a backup should always be made prior to making any changes to the registry. To change the default settings for the length of your workday or work week, log off of Outlook, open the registry, and locate the* HKEY_CURRENT_USER\Software\Microsoft\Office\9.0\Outlook\ Options\Tasks *key. To change the length of your workday, modify the Value data of the DWORD UnitsPerDay. Outlook uses minutes to determine the length of both days and weeks. Therefore, you'll have to convert the desired length of your workday to minutes (the value for an eight-hour day is 480). To change the work week settings, modify the Value data of the UnitsPerWeek DWORD, again using minutes. When you exit the registry editor and log back on to Outlook, the change will be effected.*

The final set of options affecting tasks is also accessed from the Advanced Options dialog box. Click the Advanced Tasks button to open the Advanced Tasks dialog box.

MANAGING TIME
& DETAILS

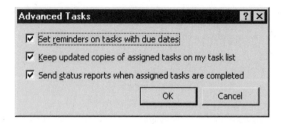

The Advanced Tasks dialog box includes the following options:

- **Set reminders on tasks with due dates**   Check this option to automatically set reminders for all new tasks that include due dates. The reminder is automatically set using the default setting from the Reminder Time option located on the Preferences tab of the Options dialog box.

- **Keep updated copies of assigned tasks on my task list**   This option appears on all task requests. Checking it here automatically checks the option on all new task request forms. Since it's likely you'll want to remain informed about a task you assign, it's a good idea to leave this option checked.

- **Send status reports when assigned tasks are completed**   If you want to receive notification in the form of a status report when an assigned task is marked complete, check this option. Again, all this does is ensure that the option of the same name on the task request form is automatically checked.

Once you've made all the necessary changes to task options, close all the dialog boxes and return to the active Outlook window. The changes should take effect immediately.

Exam | MOUS Exam Objectives Explored in Chapter 13

Objective	Activity	Heading
OL2000.6.1	Create and update one-time tasks	"Creating Tasks"
OL2000.6.2	Accept and decline tasks	"Responding to Task Assignments"
OL2000.6.3	Organize tasks using categories	"Keeping Track of Tasks with Categories"
OL2000.6.4	Assign tasks to others	"Assigning Tasks"
OL2000.6.5	Create tasks from other Outlook components	"Creating Tasks from Other Outlook Folders"
OL2000.6.6	Change the view for tasks	"Using Tasks Views"

The
Complete
Reference

Chapter 14

Using the Journal

The Outlook Journal offers a means of keeping track of your Outlook activities and Office documents with little or no effort. Items you can record in the Journal folder include e-mail messages, meeting requests, task requests, Word and Excel documents, and more. To make journaling even easier, Outlook provides an AutoJournal feature that takes over and does most of the work for you.

Adding Journal Entries

You can add Journal entries either by enabling the AutoJournal feature or by creating entries manually. As good as AutoJournaling is, it doesn't fully automate the Journal entry process. There are some items not included in AutoJournaling. Therefore, you may have to create some Journal entries manually even if you turn AutoJournaling on.

| Note | *The first time you open the Journal folder by clicking the Outlook Bar shortcut in the My Shortcuts group or the Journal folder in the Folder List, a dialog box displays informing you that you can also use the Activities tab on each contact item for tracking e-mail and other activities. This is a handy feature that may negate the need for using the Journal altogether. Review the features of both and decide for yourself.* |

Configuring Automatic Journaling

By default, AutoJournaling is turned off. If you plan to use the Journal to record items and documents for some or all of your contacts, you'll want to turn it on and save yourself the time and effort of recording Journal entries manually.

| Note | *Automatic journaling of Microsoft Office documents only works with Office 2000 programs (Word 2000, Excel 2000, and so on). It does not work with Office 97 applications since they store their log files in different locations.* |

To automate the journaling process, choose Tools | Options to open the Options dialog box. Then click the Journal Options button on the Preferences tab to display the Journal Options dialog box.

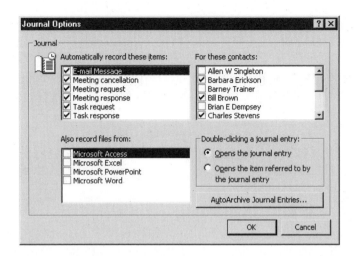

Indicate the items and documents you want recorded by checking the appropriate selections in both the Automatically Record These Items list and the Also Record Files From list. Then move to the For These Contacts list and choose the contacts for whom the selected items and documents will be recorded.

Tip *Although selecting some of the Microsoft Office documents for AutoJournaling might sound like a good idea, it can often be more trouble than it's worth. Every Office document of the type selected is recorded in the Journal, regardless of whether or not it relates to any other information in Outlook. As a result, your Journal can quickly become cluttered with everything from a letter to Mom to your first chapter of the great American novel.*

The next set of options enables you to determine what happens when you double-click a Journal entry. By default, double-clicking a Journal entry opens the entry itself. However, you can change that by selecting Opens The Item Referred To By The Journal Entry. The next time you double-click a Journal entry, the item or document referred to in the entry will open instead. For example, by default, double-clicking a Microsoft Word Journal entry opens the Journal entry containing a shortcut to the associated Word document. Changing the default double-click option results in the Microsoft Word document itself opening when you double-click the Journal entry.

The last option, the AutoArchive Journal Entries button, provides access to the AutoArchive tab of the Journal Properties dialog box. Here you can set the AutoArchiving options for the Journal folder. For more information on AutoArchiving see "Configuring AutoArchive Settings" in Chapter 18.

Warning! This tip involves editing the Windows registry, which should be performed by experienced users only. Modifying the registry can have unexpected results that may adversely affect the operation of your installed hardware and software. You can change a number of Journal settings by modifying the values for HKEY_CURRENT_USER\ Software\Microsoft\SharedTools\Outlook\Journaling subkeys. The numeric values AutoJournaled, Enabled, and JournalByContact can be set to off (0) or on (1). Some keys, such as Letters and Notes, are included only to ensure they appear on the Entry Type list, therefore, setting their options has no affect on them. They cannot be AutoJournaled regardless of their settings.

The beauty of AutoJournaling is that you don't have to do anything after you set the AutoJournal options. As long as the items, documents, and contacts have been selected in the Journal Options dialog box, any time you create a selected item or document for an indicated contact the Journal entry is recorded automatically.

Creating Journal Entries Manually

Unfortunately, not all Outlook items are eligible for AutoJournaling. Phone calls, notes, letters, faxes, tasks, and appointments are among the Outlook items that cannot be journaled automatically. Consequently, if you want these items entered in the Journal folder you'll have to create the Journal entries manually.

If you use the Journal a lot, you may want to move its shortcut from the My Shortcuts group on the Outlook Bar to the Outlook Shortcuts group. Open the My Shortcuts group and drag the Journal icon to the Outlook Shortcuts group. When the Outlook Shortcuts group opens, drop the Journal shortcut above or below an existing shortcut.

The process is not difficult, therefore creating manual Journal entries is more of a nuisance than an onerous task. From within the Journal folder, click the New button on the Standard toolbar or press CTRL-N to open a new Journal entry form (see Figure 14-1).

You can also create a new Journal entry by right-clicking a blank spot in the Information viewer and selecting New Journal Entry from the shortcut menu.

Figure 14-1. *Creating a manual Journal entry is as easy as filling in the blanks*

Enter a brief description of the Journal entry in the Subject field. Make it short and to the point so you can easily identify it later. Next, select the type of entry you're making from the Entry Type drop-down list.

Warning! *This tip involves editing the Windows registry which should only be done by experienced users. You can create custom entry types by adding them to the Windows registry. Locate the HKEY_CURRENT_USER\Software\Microsoft\SharedTools\ Outlook\Journaling key and add a subkey for each new entry type. Give the new key an appropriate name (for example, Life Event, Equipment Service, Promotion, and so on). Next, add a string value named Description. For the string's Value Data, enter the text you want to appear in the Entry Type drop-down list. Close the registry and return to the Journal. The next time you open a Journal entry and display the Entry Type drop-down list, you'll find the new entry type listed.*

If the Journal entry is associated with a specific company, enter its name in the Company field. By default, the Start Time field contains today's date and the current time (according to your computer's clock). If you're recording an event that happened earlier, you can enter a different date and time or use the pop-up calendar and drop-down time list in the Start Time field.

For keeping track of the amount of time you spend on an activity, you can activate the timer by clicking the Start Timer button. When you're finished with the call, meeting, or other activity, you can click Pause Timer to stop the timer. Time is recorded in one-minute increments in the Duration field. If you're making a record of an event that took place earlier, you can manually enter the time in the Duration field. Use the Notes field to keep track of phone calls, meeting notes, and miscellaneous information related to the entry.

To associate the Journal entry with one or more contacts, click the Contacts button and choose the contacts from the Select Contacts dialog box. If you're using categories to organize your Journal entries, you may want to assign the entry to a category by clicking the Categories button and selecting the appropriate category from the Categories dialog box. The final option on the Journal entry form is the Private option. If you share your Journal folder and want to prevent others from seeing this entry, check the Private option.

MOUS EXAM PRACTICE

In this section you learned to create Journal entries manually. Begin by trying the various methods for opening a new Journal entry form, including the shortcut key CTRL-SHIFT-J, the New button drop-down list, and CTRL-N shortcut from within the Journal folder. Next, fill out the form with the appropriate information. Finally, use the timer feature to track the duration of the activity.

Adding Attachments to Journal Entries

Journal entries, like most Outlook items, can contain attachments as well as information. For example, suppose you're recording notes to send to co-workers who were unable to attend an important meeting. You might want to include appointment items, contact records, Word documents, Excel spreadsheets, and e-mail messages related to the topics discussed at the meeting. It's easy if you create a Journal entry for the meeting and insert the necessary items as attachments.

Unlike most other Outlook items that offer several choices for inserting attachments, the Journal entry form provides a single choice, Object, on the Insert menu. Objects include such things as images, documents, spreadsheets, charts, ActiveX controls, and so on. To include an object in a document, place your cursor in the Notes field of the Journal entry form and choose Insert | Object to display the Insert Object dialog box.

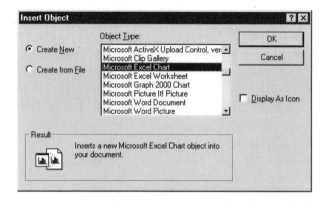

To create a new object, select the type of object you want to create from the Object Type list and click OK. This opens the program associated with the object type so you can create the object. To insert an existing object, select Create From File and click the Browse button to locate the desired file. By default, Outlook embeds the object in the Journal entries. This means that the object is included in the entry form and can be edited in the form as long as the program associated with the object is installed on your computer. Changes made to an embedded object are not reflected in the original object. To retain the relationship between the inserted object and the original object, check the Link option.

The fact that the Insert menu lacks choices other than Object doesn't mean you're limited to inserting only objects as attachments. You can add all the Outlook items you want to a Journal entry by using the drag and drop method.

Start by minimizing all open Windows applications except Outlook. Next, open the Journal entry to which you want to attach one or more Outlook items. Right-click a blank spot on your Windows taskbar and select Tile Windows Vertically to place Outlook and the open Journal entry side by side on the screen. Open the Outlook folder containing the item to attach, locate the item, drag it to the Journal entry, and drop it in the Notes field. Repeat the process until all your attachments are added. By default, dragging and dropping an item inserts a copy of the item in the Journal entry. To move the item from the original folder to the Journal entry, hold down the SHIFT key while dragging the item.

Note

Keep in mind that when you insert attachments you're attaching the actual object, file, or item, not merely creating a link. Therefore, the size of the Journal entry is increased by the size of the item you're attaching.

MANAGING TIME
& DETAILS

You can also add computer files of any type by using this procedure. However, instead of opening an Outlook folder, go to Other Shortcuts on the Outlook Bar and choose My Computer. You can then select files from anywhere on your local or network drives.

Using Outlook Items to Create Journal Entries

Creating Journal entries from other Outlook items is accomplished by dragging the item to the Outlook Bar or Folder List and dropping it on the Journal shortcut or folder. A new Journal entry opens using the item's subject as the Journal entry subject and selecting an appropriate entry type based on the item type. In addition, a shortcut to the original item is included in the Notes field of the Journal entry.

If you right-drag the item and drop it on the Journal shortcut or Journal folder, a shortcut menu appears offering you several options. You can create a new Journal entry and include the dragged item as a shortcut or an attachment.

Viewing Journal Entries

By default, Journal entries are displayed in the By Type timeline view. Timeline views, of which the Journal has several, display information along a horizontal time scale, letting you view Journal entries in relation to their start times. The timeline views go one step further and organize Journal entries by groups within the time scale (see Figure 14-2).

To fine-tune a timeline view, you can take advantage of one of the three variations offered for each timeline view: Day, Week, or Month. The Day view breaks each day on the timeline into 24 one-hour sections. This enables you to view the activities for any given day on an hour-by-hour basis. The Week view, which is the default, divides the timeline by days. The final variation, Month, also breaks the timeline up into days. However, each section is much smaller, permitting a larger number of days to be displayed at once. As a result, only the Journal entry icons appear in this view. To see the subject, you must open the Journal entry. To switch between the timeline view variations, click the appropriate button on the Standard toolbar, as shown in Figure 14-2.

To use a timeline view effectively, you should familiarize yourself with its features. You can navigate a timeline view by scrolling left and right through dates and up and down through groups of Journal entries. You can also change dates by clicking the day or month header and selecting a new date from the pop-up calendar that appears.

Another handy feature is the capability to select all entries in a group by right-clicking the group header. A shortcut menu then appears, providing you with a number of commands that affect the selected Journal entries.

In addition to timeline views, the Journal contains several table views you can use. Table views display the Journal entry information in the rows and columns format similar to a spreadsheet layout.

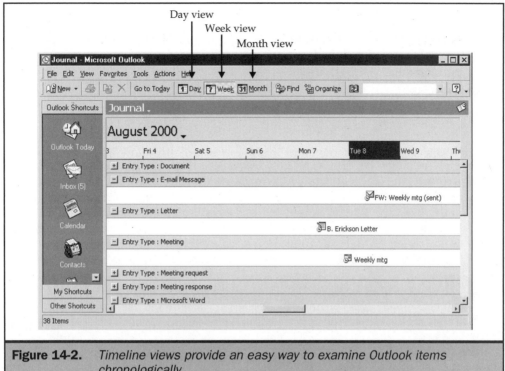

Day view
Week view
Month view

Figure 14-2. *Timeline views provide an easy way to examine Outlook items chronologically*

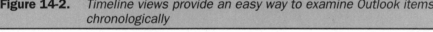 *You can't sort the table views by Contact or Category. However, you can still organize a table view using those fields. Right-click the Contact (or Category) field header and choose Group By This Field from the shortcut menu.*

Both timeline and table views have many features in common with other Outlook views. Right-clicking the headers (whether field or date) displays a shortcut menu with commands that affect the view. Double-clicking a blank spot on the Information viewer opens a new Journal entry form. For more information on working with Outlook views, see Chapter 22.

Using Timeline Shortcuts

The timeline view offers a unique environment and a number of helpful keyboard shortcuts for getting around the view quickly and easily without using the mouse. There are three groups of shortcuts you can use, depending on the focus of your actions. The first group affects the time scale itself. The next group of shortcuts works on items you've selected, and the third group applies to item groups that are selected.

MANAGING TIME
& DETAILS

To move around on the time scale, use the following shortcuts:

- **TAB key**   Press the TAB key to move from the top date header to the smaller date header, and then to the first item group header. Press SHIFT-TAB to cycle through them in the opposite order.

- **Arrow keys**   The right and down arrow keys move you forward through the time increments on the selected date header. Use the left or up arrow key to move backward through the time increments on the selected header.

When you select one or more items in an item group, the following shortcuts apply:

- **Arrow keys**   The right and left arrow keys move you forward and backward, respectively, through the displayed items and the group header. To select multiple adjacent items, hold the SHIFT key and press the right or left arrow key. You can even select multiple non-adjacent items by holding the CTRL key down and pressing the right or left arrow key to move through the items. When you reach an item you want to select, press the SPACEBAR. Continue holding the SHIFT key to move to the next item you want to select.

- **ENTER key**   Press ENTER to open the selected item.

- **ESC key**   Press the ESC key to close an open item.

- **HOME key**   Pressing the HOME key selects the first item in the group. To move to the first item without selecting it, hold the CTRL key and press the HOME key.

- **END key**   To select the last item in the group press the END key. To move to the last key without selecting it, hold the CTRL key while pressing the END key.

The final collection of shortcut keys is for working with item groups:

- **Arrow keys**   The up and down arrow keys move you from group to group either up or down. The right and left arrow keys expand (right) and collapse (left) the groups.

- **ENTER key**   When an item group is selected, pressing the ENTER key will either expand or collapse it, depending on its current state.

- **Plus and minus keys on the number pad**   The plus (+) key on the number pad expands the selected group, and the minus (-) key collapses it.

If you're not a fan of keyboard shortcuts, you can rely on your mouse to get you around.

Using the Preview Pane

To preview Journal entries without opening them, you can activate the Preview Pane. Choose View | Preview Pane to split either a timeline or table view into two panes. The top pane retains the Journal items and groups, while the bottom pane contains the

Preview Pane. Select an item in the top pane to display its information and contents in the Preview Pane. The Preview Pane header holds the Subject, Entry Type, Start Time, and Contact information. The body of the Preview Pane displays the contents of the Notes field, including text and attachments. To hide the Preview Pane, right-click the Preview Pane header and select Preview Pane. You'll also notice that you can hide header information and display Preview Pane options as well. For detailed information on setting Preview Pane options, see Chapter 22.

Turning on AutoPreview

Another useful viewing feature is AutoPreview, available in table views only. The AutoPreview feature displays the first few lines of each Journal entry's Notes field in the view. Choose View | AutoPreview to turn the AutoPreview feature on. To turn it off, repeat the process.

Printing Journal Entries

Printing Journal entries is easy. As a matter of fact, your choices are somewhat limited, which means you'd have to work at making it difficult. The first thing to note is that you can't print a timeline view. Therefore, printing in the Journal folder is restricted to printing items and printing table views.

Although you can't print a timeline view from Outlook, you can export the data to an Excel file using the Import and Export Wizard. You can open the file in Excel and create a Gantt chart, which you can then print from Excel. Like timeline views, Gantt charts are graphical representations of data displayed chronologically on a horizontal timeline.

To print an item in either type of view, right-click the item and select Print from the shortcut menu. You can also open the item and click the Print button on the Standard toolbar.

To print a table view, press CTRL-P, click the Print button on the Standard toolbar, or choose File | Print to display the Print dialog box, shown in Figure 14-3.

Select the printer to use from the Name drop-down list. Click the Properties button to set options for the selected printer. Check your printer manual for information on setting printer options. Move to the Print Style list and choose Table.

You can use the Memo style to print one or more selected items from either a table or timeline view. Each item prints on its own page and includes all fields that contain data.

If you want to include only selected rows in the printout, click Only Selected Rows, otherwise leave All Rows selected. To use the Only Selected Rows option, you must have first selected one or more rows in the view, prior to opening the Print dialog box. Next, select the pages you want to print and the number of copies. If you're printing

Figure 14-3.   *Use the Print dialog box to set your print options*

more than one copy of a multipage job, you can elect to have Outlook collate the copies for you by checking the Collate Copies option. When all the options are set, click OK to commence printing.

MOUS Exam Objectives Explored in Chapter 14

Objective	Activity	Heading
OL2000.5.4	Manually record an activity in a journal	"Creating Journal Entries Manually"

The Complete Reference

Outlook 2000

Chapter 15

Using Notes

Outlook notes items have gained the reputation for being the electronic equivalent of paper sticky notes. This description of the notes items is based on two things: their appearance, which faithfully mimics that of a yellow sticky pad note, and the ability to "stick" them on other Outlook items. What these electronic scraps are especially handy for is jotting down temporary information you use once and discard, or quick notes you can later transfer to a permanent residence in a contact or appointment item.

Creating Notes

Like so many other tasks in Outlook, there is a variety of ways to create a new note. You can press CTRL-SHIFT-N, or choose File | New | Note from any Outlook folder. If you're in the Notes folder, you can click the New button on the Standard toolbar, press CTRL-N, or right-click a blank spot on the Information viewer and select New Note. Whichever method you choose, you end up with a small yellow square like the one in Figure 15-1.

   You can also create notes by dragging other Outlook items to the Notes shortcut on the Outlook Bar or to the Notes folder in the Folder List. The information from the dragged items appears in the body of the newly created notes.

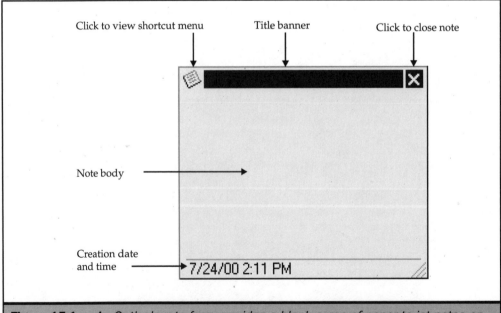

Figure 15-1.   *An Outlook note form provides a blank scrap of paper to jot notes on*

As soon as you open a new note form you can start typing. Begin by entering a title for the note. Make it brief and descriptive. Press the ENTER key to separate the title line from the body text of the note. Anything appearing on the first line (before the first hard return—an invisible formatting character is created when you press the ENTER key) appears in the Information viewer as the note title when the note is selected.

Note   *The title banner does not physically display the note title. However, pausing your mouse pointer over the title banner causes the note title to appear in a small pop-up box similar to a ToolTip.*

After you enter the note title and press the ENTER key, begin typing the body of your note. Type as much information as needed. The note form is a simple text editor, which means it word-wraps, employs Cut, Copy, and Paste commands, and continues to add new lines as you type. The only thing that is somewhat disconcerting about it is the lack of a scroll bar. As your text exceeds the visible space in the note, new lines are added and the existing text scrolls up. However, no scroll bar appears to alert you to the fact that you can scroll through the text. Fortunately, you can scroll up and down by using the arrow keys to move the cursor through the text. In addition, the PAGE UP and PAGE DOWN keys function as expected in a text editor.

Note   *Only the first 255 characters of a note title appear in the Icon view when the note is selected. Anything beyond 255 characters is cut off in the title. It still appears in the note itself, but not in the note title. Remember, the title is all the text on the first line preceding the first hard return.*

To edit an existing note, double-click the note in the Information viewer and make the necessary changes. When you're finished editing, click the X in the upper-right corner to close the note. There's no need to save the note since closing a note also saves it. Although notes are generally used for jotting short bits of information, they can hold quite a bit of data. An individual note can contain up to 29,919 characters.

If you decide a note is no longer serving any useful purpose, you can eliminate it by selecting it and pressing DELETE, or by clicking the Delete button on the Standard toolbar. You can also right-click the note and select Delete from the shortcut menu.

MOUS   **MOUS EXAM PRACTICE**
In this section, you learned how to create and modify notes. Now create a couple of notes items from other Outlook folders using the CTRL-SHIFT-N method. From within the Notes folder, use each of the various methods available for creating new notes. You might also try dragging different Outlook items to the Notes folder to see how the information is added to a new note. After you've created a number of notes items, try your hand at editing them. Open them, modify their contents, and close them.

MANAGING TIME
& DETAILS

Managing Notes

Outlook notes are straightforward and uncomplicated, which makes managing them relatively simple. However, they are Outlook items, and as such, inherit many of the features of their more sophisticated siblings. Therefore, you still have a variety of options when it comes to organizing and viewing notes.

Organizing Notes

Outlook is an information manager, which means that organizing every piece of information, including notes, is a priority. Like other items, notes begin to lose their effectiveness if they are allowed to proliferate with wild abandon. To ensure that notes retain their usefulness, Outlook provides a number of ways you can organize them as they accumulate.

Assigning Notes to Categories and Contacts

Using category and contact assignments can make sorting, filtering, and viewing notes a snap. Category assignments provide a quick and easy way to separate notes into related groups. The process of assigning notes to categories is similar to that of assigning other Outlook items to categories, as you'll see if you follow these steps:

1. Open the Notes folder.

2. Select the note(s) you want to assign to one or more categories.

3. Right-click any one of the selected notes and choose Categories from the shortcut menu to display the Categories dialog box.

You can also choose Edit | Categories from the Menu bar to display the Categories dialog box.

4. Check the categories to which you want the selected notes assigned.

Tip

If any of the selected notes already have category assignments, they appear as checkmarks in gray boxes. This does not mean all selected notes (unless only one note is selected) are assigned to the checked category. For example, one or more notes in the preceding illustration are already assigned to the Business and International categories. To assign all selected notes to the category, remove the checkmark and add it again. The gray box turns white indicating the assignment affects all selected notes.

5. Click OK to save the category assignments and return to the Notes folder.

You can also categorize individual notes during creation or editing. While the note is open, click the note icon in the upper-left corner of the note and choose Categories from the shortcut menu. This displays the Categories dialog box. Follow the steps outlined earlier to make category assignments.

Linking contacts to notes is great for quick notes you plan to add to a contact record at a later time. If you forget to transfer the information, having a link to the contact makes it very easy to match the note with the contact and update the contact record, regardless of how much time has elapsed.

Linking a contact to a note is even easier than assigning a note to a category, however, you can only link one note at a time. Open the note you want to link and click the note icon in the upper-left corner. From the shortcut menu, select Contacts to open the Contacts For Note dialog box.

Click the Contacts button to display the Select Contacts dialog box. Choose the contact(s) that you want to link to the note and click OK to return to the Contacts For Note dialog box. Click Close to add the link(s) and return to the note.

If you decide to add the note information to the contact record, open the note and copy the text. Then click the note icon and select Contacts from the shortcut menu. Double-click the contact to open the contact record. Paste the note text into the note field of the contact record.

MANAGING TIME & DETAILS

Using Organize to Manage Notes

The Organize feature is available throughout Outlook, and the Notes folder is no exception. You can use Organize to move notes to other folders and to switch views. To move notes, click the Organize button on the Standard toolbar to display the Organize pane in the Information viewer.

Select the notes you want to move and choose a target folder from the Move Note Selected Below To drop-down list in the Organize pane. Then click the Move button to complete the move.

To create a new folder, click the New Folder button in the top-right corner of the Organize pane.

Sorting and Filtering Notes

Notes, like other Outlook items, can be sorted and filtered using the sort and filter features. Applying a filter to notes enables you to establish certain criteria which a note must meet to remain visible. All notes not meeting the criteria you set are hidden while the filter is applied. The process is very similar to that used for sorting and filtering other Outlook items. There are a couple of minor differences that will be covered here.

To filter your notes, right-click a blank spot in the Information viewer and select Filter to open the Filter dialog box.

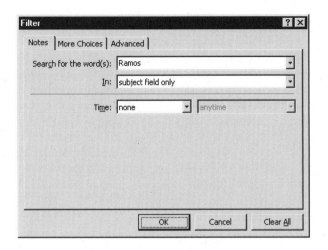

As you can see, the opening tab is called Notes. This is because the first tab of the Filter dialog box is automatically customized for each folder in which it's used. Enter the text you want to use as the search criterion in the Search For The Word(s) field. From the In drop-down list, select the field in which to search for the text. You'll find the selection is rather limited. You can choose Contents Only or Subject Field Only. The Contents Only selection applies to the body of the note, while the Subject Field Only applies to the note title. Since the title is also considered part of the contents, any text included in the title will be found regardless of which selection you make.

The last option on the Notes tab is Time. Use this option to filter notes based on the date they were created or modified. Select Created or Modified from the Time drop-down list. From the second Time drop-down list, select the timeframe to use.

Note *The created and modified dates and times for non-Personal Folder items are determined by the Microsoft Exchange Server, not the local user's computer. However, the Time option uses the local computer's clock. Therefore, if the clock on the server is different than the clock on the user's computer, the Time option may not work as anticipated.*

Click OK to apply the filter. All records not matching the filter criteria are hidden. Filters are applied only to the views in which they are created. Therefore, if you switch to another view all your notes will be visible. It's a good idea to remove a filter when you're finished using it to ensure you don't return to the view at a later time and think half your notes are gone.

Note *When you apply a filter in a table view, (Filter Applied) appears in the Folder banner, alerting you to the fact that a filter has, indeed, been applied. However, when you apply a filter to an icon view, there is no onscreen indication that a filter has been applied, other than missing notes.*

To remove a filter, return to the Filter dialog box and click the Clear All button. See Chapter 22 for complete details on using the other Filter dialog box tabs.

Sorting the Notes folder is even easier. The first thing to understand is that sorting applies to the entire folder, not just the current view of the folder contents. Therefore, when you sort your notes, the same sort order is carried over when you change views.

In an icon view, you must use the Sort dialog box, which can be accessed by choosing View | Current View | Customize Current View and clicking the Sort button on the View Summary dialog box. You can then select up to four fields on which to base the sort order. For details on using the Sort dialog box, see Chapter 22. You can also open the Sort dialog box by right-clicking a blank spot on the Information viewer.

A table view in the Notes folder can be sorted quickly and easily by clicking the field headers at the top of the Information viewer. Click the header of the field you want to sort the view by. The first time you click a header, the sort order is ascending (from A to Z). Click the header a second time to reverse the sort order. A small, recessed triangle indicates whether the order is ascending (upward triangle) or descending (downward triangle). You can sort using multiple fields by holding down the SHIFT key while clicking the field headers.

You can also sort by right-clicking a field header and selecting Sort Ascending or Sort Descending from the shortcut menu.

Since some sort order is necessary, you cannot remove a sort order, merely change it.

MOUS EXAM PRACTICE
In this section, you learned a variety of techniques for organizing your notes. Begin your practice by assigning notes to categories. Then use the Contacts command to link some of the notes to different contacts. Use the Organize feature to move notes between folders. Remember, only notes folders can accept notes items. Next, apply one or more filters to different Notes folder views. After you master the Outlook Filter feature, sort the Notes folder on a single field. Then try multiple fields. In each case, change the sort order from ascending to descending to see how the notes are affected.

Viewing Notes

As your inventory of notes grows, you may find that you need to change the way you view your notes. With only a handful of notes to manage, the default view (the Icon view with large icons) is probably sufficient. However, if you amass a large number of notes, you'll soon discover the limitations of the default view. By customizing the Icon view and taking advantage of the other standard views, you'll quickly overcome those limitations.

Customizing Icon Views

As you can see in Figure 15-2, the default Icons view displays each note in the Information viewer with a large icon and the first 25 characters of the note title.

Figure 15-2. *The Icon view becomes a little chaotic as your notes multiply*

The sort order of the Icons view is by creation date and time, with the most recently created note appearing in the top-left corner of the Information viewer. If the note title is longer than 25 characters, highlighting the note displays up to 230 additional characters of the title. To see the note body, or anything beyond the total of 255 title characters, you'll have to open the note by double-clicking it.

The Icons view is fine until you start to add a substantial number of notes, after which it becomes rather cluttered and hard to use. To restore some order, you can take advantage of the following customization options available only to the Icons view:

- **Large Icons**   This is the default option applied to the Icons view. It displays a large icon for each note in the Information viewer.

- **Small Icons**   This option replicates the default view, but replaces the large icons with small icons. The notes are still ordered (by Created date) from left to right.

- **List**   The List option does two things. It uses small icons and displays notes from top to bottom (by Created date), using multiple columns when necessary.

You can apply any of the preceding options to the Icons view by clicking the appropriate button on the Standard toolbar or right-clicking a blank spot in the Information viewer and making your selection from the shortcut menu. The same commands are also available on the View menu.

Switching Views

Even with the customization options, the Icons view may not be suitable for your needs. Therefore, Outlook provides a number of standard views in addition to the Icons view. To switch views, choose View | Current View and select the desired view from the submenu that appears. Outlook offers the following views for your viewing pleasure:

- **Icons** This is the default view, in which notes are displayed with large icons and titles. The default sort order is by the Created date field, and notes are arranged from left to right.

- **Notes List** This table view presents notes in a straight list format with Icon, Subject, Created, and Categories fields displayed.

- **Last Seven Days** This table view is identical to the Notes List view, but displays only those items created or modified within the last seven days. Keep in mind that in a Microsoft Exchange Server network the Created and Modified dates are assigned by the server, not the local computer for all non-Personal Folder items. If there's a difference between the server's clock and your local computer's clock, this view may not produce the results you expect.

- **By Category** If you assign notes to categories, use this view to group all notes by category assignments. Category groups appear alphabetically.

- **By Color** If you use color to distinguish notes from one another, use this view to separate them by the color applied.

In addition to using the View menu to switch views, you can also use the Organize feature. Click the Organize button on the Standard toolbar to display the Organize pane. Then click the Using Views link to display the views options.

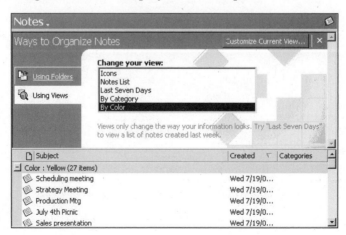

From the Change Your View list, select the view you want to use. You can even modify the currently selected view by clicking Customize Current View to display the View Summary dialog box. To close the Organize pane, click the Organize button again. For more information on customizing Outlook views, see Chapter 23.

Just as easy to use and requiring less space than the Organize pane is the Current View drop-down list, found in the Advanced toolbar. Right-click anywhere on the Standard toolbar and click Advanced to display the Advanced toolbar.

Using the Preview Pane

A handy device you can use to enhance the current view is the Preview Pane, shown in Figure 15-3.

To access the Preview Pane, choose View | Preview Pane from the Menu bar. The Information viewer is split horizontally into two panes. The top displays the current view, and the bottom displays the contents of the selected note. In addition, the Preview Pane header also contains the Subject (title) and the Created date. To close the Preview

Figure 15-3.   *Use the Preview Pane for a quick glimpse of the note's contents*

Pane, right-click the Preview Pane header and click Preview Pane. While you're there, you'll also notice additional Preview Pane options. See Chapter 22 for details on setting these options.

Using AutoPreview

The AutoPreview feature, which is available only in table views, reveals the first few lines of the note in addition to the other information normally displayed in the view. It provides a quick and easy way to scan your notes to find a tidbit of information or to determine the note's usefulness. See Figure 15-4.

To activate the AutoPreview feature, open a table view and choose View | AutoPreview from the Menu bar. The first few lines of the notes are displayed in blue. To turn off AutoPreview, choose View | AutoPreview a second time.

Figure 15-4.   *Using AutoPreview gives you a quick glimpse of each note's contents*

MOUS EXAM PRACTICE
In this section, you saw a variety of ways to view your notes information. Start your practice with the default Icons view and change it using the Small Icons and List commands. Then switch to a table view by making a selection from the Current View submenu. Open the Organize pane and use the Using Views feature to open another table view. While in a table view, apply the AutoPreview feature. From either the Icons view or a table view, activate the Preview Pane.

Customizing Notes

As simple and uncomplicated as notes are, there is still a number of things you can do to customize the way they look and behave. You can change both their color and their size to make them easier to distinguish and use. In addition, you can choose from several options that set defaults for the Notes folder.

Colorizing Notes

Colorizing can be very helpful in separating notes into easily distinguishable groups, especially if you use the Icons view. Changing a note's color changes not only the color of the icon, but the background of the note itself as well. To change the color, select one or more notes. Then right-click any of the selected notes and choose Color to display a submenu of color choices. Select the color you want to use for the selected note(s). Immediately, the notes icons in the current view change to the selected color. If you open any of the affected notes, you'll see the note background is also changed.

Resizing Notes

Although notes accept a large amount of text without resizing, you may find that you want to view more of the note's content by enlarging the note. Or, conversely, you may have a small note that requires less room and can therefore be reduced in size. Whichever your choice, the process is the same. Use your mouse pointer to grab any one of the sides or corners and drag in the appropriate direction. You can begin dragging when the mouse pointer turns into a double-pointed arrow.

MANAGING TIME & DETAILS

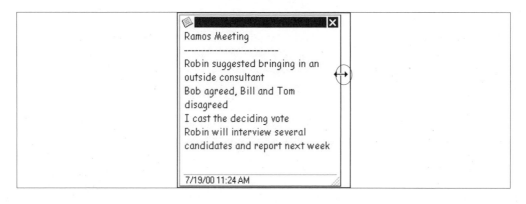

Dragging away from the note center enlarges the note. Dragging toward the note center reduces the note. To expand the width and height at once, drag the lower-right corner.

You can also modify the size of a note by double-clicking its title banner to maximize and restore it. When you maximize a note, it fills your screen. Restoring it returns it to its original size.

Setting Notes Options

There are several options you can utilize to set some of the default values for your Outlook notes. The first set of options controls the default appearance of new notes, the second determines whether the creation/modification date and time are displayed in notes. Setting these options is a breeze if you follow these steps:

1. Choose Tools | Options from the Menu bar to display the Options dialog box.

2. Click the Notes Options button on the Preferences tab to display the Notes Options dialog box.

3. Set the desired options. Your choices include:

- **Color** As you saw the moment you created your first note, the default color for new notes is yellow, in keeping with the sticky note tradition. However, if you prefer something a little more (or less) exciting, select a different color from this drop-down list. Existing notes are not affected. However, any new notes you create will be the color chosen here.

- **Size** If you find the size of new notes to be inadequate, change it to something smaller or something larger by changing this option.

- **Font** In a fit of lightheartedness, the Outlook programmers decided to use the 10-pt. Comic Sans MS font as the default. If you prefer something different, or you'd like to change the size or color of the font, click the Font button to display the Font dialog box. Select the font, font style, font size, and color you want displayed in your notes. Click OK to return to the Notes Options dialog box.

4. Click OK to save the new settings and return to the Options dialog box.

5. Click the Other tab on the Options dialog box to access additional options.

6. Click the Advanced Options button to view the Advanced Options dialog box.

7. Check When Viewing Notes, Show Time And Date to display the creation/ modification date and time in notes. Remove the checkmark to hide the date and time in notes.

8. Click OK to return to the Options dialog box.

9. Click OK to close the Options dialog box and return to the active Outlook window.

Upon opening the Notes folder, you will not immediately see any evidence of change, since the first set of options only affects notes created after the options are set, and the date and time option only affects notes' contents.

MOUS EXAM PRACTICE

In this section, you learned to customize your notes to change their appearance for aesthetic and practical purposes. Start your practice by changing the color of existing notes. Try organizing your notes by color. Next, change the size of individual notes by dragging their sides and corners, then double-click the title banner to maximize the note. Finally, change the default options for new notes and the date and time option for all notes.

Using Notes

By now you've probably gotten an idea of what you can use Outlook notes for, but this section will take you through some of the specific features that make putting notes to work for you even easier.

Creating Other Outlook Items from Notes

The first thing to remember is that drag and drop is alive and well in the Notes folder. You can drag a Notes item to any other Outlook folder and drop it to create a new item of that folder type. In addition, the contents of the note are included in the newly created item. For example, if you drag a note to the Contacts folder, a new contact form opens, with the note contents entered in the contact form Notes field. Not only is the body of the note added, but also category and contact assignments as well as creation/modification date and time.

You can drag the note to either an Outlook Bar shortcut or to the appropriate folder in the Folder List. If you right-click and drag a note to a different folder, you get a shortcut menu with several of options when you drop the note. Your choices include creating a new item with a copy of the note as text, as an attachment, or as a shortcut, or you can move the note and include it as an attachment.

Saving Notes as Text or RTF Files

If you want to exchange information contained in an Outlook note with a non-Outlook user, you can use the Save As command to save the note as a text (.txt) file or as a Rich Text Format (.rtf) file. Text files are almost universally readable, and Rich Text Format files are readable by users of most popular word processors. To save a note in either format, select the note and choose File | Save As from the Menu bar to open the Save As dialog box, shown in Figure 15-5.

From the Save In drop-down list, select the location for the saved file. Move to the Save As Type drop-down list and select Text Only (*.txt) or Rich Text Format (*.rtf) depending on your preference. Ignore the other choices as they're unsuitable for notes. Click the Save button. You can now transfer the files to disk or send them via e-mail to non-Outlook users, who can open and view their contents in a compatible text editor or word processor.

Forwarding Notes

Another handy feature the Notes folder offers is the ability to instantly create a new e-mail message with the selected note included as an attachment. The feature is called Forward and can be accessed a number of ways.

Select one or more notes from the Information viewer. Then right-click any of the selected notes and choose Forward from the shortcut menu. A new e-mail message form appears with the notes added as attachments. If multiple notes are selected, nothing appears in the Subject line of the message, but the icons appear in the notes box. If only a single note is selected, the Subject line includes FW:, followed by the note title.

Figure 15-5.   *Use the Save As dialog box to convert Outlook notes to text files*

You can also select the notes to forward and press CTRL-F or choose Actions | Forward from the Menu bar. You can forward an open note by clicking the note icon in the upper-right corner and selecting Forward from the shortcut menu.

MOUS EXAM PRACTICE
In this section, you've learned to employ features that enable you to extend the usefulness of notes. Begin your practice by using existing notes to create other Outlook items. Use the drag and drop method, then try the Using Folders feature in the Organize pane. Next, save your notes both as text files and Rich Text Files. Send them to co-workers and friends and see if they are able to open and read them. Finally, use the Forward command to send the notes themselves to other Outlook users.

Printing Notes

Printing notes is one of the easiest tasks you'll ever perform in Outlook. All you have to do is select a note in any view, right-click, and select Print from the shortcut menu. Outlook immediately prints the note in the memo style using your default printer.

Note   *Selecting multiple copies and using the Print command on the shortcut menu causes the Print dialog box to open. From this dialog box, you can select the desired print style, Table or Memo.*

If you want to have more control over your print job, select one or more contacts and click the Print button on the Standard toolbar to display the Print dialog box. Here you can designate the printer to use, modify the print style, determine the number of copies printed, and more.

You can print open notes by clicking the note icon in the upper-left corner and selecting Print from the shortcut menu. The Print dialog box appears, enabling you to set the options for the print job.

MOUS Exam Objectives Explored in Chapter 15

Objective	Activity	Heading
OL2000.8.0	Use notes	"Using Notes"
OL2000.8.1	Create and edit notes	"Creating Notes"
OL2000.8.2	Organize and view notes	"Organizing Notes" "Viewing Notes"
OL2000.8.3	Customize notes	"Customizing Notes"

The Complete Reference

Part V

The Microsoft Exchange Server Advantage

The
Complete
Reference

Chapter 16

Sharing Information

In addition to being able to exchange Outlook items with other users via e-mail, and to share free/busy information with ease, Outlook users on an Exchange server have a number of features at their fingertips that allow for even more extensive data sharing. Since Outlook information is folder based, these methods all involve sharing one type of Outlook folder or another. The three basic types of folders available in Outlook are:

- **Private folders**   Although there are several types of private folders in Outlook, only your server-based mailbox folders can be shared directly with other users. Since personal folders and all offline folders are stored on your local hard drive rather than the server, they cannot be shared directly (see "Using Net Folders" for information on indirect sharing of personal folders). Private mailbox folders can be shared either by giving another user delegate privileges or by assigning permissions.

- **Public folders**   Public folders exist for the express purpose of sharing information between Outlook users. They can be created by individuals with the necessary permissions, who then decide which users get access to the folders.

- **Net folders**   Personal folders designated as Net folders can be shared by copying the folder to each user's location and exchanging updates. Net folders enable Outlook users to share folders across the Internet as well as across the local area network (LAN).

Sharing Private Folders

All users on an Exchange server network have the option to allow other users to access their mailbox folders. If you're asking why anyone would open him- or herself to such an invasion of privacy, there are a couple of things to consider. To begin with, sharing your private folders doesn't mean opening the doors and letting everyone on the network rummage around in your mailbox. You, and you alone, determine who has access and precisely how much access each user receives. The second thing to consider is the convenience it affords you. By giving other users limited access, you can allow them to view information you would normally have to either send them or relay to them in some other manner. For example, if you have a custom journal folder in which you're tracking a particular project, you can give everyone on the team permission to view that folder. Or if you're busy enough to have a trusted assistant, you might want to give him or her the ability to schedule appointments, respond to meeting requests, and handle tasks for you. Remember, you can create new folders for the special projects and share them, rather than your primary mailbox folders.

Outlook offers two methods for giving other Outlook users access to your mailbox folders. You can either use the Delegate Access feature or assign users permissions to individual folders. The methods are similar in that they give an individual user specific permissions to a single folder. However, which method you use depends on your needs. The primary differences between delegate access and folder permissions are the folders on which each works, the ease of applying one over the other, and the level of permissions granted.

■ **Delegate access**   You can give any user delegate access to six primary Outlook folders: Calendar, Tasks, Inbox, Contacts, Notes, and Journal. This is handy for granting access to multiple folders in a single operation. Unfortunately, delegate access is limited to those six folders. In addition, the permissions you provide are more limited than those available when you assign permissions to individual folders, with one exception. No matter which level of permission (except None) you assign a delegate, it always includes the ability to send items on your behalf (the From field reads "From: [delegate's name] on behalf of [your name]").

■ **Folder permissions**   Folder permissions are not as easy to apply, since you must apply them one folder at a time. However, by assigning permissions to individual folders, you have the ability to control more precisely which permissions each user is assigned. In addition, your choice of permissions is greater.

Delegating Access to Your Data

When the need arises, you'll find that assigning delegate access privileges is easy. Simply choose Tools | Options to open the Options dialog box. Then click the Delegates tab to display the available options as seen in Figure 16-1.

Note   *If you don't see a Delegates tab in the Options dialog box, it's because you don't have the Delegate Access add-in installed. To install the add-in, have your original CD handy, choose Tools | Options, select the Other tab, click the Advanced Options button, click Add-In Manager, check Delegate Access, and click OK. At this point, either the add-in will install or you'll be instructed to insert the CD.*

To give a user permission to act as a delegate on your behalf, click the Add button to open the Add Users dialog box, which displays all the users in the Global Address List. Select the user(s) you want to assign delegate permissions to, and click the Add button. Click OK to open the Delegate Permissions: [user name] dialog box shown in Figure 16-2.

Note   *If the Delegate Permissions dialog box does not appear, and the user is simply added to the Delegates list on the Delegates tab, it means you've designated personal folders as your default delivery location. To assign delegate permissions, your default delivery location must be your server-based mailbox. To change the default delivery location, choose Tools | Services, click the Delivery tab, and select your mailbox from the Deliver New Mail To The Following Location drop-down list. You'll have to exit Outlook and restart it before the change takes effect.*

As you can see in Figure 16-2, six primary folders appear, each with its own drop-down list of permissions. By default, the Calendar and Tasks folders have Editor

THE MICROSOFT
EXCHANGE SERVER
ADVANTAGE

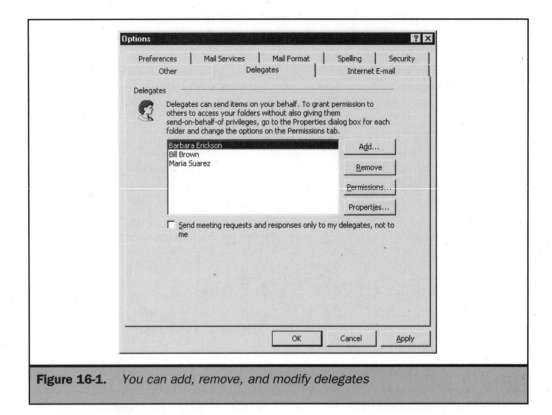

Figure 16-1. *You can add, remove, and modify delegates*

permissions already applied. The reason for both is that without permission to access the Tasks folder, a delegate who opens your Calendar folder will see his or her own TaskPad in the Day/Week/Month view, not yours. You can reset these or any other folder permissions by making the appropriate selection from the drop-down list. Your choices for permissions include the following:

- **None**   With the delegate permissions set to None, the user has absolutely no access to the indicated folder whatsoever.

- **Reviewer**   Assign Reviewer permissions to a delegate you want to authorize to read folder items and respond to them on your behalf. A user with Reviewer permissions can open items in the folder, but cannot create new items or modify existing items.

- **Author**   A user with Author permissions can both read and create items in the designated folder. As with all permissions, except None, an Author can also send and respond to items on your behalf. What a user with Author privileges cannot do is modify or delete existing items.

- **Editor**   An Editor is at the top of the delegate food chain, with permissions to read, create, modify, and delete items in the folder.

Figure 16-2.   *Setting up delegate permissions is a snap*

Make sure the folder to which you're assigning delegates doesn't have Show Home Page By Default For This Folder checked on the Home Page tab of the folder's Properties dialog box. None of the delegate permissions allows a delegate to show, hide, or disable the folder home page, which means the delegate won't be able to view the contents of the folder.

In addition to permissions, there are a few additional options on the Delegate Permissions dialog box:

- **Delegate receives copies of meeting-related messages sent to me**   This option is related to and dependent on the Calendar permissions. If you assign Editor permissions to a delegate, this option becomes available. When checked, it creates and sends the delegate a copy of any meeting-related e-mail you receive.

- **Automatically send a message to delegate summarizing these permissions**   Check this option to automatically notify a new delegate, via e-mail, of the permissions you've assigned.

- **Delegate can see my private items**   By default, delegates can see all items in a folder for which they have permissions, except items marked private. Check this option if you want the selected delegate to view all your items, including those marked private.

Once you're finished setting permissions and options, click OK to save the settings and return to the Delegates tab of the Options dialog box. Continue to add or modify delegates as needed. When you're done, click OK to close the Options dialog box and return to the active Outlook window.

Although the Delegate Permissions dialog box offers a limited set of permissions, you can customize them by opening the Properties dialog box for the folder and modifying the delegate's permissions. You'll find the delegate has been added to the Permissions tab of the folder's Properties dialog box. After you modify the permissions and return to the Delegate Permissions dialog box, note that the user's permissions now read "Custom."

Setting Folder Permissions

While assigning delegate access is convenient, and provides other users with the ability to send e-mail on your behalf, it's not nearly as powerful as setting individual folder permissions. Setting folder permissions enables you to tailor the permissions for each user much more precisely. In addition, you can assign owner permissions that allow the user to do everything with the folder that you yourself can do. However, unless you assign owner permissions to a user, he or she will not be able to send e-mail on your behalf.

To set folder permissions, right-click the folder and select Properties from the shortcut menu to open the folder's Properties dialog box. Then click the Permissions tab to view the permissions options. See Chapter 18 for detailed information on setting folder permissions.

Creating and Using Public Folders

Public folders are similar in many ways to private folders. They are containers used to store Outlook items or files, they possess most of the same properties and options, and they can be created, deleted, and modified by anyone with the proper permissions. Public folders are unlike private folders in that they are not part of the owner's mailbox, they reside on a public folder server (which may or may not be the same server the owner's mailbox is on), and their main purpose in life is to store information for public viewing and consumption.

Public folders are great for providing users with a forum in which they exchange ideas and opinions by posting messages on a given topic. If you want to disseminate company-wide information without actually passing it around, you can create public folders and post notices, policies, and other related information. You can even create public folders to share files and Outlook items and information.

Creating Public Folders

By default, creating public folders is a privilege assigned to every user on the Exchange server network. However, most administrators will quickly put an end to that to prevent the chaos that usually ensues. Therefore, you will only be able to create public folders if you have been assigned that right by your system administrator.

If you have the necessary rights, start by pressing CTRL-SHIFT-E to open the Create New Folder dialog box, shown in Figure 16-3.

You can also right-click All Public Folders in the Folder List and choose New Folder to display the Create New Folder dialog box.

Give the folder a unique, descriptive name by entering it in the Name field. Then, from the Folder Contains drop-down list, select the item type you want the folder to store. Like private folders, public folders can store only one type of Outlook item. The next step is to select a location for the new folder. Since this is to be a public folder, you must select All Public Folders or one of its subfolders. You cannot select Public Folders or Favorites. If you do, Outlook politely informs you that you can't do it when you click OK to create the folder.

Favorites is a special folder that holds copies of the existing public folders you use most frequently. You can add any existing public folder to Public Folders\Favorites by dragging the existing folder and dropping it on Favorites.

After you've made your selections, click OK and the new folder is created. That's all there is to it.

Figure 16-3.   *Creating a public folder in the Create New Folder dialog box*

Setting Public Folder Properties

Public folders, like private folders, have a number of options you can set to customize the way the folder looks and works. Accessing these options is the same for both public folders and private folders. Open the Folder List and right-click the public folder to open its Properties dialog box.

 What you see depends not only on your permissions (owners see all available tabs), but also on the location of the public folder. Only folders located in the Public Folders\Favorites folder have Favorites and Synchronization tabs.

The similarity between public and private folder properties does not end with the method of accessing them. It also extends to who is permitted to modify folder settings. To edit a public folder's properties, you must have owner permissions. If you're not an owner, you'll only be able to view the General, Home Page, and Summary tabs, none of which you can change. The Summary tab indicates the owner and displays your permissions for the folder.

The majority of public folder properties are identical to those found in private folders. The major differences lie in the fact that you cannot AutoArchive public folders, and you can only designate public folders located in the Public Folders\Favorites folder as offline folders. The remainder of this section discusses the settings unique to public folders. For detailed information on private folder properties and permissions, see Chapter 18.

Setting Administrative Options

As you can see in Figure 16-4, the Administration tab of a public folder contains a number of options, all but one of which are available only in public folders. The first option, Initial View On Folder, is the only one available in both public and private folders. The remaining options are grayed out in private folders.

The Administration options available in public folders include the following:

- **Initial View On Folder**   This option sets the default view that displays the very first time the user opens the folder. If the user never switches views, the designated view appears every time the folder opens. However, once the user switches to another view, this option no longer applies to the folder for that particular user. It still applies to other users who haven't yet opened the folder and switched to another view. As you can tell by the view names, all but Normal are applicable only to folders containing mail items.

- **Drag/Drop Posting Is A**   Use this option to change the default action resulting when you drag a mail item to the public folder and drop it. If you select Move/Copy, the item is simply moved or copied, depending on your choice. However, if you select Forward, the item is posted to the folder as a forwarded item. The original subject line is preceded by FW, indicating that it is a forward, and the From field contains your name, as the forwarder. This field has no effect on item types other than mail.

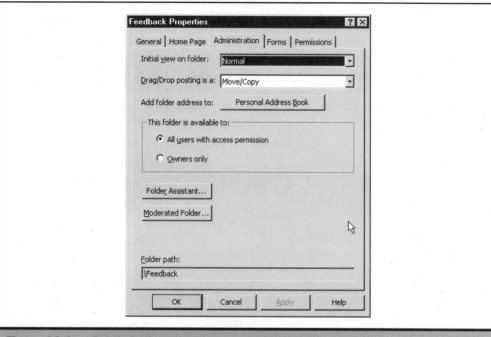

Figure 16-4.   *Public folder owners have a variety of administrative options at their disposal*

- **Add Folder Address To**   This option enables you to add the selected folder to your Personal Address Book by clicking the Personal Address Book button. While you can add any folder type to the Personal Address Book, posting an e-mail message to a folder other than a mail folder doesn't make much sense. Therefore, you'll probably only use this option for public folders that contain mail items.

- **This Folder Is Available To**   You can use this option to block access to the folder by everyone except those with owner permissions. Although you can do the same thing by resetting default and individual permissions, this gives you a means of shutting off access quickly and temporarily. It comes in handy when you're performing basic maintenance on the folder, such as editing the folder design. All posts to the folder are bounced back to the sender(s) until you change the option.

- **Folder Assistant**   Click this button to display the Folder Assistant dialog box, which lets you establish rules for handling items posted to the folder. You can create rules to return posted items to senders, automatically delete the items, forward them, or even respond to them with automatic replies. The rule criteria include From, Sent To, Subject, Message Body, Attachments, Size, Received Date, Importance, and Sensitivity.

THE MICROSOFT
EXCHANGE SERVER
ADVANTAGE

- **Moderated Folder** If you use a public folder as a forum for a particular subject, you may want to control the messages that are posted to the folder. To ensure that only those messages that are truly on topic get posted, you can designate the folder a moderated folder and have all messages sent to a moderator who reviews the messages before posting them. Click the Moderated Folder button to open the Moderated Folder dialog box, which contains options for enabling the moderated folder option and assigning moderators. You can even choose to generate an automatic response to new items received by the moderator.

- **Folder Path** This field, which indicates the location of the folder on the server, is informational only.

When you're finished setting Administration options, click OK to save the changes and return to the active Outlook window.

Setting Favorite Options

The Favorite tab, which is found only in the Properties dialog boxes of public folders located in the Public Folders\Favorites folder, lets you automate the process of adding copies of newly created subfolders to the Public Folders\Favorites folder. As you can see in Figure 16-5, the Favorite tab contains only a single option.

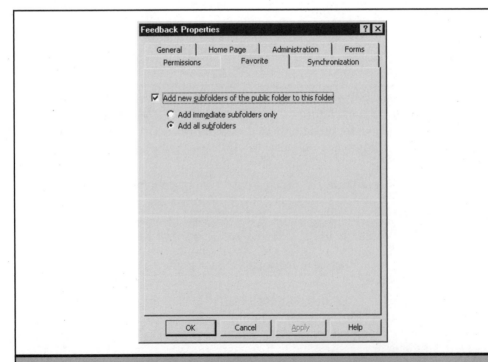

Figure 16-5.   *Adding copies of subfolders to the Public Folders\Favorites folder couldn't be any simpler*

If you want new subfolders of the selected folder to be automatically copied to the Public Folders\Favorites folder, check the Add New Subfolders Of The Public Folder To This Folder option. Although you have two choices for this option, they are meaningless. No matter which you select, the results are the same. Subfolders are added as long as you check the Add New Subfolders Of The Public Folder To This Folder option.

Using Public Folders

Using public folders isn't all that different from using private folders. For all folders except mail folders, select the folder in the Folder List and press CTRL-N to open a new form of the type appropriate for the selected folder. Fill out the form, and click Save And Close to save the new item in the selected folder. If you're in a public mail folder, pressing CTRL-N simply opens a standard e-mail message form. Sending an e-mail message from a public folder does nothing more than send the message to the recipient. Nothing is retained or stored in the public folder.

The most common use of public mail folders is for the purpose of posting messages related to a common topic, much like an Internet newsgroup. Posting simply adds the message to the folder. To post a message, open the public mail folder and press CTRL-SHIFT-S. A blank default post form appears. This is the form designated as the default form on the General tab of the folder's Properties dialog box. To use the standard post form shown in Figure 16-6, fill in the Subject line, type your message, and click Post to save it to the folder.

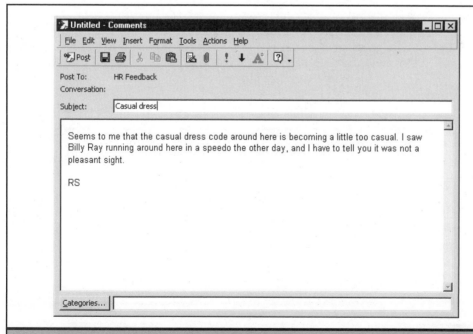

Figure 16-6.   *The standard posting form is a convenient way to post your message*

If the folder is unmoderated and you have permissions that allow you to both read and create items, you'll see your posted item almost immediately. If the folder is moderated, you may receive a reply informing you that each item must first be reviewed. Your post won't appear in the folder until after the moderator reviews and approves your message.

In addition to using CTRL-SHIFT-S, you can also click the New button on the Standard toolbar to open a blank post form. If the folder has custom forms attached to it, you can also post by opening the Actions menu and selecting one of the forms that appear at the bottom of the menu.

To read a message posted to a public folder, open the folder and double-click the message. As with a regular message, you have several options for dealing with a post. The Standard toolbar on the post form contains buttons that enable you to reply to or forward the post.

To post a response to the message, click the Post Reply button to open a reply form identical to the original post form. Enter a subject and include your response. Click Post to post it to the public folder. If you want to respond directly to the poster of the message, click the Reply button. This opens a standard e-mail message form with the poster's address entered in the To field, and RE added to the Subject line. Add your response and send the message. You can also forward a posted message to others. Click the Forward button, enter the recipient(s), type a message if you wish, and send it on its way. Forwards and direct replies to senders have no effect on the posted messages or the public folder.

Users with the proper permissions can also delete posted items from a public folder. Right-click the item and select Delete from the shortcut menu. You can also select the posted item(s) and press DELETE or click the Delete button on the Standard toolbar. You'll notice when you delete a posted item that the confirmation dialog box indicates the deletion is permanent. Posted items that are deleted are not transferred to the Deleted Items folder as are other deleted items.

  The Tools menu contains a Recover Deleted Items command, but unfortunately, due to a bug in the program, the command doesn't work. Therefore, you cannot recover posted items you delete. Once you click Yes when asked if you're sure, they're gone for good.

Using Net Folders

As handy as public folders are, they have one major limitation: they're restricted to users on the Exchange server network. If you want to share a folder with another Outlook user across the local area network or the Internet, you're out of luck—unless, that is, you have the Net Folders add-in installed. Net folders let you share personal folders with users on the local area network and over the Internet.

To use Net folders, you must have personal folders added to your profile. If you haven't already added them, see Chapter 17 for details on adding personal folders. In addition, you must have the Net Folders add-in installed. Although the Add-In Manager (Tools | Options | Other | Advanced Options | Add-In Manager) indicates that the Net folders component is installed, it isn't. By default, the add-in is set to be installed on first use, which means that the first time you attempt to use Net folders, Outlook will ask if you want to install the add-in. Have your original CD handy, and follow the onscreen instructions.

Understanding Net Folders

Net folders are personal folders shared between users who can exchange e-mail with one another. To begin with, one user creates a master folder and offers access to others by sending them invitations to the newly created Net folder. If the users who receive the invitations accept the offer and subscribe, the master folder is then duplicated on their systems. Any changes made to the folder by users with the proper permissions are automatically updated on all subscribers' systems using hidden e-mail messages.

Net folders, while relatively easy to use, have a number of quirks that can drive you crazy if you're unaware of them. To ensure you can use Net folders and retain your sanity at the same time, take heed of the following issues:

- Everyone using Net folders must be running Outlook 2000 or Outlook 98.

- Non-Outlook users can subscribe, but will only receive e-mail messages in their inboxes. No folder will be created, and no Outlook items other than e-mail messages will be useable by the non-Outlook subscriber.

- All e-mail messages must be composed and sent in Rich Text Format (RTF).

- If you change your default delivery location, Net folders no longer update. You must re-share all Net folders. This is a bug. Outlook fails to transfer the hidden folder used to process Net folders. Re-sharing the Net folders recreates the hidden folder in the new delivery location.

- Opening another user's shared Calendar in Day/Week/Month view displays your TaskPad even though you have permissions to the user's Tasks folder as well. That's just the way it is. You'll have to open the shared Tasks folder to see the user's tasks.

After you've familiarized yourself with the manner in which Net folders function, you can start creating them and sharing your information with others.

Creating Net Folders

To make creating Net folders as easy as possible, Outlook provides the Net Folder Wizard. To launch the wizard, open the Folder List and select the personal folder you want to share. Then choose File | Share | This Folder to start the Net Folder Wizard. The opening screen is informational only, so you can scan it and move on. Click Next to proceed to the Member List screen, shown in Figure 16-7.

Click the Add button to open the Add Entries To Subscriber Database dialog box, which looks suspiciously like the Select Names dialog box used to address e-mail messages. From the Show Names From The drop-down list, select the address book to use. Then choose the user(s) to add to the subscriber database. Click OK to add the users and return to the Member List screen. As you can see in Figure 16-7, each user added to the Member List automatically receives Reviewer permissions. To change the permissions, select the member and click the Permissions button to display the Net Folder Sharing Permissions dialog box.

Figure 16-7.   *The Net Folder Wizard takes the work out of setting up Net folders*

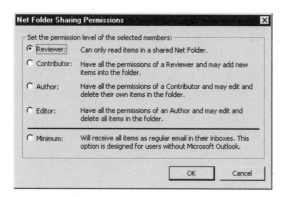

The available permissions are self-explanatory. Choose the appropriate permission level for the selected member.

You can assign the same permission level to multiple members by selecting the members before clicking the Permissions button.

If you add a user by mistake and want to remove him or her, simply select the user and click the Remove button. After you've added all the members and assigned the appropriate permission levels, click Next to proceed to the description screen. Enter a brief description of the folder and click Finish (clicking Next takes you to an informational screen informing you that you're finished). Outlook immediately starts updating the subscriber list and sending invitations.

Subscribing to Net Folders

When you're on the receiving end of a Net folder invitation, you'll get an e-mail message similar to the one shown in Figure 16-8.

As you can see in Figure 16-8, the Net folder invitation provides details on the owner, the folder name, what to do if the Accept button doesn't appear on the invitation, and more. The invitation explains how Net folders work and what happens if the recipient accepts the invitation. It also indicates the permission level assigned to the recipient, as well as descriptions of all permission levels and what rights each level grants.

If you receive such an invitation, click Accept to subscribe to the Net folder and add it to your Folder List. If you want to specify the location and name for the Net folder, click the Local Folder Name button to display the Select A Folder dialog box. Select the folder you want to use or click New to create a new folder. Click OK to return to the invitation. Click Accept to subscribe to the Net folder. Within a short time, the Net folder appears on your Folder List in the location you specified.

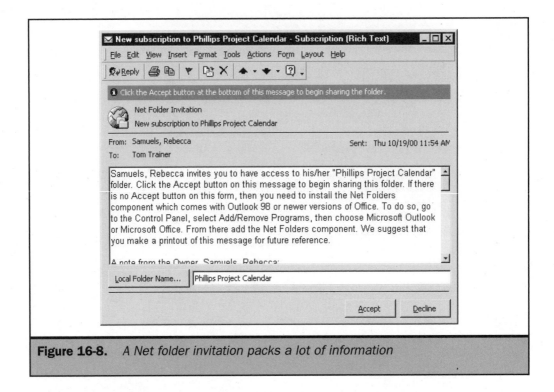

Figure 16-8.   *A Net folder invitation packs a lot of information*

If you don't want to subscribe to the Net folder, click the Decline button. You're asked to confirm your decision to not subscribe. Click OK to decline the invitation. Nothing else is needed.

Setting Net Folder Properties

Net folders, like other Outlook folders, have a number of options the owner can set. With the exception of sharing options, the Net folder properties are identical to those of personal folders. See Chapter 18 for more information on setting personal folder options.

To set the sharing options, right-click the Net folder and select Properties from the shortcut menu. Next, click the Sharing tab to display the sharing options, shown in Figure 16-9.

As you can see in Figure 16-9, the Sharing tab contains a variety of options, including the following:

■ **Net folder description**   Enter a clear and concise description of the folder contents. The better your description, the less confusion for invitees and subscribers.

Figure 16-9. *The Sharing options enable the owner to customize the update and journaling settings*

■ **Updates will be sent out every**   This option lets you decide how often to send automatic updates to subscribers.

■ **Verify contents of member folders**   Use this option to make sure all subscribers are receiving updates. When enabled, it compares the owner's file with all subscriber versions to ensure they match. If you're confident that the mail delivery systems used by all subscribers are totally reliable, you can select Never to eliminate verification altogether. If, however, you want to be on the safe side, select At Least Every and enter the desired time interval between verifications.

■ **Update size cannot exceed**   If you want to minimize the amount of space and time utilized by updates, you can limit their size. You may want to designate a size limit if you find that subscribers are including a lot of items with large attachments in the folder.

■ **Journal events for this folder**   You can track all changes made to the Net folder by checking this option. All activities in the folder are recorded in your Journal folder.

■ **Send Updates Now**   If you want to get important updates out to all subscribers without waiting for the automatic update, click the Send Updates Now button. Any changes you've made to the folder since the last update are sent immediately.

■ **Stop Sharing This Folder**   If you want to cancel the membership of all subscribers and convert the Net folder to a personal folder, click the Stop Sharing This Folder button. An informational dialog box appears, informing you that this action will unsubscribe all members. In addition, e-mail messages are sent to all subscribers, informing them that they will no longer receive updates. Click Yes to complete the action.

When you're finished setting the Net folder's sharing options, click OK to save the new settings and return to the active Outlook window.

If you're a subscriber, you'll also find some sharing options on the Sharing tab of the Net folder's Properties dialog box. However, a subscriber's options are limited to setting the time interval and size of updates, sending updates immediately with the Send Updates Now button, and unsubscribing by clicking the Cancel Membership button.

The
Complete
Reference

Outlook 2000

Chapter 17

Working Offline or on the Road

The advantages of using the C/W configuration of Outlook while being connected to an Exchange server are numerous. The ability to send and receive mail, share folders and files, and have access to public folders are just a few of the benefits. However, what happens when you can't connect to the Exchange server? Suppose you take a business trip or just want to work at home. And there's always the possibility that the Exchange server will be down and you won't be able to log on. Fortunately, there are ways to have your cake and eat it too when you use the C/W configuration of Outlook with Microsoft Exchange Server. Outlook provides two features that enable you to continue working even when you're not directly connected to the Exchange server. They are offline folders and Remote Mail.

Offline folders permit you to maintain exact duplicates of your mailbox folders on your hard disk. Unlike personal folders, offline folders are bi-directional. In other words, when you update offline folders, information is replicated in both sets of folders to ensure that offline folders and mailbox folders are the same. All you have to do is dial in to the Exchange server and synchronize your offline folders with your mailbox folders. Any changes that have been made to your mailbox folder, such as newly arrived e-mail and changes made by a delegate, are downloaded to your offline folders. At the same time, any changes you've made to the offline folders are uploaded to the mailbox on the server.

Remote mail, on the other hand, lets you dial in to the Exchange server (or Internet e-mail account) and send and retrieve e-mail while on the road. Remote mail has the added advantage of letting you download message headers only, thereby permitting you to pick and choose the messages you want to retrieve.

Using either of these features enables you to continue to reap the benefits of the Microsoft Exchange Server even when you're not able to maintain a constant connection.

Using Offline Folders

Offline folders are the key to working when a connection to the Exchange server is unavailable. Offline folders are, as stated earlier, exact replicas of mailbox folders, whose identicalness is maintained by performing periodic synchronizations with the server-based mailbox folders.

When you enable offline folders, a special offline folder file with an .ost extension is created. By default, all the primary folders (Calendar, Contacts, Deleted Items, Drafts, Inbox, Journal, Notes, Outbox, Sent Items, and Tasks) in your mailbox are included. You cannot selectively choose which primary folders to include as offline folders. It's all or nothing. You can, however, select individual custom folders you create, as well as public folders for which you have permissions.

The size of your offline folder file reflects the combined size of your primary mailbox folders and any other folders you choose to include. Offline folders, like personal folders, have a size limit. As a matter of fact, both have the same size limitations, which are actually quite generous. An offline folder file (.ost) can contain a maximum of 16,384 folders, each of which can contain a maximum of 16,384 items. In addition, the total size of the file cannot exceed two gigabytes (2GB). However, unlike personal folders, there is no option to increase the number of items a folder can hold.

Enabling Offline Folders

Before you can use offline folders, you must first set them up. To configure offline folders, choose Tools | Synchronize | Offline Folder Settings. If offline folders have not yet been enabled, a dialog box appears informing you of the fact and asking if you want to configure them now. Click Yes and the Offline Folder File Settings dialog box shown in Figure 17-1 opens.

The first thing to do is change the name of the .ost file. By default, the offline folder file is named outlook.ost. If you have more than one profile, or if you share the computer with other users, you'll end up with a series of .ost files named outlook.ost, outlook1.ost, outlook2.ost, and so on. To avoid confusion, give the file a more easily identifiable name. Make life simple and use your profile name (rsamuels.ost, or rebeccas.ost).

The next and last thing to do at this stage is select the encryption setting. Your choices include:

- **No Encryption**   Select this and the file is saved without encryption. The file size and compression ratio are almost identical to a compressible encryption file.

Figure 17-1.   *Setting up offline folders is easy: name your offline folder file and select an encryption type*

THE MICROSOFT
EXCHANGE SERVER
ADVANTAGE

■ **Compressible Encryption**   This is the default setting, which provides a certain amount of security while also offering the ability to significantly reduce the size of the file using file compression software such as WinZip. In a quick test, a 5622KB .ost file was reduced to 1132KB using WinZip 8.0.

■ **Best Encryption**   If security is your first concern, select this setting. It provides a higher degree of encryption. The price you pay is a less compressible file. Using WinZip 8.0 to compress a 5648KB file resulted in a zipped file of 4075KB.

■ **Compact Now**   This option is not available until after you've enabled offline folders and created the .ost file. When you return to the Offline Folder File Settings dialog box you can use this button to compress your offline folder file manually. Although the file is compressed as you work, this button comes in handy by letting you compact the file immediately after deleting a large number of items.

■ **Disable Offline Use**   Like the previous option, this one is only available after offline folders have been enabled. You can use it to entirely disable offline folders, or you can use it to change the folder name or the encryption settings. When you click this button, Outlook warns you that you won't be able to work offline. If you click Yes, offline folders are disabled.

When you're done, click OK to create the new file. A dialog box appears, asking if you want to create the file. Answer affirmatively, and Outlook creates the file and opens the Offline Folder Settings dialog box.

Setting the All Folders Options

As you can see in Figure 17-2, the Offline Folder Settings dialog box contains two tabs, All Folders and Quick Synchronization.

From the folders tree view on the All Folders tab, select the non-default folders you want included in offline folders. The primary Outlook folders are automatically included and cannot be excluded. Any attempt to deselect a primary folder results in a message informing you that you cannot deselect default folders. If you have custom folders that you want included, you must check each one to make sure it's included in the offline folder file. You can even add filters to individual folders. Select the folder and click the Filter Selected Folder button to display the Filter dialog box. See Chapter 22 for more information on creating filters.

The All Folders tab also contains a number of options you can use to extend the usefulness of offline folders. The All Folders options include the following:

■ **Download offline address book**   If you want to keep a copy of the offline address book in your offline folders, check this option. By default, the Exchange server uses the entire Global Address List (GAL) as the offline address book. However, starting with Microsoft Exchange Server 5.5, administrators were given the ability to create subsets of the Global Address List to use as offline address

Figure 17-2.   *You decide which non-default folders are available offline*

books. This can be a great help, especially to mobile users who have neither the need nor the space for the entire Global Address List.

- **Settings**   Click the Settings button to display the Offline Address Book dialog box. Here you'll find the following options for customizing the offline address book:

  - **Download changes since last synchronization**   Unless there have been a large number of deletions in the offline address book, you'll probably want to leave this setting enabled. When it's checked, only new and changed entries are downloaded during a synchronization. Since downloading an entire Global Address List can be quite time consuming, it's best to do so only when absolutely necessary.

  - **Information to download**   Decide how much information you want to download. You'll probably want to select Full Details, unless a lot of detailed information is maintained in the Global Address List, in which case downloading may take quite a while.

- **Choose address book**   If your administrator has created subsets of the Global Address List, they'll be listed here. Select the one you want to use. If the administrator has not created any subsets, or if the server is running Exchange 4.0 or 5.0, neither of which allows the creation of subsets, you'll have one choice only—the entire Global Address List.

- **Synchronize forms**   If you use custom forms with Outlook, check this option to include those forms in the offline folder file.

- **Synchronize folder home pages**   If you've assigned home pages to any of your folders you can include them in the offline folder file by checking this option.

- **Download Options**. Download options enable you to limit the size of messages that are included in the offline folder file. The option has two parts:

  - **Don't download messages larger than _ KB**   This option creates an Inbox subfolder called Large Messages, and adds a Large Message Rule to the Rules Wizard. This rule automatically moves messages larger than 50KB (or whatever size you indicate) to the Large Messages folder as soon as they arrive in your Inbox. Therefore, when you synchronize, the large messages are no longer in your Inbox and are not transferred. You could, of course, designate the Large Messages folder as an offline folder, but that would defeat the whole purpose. One last thing: you can modify the size rule anytime by opening the Rules Wizard and editing the Large Message Rule j ust as you would edit any other rule.

  - **Exceptions**   These options, which you can use to create exceptions to the size limit rule, are self-explanatory.

Note   *The download options do not apply to existing messages in your Inbox, only new messages that arrive after you create the offline folder file and set the options in the Download Options dialog box.*

Just for the record, there are a number of alternative methods to open the Offline Folder File Settings dialog box:

- Choose Tools | Services, double-click Microsoft Exchange Server, select the Advanced tab of the Microsoft Exchange Server dialog box, and click the Offline Folder File Settings button.

- Right-click Outlook Today and select Properties For "Mailbox – [your profile name]…", click the Advanced button on the Mailbox Properties dialog box, select the Advanced Tab of the Microsoft Exchange Server dialog box, and click the Offline Folder File Settings button.

- Right-click one of the primary Outlook folders, select Properties, click the Synchronization tab of the folder's Properties dialog box, set the This Folder Is Available option to When Offline Or Online. As soon as you click OK or

Apply, a dialog box appears informing you that you must first configure offline folders. Click Yes and the Offline Folder File Settings dialog box appears. If you don't get a message instructing you that you must first enable offline folders, it means they're already enabled and you can move on to setting synchronization options.

■ Open the Windows Control Panel, double-click the Mail (Mail and Fax) applet, double-click Microsoft Exchange Server, select the Advanced tab of the Microsoft Exchange Server dialog box, and click the Offline Folder File Settings button.

Configuring the Quick Synchronization Feature

The second tab in the Offline Folder Settings dialog box is the Quick Synchronization tab, which contains options for configuring the Quick Synchronization feature. This feature lets you create custom groups of folders for synchronization for those times when a full synchronization is unnecessary. This is especially useful for reducing the amount of time spent synchronizing, as well as the disk space taken up by the offline folder file. The groups you create here appear on the Tools | Synchronize submenu. By default, the Quick Synchronization tab shown in Figure 17-3 contains one custom group that includes the Mail and Calendar folders, since they are the most frequently used folders.

Figure 17-3. *Create folder groups for time-saving offline folder synchronizations*

THE MICROSOFT
EXCHANGE SERVER
ADVANTAGE

To create a new folder group, click the New button to display the Quick Synchronization Group dialog box.

Enter a name for the new group and click OK to create the group. The next item of business is to add folders to the group. Click the Choose Folders button to open the Choose Folders dialog box. Check the folders you want to include in the new group and click OK to return to the Quick Synchronization tab. That's all there is to it.

You can modify an existing group by changing its name, selecting different folders, or deleting the group entirely. Select the group and click Rename to display the Quick Synchronization Group dialog box, in which you can change the group name. If you want to delete a group, select it and click the Remove button. Be advised, you get no warning. It is deleted immediately. If you change your mind, you'll have to recreate it from scratch.

In addition to creating and modifying groups, the Quick Synchronization tab also offers the opportunity to include the offline address book, forms, and folder home pages in the Quick Synchronization. If you want to include any of these items when you synchronize using any of the folder groups you create here, check the appropriate option on the Quick Synchronization tab. When you're through, click OK to save the changes and return to the active Outlook view.

Setting Connection Options

If you plan to work offline, you'll want to set the Connection Options to ensure that the choice to work offline or online is yours to make. By default, Outlook assumes you want to log on to the Exchange server. Therefore, if you want Outlook to give you the option to work online or offline, you'll have to modify the connection settings. To access the settings, choose Tools | Services to open the Services dialog box. Then double-click Microsoft Exchange Server to display the Microsoft Exchange Server dialog box, shown in Figure 17-4.

From the When Starting section on the General tab, select Manually Control Connection State. This makes additional connection settings available. Check the Choose The Connection Type When Starting option. With this option checked, each time you start the program, Outlook asks if you want to connect to the network or work offline. Once you check the Connection Type When Starting option, you can ignore the next one, Default Connection State. The selection you make in the Default Connection State determines how Outlook starts. However, it only applies if you

Figure 17-4. *The connection settings are the only options you can change on the General tab*

choose not to have Outlook prompt you for a connection type by checking the previous option. The first choice automatically connects you to the network when you start Outlook; the second choice starts Outlook offline. The last option, Seconds Until Server Connection Timeout, lets you determine how long Outlook should attempt to make a connection before alerting you that it is unable to connect.

Creating a Dial-Up Networking Connection

If you plan to work offline and synchronize from a remote location, you'll want to set up a dial-up networking connection through which you can log on to the Exchange server and synchronize your offline folders. You'll also need a dial-up networking connection if you plan to use Remote Mail, which is discussed later in this chapter.

To create a dial-up networking connection, choose Tools | Services, and double-click Microsoft Exchange Server to open the Microsoft Exchange Server dialog box. Then click the Dial-Up Networking tab to configure Outlook for dial-up networking. If you have an existing dial-up networking connection that you want to use, select it from the Dial Using The Following Connection drop-down list. If you don't have a dial-up networking connection, click New to launch the Make New Connection Wizard, which walks you through creating a new connection. Check with your network administrator for the correct phone number to use.

After you create the dial-up networking connection, select the desired logon option. When you dial in, you'll have to log on to the network before gaining access to the Exchange server. You can elect to log on manually or automatically, depending on which option you choose:

- **Display connection dialogs at logon**   If you select this option, each time you log on to the network using the dial-up networking connection, you'll have to enter your logon information.

- **Use the following settings at logon**   If you'd prefer to log on automatically, choose this option and enter your user name, password, and domain name. The only danger with using this option is that anyone else who has access to your computer will also be able to log on without having to know your user name or password. Ask your administrator for the domain name.

- **Do Not Dial, Use Existing Connection**   This final option disables the dial-up networking connection. Check it if you're already connected to the Exchange server using a different connection. You might use this option if you're working offline because the Exchange server is down. Outlook will then attempt to use your normal network connection to perform manual or automatic synchronizations. The first time you successfully synchronize, you'll be alerted to the fact that the Exchange server is back up.

Synchronizing Offline Folders

Synchronizing offline folders is the process of connecting to the Exchange server and making your mailbox folders and your offline folders exact replicas of one another. This is accomplished by copying any new items in either folder to the other. In addition, items deleted in one folder are deleted in the other. Finally, any modified items are copied from the folder with the most current version of the item, replacing the older version of the item in the other folder. For example, suppose you create a new contact on the server, delete an e-mail message on the server, and change the start time for an appointment in your offline folders. When you synchronize, the new contact is copied from the server to the offline folder file, the e-mail message is deleted in the offline folder, and the modified appointment is copied from the offline folder to the sever, where it replaces the original.

You can connect to the Exchange server either through your local area network (LAN) or through a dial-up networking connection. However, be advised that synchronizing offline folders over a dial-up networking connection may be much slower than connecting to the LAN. You may even experience timeouts. If that's the case, you might be better off using Remote Mail to download your e-mail messages, and wait until you can connect to the Exchange server through the LAN before synchronizing.

One more thing: when you first enable offline folders, a synchronization is automatically performed as you exit Outlook regardless of whether you set the option to synchronize when exiting. This ensures that you have a working set of offline folders to start with. Thereafter, all synchronizations are performed according to the options you set (or don't set). You can choose to have Outlook perform automatic synchronizations, or you can manually synchronize when you're in the mood.

Whichever method you choose, Outlook creates a synchronization log in an e-mail message and sticks it in your Deleted Items folder. The log idea is great, but the Deleted Items folder seems like a strange place to put it. Who thinks to go looking in the Deleted Items folder for something new? Not only that, quite a few folks clean out the Deleted Items folder without even giving it a second glance. At any rate, the log is there. If you run into any synchronization problems, check the log for the error code(s). Armed with the error code(s), you can contact your administrator for a solution.

Using Automatic Synchronization

The Mail Services tab of the Options dialog box (Tools | Options) seen in Figure 17-5 contains one option to enable (or disable) offline folders, as well as several options to automate the synchronization process.

Figure 17-5.   *You can automate synchronization whether you're online or offline*

THE MICROSOFT EXCHANGE SERVER ADVANTAGE

You'll find the following offline folder related options on the Mail Services tab:

- **Enable offline access**   This aptly named option turns on offline folder access and makes the synchronization options available. Deselecting this option turns off all synchronization options and makes the offline folders unavailable when you're offline. As soon as you configure offline folders, this option is automatically checked.

- **When online, synchronize all folders upon exiting**   With this option checked, Outlook automatically synchronizes all folders (selected in the Offline Folders Settings dialog box) each time you exit Outlook.

- **When online, automatically synchronize all offline folders every _ minutes**   If you want to continuously update your offline folders while you're working online, check this option and enter the number of minutes between synchronizations. This comes in handy if your server is experiencing problems and going down frequently. If you get bounced off the network, you can keep working offline with up-to-date information.

- **When offline, automatically synchronize _ every _ minutes**   If you get a lot of e-mail or share your folders with others who make frequent changes, you may want to check this option, select a folder group, and enter a time interval for the automatic synchronization. It ensures that you always have the most up-to-date information while you're working offline. Outlook automatically connects to the server using the designated dial-up networking connection at the specified time interval and automatically synchronizes the selected folder group

- **Offline Folder Settings**   Click this button to open the Offline Folder Settings dialog box. See the "Enabling Offline Folders" section earlier in this chapter for details on configuring Offline Folder Settings options.

When you're finished configuring the synchronization options, click OK to save your changes and return to the active Outlook view.

Synchronizing Manually

If you're one of those folks who still prefers a standard transmission over an automatic so you have complete control over your car, you may prefer manual synchronization of your offline folders as well. Synchronizing manually gives you the option to synchronize all offline folders, a single folder, or a folder group. In addition, you can synchronize any time you get the urge.

To synchronize manually, choose Tools | Synchronize to display the submenu of synchronization options, shown next.

```
 1 Mail and Calendar

 All Folders            F9
 This Folder

 Offline Folder Settings...

 Download Address Book...
```

By default the submenu contains a single folder group, Mail and Calendar. However, if you create other groups, they are added to the submenu as well. Clicking a folder group synchronizes only those folders included in the group. In addition to the folder group(s), the submenu contains the following commands:

- **All Folders**   Use this command to synchronize all folders designated as offline folders in the Offline Folder Settings dialog box. You'll also note that the command has a shortcut key assigned to it. By pressing F9 you can dispense with the menu, and perform a manual synchronization of all folders from anywhere in Outlook.

- **This Folder**   To synchronize the currently open folder, use this command. If the folder you're in is not designated as an offline folder, this command is grayed out.

- **Offline Folder Settings**   After offline folders have been enabled and configured, this command opens the Offline Folder Settings dialog box. See "Enabling Offline Folders" earlier in this chapter for more information on setting options in the Offline Folder Settings dialog box. If you haven't yet configured offline folders, this command takes you to the Offline Folder File Settings dialog box, in which you can set up offline folders.

- **Download Address Book**   This command opens the Offline Address Book dialog box, which provides options for downloading the offline address book. See "Setting the All Folders Options" earlier in this chapter for details.

Note   *If you're connected to the Exchange server, synchronization takes place as soon as you click the desired command. However, if you're working offline, Outlook must first connect to the Exchange server using the dial-up networking connection selected in the Dial-Up Networking tab of the Microsoft Exchange Server. Once the connection is established, synchronization proceeds.*

As you can see, manual synchronization involves nothing more than selecting the appropriate command and letting Outlook do the rest. As the synchronization is occurring, you'll see its progress being reported in the Outlook window status bar.

THE MICROSOFT
EXCHANGE SERVER
ADVANTAGE

Using Remote Mail

Before going any further, it's important to note that while Remote Mail has some advantages for mobile users, it also has a number of drawbacks. Therefore, when considering whether to use Remote Mail it's best to take a look at the whole picture before deciding.

Its advantages are easy to spot. You can send and receive your server-based e-mail while on the road, and by downloading only headers, you can decide which messages you want to retrieve. This can save time and money when using a dial-up networking connection. Unfortunately, the flip side of the coin is not so attractive. The two main disadvantages are:

- **Default delivery to personal folders** You must have a personal folders information service added to your profile and designated as your default delivery location. Unless you always download headers and elect to retrieve copies only, the entire contents of your Inbox are transferred from the server to your personal folders. This means you'll have to transfer them back to the server when you return to your normal Exchange server connection. It also means that if you try organizing them by placing them in subfolders you'll have to transfer the contents of each of those subfolders.

- **Remote Mail filters** These filters are so poorly designed as to be more of a detriment than a help. They do not work when you send and receive all messages or when you download headers. They only work after you download the headers, mark the messages for retrieval, and download. The filters then apply to all the marked messages. However, if the messages you marked don't match the filter criteria, you're out of luck. The filter overrides your selection. By forcing you to mark the messages first, Remote Mail is, in effect, making you do your own manual filtering, and then ignoring your choices by applying the automatic filter. The time for these filters to work is when you send and receive all messages, not after you've decided which messages you want to retrieve.

Note   *Remote Mail filters only work on your Exchange server mailbox, not on Internet e-mail accounts you access with the Remote Mail feature.*

If you're going to use Remote Mail, your best bet is to set up a separate Outlook profile. Add personal folders to it and designate them as the default delivery location. Use this profile while you're on the road, and use your regular profile when you return to your normal Exchange server connection. You'll still have to transfer the Inbox contents (unless you always retrieve copies only), but at least you won't have to keep switching delivery locations.

The other thing you may want to do is ignore the Remote Mail filters and set up rules on your server-based mailbox instead. Have those rules channel into your Inbox only the mail you normally want while on the road. When you use Remote Mail on the road and retrieve your messages, the filters will already have been applied back at the server. In the event you decide you want to get those messages that have been filtered out, you can reconnect using your regular profile and perform a synchronization that includes the mail folders in which the filtered messages are stored.

To use Remote Mail, you need to create a dial-up networking connection and then set the Remote Mail options. For information on setting up a dial-up networking connection, see "Creating a Dial-Up Networking Connection" earlier in this chapter.

Configuring Remote Mail

If you plan to use Remote Mail, you must have a personal folders service added to your profile. See the section entitled "Using Personal Folders" later in this chapter for information on configuring personal folders. In addition, you must designate personal folders as the default delivery location (Tools | Services | Delivery).

Once you've added personal folders and set the delivery location, choose Tools | Services, and double-click Microsoft Exchange Server to open the Microsoft Exchange Server dialog box. Click the Remote Mail tab to display the Remote Mail configuration options, shown in Figure 17-6.

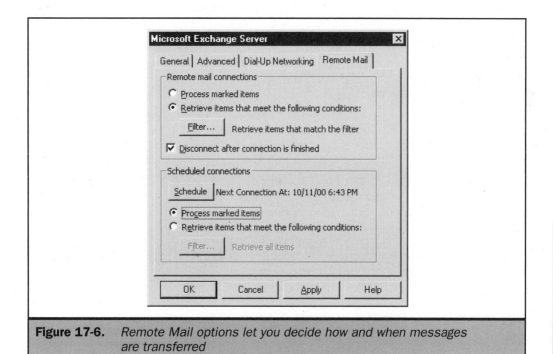

Figure 17-6.   *Remote Mail options let you decide how and when messages are transferred*

As you can see in Figure 17-6, you have a variety of options that let you customize the manner in which Remote Mail transfers e-mail messages. If you look closely, however, you'll see that there are only two sets of options, both of which contain similar choices.

- **Remote mail connections** The options in this section apply when you manually send and receive Remote Mail:

  - **Process marked items** Choose this option if you plan to manually select individual e-mail messages for download.

  - **Retrieve items that meet the following conditions** If you want to automate the process by creating a filter that determines which messages are downloaded, choose this option.

  - **Filter** The Filter button only becomes available when you select the previous option. Click the button to display the Filter dialog box. Since it only applies to messages, it is less sophisticated than the Filter dialog box used to customize Outlook views. However, it still provides a variety of filtering criteria. If the simple options in the Filter dialog box aren't sufficient, click the Advanced button for more options. Be advised that the filter applies only to those messages whose headers you download first and then mark for retrieval. The filter overrides any selections you make in marking headers. Remote Mail filters do not apply when you use the Send and Receive commands.

  - **Disconnect after connection is finished** To reduce the risk of keeping the connection open after you finish downloading your messages, you can check this option and Outlook will automatically close the connection after Remote Mail is finished.

- **Scheduled connections** The options in the Scheduled Connections section enable you to automate Remote Mail by setting a schedule for an automatic connection. Clicking the Schedule button displays the Schedule Remote Mail Connection dialog box, which lets you set a schedule based on a precise time of day, a time interval, or both. Note, however, that the earliest time takes precedence. For example, suppose you check the At option and set the time to 12:15 P.M., and then check the Every option and indicate you want a scheduled connection every hour. If you set these options at 9:00 A.M., the first connection will occur at 10:00 A.M., not 12:15 P.M. As soon as you set a scheduled connection, the remaining options become available. The Process Marked Items, Retrieve Items That Meet The Following Conditions, and Filter options are identical to those in the Remote Mail Connections section.

When you're finished setting the Remote Mail options, click OK until you return to the active Outlook window. You're now ready to begin using Remote Mail to send and receive e-mail.

Sending and Receiving E-mail

When it comes to retrieving your e-mail using Remote Mail, you have several options, all of which appear on the Tools menu. Although only one is called Remote Mail, there are a couple of others you can use as well. However, depending on where you are when you access the Tools menu you may see some, all, or none of the Send and Receive commands. To be on the safe side, open the Inbox folder, from which all Send and Receive commands are available. Here's what you'll find on the Tools menu:

- **Send**   Use this command to send outgoing e-mail without retrieving any incoming messages. Unfortunately, it sometimes seems not to know the difference between sending and receiving when connecting to the Exchange server, and retrieves as well.

- **Send/Receive**   Clicking this command displays a submenu with additional choices. The standard menu items are All Accounts, Microsoft Exchange Server, and Free/Busy Information. If you have Internet e-mail accounts added to your profile, they appear as menu items as well. Select the appropriate item and everything is sent and retrieved.

- **Remote Mail**   Clicking the Remote Mail command displays a submenu with a number of Remote Mail commands.

    - **Connect**   This launches the Remote Connection Wizard that lets you choose the e-mail service and the type of e-mail exchange you want to perform. You can send and receive all mail or just download the headers.

    - **Disconnect**   When you're through sending and receiving, you can use this command to manually break the connection.

    - **Mark to Retrieve**   After you download headers, select the messages you want to retrieve, and use this command to mark them for retrieval.

    - **Mark to Retrieve a Copy**   If you want to leave the original message on the server and only retrieve a copy, use this command. This is very handy for server-based e-mail. When you return to your normal Exchange server connection, you won't have to bother transferring everything from your personal folders Inbox to your server-based Inbox.

    - **Delete**   This command deletes the selected message or header. Deleting a header does not delete the original message on the server.

    - **Unmark**   Use this command to unmark selected messages that have been marked.

    - **Unmark All**   This command unmarks all marked messages regardless of whether or not they've been selected.

THE MICROSOFT
EXCHANGE SERVER
ADVANTAGE

■ **Remote Tools**   Click this command to display the Remote toolbar, which
contains all the same commands found on this menu, with the exception, of
course, of Remote Tools (even with advanced computer technology you still
can't lift yourself by your own bootstraps).

Since the Remote Connection Wizard is the "official" method for sending and
receiving Remote Mail, it deserves a closer look. Begin by choosing Tools | Remote
Mail | Connect to launch the wizard, shown in Figure 17-7.

Check the e-mail account(s) you want to work with remotely. If you have more
than one dialing location set up, check the Confirm Before Connecting option. Click
Next to move to screen two. As you can see in Figure 17-8, you can elect to send and
receive all e-mail, or you can download headers and selectively send messages
currently in your Outbox.

To send and retrieve all e-mail in the selected accounts, choose Retrieve And Send
All New Mail. If you want to selectively send outgoing messages and download
incoming headers, choose Do Only The Following and make the appropriate selections
from the list. One thing to note: no matter what else you select, you must download
headers. In other words, you cannot choose to send some or all outgoing messages, and
not download headers. If you checked the Confirm Before Connecting option on the
opening screen, you can click Next to select the dialing location. Otherwise click Finish
to complete the e-mail exchange.

After Remote Mail is finished, return to the Inbox to read your messages or review
the downloaded headers. If you downloaded headers, select the ones you want to

Figure 17-7.   *You can choose as many or as few e-mail accounts as you wish*

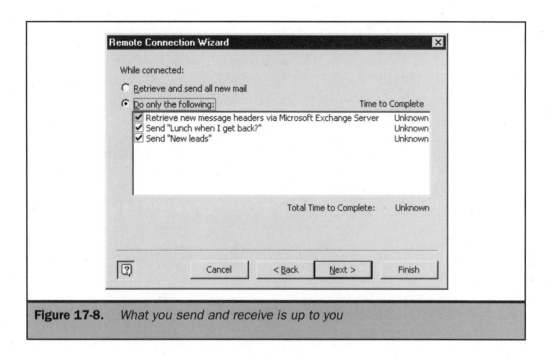

Figure 17-8.   *What you send and receive is up to you*

retrieve and click the Mark button or the Mark To Retrieve A Copy button on the Remote toolbar. You can also right-click messages and make your selection from the shortcut menu, or you can choose Tools | Remote Mail | Mark.

If you download headers from an Internet e-mail account, the attachment icon is missing from the headers of messages with attachments. One way to work around this limitation is to add the Size field to the Inbox Messages view. Since most messages are relatively small, the size of a message can be a good indicator of the presence (or absence) of an attachment. See Chapter 22 for more information on customizing views.

To retrieve the messages, return to the Remote Connection Wizard by choosing Tools | Remote Mail | Connect. Select the desired e-mail account(s), and choose Do Only The Following. All the messages you marked for download appear in the list. If you change your mind about any of them, you can deselect them in the list and they will not be downloaded. Click Finish to download those messages you've selected.

Using Personal Folders

If you read the previous section on Remote Mail, you already know that personal folders are necessary to take advantage of the Remote Mail feature. In addition to using personal folders for Remote Mail, you can also use them to store important Outlook items that you want to remove (or copy) from your server-based mailbox, but don't want to archive. If you have personal folders added to your profile, you can move and copy Outlook items between your mailbox and your personal folders with ease. Unlike archive folders, the personal folders are always available on your Folder List after you add them.

Adding Personal Folders

Adding personal folders is easy. They are considered an information service, and as such are added to your profile through the Services dialog box. Choose Tools | Services to open the Services dialog box (see Figure 17-9).

Click the Add button to open the Add Service To Profile dialog box.

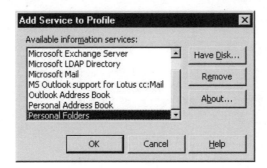

Select Personal Folders and click OK to display the Create/Open Personal Folders File dialog box. Enter a name for the file in the File Name field. Be sure to make it unique and easily identifiable. It's actually a good idea to give it the same name as your profile to avoid confusion. If you previously created a personal folder file, select it from the list or use the Look In drop-down list to locate it. Click Open to display the Create Microsoft Personal Folders dialog box, shown in Figure 17-10.

The text you enter in the Name field appears in the Outlook Folder List, as well as in the Services dialog box. The Encryption setting lets you decide just how much security you want applied to the file. For most users, Compressible Encryption is a good choice.

Adding a password is a good idea, especially if you share the computer with other users. Enter a password, then enter it a second time to make sure you haven't made any typos. You can check the Save This Password In Your Password List to save yourself the trouble of having to enter it each time you want to access the personal folders. However, this means that anyone who logs on using your profile will also have complete access to your personal folders.

Personal folders are similar to offline folders in that they have the same size limitations. Personal folders cannot exceed 2 gigabytes (GB) nor can they contain more than 16,384 folders, each of which is limited to no more than 16,384 items. However, unlike offline folders, personal folders can be modified to hold more items per folder. See the next section for more information.

Figure 17-9. *The Services dialog box displays all your existing services*

Figure 17-10. *Set up your personal folders to suit your needs*

Setting Personal Folder Options

To change personal folder properties, open the Services dialog box (Tools | Services) and double-click the Personal Folders information service on the Services tab to open the Personal Folders dialog box shown in Figure 17-11.

You'll find the following options in the Personal Folders dialog box:

- **Name** Once again, you have the opportunity to change the name of this set of personal folders.

- **Path** This field is informational only and cannot be changed. It displays the path to the .pst file for this set of personal folders.

- **Encryption** This field is also unchangeable, and here for informational purposes only. It displays the level of encryption selected when the file was created.

- **Change Password** If you want to change your password (which you should, on a regular basis), this is the place to do it.

- **Compact Now** Deleting Outlook items leaves a lot of empty space in a .pst file, but does not reduce the size of the file. Click the Compact Now button to recoup that empty space and shrink the size of the file.

Figure 17-11.   *Customizing personal folders is easy*

- **Allow upgrade to large tables** Checking this option increases the number of items an individual folder in the .pst file can hold, from 16,384 to 65,536.
- **Comment** Use this text field to add any miscellaneous information you want.

Once you've configured your personal folder options, you're ready to use them. You can create, copy, move, and delete items in personal folders just as you can in your mailbox folders. However, remember, personal folders information is stored locally on your hard disk, not on the server. Therefore, unless you've designated your personal folders as the default delivery location (Tools | Services | Delivery), you'll probably want to do all your work in your mailbox folders and use the personal folders for storing important information you want safe and available any time.

The Complete Reference

Part VI

Getting More Out of Outlook

The
Complete
Reference

Outlook
2000

Chapter 18

Organizing and Managing Folders

In case you hadn't noticed, everything in Outlook revolves around folders. Whether it's e-mail, scheduling, or contact management, each Outlook component is a folder. Folders are, in fact, nothing more than containers for holding related pieces of information. In addition to the information itself, Outlook folders contain two things: forms for entering information and views for displaying information. In this chapter, you'll learn to create, move, copy, delete, and modify folders.

Folders Overview

Each Outlook folder is unique in that it can hold only one type of Outlook item. For example, you cannot store appointment items in a mail folder or vice versa. When you create a folder, you must designate the type of item it will hold. Once you make that decision, you cannot change it.

When you attempt to move an item into a folder of a different type, the item you move is converted to the item type normally stored in the target folder. For instance, if you drop a task item in an e-mail folder, you end up with an e-mail message that includes the task information. Drop an e-mail message into a note folder and you end up with a new note that contains the e-mail message information.

The folder hierarchy begins with the Outlook Today folder, which is actually the mailbox itself. The level below the mailbox contains the primary folders: Calendar, Contacts, Deleted Items, Drafts, Inbox, Journal, Notes, Outbox, Sent Items, and Tasks. Personal and public folders, when added, are on a par with the mailbox.

Tip   *You can use the BACKSPACE key to move up through the folder hierarchy one level at a time. For example, if you're in one of the primary folders, pressing the BACKSPACE key takes you to Outlook Today.*

To view the existing folder hierarchy, open the Folder List by choosing View | Folder List. If the Advanced toolbar is displayed, you can click the Folder List button to display the Folder List (see Figure 18-1).

Tip   *You can also click the current folder name on the Folder banner. Use this option to toggle the Folder List on and off for a quick peek. It drops the list on top of the Information viewer and obscures whatever you're working on. To keep the Folder List permanently in view, click the yellow pushpin in the top right corner. This also incorporates the Folder List into the Information viewer so all the folder information is visible.*

As you can see in Figure 18-1, subfolders are indicated by a plus or minus sign to the left of the parent folder. A plus sign indicates the subfolders are currently collapsed; a minus sign indicates they are expanded.

Figure 18-1. *The Folder List provides a tree-like view of the Outlook folder hierarchy*

Working with Folders

The first order of business is to access the contents of the individual folders. Outlook provides a couple of different ways to do this. You can use the Outlook Bar or the Folder List to open an Outlook folder. By default, all primary Outlook folders are represented on the Outlook Bar by a shortcut. However, not all folder shortcuts are in the Outlook Shortcuts group. Some are located in the My Shortcuts group, which means you may have to open that group to access shortcuts to some primary Outlook folders. The Folder List, on the other hand, contains all existing folders. The only problem here is that you have to display the Folder List to use it. Take your pick: both the Outlook Bar and the Folder List work equally well. It's just a matter of preference. In addition to clicking the shortcut or folder name, you can right-click either and select Open. It hardly seems worth the extra trouble. What does make the extra effort worthwhile is right-clicking and selecting Open In New Window when you want to display a folder in a separate window.

Before moving on, it's important to note that for many folder operations outlined in the upcoming sections, you must either be the owner of the folder or have permissions that enable you to create, edit, or delete items as needed.

Creating Folders

When you begin using Outlook, you start with a framework of primary folders that take care of your basic e-mail and information management needs. As you utilize more and more features, you may find that the initial handful of folders just isn't enough to organize all your data.

The first place you'll probably encounter a need for new folders is in organizing your e-mail. Just as with your paper correspondence, you'll want to retain copies of important e-mail messages. And as with your hard copy correspondence, you'll find it much easier to track your e-mail messages if you file them with other related messages in separate, clearly labeled folders. When that time comes, simply create new folders for all the different categories of e-mail you save.

When you create new folders, save yourself time and aggravation by planning a logical hierarchy before you start. For example, if you're creating folders to hold e-mail, put them under the Inbox. If you're going to keep track of vendor e-mail, create a Vendor subfolder in the Inbox, then create a separate subfolder for each vendor.

While it would make sense to place new e-mail folders under the Inbox, there is no hard and fast rule that says you must. You can create new folders on the same level as the primary folders or under any existing folder you choose. You can even add subfolders that contain different items than the parent folder.

To create a new folder from anywhere within Outlook, press CTRL-SHIFT-E to display the Create New Folder dialog box, shown in Figure 18-2.

Enter a name for the new folder and select the item type from the Folder Contains drop-down list. Move to the Select Where To Place The Folder display list and choose the parent folder for the new folder. You can place the new folder on any level except the first level. Only the mailbox, personal folders, and public folders can reside on the top level. Click OK to create the new folder.

Here are a few other ways to create a new folder:

- Choose File | New | Folder from the Menu bar.
- Click the down arrow to the right of the New button on the Standard toolbar, and select Folder from the drop-down menu.
- Right-click the Folder banner of the current folder and select New Folder from the shortcut menu.
- Right-click a folder in the Folder List and select New Folder from the shortcut menu.

Figure 18-2.   *Creating new folders in Outlook is easy*

Tip   *If you happen to be a folder fanatic, you may want to add the Folder (or New Folder; they're the same) command to one of your toolbars or menus. Right-click a visible toolbar and select Customize to open the Customize dialog box. Click the Commands tab and select File in the Categories list. Now drag the Folder (or New Folder) command and drop it on the toolbar or menu of your choice. For more on customizing toolbars and menus, see Chapter 23.*

When you create a new folder, Outlook immediately asks if you want to add a shortcut for the new folder to the Outlook Bar.

Unless this is a folder you plan to use regularly, you probably don't need a shortcut for it. As a matter of fact, most new folders will probably not require a shortcut on the Outlook Bar. Therefore, you might want to check the Don't Prompt Me About This

Again option to avoid having to answer the question every time you create a new folder. Not only that, adding a shortcut is so easy, you can do it any time you want. Just open the Folder List, drag the folder to the Outlook Bar, and drop it between two existing folders. To remove a shortcut, right-click the shortcut and select Remove From Outlook Bar from the shortcut menu.

As soon as you create a new folder, it's added to the Folder List on the level you indicated when creating it. Outlook automatically sorts the Folder List alphabetically by folder name so the new folder appears accordingly. Unfortunately, you cannot set a different sort order nor can you sort the list manually.

MOUS EXAM PRACTICE
Creating a new folder is easy, but requires some planning and can be done using a variety of methods. Begin by planning a logical structure for a series of new folders. Then use the various methods to create each new folder. Try creating and removing Outlook shortcuts for the new folders.

Copying Existing Folders

You can also create a new folder by making a duplicate of an existing folder. This is an easy way to create a new folder that contains many of the same settings as an existing folder. The settings transferred depend to some extent on the folder type. For instance, contacts folders that are copied include general settings, home page settings, Outlook Address Book settings, activities settings, permissions settings, forms settings, and administration settings—actually, everything but the synchronization settings.

Note *Custom views are not transferred when a copy is made. If, however, a custom view was created to be used with all folders of the type you're now copying, the view will appear in the copied folder's Current Views list.*

The only potential problem associated with using the Copy command is that you also duplicate the contents of the source folder. In some cases, this may be an advantage rather than a problem. Suppose, for example, you want to split your Contacts folder into a business contacts folder and a personal contacts folder. Using the Copy command enables you to create two new folders with most of the settings of the original folder as well as all the contacts. You can then filter out the non-business contacts from the business folder and delete them, and your business contacts folder is ready. Do the same for your personal contacts folder and you're finished.

The quickest way to copy a folder is to open the Folder List and right-drag (hold down the right mouse button instead of the left when dragging) the folder to a new location. Drop it on the target folder and select Copy from the shortcut menu.

If you prefer to use a method other than drag and drop, you can use the Copy command. Start by displaying the Folder List. Next, right-click the folder you want to copy, and select Copy [folder name] from the shortcut menu to open the Copy Folder dialog box.

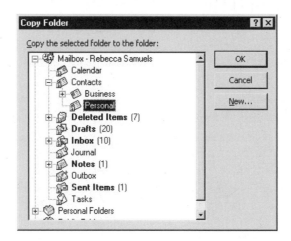

Note   *You can also copy a folder by clicking an Outlook Bar shortcut to open the desired source folder. Then choose File | Folders | Copy [folder name] from the Menu bar to display the Copy Folder dialog box.*

From the Copy The Selected Folder To The Folder display list, choose the folder under which you want the copy placed. The folder you select here becomes the parent folder of the copied folder. If you want to create a new parent folder, click the New button and follow the instructions for creating a new folder. When you've selected the parent folder for your copy, click OK to create the copy and return to the active view. At this point, you can adjust the folder's contents and settings as necessary.

Using the Copy Folder Design Command

The Copy Folder Design command is a hybrid command that does not create a new folder, but rather, replaces some design elements of an existing folder with those of a different existing folder. You can use the command in conjunction with the New Folder command to create a customized folder. Unlike the Copy command, Copy Folder Design does not transfer the same group of customized settings to the target folder.

Note   *To use the Copy Folder Design command, the Exchange Extensions Commands Add-in must be installed. To check or to install the Exchange Extensions Commands Add-in, choose Tools | Options | Other | Advanced Options | Add-In Manager.*

Begin by opening the Folder List and selecting your target folder. Next, choose File | Folder | Copy Folder Design to display the Copy Design From dialog box, shown in Figure 18-3.

Select the source folder from the Copy Design From This Folder list. As soon as you select a source folder, the Copy Design Of options become available. Check the appropriate option(s) from the following:

- **Permissions** Any permissions setting you've configured in the source folder will be duplicated in the Permissions tab of the target folder's Properties dialog box.

- **Rules** If the source and target folders are mail folders, any message handling rules in the source folder are applied to the target folder.

- **Description** The only thing transferred when this option is checked is the text entered in the Description field on the General tab of the source folder's Properties dialog box.

- **Forms & Views** Any custom forms and custom views associated with the source folder are transferred to the target folder.

Figure 18-3.   *You decide which properties to transfer to the new folder*

Tip

A bug in the original release of Outlook prevents three settings that should be transferred from actually being transferred. They include the When Posting To This Folder, Use option and the Automatically Generate Microsoft Exchange Views option, both of which are found on the General tab of the folder's Properties dialog box. The third option that fails to transfer is the Only Show Views Created For This Folder option, found in the Define Views For [folder name] dialog box (View | Current View | Define View). This bug was fixed in the initial Microsoft Office 2000 Service Release update. You can download or order the update from the Microsoft Web site (http://officeupdate.microsoft.com). Since quite a few problems were reported with the first release, SR-1, make sure you get SR-1a or later.

Regardless of whether you check the Description option, the text entered in the Description field located on the General tab of the source folder's Properties dialog box appears in the Description window at the bottom of the Copy Design From dialog box. This is informational only and cannot be edited from within the Copy Design From dialog box. Click OK to complete the process.

Because the new settings transferred by the Copy Folder Design command replace any existing settings in the target folder, Outlook alerts you to the fact and asks for confirmation. Click Yes to complete the folder design transfer, or click No to return to the active view and start over.

Moving Folders

Once you begin taking advantage of the folder system used by Outlook, you'll find there are times when you want to move a folder from one location to another. For example, suppose you have separate Inbox subfolders for two companies you do business with and they merge. You'll probably want to create a new folder for the newly formed company and add the existing folders to it as subfolders.

By far the easiest method of moving a folder is a simple drag-and-drop procedure. Grab the folder you want to move, and drop it on the folder to which you want it moved. That's all there is to it. One word of caution. Don't bother trying to move any of the primary Outlook folders (Calendar, Contacts, Deleted Items, Drafts, Inbox, Journal, Notes, Outbox, Sent Items, and Tasks). They cannot be moved under any circumstances.

Note

If you right-drag a folder and drop it on a new location, a shortcut menu appears offering you the opportunity to move or copy the folder.

If you're not a drag-and-drop fan, there is another way to accomplish the task of moving a folder. Open the Folder List and right-click the folder you want to move. From the shortcut menu, select Move [folder name] to open the Move Folder dialog box, shown next.

From the Move The Selected Folder To The Folder display list, choose the folder to which you want the selected folder moved. The folder you pick here becomes the parent folder of the folder you're moving. If you want to create a new folder into which to move the selected folder, click the New button and follow the instructions for creating a new folder. After you select the target folder, click OK to complete the move and return to the active view.

 You can also select the folder and choose File | Folder | Move [folder name] to open the Move Folder dialog box.

Regardless of which method you use to move the folder, nothing changes except the folder's location in the folder hierarchy. No contents, settings, or views are added or left behind. Everything is the same after the move as before the move.

Renaming Folders

Occasionally what seems like a good name for a folder turns out to be confusing or misleading and you find yourself wishing it had a different moniker. Fortunately, the solution for this dilemma is simple: rename the folder. Well, it's as simple as you choose to make it. Like most other tasks in Outlook, there are a couple of different ways to rename a folder.

The easiest method is to click the folder name in the Folder List and press F2 to turn on the edit mode for the folder name field. You can then edit the existing name or type a new name over the old name. To save the change, press the ENTER key when you're done. Right-clicking the folder name and selecting Rename [folder name] also turns the edit mode on. You could even highlight the folder name and choose Folder | Rename [folder name] from the Menu bar if you were so inclined.

Although you can also change the name of the shortcut in the Outlook Bar, don't confuse this with renaming the folder. The two procedures are distinct from one another. Changing the shortcut name has no effect on the folder name and vice versa.

If you insist upon using the most complicated method available, right-click the folder in the Folder List, select Properties from the shortcut menu, edit the name field on the General tab of the folder's Properties dialog box, and click OK to save the change. If you try any of these methods on the primary Outlook folders, you'll find they don't work. The reason is simple. You can't rename the primary folders.

Deleting Folders

When a folder outlives its usefulness, you can do a little housekeeping and remove it. Not only will this eliminate some unnecessary clutter in Outlook, it will also reduce your risk of exceeding any space limitations imposed by your administrator.

Deleting a folder is easy: select it in the Folder List and press DELETE. A confirmation dialog box appears asking if you really want to delete the folder, its contents, and any subfolders it may have hanging around. Unless you were just kidding when you hit the DELETE key, click Yes.

There are a number of other methods you can use to delete a folder:

- Select the folder in the Folder List, and click the Delete button on the Standard toolbar.

- Drag the folder to the Deleted Items shortcut on the Outlook Bar, or to the Deleted Items folder in the Folder List.

- Right-click a folder in the Folder List and select Delete [folder name] from the shortcut menu.

- Select the folder in the Folder List, and choose File | Folder | Delete [folder name].

 In most cases you'll be asked to confirm your decision to delete the folder. As long as you're sure about the decision, answer affirmatively.

Deleting a folder deletes the entire contents of the folder as well as any subfolders and their contents. Therefore, it would behoove you to not take this action lightly. Fortunately, even if you make a mistake or change your mind, you can save the deleted folder(s) from the clutches of oblivion by opening the Deleted Items folder and moving them back to their original location.

If you change your mind, but have already emptied the Deleted Items folder, don't despair. You may still be able to retrieve your deleted folders. Open the Deleted Items folder and choose Tools | Recover Deleted Items to open the Recover Deleted Items From dialog box. Select the folder(s) to recover and click the Recover Selected Items button. To permanently delete the items so they cannot be recovered using the Recover Deleted Items command, click the Purge Selected Items button.

Note *Your administrator determines the length of time deleted items remain on the server before being permanently deleted. Therefore, if the retention time has expired, the Recover Deleted Items command will not help. However, since any administrator worth his or her salt backs up the server regularly, you may still be able to recover your deleted folder(s) if you ask nicely (and infrequently).*

Archiving Folders

One of the advantages Outlook offers is the ease with which it enables you to store all your information. One of the disadvantages of Outlook is the ease with which it enables you to store all your information. Confused? Well, don't be. The problem is that most administrators limit the amount of space allocated to your mailbox. Chances are, you will eventually run up against that limit and have to do some serious housecleaning. Rather than waiting for that eventuality, you can take advantage of the Outlook archiving features to perform regular housekeeping chores on some or all of your folders.

The archiving feature, which uses rules you establish to move folder items into a special archive folder located on your local hard drive, comes in two flavors: automatic and manual. For a complete discussion of both methods, see the sections on archiving e-mail in Chapter 5.

Modifying Folder Properties

Folders are complex creatures and as such have quite a few settings you can apply to make them behave the way you want. These settings—also called properties—can be found in the folders' Properties dialog boxes. To access a folder's Properties dialog box, right-click the folder in the Folder List or the shortcut in the Outlook Bar, and select Properties from the shortcut menu.

With the exception of the contacts folders, the settings available in the folders' Properties dialog boxes are the same as those in the Current Customers Properties dialog box shown in Figure 18-4.

See Chapter 9 for a complete discussion of the Activities and Outlook Address Book tabs, which are available only in contacts folders' Properties dialog boxes.

Note *Personal folder and public folder Properties dialog boxes contain some, but not all of the tabs described in this section.*

Current Customers Properties

| Administration | Forms | Permissions | Synchronization |
| General | | Home Page | AutoArchive |

Customers

Type: Folder containing Mail Items
Location: Inbox
Description:

This folder contains email from our current customers. It does not contain email from previous customers, or from any potential customers with whom we are currently negotiating.

When posting to this folder, use: Post

☑ Automatically generate Microsoft Exchange views

Folder Size...

| OK | Cancel | Apply | Help |

Figure 18-4. *The folder's Properties dialog box enables you to customize a multitude of settings*

To open a folder's Properties dialog box, right-click the folder in the Folder List and select Properties from the shortcut menu. As you can see, the Current Customers Properties dialog box contains seven tabs, each of which contains related options. These options enable you to set everything from folder permissions to AutoArchive rules to the default form used to input data into the folder.

Setting General Options

The options on the General tab are fairly simple and uncomplicated. The tab contains five basic options that enable you to change the folder name, designate the default input form, and more. The options you'll find here include:

- **Folder name** Although there is no label for this field that says "Folder name," that is precisely what the first field at the top of the tab is. You can change the folder name of any folder you create, by editing or typing over the existing name. You cannot, however, change the folder name of any of the 11 (counting Outlook Today) primary Outlook folders.

- **Description** This field is a text box in which you can enter anything you want. If you create a series of subfolders with similar names, you might use this field to add some descriptive text that will help you easily identify each folder.

- **When posting to this folder, use** From this drop-down list, you can select a different form to use as the input form for the folder. If you leave the selection as is, Outlook automatically uses the default input form. The default forms are Post for mail folders, Appointment for calendar folders, Contact for contacts folders, Journal Entry for journal folders, and Note for notes folders. To use a custom form, select Forms from the drop-down list to open the Choose Form dialog box. There you can choose a form from either the Standard Forms Library or the Personal Forms Library. The custom forms must, of course, be compatible with the folder type.

- **Automatically generate Microsoft Exchange views** If you share folders with Microsoft Exchange users, you'll want to check this option to ensure that views you create for this folder are available to those users as well.

- **Folder Size** Click this button to display the Folder Size dialog box, which provides the folder name, the folder size, the combined size of the selected folder and its subfolders, and a listing of each subfolder and its size.

After you set the General tab options, you can click the Apply button to put the options into effect without having to close the Properties dialog box. If you're finished setting options, you can click the OK button to apply the changes and close the Properties dialog box at the same time.

Adding a Folder Home Page

An interesting feature unique to Outlook 2000 is the ability to assign a home page to each folder. You can designate any Web page on the Internet, your company's intranet, or even an HTML document on your network or local hard drive. Whether you want to check the company intranet or just like to peruse the latest stock prices before you get started each day, you can make sure the Web page of your choice displays when you open a folder.

Assigning a Web page as the home page for one of your folders is easy. Open the folder's Properties dialog box and click the Home Page tab to display the Home Page options, shown in Figure 18-5.

The fist thing you need to do is enter the URL or path of the Web page in the Address field. If you want to add an Internet address, type it in using the standard URL format: http://www.domainname (http://www.osborne.com). For a file on a local or network drive, use the file format: file:driveletter:\folder\filename (file:C:\My Documents\mydogsparky.htm). If you don't know the path, click the Browse button

Inbox Properties

Administration	Forms	Permissions	Synchronization
General		Home Page	AutoArchive

☐ Show home page by default for this folder

Address:

http://www.nytimes.com

Browse...

Restore Defaults

Outlook will download these pages for offline viewing and
check for updates whenever this folder is synchronized.

Offline Web Page Settings...

| OK | Cancel | Apply | Help |

Figure 18-5. *Enter a URL or select a Web page from a local or network drive*

to open the Find Web Files dialog box. It's identical to other Windows Find or Open dialog boxes. Locate the file you want by using the Look In drop-down list. Once you find the file, select it and click OK to add it to the Address field on the Home Page tab.

As soon as you enter a URL or path in the Address field, the Show Home Page By Default For This Folder option becomes available. If you check this option, the Web page you assign in the Address field displays automatically every time you open the folder. If you leave the option unchecked, the folder displays normally. You can then display the Web page by opening the folder and choosing View | Show Folder Home Page from the Menu bar.

The next button on the Home Page tab is the Restore Defaults button. If you decide that you no longer want a home page to display or you simply want to start from scratch, click the Restore Defaults button to wipe the Home Page options clean.

If you've enabled offline folders and set the This Folder Is Available option on the Synchronization tab to When Offline Or Online, you'll find one more option on your Home Page tab. It's the Offline Web Page Settings button, which when clicked displays a Properties dialog box for the specific Web page entered in the Address field (see Figure 18-6).

Figure 18-6.   *Keep your home page up to date with offline Web page settings*

As you can see in Figure 18-6, the Web page Properties dialog box has three tabs, each of which contains one or more options for synchronizing the Web page for offline use.

   If your home page is a file on a local or network drive, you'll only see a single tab, the Web Document tab.

If your home page is a URL, you'll see the following three tabs:

■   **Web Document**   In addition to information about the Web page, you'll also find a single option here. By default the option, Make This Page Available Offline, is checked. In theory, deselecting this option removes the Web page from your offline folders. However, in reality, the option appears to do nothing. The next time you return to the dialog box, the option has re-enabled itself and the Web page continues to appear whether you're working offline or online.

■   **Schedule**   The Schedule tab lets you decide whether to synchronize your home page manually or automatically using a schedule of your choosing. To create a new schedule, click Add and enter a name and simple schedule. To create a more sophisticated schedule, select a schedule and click the Edit button to display the dialog box of the same name as the schedule. This dialog box includes options enabling you to set extremely complex synchronization schedules for all offline Web pages.

■ **Download** The Download tab offers options for determining the amount of content that is downloaded when offline Web pages are synchronized. You can indicate the level of linked pages to download as well as the type of content to download (or restrict). You can even have Outlook automatically send an e-mail message to a designated address each time the Web page changes.

When you're finished setting the Home Page options, click Apply and move on to another tab, or click OK to save the changes and return to the active view.

The addition of a home page to a folder makes several new Outlook commands available when the home page is displayed in the Information viewer. To display the home page, choose View | Show Folder Home Page.

■ **Open in Default Browser** This command, which is found on the File menu when the home page is displayed in the Information viewer, opens the folder home page in your default Web browser in a separate window.

■ **Outlook Bar Shortcut to Web Page** With the folder home page displayed, choose File | New | Outlook Bar Shortcut To Web Page. A dialog box appears, informing you that the shortcut will be added to the bottom of the My Shortcuts group. Click OK to add the shortcut. The next time you click the shortcut, the Web page opens in your default browser.

■ **Send Web Page by E-mail** To use this command, first display the home page. Then choose Actions | Send Web Page By E-mail to create a new e-mail message with the home page included. If your default message format is Plain Text or Rich Text, the Web page is included as an attachment. If your default message format is HTML, the Web page is pasted into the message.

Configuring AutoArchive Settings

If you have a hard time keeping up with your Outlook housekeeping chores, you might want to give AutoArchive a try. It moves aging Outlook items to a special archive folder at regularly scheduled intervals, thereby freeing up space in your mailbox. If you don't care about saving the items, you can instruct AutoArchive to delete them instead. You can create custom AutoArchive schedules and instructions for each folder by setting options on the AutoArchive tab.

Here's what you'll find:

■ **Clean out items older than** Check this option to enable AutoArchiving for this folder. Then enter the aging criteria for AutoArchiving individual items.

- **Move old items to**   If you want to save items that meet the aging criteria, enter the path to the archive file. To locate an existing archive file, click the Browse button.

- **Permanently delete old items**   If you don't want to save items that meet the age criteria, you can select this option and have AutoArchive delete them rather than move them to the archive file.

When you're finished setting the AutoArchive options, click Apply and move to the next tab, or click OK to return to the active view.

Setting Administration Options

The first thing to note about the Administration tab is that you won't see it unless the Exchange Extensions Property Pages add-in is installed. To install the add-in, choose Tools | Options to display the Options dialog box. Then click the Other tab and click the Advanced Options button to open the Advanced Options dialog box. Click the Add-In Manager button to display the Add-In Manager dialog box. Check the Exchange Extensions Property Pages option and click OK.

The next thing to note about the Administration tab is that unless you're in a public folder of which you're the owner, or to which you possess owner permissions, there's not much you can do with it. When you select the Administration tab in a private folder, the only option available to the folder owner or a user with owner permissions is the Initial View On Folder option. While you can use this option in a private folder as well as a public folder, there's really not much point unless you've given other users permission to view the private folder.

The Initial View On Folder option sets the default view that displays the very first time the user opens the folder. If the user never switches views, the designated view appears every time the folder opens. However, once the user switches to another view, this option no longer applies to the folder for that particular user. It does still apply to other users who haven't yet opened the folder and switched to another view.

By default, five selections appear on the drop-down list, regardless of the type of folder you're in. Four of the five default selections (Group By From, Group By Subject, Group By Conversation Topic, and Unread By Conversation) can be applied to mail folders only. So don't drive yourself crazy trying to apply them to a contacts folder or a calendar folder. The remaining selection, Normal, uses the standard form for the selected folder type.

The Initial View On Folder option is used mainly in conjunction with custom views to bring some facet of the folder information to the attention of all users on their initial visit to the folder. For example, you might create a custom view that groups items by the Modified date, thus ensuring every user sees the most recent additions to the folder upon his or her initial visit. Or you might just want to make all users aware that you've created a new view so they can take advantage of it if they so desire.

The remaining options on the Administration tab apply to public folders only and are therefore covered in Chapter 16.

Associating Forms with Folders

You can associate custom forms with any folder for which you are the owner or for which you have owner permissions. All you have to do is use the Forms Manager, which can be accessed from the Forms tab of the folder's Properties dialog box, as seen in Figure 18-7.

Like the Administration tab, the Forms tab requires the Exchange Extensions Property Pages add-in and owner permissions. Without both, the tab does not appear on the folder's Properties dialog box.

To find out whether the Exchange Extensions Property Pages add-in is installed, check the Add-In Manager dialog box. Start by choosing Tools | Options to display the Options dialog box. Then click the Other tab, and then the Advanced Options button to open the Advanced Options dialog box. Finally, click the Add-In Manager button to display the Add-In Manager dialog box. If the Exchange Extensions Property Pages option is checked, the add-in is installed. If it's not checked, click the check box to enable the option, and click OK. This will install the add-in.

Figure 18-7. *Control folder input with only the forms you want used*

If the problem is the lack of owner permissions, the only thing you can do is request that the folder owner provide you with the necessary permissions. One last thing. Even if you're the folder owner, or a user with owner permissions, the Allow These Forms In This Folder options are not available unless the folder is a public folder. In private folders these options are grayed out.

Now, on to associating forms with the folder. The first order of business is to link custom forms to the folder. To start, click the Manage button to display the Forms Manager dialog box, shown in Figure 18-8.

You can also access the Forms Manager by choosing Tools | Options | Other | Advanced Options | Custom Forms | Manage Forms.

As you can see in Figure 18-8, the Forms Manager has two Set buttons and two display windows. The premise is simple: display existing forms in the left pane and move them to the right pane to associate them with the current folder (whose name appears next to the right Set button). When accessed from the Forms tab, only the left Set button is active. The right Set button is disabled to ensure you only associate forms with the currently selected folder. Click the left Set button to open the Set Library To dialog box (see Figure 18-9).

You can elect to use forms contained in a forms library or forms already associated with another folder. To use forms from a forms library, open the Forms Library drop-down list and select the desired library.

Note   *In reality, each folder contains its own forms library. When you associate a form with a particular folder, you are really placing a copy of the form in the folder's forms library.*

Figure 18-8.   *The Forms Manager takes the work out of associating forms with folders*

Figure 18-9.   *Select the library or folder containing the custom forms you want
to use*

To use forms associated with a folder, select the particular folder from the Folder
Forms Library display list. Click OK to return to the Forms Manager, where forms from
the library or folder you selected now appear in the left pane. As you can see in Figure
18-8, the name of the selected library (or folder) appears to the left of the Set button,
and all the associated forms are displayed beneath it.

Tip   *Outlook folders are limited to a single Outlook item type or message class. This means
that forms associated with the folder must belong to a compatible message class. In spite
of the fact that the Forms Manager allows you to add non-compatible forms to a folder's
forms library, you will not be able to use them. To determine a form's message class,
select the form and click the Properties button. The Message Class field indicates the
selected form's message class.*

The next step is to choose the form(s) to link with the selected folder and make the
association. From the left pane, select one or more forms, and click the Copy button to
move them to the right pane. That's all there is to it. Once you click Close, the association
is complete.

There are a number of other options in the Forms Manager, including the following:

■ **Update**   If changes have been made to forms since you first associated them
   with the folder, you can update the copies in the folder's forms library by
   selecting them and clicking the Update button. The forms originally associated
   with the folder are replaced by the most recent versions.

- ■ **Delete**   To remove a form from either list, select it and click the Delete button. Use this one carefully. Deleting a form from the right list simply deletes the copy placed in the folder's forms library. However, deleting the form from the left pane actually deletes the original form. If you mistakenly delete the original form, you'll have to recreate it from scratch.

- ■ **Properties**   You can use this button to modify some of the form properties, such as name, category assignments, contacts, and comments. In addition, you can see non-editable information such as version, form number, the type of operating systems with which the form is compatible, and the message class to which the form belongs.

- ■ **Show Categories**   If the form has been assigned to categories and/or subcategories, checking this option changes forms lists to display available forms grouped by categories and subcategories.

- ■ **Install**   Use this button to add custom forms from a form setup file (.cfg) or a form message file (.fdm). This option is used in conjunction with the next option, Save As, which saves a selected form to one of the two form file formats. This enables you to share custom forms with other Outlook users.

- ■ **Save As**   Select the form to save and click this button to display the Save As dialog box. Choose a target folder in which to save the form, enter a filename, select the file format (.fdm, or .cfg), and click Save. You can now send the file to any other Outlook user, who can add it to his or her forms library by using the Install command.

You'll also notice in Figure 18-8 that the Forms Manager dialog box contains a section called Description. Here you'll see some of the properties of the selected form. This can be helpful in comparing copies in a folder's form library with the originals to determine if the folder contains the most current version of the form.

After you've associated forms with the folder and clicked Close, you return to the Forms tab, where the associated forms now appear in the Forms Associated With This Folder list. If you're in a public folder, the Allow These Forms In This Folder options are available. Select the appropriate option to determine which forms can be used in this folder. The options are self-explanatory.

Giving Others Permission to Access Folders

The Permissions tab of the folder's Properties dialog box is another of the tabs that requires the Exchange Extensions Property Pages add-in and owner permissions. Without them, the Permissions tab does not appear. See the previous section, "Associating Forms with Folders," for information on installing the Exchange Extensions Property Pages add-in.

If you have the Exchange Extensions Property Pages add-in installed, but do not have owner permissions to the folder, you'll see a Summary tab instead. This tab displays the current permissions settings for the folder, but does not permit you to make any changes to the settings.

Setting permissions for a folder determines the ability other users have to access and modify the folder and any items it contains. Initially, only the original folder owner can grant permissions to other users. However, by assigning owner permissions to another user, a folder owner can give another user the same rights the owner has.

To access a folder's Permissions tab, right-click the folder shortcut in the Outlook Bar to open the folder's Properties dialog box. Then click the Permissions tab, which provides a variety of options that let you designate which users are allowed access to the folder (see Figure 18-10).

The first thing to decide is what the permissions setting is going to be for the bulk of users. As you can see in Figure 18-10, the only user listed is Default. This covers everyone with access to the folder except those users for whom you add customized permissions. You'll also notice that the role set for Default is None. This means that no one, except the owner, has permission to access the folder. You can change the role, or you can create your own custom role by setting the various options in the Permissions section. In addition to setting roles and permissions for the Default user, you can also add individual users to whom you want to give special permissions.

Giving a specific user special permissions requires adding the user to the Permissions tab and assigning the desired role or setting custom permissions. To add a user, click the Add button to display the Add Users dialog box, shown in Figure 18-11.

Figure 18-10.   *Setting folder permissions is easy with the wealth of options at your disposal*

Figure 18-11. *The Add Users dialog box displays users from your Global Address List*

Since users must be on the Microsoft Exchange Server network to access server folders, you won't find users from your Outlook Address Book or Personal Address Book listed. The only selections available in the Show Names From The drop-down list are the Global Address List, which displays everyone in the organization, and address lists for individual sites in the organization.

Select the user(s) to whom you want to give special permission for accessing and using the folder, and click the Add button. Next, click OK to add them to the Permissions tab. Now you're ready to assign roles and set permissions.

Start with Default. Then set the permissions for each user you added. For most of your users, the standard roles, which include the following, should suffice:

- **Owner** If the folder is part of your mailbox, or a folder that you created, you will automatically have owner rights. The original owner can also give other users Owner rights. Owners can add and remove users, assign permissions, and do pretty much anything they want to with the folder. Careful consideration should be used before assigning the Owner role to users.

- **Publishing Editor** Assign this role to users to give them the ability to read, create, modify, and delete all folder items. In addition, Publishing Editors can create subfolders.

- **Editor** An Editor can create, read, modify, and delete all items in the folder, but cannot create subfolders.

- **Publishing Author**   A Publishing Author has the same rights as the Publishing Editor with one exception. The ability to modify and delete items is limited to those items created by the Publishing Author.

- **Author**   This role gives the user rights similar to those of an Editor. The Author can create, read, modify, and delete items. However, modifying and deleting is limited to those items created by the Author.

- **Nonediting Author**   This role enables the user to read and create items. Deleting is limited to only those items created by the Nonediting Author, while editing is (as the name implies) completely forbidden regardless of who created the item.

- **Reviewer**   A reviewer gets to sit on the sidelines and watch the action without participating. Reviewers can view the folder and read items, but that's it. No creating, editing, or deleting is allowed.

- **Contributor**   The only permission granted to a Contributor is the right to create items. No reading, editing, or deleting is allowed.

- **None**   Not only can't you use the folder when assigned this role, you can't even see it. None means none—no reading, creating, editing, deleting, or even peeking is allowed!

Tip   *You can set roles and permissions for more than one user by selecting multiple users and making your choice from the Roles drop-down list, or by checking the desired permissions options. Of course, the selected users will all have identical permissions.*

In addition to the predefined roles found on the Roles drop-down list, you can create your own custom role known, appropriately, as Custom, by selecting the individual permissions you want to give a particular user. The permissions you can assign include:

- **Create Items**   This gives the user permission to create folder items.

- **Read Items**   With Read Items permission assigned, a user can view the folder and open any folder item.

- **Create Subfolders**   Check this option to give the user permission to create subfolders of the folder.

- **Folder Owner**   Contrary to what the option implies, and the Help file states, checking this option alone does not automatically grant the selected user Owner permissions. What it does do, however, is enable the user to set his or her own permissions. There's only one small catch. You must also provide Read Items permission so the user can open the resource Calendar folder to gain access to the Permissions tab of the folder properties.

- **Folder Contact**   Check this option to designate the selected user as a folder contact. This means the selected user will receive copies of automatic notifications from the folder or sent to the folder.

- **Folder Visible**   This misleadingly named option does not, by itself, make the resource Calendar folder visible. It requires that the Read Items option be checked as well. By itself, the Folder Visible option only makes the folder's free/busy time available in the Attendee Availability tab of meeting and meeting request forms.

- **Edit Items**   Fortunately, this permission is aptly named and enables the user to edit Calendar items according to the Edit Items option selected. The options are None, Own, and All. None speaks for itself. Own lets the user modify only those items he or she has created. All lets the user change any Calendar item regardless of its origin.

- **Delete items**   The Delete Items permission is identical to the Edit Items permission except that it enables the user to delete items from the folder. The options provide the same permission types as the Edit Items options.

In addition to adding users and setting permissions, you can also delete users. Highlight the user(s) you want to eliminate and click the Remove button. Outlook deletes the user without warning (or confirmation) as soon as you press the DELETE key. Therefore, if you accidentally delete a user, you'll have to re-add him or her. If you happen to delete the Default user, don't worry. Just click the Apply button and the Default user is back with, you guessed it, the default setting of None.

Configuring Synchronization Settings

If you work offline, you'll undoubtedly find yourself setting the Synchronization tab options on occasion. However, before you can do that you must have offline folders enabled. This requires checking the Enable Offline Access option on the Mail Services tab of the Options dialog box (choose Tools | Options). See Chapter 17 for more information on enabling and using offline folders.

You can also enable offline access by checking the Enable Offline Use option on the Advanced tab of the Microsoft Exchange Server dialog box. Choose Tools | Services to display the Services dialog box, then double-click Microsoft Exchange Server.

Before proceeding, there are a couple of things you should understand about offline folders and synchronization. First, when you enable offline folders, all the primary Outlook folders (Calendar, Contacts, Deleted Items, Drafts, Inbox, Journal, Notes, Outbox, Sent Items, and Tasks) are included automatically. You cannot choose to make some available offline and others not available offline, as you can with folders you create yourself. Another thing to note is that public folders can only be used offline if they are in your Public Folders/Favorites folder. If you open the Properties dialog box for a public folder that is not in the Favorites folder, the Synchronization tab doesn't appear.

As you can see in Figure 18-12, the Synchronization tab contains two options, This Folder Is Available, and Filter. In addition to the options, the tab also contains statistics for the folder, indicating the date of the last synchronization, as well as the number of items in the folder and in the offline folder.

The first option, which is available in all folders before offline access is enabled, is only available in non-primary folders after offline access is enabled. This is because you cannot selectively exclude primary Outlook folders from offline access. Therefore, the only purpose this option serves in a primary folder is to permit you to enable offline access directly from the Synchronization tab. With offline access disabled, setting the This Folder Is Available option to When Offline Or Online, and clicking OK or Apply, prompts Outlook to ask if you want to enable offline access.

In a non-primary folder, selecting When Offline Or Online ensures the individual folder is included each time you perform a full synchronization. To exclude a non-primary folder, set the This Folder Is Available option to Only When Online.

In the event you only want a portion of the file's contents while you're offline, you can use the Filter button to specify which folder items are synchronized. Sometimes you don't need or want the entire contents of a folder. For example, if you're going on the road and have a large Contacts folder, but limited storage space on your laptop, you can elect to synchronize only your business contacts and not your personal contacts

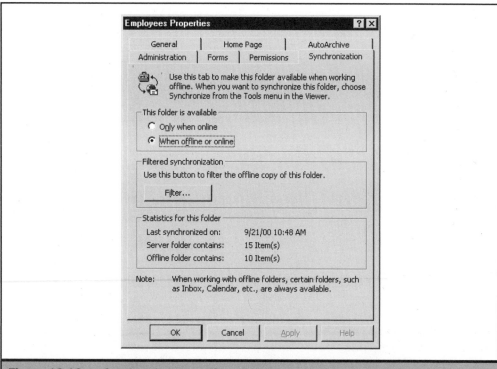

Figure 18-12. *Synchronize your offline folders so you can keep working when the server is down or you're on the road*

(if you've assigned them to categories). Click the Filter button to display the Filter dialog box, and set the desired filter criteria. See the section entitled "Adding and Applying Filters" in Chapter 22 for more information on using filters.

Exam MOUS Exam Objectives Explored in Chapter 18

Objective	Activity	Heading
OL2000.2.1	Create folders	"Creating Folders"

The Complete Reference

Chapter 19

Advanced E-mail Techniques

Outlook has a host of clever automated procedures that provide a lot of additional power while, at the same time, eliminating a lot of the work. A simple one-time setup process creates permanent customized functions you can use over and over.

Adding Signatures to E-mail

A signature is text you create and save so you can automatically add it to e-mail you compose. You use an electronic signature very much the same way you use your written signature. The difference is that your electronic signature can contain a wealth of information in addition to your name. You can also provide your title, company name, address, phone number, and any other information you consider pertinent. It's certainly easier to use a boilerplate than to type all that data every time you compose a message. Some people use a signature to sign off with a joke, a bit of philosophical wisdom, or a blatant political rally cry. In fact, some people get carried away and create signatures that are longer than most of the messages they send. Your taste, and the sensibilities of the people who receive your mail, should determine your signature contents. You can create as many signatures as you wish, and append the appropriate one to each message you create.

Creating Signatures

Creating and saving signatures is a snap; coming up with the appropriate words is the hard part. When you've decided on the text for your signature, begin by choosing Tools | Options and moving to the Mail Format tab of the Options dialog box. Click the Signature Picker button, located at the bottom of the tab, to open the Signature Picker dialog box.

Check the default message format at the top of the dialog box before you begin designing your signature. Outlook uses the same format for your signature.

Selecting the Signature Design Options

When you're designing your first signature, there are no signatures to pick, of course, so click New to open the Create New Signature dialog box, shown in Figure 19-1. Enter a name for this signature, and then select one of the following options:

- **Start with a blank signature** Select this option to create a signature from scratch. You can type the signature or cut and paste it from an existing document.

- **Use this existing signature as a template** This choice becomes available only after you create your first signature. You can then use it to create variants of your signature, without having to start from scratch.

- **Use this file as a template** This option allows you to use text previously saved as a Rich Text Format (RTF) file. Enter the path to the file or click Browse

Figure 19-1.   *Start by giving your signature a name that reflects its contents*

to locate the file on your hard drive. Most word processors (including Microsoft Word) provide an option for saving a file in RTF format.

Click Next to begin working on your signature in the Edit Signature dialog box.

Creating and Designing Signature Text

If you chose an existing signature or a template file, the text is already in the text box. If you elected to start with a blank signature, you must type (or paste) the text for the signature (see Figure 19-2).

Once you've inserted the text, you can polish it up using one of the following options:

- ■ **Font**   Click Font to open the Font dialog box, where you can change the font, font size, font style (bold, italic, and so on), color, and effects such as underline or strike-through.

- ■ **Paragraph**   Click the Paragraph button to display the Paragraph dialog box, which gives you options to align the text to the left, center, or right. You can even add bullets if the text in your signature calls for it.

- ■ **Clear**   Use the Clear button to delete the text and start again.

- ■ **Advanced Edit**   The Advanced Edit button lets you use an editor other than the Outlook text editor to format your signature. As soon as you click it, Outlook launches the appropriate application. For plain text signatures, Notepad opens; for other signature types, Microsoft Word opens. If your default message format (and

Figure 19-2. *Plain text signatures have no formatting options, but they work for every type of message (plain text, RTF, or HTML)*

therefore your signature) isn't plain text, Outlook offers plenty of formatting options (the Font and Paragraph buttons are accessible). Select some or all of the signature text and use the buttons on the dialog box to spiff up the formatting.

 Formatted signatures don't retain their formatting when you attach them to plain text messages.

Click Finish to save the signature and return to the Signature Picker dialog box. If you don't want to create another signature (by clicking New) or attach a vCard (discussed next), choose OK twice to close all the dialog boxes.

Attaching a vCard

You can attach a vCard to your signature by choosing one from the drop-down list in the dialog box. If you don't have an appropriate vCard, click New vCard From Contact to create one. See Chapter 8 for more information on creating vCards.

Editing and Removing Signatures

When the need arises you can return to the Mail format tab of the Options dialog box to edit or delete an existing signature. Click the Signature Picker button to open the

Signature Picker dialog box used to create the original signature. As you can see in Figure 19-3, all signatures you've created are displayed in the Signature list.

Select a signature (Outlook shows you its contents in the Preview box) to perform either of the following tasks:

- Click Edit to open the Edit Signature dialog box (the same one you used to create the signature). All the edit and formatting options that were available when you created the signature are available again. Click OK when you finish making your changes.

- Click Remove to delete the signature from your collection. Outlook asks you to confirm that you want to permanently remove the signature.

Choosing a Default Signature

When you leave the Signature Picker dialog box, the last signature selected automatically becomes the default signature. If you want to change the default signature, you can make a different selection from the Use This Signature By Default drop-down list. In addition, you can instruct Outlook when to use or withhold the default signature (see Figure 19-4).

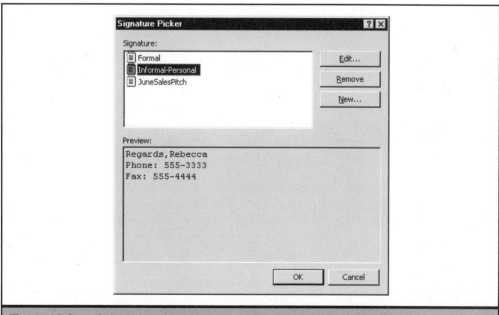

Figure 19-3.   *Select the signature you want to view, edit, or delete*

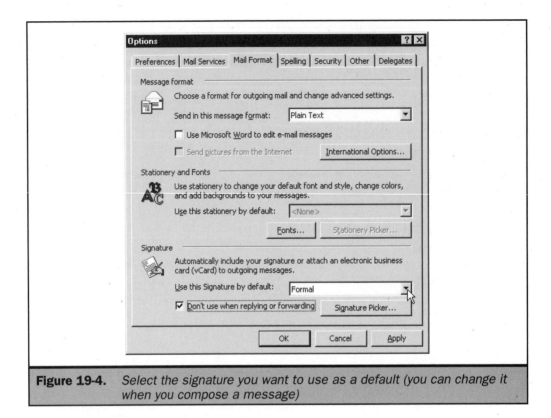

Figure 19-4.   *Select the signature you want to use as a default (you can change it when you compose a message)*

If you want to decide on a signature each time you create a message, select None from the drop-down list.

   Each time you return to the Signature Picker dialog box to edit, remove, or create a signature, the signature that's selected when you leave the dialog box becomes the new default. Be sure to check the default signature on the Mail Format tab before clicking OK to close the Options dialog box.

You can also choose whether or not you want to use a signature when you're replying to an E-mail message or forwarding a received message to another recipient. By default, Outlook selects the option Don't Use When Replying Or Forwarding. If you want to use your signature all the time, click the check box to remove the checkmark.

If you opt to use signatures when you reply to or forward a message, you may find that a signature containing multiple fonts, or font attributes applied to text (such as bold or italic), appears as plain text in a reply. This happens when the format type of the original message is plain text. Outlook automatically forces the format of the reply to match the original message. The signature itself hasn't changed.

Using Signatures in Messages

After you create a signature, Outlook assumes you want to use it. If you selected anything but None as the default signature, your default signature appears automatically whenever you open a new message window.

Create the message as usual. Be sure your insertion point is above the signature as you enter the text of your message. If you decide you don't want to use the signature in the current message, select the text of the signature and delete it.

    If you find you're deleting signatures more often than using them, save yourself some work by returning to the Mail Format tab of the Options dialog box and selecting None as the default signature. Then just insert a signature when you want to use one.

You can insert a signature manually if you selected None as the default signature, or if you have multiple signatures and want to choose a different (from the default) signature for the current message.

Position your insertion point where you want the signature to appear (usually at the end of the message) and click the Signature button on the Standard toolbar. You can also choose Insert | Signature to display a submenu that lists all your signatures. Select the one you want to use.

Tip *The Signature submenu holds a maximum of ten signatures. If you've created more than ten signatures, and you don't see the signature you want to use, click More on the submenu to open the Select A Signature dialog box to see a complete list.*

If you're replacing an existing signature, you might want to highlight the existing signature first so the new signature is inserted over the old one, thus eliminating the possibility of ending up with two signatures.

MOUS *MOUS EXAM PRACTICE*
In this section, you learned to create, format, edit, and use signatures. Begin by creating several different signatures. Customize each one using the formatting features available for your default message format. Then set one of the signatures as your default signature. Next, compose an e-mail message to see how the default signature appears. Finally, manually change the signature from the default to one of the other signatures you created. Send yourself and your co-workers messages with the signatures to see how they appear when received.

Dealing with Junk Mail

Junk e-mail (more commonly known as *spam*) is an annoying problem that keeps growing. One serious problem with junk e-mail is that it usually costs the recipient more than it costs the sender (which is the opposite of the financials attached to junk mail that's delivered by the USPS). Whether you believe in the axiom that your time is worth money, or you actually pay by the minute for Internet access, the time spent waiting for junk mail to download to your Inbox and the time spent deleting it become significant as more and more junk mail arrives.

Outlook offers some assistance as you attempt to dodge the streams of junk mail that invade your mailbox.

Setting Filter Actions

You can have Outlook automatically filter junk mail as it arrives in your Inbox. In addition, you can configure automatic actions (such as delete, move to another folder, and so on) when the filter identifies junk mail. Outlook actually defines two types of undesirable e-mail: junk mail and adult content mail. To set up your junk mail filters, display your Inbox and click the Organize icon on the toolbar (or choose Tools | Organize). Then choose Junk E-Mail to see the window shown in Figure 19-5.

Figure 19-5.   *Take advantage of the automatic options available for getting rid of junk e-mail*

Outlook keeps a list of key words and phrases, and examines your incoming e-mail to see if those words exist in any message. If so, the message is deemed to be unsolicited junk mail, and the actions you specify are taken. If you wish, you can specify one action for junk messages and a different action for adult content messages.

Color Junk Mail Listings

By default, Outlook offers to change the color of the Inbox listing of any junk or adult content message. Select a color from the drop-down list; you can choose the same color for both types of filtered messages, or select a different color for each in order to identify the message type more easily. When you've selected the colors you want to use to identify these messages, click Turn On to save your configuration options.

The filtered messages remain in your Inbox, so you can decide whether you want to open a message (just to check), manually move the message to another folder, or manually delete the message.

Move Junk Mail

You can have Outlook automatically move your junk mail to another folder instead of sending it to your Inbox. To do so, select Move from the drop-down list next to the word "Automatically," and the drop-down list in the second box changes to a list of folders. Select the Junk E-Mail folder, the Deleted Items folder, or Other Folder (which opens a dialog box that displays all your Outlook folders so you can select one, or create one). Then click Turn On to save your configuration options.

 If you select the Junk E-mail folder, and that folder doesn't already exist, Outlook automatically opens the Create New Folder dialog box. As occurs whenever you create a new folder, you're also offered the opportunity to place a shortcut to the folder on your Outlook Bar.

You can't edit or view the files Outlook uses to track the words that filter spam, but you can see documentation that explains those files. The documentation file is named Filters.txt, and it's located in C:\Program Files\Microsoft Office\Office. Unfortunately, the file on your hard drive is probably incorrect (Microsoft knows about this problem). You can see an accurate copy of the documentation file at http://officeupdate.microsoft.com/Articles/newfilters.htm. Use the File | Save As command on your browser to save this file to your hard drive.

Adding Senders to the List of Junk Purveyors

Outlook's filtering mechanism is helpful, but not fail proof. It's certainly possible to receive a great deal of junk mail that slips through the filters because the words and phrases that kick off the filters may not be contained in some junk mail.

To help filter junk, you can maintain a list of senders so that mail from those senders is also filtered.

Add a Sender from a Message Listing

If you receive junk mail or adult content mail, right-click the message listing in your Inbox and choose Junk E-Mail from the shortcut menu. Then choose Add To Junk Senders List, or Add To Adult Content Senders List from the submenu. You can also choose Actions | Junk E-mail to display a submenu with the same choices.

 You cannot use this technique if the From field on the message is blank; Outlook issues the error message, "The operation failed. An object could not be found."

View and Update Your Junk Senders List

To view or edit the list of junk senders, display your Inbox and click the Organize icon on the toolbar (or choose Tools | Organize). Choose Junk E-Mail and scroll to the bottom of the Organize window and click the Click Here link. Then click Edit Junk Senders or Edit Adult Content Senders.

The Edit Junk Senders or Edit Adult Content dialog box opens, displaying the names of all the senders currently in the list.

To add a sender, click Add and enter the sender's name as it appears on e-mail messages. If you want to modify a name on the list, select the listing and click Edit. To remove a sender from the list, select the listing and click Delete. When you're finished working with the Sender list, click OK to return to the active window.

Note   *You can also have an Exception List, which means that you can fine tune the filters so they permit mail that meets your exception criteria to slip through the filter. This is useful if your mother sends you e-mail that contains phrases found on Outlook's "hit list." Creating and maintaining an Exception List is covered in the next section, "Using the Rules Wizard."*

Using the Rules Wizard

The Rules Wizard is an automated organizer, helping you manage your e-mail so that messages you send and receive are handled properly without the need for you to do any work. All you have to do is tell the wizard about a rule ("when my brother sends me a message, forward it to my sister if the subject line has the word loan in it"), and you can rest assured that the wizard will carry out the rule flawlessly and automatically.

Understanding Server and Client Rules

Some rules you create can be implemented on the Exchange server, even when you're not logged in to the server. These are called server-based rules. In order to qualify as a server-based rule, all the elements of the rule must exist on the server. For example, if a rule involves moving messages to server-based folders, the rule is server based since all mail is initially received at the server, and the destinations indicated in the rule are folders, which are also located on the server.

Other rules must wait for you to open Outlook and log on to the server before they're implemented, and these are called client-only rules. For example, if you instruct the wizard to move a message to a folder in your Personal Folders list, or to forward a message to a recipient in your Personal Address Book, the wizard can't complete its work until those entities are available as a result of your logon.

When you create a rule, the wizard notifies you if the rule is a client-only procedure.

Creating a Rule

To create a rule, you must give the wizard some guidelines (it's a wizard, not a mind reader):

- When to apply the rule (when messages arrive, when you send a message, when a message contains certain words).

- What to look for in the message (a certain sender, certain recipients, a certain word in the subject field or message body).

- What to do when a message matches the criteria (move it, delete it, forward it, play a musical tone).

You can create a rule by stepping through the wizard windows, or by finding a message on which the wizard can base a rule.

If you manage junk mail by filtering as described in the previous section, you've already begun using the Rules Wizard.

Creating a Rule with the Wizard

To create a rule by stepping through the wizard windows, choose Tools | Rules Wizard. When the Rules Wizard opens, all existing rules are listed. If you haven't yet created a rule, the list is blank.

To create a rule, click the New button in the Rules Wizard window. The first thing the wizard needs to know is the type of rule you want to create (see Figure 19-6).

Some types of rules require you to specify the details, and the wizard provides an underlined link you can click to fill in the necessary data. For example, if you select the rule type "Move new messages from someone," the bottom pane displays two underlined links:

- **People or distribution list**   Click this link to open a dialog box that has all the names in your address lists. You can select the sender(s) to whom this rule applies or enter a new sender.

- **Specified folder**   Click this to open a dialog box that displays all the folders in your Outlook system. Select the folder into which you want to move the messages that apply to your new rule.

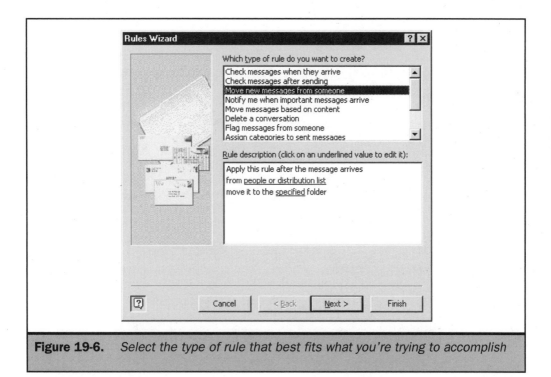

Figure 19-6. *Select the type of rule that best fits what you're trying to accomplish*

After you select the type of rule and fill in the required information (if the rule requires information), click Next.

In the next wizard window, select the conditions that must exist to activate the rule. The list that appears in this window varies, depending upon the type of rule you selected in the first wizard window. For example, Figure 19-7 shows the conditions offered for the rule type "Move messages based on content."

Some of the conditions may require you to enter data. For example, if you're creating a rule based on words or phrases in the subject line or the message body (or both), click the appropriate link in the wizard window to enter the specifics. Some specifics can include multiple entries.

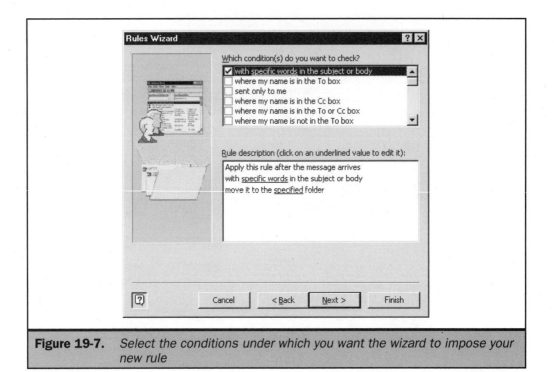

Figure 19-7.   *Select the conditions under which you want the wizard to impose your new rule*

Continue to click Next to move through the wizard windows; the contents vary depending upon the type of rule you're creating, and the conditions you've set for the rule. You can also tell the wizard about exceptions to the rule (for example, you might want to ignore a rule based on the sender if a certain word appears in the subject line). The last wizard window asks you to name the rule (choose a name that's descriptive) and asks if you want to turn the rule on now. Click Finish when you've completed this final wizard window.

Note   *The final wizard window may also ask if you want to run the rule against a folder, which means you can apply the rule to messages already in that folder.*

Creating a Rule from a Message

If you receive a message from someone and decide that further messages from that person should be handled via a rule, you can create that rule by using the message as a template. Begin by selecting the message listing in your Inbox or any other folder. Then click the Organize icon on the toolbar, or choose Tools | Organize to open the Organize window. Now find the item named Create A Rule, which already has information filled in using data from the message you originally selected.

Finally, change details as desired, and click Create. Your rule is saved, and Outlook offers to run the rule against the currently selected folder to see if any other messages match the criteria.

Managing Rules

After you create rules, you can edit, remove, and manage them from the Rules Wizard dialog box (see Figure 19-8). To open the Rules Wizard, choose Tools | Rules Wizard.

Figure 19-8. *You can modify, delete, disable, and re-order your rules in the Rules Wizard dialog box*

The opening window of the Rules Wizard provides an opportunity to fine tune the way the wizard processes rules:

- To temporarily stop applying a rule, click the rule's check box to remove the checkmark. When you want to re-apply the rule, click the blank check box to insert a checkmark (it's a toggle).

- To permanently remove a rule, select its listing and choose Delete.

- To change the specific data that kicks off the rule, select the rule's listing, and then select the appropriate link in the bottom of the dialog box.

- To change the name of a rule, select its listing and choose Rename.

- To change the way the rule works, select its listing and choose Modify. The original wizard process runs again so you can make changes to the rule's configuration.

- To change the order in which rules are applied, select a rule and use the Move Up and Move Down buttons to change its position in the list.

When you're through, click OK to save the changes and return to the active window.

Configuring the Order of Rules Processing

The fact that rules are processed in a certain order can lead to confusion and even problems. There are two sets of parameters the wizard uses when applying rules:

- Rules are applied in the order in which they appear in the Rules Wizard list.

- All server-based rules are applied (in order) before any client-based rules are applied (in order).

The server-based rules before client-based rules approach is in effect even if you're logged on. If you're not logged on, only the server-based rules are applied until you log on, at which point the client-based rules are applied.

You can face a real dilemma as a result of this ordered procedure, because it means that after the wizard applies a rule, it moves to the next rule and applies it, and that may mean that the second rule is applied to the messages that were already affected by the first rule. Sometimes that's okay, and sometimes it's not. For example, suppose you create the following two rules:

- Messages in the Inbox that are from a sender named John Doe are forwarded to Jane Roe (who handles the John Doe account and must be kept informed), and the original message is deleted from your Inbox.

- Any message with the word "advertisement" in the subject line is deleted.

If you receive a message from John Doe with the sentence "I like the advertisement you designed" in the subject line, and the rules are applied in the order indicated here, you have no problems. However, if the rules are applied in reverse order, Jane Roe never sees the message—it's deleted from the Inbox before the second rule is applied, and therefore isn't available for the actions included in the second rule.

If you have a lot of rules, especially if they're complicated (perform more than one action), you risk having rules applied improperly or not at all. There are a few guidelines to keep in mind as you manage rules:

- Give careful thought to the order in which rules are applied, using the Rules Wizard window to change the order when necessary.

- Take advantage of the action "stop processing more rules," (in the What Do You Want To Do With The Message? option) which is available for every rule you create. Selecting this choice tells the Rules Wizard that all messages impacted by the current rule are not to undergo processing by any rules that follow this rule.

Note   *The "stop processing more rules" action isn't an absolute cure, because sometimes you may create rules that are specifically designed to work with each other, each rule enhancing (or further filtering) the work of the previous rule.*

Rules for Meeting and Task Requests

The Rules Wizard is perfectly happy to apply rules against meeting requests and task requests (after all, they're messages), but you must configure the rule properly. You can only set up rules that affect incoming meeting and task requests; you cannot apply rules to task and meeting requests you send to others.

To set up a rule that's specific to such requests, choose the following options in the Rules Wizard:

1. Choose "Check messages when they arrive" as the type of rule. Click Next.

2. Choose "uses the form name form" as a condition, and then click the form name link to choose the form.

3. In the Choose Forms dialog box that opens, select Application Forms from the drop-down list at the top of the dialog box.

4. Select Meeting Request or Task Request (or both) and click Add, then click Close to return to the Rules Wizard.

5. Choose the actions you want to apply to these messages.

Bear in mind a couple of things. One, the tracking features don't work if you move messages out of the Inbox into another folder with a rule. Two, moving a message to a special folder with a rule doesn't work the way it does when you manually move or drag a message. For instance, moving a meeting request to your Calendar folder with a rule doesn't automatically create an appointment.

Running Rules Manually

Usually you create a rule as a result of having performed a task manually many times. For example, you've manually been moving all the messages from your brother to a folder named Family Mail, or all the messages with the word "budget" in the subject line to a folder you created to store mail about the company budget.

While rules take care of the new, incoming mail, they aren't retroactive. In other words, rules take effect "from here on," processing actions against messages that arrive or are sent after the rule is created, but not affecting messages already contained in the folders to which the rules apply.

Starting with Outlook 2000, you can run a rule against existing messages, which provides a nifty way to clean up your Inbox or other folders automatically instead of manually. Here's how to run your rules manually:

1. Choose Tools | Rules Wizard.

2. Click Run Now to open the Run Rules Now dialog box shown in Figure 19-9.

3. Select the rules you want to run.

4. If necessary, change the folder you want to run the rules against by clicking Browse and selecting a new folder. Also specify whether you want to run the rules against any subfolders.

5. Use the drop-down list at the bottom of the dialog box to select the messages for which you want to apply these rules: all messages, unread messages, or read messages.

6. Click Run Now, then click Close.

The rules are applied. (Outlook doesn't display any messages, everything happens behind the scenes.)

Tricks, Tips, and Troubleshooting for Rules

It's not possible to go over every possible criteria selection, and the resulting actions you might select as you create rules. As a remedy for this lack of ability to discuss every possible permutation and combination you could invent, it seems prudent to present some helpful information (based on problems that are frequently encountered).

Automatically Forwarding Messages

One of the actions available to you when you create a rule is the ability to forward a message that meets certain criteria. However, unlike the sequence of events that occur when you forward a message yourself, no copy of the forwarded message is sent to your Sent Items folder.

Figure 19-9.   *Catch up with old messages by applying rules against them*

This means you have no way of determining whether the message was forwarded (except by calling the recipient). Unfortunately, this is one of those Outlook design issues that requires you to have blind faith that the Rules Wizard did what you commanded.

BCC Is Not an Available Criterion

You cannot ask the wizard to filter incoming mail that has your name on the BCC field. If you are creating a rule for outgoing mail, you cannot ask the wizard to select a message on the basis of a name in the BCC field.

From E-Mail Address Versus Reply to E-mail Address

Some e-mail messages you receive may have both a From field and a Reply To field. If you reply manually, the message is sent to the Reply To address. However, if you create a rule that has Reply as an action, the message is sent to the name in the From field.

Moving Messages to Deleted Folders

If you create a rule that moves certain messages to another folder, and you delete the folder, the rule is supposed to stop functioning. However, you'll probably find that the rule continues to apply the action, moving messages into the deleted folder.

This occurs because a folder, like a message, is not permanently deleted until you delete it from the Deleted Items folder. When you delete a folder, it becomes a subfolder of the Deleted Items folder until you empty the Deleted Items folder. At that point, the rule will cease to function.

Creating Rules That Support OR as the Condition

Outlook does not offer any OR conditions in the Rules Wizard. This means you cannot create a rule that says "move a message to the Family Stuff folder if it is from Joe Blow OR has the word birthday in the subject field." If you select those two criteria in a rule, a message must meet both criteria in order to kick off the action of moving the message to the folder.

Sometimes you want to check for messages that have either of two criteria, but not both. The solution is to create two separate rules, and in each rule you must specify one criterion and specifically exclude the other. The Rules Wizard provides an opportunity to create exclusions in the next-to-last wizard window.

Automatically Assigning Categories

You can create a rule in which messages that meet your criteria are assigned to a category. This is handy if you use categories to track and sort messages. However, the Rules Wizard doesn't check up on you. If you haven't created the category, the wizard doesn't remind you to do so, it just ignores the problem and the rule.

   Any rule that involves assigning a category is automatically a client-based rule.

Rules Wizard Error Messages

Some of the error messages the Rules Wizard displays are important, some are misleading, and some can be ignored. Here are a few error messages you may see when you are creating a rule:

- **There is not enough space on the Microsoft Exchange Server to store all of your rules. The rules that failed to upload have been deactivated**.   Microsoft Exchange Server allocates 32KB of your mailbox for rules. That should be enough space to hold about 25–30 rules. In addition, that space holds any auto replies you create for "out-of-office messages." While it's unlikely that you'd ever create enough rules to reach the maximum size limit, it's always a good idea to be efficient in the way you create rules. One of the most commonly applied inefficiencies is listing a great many names in the criteria. If you want to filter a message based on whether or not it came from (or is sent to) a large group of users, create a distribution list with those user names before you create the rule, then use the distribution list in the rule. The server stores only the name of the distribution list within the rule (the distribution list is expanded when the rule runs). This only works with names and distribution lists based on the Global Address List. If you use a distribution list based on your Personal Address Book, or your Contacts database, the names are stored individually (so it's useless to create the distribution list just for the rule). In that case, even creating one rule may fill your server space if the rule criteria involves more than 30 names.

■ **This rule could not be created. Check your folder permissions**. This error message appears if you select Run Rule Now on the last wizard page, and then cancel the manual run process. Don't worry, the error message is specious, and the rule is created.

■ **The file name, location, or format is not valid**. This error message can appear if you choose to start an application as the action for a rule. If the error appears, it means you added a parameter to the command that opens the application. For example, you may have created a rule that opened Microsoft Word when a message arrived from Zeke, because you save every word Zeke writes in a Word file named ZekesThoughts.doc. To accomplish this, you used the command **winword "c:\my documents\zekesthoughts.doc"**. This command works fine from a command line (Word opens with ZekesThoughts loaded), but the Rules Wizard does not know how to handle the parameters. The solution is to give the wizard the filename instead of the program's executable file. This trick works as long as the file extension is linked to the application you want to run. To accomplish this, when the Rules Wizard displays the dialog box to choose the application, change the file type to All Files and move to the folder that contains the file you want to load. Select that file and continue with the Rules Wizard process. The Rules Wizard does not catch on, and you won't see an error message saying "hey, that's not an application." (If the file you want to open automatically isn't registered with a software program, or isn't registered for the software you want to run, create a shortcut for the application and put the appropriate parameters for opening the file in the shortcut. Then point to the shortcut when you create the rule.)

Using the Out of Office Assistant

The Out of Office Assistant is primarily designed to generate automatic replies to messages sent to you when you're not in your office and you're not checking e-mail. This is not the same as being out of the office and checking in from a remote location, because in that case you generally continue to check your e-mail. The automatic reply is usually worded to explain that you're out of the office.

In addition to generating an automatic reply, you can set rules to handle incoming messages automatically. This is useful if mail arrives that can't wait until your return to the office, and must be forwarded to someone else or otherwise managed automatically.

The automatic reply and the rules you establish don't work until you specifically notify the Out of Office Assistant that you're out of the office.

A bug in Microsoft Exchange Server 5.5 prevented the activation of the AutoReply when users created a rule that was configured as the last rule to process (a selection named "Do not process subsequent rules" is available when you create rules; it's discussed later in this chapter). The Out of Office AutoReply itself is a rule and is considered to be the last rule in the list of rules. If a user-created rule is configured to name itself the last rule, the AutoReply doesn't kick in. A fix is now available from Microsoft. You can get information about the problem and find a link to the fix in Knowledge Base Article Q248456.

Creating the AutoReply Message

The AutoReply message is created in the Out of Office Assistant dialog box, which you open by choosing Tools | Out of Office Assistant. Enter the message in the text box, as shown in Figure 19-10.

The AutoReply message isn't sent until you select the option I Am Currently Out Of The Office. This means you can create the AutoReply message at any time and implement it only when it's needed.

If an AutoReply is the only rule you want to set for the times you're away from the office, click OK; that's all you have to do. Remember to select the option that indicates you're out of the office when you want to implement this feature.

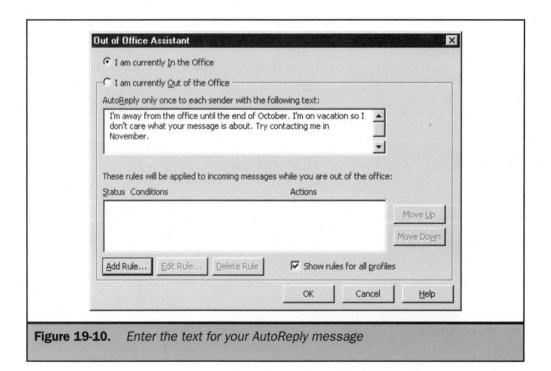

Figure 19-10.   *Enter the text for your AutoReply message*

Here are a few things you should know about the way AutoReply works:

- AutoReply kicks in automatically when you tell the Out of Office Assistant you're out of the office, even if you don't enter text (senders receive a blank message).

- Each sender receives only one AutoReply. Outlook keeps track of the senders so that the first message from any sender kicks off an AutoReply. Subsequent messages from the same sender do not generate an automatic response.

- The list of senders who received the AutoReply message is cleared when you notify the Out of Office Assistant that you are back in the office.

- The text in the Subject field of your AutoReply is: Out of Office AutoReply: *<original subject text>*.

Creating Out of Office Rules

Suppose something's going on that can't wait until you return from your vacation. Perhaps there's a project you're running that can't stop just because you're absent. You'll want to forward messages concerning the project to another person in the company. Fortunately, in addition to creating an AutoReply (or instead of using an AutoReply), you can set rules to handle messages while you're out of the office.

To create a rule, choose Add Rule in the Out Of Office Assistant dialog box. The Edit Rule dialog box opens (see Figure 19-11).

Use these guidelines as you create rules:

- Rules must be server-based; you cannot move a message to any folder that isn't in your server-based mailbox.

- You can have multiple conditions in a single rule.

- You can have multiple actions in a single rule.

- You can create multiple rules.

- Multiple rules are applied in the order in which they're listed.

Specifying Conditions for a Rule

The Out of Office Assistant provides several fields you can use to set the conditions for a message in order to qualify the message for this rule. Multiple entries are separated with a semicolon, and unlike the Rules Wizard, multiple entries indicate an OR condition for that field. A message doesn't have to match all the data you enter in any given field, it just needs to match one entry. However, if you enter data in more than one field, messages must match at least one entry in each field to qualify for the rule.

- **From** Enter the names of senders, either by clicking the From button and selecting names from a list, or by typing the name directly in the From box. Separate multiple names with a semicolon, and click Check Names to make sure the name you typed has a match in your address lists.

- **Sent To**   Specify whether the message is sent directly to you, copied to you, or both. You can also further qualify the message by including additional names that must appear in the To field of the message. Click the Sent To button to select the name(s) from an address list, or enter the name(s) directly and check them against your list by clicking Check Names. Separate multiple names with a semicolon.

- **Subject**   Enter a word or phrase that must appear in the Subject field. Separate multiple words or phrases with a semicolon.

- **Message body**   Enter text that must appear in the body of the message. Separate multiple strings of text with a semicolon.

Setting Advanced Criteria

Click Advanced to use the additional qualifiers available in the Advanced dialog box, shown in Figure 19-12.

Figure 19-11.   *The top half of the dialog box is for setting conditions; the bottom half is for designing actions that take place when those conditions are met*

Figure 19-12.   *You can narrow the criteria further with the choices in the Advanced dialog box*

Most of the choices on the Advanced dialog box are self-explanatory, but a few bear some discussion.

Selecting the Only Items That Do Not Match These Conditions option provides a way to create a counterbalancing rule. For example, after you create a rule that specifies conditions based on certain senders and causes those messages to be forwarded to your boss, you may decide you want all other messages forwarded to your assistant. Create a rule in which the conditions are the same as the first rule, changing the person to whom the messages are forwarded. Finally, click the Advanced button and select the Only Items That Do Not Match These Conditions option.

Another clever use for the counterbalancing rule also provides a method of keeping your mailbox from becoming massively crowded while you're away. Create a rule that moves all messages with "urgent" in the Subject field to a folder you create in your server-based mailbox (name the folder Urgent or something similar). Then create a counterbalancing rule (messages that do not have "urgent" in the Subject field), and use the Reply With action and the Delete action (explained in the next section) to both send a message to the sender and delete the message from your mailbox. In the text of your Reply, explain what's going on. For instance, you might say, "If it's urgent that I see this message as soon as I return, please resend it with the word "urgent" in the Subject field. Otherwise, please send the message again after my return because the message you sent has been automatically deleted."

Configuring the Actions

When a message meets any of the criteria you set, an action results. You configure the action in the same Edit Rule dialog box in which you configured the conditions. Most of the actions are self-explanatory, but the following bear some discussion:

- **Reply with**　Select this option and click Template to open a standard message form. Enter text, insert an attachment if you wish, and add any additional recipients to the TO or CC fields. Then choose Save & Close. This reply is sent to the sender(s) named in your rule.

- **Custom**　This option initiates a third-party program you installed. Programs that perform special rule-based functions are available from several sources. Try http://www.slipstick.com for custom programs and links to other Web sites with custom programs.

- **Do not process subsequent rules**　You can select this option to make this rule the last rule that's used, regardless of its position in the list of rules. However, it's best to select this option only for the last rule in a list of rules.

When you've finished configuring the rule, click OK to return to the Out of Office Assistant dialog box, where your rule is listed.

By default, the rule has a checkmark, indicating that when you tell the Out of Office Assistant you're away, the rule runs. You can deselect the checkmark for any rule you don't want to run while you're away.

If you have multiple profiles for logging on to Outlook, and you've created Out of Office Assistant rules on more than one profile, select the Show Rules For All Profiles option to have access to all the rules you've created.

You can edit or delete a rule by selecting its listing and clicking the appropriate button. You can even change the order of the list of rules by selecting a rule and using the Move Up and Move Down buttons.

Saving Time with Templates

Everyone who uses e-mail finds that he or she creates the same or similar messages frequently. For example, you may send a meeting request with basically the same contents to the same list of recipients whenever you need to meet about some department business, or you may send an e-mail message to the same person or group about a certain topic.

Any message that is essentially the same as a previous message can be turned into a template, which means you need only open the message form, change one or two items, and send the message. This is far easier than creating the message from scratch over and over. Templates work with all the Outlook message forms: e-mail messages, task requests, and meeting requests.

Creating a Template

To create a template, open a blank message form and enter the header information (recipients and subject). If this is an e-mail message form (rather than a task request or a meeting request), enter the message text. Figure 19-13 is an example of a message that's set up to be a template.

Instead of choosing Send, take these steps:

1. Choose File | Save As to open the Save As dialog box.

2. Select Outlook Template (.oft) from the drop-down list in the Save As Type field.

3. The folder in the Look In text box changes to the folder in which Office templates are located. The filename is the subject line of the message.

4. Choose Save.

5. Close the message window by clicking the X in the upper-right corner, or by choosing File | Close.

6. If Outlook asks if you want to save changes, click Yes.

7. If Outlook asks if you want to send the message now, choose Yes or No depending on the circumstances.

If you're creating a template from an e-mail message form, you also have the opportunity to save the message in your Drafts folder. It's a good idea to do so because this gives you an additional (and easy to get to) copy of the template.

You can create as many templates as you need, using any of the Outlook message forms.

Using a Template

Sending a message from a template is as easy as opening the template, making any minor changes that might be necessary, and clicking the Send button. This is certainly faster and easier than selecting recipients and typing text in the message box.

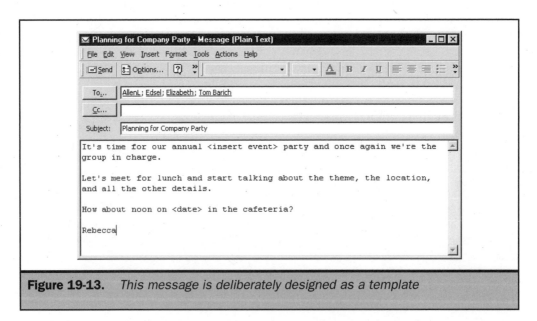

Figure 19-13.   *This message is deliberately designed as a template*

GETTING MORE OUT OF OUTLOOK

Choose File | New | Choose Form to open the Choose Form dialog box. Select User Templates In File System (or the folder in which you saved the template) from the Look In drop-down list, and double-click the template you want to use. This opens the template. Make any necessary changes in the message and click Send to transmit the message.

The magic of all this is that when you selected the template, Outlook didn't open your template, it opened a blank message form based on your template. The changes you made were to the message, not the template. No matter what you do to a message based on a template, the template itself remains exactly the way it was when you originally saved it.

Unfortunately, this also has a small downside. You can't edit a template, so if you want to make changes you must start all over. If you want to delete a template, you must exit Outlook and use Windows Explorer or My Computer to find the file and delete it.

MOUS EXAM PRACTICE
In this section, you learned to create and use templates for composing e-mail messages. To ensure you understand the process, create a variety of mail messages, meeting requests, and task requests and save them as templates. Then open them and send messages to your co-workers and friends using the templates.

Exam ▼ MOUS Exam Objectives Explored in Chapter 19

Objective	Activity	Heading
OL2000.1.13	Add a signature to e-mail	"Adding Signatures to E-mail"
OL2000.1.15	Use mail templates to compose mail	"Saving Time with Templates"

The
Complete
Reference

Chapter 20

Using Outlook with Other Applications

Outlook not only provides a comprehensive set of self-contained e-mail and information management features, but also a number of features that offer tight integration with other software applications. Since Outlook is part of the Microsoft Office suite, it naturally plays well with other Office applications. In addition, the import and export feature affords Outlook users the opportunity to exchange and utilize information from a wide range of other software applications.

Working with Office Applications from Within Outlook

As you might expect, Outlook and its Office siblings are close. So close, in fact, that you can perform a variety of operations from within Outlook that work directly with other Office applications. For example, you can create a single letter or entire mail merge in Word using the Outlook Contacts folder. In addition, you can use Word as your e-mail editor, even if it's not configured to be the default e-mail editor, by employing the New Mail Message Using command found in Outlook. To take advantage of the ties between Outlook and other Office applications, you must, of course, have the other applications discussed here installed on your computer.

Using the Outlook Contact Database for Mail Merge

Outlook 2000 is the first version of Outlook that includes a true mail merge feature. Previous versions of Outlook required you to access the Outlook contact database and perform the mail merge from within Word. Now you can let Outlook do all the work. Not only that, you can even use the mail merge feature to create personalized e-mail messages and electronic faxes to your contacts.

To begin, open the Contacts folder. If you don't want to include all the contacts in the mail merge, apply a filter to display only those contacts you want included. For more information on applying filters, see Chapter 22. You can also select individual contacts for inclusion by holding down the CTRL key and clicking the desired contacts. After you've selected the contacts, choose Tools | Mail Merge to open the Mail Merge Contacts dialog box, shown in Figure 20-1.

As you can see in Figure 20-1, the Mail Merge Contacts dialog box contains a number of customization options:

- **Contacts**   Select All Contacts In Current View to include all contacts currently visible. If you've already applied a filter, only those contacts that matched the filter criteria are included. If you applied no filter, all the contacts in the folder are included. If you manually selected contacts to include, choose Only Selected Contacts. Any filter you applied is ignored in favor of those selected contacts.

Figure 20-1.   *Mail merge was never this easy*

- **Fields to merge**   Your choices here are to include all contact fields or just those
  that appear in the current view. If you're thinking this means that the fields you
  select here are going to be inserted into the mail merge document, don't worry.
  It simply indicates which fields will be made available for insertion in the merge
  document. Therefore, you might want to select All Contact Fields to be on the safe
  side. You may have to scroll a little more to find what you're looking for, but that
  way you'll be sure not to miss a field you want to include.

- **Document file**   This option lets you create a new merge document or use an
  existing document. To create a new merge document from scratch, select New
  Document. If you already have an existing merge document you want to reuse,
  select Existing Document, and click the Browse button to locate it. This comes in
  handy not just for reusing a document created previously, but also for modifying
  an existing document for a different use. For example, if you have an existing
  document used to notify customers of a change in your pricing policy, you could
  easily modify it, and create a new merge document to notify vendors of a change
  in your purchasing policies. Save it with a new name and you've got a new merge
  document with a fraction of the effort.

- **Contact data file**   If you've applied a filter or manually selected individual contacts, you may want to save this particular group of contacts for future use by creating a contact data file and saving it to your hard disk. Enter a path and name for the new file, or click the Browse button to select a location.

- **Document type**   From the Document Type drop-down list, you can select one of four merge document types: Form Letters, Mailing Labels, Envelopes, or Catalog. The first three are self-explanatory. The fourth, Catalog, is a single document displaying the selected fields for each contact. The catalog type is used to create everything from simple phone or address lists to complex reports detailing a wealth of information about each contact.

- **Merge to**   This drop-down list provide three or four (if you have a faxing service installed) output options. You can elect to create a new Word document (New Document), send the information to your default printer (Printer), send the information to each contact via e-mail (E-mail), or fax the information to each contact (Fax).

Note   *If you select E-mail from the Merge To drop-down list, an additional field appears, Message Subject Line. The text you enter here appears in the Subject line of each e-mail message created.*

After you set all your mail merge options, click OK to launch Word and complete the mail merge process. No matter which mail merge selections you make, Word opens with a blank document and the Mail Merge toolbar displayed, shown in Figure 20-2. If you select Mailing Labels or Envelopes, however, the Mail Merge Helper dialog box appears also. You have to let Word know the type of labels or envelopes you want to use by clicking Setup and making your choice.

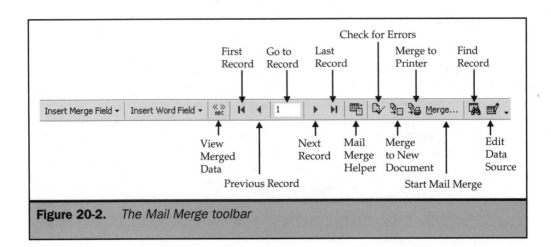

Figure 20-2.   *The Mail Merge toolbar*

The next step for any document type is to add fields to the merge document. Contact fields are available for all merge documents. However, form letters provide an additional choice of Word fields. Although the following set of instructions applies specifically to Form Letter and Catalog document types, you can utilize much of the information to complete a merge for Mailing Labels and Envelopes as well.

Click the Insert Merge Field button to display a drop-down list of contact fields. To include Word fields, click the Insert Word Field button. From the list, select the field you want to include in the document. The new field appears in the document at the blinking cursor. Be sure to place the cursor in the appropriate position before selecting a field. For example, if you're including a business address, and want city, state, and zip code to appear on a single line, add Business_Address_City followed by a comma and a space, then add Business_Address_State followed by a space, and finally, add Business_Address_Postal_Code. The line should appear like this:

<<Business_Address_City>>, << Business_Address_State>>
<<Business_Address_Postal_Code>>

You can intersperse text anywhere you want. For example, you might start a letter with a salutation that looks something like this: Dear <<Full_Name>>, or Hi <<First_Name>>. You can create the body of your letter, e-mail, or fax as you would normally. Again, you can add fields as needed. Perhaps you're sending a notice to inform your vendors of the new buyers they should contact. If you have a custom field in your contacts database called Buyer, you might add a line to the message that states "In the future <<Buyer>> will be handling your account."

If you want to take a sneak peek at your merge document before completing the merge, click the View Merged Data button. It's a toggle switch that displays the actual data for each field in the document the first time you click it. Click it a second time and the data disappears, and the field names return. While in the data view, you can cycle through all the contacts included in the merge by clicking the various record buttons.

The next step is to perform the merge. Click the Start Mail Merge button to open the Merge dialog box:

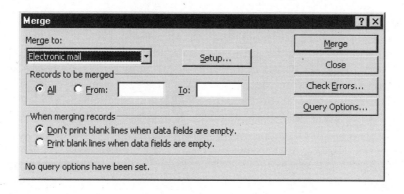

The Merge dialog box contains the following options you can use to customize the final merge document(s):

- **Merge to**   In case you've changed your mind since you started the merge back in Outlook, you can choose a different document type for the merge. You'll find New Document, Printer, Electronic Mail, and Electronic Fax (if fax is installed) on this drop-down list.

- **Setup**   This button is only available when you select Electronic Mail or Electronic Fax from the Merge To drop-down list. Clicking the Setup button displays the Setup dialog box, which lets you choose the field that contains the e-mail address or fax number to be used to address the final documents. You can also change the Subject line and elect to send the merged document as an attachment.

- **Records to be merged**   This option gives you an opportunity to narrow the selection of contact records included in the merge. Select All to include all records initially selected. If you want to include a subset of the records you chose in the beginning, click From and enter the record numbers of the first and last record to include in the From and To fields. You can determine the record numbers by returning to the merge document, clicking the View Merged Data button, and cycling through the records.

- **When merging records**   This option enables you to eliminate the printing of blank lines when no data appears in the field for a particular record. You'll probably want to stick with Don't Print Blank Lines When Data Fields Are Empty. It makes for a neater and more professional-looking merge document.

- **Merge**   When you're ready to perform the merge, click this button.

- **Close**   If you want to work on the merge document a little more, click this button to close the Merge dialog box. You can always return when you're ready.

- **Check Errors**   Click this button to run an error check on the merge. The Checking And Reporting Errors dialog box opens, offering you several choices. You can simulate the merge and log the errors in a new document, run the merge and simply report the errors as they happen, or run the merge and log any errors that occur in a new document. Since performing a large merge can be time consuming, you might want to run a simulation first. This is especially true if you're sending the finished documents to the printer, e-mail, or fax. If you elect to run the merge and get a blow-by-blow report, some problems are bound to slip by before you can stop the merge, and you'll have to start all over again. If you choose to run the merge and dump the errors into a log file, you won't know about the problems until it is over and too late to stop it.

- **Query Options**   The Query Options button gives you access to the Query Options dialog box, which offers the opportunity to filter the contact records and to sort them. This can be very helpful if you want to create subsets of the merge, and if you want to ensure the merge is created in a particular order.

It is a life saver if you're printing a large number of labels that you plan to mail out. To get the best mailing rates at the Post Office, you've got to pre-sort your mail by zip code. Just click the Sort Records tab, scroll down the Sort By list, and select the appropriate zip code field.

After you set all the Merge options, it's time to perform the merge and create the final document(s). Click the Merge button, sit back and relax (with your fingers crossed, of course), and let Word and Outlook do the rest. What you end up with depends on the choices you made along the way:

- **New Document** If you chose to produce a new document, Word creates a new document containing form letters, labels, envelopes, or catalog entries for each contact.

- **Printer** If you sent the document to the printer, the Print dialog box appears. Set your printer options, click Print, and your final documents appear in hard copy.

- **E-mail** An e-mail message is created for each contact and immediately placed in the Outlook Outbox. The next time the Exchange server does a sweep, or the next time you send e-mail, the messages are dispatched.

- **Fax** If you performed a fax mail merge, the resulting documents are passed on to the installed fax application and immediately sent to the selected contacts.

If you created a new document, save or print it before closing Word and returning to Outlook to continue working.

Using Contacts to Create Letters with Word

In addition to utilizing contact information for creating mail merge documents, you can also use it to create letters in Word. The process is relatively simple. Open the Contacts folder and select the contact to whom you want to write the letter. Next, choose Actions | New Letter to Contact. This opens Word and launches the Letter Wizard shown in Figure 20-3.

Follow the wizard instructions to create the letter. When you proceed to Step 2, the Recipient Info tab, you'll see that the selected contact's name and address have been inserted in the Recipient's Name and Delivery Address fields, respectively. When you complete the Letter Wizard, Word creates a letter with the designated headings, salutation, and closing. Add the contents, perform any necessary customizing or proofing, and send it on its way.

Using the New Mail Message Using Command

Another handy command you can employ to take advantage of other Office applications from within Outlook is the New Mail Message Using command. It enables you to create and send, via e-mail, a document from any of the installed Office applications, without having to leave Outlook.

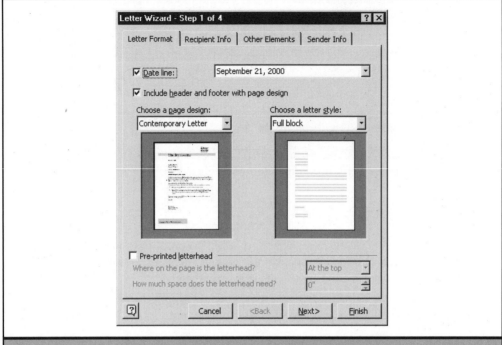

Figure 20-3. *The Word Letter Wizard walks you through the process of creating a letter*

To use the command, open the Inbox and choose Actions | New Message Using | Microsoft Office. This displays the Microsoft Office submenu containing all the Office applications (except Outlook) currently installed on your system. Select the application of your choice to launch the application with a mail message form opened, and a document of the type associated with the application embedded in the message body (see Figure 20-4).

Note *Only the data from the document is embedded in the message, not the document itself. Therefore, when you receive a message containing such information you can read it, but you cannot manipulate it as you can a document that's included in a message as an embedded object.*

Enter recipients' addresses in the To and Cc fields, and then enter a brief description of the message in the Subject line. You cannot enter a message to accompany the document data. However, you can set some options. If you take a close look at Figure 20-4, you'll see the message has a toolbar with additional options. You can add a file attachment, set the priority, flag the message, and more.

Figure 20-4.   *Using the Microsoft Excel Worksheet command opens Excel and embeds a worksheet in the message body*

> **Tip**
> *The default message form only permits you to insert file attachments in the message. By modifying the Windows registry, you can add the ability to include Outlook items as well as files. Warning! Since editing the Windows registry can adversely affect your system, only experienced users should make modifications. All users, regardless of experience, should back up the registry before making any changes. Locate the `HKEY_CURRENT_USER/Software/Microsoft/Office/9.0/Outlook` key, and add a new DWORD Value. Name it **ExtendedEnvelopeUI**, and give it a Value Data of **1**. The next time you open a message form in Word, you'll see an Item button on the toolbar for inserting Outlook items as attachments. You'll also find an HTML and a Plain Text button on the message toolbar. You can use these to change the message format.*

The next step is to add the data to the Office document (worksheet, table, and so forth). Since you're starting with a blank document, you can either add the data manually or cut and paste it from another document. If you open an existing document, you lose the message form. However, you can still send an existing document by opening it and then clicking the E-mail button on the application's Standard toolbar. This opens another message form containing the document.

When you've addressed the message form and entered the necessary information into the document, you can send the message by clicking the Send button. The name of the Send button varies depending on the Office application. For example, in Word it's called Send A Copy, while in Excel it's called Send This Sheet. After the message is sent, the Office application remains open with the document still active. However, the message form is no longer available. You can now choose to save, modify, or discard the document.

Using the Office Clipboard

Another nice thing about the closeness of the Office applications is their ability to share the Office clipboard. Similar to the Windows clipboard, the Office clipboard allows you to copy text and graphics from a document and store them for later use in the same document or an entirely different document. However, unlike the Windows clipboard, the Office clipboard accepts multiple items.

Note

While you can copy from any source that supports copying and cutting, you can only paste items from the Office clipboard into Office applications (Microsoft Word, Excel, Microsoft Access, Microsoft Outlook, or PowerPoint).

The basic operation of the Office clipboard is no different from that of the Windows clipboard. The Copy, Cut, and Paste operations can be performed by selecting the text or graphic and pressing CTRL-C, CTRL-X, and CTRL-V, respectively. You can also use the Copy, Cut, and Paste commands found on the Edit menu. You'll even find the commands available on a shortcut menu when you right-click selected text or objects.

The Office clipboard is available in all forms except the Note form. To display the Office clipboard, right-click anywhere on the form's toolbar and select Clipboard from the shortcut menu. You'll note that each item copied or cut to the clipboard appears as a page with an Outlook icon in the top left corner. To view the first 50 characters of the item, pause your mouse pointer over it.

With the Office clipboard open you can perform a number of operations. You can copy an item by selecting it and clicking the Copy button on the clipboard. To paste an item from the clipboard, place your cursor in a text field in the form and double-click the item on the clipboard. If you have multiple items on the clipboard and want to paste them all at once, click the Paste All button on the clipboard. Finally, if you want to remove all data on the clipboard, click the Clear Clipboard button.

The clipboard can hold a maximum of twelve items. Once you exceed that number, each succeeding item causes the earliest item on the clipboard to be removed to make room for the new item.

Since the Office clipboard is a toolbar, you can dock it if you want. Either drag it to one of the four sides of the form window or nestle it up against a visible toolbar. When you drop it, you'll see that it becomes docked. You can also double-click its title bar to dock it.

To close the Office clipboard, click the small X in the upper right corner or right-click the Clipboard toolbar and deselect Clipboard from the shortcut menu.

MOUS EXAM PRACTICE
Getting up to speed with the Office clipboard is easy. Begin by opening a form and displaying the clipboard by right-clicking the toolbar and selecting Clipboard. Next, highlight a bit of text and copy it to the clipboard using a standard method. Then copy another piece of text using the Copy button on the clipboard. Try your hand at pasting by placing the cursor in a text field and double-clicking one of the clipboard items. Next, try pasting all the items by using the Paste All button. When you're through practicing, click the Clear Clipboard button to remove all items.

Outlook Commands Available in Office Applications

The integration between Outlook and the Office applications works both ways. In addition to accessing Office applications from Outlook, you can also take advantage of Outlook while working in other Office programs. The two major functions you can perform in other Office applications are sending e-mail and posting documents to Exchange server folders.

Sending E-mail

While working in most Office applications, you can send the document you're working on with little or no fuss. Rather than open Outlook, create a new message, and attach the document, you might just as well use one of the Send To commands available on the File menu of Word, Excel, Access, or PowerPoint.

Either open an existing document or create a new one in the application of your choice. When you're ready to send it, choose File | Send To. You'll find two mail commands on the drop-down menu that appears: Mail Recipient and Mail Recipient (As Attachment). Select the one that meets your needs.

- ■ **Mail Recipient**   Use this command to open a message form in the application and embed the document information (not the document itself) in the body of the message.

- ■ **Mail Recipient (As Attachment)**   This command opens a new Outlook e-mail message form with the document already inserted as an attachment.

Enter the desired recipient(s) in the To, Cc, and Bcc fields, and type a brief description in the Subject field. If you don't see the Bcc field and want to use it, choose View Bcc Field from the form's Menu bar. If you're sending the document as an attachment, type your message. Set any options you want and click the Send button. If you use the Mail Recipient command, the name of the Send button will vary depending on the application you're in.

You can also send e-mail messages from Word by choosing File | New to open the New dialog box. By the way, if you're a shortcut key fan you'll probably be tempted to use the CTRL-N shortcut. Don't bother. It simply opens a blank document, not the New dialog box. When you've finally got the New dialog box open, click the General tab and then double-click the E-mail Message icon. An untitled message form opens. Fill it out and send it. That's all there is to it.

Posting Office Documents to Public Folders

If you use public folders, you'll find this feature quite useful. It is common to post not only messages in public folders, but documents as well. You may have a white paper, budget report, or list of ideas you want to get feedback on. Rather than post a message with the document attached, you can post the document itself directly to the public folder. This feature is available in Word, Excel, and PowerPoint.

Begin by opening one of the just-mentioned Office applications, and opening an existing document or creating a new one. When your document is ready for primetime, choose File | Send To | Exchange Folder to open the Send To Exchange Folder dialog box, shown in Figure 20-5.

Select the public folder to which you want the current document posted, and click OK. Unfortunately, the folder icons in the Send To Exchange Folder dialog box are all identical. Therefore, you cannot distinguish between the various folder types (mail, contacts, appointments, and so on). So be sure you know the name of the public folder you want to post to before you start out.

While you can post to any folder type, including Mailbox and Personal folders, it doesn't make a lot of sense to post documents to anything other than public folders that contain mail items. When you post to other folder types, the results are generally impractical. For example, nothing appears in a Calendar folder, and a no-name contact record appears in a Contacts folder. No matter where you post it, double-clicking the item launches the associated application and opens the document.

Figure 20-5.   *The Send To Exchange Folder dialog box brings your Outlook Folder List to you wherever you are*

Importing and Exporting Data

The wealth of information that abounds in today's information society is impressive, to say the least, but can easily become overwhelming. Part of the problem is the variety of sources from which that information emanates. Just look at the number of different programs available for handling contact information. Some people use address book software, others use personal information managers, some use spreadsheets or databases, some use contact mangers, others use the address books in their e-mail software, and then there are those who use address lists compiled in word processing documents. The same goes for e-mail, appointments, and other bits of information.

While Outlook doesn't work directly with most major applications outside the Office suite, you can still make use of Outlook information in other programs, and vice versa. The way to accomplish this is by exchanging data using the Outlook Import And Export feature. When you import information from other programs, Outlook converts it to a format that Outlook can understand. When you export Outlook information, Outlook converts it to a format that other applications can work with.

Importing Data into Outlook

If you happen to be starting out with Outlook and pulling together all your bits and pieces of information from a variety of programs, or if you're gathering information from others who use different software, you'll be glad to know that Outlook has a powerful import feature.

Outlook may be smart enough to convert the data you want to import, but it will need a little help in identifying it. Therefore, the first thing you need to know is the format of the information you want to bring into Outlook. Other than that, you only need access to the file(s) containing the data. Choose File | Import And Export to start the Import And Export Wizard, shown in Figure 20-6.

The opening screen provides a number of import options, including:

- **Import a VCARD file (.vcf)** vCards have become the standard for sharing contact information in a business card format over the Internet. If you receive and store vCard files from the Internet, you can import them into your Outlook contacts database using this option.

- **Import an iCalendar or vCalendar file (.vcs)** iCalendar and vCalendar are used to exchange calendar information via the Internet. Use this option to import either format into the Outlook Calendar folder.

- **Import cc:Mail Archive** To import a cc:Mail archive file into Outlook, use this option. It comes in handy for those folks moving from a cc:Mail system to an Exchange server system.

- **Import from another program or file** This is one of the more popular import actions, simply because it enables you to import data from a wide range of programs including contact managers, PIMs, spreadsheets, databases, text files, and more. As soon as you select this option and click Next, you're presented with a list of file types you can import.

- **Import Internet Mail Account Settings** If you're switching your Internet e-mail to Outlook from another e-mail client, you can use this option to import the settings from the existing e-mail account into Outlook. Selecting this option and clicking Next launches the Internet Connection Wizard, which searches your hard drive for existing Internet e-mail accounts and lets you select the one whose settings you want to transfer to Outlook. When you finish with the Internet Connection Wizard, Outlook adds the new account to your profile.

- **Import Internet Mail and Addresses** Often used in conjunction with the previous option, this one makes the transfer of e-mail and recipient addresses relatively painless. Rather than leave all your existing e-mail and recipient addresses behind, this option allows you to bring them into Outlook. There's nothing worse than having to bounce back and forth between two e-mail programs looking for an important piece of e-mail or an address. After selecting this option, click Next to see a list of supported e-mail programs. Before the import completes, Outlook displays an Import Summary dialog box, indicating how many messages, addresses, and distribution lists were imported. Oh yes, one more thing. If you import from Outlook Express, you can also include any mail-handling rules you may have created.

> **Tip** *Importing third-party file formats such as Ecco and ACT! requires that the original application be installed on your computer. If you're importing data provided by another user who has the application running, ask the user to export the data into a format Outlook can import directly, such as text delimited, Word, Excel, or Access.*

Since most of the Import And Export Wizard screens are self-explanatory, there's no need to go through each one here. However, there are a few things that may need clarification. Those are covered next.

Import/Export Engine

The first time you attempt to import data either from a cc:Mail archive file (Import cc:Mail Archive) or from another application (Import From Another Program Or File), you'll run into an error message indicating that the Import/Export engine is not installed. The dialog box asks if you want to install it now. Since the Import/Export engine is the translator needed to convert the imported data into a format Outlook can use, it's in your best

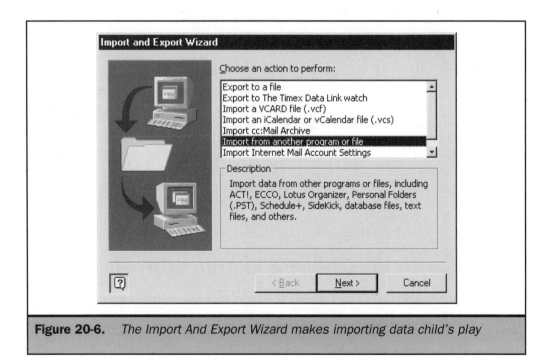

Figure 20-6. *The Import And Export Wizard makes importing data child's play*

interest to answer yes. However, before doing so you should grab your original Office CD and insert it in the CD-ROM drive. All you have to do after that is follow the onscreen instructions.

While the Import/Export engine may sound like a single utility, it is not. It's actually a collection of file converters. So even if you say yes and install the Import/Export engine for one file type, the others are not installed. Therefore, if you plan to import a variety of different file formats, you might want to install all the converters at once. Insert your original CD in the CD-ROM drive and start the Office or Outlook setup routine. You can use the Add/Remove Programs applet in the Windows Control Panel (Start | Settings | Control Panel) or double-click Setup.exe on the root of the CD. When the installer is running, go to the Add Or Remove Features section, and expand the Microsoft Outlook For Windows features by clicking the plus sign (+) to its left. Click the down arrow next to Importers And Exporters to display the installation choices for import and export converters. Select Run All From My Computer, and click the Update Now button. All the converters are installed and you are returned to the active window.

Mapping Fields

Field mapping is one of the most important, and most confusing (the first time you use it), features of the Outlook import process. It provides an accurate way to import address book and other database information even if Outlook and the source program use different names for the same fields. For example, the Ecco personal information manager calls the field that holds your work phone number Work #, while the same field in Outlook is called Business Phone. The Outlook file converters are pretty good about recognizing commonly used fields, such as name, company, address, phone number, and so on. However, there's no way the converters can recognize custom fields or obscure fields not used in Outlook. When you run across fields of this nature you're going to have to give Outlook a hand, which is where field mapping comes in.

When you map fields, you're simply telling Outlook which fields from the incoming file match up with existing Outlook fields. This way, if the imported file has a custom field called Company URL, you can instruct Outlook to dump the data from that field into the Outlook Web Page field. You get the opportunity to map fields when you reach the Import A File screen, which resembles the one shown in Figure 20-7.

Select the action that requires field mapping and click the Map Custom Fields button to open the Map Custom Fields dialog box, shown in Figure 20-8.

As you can see in Figure 20-8, fields from the imported file are displayed in the left pane, while fields from Outlook appear in the right pane. The left pane has a single column, Value, which contains the names of the fields in the imported file. The right pane has two columns, Field and Mapped From. Field is the name of the Outlook field, and Mapped From is the name of the imported field that the Outlook converter has matched up with the Outlook field. Your job as a custom field mapper is to ensure that the matching is correct and to match any fields the converter couldn't. That's not to say, however, that every field must be mapped. If there's data you don't want to import, you can choose not to map the field or even remove the mapping already done by the converter.

Figure 20-7.   *You can customize field mapping and the data destination*

Figure 20-8.   *Matching fields is easy in the Map Custom Fields dialog box*

However, for those fields that you want mapped, the task is pretty easy. In the left pane, locate the field you want to map, and drag it to the right pane. Now find the Outlook field you want it mapped to and drop it on the Outlook field name. The imported field name instantly appears in the Mapped From column. To unmap a field, simply drag the Outlook field name from the Field column on the right and drop it anywhere in the left pane. The association is immediately terminated, and the field name disappears from the Mapped From column. You can even change the mapping by dropping a different import field onto an Outlook field, without first removing the existing mapped field. The new one replaces the old association.

If you want to see the actual data, rather than the field names, click the Next button. Immediately, the field names in both the Value column on the left, and the Mapped From column on the right are replaced by the information from the imported fields. Each time you click Next, you see the data from the next record. When you're finished mapping, click OK to return to the Import A File Wizard. If you're ready to complete the import, click Finish and you're on your way.

Exporting Outlook Data

The flip side of importing is, of course, exporting. Exporting Outlook data involves converting it to a format that other programs can utilize or import. It's handy for sharing information with friends and colleagues who happen to use software other than Outlook for their information management needs.

When it comes to exporting Outlook data, the process is similar to importing. You begin by choosing File | Import And Export to start the Import And Export Wizard. However, unlike the import feature, export has only two options, Export To A File and Export To The Timex Data Link Watch. The second is used only to export Outlook data for use with a Timex Data Link watch and is self-explanatory.

The first option, Export To A File, is for all your other export needs. As soon as you select Export To A File and click Next, the wizard displays a list of file types to which you can convert Outlook information. Your choices include the following file types:

- **Comma Separated Values (DOS)**   Use this type to create a text file in which each field is delimited (separated) by commas. The delimiter lets other programs know where one field ends and the next begins. This format uses the ASCII character set, which is compatible with DOS programs as well as Windows programs.

- **Comma Separated Values (Windows)**   This option is the same as the first, except that the file created uses the ANSI character set compatible with Windows programs, but not with DOS programs.

- **dBase**   To those who were around in the days before Microsoft dominated the desktop software world, dBase is a familiar name. It was, for many years, the most popular database product around. As a result, its .dbf file format is still considered a standard for many database products.

■ **Microsoft Access**   Use this option to export Outlook data into the .mdb file format used by Microsoft Access.

■ **Microsoft Excel**   To use Outlook data in an Excel worksheet, choose this option. It dumps the Outlook data into an Excel-compatible file with an .xls extension.

■ **Microsoft FoxPro**   FoxPro, which has been around for quite a while, uses a variation on the .dbf format. Although the extension is the same, it differs from the dBase .dbf format, so don't confuse the two. Be sure to use this option for exporting Outlook data for use with FoxPro.

■ **Personal Folder File (.pst)**   If you want to share your Outlook information with another Outlook user, you can export your mailbox or other folders to a .pst file, which another user can then open in Outlook by adding it to his or her profile. It's also an easy way to create personal folders for yourself from your mailbox folders.

■ **Tab Separated Values (DOS)**   This format, sometimes referred to as TSV, is the same as the Comma Separated Values (DOS) format, except that the field delimiter is a tab character (the invisible formatting character created when you press the TAB key) rather than a comma.

■ **Tab Separated Values (Windows)**   This is the same as the Comma Separated Values (Windows) format, except that a tab is used as the delimiter instead of a comma.

After you make your selection, click Next to view the export folder screen, which contains a tree-like view of your Outlook folders. Select the folder from which you want to export your Outlook information, and click Next. No matter which file type you selected in the beginning, the next screen offers you a chance to locate and name the target file into which you want the Outlook data stored.

If you're exporting to a .pst file, you get added options for handling duplicate records, and you're almost at the end. Clicking Finish creates the .pst file and presents you with a Create Microsoft Personal Folders dialog box in which you can set the configuration options for the new .pst file.

For all other file types, the next step after designating the target folder is to click Next, which brings up the actions screen. Here you get the opportunity to map custom fields. When you're finished with your field mapping chores, click Finish to create the new file.

One last thing: all information from the selected Outlook folder is exported even if a filter is applied at the time the export takes place. For example, suppose you're exporting your Contacts folder to an Access database format, and you decide you only want to export information on your customers. You might think that by first filtering out all the non-customer contacts in the Contacts folder you could limit the export to customers only. Unfortunately, while it is a good thought, it doesn't work that way. Outlook ignores all filters and dumps the entire contents of the selected folder into the target folder. The easiest way to export a subset of one of your folders is to apply a filter and move or copy the desired Outlook items to a new Outlook folder. You can then export the new folder rather than the original folder.

Exam | MOUS Exam Objectives Explored in Chapter 20

Objective	Activity	Heading
OL2000.1.16	Integrate and use mail with other Outlook components	"Sending E-mail"
OL2000.4.7	Use the Office clipboard	"Using the Office Clipboard"

The Complete Reference

Chapter 21

Using Outlook to Access the Internet

Since the Internet is quickly becoming an inescapable part of everyday life, it's no surprise that Outlook 2000 provides direct access to the Internet. As a matter of fact, you can't even run Outlook 2000 without installing Internet Explorer 4.01 or higher. It's this tight integration with Internet Explorer that enables Outlook to associate Web pages with folders, act as a Web browser, and utilize Internet Explorer Favorites. In addition, Outlook also integrates with Outlook Express to create the Outlook Newsreader, which lets you access Internet newsgroups from within Outlook. You can even conduct online meetings over the Internet from within Outlook by taking advantage of its ability to integrate with Microsoft NetMeeting.

Viewing Web Pages in Outlook

Before going any further, there is one thing you should be aware of. When you connect to a secure Web site, Outlook does not display the lock icon in the status bar that usually indicates that your communication with the site is encrypted. Nor does it display a notice when you enter or leave a secure site, even if you have the notice enabled in your Internet Options. Therefore, it is recommended that you use Internet Explorer or another browser outside of Outlook for conducting sensitive or financial transactions over the Internet.

If you've already connected to a secure site in Outlook and want to use your default Web browser to ensure your communication is encrypted, choose File | Open In Default Browser to launch your default Web browser and open the current Web page.

If you're just doodling around, checking the news, stock quotes, or the latest fashion trends on the Internet, you can do so without ever leaving the Outlook environment. You can even associate Web pages with individual Outlook folders by creating a home page for each folder. (See Chapter 18 for more information.)

Using Favorites

Getting on the Web from Outlook is almost too easy. All you need is an Internet connection, Outlook, and your mouse. When you install Outlook, it searches out and adds existing bookmarks from Internet Explorer to the Outlook Favorites menu. If you want to visit one of those links, simply establish an Internet connection, open the Favorites menu, click the desired link, and you're off. If the Web page is available, it opens in the Information viewer, replacing the current folder view. You can now view the page, click links, fill out forms, and do what you would normally do in a Web browser.

You can follow the progress of the page as it's downloading by keeping an eye on the Outlook window status bar. The page being loaded is indicated on the left side of the status bar, and a Loading icon appears on the right side.

Adding Web sites to the Favorites menu is also quite easy. Open the Web page you want to add and choose Favorites | Add To Favorites to display the Add To Favorites dialog box, shown in Figure 21-1. Select the folder in which you want to place the Web page shortcut, or create a new folder by clicking the New Folder button on the dialog box toolbar.

Tip

The name given to the shortcut created when you add a Web page to your Favorites folder is taken from the Web page title, which in many cases is long, drawn out, and often confusing. To give the shortcut a more easily identifiable name, change the File Name information to something you'll quickly recognize.

Click Add to create a shortcut for the Web page in the selected folder, and return to the active window. The next time you want to access the Web page, open the Favorites menu and select the shortcut to return to the associated page.

Figure 21-1. *The Add To Favorites dialog box resembles a Windows Save As dialog box*

Using the Web Toolbar and Web Commands

As soon as you open a Web page or Web document in Outlook, the Web toolbar immediately appears.

As you can see, the Web toolbar contains a number of standard browser commands that make navigating the Web easy. The default buttons on the Web toolbar include:

- **Back** Click this button to return to the previously viewed Web page. This button will not take you back to an Outlook folder, even if that was the last thing you viewed in the Information viewer. It will take you to the last Web page you visited prior to displaying the folder.

- **Forward** The Forward button works the same as the Back button. It simply takes you in the opposite direction. It becomes available after you open at least two Web pages and return to one previous page.

- **Stop Current Jump** Click the Stop Current Jump button to halt the downloading of the currently selected Web page.

- **Refresh Current Page** Web pages are constantly being updated. To be sure you're viewing the latest version, click the Refresh Current Page button.

- **Start Page** If there's one thing you can say about Microsoft programmers, it's that they're consistently inconsistent. With the tight integration between Outlook and Internet Explorer, you'd think they would, as a matter of course, name the standard toolbar buttons the same in both programs. But, of course, you'd be wrong. The Start Page button is everyone else's Home Page button. Fortunately, it works the same, and takes you to the home page designated in your Internet Options, which are accessible from the Windows Control Panel or the Internet Explorer Tools menu.

- **Search the Web** If you don't have a favorite search engine, click this button and Outlook whisks you away to the Microsoft Web site that houses a bevy of search engine, directory, and references site links.

■ **Address**   Enter the URL of the Web site you want to visit or view the address of the currently displayed Web page. The drop-down list contains the addresses of recently visited Web pages.

In addition to displaying the Web toolbar, opening a Web page in Outlook also adds several commands to the menu system. The following commands are available when you display a Web page in Outlook:

■ **Open in Default Browser**   Located on the File menu, this command opens the Web page currently displayed in Outlook in your default Web browser.

■ **Outlook Bar Shortcut to Web Page**   Choose File | New | Outlook Bar Shortcut To Web Page to add a shortcut to the Outlook Bar for the currently displayed Web page. By default, the new shortcut is added to the My Shortcuts group.

■ **Send Web Page by E-mail**   Use this command, found on the Actions menu, to create a new e-mail message. If your default e-mail format is Plain or Rich Text, the currently selected Web page is inserted into the e-mail message as an HTML file attachment. If your default message format is HTML, the Web page is pasted into the message body.

Since the Web toolbar is by no means overcrowded, and these commands can be useful when viewing Web pages, you might want to add at least two of them to the Web toolbar for quick access when surfing the Internet in Outlook. You might want to add only two because the Microsoft programmers forgot to add Outlook Bar Shortcut To Web Page to the Commands tab of the Customize dialog box. To add the others, right-click any toolbar, select Customize, and click the Commands tab. Select the File category to locate the Open In Default Browser command. You'll find the Send Web Page By E-mail command in the Actions category. Drag the command of your choice to the Web toolbar and drop it between two existing buttons.

Caution   *In the event you get wild and crazy and decide to move the Outlook Bar Shortcut To Web Page command from the New menu to the Web toolbar, be careful. If you accidentally drop it along the way, you will not be able to get it back again without running the Detect And Repair command. Losing a command usually isn't a problem since there's (almost) always a permanent copy in the Customize dialog box. However, in this case there is no permanent copy, so you'll be minus the command unless you run Detect And Repair, which requires your original CD and, in some cases, a fair amount of time.*

Outlook Web Tricks

In addition to letting you assign Web pages to folders, browse the Web, and send Web pages via e-mail, Outlook has a couple of other Web tricks up its sleeve.

Opening Web Pages Automatically

Although Outlook can't get your first cup of coffee in the morning, it can make sure your favorite Web site is waiting for you when you return from the coffee room. All you need is an established Internet connection and a URL, and you're all set.

Begin by creating a new appointment. Enter a brief description in the Subject line. If you like to read the *New York Times* with your coffee when you get to work, enter something like **Open NY Times Web site**. Click the Recurrence button on the appointment form toolbar, and fill in the desired information. Using the *New York Times* example, you might make the recurrence pattern Daily, and select Every Weekday. If you get to work at 8:00 every morning, you might make the start time 8:05A.M. Set a start date and click OK to save the recurrence information and return to the appointment form.

Now check the This Is An Online Meeting Using option, and select NetShow Services from the drop-down list to the right of the option. The Event Address field appears. Enter the URL of the Web site you want to open. In the earlier example, it would be http://www.nytimes.com. The last thing you must do is set a reminder to trigger the action. Check the reminder option and enter or select 0 minutes. Click Save And Close and you're done. When the next due date and time arrive, the Outlook launches your default Web browser and opens the designated page.

Sending Pictures from the Internet

As discussed earlier in this chapter, you can send Web pages via e-mail, using the Send Web Page By E-mail command. Unless your default mail format is HTML, you may not be aware that you can also elect to send pictures with the Web page. This enables the recipient to view the Web page, including pictures, even if he or she isn't connected to the Web. Simply sending a Web page by e-mail sends the text and pointers to the pictures on the Web site, but not the pictures themselves.

Note   *The only downside to using this command is that it increases the size of the message substantially. Images require a lot more storage space than text, therefore, you may want to use this option sparingly.*

To include pictures with a Web page, make HTML your default mail format first. Then open (in Outlook) the Web page you want to send. Choose Actions | Send Web Page By E-mail to create a new e-mail message with the Web page included in the body. From the message form toolbar, choose Format | Send Pictures From The Internet. Enter your recipients, any message you want to include, and click Send. Using this command, you can send completely viewable Web pages to individuals who don't have Internet access.

Launching Your Default Web Browser

Unlike the Open In Default Browser command, which requires that you have a Web page already open in Outlook, the Web Browser command launches your default browser anywhere within Outlook, and at any time. From any folder, choose View | Go To | Web Browser. Your default browser launches and attempts to open the Web page designated in the browser as the home page.

Using the Outlook Newsreader

Newsgroups are specialized forums comprised of messages posted to a news server by users with a common interest in the newsgroup topic. If you know how to find and use them, newsgroups can provide a wealth of information. Although Outlook does not technically have its own newsreader, it borrows the one from Outlook Express and uses it as if it were its own. This feature is another example of the tight integration between Microsoft products.

Making Outlook Your Default Newsreader

The first order of business is to make Outlook your default newsreader. You can do this either through the Internet Options applet in the Control Panel or through the Internet Options found in Internet Explorer. From within Internet Explorer, choose Tools | Internet Options to open the Internet Options dialog box. Then click the Programs tab to display the default programs used for Internet access (see Figure 21-2).

From the Newsgroups drop-down list, choose Microsoft Outlook. Click OK to save your settings and return to the active view. Return to Outlook and choose View | Go To | News to start the Internet Connection Wizard, shown in Figure 21-3.

Note   *If your current version of Outlook Express replaced an earlier version, a dialog box may appear informing you that mail will be converted from the old version to the new. Click OK to proceed.*

Enter the name you want to be used when you post to any newsgroups using the Outlook Newsreader. Click Next to move to the Internet e-mail address screen. Enter your Internet e-mail address and click Next to continue. The screen that appears asks for the name of your news server. This information is provided by your Internet service provider (ISP) or by your system administrator if your access to the Internet is through a local area network (LAN). Enter the appropriate name server information. If the server requires a user logon and password, check the My News Server Requires Me To Log On option. Click Next to proceed. If you left the My News Server Requires Me To Log On option unchecked, you immediately jump to the final screen informing you the setup is complete.

Figure 21-2.   *Outlook must be selected as your default program for Newsgroups*

If you checked the option, the next screen asks for your account name and password. By checking the Remember Password option, you can instruct Outlook to remember your password so you don't have to enter it each time you log on.

Caution   *While using the Remember Password option may save you a little time and effort each time you log on, it also means that anyone with access to your computer can log on as you, without having to know your password.*

The final option on the Internet News Server Logon screen is the Log On Using Secure Password Authentication (SPA) option. If your ISP requires SPA, check this option. Click Next to view the final screen, and then click Finish to complete the account setup. Outlook asks if you would like to view a list of the newsgroups available on the account you've just created. If you're connected to the Internet, click OK to download the list of newsgroups. When you're finished downloading, you should see a Newsgroup Subscriptions dialog box similar to the one in Figure 21-4.

Internet Connection Wizard	

Your Name

When you post a message to a newsgroup or send an e-mail message, your display
name will appear in the From field. Type your name as you would like it to appear.

Display name: Rebecca Samuels

For example: John Smith

< Back   Next >   Cancel

Figure 21-3.   *The Internet Connection Wizard makes setting up the Outlook
Newsreader quick and easy*

All the newsgroups on the news server are displayed in the All tab of the dialog box.
To search for specific groups, type a keyword in the Display Newsgroups Which Contain
field. You don't have to do anything more. The search is conducted as soon as you stop
typing. Select any newsgroups to which you want to subscribe, and click the Subscribe
button. Subscribing adds the selected newsgroup(s) to your Outlook Newsreader folders
list. Since most news servers contain a large number of newsgroups, subscribing
eliminates the need to scour the entire list each time you want to visit a newsgroup.

The Subscribed tab lists all newsgroups to which you are currently subscribed.
The New tab lists any new newsgroups added to the news server since the last time
you downloaded. When you're done subscribing (or unsubscribing), click OK to close
the Newsgroup Subscriptions dialog box and return to the Outlook Newsreader,
shown in Figure 21-5.

Reading Newsgroup Messages

After you download and subscribe to newsgroups, the next step is to download
messages, read them, and if you're so inclined, post messages of your own. To
download messages, click the newsgroup of your choice in the Folders list. As long
as you have an Internet connection established, the Outlook Newsreader automatically

Figure 21-4.   *Select the specific newsgroups to which you want to subscribe*

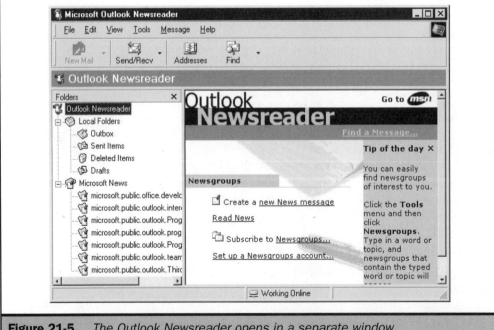

Figure 21-5.   *The Outlook Newsreader opens in a separate window*

starts downloading the messages contained in the selected newsgroup. As you can see in Figure 21-6, the top half of the right pane displays the list of messages, while the bottom pane provides a preview of the selected message. It's very much like the Outlook Inbox with the Preview Pane turned on.

You can scroll through the messages, displaying them in the Preview Pane as you go, or you can open a message in a separate window by double-clicking the message in the top pane. You can also right-click a message and select Open from the shortcut menu. One last thing about messages. You'll see a plus (+) sign to the left of some messages. This indicates the message has responses, which you can view by clicking the plus sign. This is similar to grouping by conversation in the Outlook Inbox, but it is done automatically when someone responds to a specific message.

Synchronizing Newsgroups

To make life simple, you can have the Outlook Newsreader automatically synchronize the newsgroups to which you subscribe to keep them up to date. In the Folders list, click the newsgroup account you want to synchronize. The synchronization window appears in the right pane (see Figure 21-7).

The synchronization window displays all the newsgroups to which you are subscribed for the selected newsgroup account. In addition, the synchronization

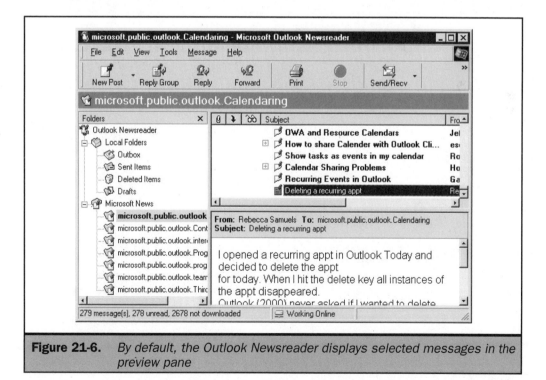

Figure 21-6. *By default, the Outlook Newsreader displays selected messages in the preview pane*

Figure 21-7. *Let the Outlook Newsreader do the work by synchronizing newsgroups automatically*

window also contains the following three buttons, which appear here in the order they are generally used when performing your first synchronization:

- **Settings** Click the Settings button to set the synchronization options for the selected newsgroup. The Settings drop-down menu which appears contains four options:

  - **Don't Synchronize** This is the default setting. It results in no action on the newsgroup for which it's set. Nothing new will be downloaded during a synchronization.

  - **All Messages** Select this option to download all messages, including headers and bodies. This will make accessing the messages a little quicker, but will also take up additional disk space since the messages are stored on your local computer. On the other hand, if you can afford the disk space, this is a handy way to access the messages when you're offline. You can always go into the newsgroup properties (right-click the desired newsgroup and select Properties) and delete all the downloaded messages.

- **New Messages Only** Rather than clutter up your newsreader with all the messages, you can elect to download only new messages that have been posted since your last download.

- **Headers Only** This is the quickest method, and it requires a minimum of local hard disk space, since the message bodies are left on the server and only accessed when you select the associated header.

■ **Newsgroups** This button activates the Newsgroups Subscription dialog box, where you can subscribe or unsubscribe to newsgroups as you choose.

■ **Synchronize Account** Click this button to download the most current messages for all newsgroups to which you are subscribed in the selected account. The manner in which the synchronization is performed depends on your selection in the Settings menu, displayed when you click the Settings button.

After you select the setting for each newsgroup, you can turn the setting on and off by checking or removing the checkmark in the box next to the setting name in the newsgroup list.

In addition to using the Synchronization window, you can also perform a synchronization by selecting the newsgroup account you want to synchronize and choosing Tools | Synchronize All. A synchronization is performed based on the settings already established. To synchronize a single newsgroup, select the newsgroup in the Folders list and choose Tools | Synchronize Newsgroup. The Synchronize Newsgroup dialog box appears, enabling you to choose a one-time setting for synchronizing this newsgroup.

The default setting you've chosen for this newsgroup does not change. When you return to the Synchronization window you'll see the default setting is still in effect, regardless of what you selected in the Synchronize Newsgroup dialog box.

Creating News Accounts

Creating a news account is simple. As a matter of fact, that's exactly what you did when you first opened the Outlook Newsreader. To create another news account, choose Tools | Accounts to display the Internet Accounts dialog box.

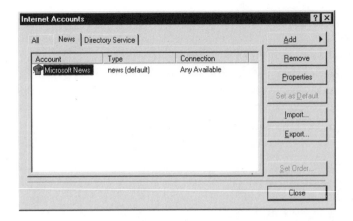

Click the Add button and select News to open the Internet Connection Wizard. Refer to the instructions in the section entitled "Making Outlook Your Default Newsreader," earlier in this chapter. When you return to the Internet Accounts dialog box, click Close to return to the Outlook Newsreader.

Posting to Newsgroups

Subscribing to a newsgroup generally means that the topic covered is of interest to you. Therefore, it's not unreasonable to expect that you may want to post a message of your own to the newsgroup. You may want to ask a question, supply an answer to a question already posted, or simply add your two cents to an ongoing discussion. Whatever your reason, posting to a newsgroup is easy.

The manner in which you post to a newsgroup is very similar to sending e-mail. There are a number of actions you can take to post to a newsgroup. The following Standard toolbar buttons make the most common forms of posting just a mouse click (or two) away.

- **New Post**   Select the newsgroup you want to post to, and click this button to open a new message form addressed to the selected newsgroup. Enter a brief and concise Subject line that makes the message contents clear. Then type your message, and send it on its way by clicking Send.

- **Reply Group**   If you want to respond to a particular message on the newsgroup, select the message and click Reply Group. This opens a new message addressed to the newsgroup, but with the Subject line already filled in, indicating this is a response to the selected message. In addition, the contents of the original message are pasted into the body of your new message, and set off by the greater than (>) symbol, indicating they are not part of your response. Enter your message above the pasted information and click Send. When the message is posted to the newsgroup, it appears as part of the conversation thread beneath the message to which you are responding.

- **Reply**   If you don't want to respond to the newsgroup, but would rather reply to the sender of a specific message privately, select the message and click the Reply button. This opens a message similar to the Reply Group message. The difference is that this one is addressed to the sender of the original message, not to the entire newsgroup.

- **Forward**   If you find a posting of particular interest, you can forward it to someone else who may share your interest. Select the message and click the Forward button to open a new message form with the Subject line filled in and the contents of the original message pasted in the body. Add the desired recipient(s) and send it on its way.

Note

It's important to always keep in mind that newsgroups are usually very targeted. Therefore, your posts should be relevant to the group. Sharing your favorite Hamburger Helper recipes on a gourmet cooking newsgroup is not going to make you one of the more popular members of the group. Also, keep in mind that it is a public forum and basic social amenities should be observed.

In addition to the toolbar buttons, you'll find other commands for posting on the Tools menu. As a matter of fact, there are a lot more commands of all types on the Outlook Newsreader menus. Spend a little time experimenting and you'll learn all kinds of interesting and helpful things about the program.

Using NetMeeting

NetMeeting is a sophisticated piece of software from Microsoft that allows you to communicate in real time with others over the Internet. This means you can place calls over the Internet, chat online, and even conduct virtual meetings online. It's the online meeting part that is of particular interest to Outlook users.

NetMeeting works hand in hand with Outlook to enable you to schedule and conduct online meetings without leaving the Outlook environment. If meeting participants have the requisite hardware installed, you can even include audio and video in your online meetings. In addition to having the necessary audio and video hardware, a fast LAN or Internet connection is recommended for utilizing audio and video in a NetMeeting environment.

NetMeeting is part of Internet Explorer. If you're running Windows 98 or Windows 2000, you automatically have NetMeeting since Internet Explorer is now an integral part of both operating systems. If you are running Windows 95 or Windows NT, you can download Internet Explorer from the Microsoft Web site. Even if you already have NetMeeting installed, you may want to upgrade to the latest version, which you can also download from the Microsoft site.

NetMeeting enables you to phone, chat, and meet online by using Internet Locator Servers (ILS) and Uniform Location Services (ULS). Each meeting participant logs on to an ILS or ULS server, which keeps track of the basic information required to make a NetMeeting connection. The first item it notes is that a user is online. The second piece of information required is the user's IP address. Since most users access the Internet through an ISP, which assigns a different IP address each time, there is no way to determine the IP address until the user logs on. This is where the ILS or ULS server comes into the picture. Once you log on to the ILS/ULS server, it (obviously) knows you're online and takes note of your current IP address. You can then communicate with others who are also logged in.

Since covering NetMeeting thoroughly would require a lot more room than is available here, the sections that follow will take you through the basics of setting up, scheduling, starting, and joining NetMeetings. For additional information, tips, tricks, and more, there are a number of Web sites dedicated to NetMeeting. The following is just a small sample of what's out there. Keep in mind when attempting to use these links that the Internet changes rapidly, and by the time you read this, some of the sites may have changed.

- **Meeting by Wire**   http://www.meetingbywire.com/. This site has a good beginners' overview of NetMeeting as well as tips and tricks for the more experienced user.

- **NetMeeting Zone**   http://www.netmeeting-zone.com/. News, tips, information, and more is what you'll find at the NetMeeting Zone.

- **NetMeetingHQ**   http://www.netmeetinghq.com/. If you're looking for a good listing of ILS servers, check out the NetMeetingHQ site.

- **Microsoft NetMeeting Web site**   http://www.microsoft.com/windows/ NetMeeting/. Surprisingly, most of what you find at Microsoft's site is marketing hype, with a dash of helpful information thrown in here and there.

Configuring NetMeeting

While NetMeeting works with Outlook, it is not part of Outlook. It is a separate Microsoft application provided with Internet Explorer, which means you must set it up to work with Outlook.

To configure NetMeeting from within Outlook, choose View | Go To | Internet Call | Internet Call. This launches the NetMeeting Wizard, which walks you through the process of setting up NetMeeting to work with Outlook. The opening screen is purely informational. When you're done reading, click Next, which brings you to the personal information screen. Enter your first and last names and your e-mail address. The remaining information is strictly optional.

Caution   *If you plan to use NetMeeting for chatting with strangers, do not provide any personal information that may put you at risk.*

Click Next to proceed to the directory server screen. You can accept the default, Microsoft Internet Directory, or type in a different ILS server. The wizard screens described here are found in Windows 98, which comes with NetMeeting 3.0, and in Windows 2000, which comes with NetMeeting 3.01. If you're using an earlier version of NetMeeting, your screens will be somewhat different.

Note   *Microsoft shut down all its ILS servers and redirected the Microsoft Internet Directory to the MSN Messenger Service. Be advised, however, that to use it you will have to sign up for a (free) Hotmail account.*

To make sure your name does not appear in the directory server indicated in the previous option, check the Do Not List My Name In The Directory option. Displaying your name in the directory enables all other users logged into the directory server to place calls to you. Click Next to move to the connection screen. Indicate the connection type (and speed, if applicable), and click Next. The NetMeeting Wizard now offers to add a NetMeeting shortcut to both your desktop and your Quick Launch bar. Check the one(s) you want and click Next.

If your computer has a sound card, you'll see the Audio Tuning Wizard. Follow the instructions for configuring your sound card to work with NetMeeting. After you make the adjustments for speaker and microphone volumes, click Finish. NetMeeting starts and you're ready to begin. The remaining sections on NetMeeting assume you've already established an ILS or ULS server to which all users have access.

Scheduling a NetMeeting

Scheduling a NetMeeting in Outlook is practically the same as scheduling any other meeting. Begin by opening a new meeting request form and filling in the basic information. See Chapter 12 for detailed information on scheduling meetings and using meeting request forms. Check the This Is An Online Meeting Using option, and select NetMeeting from the drop-down list. As you can see in Figure 21-8, checking the online meeting option adds a number of new fields to the meeting request form.

The following fields are added to the meeting request form for a NetMeeting:

■ **Directory Server**   Enter the directory server you want everyone to connect to for the meeting. If you've registered with multiple servers, choose the one for this meeting from the Directory Server drop-down list.

■ **Automatically start NetMeeting with Reminder**   Check this option to have Outlook automatically connect to the directory server when the reminder activates. If you choose this option, be sure to set the reminder time to 0 minutes so the meeting doesn't start before its scheduled time. Some participants may not be ready. If you use this option, you may want to create a separate appointment for this meeting and set a reminder to go off before the scheduled meeting time.

- **Organizer's e-mail**   Outlook automatically completes this field with the address you entered in the personal information screen of the NetMeeting Wizard.

- **Office document**   If you want to review or collaborate on an office document, enter the document path here. Use the Browse button to locate the document if you're unsure of the exact path. If you choose this option, the standard NetMeeting application does not open. Instead the office document opens with an Online Meeting toolbar floating in the document.

Complete the rest of the form as you would any other meeting request form and click Send when you're finished. Each participant will receive an invitation via e-mail.

Figure 21-8.   *A NetMeeting requires additional information*

Starting a NetMeeting

If you set the option to start the NetMeeting automatically when the reminder pops up, there's nothing to do but sit back and wait. At the appointed time, the reminder appears and NetMeeting takes over and logs on to the Internet. Each participant also sees a reminder which provides a Join NetMeeting button.

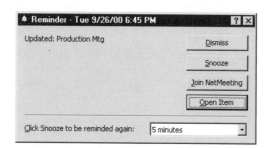

As long as he or she has NetMeeting installed and configured, and has established an Internet connection, clicking the Join NetMeeting button logs the participant on to the NetMeeting directory server.

 Since reminders are handled locally, the clocks on the users' PCs determine when the reminders go off. If all clocks are not set for the same time, participants will be signing on early or late.

To start a NetMeeting manually, right-click the meeting item in the Calendar folder and select Start NetMeeting from the shortcut menu. You can also open the meeting item and choose Actions | Start NetMeeting from the Menu bar.

Joining a NetMeeting

As indicated in the previous section, joining a NetMeeting set to start automatically when a reminder launches is as easy as clicking the Join NetMeeting button on the reminder. To join a NetMeeting in progress, without the help of a reminder, right-click the item in the Calendar folder and select Join NetMeeting from the shortcut menu. If the meeting item is open, choose Actions | Join NetMeeting.

NetMeeting Tools

As long as all participants have the appropriate hardware installed, audio and video communications are available. However, a NetMeeting can be conducted without either by using the remaining tools, which can replace audio and video communications or enhance them. The following NetMeeting tools enable participants to communicate and collaborate with other participants:

- **Share Program** If you want to make an application on your computer available to others in the meeting, use the Share Programs tool. It enables you to select any currently running application and share it with others. In addition, you can even let them take control of the application if you choose. You can start an application during the NetMeeting session and share it.

- **Chat** If audio communication is unavailable for some or all of the participants, using the Chat feature will certainly come in handy. With this tool you can type instant messages to any or all participants. You can even save transcripts of the messages for future reference.

- **Whiteboard** This mini paint application provides a way for all participants to share graphical representations with one another. Whether you want to draw a map or sketch a new design, the whiteboard is the perfect tool.

- **Transfer Files** At any time during the meeting, you may find you want to exchange files with other meeting members. Simply click the Transfer Files button, locate the files, and send them on their way.

All the communication and collaboration features available in NetMeeting make it an ideal tool for conducting important meetings when participants are unavailable for a face-to-face meeting. For some meetings, in which the goal is to review or collaborate on an Office document, NetMeeting may be better than a face-to-face meeting.

The Complete Reference

Chapter 22

Working with Views

W─ithout folder views, Outlook would be about as useful as a VCR without a
television set. All the information might be there, but you'd never be able to
see it. Each Outlook folder comes with a number of standard views that
present the folder contents in a variety of ways. In this chapter, you'll discover not only
what types of views are available, but also how you can navigate, customize, and even
create your own views.

Understanding Views

Although each Outlook folder has anywhere from five to ten different standard views,
they all fall into one of five view types. To use, create, and customize Outlook views you
should understand what a view is, as well as the different types available and their uses.

To begin with, a view is the structure within which folder information is displayed.
At the minimum, views consist of at least one piece of information about one or more
items or files contained in the folder. Complex views can consist of multiple fields
(name, address, phone number, and so on), as well as special sort, filter, group by, and
font settings. All Outlook views belong to one of the following types:

- **Icon**   An icon view is one in which Outlook items or computer files are
  represented by their associated icons. The icon and all or part of the item or
  filename are displayed. The default Notes folder view is an icon view.

- **Day/Week/Month**   This type of view, which, not surprisingly, is ideal for
  Calendar folder items, displays items in a calendar format of the variety you'd
  find in a daily planner. This is the default view for the Calendar folder.

- **Card**   A card view presents information in a format similar to a Rolodex or
  other address card. As you might guess, Contacts folder information is best
  suited for a card view.

- **Timeline**   For viewing information in relation to time or dates, a timeline view
  is the answer. Each item in the view is displayed in chronological order along a
  time scale divided into hours or days.

- **Table**   By far the most common view type in Outlook, the table view displays
  information in a row and column format. Rows represent individual records
  (items), and columns represent fields (details about the items).

Some view types, such as day/week/month and card, are almost exclusively used
to display specific types of information, while others, such as table views, are versatile
enough to display any type of information. The type of view you choose depends on
the results you want to achieve. For example, if you want to view detailed information

about each of your contacts, you would probably use a card view. However, if you want a simple phone listing of your contacts, you would almost certainly use a table view.

Navigating Views

Utilizing folder views involves two things: switching between views and getting around in a view once you arrive. There are several methods for navigating between folder views, some easy and others even easier. The same goes for navigating within a view. Of course, how you get around in the view depends to some extent on the type of view you're using.

Switching Views

You can switch views by choosing View | Current View to display the submenu of available views. Then select the view of your choice. This method is fine if you only occasionally switch between views. However, if you're an inveterate view switcher you'll want to add the Advanced toolbar to the Outlook window. The Advanced toolbar provides a Current View drop-down list, which makes changing views a snap.

Current View

To add the Advanced toolbar to all Outlook folders, right-click the Standard toolbar and select Advanced from the shortcut menu that appears. To remove a toolbar, deselect it from the shortcut menu to eliminate the checkmark. After you add the Advanced toolbar, you can switch views simply by opening the Current View drop-down list and selecting the view you want to see.

If you're a view switcher, but you don't want to waste valuable real estate by adding the Advanced toolbar to your Outlook window, there's an alternative. You can add a Current View button to your Standard toolbar that displays a menu of all available views when clicked. Right-click a toolbar and choose Customize from the shortcut menu to open the Customize dialog box, then click the Command tab, select View in the Categories list, and drag the Current View command to the Standard toolbar. Drop the command where you want it. See Chapter 23 for details on adding and removing toolbar buttons.

You can also use the Organize feature to switch views. In any Outlook folder, click the Organize button on the Standard toolbar to display the Organize pane. Click the Using Views link to display the Change Your View list box containing all available views.

From the Change Your View list box, select the view you want to switch to. When you're through, click the Organize button again or the small X in the top right corner of the Organize pane to close it.

Navigating Within Folder Views

Getting around in a folder view is a snap. The most difficult task is deciding whether to use the mouse or the keyboard. Using the mouse is pretty straightforward. Click an item to select it. Double-click an item to open it. Moving through the view is a simple matter of using the scroll bars. When it comes to the keyboard you'll find each view type has a variety of keystrokes and shortcuts that enable you to get around without using the mouse at all.

Table, Card, and Icon Views

Although table, card, and icon views are quite different to look at, they have one thing in common: the way you navigate them. Whether you use the mouse or the keyboard, the method is identical in all three—well, almost. The truth of the matter is, there are two types of table views, which complicates things a little. Using the mouse is the same. However, using the keyboard is a little different depending on the view type. Using a shortcut on table views with editable fields sometimes produces a different result than using the same shortcut on a table view with non-editable fields. Card and icon views use the same shortcuts used by table views with non-editable fields.

Note *Editable fields are those that you can edit in the view, without having to open the item. You can turn editing on or off by checking or removing the checkmark from the Allow In-Cell Editing option in the view's Other Settings dialog box.*

Some keystrokes are obvious, such as using the UP ARROW and DOWN ARROW keys to move from one item to the next. The PAGE UP and PAGE DOWN keys also perform as expected, taking you to the item at the top or bottom of the screen, respectively. However, as you can see in Table 22-1, other keystrokes are not quite so obvious (nor are they always what the Outlook help file claims them to be).

Keystroke	Action in Table Views with Editable Fields	Action in Table Views with Non-Editable Fields, Card Views, and Icon Views
CTRL-SPACEBAR	Delete the entry in the selected field.	Select or deselect the active item.
ENTER key	Open the selected item.	Open the selected item.
LEFT ARROW key	Move one field to the left.	Move to the previous item. In a card view, this moves to the adjacent item in the next column to the left.
RIGHT ARROW key	Move one field to the right.	Move to the next item. In a card view, this moves to the adjacent item in the next column to the right.
HOME key	Move to the first editable field in the item record.	Select the first item in the view.
END key	Move to the last editable field in the item record.	Select the last item in the view.
CTRL-HOME	Move to the first item in the view and select it.	Move to the first item in the view (does not select it).
CTRL-END	Move to the last item in the view and select it.	Move to the last item in the view (does not select it).
SHIFT-UP ARROW	Select the current item and the item above. Continuing to hold the SHIFT key while pressing the UP ARROW key extends the selection one record at a time. This also deselects records previously selected using the SHIFT-DOWN ARROW shortcut.	Select the current item and the item above. Continuing to hold the SHIFT key while pressing the UP ARROW key extends the selection one record at a time. This also deselects records previously selected using the SHIFT-DOWN ARROW shortcut.

Table 22-1.   *Shortcut Keys for Navigating Table Views*

Keystroke	Action in Table Views with Editable Fields	Action in Table Views with Non-Editable Fields, Card Views, and Icon Views
SHIFT-DOWN ARROW	Same as SHIFT-UP ARROW except the action moves in the opposite direction.	Same as SHIFT-UP ARROW except the action moves in the opposite direction.
CTRL-SHIFT-HOME	Select all items from the current item to the first item.	Select all items from the current item to the first item.
CTRL-SHIFT-END	Select all items from the current item to the last item.	Select all items from the current item to the last item.
CTRL-A	Select all items in the view.	Select all items in the view.
CTRL-UP ARROW	Move up one item without deselecting the current item(s), but without extending the selection to the next item.	Move up one item without deselecting the current item(s), but without extending the selection to the next item. Use this in conjunction with CTRL-SPACEBAR to select non-adjacent items.
CTRL-DOWN ARROW	Same as CTRL-UP ARROW except action moves downward.	Same as CTRL-UP ARROW except action moves downward.

Table 22-1.   *Shortcut Keys for Navigating Table Views* (continued)

In case you're wondering, table views in mail, journal, and notes folders contain non-editable fields by default, while table views in calendar, contacts, and tasks folders contain editable fields by default.

If you have Group By settings applied to a folder view you can use some additional keystrokes for working with the groups. To expand a group, press the RIGHT ARROW key or the ENTER key. Once the group is open, press the DOWN ARROW key to select the first item in the group. To collapse the group, use the LEFT ARROW key or the ENTER key.

Day/Week/Month Views

At first glance, the day/week/month view seems to be rather complex (navigationally speaking) since it contains three different elements to navigate: the Appointment area, the Date Navigator, and the TaskPad. However, once you break it down into its component parts, it's actually pretty simple. To begin with, the Date Navigator relies entirely on the mouse or on actions taken in the Appointment area. Next, the TaskPad is nothing more than a table view with editable fields, which means you can refer to Table 22-1 for keystrokes to use. That leaves only the Appointment area, which does have its own set of shortcut keys (see Table 22-2).

You may find some slight variations in these keystrokes and shortcuts as you move from one subview (day view, week view, or month view) to another.

Keystroke	Action
ALT-1	Displays the day view.
ALT-2 through ALT-9	Displays two through nine days in the Appointment area.
ALT-5	Displays the work week view.
ALT-0	Displays ten days in the Appointment area.
ALT-- (minus sign)	Use the hyphen or the minus sign to display the week view.
ALT-= (equals sign)	Displays the month view.
TAB	Move to the next appointment in the Appointment area.
SHIFT-TAB	Move to the previous appointment in the Appointment area.
CTRL-TAB or F6	Move between the Appointment area, the TaskPad, and the Folder List.
LEFT ARROW or RIGHT ARROW	Move to the previous or next day.

Table 22-2. *Shortcut Keys in the Appointment Area*

Keystoke	Action
ALT-LEFT ARROW or ALT-RIGHT ARROW	In the week, month, or day (with multiple days displayed) view, this shortcut moves t he selected appointment item to the previous (LEFT ARROW) or next (RIGHT ARROW) day.
ALT-DOWN ARROW or ALT-UP ARROW	With no item selected, this shortcut moves you to the same day of the next week (DOWN ARROW) or to the same day of the previous week (UP ARROW). With an item selected, it moves the item to the same day of the next or previous week.

Table 22-2. *Shortcut Keys in the Appointment Area* (continued)

Timeline Views

Timeline views, which display items in chronological order, also have their own navigational keystrokes. Like table views, Group By settings can be applied to timeline views, which means they also have additional shortcuts that can be used when items are grouped. See Table 22-3 for a listing of shortcuts you can use in a timeline view.

Keystroke	Action
LEFT ARROW	Select the previous item.
RIGHT ARROW	Select the next item.
ENTER	Open the selected item(s).
CTRL-SPACEBAR	Select or deselect the active item.
SHIFT-LEFT ARROW	Select the current item and the previous item. Continue to hold the SHIFT key while pressing the LEFT ARROW key to extend the selection.
SHIFT-RIGHT ARROW	Select the current item and the next item. Continue to hold the SHIFT key while pressing the RIGHT ARROW key to extend the selection.

Table 22-3. *Navigational Shortcuts Used in a Timeline View*

Keystroke	Action
CTRL-LEFT ARROW	Move to the previous item without deselecting the current item. Use in conjunction with CTRL-SPACEBAR to select non-adjacent items.
CTRL-RIGHT ARROW	Move to the next item without deselecting the current item. Use in conjunction with CTRL-SPACEBAR to select non-adjacent items.
HOME	Select the first item in the view.
END	Select the last item in the view.
CTRL-HOME	Move to the first item in the view.
CTRL-END	Move to the last item in the view.

Table 22-3. *Navigational Shortcuts Used in a Timeline View* (continued)

The keystrokes used to navigate timeline groups are identical to those used in a grouped table view. Press the RIGHT ARROW key or the ENTER key to expand a group. Once the group is open, press the DOWN ARROW key to select the first item in the group. Press the LEFT ARROW key or the ENTER key to collapse the group.

Customizing Folder Views

Folder views, like almost everything else in Outlook, are highly customizable. Although some views are more equal than others when it comes to customization, all views permit you to make some modifications. You can change everything from the fields displayed to the colors and fonts in which they're displayed. Most customizing in folder views is done using one of five customization features. As you can see in Table 22-4, the available features depend on the view type.

Unlike previous versions of Outlook, which asked if you wanted to save changes to views, Outlook 2000 automatically saves the changes without your consent. Therefore, if you plan to make extensive changes to a view you might want to create an entirely new view using the selected view as the basis. See the section entitled "Creating New Views" later in this chapter for more information.

To access the customization options, regardless of the view you're in, you can use the Customize Current View command to open the View Summary dialog box. As you can see in Figure 22-1, the View Summary dialog box contains buttons for each of the

Customization Feature	Table View	Day/ Week/ Month View	Card View	Timeline View	Icon View
Adding and removing fields	X	X	X	X	
Grouping	X			X	
Sorting	X		X		X
Filtering	X	X	X	X	X
Fonts and other settings	X	X	X	X	X
Automatic formatting	X		X		

Table 22-4. *Customization Options Available for Outlook Views*

Figure 22-1. *The View Summary dialog box is your view customization headquarters*

different customization features. To open the View Summary dialog box, choose View | Current View | Customize Current View. You'll also find the Customize Current View command on the shortcut menu that appears when you right-click a field header in a table view or a blank spot in any view.

You'll also notice in the View Summary dialog box that a brief description of the feature's current state appears next to each button. Knowing what customizations have already been applied can help you determine additional customizations that need to be added.

Adding and Removing Fields

In all but the icon view, you can modify the fields that appear in folder views. Table and card views permit you to add and remove as many fields as you choose, while the day/week/month and timeline views only permit minor field changes. Depending on the view type, you may have more than one way to achieve your field modifications. In all views that permit field changes, you can utilize the Customize Current View command to access the dialog box containing the available fields. Table fields have an additional feature called the Field Chooser from which fields can be added directly to the view.

Using the Customize Current View Command

To add or remove fields in a view, use the Customize Current View command to open the View Summary dialog box seen previously in Figure 22-1. Depending on the current view type, you may have as many as three options for accessing the Customize Current View command. From any folder view, you can choose View | Current View | Customize Current View, or right-click a blank spot in the Information viewer and select Customize Current View from the shortcut menu. In a table view with column headers, right-click a column header and choose Customize Current View from the shortcut menu.

In the View Summary dialog box, click the Fields button to display the Date/Time Fields dialog box or the Show Fields dialog box. The dialog box you see depends on the view type from which you invoke the Customize Current View command. From the Day/Week/Month view you'll see the Date/Time Fields dialog box. Accessing the Customize Current View command from a table view displays the Show Fields dialog box.

The Date/Time Fields dialog box is simple and straightforward (see Figure 22-2). It only permits you to change the Start and End fields in the view and, naturally, limits your choices to date or time fields. From the Select Available Fields From drop-down list, choose the type of fields you want to use. The fields are then displayed in the Available Date/Time Fields list. Select a field and click the Start or End button to change the associated field. Click OK twice to save the changes and return to the active view.

As you can see in Figure 22-3, the Show Fields dialog box provides not only more fields to choose from, but also more options. The Show Fields dialog box is similar to

Figure 22-2.   *Use the Date/Time Fields dialog box to modify the fields used in calendar and timeline views*

Figure 22-3.   *The Show Fields dialog box lets you add and remove fields from table and card views*

the Date/Time Fields dialog box in that it contains a drop-down list of field types and a display list of available fields for the selected field type. The remaining options are unique to the Show Fields dialog box.

You can bypass the View Summary dialog box altogether, and display the Show Fields dialog box in table or card view by right-clicking a blank spot in the view and selecting Show Fields.

Begin by selecting the field type from the Select Available Fields From drop-down list. If you want to add a field to the current view, select the field in the Available Fields list and click the Add button. Unlike the Add button in the Date/Time Fields dialog box, this Add button does not replace the existing field, but rather adds the selected field to the list of fields currently included in the view. To remove a field, select it from the Show These Fields In This Order display list and click the Remove button.

By selecting a field in the Show These Fields In This Order list before adding a field, you can determine the new field's placement (below the selected field). You can also add or remove a field by double-clicking it in the appropriate list.

In addition to adding and removing fields, you can also change the order in which the fields appear in the view by using the Move Up and Move Down buttons. Highlight the field(s) you want to move and click the appropriate button. Moving a field up in the list moves it to the left in the table view itself, and moving it down in the list moves it to the right in the table view. You'll also notice two buttons in Figure 22-3 that are grayed out, Properties and Delete. These options are only available for custom fields. As you might suspect, they show the custom field properties and enable you to delete a custom field. You can even add a new field by clicking the New Field button to open the New Field dialog box.

New Field	? ✕
Name:	Sales Lead
Type:	Yes/No ▾
Format:	Icon ▾
	OK Cancel

Give the field a name, select the type of field you want to add, and choose a field format. For more information on creating custom fields, see Chapter 24. When you finish making your selection(s), click OK twice to effect the change(s) and return to the current view.

Using the Field Chooser

Outlook table views have an additional tool available for adding and removing fields, called the Field Chooser. As you can see in Figure 22-4, the Field Chooser is a small dialog box holding buttons (headers, actually) that represent fields. The field type selected in the drop-down list at the top of the dialog box determines the fields that appear.

To access the Field Chooser, right-click a column header in the table view and select Field Chooser from the shortcut menu. You'll also find a Field Chooser button on the Advanced toolbar, which you can display by right-clicking the Standard toolbar and selecting Advanced from the shortcut menu.

By default, Frequently-Used Fields (the most commonly used fields for the folder type) are displayed. If the field you want isn't there, select another field type from the drop-down list. When you find the field you're looking for, drag it to the position on the header bar where you want it to appear and drop it. As you move the field across the header bar you'll see a pair a red arrows appearing between existing headers you're near. The red arrows indicate the spot in which a new field will land if you drop it. Select the desired position for the new field and let it go. The headers on either side move to make room for the new column.

Figure 22-4.   *The Field Chooser provides a quick way to add fields to a table view*

You can display (but not modify) a field's properties by double-clicking the field in the Field Chooser.

The Field Chooser, like the Show Fields dialog box, enables you to add a custom field by clicking the New button and entering the appropriate information in the New Field dialog box. You can also delete custom fields by highlighting the custom field you want to eliminate and clicking the Delete button. When you're finished adding fields to the view, click the X in the top right corner of the Field Chooser to close it.

Working with Fields in Table Views

Table views provide a quick and easy way to rearrange and delete fields without having to bother with the Show Fields dialog box, which is the only way you can move and delete fields in non-table views. In table views you can use drag and drop to move field headers from one position to another or delete them altogether.

Grab the field header you want to reposition, and drag it to a new location. As you move the field over the header bar, red arrows appear at the next spot on which you can drop the header. You can release the field as soon as the arrows appear, and the header squeezes into the location indicated by the arrows. Removing a field from the view is even easier. Simply drag the field header into the Information viewer, and drop it. It disappears immediately.

Of course, the field has not been permanently deleted, simply removed from the current view. If you change your mind and want the field to reappear you can open the Field Chooser and drag the field back onto the view. See the previous section "Using the Field Chooser" for details.

Defining the Sort Order

Sorting is one of Outlook's most useful features. It enables you to arrange all the items in the view in a manner that makes finding information fast and effortless. Depending on the type of view you plan to sort, you may have more than one way to perform a sort. All view types that support sorting (table, card, and icon) can be sorted using the Sort dialog box. In addition, table views can be sorted from directly within the view by clicking field headers.

One thing to be aware of is that regardless of which method you employ, some fields cannot be used as sort criteria. When you attempt to sort by Company, Categories, Contact (as opposed to Contacts), Notes, or Read you receive an error message informing you that "You cannot sort by this field." There is no apparent reason for this anomaly.

Using the Sort Dialog Box

The Sort dialog box, seen in Figure 22-5, enables you to sort by as many as four different fields, either in ascending (A-Z) or descending (Z-A) order.

Figure 22-5.   *Applying a sort is easy when you use the Sort dialog box*

The easiest way to open the Sort dialog box is to right-click a blank spot in the Information viewer and select Sort from the shortcut menu. If you can't find a blank spot, choose View | Current View | Customize Current View and click the Sort button in the View Summary dialog box.

Once you have the Sort dialog box open, choose the field type for the first sort criterion from the Select Available Fields From drop-down list. From the Sort Items By drop-down list, select the first field on which you want to base the sort. Click Ascending or Descending to determine the order of the sort. If you want to use a secondary sort, repeat the process using the Then By drop-down list. You can add up to four sort criteria using the additional Then By options. When you're finished, click OK (once or twice, depending on how you accessed the Sort dialog box) to apply the sort and return to the current view.

If you've selected fields that are not already in the view, Outlook asks if you want to add them at the same time. Click Yes to add the field and apply the sort, No to leave the field out and still apply the sort, or Cancel to halt the process and start over. To remove the currently applied sort, open the Sort dialog box and click the Clear All button to remove all sort criteria.

Sorting Table Views

Sorting in table views is a breeze. You don't even have to open the Sort dialog box. Simply click a field header to sort the view by the field it represents. The first time you click a field header the sort order is ascending. Click the header a second time to reverse the order and make the sort descending. Whatever the current sort order is, clicking the header reverses it. You can tell if a field is being used to sort the view by the appearance of a small embossed triangle on the header. The direction in which the triangle points, indicates the sort order (up for ascending, down for descending).

You can also sort the view by multiple fields. Set the order for the first field by clicking its header. Then hold down the SHIFT key and select additional column headers to use their fields for subsorts. To reverse the sort order of a secondary sort, click the header again while holding down the SHIFT key. This method, like the Sort dialog box, limits you to four fields for sorting. If you attempt to use a fifth field, Outlook informs you that you're using "Too many sort levels."

The one thing you can't do using the field headers that you can do using the Sort dialog box is sort by fields that are not included in the view. You'll have to add them first. See the earlier section titled "Adding and Removing Fields."

There's one last method you can use to sort a table view. Right-click the header of the field you want to sort by and choose Sort Ascending or Sort Descending. If a sort is already applied using that field, the appropriate command will already be selected on the shortcut menu.

Adding and Applying Filters

Filters are handy devices that hide (filter out) records that fail to meet search criteria you enter in the Filter dialog box. For example, if you have a ton of messages in your Inbox and you're looking for messages from a certain individual, you can filter out all e-mail messages except those from that person. To access the Filter dialog box, right-click a blank spot in any view type (filtering is supported by all views), and select Filter from the shortcut menu. You can also choose View | Current View | Customize Current View and click the Filter button in the View Summary dialog box.

The first tab of the Filter dialog box varies depending on the folder in which you happen to be when you open the Filter dialog box. The tab is named for the folder, and the options are tailored to that folder type. The Filter dialog box shown in Figure 22-6 is from the Inbox folder. For information about the opening tab in other folder types, see the chapter covering that particular folder.

Using the More Choices Tab

The remaining two tabs are identical regardless of which folder you're in when you invoke the Filter dialog box. The second tab, shown in Figure 22-7, is the More Choices tab.

Figure 22-6. *Each folder determines the name and options on the opening tab of the Filter dialog box*

Figure 22-7. *More Choices is just what you get when you click the More Choices tab*

The More Choices tab offers a variety of filtering options using basic fields common to most Outlook items. These options include:

- **Categories**   Anyone who uses categories will appreciate this one. Enter the category you're looking for. Be advised, however, that performing a search that includes multiple categories locates not only messages assigned to both, but also messages assigned to either. Outlook adds an implied OR between multiple selections in this field. There's nothing you can do about it, so you'll just have to learn to live with it.

- **Only items that are**   This is a great way to find only items you've read or only items you haven't. Use the drop-down list to make your selection.

- **Only items with**   If you want to find items based on the fact that they do or do not contain attachments, this is the option for you.

- **Whose importance is**   When time is short and you have a lot to do, you may want to filter out everything but the most important stuff. In that case, use this option to search for those of high importance.

- **Match case**   If you've entered text in the Search For Word(s) field on the opening tab, you can use this option to search for only those instances of the word(s) that match the exact case of the text you entered. Check the option to enable it.

- **Size (kilobytes)**   This option can be helpful if you know that you received a rather large attachment with your message. Indicate an operator (equals, between, less than, or greater than) and the size.

Using the Advanced Tab

The third and last tab, shown in Figure 22-8, lets you create custom criteria based on almost any field in Outlook. The way it works is simple. You select a field to base the criteria on. Then you enter a condition that must be met by the record(s) you want to see when the filter is applied. All records that do not meet the condition(s) are filtered out, and temporarily hidden from view.

Begin by clicking the Field button to display a drop-down menu of field types. Selecting the field type displays a submenu containing the available fields for that type. Now select the field you want to use for the first advanced filter criterion. The field appears in the text box below the Field button. The next thing to do is establish the condition to be met. Select a conditional operator from the Condition drop-down list. Depending on the field type you select, the operators vary. For text fields, your choices include operators such as Contains and Is(Exactly) that work on alphanumeric data. Date fields accommodate conditional operators such as Anytime, Yesterday, and Today. Conditional operators for numeric fields include such things as Equals, Is At Least, and Is More Than. You'll find even more variations, but as with these, most are self-explanatory.

Figure 22-8.   *The Advanced tab lets you build your filter criteria from scratch*

After you select the condition, move to the Value field. Enter the data you want the conditional operator to evaluate when determining whether the record qualifies. If you select Is Empty or Is Not Empty, no Value field entry is necessary (or permitted) since the operator is Boolean. Either the condition is met or it's not.

*When entering data in the Value field you can use And and Or operators between values. For example, to find all messages that contain lunch and Mario's (Meet Bill for lunch at Mario's) in the subject line, enter **lunch and Mario's** in the Value field. However, if you're looking for messages that contain either in the subject line, enter **lunch or Mario's**.*

Once you've entered the information in the appropriate fields, click Add To List to add the new filter criteria to the Find Items That Match These Criteria display list. Add as many conditional statements as you need, and click OK to apply the filter.

If you add multiple conditions there is an implied "and" between all statements. Therefore, only those items that meet the conditions of all statements are displayed.

To remove filter criteria, you can select the statement to eliminate, and click the Remove button. If you want to remove the entire filter, click the Clear All button.

Grouping Items

The Outlook Group By feature, which is available in both table and timeline views, enables you to create sets of items that all have one or more things in common. For example, to quickly find vendors, customers, and employees you might create groups based on categories in your Contacts folder. You could further break down the contacts by creating a subgroup based on the Company field.

As with most Outlook features, there are a couple of ways to create groups, depending on the view you're in. You can create groups in both the timeline view and the table view by setting options in the Group By dialog box. Table views offer two additional methods. You can use the Group By This Field command or the Group By Box command. Both beat the Group By dialog box hands down for quick and easy grouping.

Using the Group By Dialog Box

To access the Group By dialog box seen in Figure 22-9, in either a timeline view or a table view, right-click a blank spot on the Information viewer and select Group By from the shortcut menu.

Figure 22-9. *The Group By dialog box works in a similar fashion to the Filter dialog box*

Another method you can use in either view is to choose View | Current View | Customize Current View and click the Group By button in the View Summary dialog box. In a timeline view you have one additional method. Right-click the timeline bar or date header and select Group By from the shortcut menu.

Once you open the Group By dialog box, you'll find it's similar to the Filter dialog box. You can group items by up to four different fields, and you can elect to sort items in the groups either in ascending or descending order. Begin by choosing the field type from the Select Available Fields From drop-down list. Then, from the Group Items By drop-down list, select the field you want to use for the first group. If the field is already in the view, the Show Field In View option appears with a checkmark. If the field is not currently displayed in the view, check the option to include the field. Next, indicate whether you want the group sorted in ascending or descending order. If you want to create subgroups, repeat the process in one or more of the next three Then By fields.

Note *When you create a group based on a field that can contain multiple values, such as Categories, an item assigned to multiple categories will appear in all groups to which it is assigned.*

The final option (not counting Clear All) in the Group By dialog box is Expand/Collapse Defaults. This field contains a drop-down list with three choices for the manner in which you want the groups displayed.

- ■ **All expanded** When you apply the Group By settings, each of the groups is expanded to display all items within.

- ■ **All collapsed** Select this option to collapse all groups so that none of the items shows.

- ■ **As last viewed** If you change sort order or Show Field In View options and reapply the Group By settings, the expanded/collapsed state of the view is retained.

Click OK (twice if you accessed the Group By dialog box from the View Summary dialog box) to save the settings and create the groups.

Note *If you find that you have more than one group with the same name, it's probably the result of grouping by a text field, such as Subject or Company, in which the text entry is followed by one or more (unintentional) spaces. Grouping requires an exact match of characters and considers spaces to be valid characters. Luckily the Group By feature is not case sensitive, so you can go to town with capitalization, or the lack thereof.*

Working with groups is easy. Click the plus sign to the left of the group header to expand the group. Click the minus sign to collapse the group. To sort groups, use the sort options in the Group By dialog box. To sort items within the groups, use the options in the Sort dialog box. If you want to remove all Group By settings, return to the Group By dialog box and click Clear All.

Alternate Group By Methods

Table views, which are the most prevalent views found in Outlook, provide a couple of alternatives to the Group By dialog box. These alternatives consist of a pair of commands found on the shortcut menu that appears when you right-click a column header. As with many options found only in table views, they are quicker and easier to use than dialog box settings. However, they are also less powerful.

Tip *If you have the Advanced toolbar displayed, you can access the Group By box by clicking the Group By Box button. If on the other hand you don't want to take up space with the Advanced toolbar, but would like to have a Group By Box button on your Standard toolbar, you can add one. Open the Customize dialog box and drag the Group By Box command to the Standard toolbar. See Chapter 23 for more information on customizing toolbars.*

Since both commands use the Group By box, the first command to consider is the Group By Box command itself. Right-click any column header and select Group By Box to display the Group By box above the column headers. As you can see in Figure 22-10, the box contains an information box indicating that you should "Drag a column header here to group by that column."

Figure 22-10. *The Group By box offers a quick drag-and-drop method of creating groups*

It's that simple. Drag the column header of the field on which you want to base your first grouping, and drop it in the box. To create subgroups, drag another header and drop it in the Group By box. The result, seen in Figure 22-11, is that a copy of each header is placed in the Group By box, and the table view is grouped by those fields.

If you look closely you'll note that a small black line connects the headers, indicating the relationship. You can change the relationship by dragging the headers to different positions. Dragging any field to the left and dropping it when the red arrows appear places it higher in the group hierarchy. Moving it to the right demotes it. To remove a grouping altogether, drag the header out of the Group By box and drop it on the Information viewer. Contrary to what you might think, removing a header with subheaders attached does not remove the subheaders as well. They simply move up the ladder. You can sort and resort groups by clicking the column headers in the Group By box. To sort items within groups, use the column headers in the view. When you decide it's time to close the Group By box, right-click any column header and select Group By Box again.

You can open the Group By dialog box by double-clicking a blank spot in the Group By box.

Figure 22-11.   *The Group By box displays the column headers used, in the order in which they're applied*

Now that you understand how the Group By box works, you're ready to move on to the Group By This Field command. Decide which field you want to use to create a group. Then right-click its column header and select Group By This Field from the shortcut menu. The Group By box opens (if it's not already open), a copy of the column header is placed in it, and the view is grouped by the associated field. To create subgroups, you can either drag additional column headers into the Group By box, or, if you like to do things the hard way, you can choose another column header, right-click, and select Group By This Field again.

Configuring Other Settings

The Other Settings dialog box could be more appropriately named Formatting Settings, since it contains mostly font and formatting options for the view in which it's invoked. Other Settings options range from changing the fonts of headings and item entries to the color of table view grid lines and the width and height of cards in a card view.

You can open the Other Settings dialog box from any view by right-clicking a blank spot in the view and selecting Other Settings from the shortcut menu. You can also access the Other Settings dialog box from the View Summary dialog box.

Table View

Table views, which are widely used throughout Outlook folders, contain an extensive group of Other Settings options. As you can see in Figure 22-12, the Other Settings dialog box options include font options, grid line options, and a handful of options dealing with columns, cells, and the AutoPreview feature.

 Some table views offer a third method of accessing the Other Settings dialog box. If the table view contains a "new item" row at the top, you can right-click it and select Other Settings from the shortcut menu.

The options available in a table view Other Settings dialog box include the following:

- **Column headings** The Font option in this section changes the font used in the column headings. Click the Font button to display the Font dialog box. Here you can modify the font, font style, and font size used to display header information. The other option found in the Column Headings section is Automatic Column Sizing. When checked, this option forces the resizing of all columns to make them fit within the visible window.

- **Rows** You can use the Font option in the Rows section to change the font used in the fields contained in each row. One thing to note: font settings applied in the Automatic Formatting dialog box take precedence over font options set here. The other options found in this section include Allow In-Cell Editing, which when checked enables you to modify field contents in the view, and Show "new item" Row. The Show "new item" Row option adds a blank

Figure 22-12. *Other Settings options in table views are wide ranging*

row at the top of the view, in which you can enter information to create a new folder item, or which you can double-click to open the item form associated with the folder.

- **AutoPreview** The Font button here enables you to modify the font used in the AutoPreview feature. The other three options let you determine if and how the AutoPreview feature works.

- **Grid lines** Grid lines are the lines separating both fields and columns in some table views. If you check the Phone List view of the Contacts folder, you'll see a table view with grid lines turned on. Now take a look at the Messages view of the Inbox to see what a table view without grid lines looks like. Your Grid Lines choices include the type and color of the grid lines as well as an option to shade (or not shade) group headings. The Shade Group Headings is checked by default for a good reason. It's much easier to distinguish group headings from group items when the headings are shaded.

- **Preview Pane** This is a simple option that displays the Preview Pane when checked. It also enables the Hide Header Information option. To display the Preview Pane without header information, check this option.

Once you've set all the Other Settings options, click OK (twice if you used the View Summary dialog box) to return to the view, which now sports the new "other settings."

Day/Week/Month View

When you access Other Settings from within a day/week/month view, the dialog box that appears is the Format Day/Week/Month View dialog box, shown in Figure 22-13.

The Format Day/Week/Month View dialog box contains font options to change the appearance of time displays as well as information in each of the three subviews (Day, Week, and Month). The font options all work the same for each subview. Click the button to open the Font dialog box and change the font, font style, and font size as needed. In addition to font options, the Format Day/Week/Month View dialog box also contains a number of other options, including:

- **Time scale**   The Appointment area in the day view displays appointment blocks based on the Time Scale settings. By default the Time Scale is set to 30 minutes. If most of your appointments are longer or shorter, you can change the Time Scale settings to fit your needs.

- **Show time as clocks**   This field is found both in the Week and Month sections. Besides being unbearably cute, it does offer one advantage. When checked, both the start and end times are displayed in the week and month views.

- **Show end time**   This option also appears in the Week and Month sections. When the Show Time As Clocks option is checked, this option displays the end time of appointments as well as the start time.

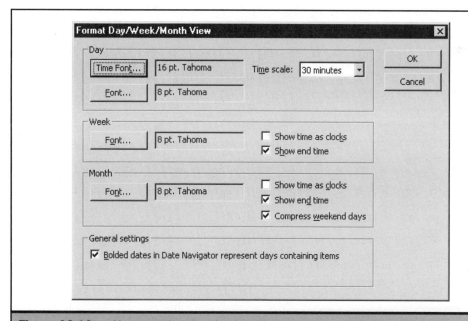

Figure 22-13.   *You can give the day/week/month view a whole new look*

- **Compress weekend days**   Figuring that most work weeks are Monday through Friday, Outlook saves space in the month view by forcing Saturday and Sunday to share a single day block, thereby eliminating the need for an additional column. If you want Saturday and Sunday to each have its own column, remove the checkmark from this option.

- **Bolded dates in Date Navigator represent days containing items**   With this option checked, any dates for which appointments or events are scheduled appear bolded in the Date Navigator.

When all options are set to your satisfaction, click OK (twice if you used the View Summary dialog box to access the Format Day/Week/Month View dialog box) to save the changes and return to the current view.

Card View

The Format Card View dialog box seen in Figure 22-14 is displayed when you select Other Settings from the shortcut menu or the View Summary dialog box in a card view.

As you can see, the Format Card View dialog box contains font options for changing both the headings and body of individual cards. These options work like other font options. Click the appropriate Font button to open the Font dialog box. Make the desired changes to the font and click OK to return to the Format Card View dialog box. Other options for formatting the card view include:

- **Allow in-cell editing**   With this option checked, you can edit individual fields in the card view without having to open the item form.

- **Show empty fields**   By default, Outlook hides fields in the card view that contain no data. If you want to see all fields in the view regardless of their contents (or lack thereof), check this option.

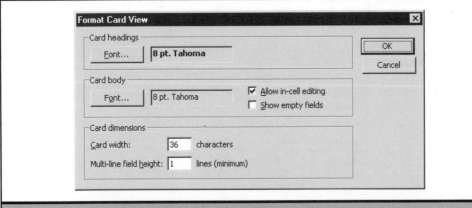

Figure 22-14.   *You can spruce up your card views with the Format Card View dialog box*

- **Card width** This option enables you to change the width of cards appearing in the view. In theory you can make the card as small as three characters or as large as 1,000 characters wide. However, neither end of the spectrum is practical. At the low end, only the first three characters of each line appears. At the high end, the width is limited by your window size and display settings. At full screen with a screen resolution of 800 × 600, the maximum width of a card is around 124 characters (it may vary depending on your video card). If your resolution is higher, the maximum will be higher as well. If your resolution is lower, the maximum will follow suit.

- **Multi-line field height** This option controls the minimum number of lines displayed in a multi-line field such as Address. The number must be between 1 and 20. Be aware, however, that if you raise the minimum to more lines than the field actually holds, blank lines are displayed to make up the minimum, even if Show Empty Fields is disabled.

Tip *You can also change the card width by grabbing one of the vertical borders between columns of cards and dragging it to the left to reduce or to the right to increase the card size.*

When you're finished setting Format Card View dialog box options, click OK (twice if you used the View Summary dialog box) to save the options and return to the active view.

Timeline View

The Format Timeline View dialog box, shown in Figure 22-15, appears when you select Other Settings from within a timeline view. As you can see, the Format Timeline View dialog box contains Fonts, Scales, and Labels options.

The font options apply to both time scales in the view, as well as the items that appear in the view. To change the font options, click the appropriate font button and make the necessary changes in the Font dialog box. The remaining options include:

- **Show week numbers** Check this box to add the week number (Week 1 through Week 52) to the view. How this works depends on whether you're in the day, week, or month timeline view. In the day and week views, the week number is added to the upper scale. In the month view, the week number replaces the days of the week in the lower scale.

- **Maximum label width** This option lets you put a limit on the number of characters that can be displayed in an item label that appears in the view. Although the field permits you to enter any number up to 9999, it will not accept anything beyond 132 regardless of your display settings. If you enter a number larger than 132, Outlook automatically resets the option to 132.

Figure 22-15.   *Use the Format Timeline View dialog box to apply custom formatting to your timeline view*

■ **Show label when viewing by month**   By default, item labels are not displayed in the month view. Check this option to turn labels on in the month view.

While you have the Show Label When Viewing By Month option to turn labels on or off in the month view, no such option exists for the day and week views. However, you can get around that by setting the Maximum Label Width option to zero to turn item labels off. If you want to turn them on again, return to the Format Timeline View dialog box and reset the Maximum Label Width to 80 or a length of your choice.

Click OK until you return to the active timeline view. All your changes will be saved and applied to the current view.

Icon View

The icon view is the only view that does not provide font formatting options when the Other Settings command is used. Instead, the Format Icon View dialog box that appears offers options for the size and placement of icons within the view (see Figure 22-16).

There are only two sets of options in the Format Icon View dialog box: View Type and Icon Placement. The View Type options include Large Icon, Small Icon, and Icon List. They are pretty much self-explanatory, but a little additional information might be helpful. It doesn't take a rocket scientist to figure out that the difference between the Large Icon and Small Icon options is the size of the icon. However, the difference between the Small Icon and the Icon List is a little less obvious. Both use small icons.

Figure 22-16.   *Sizing and arranging icons is what the Format Icon View dialog box is all about*

However, the arrangement of icons in the Small Icon view is, by default, from right to left, while in the Icon List the arrangement is from top to bottom.

The next option, Icon Placement, is available only if Large Icon or Small Icon is selected in the first option. This option enables you to change the arrangement of items in the view:

- **Do not arrange**   Use this option to let the little critters lay where they fall. No order is imposed on them at all, unless you do it yourself.

- **Line up icons**   This option imposes a limited amount of order by lining each item with the nearest grid line of the invisible grid present in all icon views. You can see this option in action by setting the option and returning to the view. Then move an icon and let it go. Unless you happen to be right on a grid line, the icon "snaps" to the grid line closest to the spot where you drop it.

- **AutoArrange**   This feature automatically arranges icons in rows from left to right.

- **Sort and AutoArrange**   Use this option in conjunction with the Sort feature to automatically arrange items in rows based on Sort criteria you specify.

Once you set all the Format Icon View dialog box options, click OK until you return to the active view.

Using Automatic Formatting

Automatic formatting, which is only available for table and card views, enables you to set options that apply formatting to an item when the item meets certain conditions you specify. An example of Automatic Formatting can be seen in the task list. When a task becomes overdue, it automatically changes to red. This is the result of an Automatic

Formatting rule that stipulates any task whose due date is earlier than today's date must be dressed in a red font. You might create your own rule to turn e-mail messages from the boss bright blue, to ensure you don't accidentally miss one.

You can create your own rules or modify existing rules. You can do anything you want to your own rules. However, your ability to modify rules that come predefined with the view is limited to turning them on and off, and to changing the font. What you cannot do is change the conditions upon which these rules are based.

To create an Automatic Formatting rule, begin by opening the Automatic Formatting dialog box. Right-click a blank spot in the view and select Customize Current View to open the View Summary dialog box. Next, click the Automatic Formatting button to display the Automatic Formatting dialog box. Figure 22-17 shows the Automatic Formatting dialog box from the Simple List view in the Tasks folder. As you can see, the view has a number of predefined formatting rules already in place.

The first thing you'll notice is that all the existing rules have a check box next to them. To turn a rule on, add a checkmark. To turn a rule off, remove the checkmark. As mentioned earlier, you can only change the font formatting on predefined rules. Until you create a new rule, that's all you have. Therefore, you might as well get to work and create a new rule.

Click the Add button to add a new rule. An "untitled" rule appears in the Rules For This View display list, and all three options at the bottom of the dialog box become available. Enter a name for the new rule in the Name field. Click the Font button to

Figure 22-17.   *Let Outlook do all the work for you when it comes to making special items stand out*

open the Font dialog box. Select the font, font style, font size, font color, and any effects you want the text to have, and click OK to return to the Automatic Formatting dialog box.

Be sure not to duplicate the font formatting already set for an existing rule. If you do, you'll have no way to distinguish items formatted by the old rule from items formatted by the new rule.

The last step in creating the rule is to establish the conditions that will trigger the rule. Click the Condition button and you'll be amazed at what appears—the Filter dialog box. That's right, you use the Filter dialog box to determine the criteria the new rule uses. The filter is not actually applied to the view. When new items are created in the folder or arrive by other means, they are tested against the filter criteria. Those that meet the conditions receive the designated formatting. Those that don't, slide by untouched. For detailed information on creating filters, see the section earlier in this chapter entitled "Adding and Applying Filters."

If you want to modify an existing rule, select it and make the necessary changes using the three options at the bottom of the Automatic Formatting dialog box. You'll find that when editing one of the predefined rules, the only change you can make is to the Font used. Deleting a rule is as easy as selecting it and clicking the Delete button. As you might have guessed, you cannot delete predefined rules, nor can you rearrange the order of predefined rules. Since the order in which rules appear in the list determines the order in which they're processed, this means that predefined rules are always processed first. Any rules you create you can reorder by selecting the rule and clicking the Move Up or Move Down button.

When you're finished, click OK until you return to the active view. If you created a new rule or modified an existing rule, you'll see the results immediately.

Modifying Columns

Columns found in table views can be relocated, widened, narrowed, renamed, and formatted. Moving columns and changing their width can both be accomplished using the column headers. To move a column from one position to another, drag the column header left or right until a pair of red arrows appear. Drop the header, and the column appears at the location indicated by the arrows. To change the width of a column, move your mouse pointer to the right border of the column header and drag the border left to shrink the column or right to enlarge it.

Format Columns

If you're big on one-stop shopping, you might want to check out the Format Columns dialog box, shown in Figure 22-18.

To open the Format Columns dialog box, right-click a field header and select Format Columns from the shortcut menu. As you can see, the Format Columns dialog box has a variety of options for customizing table view columns. To apply the

Figure 22-18.   *The Format Columns dialog box can fill all your column-formatting needs*

formatting, select a field from the Available Fields list and set the desired options from among the following:

- **Format**   If the field is capable of being displayed in more than one format, you can select the format of your choice from the Format drop-down list. For example, the Attachment field can be displayed as an icon (the default), Yes/No, On/Off, or True/False.

- **Label**   You can change the text that appears in the column header by using the Label option. This does not change the name of the field nor does it change the label in any other table view in the folder.

- **Width**   If you want to set the column to a precise width, you can select Specific Width and enter the number of characters wide you want the column to appear. If you want Outlook to automatically adjust the column to accommodate the longest field entry or the column name, whichever is longer, select Best Fit.

- **Alignment**   The Alignment option applies to the text within the column. Setting the alignment to Left forces all field entries to snuggle up to the left side of the cell. Center places the entries in the center of the cell, and Right pushes them up against the right side of the cell.

You can apply formatting to as many fields as you want. When you're finished, click OK to return to the active view and apply the changes.

Best Fit

The Best Fit command, which appears in the Format Columns dialog box described in the previous section on column formatting, also comes as a standalone command. In a table view, right-click the header of the column you want to adjust and select Best Fit. Outlook automatically makes the column wide enough to display the entire column name or the longest field entry in the column, whichever is longer.

Since card views also contain columns, although of an entirely different nature, the Best Fit command can also be accessed in them. Card view columns are simply there to keep the individual cards from spilling over onto one another. All columns are identical in size. Therefore, resizing one automatically resizes all.

The Best Fit command works a little differently in a card view than it does in a table view. Rather than adjusting column size to accommodate the contents, it adjusts column size to prevent partial columns from appearing in the view. If three and a half columns are showing when you apply the Best Fit command, Outlook resizes them to fit three entire columns in the view. To use the Best Fit command, right-click a blank spot in one of the columns (including the partial column) and select Best Fit from the shortcut menu.

Removing Columns

Removing columns is easy and painless. All you have to do is drag the column header into the Information viewer, and poof! It's gone. Of course, it's not gone for good. You can open the Show Fields dialog box or the Field Chooser and put it back any time you want. If you're allergic to dragging and dropping, you can always right-click the header of the column you want to delete, and select Remove This Column.

Removing View Customizations

If, after customizing a view, you find that you want to remove the customizations and return the view to its original state, you can do so without a great deal of trouble. As a matter of fact, you can do it a couple of different ways. One restores a single view, and the other restores all folder views to their defaults.

To return a single view to its pre-customized state, open the folder where it's used, and choose View | Current View | Define Views to open the Define Views dialog box. Select the view you want to restore and click the Reset button. Outlook immediately wants to know if you really mean it or if you're just kidding around. If you really mean it, click OK and all customizations are removed, and the view returns to its natural state. Click Close to return to the active view.

If you decide it's time to do some serious housekeeping and return everything to its original condition, you'll have to exit Outlook and restart it using a command line switch.

Caution *Not only does this method remove all customizations to predefined Outlook views, it also removes all custom views you've created. Therefore, do not use this method unless you either have no custom views or you wish to delete them all.*

If you're ready to remove all custom views and all customizations to predefined views, choose File | Exit And Log Off from the Menu bar. This closes Outlook and logs you off the Exchange server. Now click Start | Run to open the Run dialog box. Enter **Outlook/CleanViews** in the Open field. Click OK to restart Outlook using the CleanViews switch. Outlook opens with all folder views restored to their original condition.

Customizing Outlook Today

Outlook Today is a Web page that provides a quick overview of your most important Outlook information. By default, Outlook Today displays appointment items due for the next five days, your entire task list, and the number of unread messages in your Inbox, Drafts folder, and Outbox. A quick check here before starting your day can give you a good idea of what's on your plate (see Figure 22-19). To open Outlook Today, click the Outlook Today shortcut in the Outlook Bar.

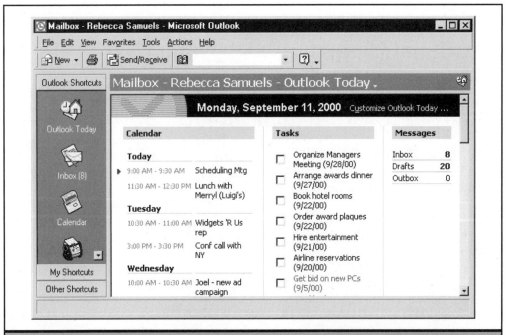

Figure 22-19. *For a quick look at your day, check the Outlook Today page*

> *If you're in any of the primary Outlook folders (Inbox, Calendar, Tasks, and so on)
> you can open Outlook Today by pressing the BACKSPACE key. Since Outlook Today is
> at the top of the folder hierarchy, and the BACKSPACE key moves you up one level in
> the hierarchy each time you press it, it will always take you to Outlook Today as long
> as you're in one of the primary folders.*

Using the Customize Outlook Today Page

Of course, your notion of what comprises important information might not coincide with
that of the Outlook programmers. Therefore, you may want to take advantage of the
customization options available, and make a few changes to your Outlook Today page.

Begin by clicking the Customize Outlook Today button in the top right corner of the
Outlook Today page to open the Customize Outlook Today page, shown in Figure 22-20.

Figure 22-20. *Use the Outlook Today customization options to control the
appearance and content of the Outlook Today page*

As you can see, the Customize Outlook Today page contains five sets of options, which include the following:

- **Startup**   This one's simple. Check it if you want Outlook to open to the Outlook Today page every time you start up. This option actually resets the Startup In This Folder option found in the Advanced Options dialog box (Tools | Options | Other | Advanced Options).

- **Messages**   The name of this option is somewhat misleading since it can apply to any Outlook item, not just messages. In reality, it simply displays the folder name and the number of unread items contained in the folder. Click the Choose Folders button to open the Select Folder dialog box. Then check the folder(s) you want to include in the Messages section of Outlook Today.

- **Calendar**   By default, the Calendar section of the Outlook Today page displays appointment items for today and the next four days (for a total of five). You can change this to any number between 1 and 7.

- **Tasks**   When it comes to tasks, your options are more extensive:

  - **In my task list, show me**   You can begin by deciding whether you want to display all tasks or only those due today. In addition, you can choose whether or not to include tasks without due dates.

  - **Sort my task list by**   You can set a primary sort and a secondary sort to determine the order in which tasks display in Outlook Today. Select the field(s) by which you want the items sorted and then choose Ascending (A-Z) or Descending (Z-A) for each sort you enable.

- **Styles**   If you want to gussy up your Outlook Today page, you can select from five different styles. If you choose a style from the drop-down list, you'll see a fair, if somewhat tiny, representation of what the style looks like in the Preview Pane below the option.

After you make your selections, click the Save Changes button in the top right corner of the page to apply the changes and return to the Outlook Today page. One more thing: if you want to disable Outlook Today, simply right-click the Outlook Today shortcut in the Outlook Bar, and select Properties to open the Mailbox Properties dialog box. Click the Home Page tab and remove the checkmark in the Show Home Page By Default For This Folder option.

Using Advanced Techniques

As with many options in Outlook, you can also change the Outlook Today customization options from within the Windows registry.

Only experienced users should edit the Windows registry. Modifying the registry can produce unexpected results, including system crashes from which you may not be able to recover. Always create a backup copy of your registry before making any changes.

You'll find most of the Outlook Today customization options in the `HKEY_CURRENT_USER\Software\Microsoft\Office\9.0\Outlook\Today` key, and the rest in its `\Folders` subkey. Well, you'll find them there if you've opened the Customize Outlook Today and clicked the Save Changes button at least once. The fact that you can change these options in the registry doesn't necessarily mean you should. With one exception, there's no real benefit to setting the options in the registry rather than on the Customize Outlook Today page.

The exception is the CallDays value (Show This Number Of Days In My Calendar on the Customize Outlook Today page). Using the drop-down list provided in Outlook, the maximum numbers of days you can display in the Outlook Today Calendar section is seven. You can squeeze one more day out of it by changing the CallDays Value data to 8. Unfortunately, entering any number larger than 8 still nets you only eight days in the Calendar section.

You can also override the default Outlook Today page and replace it with a Web page by adding a String Value to the `HKEY_CURRENT_USER\Software\Microsoft\Office\9.0\Outlook\Today` key, and naming it Url. Enter the location of the Web site in the Value data. You can use a typical URL format such as http://www.osborne.com.

Using the same method, you can also replace the Outlook Today page with one of your own. However, it is a much more complex operation, requiring both an Outlook Today page (outlook.htm) and a Customize Outlook Today page (custom.htm) located in the same folder. If you're interested in learning more you can download OutToday.exe from the Microsoft Office Resource Kit Web site (http://www.microsoft .com/office/ork/2000/appndx/toolbox.htm). It provides detailed instructions on modifying and creating custom Outlook Today pages. You can even download sample Outlook Today pages that you can use as a basis for your custom pages. You'll find them in the OutExmpl.exe file on the same page.

The Internet (including Microsoft's Web site) is in a constant state of flux. Therefore, by the time you read this, the URL may have changed or the information may have been removed.

One more thing. If you're an inveterate tinkerer, you can also add a DWORD value to the `HKEY_CURRENT_USER\Software\Microsoft\Office\9.0\Outlook\Today` key and name it Disable. A Value data of 1 turns off the Outlook Today page, and a Value data of 0 turns it on.

Creating New Views

While customizing views is great, sometimes you may want to retain an existing view, and create a completely new view from scratch. Nothing to it. Open the folder in which you plan to use the view. Next, grab your mouse and head for View | Current View | Define View to open the Define Views dialog box (see Figure 22-21).

If you don't use the Define Views command often enough to warrant adding it to a toolbar, but enough to find its default location annoying, you can move it to a more convenient location, such as the View menu. Open the Customize dialog box. Then, while the Customize dialog box remains open, choose View | Current View to display both the View menu and the Current View menu. Now drag the Define Views command from the Current View menu to a spot on the View menu and drop it. You can use this method to move commands from and to any menus.

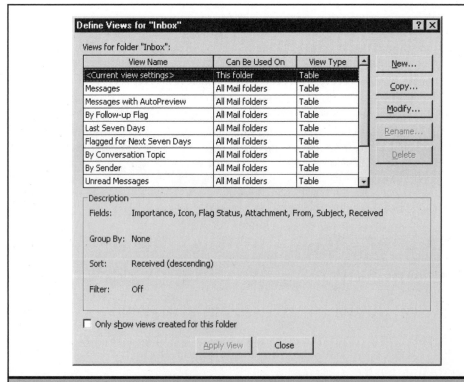

Figure 22-21.   *Create your own custom views in the Define Views dialog box*

To create a new view, you have two choices. You can either create a new view from scratch, or you can make a copy of an existing view and customize it to suit your needs. The advantages of copying an existing view are obvious if the new view will contain a large number of features already found in the existing view.

Creating a View from Scratch

To create a brand new view, click the New button in the Define Views dialog box to open the Create a New View dialog box, as shown in Figure 22-22.

Give the new view a brief, descriptive name. Then select the view type from the Type Of View list. The Can Be Used On option provides you with the opportunity to restrict or share the new view depending on your needs. To make the new view available to anyone who has access to the folder in which the view is created, choose This Folder, Visible To Everyone. To make it available only in the folder in which it's created, but hide it from everyone who has access to the folder except yourself, select This Folder, Visible Only To Me. The final choice makes it available in all folders of the type in which the view is being created.

When you've made your selection, click OK to open the View Settings for [name of new view] dialog box (really the View Summary dialog box with a new name). Here you can add Fields, and apply Group By, Sort, Filter, Other Settings, and Automatic Formatting (if they're all available) settings to your new view. See the sections on each of these features earlier in this chapter for detailed information.

Figure 22-22.   *Make sure the view name accurately describes the new view*

After you set all the options and return to the Define Views dialog box, you'll find the new view at the top of the Views For Folder [name of folder] display list. Click Close and your new creation is ready for primetime viewing. The next time you open the Current View menu, the new view appears at the top of the menu.

Using an Existing View

Sometimes there's no need to reinvent the wheel. You may have an existing view that's almost right for the job, but not quite. In that case, the simplest method is to make a copy of the existing view and customize it. Before you begin, open the Outlook folder in which you want the new view to appear. Choose View | Current View | Define Views to open the Define Views dialog box seen previously in Figure 22-21. Next, select the existing view on which to base the new view. Now click the Copy button. The Copy View dialog box appears.

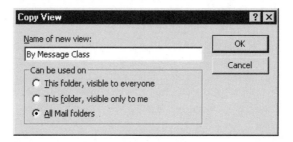

Give the new view an easy-to-identify name. Then select the appropriate Can Be Used On option. The first option makes the view available in the current folder to anyone with access. The second option also makes it available in the current folder, but only to you. The third option makes it available in all folders of the current folder's type and to anyone with access to those folders.

Click OK to open the View Summary dialog box. Here you can customize the existing Fields, Group By, Sort, Filter, Other Settings, and Automatic Formatting settings. See the sections earlier in this chapter on each of those features for more information.

When you return to the Define Views dialog box, the new view appears on the Views For Folder [folder name] list. Click Close to save the new view and return to the active view. When you access the Current View menu, you'll find your new view listed there as well.

Deleting Views

To ensure you don't do something you may later regret, Outlook permits you to modify but not delete the predefined views that come with it. However, Outlook couldn't care less if you decide to eliminate one of your own creations. All you have to do is open the folder in which the view resides and choose View | Current View | Define Views to open the Define Views dialog box. Then select the offending view and click Delete (if there's no Delete button, it means you've selected a "real" view). Outlook asks for confirmation. If you're sure about your action, click OK, and your view is history.

If you delete the current view, it remains onscreen when you close the Define Views dialog box. Don't worry, it's not really there. Switch views and it disappears, never to be seen again. It also disappears from the Current View menu.

The Complete Reference

Chapter 23

Customizing Outlook

I f you're a history buff, you'll probably remember that Henry Ford once proclaimed
that customers could buy his cars in any color they wanted, as long as it was black.
Well, those days are long gone. Today, everything from your toaster to your
minivan has a wealth of options. Outlook, like the other tools that help you deal with
today's fast paced life, has more than its fair share of options. Other chapters in this
book cover options specific to individual Outlook folders or features. This chapter,
on the other hand, is devoted to application-wide options that make Outlook do your
bidding at every turn.

Basic Customization

In addition to its many advanced options, Outlook provides a number of basic options
both for starting Outlook and for determining how it works after it launches. The
startup options let you decide whether you want special commands to run as Outlook
opens. The global options affect the way certain features operate throughout all folders
within Outlook.

Customizing the Outlook Startup

As you might suspect, the best place to start is at the beginning. In the case of
customization options, the beginning starts even before you have Outlook running.
In addition to the multitude of options that determine how Outlook performs, there
is also a set of options, called command-line switches, that determine how Outlook
starts. Using command-line switches, you can tell Outlook upon starting to open a
certain folder, automatically reset all views to their original state, or even address an
e-mail message to a specific individual.

A command-line switch has two components: the path to the Outlook executable
file (Outlook.exe), and the command-line switch itself. If you accepted the default
target folder for Outlook when you installed it, the path to Outlook.exe is "C:\Program
Files\Microsoft Office\Office\Outlook.exe".

Note   *When entering the path in a command-line switch, be sure to put the entire path within
quotation marks to preserve long filenames.*

Therefore, a command-line switch to start Outlook and automatically open an e-mail
message form would appear like this:

```
"C:\Program Files\Microsoft Office\Office\Outlook.exe" /c ipm.note
```

See Table 23-1 for a listing of useful command-line switches.

To Do This	Use This Switch	Example
Hide the Outlook Bar	/folder	Not applicable
Display the Outlook Bar	/explorer	Not applicable
Open Outlook to a specific folder	/select Outlook:<foldername>	/select outlook:calendar
Display the specified file folder	/select "path\folder name"	/select "C:\My Documents"
Create a new Outlook item using the specified message class. You can use Outlook forms or other valid MAPI forms. This switch does not launch Outlook. It simply creates the form and sends or saves it when you click the appropriate button.	/c <messageclass>	/c ipm.note (e-mail) /c ipm.stickynote (Note) /c ipm.appointment (appointment) /c ipm.task (task) /c ipm.contact (contact) /c ipm.activity (journal entry) /c ipm.post (post)
Create and send a message addressed to a specific recipient, without opening Outlook. This switch does not launch Outlook. It simply creates the message and sends it when you click Send.	/c ipm.note /m <full e-mail name>	/c ipm.note /m rsamuels@mindspring.com
Use in conjunction with /c <messageclass> to create a new item with the specified file as an attachment. This switch does not launch Outlook. It simply creates the form and sends it when you click Send.	/a "path/file name"	/c ipm.note/a "C:/My Documents/my.doc" (creates a new e-mail message and attaches my.doc)
Check to see if Outlook is the default program for mail, news and contacts. If it is, nothing happens. If it's not, Outlook informs you and asks if you want to register it as the default.	/checkclient	Not applicable

Table 23-1. *Outlook Command-line Switches*

To Do This	Use This Switch	Example
Launch Outlook and reset free/busy time for all existing appointments. This command regenerates the .prof file containing free/busy data. Used when free/busy data displays incorrectly.	/CleanFreeBusy	Not applicable
Launch Outlook and regenerate existing reminder data. To fix reminders that are not activating at the correct times.	/CleanReminders	Not applicable
Launch Outlook and delete saved searches from the Exchange server.	/Cleanfinders	Not applicable
Launch Outlook and restore default folder views. Be careful. This one deletes all customizations, including new views.	/CleanViews	Not applicable
Launch Outlook and restore missing Outlook folders. Works on the default delivery location.	/ResetFolders	Not applicable
Launch Outlook and restore the Outlook Bar to the default setting. This removes all customizations.	/ResetOutlookBar	Not applicable
Launch Outlook and disable the Preview Pane feature. Removes the option from the View menu.	/NoPreview	Not applicable

Table 23-1. *Outlook Command-line Switches* (continued)

To Do This	Use This Switch	Example
Launch Outlook and launch Outlook in Safe mode. No extensions, Preview Pane, or toolbar customizations are loaded. This does not remove any of these items, it merely prevents them from loading.	/Safe	Not applicable
Launch Outlook and display the Profiles dialog box, even if you have the Always Use This Profile option checked on the Mail Services tab of the Options dialog box (Tools | Options).	/Profiles	Not applicable
Launch Outlook and use a specific profile, even if another is set as the default. Use quotation marks around profile names that include spaces.	/Profile <profilename>	/Profile "Rebecca Samuels"

Table 23-1.   *Outlook Command-line Switches* (continued)

There are several methods for using command-line switches:

■ **Run**   Open the Run dialog box (click Start \| Run) and enter the command-line switch in the Open text box.

■ **Create a desktop shortcut**   Right-click on the desktop and select New \| Shortcut. Enter the command-line switch (both the Outlook.exe path and the switch) in the Command Line field. Give the shortcut an appropriate name and click Finish to save it. Since you're using the Outlook.exe file, the shortcut automatically uses the Outlook icon, therefore you don't have to include any reference to Outlook in the shortcut name. The next time you use the shortcut, Outlook starts according to the command-line switch used.

- **Start menu shortcut** You can add a shortcut to the Start menu by right-clicking the Windows taskbar, selecting Properties, clicking the Start Menu Programs tab, and clicking Add to display the Create Shortcut dialog box. Enter the command line, select the folder (menu) in which to place the shortcut, give the shortcut a name, and click Finish.

- **Office Shortcut Bar** Create a shortcut using either of the previously described methods. Then drag the new shortcut and drop it on the Office Shortcut Bar.

- **MS DOS Prompt** You can open an MS DOS window by using the MS DOS Prompt command. Then type the complete command-line switch at the prompt and press the ENTER key.

Command-line switches come in handy for dealing with the consequences of electronic mishaps. When certain Outlook files are corrupted due to hard disk or other problems, you can frequently remedy the situation by starting Outlook with one of the command-line switches found in Table 23-1, such as /ResetFolders or /CleanFreeBusy.

In addition, command-line switches can be very useful when incorporated into shortcuts. You can create a series of different shortcuts, each with its own specific command-line switch. This way you can have a shortcut to open Outlook any number of different ways.

> **Tip** *You can add a desktop (or Start menu) shortcut to the Outlook Bar by dragging it from the desktop to the Outlook Bar. This enables you to add command-line switches to the Outlook Bar. For example, magazine and book editors might create a shortcut to send submission/author guidelines in response to proposals they receive. Simply create a desktop shortcut that opens a blank e-mail message and attaches the desired file. The command line in the shortcut would look something like this; "C:\Program Files\ Microsoft Office\Office\Outlook.exe" /c ipm.note/a "C:\My Documents\ AuthorGdlns.doc". After you create the desktop shortcut, drag it from the Windows desktop to Outlook and drop it on the Outlook Bar. One caveat: not all command-line switches will run from within Outlook.*

Setting Outlook Global Options

In addition to the many options specific to individual folders or features, Outlook offers a variety of options to customize global features that apply throughout Outlook. You can access the Options dialog box shown in Figure 23-1 by choosing Tools | Options from the Menu bar.

Figure 23-1. *Outlook options are plentiful*

Note *Depending on your particular setup, the Options dialog box may contain additional tabs.*

As you can see in Figure 23-1, the Options dialog box contains a tab called Other. This tab is of particular interest to anyone desiring to set global options. It contains a variety of global options affecting numerous Outlook features, including AutoArchiving, tasks, the Outlook startup, reminders, and more.

In addition, there is a Spelling tab that lets you set some rules for how the Outlook spell checker performs its duties.

Customizing the AutoArchive Feature

The AutoArchiving feature, discussed in detail in Chapter 5, has several general options that control the way AutoArchiving behaves. After you open the Options dialog box (Tools | Options), click the Other tab. Then click the AutoArchive button to display the AutoArchive dialog box.

The options in the AutoArchive dialog box work in conjunction with the AutoArchive settings in the individual folders. Before any individualized folder settings work, you must first turn AutoArchiving on here and set the remaining options. Once AutoArchiving is enabled, you can open each folder's Properties dialog box, turn on AutoArchiving for the particular folder, and modify the other settings as needed.

 By default, only the Calendar, Tasks, Journal, Sent Items, and Deleted Items folders have AutoArchiving turned on.

The general AutoArchiving options found on the AutoArchive tab include:

- **AutoArchive every _ days**   Check this option to turn AutoArchiving on. Then set the number of days between AutoArchiving sessions.

- **Prompt before AutoArchive**   Check this option if you want Outlook to ask before it performs an AutoArchive operation.

- **Delete expired items when AutoArchiving (e-mail folders only)**   If you want to move e-mail messages that have expired to the Deleted Items folder after AutoArchiving is finished, check this option. As you can tell from the option name, it only works on folders containing e-mail messages.

- **Default archive file**   Indicate the path and name of the file in which you want to store archived items. Enter the path and filename or click the Browse button to locate the file. You can override this setting for individual folders by setting a different archive file in each folder's Properties dialog box.

When you're finished, click OK to save the settings and return to the Options dialog box. Click OK again to close the Options dialog box and return to the active view.

Setting General Options

At first glance, the General options don't appear to amount to much. Located on the Other tab, the General options include a single option and a button. However, as you

Figure 23-2. *The General options appear deceptively modest at first glance*

undoubtedly know, looks can be deceiving and, in this case, certainly are. Begin by choosing Tools | Options to open the Options dialog box. Then click the Other tab to display three sets of miscellaneous options (see Figure 23-2).

The single General option is Empty The Deleted Items Folder Upon Exiting, which, when checked, causes Outlook to delete everything in the Deleted Items folder when you exit Outlook. This is an easy way to keep your Deleted Items folder uncluttered. But it also means that your access to deleted items will be somewhat limited. Once you clean out the Deleted Items folder, the only way you can retrieve those items is to use the Recover Deleted Items command, by opening the Deleted Items folder and choosing Tools | Recover Deleted Items. Remember, deleted items on the server are periodically eliminated by the administrator to save storage space. Therefore, the deleted items may or may not be there when you go looking for them.

The Advanced Options button opens the Advanced Options dialog box, shown in Figure 23-3. In addition to having a number of advanced options, this dialog box also contains five additional buttons, each providing access to another dialog box of options.

Figure 23-3. *The advanced options include everything from startup folder options to the COM Add-Ins Manager*

The options you can set in the Advanced Options dialog box include:

- **Startup in this folder** From the drop-down list, select the folder you want Outlook to display on startup.

- **Warn before permanently deleting items** Check this option if you want Outlook to alert you when you're about to delete an item permanently (as opposed to just moving it to the Deleted Items folder). You will be prompted when you attempt to delete an item from the Deleted Items folder itself, or when you go to empty the Deleted Items folder. You'll also be notified if you use the SHIFT-DELETE shortcut key to permanently delete a selected item.

- **When selecting text, automatically select entire word** Check this box to change text selection in a text box from a single character at a time to a single word at a time. However, this option doesn't kick in until you've selected at least one word. For the first word, selection is one character at a time. After the first word is selected, each subsequent word (and its trailing space) is selected as soon as you select the first character of the word.

- **Provide feedback with sound** If you want Outlook to play a sound when you perform certain actions, check this option. Unfortunately, without the Office 2000 sounds, which you have to download from Microsoft's Web site, this option doesn't work. To download the sounds, establish an Internet connection and choose Help | Office On The Web to go to the Office Update Web site. Choose your country, then click the Downloads link, and download the Microsoft Office Sounds for Office 2000 file (sounds.exe). It only takes a couple of minutes, so it's no big deal. Double-click the sounds.exe file after you download it, and a wizard walks you through the installation. One more thing: if you have other Microsoft Office 2000 applications installed, they all inherit the sounds as well. It's all or nothing. Turn sounds on in one application, and they all have sound. Turn sounds off in one application, and none of them have sound.

- **Date Navigator**   This option lets you change the font used in the Date Navigator. Click the Font button and select the font, font style, and font size.

- **When viewing Notes, show time and date**   If you want the date and time the note was created or last modified to appear at the bottom of each note, check this option.

- **Task working hours per day**   Enter the number of hours your workday comprises. Outlook uses this number to calculate the number of days in the Total Work and Actual Work fields located on the Details tab of task forms. For example, if you enter 8 as the Task Working Hours Per Day, and then enter 16 in either the Total Work or the Actual Work fields, Outlook converts it to 2 days.

- **Task working hours per week**   This is the same as the previous option except it applies to the work week. Therefore, if you enter 40 hours here, and 80 hours in the Total Work or Actual Work fields, Outlook converts it to 2 weeks.

- **Reminder Options**   Click this button to display the Reminder Options dialog box. Here you'll find three self-explanatory options that let you choose whether you want a visual or aural cue when reminders come due.

- **Add-In Manager**   Click the Add-In Manager button to open the Add-In Manager dialog box, which contains a list of all the add-ins currently installed. To enable an add-in, place a checkmark in the box. To disable an add-in, remove the checkmark.

- **Advanced Tasks**   The Advanced Tasks button provides access to the Advanced Tasks dialog box, which contains three options. See Chapter 13 for a detailed explanation.

- **Custom Forms**   Click this button to open another Options dialog box containing additional buttons that provide access to the Forms Manager, Web services options, and network logon passwords. In addition, the Options dialog box contains a single option for designating the amount of hard disk space available for the storage of custom forms. Reserve as much space as you think you'll need.

  - **Manage Forms**   Clicking the Manage Forms button opens the Forms Manager, which is covered in detail in Chapter 24.

  - **Web Services**   The Web Services dialog box, which appears when you click this button, offers a couple of options for using Outlook Web Access (OWA) to open messages and forms not recognized by Outlook. OWA enables users to connect to the Exchange server with a browser and is generally employed by non-Outlook users. In this case, Outlook takes advantage of OWA by launching your default Web browser and displaying the unrecognized form in HTML format. Check the first option to enable this feature. Then indicate the location of your Web server. To have Outlook to ask before opening such forms, check the Prompt User Before Opening Each Form option. If your administrator has established a Web page library of HTML forms, you can add a Web Form command to the Actions menus of mail folders by checking the Activate Web Forms Link On Actions Menu option. Then enter the URL of the Web page forms library.

■ **Password**   This button opens the Change Windows NT Password dialog box, which allows you to change your password to log on to the network. You'll need your user name, the name of the domain you log on to, and your current password.

■ **COM Add-Ins**   Click this button to display the COM Add-Ins dialog box, which enables you to add and remove COM add-ins that provide added functionality to Outlook through the use of executable (.exe) and Dynamic Link Library (.dll) files. You'll find a selection of COM add-ins on the Microsoft Office Update Web site (http://officeupdate.microsoft.com/).

After you finish setting all the advanced options, click OK until you return to the active Outlook window.

Customizing the Spell Checker

Unless you're a spelling bee master and unerring typist, you'll probably find the Outlook spell checker quite useful. Since most folks make an occasional mistake or two, whether it's spelling or simply a typo, having a spell checker handy is helpful, especially when preparing important correspondence.

Note	*The spell checker is part of the shared Office proofing tools. Consequently, the proofing tools must be installed for the spell checker to work in Outlook. You may have to return to the Add/Remove applet in the Control Panel and install the proofing tools from the Office CD.*

It's important to remember that, as far as the Outlook spell checker is concerned, any word not appearing in either the default dictionary or the custom dictionary is misspelled. Since the combined dictionaries cannot possibly contain every word in the language, you will encounter many correctly spelled words that Outlook considers misspellings.

The Outlook spell checker comes with quite a few options, all of which can be found on the Spelling tab of the Options dialog box, shown in Figure 23-4.

GETTING MORE OUT OF OUTLOOK

Figure 23-4. *You can even develop your own custom dictionary for the spell checker*

You'll find the following options on the Spelling tab:

- **Always suggest replacements for misspelled words**   Check this option to ensure that Outlook not only flags words not found in its dictionary, but also offers suggested spellings for the flagged words.

- **Always check spelling before sending**   If you want Outlook to remember to perform a spell check even when you forget, check this option. It ensures that a spell check is run automatically before an e-mail message is sent.

- **Ignore words in UPPERCASE**   Since words entered in all uppercase letters are frequently acronyms or abbreviations, you can tell the Outlook spell checker to totally ignore them by checking this option.

- **Ignore words with numbers**   Since most words do not contain numbers, you're probably safe in telling Outlook to let words containing numbers slip by without question. However, if you're still using the hunt and peck method of typing, you may want to uncheck this one to make sure no mistake gets by unnoticed.

- **Ignore original message text in reply or forward** It's generally considered bad manners to edit another's e-mail message. Unless you're an English teacher and feel compelled to do it, you'll probably want to leave this option enabled. When checked, the spelling checker only checks your part of a message containing a reply or forward for spelling errors.

- **Edit custom dictionary** Outlook provides a custom dictionary to accommodate those words not found in the default dictionary. This is where those words that Outlook flags end up when you click the Add button. Occasionally, you may hit the Add button accidentally and wish you could remove a misspelled word from the dictionary to ensure it doesn't get by in the future. Well, here's your opportunity. It also comes in handy for adding lists of specialized words. You can cut and paste a list of technical terms so you won't have to deal with each one individually when you use it in an e-mail.

- **International dictionaries** Outlook comes with dictionaries for several different languages. If you are corresponding in a language different from the default dictionary language, choose the appropriate dictionary from the Language drop-down list.

Just so you don't think you're losing your mind, there's a bug in the spell checker that affects certain abbreviations that end with a period, such as Mr. and Mrs. In HTML messages, they may be flagged as misspelled. If you select the proper spelling from the list and click Change, the spell checker adds an extra period (Mr. becomes Mr..).

Customizing the Outlook Bar

The Outlook Bar is an extremely useful and flexible navigational tool that lets you move between Outlook folders and system folders with a single mouse click. The ability to tailor it to the way you work makes it even handier. You can change its size, hide it, add and remove shortcuts and shortcut groups, and even change the size of the shortcut icons. With a minimum amount of effort you can have it jumping through hoops in no time.

Resizing and Hiding the Outlook Bar

If you find you need more workspace in the Outlook window, one of the things you can do is resize the Outlook Bar by dragging its right border to the left. This increases the space allocated to the Information viewer (and Folder List, if it's displayed). In the event you're an ardent Folder List fan and hardly ever use the Outlook Bar, you can regain all of its space by simply hiding it.

The easiest way to hide it is to right-click a blank spot (not a shortcut) or a program group header on the Outlook Bar, and select Hide Outlook Bar from the shortcut menu.

You can also choose View | Outlook Bar from the Menu bar. When the Outlook Bar is hidden, choosing View | Outlook Bar redisplays it.

If you discover that you are unable to hide and display the Outlook Bar, or that it is improperly positioned, it may be a registry problem. Warning! Only experienced users should edit the Windows registry. All users should back up the registry before making any changes. To correct display and positioning problems with the Outlook Bar, close all programs and delete the HKEY_CURRENT_USER\Software\Microsoft\Office\ 9.0\Outlook\Office Explorer\Frame *key from the registry. After you close the registry and reopen Outlook, the registry key is rebuilt, and the Outlook window is restored to its original configuration.*

If you're so inclined, you can even add an Outlook Bar button to one of your toolbars so you can hide and display the Outlook Bar with a single mouse click. Right-click an existing toolbar and select Customize from the shortcut menu. Click the Commands tab and select View from the Categories list. Scroll down the Commands list in the right pane until you find the Outlook Bar command. Then drag the Outlook Bar command and drop it on the desired toolbar or menu bar. The next time you want to turn the Outlook Bar on or off, click the Outlook Bar button.

Adding and Removing Shortcuts

As handy as the Outlook Bar is right out of the box, its real power lies in the ability to customize it, especially by adding and removing shortcuts. You can add shortcuts for new Outlook folders you create, for Web pages, system folders, and more.

To add a shortcut to the Outlook Bar, right-click a blank spot (not a shortcut) on the Outlook Bar and select Outlook Bar Shortcut to open the Add To Outlook Bar dialog box, shown in Figure 23-5.

To add an Outlook folder, scroll through the tree view of existing folders and select the folder to which you want the new shortcut to point. If, however, you want to add a shortcut to a system folder, select File System from the Look In drop-down list first. This changes the tree view to a listing of the folders on your hard drive and network drives to which you have access. Now select the desired folder. After you select your Outlook or system folder, click OK to create the shortcut. It's automatically added to the bottom of the currently displayed shortcut group.

You can also add shortcuts to Outlook folders and system folders using the drag-and-drop method. For an Outlook folder, you must first display the Folder List. Then simply drag the folder for which you want to add a shortcut to the Outlook Bar and drop it in the desired group. You can drop the folder anywhere the black, horizontal I bar appears. The shortcut will then insinuate itself between the shortcuts on either side. To use the drag-and-drop method for a system folder (or file), open Windows Explorer, locate the file (or folder), drag it to the Outlook Bar, and drop it where you want the shortcut to appear.

Figure 23-5. *The Add To Outlook Bar dialog box provides access to both Outlook and system folders*

You can also open the Folder List, right-click an Outlook folder or a system folder (if you're currently displaying My Computer in the Folder List), and select Add To Outlook Bar from the shortcut menu.

To add a shortcut to a Web page, open the Web page in Outlook, and choose File | New | Outlook Bar Shortcut To Web Page.

Removing an Outlook Bar shortcut is a simple matter of right-clicking the offending shortcut and selecting Remove From Outlook Bar. Just to make sure you're serious, Outlook asks you to confirm the deletion. If you accidentally delete a shortcut, just follow the earlier instructions to re-create it.

Reorganizing Shortcuts

By default, the Outlook Bar is arranged to provide easy access to the most commonly used folders. However, what may be commonly used folders to one user may not be the most commonly used folders to another. For example, suppose you never use the Notes feature, but you're always accessing My Computer? Or perhaps you use Outlook for e-mail and practically nothing else. In either case you'll want to rearrange the shortcuts to suit the way you work. Whether it's to move the Notes shortcut to My Shortcuts and add the My Computer shortcut to Outlook Shortcuts, or to move the Sent Items, Outbox, and Drafts folders shortcuts to the Outlook Shortcuts group, the choice is yours.

If you can drag and drop, you can move shortcuts. Simply drag the shortcut from its current location to a new spot on the Outlook Bar. When you find just the right place for it, drop it. You can drop it anywhere the black, horizontal I bar appears. To move shortcuts between shortcut groups, use the same drag-and-drop procedure. Without letting go of the left mouse button, hover over the target shortcut group title until the group opens. Then move to the desired location and drop the shortcut group.

Changing the Size of Shortcuts

Once you begin adding shortcuts to the Outlook bar, you may find yourself spending a lot of time scrolling through all the shortcuts in a shortcut group, looking for a particular shortcut. When this happens you can start deleting some of the shortcuts you use less frequently than others. However, there's a better way that enables you to keep your existing shortcuts and reduce the scrolling at the same time.

All you have to do is resize the shortcuts in the shortcut group that's getting overpopulated. Start by displaying the shortcut group whose icons you want to resize. Now right-click the shortcut group title, and select Small Icons from the shortcut menu. The shortcuts icons are drastically reduced in size, and the text is placed to the right of the icon instead of below it. As you can see in Figure 23-6, both changes result in a dramatic increase in the amount of space available in the shortcut group.

Returning the shortcuts to their original size is a simple matter of displaying the shortcut group, right-clicking the group title, and selecting Large Icons from the shortcut menu.

Figure 23-6.   *The Outlook Bar on the left contains large icons; the Outlook Bar on the right contains small icons*

Renaming Outlook Bar Shortcuts

There's one more change you can make to shortcuts if you're so inclined: you can rename them. Suppose you're really bored and you decide that Deleted Items is much too tame for you. After a bit of serious consideration, you determine that The Terminator is a more appropriate name for the shortcut. So how do you go about making the name change? Easy. Right-click the shortcut and select Rename Shortcut, which highlights the shortcut name and activates the edit mode. You can now type an entirely new name over the existing name or simply edit the existing name. When you're through, press the ENTER key to save the name change.

Keep in mind that this operation only renames the shortcut icon, not the actual folder the shortcut points to. So even if you change the name of the Deleted Items shortcut to The Terminator, the folder that appears when you click the shortcut is still called Deleted Items.

Adding and Removing Shortcut Groups

In addition to adding and removing Outlook Bar shortcuts, you can also add and remove the shortcut groups that hold the individual shortcuts. By default, Outlook 2000 comes with three shortcut groups: Outlook Shortcuts, My Shortcuts, and Other Shortcuts. If you begin to accumulate system folder and Web page shortcuts, you may decide you need additional groups to keep all your shortcuts organized.

If you find yourself in this position, you can add your own shortcut group by right-clicking any shortcut title and selecting Add New Group. A new group, cleverly titled New Group, appears at the bottom of the Outlook Bar. The group title box is already in edit mode, so you can type in a more descriptive name and then press ENTER to save it.

| Note | *On the off chance that you get shortcut group happy and start adding them indiscriminately, you're probably going to be disappointed to hear that there is a 12-group limit. That's right, you cannot have more than 12 shortcut groups on the Outlook Bar at any one time. As soon as you reach the limit, you'll find that the Add New Group command becomes disabled.* |

To remove a group, simply right-click the group title and select Remove Group from the shortcut menu. Outlook requests confirmation that you really want to delete the group. If you click Yes, the group is immediately removed. Keep in mind that all shortcuts in the group are also deleted. Therefore, you might want to move any shortcuts before deleting the group.

To rename a shortcut group, right-click the group and select Rename Group. This puts the group title box in edit mode. You can then enter an entirely new name or edit the existing name. Press the ENTER key to save the change.

Troubleshooting the Outlook Bar

As powerful a navigational tool as the Outlook Bar is, it can occasionally become cantankerous and start acting a little weird. You may find that shortcuts stop working, error messages start appearing, or Outlook may start crashing when you click a shortcut. If you encounter such behavior, there are a couple of things you can try.

The first thing to understand is that the Outlook Bar settings are contained in two system files. The first is outlbar.inf, which contains all the Outlook Bar basic settings. The second, *profilename*.fav (for example, rebecca.fav), contains any customizations you make to the Outlook Bar. The outlbar.inf file is editable. The .fav file is not. However, only experienced users should edit the outlbar.inf, and even they should make a backup copy of it before making any changes.

If your Outlook Bar is acting up, the first thing to try is renaming the .fav file, and letting Outlook rebuild the Outlook Bar by creating a new .fav file upon startup. Close Outlook, and then use the Windows Find feature (Start | Find) to locate the .fav file and rename it.

Note *If there are multiple profiles, there will be multiple .fav files. Make sure you delete the one associated with your profile.*

A good renaming technique is to change the .fav extension to .old. For example, if your file is named rebecca.fav, change it to rebecca.old. Now reopen Outlook, which automatically generates a new .fav file with the same name as the original and rebuilds the Outlook Bar from scratch.

Note *While it's true that the command-line switch /ResetOutlookBar does the same thing, it's also true that if the .fav file wasn't the problem, all your Outlook Bar customizations are irretrievably lost.*

If this does not solve your problem, you can close Outlook, delete the new .fav file created, and rename the .old file back to .fav. The next time you start Outlook, all your customizations will be back.

If you're not comfortable with renaming files, and you don't mind losing (or haven't made) any customizations to the Outlook Bar, you can use the /ResetOutlookBar command-line switch. See the section titled "Customizing the Outlook Startup" earlier in this chapter for details on using command-line switches.

In some cases, custom views can be the culprits that cause erratic behavior in the Outlook Bar. If nothing else works you can reset all the Outlook views to their original state by using the /CleanViews command-line switch. Be advised, however, that all custom views are deleted when this switch is used.

Customizing Toolbars

Outlook toolbars are handy items to have around if you use them. They provide quick access to commands you otherwise have to select from a menu or run with a shortcut key combination. The most important thing to remember about Outlook toolbars is that they are there for your convenience. You control which toolbars are displayed, where they appear on the Outlook window, and which commands they contain. If they're not making themselves useful, you can change them, move them, or get rid of them entirely.

Outlook toolbar and menu settings are stored in the Outcmd.dat file. If you do any customization to toolbars or menus, you should back this file up regularly to ensure against losing your customizations if a problem arises that requires resetting the toolbars and menus. If you have a backup you'll be able to instantly reapply your customized settings by replacing the Outcmd.dat with the backup copy. Use the Windows Find command to locate Outcmd.dat.

One other thing about toolbars in Outlook: while a toolbar displayed in one folder appears in all other folders, the buttons that appear on the toolbar may change. Since each folder has different features, you'll find that some buttons disappear and others appear as you move from folder to folder. This is also true of changes you make. Only those commands that can be used in the current folder appear on the toolbars.

Showing and Hiding Toolbars

Toolbars, like most tools, are only useful if you have the right one for the job at hand. By default, the Menu bar (which, by the way, is technically a toolbar) and the Standard toolbar are always displayed. While you can hide the Standard toolbar, you cannot hide the Menu bar. The first order of business is to figure out where to find a toolbar when you need it. Fortunately, that's pretty easy. Right-click anywhere on the Menu bar or an existing toolbar to see a shortcut menu of the available toolbars for the current view.

Once you access the shortcut menu, you can add or remove toolbars by selecting them from the menu. Toolbars with checkmarks next to them are already visible. Remove the checkmark to hide them. Place a checkmark next to a currently hidden toolbar and it appears immediately.

You can also display and hide multiple toolbars at once by using the Customize dialog box, which you can open by right-clicking any toolbar and selecting Customize from the shortcut menu. Then click the Toolbars tab to view the available toolbars. You can also choose Tools | Customize.

Tip   *You can open the Customize dialog box by double-clicking a blank spot next to any
visible toolbar except the Menu bar.*

Check the toolbars you want to display, and uncheck those you want to hide. The
result is immediate, and the toolbar(s) appear even before you close the Customize
dialog box. You'll note that the Menu bar appears on the list of available toolbars.
However, any attempt to remove the checkmark fails. The Menu bar is the one toolbar
that must always remain visible, although the menus change with the view. When
you're through, click Close to return to the active view.

Repositioning Toolbars

The fact that the Microsoft programmers think that toolbars belong at the top of your
application window doesn't mean you have to agree. If you don't, the solution is
simple: put them where you want them.

Before rearranging your toolbars, there is one thing you should know about them.
You have two options when it comes to the manner in which you position Outlook
toolbars in the Outlook window. You can have docked toolbars or floating toolbars.

Docked toolbars are tightly snuggled up against one of the four sides of the
Outlook window or against another docked toolbar. Floating toolbars, on the other
hand, are free spirits that hang out wherever you happen to drop them on the screen.
As you can see in Figure 23-7, the only problem with floating toolbars is that they
invariably get in your way while you're working.

Docked toolbars

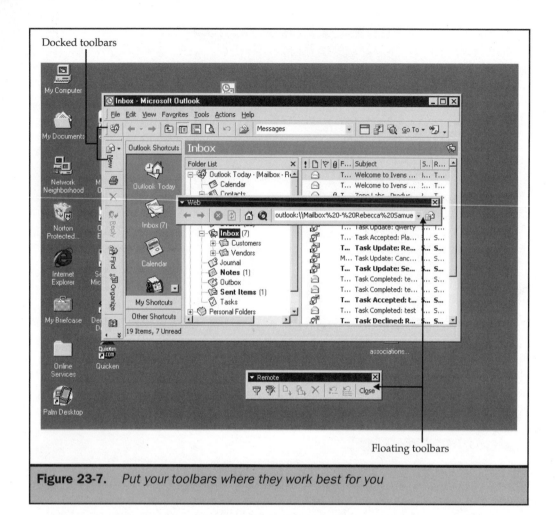

Floating toolbars

Figure 23-7.   *Put your toolbars where they work best for you*

To move a toolbar, position your mouse pointer over the toolbar handle (the raised vertical bar at the left side of the toolbar), and drag the toolbar to a new location. If you want the toolbar docked, drag it to the desired side. As soon as it's in position, it automatically docks itself. If you want the toolbar to float, drop it anywhere on the screen.

You can also change the position of docked toolbars by dragging them around. For example, if you decide that you want the Menu bar to appear below the Standard toolbar, all you have to do is grab the Menu bar handle and drag it under the Standard toolbar. They will immediately switch places.

In addition to the difference in position, floating toolbars contrast with docked toolbars in other ways. As soon as a toolbar changes from docked to floating, it sheds its move handle. Not to worry, though. You can still move it, only now you have to grab it by its title bar: the blue bar (or another color if you've changed your desktop settings) that contains the toolbar title.

Tip *You can turn a floating toolbar into a docked toolbar by double-clicking the toolbar's title bar.*

Another difference is the shape of the toolbar. When docked along the edge of the window the toolbar stretches itself out to be as unobtrusive as possible. When it becomes a floating toolbar, it's not so easy to figure out the least obtrusive position, so it assumes a rectangular shape. To make it even more manageable, you can change its dimensions by dragging any of its four sides.

Modifying Existing Toolbars

The standard toolbars that appear in the Outlook window and in Outlook input forms can be changed to suit your needs or your whims. You can add and remove command buttons, as well as rearrange their position on the toolbar. For example, if you rarely use the Find A Contact box on the Standard toolbar, but are always switching views, you might want to remove the Find A Contact command and add the Current View command.

Adding and Removing Command Buttons

Whether you're adding or removing command buttons from a toolbar, the first order of business is to display the toolbar and open the Customize dialog box. Right-click a visible toolbar and select Customize. If you want to display another toolbar, click the Toolbars tab and check the toolbar(s) you want displayed. To remove command buttons from a visible toolbar, all you have to do is drag them off the toolbar (while the Customize dialog box is visible) and drop them in the Information viewer. Don't worry, removing a command from the toolbar does not remove it from the list of available commands, simply from the toolbar.

Adding a command requires a little more effort. Click the Commands tab in the Customize dialog box to display the available Outlook commands.

From the Categories list in the left pane, select the type of command you want to add. All the commands available in that category then display in the Commands list in the right pane. Now drag the desired command from the Commands list and drop it on the toolbar in the location you want it to reside. You can drop the command when the black I bar appears and when the small square attached to your mouse pointer changes from an X to a + (plus sign). If you drop the command too soon, it disappears and you have to repeat the process.

While the Customize dialog box is displayed, you can move toolbar buttons around by dragging them from one location to another and dropping them. You can use this method to move them to a new location on the same toolbar or to a different toolbar (as long as it's displayed).

You can move, remove, and copy command buttons from a toolbar (or a menu) during normal Outlook operations, without opening the Customize dialog box. To move or remove a button, simply hold down the ALT key and drag the button to a new location or onto the Information viewer to remove it altogether. To copy a button, press ALT-CTRL and drag the button from one toolbar to another. When you drop the button, a copy is placed on the target toolbar, while the original button remains on the source toolbar.

Changing Button Icons and Text

Another nice thing about the Outlook toolbars is that you can also modify the individual toolbar buttons. With the Customize dialog box open, you can change a button's appearance, add a keyboard shortcut, and even assign a hyperlink to it.

To modify a toolbar button, display the toolbar containing the button you want to change, then open the Customize dialog box. Now right-click the button you want to customize to display a shortcut menu similar to the one seen in Figure 23-8.

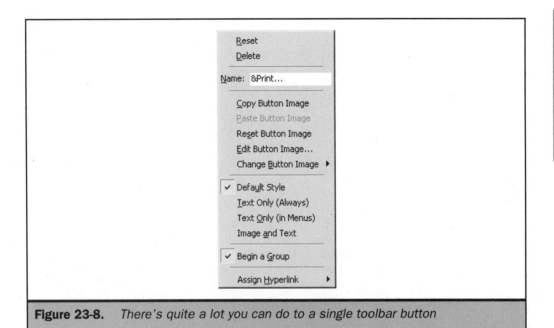

Figure 23-8.   *There's quite a lot you can do to a single toolbar button*

As you can see, there are a number of customizing options available:

■ **Reset**   Removes image, text, and hyperlink modifications, and restores the button to its original state. It does not restore style changes to buttons. If you change the style from default to Text Only (Always), selecting Reset does not change it back.

■ **Delete**   Removes the selected button from the toolbar. It has the same effect as dragging the button off the toolbar and dropping it on the Information viewer.

■ **Name**   The current name of the button appears in the Name text box. This is the text that appears when you select any of the button styles that include text. You can edit this text to suit your needs. You'll notice an ampersand (&) in some names. When used as part of a button name, it underlines and converts the character that follows to a shortcut for running the command. As you can see in Figure 23-8, the name for the Print command is &Print.... When you display the name on the toolbar button, it appears as Print.... Any time a command contains an underlined letter in its name, you can activate the command by holding down the ALT key and pressing the underlined letter. Therefore, if the Print name is displayed on the button, you can open the Print dialog box by pressing ALT-P. You can create your own shortcut keys by placing the ampersand anywhere you want it. Just be sure not to create shortcut keys that conflict with other commands.

- **Copy Button Image**   Select a button and use this command to copy the default image (not the button or the command, just the image) used on this button.

- **Paste Button Image**   Used in conjunction with the Copy Button Image command, this one pastes the copied image to another button you select.

- **Reset Button Image**   If you change your mind about a button image modification you've made, you can use this command to restore the button image to its original state.

- **Edit Button Image**   Choose a button with an image you want to modify, and click this menu command to open the Button Editor, a mini-paint program with which you can modify the image. Select a color from the palette and click a pixel (one square) to change its color. A second click removes the color. Edit the image and click OK to return to the Customize dialog box.

- **Change Button Image**   If you don't like the existing image, or if the button doesn't have one, you can use this command to add a new graphic to the button. As soon as you select this command, a submenu of alternative images appears. Click one to add it to the selected button.

- **Default Style**   The Default style for most toolbar buttons is graphic only, no text. If you've changed the button style, you can use this command to return the button to its original style.

- **Text Only (Always)**   If you find the command button icons confusing or annoying, you can select this command to display the text name on the button and eliminate the icon altogether.

- **Text Only (in Menus)**   This command allows the selected command to appear with an icon when used on a toolbar, but with text and no icon when used on a menu.

- **Image and Text**   Choose this option to always show both the icon and the text title. This can be helpful for a new user who is just learning the program.

- **Begin a Group**   Use this command to add a vertical bar to a toolbar to separate groups of buttons.

Tip   *You can also modify the width of toolbar commands that contain drop-down lists, such as Find A Contact and Current View. With the command displayed on a menu and the Customize dialog box open (it puts Outlook in the customize mode), simply drag the command box border to the left or right to change the size.*

While you have the Customize dialog box open, you can also copy a command button from one toolbar to another by pressing CTRL and dragging a clone of the button to a new location. When you're through customizing toolbars and toolbar buttons, click Close to exit the Customize dialog box and return to the active window.

Creating New Toolbars

Not only can you customize existing toolbars, you can also create your own. This comes in handy for putting together a toolbar of your favorite commands, or collections of commands you only use occasionally or only in a certain folder.

Creating a new toolbar is a two-part operation. The first step entails creating the blank toolbar. The next step is adding commands to the new toolbar.

To create a blank toolbar, open the Customize dialog box, and click the Toolbars tab. Click the New button to open the New Toolbar dialog box.

Give your new toolbar a unique, descriptive name and click OK to add it to the Toolbars tab. A blank toolbar one button wide appears next to the Customize dialog box. Look carefully or you might miss it.

Once you've got the blank toolbar, you can start adding commands immediately, or you can move the toolbar to the place you want it to sit before adding commands. Since the process is the same regardless of whether you're adding commands to a new toolbar or an existing toolbar, refer to the earlier section titled "Adding and Removing Command Buttons" for detailed instructions. The same goes for editing and moving command buttons.

Setting Toolbar Options

In addition to customizing individual toolbars and buttons, Outlook also provides several global options that affect toolbars throughout the application. You'll find these options on the Options tab of the Customize dialog box (see Figure 23-9).

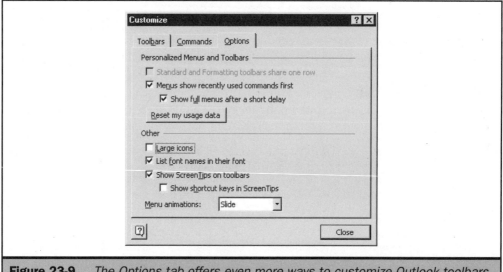

Figure 23-9.   *The Options tab offers even more ways to customize Outlook toolbars*

The toolbar options found on the Options tab include the following:

- **Standard and Formatting toolbars share one row**   This option is grayed out unless you are in a form, such as an e-mail message form, that contains a text field which permits text formatting. In that case, you can elect to display both the Standard and the Formatting toolbars on the same row to reduce the amount of space they take up.

- **Large Icons**   By default, Outlook uses small icons on the toolbar buttons. This reduces the amount of space each button takes up and provides easy access for most users. However, if you have a difficult time making out the small icons, you can check this option to display large images on those toolbar buttons that contain images.

- **List font names in their font**   The Formatting toolbar, which appears in forms that contain text boxes, such as message and note fields, contains a Font drop-down list from which you can select the font of your choice. When the List Font Names In Their Font option is checked, each font name is displayed in the list using the actual font. For example, Comic Sans MS appears on the list in the Comic Sans MS font, and Impact appears in the **Impact** font. This enables you to see what the font will look like when selected. Unfortunately, it also requires more memory and takes longer to display the list. If you're familiar with the different fonts, you can speed things up a bit by removing the checkmark for this option.

- **Show Screen Tips on toolbars** Screen Tips are those little text boxes that appear when you pause your mouse pointer over a toolbar button for a couple of seconds. They contain the toolbar name and can be quite useful for identifying buttons that contain icons only. If you display text in your buttons you may want to eliminate the Screen Tips by deselecting this option.

- **Show shortcut keys in Screen Tips** Some commands have shortcut keys automatically assigned to them. If you want the shortcut key to appear in the Screen Tip along with the command name, check this option.

The remaining options on the Options tab pertain to menus and are covered in the section titled "Setting Menu Options" later in this chapter.

MOUS EXAM PRACTICE
In this section, you learned to hide, display, customize, and create Outlook toolbars. Begin this practice session by hiding and displaying toolbars using both methods covered—right-clicking an existing toolbar, and using the Customize dialog box. Next, modify an existing toolbar by adding, removing, and rearranging command buttons. Then try your hand at creating your own custom toolbar and adding new command buttons. Finally, modify some of the toolbar options to see how existing toolbars are changed.

Using Menus

Practically everywhere you go in Outlook you can find menus that make your job a little easier. The Menu bar, which is the only toolbar you can't hide, is always with you wherever you are. Even some toolbar buttons have menus that display a list of commands. Because they disappear when not in use, menus enable you to keep a large number of commands at your fingertips without cluttering up your screen.

The Menu bar is where the bulk of the Outlook 2000 commands reside. Since the Menu bar is technically a toolbar, it has many of the toolbar properties. You can dock it, float it, change its shape, or customize it just like any other toolbar.

You can move it the way you move a toolbar, by grabbing its move handle and dropping it where you want it to go. If you place it at the edge of the screen, it docks itself and rearranges its "buttons" to accommodate its new position.

Drop it anywhere on the screen, and like a toolbar, it alters its shape and floats where you place it. You can change its dimensions by dragging any of the four edges. However, unlike the other toolbars, you cannot close the Menu bar. It must remain visible at all times. Even if you open the Customize dialog box, you cannot remove the checkmark next to Menu Bar.

Another thing to take note of is the shortcut key combinations that appear next to some of the commands. These are generally the more common commands, such as Open, Print, Copy, Paste, and so on. Shortcut keys will save you a lot of time in the long run if you memorize and use them.

Understanding Personalized Menus

While the basic menu system incorporated into Outlook has been around for quite a while, this latest version of Outlook contains a new twist: "intelligent" menus. These new, intelligent menus have been dubbed Personalized Menus by Microsoft. They begin by displaying only the most commonly used commands and hiding those commands that are less frequently accessed. During the initial period of use, Outlook tracks which menu commands you actually use. Based on your usage, Outlook then automatically "personalizes" the menus to display those commands you use most frequently, and hides those you don't use. Depending on the amount of time you spend in Outlook, it can take as little as a couple of days or as much as several weeks before you begin noticing the changes.

While this may sound good in theory, in practice it's more time consuming and annoying than helpful. It quickly becomes apparent that the changing menus cause confusion since commands are not always in the same place. In addition, there are still enough commands on the menus to ensure a certain amount of hunting for the right command. Finally, when you're searching for a command that happens to be hidden you have to wait several seconds before the full menu appears. The only way to display the full menu immediately is to click the chevron at the bottom of the personalized menu. This of course means an extra action, which is unnecessary if you forego the personalized menus.

Customizing Menus

Like toolbars, menus are quite flexible, affording you the opportunity to mold them into the power tools that best fit your work habits. You can add and remove commands, as well as move, copy, and rename them. In addition, you can reposition and even remove individual menus (but not the Menu bar itself), and add shortcut keys to menu items you use frequently.

The methods used to customize Outlook menus are identical to those used to customize Outlook toolbars. Therefore, you can refer to the section titled "Customizing Toolbars" earlier in this chapter for detailed information on customizing menus.

Creating New Menus

As with toolbars, sometimes modifying the existing menus just isn't enough. You may have a specialized need that requires a series of commands (from different categories) all grouped on one menu. In that case, you can create your own menu and fill it with exactly those commands that you need (or want). For example, if you do a lot of customizing you may want to create a Customize menu that contains commands such as Options, Customize Current View, Customize, Organize, Services, and others.

To begin, open the Customize dialog box and click the Commands tab. Scroll down and select the last item in the Categories list, New Menu. This displays the New Menu command in the Commands list on the right. As a matter of fact, it's the only command in the New Command category. Drag the New Menu command from the Commands list to the Outlook Menu bar, and drop it next to or between existing menu titles (File, Edit, View, and so on). A new menu immediately appears on the Menu bar.

The next step is to give the new menu an appropriate name. Right-click the New Menu item and enter the desired name in the Name field. If you want to add a shortcut key to the menu, include an ampersand (&) before the character you want to use as the shortcut. Using the earlier example of creating a Customize menu, you might want to use the C in Customize as the shortcut key. If so, you would enter **&Customize** in the Name field. The C then becomes underlined, indicating that you can access the Customize menu by pressing ALT-C. Make sure that your new shortcut key doesn't conflict with any existing shortcut keys.

The final step is to populate the new menu with the desired commands. From the Categories list, select the category containing the first command you want to include. Continuing with the Customize menu example, you might select Tools. Then in the Commands list, select the desired command, such as Options. Drag the command to the new menu, which opens as soon as you move the mouse pointer over the menu title. Drop the command in the box that opens below the menu as soon as the black I bar appears. Continue adding commands until you have a complete menu.

This not only works for adding new menus to the Menu bar, but also for adding new submenus to existing menus. Suppose, for example, you wanted to have a submenu on the View menu that included all the available commands for defining and customizing views. Drag the New Menu command to the View menu and drop it among the existing View menu commands. Give it an appropriate name, and then add Define Views, Customize Views, Format Columns, Sort, Filter, and other such commands to the box that opens at the right of the New Menu submenu.

Setting Menu Options

Fortunately, Outlook provides menu options that, among other things, allow you to disable the personalized menus and reset the usage information upon which personalized settings are based. To modify the options, open the Customize dialog box and click the Options tab to display the menu and toolbar options (as shown in Figure 23-9).

The options that apply to menus include the following:

- **Menus show recently used commands first** Check this option to enable personalized menus. Outlook will then track your usage of menu commands and personalize the menus by hiding commands you use infrequently. To disable personalized menus, remove the checkmark.

- **Show full menus after a short delay** This option, which is only available if the previous option is checked, automatically displays hidden commands after the menu is open for a few seconds. If you want the hidden commands to remain hidden until you click the chevron at the bottom of each menu, remove the checkmark.

■ **Reset my usage data**   If your personalized menus do not correctly reflect your usage of the menu commands, you can start the usage tracking over by clicking the Reset My Usage Data button. Outlook warns you that this action removes the record of your command usage (the file containing your usage data is C:\Windows\Application Data\Microsoft\Office\MSOutlo.pip) and restores it to its default state. If you're not sure about taking this action, you might want to make a backup copy of MSOutlo.pip. If you change your mind, you can delete the new MSOutlo.pip file, and replace it with the backup copy. Just make sure you do not delete or replace the copy of MSOutlo.pip in C:\Program Files\ Microsoft Office\Office.

■ **Menu animations**   If you enjoy computer animations, you can make the Outlook menus a little more lively by selecting an animation type from this drop-down list. By default, the selection is None. With this setting, the menus simply appear when you click the menu title. If you like having the Outlook menus appear by starting at the top left corner of the menu title and "unfolding" toward the bottom right corner of the screen until the menu is displayed, select Unfold. To have the menus appear from top to bottom in a sliding motion, select Slide. Selecting Random makes the menus appear using one of the two animations. However, which animation is used depends entirely on random chance.

When you're through setting menu options, click Close to save your new settings and return to the active Outlook view.

MOUS EXAM PRACTICE
In this section, you learned to use personalized menus, change existing menus, and create your own custom menus. Start your practice by modifying an existing menu. Add new commands, move them around on the menu, and then remove them. Next, create your own custom menu and add commands to it. Then create a submenu and fill that with commands. Finally, change some of the menu options. Be careful not to reset your usage information unless you're prepared to start the menu personalization tracking over.

Exam | MOUS Exam Objectives Explored in Chapter 23

Objective	Activity	Heading
OL2000.1.17	Customize Menu and task bars	"Customizing Toolbars" "Using Menus"
OL2000.3.9	Customize Menu and task bars	"Customizing Toolbars" "Using Menus"

The Complete Reference

Part VII

Building Outlook Applications

The
Complete
Reference

Chapter 24

Designing Custom
Forms and Fields

Although Outlook has an extensive collection of forms and fields right out of the box, there's no way that the Microsoft programmers could anticipate everyone's needs. Therefore, you'll be happy to hear that you can create your own custom forms for inputting and even receiving Outlook information (with the exception of the Notes folder). In addition, you can create new fields to hold data, and add them to your custom forms. In this chapter, you'll discover just how painless creating custom forms and new fields really can be.

Understanding Form Basics

Working with and customizing forms is a lot easier if you understand the underlying concepts. The best place to start is at the beginning of the Outlook data chain. Outlook information consists of fields, records, and folders. Fields are containers that hold individual pieces of information (Name, Company, Address, and so on). Records, more familiarly known in Outlook as items, are collections of related fields. For example, the Full Name, Job Title, Company, and other fields that pertain to a single contact in your Contacts folder, together form a record. Folders are groups of related records (and views). Forms (at last!) are the devices with which you enter, and in some cases display, Outlook information.

Forms do not contain information, they merely facilitate the input of information into fields and records. All input forms also display information when you open an individual record. Other forms, such as the Read Pages of mail message forms, exist for the sole purpose of displaying information entered using input forms (Compose Pages of message forms, in this example). One more thing to understand about Outlook forms is that you cannot create a custom form from scratch. You must use an existing form as the basis for new forms.

Planning

The level of success you achieve with form building, as with most projects, is greatly enhanced by forethought and planning. The mechanics of form building is not terribly complex. You open a form in the design mode, drag a field or a control onto the form, move it around, set its properties, publish the form, and you're done. However, if you want a form that truly meets your needs, you should take a few things into consideration.

Although custom forms are, in theory, backward-compatible, it's usually best to design a form for the least common denominator. While the form basics are the same, adding new features to a form for use in a version of Outlook that doesn't support those features means the form won't function properly in that version. Therefore if your form will be used with Outlook 2000, Outlook 98, and Outlook 97, you should design for Outlook 97—better yet, design in Outlook 97. Also, be aware that custom

Contact forms created in Outlook 2000 (or Outlook 98, for that matter) will not work at all in Outlook 97.

Note	*The Notes folder form is unavailable for customization, so you're stuck with it whether you like it or not.*

It's also a good idea to think about who's going to use the form and why. Make sure you add necessary fields and eliminate extraneous fields. Too much or too little information can make a custom form ineffective. If you plan to construct a complex, multipage form, you might consider laying it out on paper first. Ask any good craftsman about the value of working from a plan. Artists may rely on creativity, but an experienced builder won't hammer that first nail without a good blueprint.

Pages

Forms consist of one or more pages, which provide the foundation for each form. The form merely acts as a backdrop on which to place controls and fields. Most Outlook forms consist of multiple pages. The Contact form, for example, contains five pages by default: General, Details, Activities, Certificates, and All Fields. Even mail message forms, which appear to have only a single page, consist of two pages: a Compose Page for writing an e-mail message, and a Read Page for reading the contents of a received message. In reality, all forms contain multiple pages. In addition to the page(s) visible when the form is displayed, each form includes blank pages for customization, a Properties page for setting form options, and an Actions page for designating actions available to the user, such as Reply, Reply To All, and so on. These "hidden" pages become visible when you open a form in the design mode (Tools | Forms | Design A Form).

Objects

Every form must contain objects. Without objects, the form is nothing more than a blank page. There are two types of objects you can use with an Outlook form: fields and controls. Fields are the actual storage containers used to hold pieces of Outlook data, while controls are objects such as text boxes, scroll bars, and command buttons that enable users to manipulate that data. Some objects simply add informational or decorative items to the form. The Image object, which adds a graphic image to the form, is an example.

Since there's no way to make use of fields without controls, the Outlook fields you can add to a form are, in reality, prepackaged combinations of fields and controls. In other words, each "field" available from the Field Chooser is actually one or more controls, already linked (bound) to a specific Outlook field. You can create the same combination yourself by adding the controls and manually linking them to the field. The difference between manually linking controls and fields, and creating new "fields" is simply that "fields" are permanent (until you delete them), reusable combinations.

Layout

The form layout is just what you'd expect—the placement of objects (controls and fields) on the form page. As so many designers of everything from fashion to furniture have pointed out, there is a direct correlation between form (no pun intended) and function. The more organized and aesthetically pleasing your form is, the more effective it will be. Fortunately, Outlook provides a number of tools that make your form layout chores almost effortless. The layout features, which can be found on the Layout menu in the design mode, include an optional grid (turned on by default) that enables you to easily align objects on the page, plus a wealth of features to automate object alignment, spacing, layering, and more.

Designing Your Custom Form

Now that you've got the basics down, it's time to get to work. The first order of business is to select the existing form on which to base the customized form. Choose Tools | Forms | Design A Form to open the Design Form dialog box, shown in Figure 24-1.

Figure 24-1.   *Select the existing form on which to base your new form*

From the Look In drop-down list, choose the forms library containing the form. The first time you create a custom form you'll probably want to base it on one of the default forms that come with Outlook. You'll find these in the Standard Forms Library. From the list of available forms, pick the one you want to use and click Open to display the selected form in the design mode. As you can see in Figure 24-2, the form (the Message form in this case) opens displaying the first page of the form and the Field Chooser.

If you take a close look at Figure 24-2, you'll see that all the tab names except Message are enclosed in parentheses. This indicates the pages are hidden when the form is used. You can choose which pages are hidden and which are displayed when the form is used by opening the page and choosing Form | Display This Page. When the command has a checkmark next to it, the selected page will be displayed. Without a checkmark the page will be hidden during normal use.

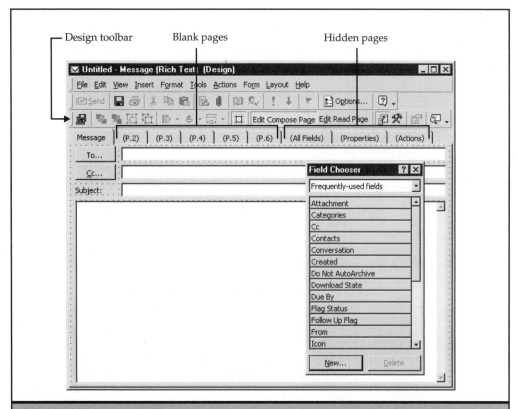

Figure 24-2. *The design mode adds a toolbar and two new menus to the form*

Using the Grid

If you want to produce a well-organized and professional-looking form, it's important to line up the objects you add to the form. The first line of defense in object alignment is the grid. As you can see in Figure 24-3, the grid is a pattern of dots on a form page that provides a frame of reference for placing objects relative to one another.

In addition to using the grid as a visual frame of reference, you can also instruct Outlook to force objects to automatically align themselves with the nearest top-left grid intersection. This feature, which is called Snap To Grid, is turned on by default. You can turn it on and off by clicking the Snap To Grid button on the design toolbar, by right-clicking the page (not an object) and deselecting Snap To Grid, or by choosing Layout | Snap To Grid.

If you find the grid too large or small, you can adjust its size by choosing Form | Set Grid Size to display the Set Grid Size dialog box, in which you can manually adjust

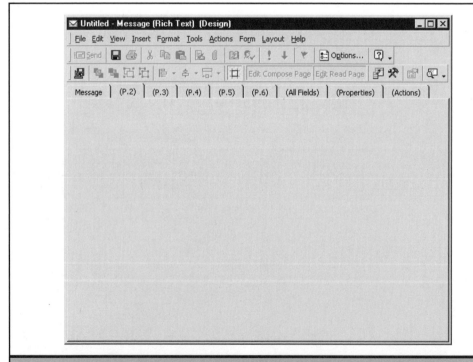

Figure 24-3. *Use the grid to facilitate object placement*

both width and height dimensions. The larger the numbers, the wider the gap between grid points.

There are a couple of other commands available for working with the grid. The first is Show Grid. This command, found on the Layout menu and on the shortcut menu that appears when you right-click a form page, shows or hides the grid depending on its state. When the command is checked, the grid appears; when the command is unchecked, the grid disappears. One thing to remember is that the Snap To Grid command remains in effect regardless of whether the grid is visible.

The other command that works with the grid is the Size To Grid command. If you have an object with one or more sides that do not extend to a grid line, you can automatically resize the object so that all sides fall on the nearest grid line. Select the object and choose Layout | Size To Grid.

Adding and Removing Fields

Most likely, customizations you perform will involve the addition of fields to the form or the removal of existing fields.

> **Note** *Before going any further, it's important to remember the distinction between pure fields (data containers alone) and the "fields" you can manipulate with the Field Chooser. The "fields" you can work with are really predesigned field/control combinations, which means that when you add a field to a form you generally end up with more than one object. For example, many "fields" include a label control and a text box control, both of which are bound to the real [data container] field.*

Removing existing fields is a simple matter of selecting the controls that make up the field and pressing DELETE, or right-clicking and selecting Delete from the shortcut menu.

> **Tip** *You can select multiple objects by holding down the CTRL key and clicking each object. You can also select multiple objects by drawing a selection box around them. Place your mouse pointer above and to the left of the topmost and left-most objects you want to include. Then hold down the left mouse button and drag the mouse pointer toward the lower-right corner of the page until you've enclosed all the desired objects in the selection box. When you let the left mouse button go, the objects completely or only partially within the selection box are automatically selected. As long as you touch an object with the selection box it will be included.*

BUILDING OUTLOOK
APPLICATIONS

Adding objects is almost as easy. You'll need the Field Chooser, shown in Figure 24-4, to add fields to your form, so be sure it's visible. If you don't see it, right-click the form page and select Field Chooser from the shortcut menu. You can also display it by choosing Form | Field Chooser.

Once you've got it onscreen, begin by locating the desired group of fields from the drop-down list at the top of the Field Chooser. Although you can use some fields from other item types, you'll generally want to use fields that belong to the same item type as the form you're working on. When you select a field group from the drop-down list, all the fields in that group appear in the Field Chooser. Locate the field you want to add to the form and drag it from the Field Chooser to the location on the form you want it to appear. When you drop the field on the form, all of its elements are selected. In other words, if the field contains a label control and a text box control, both are selected as soon as they're placed on the form. This lets you work on all the field's elements simultaneously, without disturbing their relationship to one another. If you move the field, you move all the objects; if you resize the field, you resize all the objects proportionally. However, once you select any other object on the form, the focus is transferred, and the objects are treated individually unless you select them manually as a group.

If you decide you need a new field, you can create one on the fly by clicking the New button on the Field Chooser. See the section entitled "Creating Your Own Custom Fields" for more information.

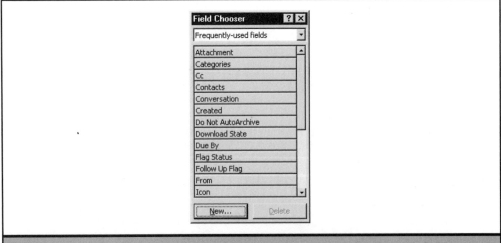

Figure 24-4.   *The Field Chooser provides access to all existing Outlook fields*

Working with Controls

Controls are objects that either display information, such as a label or graphic image, or enable a user to manipulate data in Outlook fields. The Label and the Image controls are examples of the first. The TextBox and CommandButton controls are examples of data manipulating controls. Both the Subject title and the subject textbox on a message form are controls. The title is a Label control providing information only, while the textbox, a TextBox control linked to the Outlook Subject field, lets the user input and display data from the Subject field.

Note *Although there is no official limit to the number of controls or fields you can include on a custom form, you should try to keep the number under 300 to avoid potential problems. While this sounds like a sizeable number, it can be reached more quickly than you might think, especially when you start using multiple pages in a form.*

Adding controls is a lot like adding fields. The first thing to do is right-click a blank spot on the form page and select Control Toolbox to open the Toolbox. You can also display or hide the Toolbox by clicking the Control Toolbox button on the form design toolbar.

By default, the Control Toolbox has fourteen controls plus a selector tool called Select Objects. You add controls by using one of the two available methods. You can either drag a control icon and drop it on the form, or you can click the control on the Toolbox and draw the control on the form. The difference between the two methods is in the size of the control that appears. Using the drag-and-drop method, you end up with a default-sized control. The default size varies from control to control. If you elect to draw the control on the form, your mouse pointer turns into a crosshairs pointer with an icon of the control attached. Move to the pointer to a spot on the form in which you want the top left corner of the control to appear. Click and hold the left mouse button while dragging the pointer toward the bottom right corner of the page. As you drag, a selector box appears. Drag the pointer until the selector box attains the size you want the control to be, and release the left button to create the control. When you're done, you'll end up with a control planted on the form at the location you specified and in the size you want. As you can see in Figure 24-5, the basic controls provide you with a variety of form elements.

Adding the control to the form is just the beginning. Once you have your control in place you can set its properties, move it around, resize it, add it to a control group, and more. Since most controls should be bound to fields to make them useful, the decision to use a control or a "field" from the Field Chooser depends on the type of object you're trying to create. For something like a simple textbox (TextBox) with a label (Label) it's generally easier to take an existing field or create a new field and drag it onto the form. However, if you want to create something more sophisticated, such as

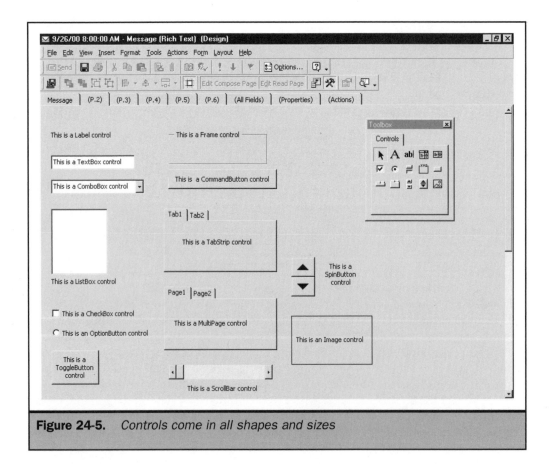

Figure 24-5.   *Controls come in all shapes and sizes*

a drop-down list (ComboBox), a display list (ListBox), or a set of radio button options (OptionButton), you'll have to use a control. The "fields" you can drag off the Field Chooser are rather limited in the default controls they use.

Setting Control Properties

Each control has an extensive set of options you can customize. These options, which can be found in the control's Properties dialog box, include everything from the control name and caption to complex validation rules. To view a control's Properties dialog box, right-click the control and select Properties from the shortcut menu. You can also click the Properties button on the form design toolbar to display the Properties dialog box. Regardless of which control you choose (a combo box control in this example), the Properties dialog box resembles the one shown in Figure 24-6.

The Properties dialog box remains the same for all standard controls with two exceptions: the MultiPage control, which only has a single tab (Display) for each page, and the Frame control, also with a single tab (Display).

Display Properties   The Display tab, seen in Figure 24-6, contains a variety of options that affect the appearance and location of the control, which in this example is a combo box to be added to a feedback post form. It provides the user with a

Figure 24-6.   *Customizing controls is easy with this extensive collection of options*

drop-down list of feedback types such as Comment, Suggestion, and Problem. The options you can set on the Display tab include the following:

- **Name**   This field lets you provide a descriptive identifier for the name. If you plan to do any VBA or VBS scripting you may want to include a control prefix so you can easily identify the control type simply by looking at the name. You can use a standard naming convention such as the one presented in Table 24-1, or create one of your own design. Just make sure you're consistent when using either one.

- **Caption**   The Caption is nothing more than a built-in label for the control. Some standard controls, like Label, CheckBox, OptionBox, ToggleButton, and CommandButton, have captions. The rest do not, which is where the Label control comes in. You add your own caption by placing a Label control next to the captionless control.

- **Position (in pixels)**   If you want to fine tune the position and size of a control, here's your chance. You can set the control's exact position by indicating the pixel intersection of the top left corner of the control. To set the control's size to within a pixel, set the Height and Width options.

Control	Prefix
CheckBox	chk
ComboBox	cbo
CommandButton	cmd
Frame	fra
Horizontal ScrollBar	hsb
Image	img
Label	lbl
ListBox	lst
OptionButton	opt
TabStrip	tab
TextBox	txt
ToggleButton	tgb
Vertical ScrollBar	vsb

Table 24-1.   *Suggested Control Prefixes*

- **Font**   Use this option to open the Font dialog box and change the font, font style, or size used to display text in the control or in its caption.

- **Foreground color**   This option determines the color of the text displayed in the control or in the control's caption. The Foreground Color drop-down list does not contain actual color choices, but rather, Windows styles to which certain colors are assigned. Unfortunately, this is not only confusing, but extremely limiting, since most of the choices are white, gray, or black. If you want to pick a color for the text used in a control, open its advanced Properties dialog box and modify the ForeColor setting. You'll still have the option of selecting colors by Window styles. However, by double-clicking the ForeColor property you can access a color palette from which to select any color you want.

- **Background color**   This option works the same as the Foreground Color option, except it applies to the control's background. If you want to choose a color instead of a style, open the advanced Properties dialog box and double-click the BackColor property to display the color palette.

- **Settings**   The Settings properties are a series of check box options that include the following:

  - **Visible**   If you want the control to appear on the form, check this option. To hide a control, deselect this option.

  - **Enabled**   By default, all controls are enabled. Removing the Enabled checkmark disables the control, which means that it no longer functions. For example, a disabled TextBox control becomes totally uneditable, a disabled ComboBox drop-down list will not display, and a disabled CommandButton will not respond to a click.

  - **Read only**   Making a control read-only means you can't edit the visible control in the form. With controls that contain text, such as a TextBox control, you won't be able to change the text, but you will be able to highlight and copy it (which you cannot do if you disable the control).

  - **Resize with form**   This option ensures that the size of the control remains relative to the size of the form. If you check this option, the control will shrink when the user reduces the size of the form, and expand when the user increases the size of the form.

  - **Sunken**   If you want the control to have a 3-D appearance that makes it look like it's recessed, this is the option for you.

  - **Multiline**   With this option checked, a text control such as a TextBox can accept multiple lines of text. If the option is unchecked, the control is limited to a single line of text.

Value Properties   The Value tab of the control's Properties dialog box, shown in Figure 24-7, which is available for all standard controls except Frame and MultiPage controls, provides quite a bit of power without requiring any coding. For this example

Figure 24-7.   *The Value tab gives you programming power without the hassle of learning to program*

we're using the Properties dialog box of a second combo box control called Severity, which is to remain hidden unless the user selects Problem from the Feedback combo box.

It offers a number of options that enable you to do more than simply add fields and objects to a form. Here's what you'll find:

- **Choose Field**   Since controls cannot store data, it's necessary to bind (link) a field to any control you want to use for data input or display. Click this button to reveal the menu of available fields you can bind to the selected control. If you want to create a new field, click the New button and enter a name, field type, and field format.

- **Type**   This setting displays the field type of the selected field from the previous option. You cannot change the field type after a field has been created.

- **Format**   Depending on the field type, you may or may not be able to change this option. For example, a text field has but a single format (Text), while a Yes/No field has four possible Format types: Yes/No, On/Off, True/False, or Icon. If the field selected in the Choose Field option has multiple formats, you'll be able to choose the format you want to use.

- **List type**   If the selected control is a ComboBox, you'll have a choice of list types. Although both list types appear to be identical, there is one difference.

A Dropdown permits the user to select one of the possible values or enter a value by typing it in. A Droplist limits the user to only those values that appear on the list.

- **Property to use**   This is the tricky (and powerful) one. It enables you to use the value of a field from one control to customize a specific property in a different control. For example, suppose you have a ComboBox called Feedback, with Comment, Suggestion, and Problem as the possible choices in the drop-down list. You might decide you want an additional drop-down list to appear whenever the user selects Problem. The purpose of the new drop-down list is to indicate the severity of the problem. This ComboBox control might be named Severity. Each control would have a corresponding field to hold the data. Now, the question is, how do you get the second control, Severity, to stay hidden unless the user selects Problem from the Feedback drop-down list? The answer: set the Severity control's Property To Use option to Visible, and then create a formula (in the Set The Initial Value Of This Field To option) that converts the value entered in the Feedback control to something that will turn the Visible property on or off in the Severity control. For the Visible property, -1 (or 1) and 0 (On and Off, respectively) are the magic numbers. Therefore, the formula has to say, *If the value in the Feedback field equals "Problem" make the value for this field (Severity) -1, otherwise make it 0.* When the user selects Comment or Suggestion from the Feedback drop-down list, the Severity control stays out of sight. However, as soon as the user selects Problem, the Severity drop-down list appears. See the Set The Initial Value Of This Field To bullet item in this section for more information on creating a formula.

- **Value**   When this option is available, you can enter a value that is applied to the property selected in the previous option, Property To Use.

- **Possible values**   This option appears only if the selected control is a ComboBox or ListBox. It enables you to specify the choices you want available to the user. Enter each item followed by a semicolon to indicate the next item belongs on a separate line in the control.

- **Set the initial value of this field to**   Check this option and enter a value or a formula in the associated textbox to be used as the value of the bound field the first time the control appears. Taking the earlier example of the Feedback ComboBox control, you might check this option and enter **Comment**. This would ensure that the Feedback drop-down list displays the Comment choice rather than a blank line, when it first appears on the form.

- **Edit**   The Edit button opens a dialog box in which you can create a formula to use in this field. The Field button displays a menu of Outlook fields you can use in the formula. The Function button displays a menu of functions you can use. In the earlier Severity control box option, the formula used was *If the value in the Feedback field equals "Problem" make the value for this field (Severity) -1, otherwise make it 0.* The actual formula is **IIf([Feedback]="Problem",-1,0**. You can enter formula information by using the buttons or typing it manually. Most of the time you'll probably use a combination of both methods.

- **Calculate this formula when I compose a new form** This calculates the formula only when the form is first created. Thereafter, the formula is ignored.

- **Calculate this formula automatically** Select this option to instruct Outlook to recalculate the formula every time there's a change in the form. Setting this option in the Severity example ensures that when the user selects Problem, the Severity control appears. If the user changes her mind and selects Comment, the formula is recalculated, and the Severity control disappears.

If you want to use the Property To Use option, but don't know the values that trigger each of the different properties, there's a way to find most of them. Close the Properties dialog box, right-click the control, and select Advanced Properties to display the advanced Properties dialog box. Select a property to view its possible values.

Validation Properties The final tab of the Properties dialog box, Validation, contains a variety of options for controlling the information a user is allowed to enter into the control. You can choose to let the user ignore the field or force him to enter something before closing or sending the form. In addition, you can determine the parameters for what information the form will accept or reject. The following options let you decide which information can be entered in the selected control:

- **A value is required for this field** Check this option if you want the user to enter something before closing the form. If the user attempts to skip the field, Outlook displays a message informing the user that "A field on this form requires a value."

- **Validate this field before closing the form** Check this option if you want to impose restrictions on the values that can be entered into the field to which the control is bound.

- **Validation Formula** You can use this field to enter a formula against which the user input will be evaluated. If the input fails to meet the formula criteria, Outlook refuses to close the form. For example, if one of your customers recently changed the company name from Easy Widgets to Value Widgets, you might add a formula that rejects Easy Widgets as input in a field that accepts company name information. Your formula would be **<>"Easy Widgets"**. If a user entered Easy Widgets in the field and tried to close the form, Outlook would respond with a message stating that the entered data is not valid.

- **Display this message if the validation fails** If you use a validation formula, it might be more helpful to the user if you create your own message to replace the generic Outlook message that says, "The data you entered for [field name] is not valid." In the Easy Widgets example, you might create a message that says, "Easy Widgets is now known as Value Widgets. Please update your customer information."

■ **Include this field for Printing and Save As**   This one means just what it says. If you check this option, the field bound to the selected control appears when you print the form or use the Save As command. If you deselect this option, the field disappears from a printout or a saved file.

When you reach this point, you should be finished setting basic properties for your control. Click OK to close the Properties dialog box and save the new control settings.

Setting Advanced Control Properties

If you want to spruce up your control by modifying more properties than the basic Properties dialog box provides, you might want to try the advanced Properties. Here you'll find an extensive collection of properties. For example, you can add a tool tip, change colors, limit the number of characters that can be entered, change the mouse pointer that appears over the control, and more.

To display the advanced Properties dialog box (see Figure 24-8), right-click the control whose properties you want to modify, and select Advanced Properties from the shortcut menu.

As you can see in Figure 24-8, the advanced Properties dialog box contains two columns of data. The left column holds the property name, while the right column contains the property value. When you select a property, its value appears in the text box at the top of the dialog box to the right of the Apply button. Depending on the property type, you can enter text, select a value from a drop-down list, or choose a file.

Figure 24-8.   *Advanced Properties include a number of properties not found in the basic Properties dialog box*

If a property has multiple possible values, you can double-click the property (name or value) to cycle through the choices. If the property uses a file as a value, as does the Picture property, double-clicking the property displays an open (Load Picture in this case) dialog box, with which you can locate and select the appropriate file.

After you change a property's value, you can click the Apply button and Outlook immediately makes the change to the control. This lets you judge the effects of your changes without having to close and reopen the dialog box.

Rearranging Controls on the Form

As handy as the Snap To Grid feature is, nothing beats auto-aligning tools for really putting controls in their place. The alignment and layering tools Outlook provides let you line up your controls any way you want, with little or no effort.

Alignment is the process of taking two or more controls and lining them up along the same imaginary line, which is determined by two things: the dominant control and the alignment type you select. The dominant control is the one to which the other selected controls align themselves. Your method of selection determines the dominant control. If you select by holding down the CTRL key and clicking, the last control selected is the dominant control. If you hold down the SHIFT key while clicking, the first control selected is the dominant control. If you draw a selector box around multiple controls, the first one selected becomes the dominant control. You can always recognize the dominant control by its white sizing handles.

After you select the controls to align, right-click any one of them and select Align from the shortcut menu to display the submenu of alignment commands. The alignment commands you can choose include Left, Center, Right, Top, Middle, Bottom, and To Grid, all of which are self-explanatory, with the possible exception of To Grid. To Grid is really nothing more than a Snap To Grid command that works on multiple fields. If the Snap To Grid feature is turned off or if you've changed the grid size, you can use the To Grid alignment command to snap all the selected controls to the nearest grid intersection.

Tip   *You'll find both alignment and layering commands on the form design toolbar.*

There's another feature similar to alignment, called spacing, which enables you to position selected objects an equal distance from one another horizontally or vertically. Select the objects you want to space and choose Layout | Horizontal Spacing or Layout | Vertical Spacing from the Menu bar.

To make form design easier, Outlook permits layering. In other words, you can place one control on top of another. This comes in handy for adding other controls to TabStrip and MultiPage controls. Since layering is permitted, it means that one control is positioned in front of or behind other controls. Sometimes this is easy to figure out (when one control partially hides another) and sometime it's not (when the top control is transparent). Fortunately, Outlook provides commands to move objects backward and forward. Right-click the control and select Bring Forward from the Order submenu to move the object one layer closer to the top of the heap (closer to you, the viewer), or Send Backward to move it one layer further away from the viewer. To bring an item to the top layer, even if it's at the bottom of the pile, select it and choose Layout | Order | Bring To Front from the Menu bar. To send it to the bottom of the pile, choose Send To Back.

Tip   *You can also use the Bring to Front and Send to Back buttons on the form toolbar.*

Moving and Sizing Controls

No matter how careful your initial placement of an object on the form, you're bound to want to move it sooner or later. You can move all standard controls except Frame and MultiPage controls by dragging them to a new location. Frame and MultiPage controls (along with the other controls) can be moved by selecting the control and placing your mouse pointer over one of the borders until the pointer turns into a four-sided arrow. You can then drag the control wherever you want. To move multiple controls at once, select them all first, then drag any one of them. The rest follow, staying in relative position to one another.

There are several ways to resize form objects. You can resize them manually by grabbing one of the sizing handles that appear when you select the object, and dragging the side or corner of the object. You can also open the Properties dialog box or the advanced Properties dialog box and enter the exact dimensions for the control. However, if you want to let Outlook do all the work, use one of these commands:

- ■ **Make Same Size**   Use this command to make one dimension of a control the same as the corresponding dimension of a different control. Select two or more objects, and choose Layout | Make Same Size to display a submenu that contains Width, Height, and Both commands. Select the appropriate command. All selected objects are resized to match the dominant control. See the earlier section entitled "Rearranging Controls on the Form" for more about dominant controls.

- ■ **Size to Fit**   This is a useful command that sizes most controls to the minimum size needed to accommodate the control or its contents. For example, using the Size To Fit command on a Label control shrinks (or expands) the Label control to fit the Caption text.

- ■ **Size to Grid**   Use this command to resize the control to fit within the closest grid lines. The control will expand or contract depending on which grid lines are closest. One side may expand while the other side contracts.

In case you're wondering, it is possible to resize multiple objects at the same time. Select all the objects you want to resize and use one of the resizing methods described here.

Grouping Controls

Grouping controls enables you to select two or more controls and temporarily join them together. After you group them, they respond as a single unit. As a matter of fact, you can no longer select them individually. This is great for moving a captionless control such as a TextBox control, and its associated Label control. Group them together and they remain in the same relative position to one another no matter how far or how often you move them.

Select the controls you want to group and click the Group button on the form design toolbar. You can also right-click one of the selected controls and choose Group from the shortcut menu. To break up a group of controls, select the group and click the Ungroup button on the form design toolbar, or right-click the group and select Ungroup from the shortcut menu. You can also choose Layout | Group.

Creating Custom Controls

If you find yourself adding and customizing the same control type over and over, you might want to add it to the Control Toolbox as a custom control. That way the next time you need it, you can just drag or draw it on the form, and all the settings will be taken care of. You can add an existing control to the Control Toolbox by dragging it to the Toolbox. As soon as you drop it on the Toolbox, it appears as an icon. When you move your mouse pointer over the new, custom control, a tool tip appears, containing "New [control type]" (a custom TextBox tool tip would say "New TextBox"). To change the tool tip and the icon image, right-click the icon and select Customize New [control type] to open the Customize Control dialog box.

Begin by entering new text for the tool tip. If you're so inclined, you can modify the icon itself by clicking Edit Picture and editing the icon one pixel at a time. If you have additional icons you can locate and select one by clicking the Load Picture button.

 You can even add control groups to the Toolbox as custom controls. Just create the group and drag it to the Toolbox.

In addition to letting you create your own custom controls, Outlook also provides a large collection of additional controls, such as a Toolbar control, an Excel chart control, and more. Right-click the Toolbox and select Custom Controls to display the Additional Controls dialog box. Check the controls you want included and click OK to add them to the Toolbox. If you start running out of room on the Toolbox, you can add more pages by right-clicking the Controls tab and selecting New Page from the shortcut menu.

Setting Form Properties

Forms, like controls, have their own properties you can set. Not surprisingly, you'll find them on the Properties tab of the form in the design mode (see Figure 24-9).

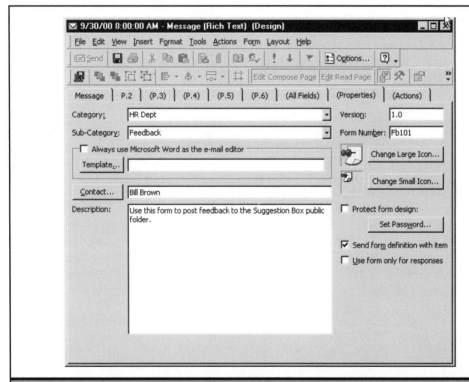

Figure 24-9. *Setting form properties makes your forms management tasks a lot easier*

Note *Some Outlook options set at the time a form is created may become part of the form's properties, even if the options are later changed. For example, creating a custom message form when your E-mail Sensitivity option (Tools | Options | E-mail Options | Advanced Options) is set to Confidential means the new form will have a default sensitivity of confidential. The only way to modify this is to change the original Outlook option and then republish the form.*

Most of the options on the Properties tab are self-explanatory. However, there are a few things you should know. To begin with, assigning forms to categories and subcategories can be quite useful, but the only place they're used is in the Forms Manager. It's always a good idea to give the form a version number, and change it each time you modify the form. This makes it much easier to keep track of the most current iteration of the form, especially if you share it with others. You might want to use a software version numbering scheme such as 1.0, 1.1, 1.2, 2.0, 2.1, and so on. The fractional increments indicate minor changes, the integer increments indicate major updates. One last thing: you may be tempted to ignore the Description field. Don't. If you create a lot of custom forms it can quickly become difficult to tell them apart, even with a good naming scheme. A brief description of what the form is used for can eliminate a lot of time wasted searching for the right form.

Testing and Publishing the Form

No matter how good your design skills, it's always a good idea to run the form before publishing it. All too often, a minor mistake can throw the whole form out of whack. To test a form before publishing, choose Form | Run This Form. A finished form, ready for use, immediately appears. Fill it out and send it or close it to make sure everything works the way you expect.

Tip *If you plan to use the new form with other versions of Outlook, it's a good idea to test it on those versions before distributing it to others. Some features may not be supported in older versions of Outlook. The time to find out is before everyone starts using the new form.*

After you've tested the form and are satisfied with it, you'll want to publish it. Do not confuse Publish with Save. In the case of forms, the Publish command works more like a standard save command than the Save command does. When you publish a form, you actually are placing a copy of it in the forms library of your choice, so you can use, edit, or distribute it at a later time. The Save command, on the other hand, saves only the current instance of the form as an item or one-off form (not a reusable form).

Tip *Rather than wait until you've finished the form, you should publish it periodically to ensure all your work doesn't go down the drain if a power failure or other mishap shuts down Outlook before you're through.*

To publish your form, click the Publish button on the form design toolbar or choose Tools | Forms | Publish Form to open the Publish Form As dialog box, shown in Figure 24-10.

From the Look In drop-down list, select the forms library in which you want to save the custom form. By default, the Personal Forms Library is selected. Depending on your plans for the form, this may or may not be the best location for the new form. When publishing a form, consider the way Outlook searches for the form when you open an item that uses it. The first place Outlook searches is the forms cache on your local computer. If you've used the form during this session, it should be there. The next place Outlook searches for a form is in the folder you're currently in. The Personal Forms Library is the third place Outlook looks. The next place Outlook scans is the Organizational Forms Library.

Therefore, if you're the only one using the form, and you usually create items from within the folder with which they're associated, you might want to publish the form to the folder in which you use it. If you're more inclined to create a new item from anywhere in Outlook, use the Personal Forms Library. If, on the other hand, you plan to share the form with other users, you'll probably want to put it in the Organizational Forms Library to simplify the update process. All users on the Exchange network should have access to the Organizational Forms Library. Therefore, any time you want to change the form you need only change the copy in the Organizational Forms Library.

After you decide where to put the form, enter a display name in the Display Name field and the name for the file in the Form Name field. Outlook assumes you want

Figure 24-10.   *The Publish Form As dialog box is similar to a Save As dialog box*

BUILDING OUTLOOK
APPLICATIONS

them to be the same, so it duplicates the Display Name information in the Form Name field. You can change it if you wish. Click Publish and the form is tucked away for future use.

Creating Your Own Custom Fields

Although Outlook provides an abundance of standard fields, there are going to be times, especially while customizing forms, when you find a need for additional fields. When that time arrives you can quickly and easily create a new field to suit your particular needs. From anywhere in Outlook, including the forms design mode, you can create a new field by opening the Field Chooser and clicking the New button to display the New Field dialog box.

Begin by giving the new field a unique name. Then designate the field type by making your selection from the Type drop-down list. Most of the field types are self-explanatory. A Text field holds text, a Numbers field holds numeric data, a Currency field holds numeric data preceded by a currency symbol. There are however, a few fields that might require a little more explanation:

- **Yes/No**   This field type is used to accept simple Yes/No, On/Off, or True/False data. It's most frequently used in conjunction with a CheckBox or ComboBox control. In its Icon format it's also used as a visual indicator in folder views (the Attachment icon in the Inbox).

- **Duration**   A Duration field is used to hold length-of-time information. It is used to record the interval of time that has elapsed or that you expect to elapse (a meeting or phone call).

- **Keywords**   Keyword fields are text fields whose primary purpose is to facilitate grouping and locating items.

- **Combination**   If you've ever wondered how a Full Name field manages to pull data from a First Name and a Last Name field and put them together, here's your answer: a Combination field. As soon as you select Combination as the field type, the Format field in the New Field dialog box changes to Formula. You can either enter a concatenation formula here or click the Edit button to display the Combination Formula Field dialog box, which provides more room to work, and a field selection button, aptly named Field. The formula can be relatively simple, as is the case with the Full Name example, for which the formula is [First Name] [Last Name]. Notice that there is no operator, such as a plus sign, between the two fields. Anything you place between the field names appears in the text box, which is why you want to make sure you don't add extraneous characters, but do leave a space between them.

■ **Formula**   You can use this field type to create a field that can draw information from multiple fields and perform calculations on them at the same time. It can also be used to conditionally draw information from other fields. When you select Formula as the field type, the Format field changes to Formula. Either enter the formula directly or click the Edit button to open the Formula Field dialog box, which provides both a Field button and a Function button.

After selecting the field type, move to the Format (or Formula) field. Select the desired format for the field or enter a formula. Then click OK to create the custom field. All custom fields are added to the user-defined fields group.

BUILDING OUTLOOK APPLICATIONS

The Complete Reference

Chapter 25

Automating Outlook with VBA

Outlook 2000 is the first version of Outlook to include Visual Basic for Applications (VBA), a version of the Visual Basic programming language specialized for automating applications. This enables you for the first time to develop macros in Outlook. Macros are miniature programs that automate actions within an application—you create the macro, and then you can call it up and run it any time you like. You can use the Outlook Tools menu or add a custom toolbar button to run the macro. However, unlike many of the other Office 2000 applications, Outlook doesn't include a macro editor, which captures keystrokes as you execute actions in the application and translates those keystrokes into program code. In Outlook, you create your macros directly with VBA code.

This chapter doesn't teach you how to program in VBA because this topic is beyond the scope of this book. Rather, it shows examples of how VBA is used to create Outlook macros. You don't need to understand VBA code to use the macros presented in this chapter, but if you have a basic familiarity with VBA code then you should be able to understand the code shown in this chapter. To learn more about programming Outlook, read *Sams Teach Yourself Microsoft Outlook 2000 Programming in 24 Hours*, by Sue Mosher (Sams, 1999). Other references are included in the "Summary" section at the end of this chapter.

So why do you want to program your own macros? Quite simply, to enhance Outlook and make it work the way you want it to work. In this chapter, you will learn how to create some useful macros that do the following:

- Insert time and date stamps and standard disclaimers into e-mail
- Insert the names and e-mail addresses of all members of a distribution list into a table in a Word document
- Import contacts from an Access database

Using the Visual Basic Editor

VBA provides two types of procedures, Functions and Subs. Functions can return a value to the procedure that calls them, but cannot themselves be macros. In VBA, a macro is defined as a Sub. There are two requirements for Subs to be macros. The first is that the Sub is public, which means that it can be seen anywhere in Outlook. The second requirement is that the Sub must not require any inputs, or arguments, when it is called. So if you can't create a macro using a keystroke recorder, as in Word, how do you create a macro in Outlook? You use the Visual Basic Editor (VBE), a tool available to all Microsoft Office 2000 programs.

To open the VBE, press ALT-F11. You can also open the VBE from a menu by choosing Tools | Macro | Visual Basic Editor. If you do not have this choice on your Tools menu, use the Office 2000 installation CD to install this component, which is an optional installation. When it is first opened, the VBE shows Project1 in the Project Explorer, the window in the upper-left corner of the VBE. When Project1 is expanded, the VBE looks similar to Figure 25-1.

Figure 25-1. *The Outlook Visual Basic Editor*

If you have ever used the VBE in any of the Office applications—or the similar Integrated Development Environment (IDE) in Visual Basic—the Outlook VBE will look familiar. The VBE has four main windows that you use when creating macros. The top left window is the Project Explorer, which is similar to the Windows Explorer and enables you to explore your Outlook project (Outlook only allows one project, and it is always named VBAProject.OTM). The bottom left window is the Properties window, where the properties of the project or selected component of the project are displayed. If you don't see the Project Explorer or the Properties window, you can open them from the View menu. The Code window at the top right of the VBE is used to enter and edit code. A Code window opens automatically when a module or class containing code is selected. The Immediate window at the bottom right is used to test and evaluate expressions and variables when debugging your macros. The Immediate window isn't shown in Figure 25-1, but can be opened from the View menu.

There are other windows that can be opened, the most important of which is the Object Browser. The Object Browser enables you to examine the components of various libraries (DLL files) and object models for Outlook, Word, Excel, and so on. An object model is the programming interface that is exposed for you to use in your programs. Any object model or library that is placed in the project's references can be examined in the Object Browser. The references for a project is the list of object models of other programs that you can use in your own code, or view in the Object Browser.

Setting Project References

Since you are programming Outlook, a reference to the Outlook object model must be set in the project. Choose Tools | References, and make sure that the Microsoft Outlook 9.0 Object Library is checked. If it isn't, scroll down the list of available references to the Microsoft Outlook 9.0 Object Library and check it. Other macros in this chapter will use the Word and Data Access Objects (DAO) object models, so also check the references to the Microsoft Word 9.0 Object Library and the Microsoft DAO 3.6 Object Library. Click OK to add the checked references. Some references are automatically added for you. When you are finished, the References dialog box should look like Figure 25-2. (Your list of references may be different.) The referenced objects are moved to the top of the list when you close the dialog box.

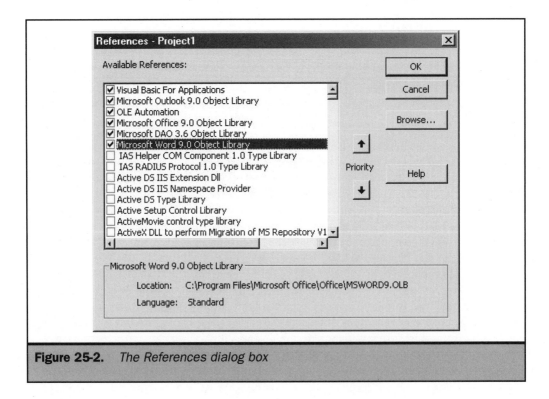

Figure 25-2. *The References dialog box*

Looking at the Object Browser

Next, use the Object Browser to show the Outlook object model. Press F2 or choose View | Object Browser to open the Object Browser. In the Project/Library list that shows <All Libraries>, select Outlook. You can enlarge sections of the Object Browser like any other window, by hovering the mouse over section boundaries and dragging it when it turns into a resizing cursor. The Object Browser now shows the Outlook object model, as seen in Figure 25-3.

We'll return to the Outlook Object Model later in this chapter, but for now, close the Object Browser by clicking on the Close Window control (the X in the top right-hand corner of most windows). Next, you will insert a code module, where you will create your macros:

1. Choose Insert | Module to insert a new code module into the Outlook VBA project.

Figure 25-3.   *The Object Browser showing the Outlook object model*

2. In the Properties window, change the name from Module1 to
basOutlook2000Macros. The "bas" prefix indicates that this module
is a Basic code module.

3. Return to the Code window.

Setting Project Options

Before putting your first lines of code into the project, you should set some options for
the project. These settings will make it easier to enter and test your macros. Choose
Tools | Options in the VBE and select the Editor tab. It is best to check all the check
boxes on the Editor tab, and set a tab width that lets the indented sections of the code
stand out without taking too much space. Figure 25-4 shows the Editor tab of the
Project Options dialog box, and Table 25-1 explains the Code Setting options in the
Editor tab.

Each tab has a Help button that explains the meaning of each choice on that tab.
Use this help to explain choices you don't understand. Auto List Members and Auto
Quick Info are particularly useful when you are entering code. They provide information
about the functions you are using while you type, and show what entries are needed to

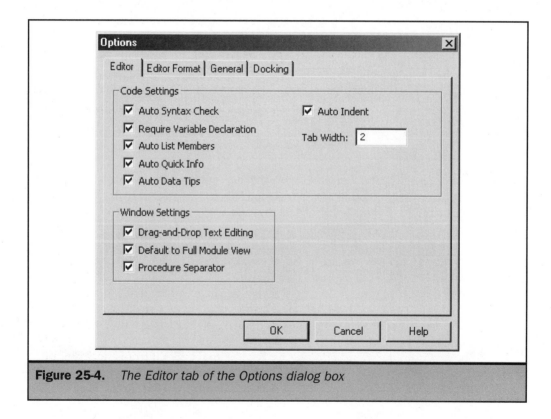

Figure 25-4. *The Editor tab of the Options dialog box*

Code Setting Option	What It Does
Auto Syntax Check	Checks if a line uses correct syntax when it is entered.
Require Variable Declaration	Requires that all variables are declared with a Dim statement. This makes it easier to ensure that all variables are of the correct types and spelled correctly in the Sub statements. Checking this option inserts an Option Explicit statement in each new code module that is created.
Auto List Members	Helps complete code statements by showing a list of permissible entries at the cursor insertion point as you type.
Auto Quick Info	Shows in-line help about functions and their parameters as you type.
Auto Data Tips	Displays the value of variables and objects when the mouse cursor is hovered over the variables and objects when testing code.

Table 25-1. *Code Setting Options in the Editor Tab of the Options Dialog Box*

BUILDING OUTLOOK APPLICATIONS

complete the code line. Auto List Members provides a list of the possible values that can be supplied to functions, and items from the list can be selected by highlighting them and pressing the TAB key. This enters the item from the list into your code.

Creating a Macro Template

Click the mouse in the new Code window and enter the following code to create a macro template. You can use this template when you create new macros, customizing it as needed. The first line declares a Sub procedure (also known as a method) named MacroTemplate. The Sub is declared to be Private, meaning that it can only be seen by other methods within the same code module. This is to prevent it from appearing in the list of macros. When you are ready to use the template, change the name of the Sub to one that is meaningful and change the Private declaration to Public.

Any text that appears after an apostrophe is considered a comment by VBA. It's good practice to add a lot of comments to your code so later you or others can easily see what the code does. You will see a lot of comments in the macros in this chapter.

```
Private Sub MacroTemplate()
  ' Change the name and make it Public to use for a macro.
```

The next line creates a variable by using the Dim statement. You should always declare all variables, which are containers for values and properties of objects. The template declares a variable for the Outlook Application object, which is required for access to all Outlook properties. You will add other variables as needed for any macro you create, but all your Outlook macros should have this declaration. Following the declaration of the Outlook Application object, the On Error GoTo statement is used to declare an error handler for any errors that might occur when the macro is run. It's a good idea to have such an error handler in your code, to display more meaningful error messages than the system would and to enable your code to terminate properly if an error occurs.

```
  ' Add other Dim statements as required.
  Dim objOutlook As Outlook.Application

  On Error GoTo ErrorHandler
```

The next line uses the CreateObject function to create an instance of the Outlook Application object and assign it to the objOutlook object variable. A common convention is to prefix all variables with an abbreviation that tells what type of variable it is. Table 25-2 shows some commonly used prefixes for variable types.

```
  Set objOutlook = CreateObject("Outlook.Application")
```

Prefix	Variable Type
Bln	Boolean (True/False or Yes/No)
Dat	Date
Db	Database
Dbl	Double precision floating point number

Table 25-2. *Common Variable Prefixes*

Prefix	Variable Type
Int	Integer (16-bit number)
Lng	Long (32-bit number)
Obj	Object
Rst	Recordset
Sng	Single precision floating point number
Str	String

Table 25-2.   *Common Variable Prefixes* (continued)

The next section of the macro template starts with the MacroExit label. Labels are indicated by ending with a colon and are points to which you can direct program execution as needed. It's always good practice to set any object variable declared in the procedure equal to Nothing, which releases it from memory. Not releasing objects is one of the main reasons that programs remain in memory when you close them, so always release all your object variables. The Exit Sub statement at the end of the exit section terminates the macro.

Note   *Only variables that are objects can be set equal to Nothing. Other variables that contain values are automatically released when the macro ends. In most cases, object variables are automatically released when the macros in which they are defined end. However, if unhandled errors occur in your code or the object variables are referenced in other code, they may not be released as expected. It's always safest to explicitly release object variables.*

```
MacroExit:
 ' Set all objects equal to Nothing to destroy them and
 ' release the memory and resources they take. Add other
 ' objects that are created.
 Set objOutlook = Nothing

 Exit Sub
```

The error handler displays a message showing the description and error number of any error that occurs. It then clears the error state and tells the program to go to the MacroExit label. Error handlers can be very complex, with tests for different error conditions and different actions to take depending on the results. However, this simple error handler is sufficient for many of the macros you will create. Finally, the End Sub statement tells VBA that the macro ends at that statement.

```
ErrorHandler:
  MsgBox "Error: " & Err.Description & vbCrLf & "Error # " _
    & Err.Number
```

Tip   *The underline character following the space at the end of the line above forms what is called a line continuation. The text on the line following the space and underline is considered by VBA to be part of the previous line. Breaking up your code lines with line continuations helps make your code more readable, since you don't have to horizontally scroll your code window to read all the code.*

```
  Err.Clear
  GoTo MacroExit
End Sub
```

The error handler is always placed at the end of the macro, after the Exit Sub line. This prevents the error handler from running when there is no error. The GoTo MacroExit line directs the macro execution to the MacroExit label, where the objects created by the macro are released by setting them equal to Nothing, and where other clean-up code may be placed. The flow of code execution for a macro is shown in Figure 25-5.

Now that you have seen the environment in which macros are created, and have seen how the framework of a macro is organized, it's time to jump in and create your first macro.

Creating a DateTime Stamp Macro for E-mail

The DateTime macro inserts a date and time stamp at the beginning of an open e-mail message. Figure 25-6 shows the sequence of actions the macro follows. This chart follows the format of the macro template flow chart, with the macro actions performed detailed for the DateTime macro.

To create this macro, use the macro template shown earlier. Change the macro name to DateTime and change the visibility (also known as scope) to Public. Additional variables are declared for Outlook Inspector and MailItem objects, and for two string variables, the last of which, strAryDateParts, is an array of strings used for the separation of the date value from the time value. An Inspector is the window that is opened when you open an Outlook item. No Outlook item can be opened without an

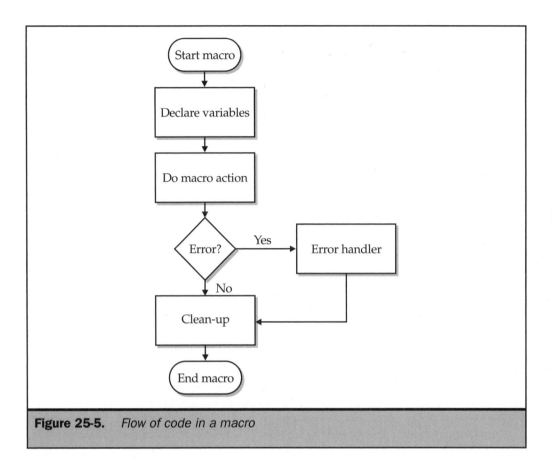

Figure 25-5. *Flow of code in a macro*

associated Inspector being opened. A MailItem is any e-mail item in Outlook. Outlook defines object types for tasks (TaskItem), contacts (ContactItem), appointments (AppointmentItem), and all other special Outlook items.

```
Public Sub DateTime()
 ' This macro requires a reference to the Outlook object model.
 Dim objOutlook As Outlook.Application
 Dim objInspector As Outlook.Inspector
 Dim objMail As Outlook.MailItem

 Dim strDateTime As String
 Dim strAryDateParts() As String
```

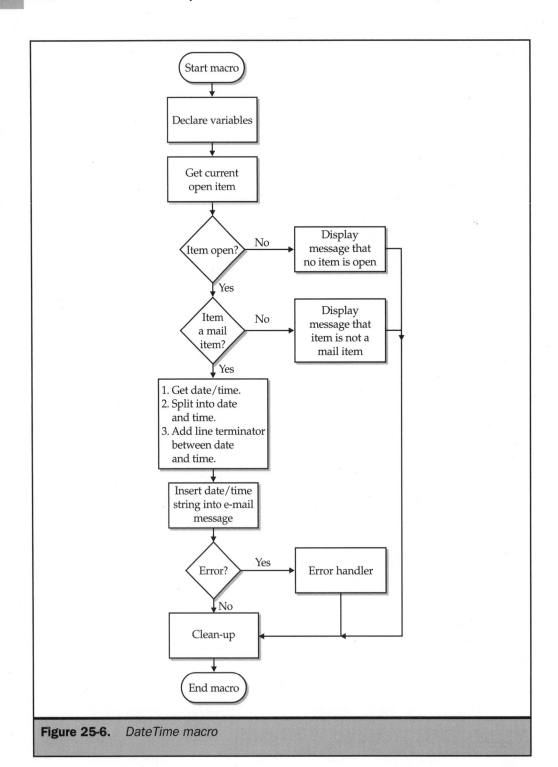

Figure 25-6. *DateTime macro*

After declaring the error handler and creating the Outlook Application object, an Inspector object is declared for the currently open item using the ActiveInspector property of the Outlook Application object. If no items are open, an error will occur and be handled by the error handler.

```
On Error GoTo ErrorHandler

Set objOutlook = CreateObject("Outlook.Application")

' The ActiveInspector is the currently open item.
Set objInspector = objOutlook.ActiveInspector
```

If an item is open, it is checked to confirm it is an e-mail item. If it is not, a message is displayed to that effect. Each item type in Outlook has a Class associated with it; the Class for mail items is olMail. The CurrentItem property of the Inspector is used to check the Class of the item, and if it is a mail item the objMail variable is assigned to it. Objects are assigned to variables with the Set keyword. Non-object variables do not use the Set keyword. This can be confusing and is often a source of errors in macros.

```
' Check and see if anything is open.
If Not objInspector Is Nothing Then
  ' See if the current item is an e-mail item.
  If objInspector.CurrentItem.Class = olMail Then
    ' Get the current mail item.
    Set objMail = objInspector.CurrentItem
```

The strDateTime variable is set to the current date and time by calling the Now() function. Then the date and time are assigned to individual elements of the string array strAryDateParts by the Split function. Split can be used to split up strings at specified characters, called delimiters. The delimiter in this case is the space character, and here the date/time string is split into only two elements. This keeps the AM/PM time designator with the time. For example, a date and time string of "7/4/2000 10:00:00 AM" is split into two strings, "7/4/2000" and "10:00:00 AM". The "7/4/2000" string is placed in element 0 of strAryDateParts, and the "10:00:00 AM" string is placed in element 1 of strAryDateParts.

```
' Get the current date and time.
    strDateTime = Now()
    ' Split the date and time at the space separator.
    ' Date goes into one array element and time into another.
    strAryDateParts = Split(strDateTime, " ", 2)
```

Array elements are referenced by a subscript number, which usually starts at 0. In the next section of the macro, the date (element 0) and time (element 1) are combined again into one string variable, this time separated by a new line. Strings are combined by using the ampersand character (&), which is referred to as string concatenation. The VBA constant for a new line is vbCrLf, which stands for a combination of the carriage return and line feed characters. The effect is the same as when you press the ENTER key when using a word processor.

```
' Combine the date and time, separated on two lines.
strDateTime = strAryDateParts(0) & vbCrLf & strAryDateParts(1)
```

The effect of combining (concatenating) the date and time strings separated by a new line combination is to place the date on the first line, followed by the time on the next line. Figure 25-7 shows the result of the macro, with the date and time on two lines.

The big text field in an e-mail item (and most other Outlook items) is called the Body property. The date and time stamp, now consisting of two lines of text, is inserted at the beginning of the body of the objMail item. A bug in Outlook causes any Outlook item to become a Rich Text Format (RTF) item when the Body property is changed.

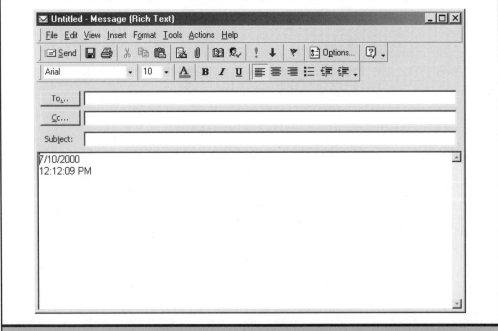

Figure 25-7. *The date and time stamp shown on two lines*

This is no problem when the recipient of the e-mail also uses Outlook, but can cause problems when other mail clients are used. Workarounds for this problem have been developed, but they use advanced techniques and other object libraries that aren't covered in this book.

```
' Add the date and time stamp to the beginning of the e-mail.
objMail.Body = strDateTime & objMail.Body
```

The first Else clause is executed only if the test for the item being an e-mail item fails, and the test displays a message that the item is not an e-mail item. The final Else clause is executed if no item is open. All If statements end with an End If statement. Else and ElseIf statements between If and End If statements are optional and provide alternate paths for program execution when the test for an If statement fails.

```
Else
    ' Show error message with only the OK button.
    MsgBox "This is not an e-mail item"
  End If
 Else
   ' Show error message with only the OK button.
   MsgBox "No item is open"
 End If
```

The remainder of the macro sets all object variables equal to Nothing and exits. Notice that only object variables are set equal to Nothing—strings and other variable types are not. The standard error handler follows the Exit Sub statement.

```
MacroExit:
  ' Set all objects equal to Nothing to destroy them and
  ' release the memory and resources they take.
  Set objOutlook = Nothing
  Set objInspector = Nothing
  Set objMail = Nothing

  Exit Sub

ErrorHandler:
  MsgBox "Error: " & Err.Description & vbCrLf & "Error # " _
    & Err.Number
  Err.Clear
  GoTo MacroExit
End Sub
```

Executing a Macro

Now that you have created your first macro, it's time to test it. Create a new e-mail item by choosing Actions | New Mail Message (or CTRL-N), and choose Tools | Macro | Macros to open the Macros dialog box. You can also use the key combination ALT-F8 to open the Macros dialog box, which should look similar to Figure 25-8. Highlight DateTime and click the Run button. The current date and time are inserted in the open e-mail item. Congratulations, you have created and executed your first macro.

To save the macro and your work in the VBE, click the disk icon on the toolbar in the VBE or select Save from the File menu.

Adding a Macro to a Toolbar Button

In addition to running macros from the Macros dialog box, you can put macros that you run frequently on a toolbar or menu. The procedure is similar to the toolbar and menu customizations you learned about in Chapter 23. In the Customize dialog box, select the Macros category in the Commands tab. The available macros appear in the Commands list on the right. Drag the macro you want to add to the toolbar or menu, and it's ready for use.

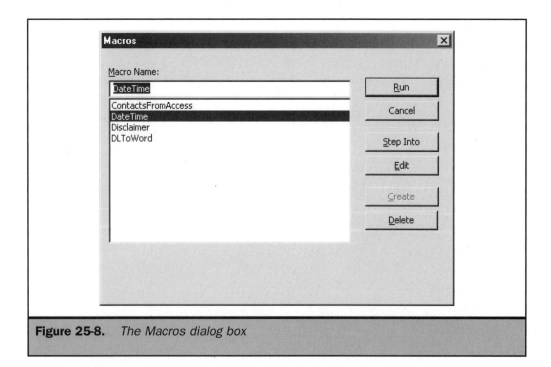

Figure 25-8. *The Macros dialog box*

> *When you add a macro, such as DateTime, to a toolbar or menu, it is listed as Project1.DateTime. You can right-click the macro button in Customize mode and change the name to DateTime (or anything else you want).*

Creating the Disclaimer Macro

The next macro is very similar to the DateTime macro. It inserts a standard disclaimer into an e-mail message, but this time the insertion is at the end of the message. Only the sections of the macro that are different than the DateTime macro will be explained. Here is the macro in its entirety:

```
Public Sub Disclaimer()
    ' This macro requires a reference to the Outlook object model.
    Dim objOutlook As Outlook.Application
    Dim objInspector As Outlook.Inspector
    Dim objMail As Outlook.MailItem

    Dim strDisclaimer As String

    On Error GoTo ErrorHandler

    ' Create the disclaimer string.
    strDisclaimer = "The information contained in this message " _
        & "constitutes privileged and confidential information " _
        & "and is intended only for the use of and review by " _
        & "the recipient designated above."
    ' Add a blank line between the e-mail text and the disclaimer.
    strDisclaimer = vbCrLf & strDisclaimer

    Set objOutlook = CreateObject("Outlook.Application")

    ' The ActiveInspector is the currently open item.
    Set objInspector = objOutlook.ActiveInspector

    ' Check and see if anything is open.
    If Not objInspector Is Nothing Then
        ' See if the current item is an e-mail item.
        If objInspector.CurrentItem.Class = olMail Then
            ' Get the current mail item.
            Set objMail = objInspector.CurrentItem
```

The existing DateTime macro added the text to the beginning of the message. The code for the disclaimer macro adds the disclaimer to the end of the message. The difference is in how the string added by the macro is inserted into the message body. If the string that is combined with the body is first, it appears before the text in the body (objMail.Body = strDateTime & objMail.Body). If the string that is combined with the body appears second, it appears after the text in the body (objMail.Body = objMail.Body & strDisclaimer). The ampersand character is used to concatenate (combine) two strings together.

```
' Add the disclaimer to the end of the e-mail.
      objMail.Body = objMail.Body & strDisclaimer
    Else
    ' Show error message with only the OK button.
      MsgBox "This is not an e-mail item"
    End If
  Else
    ' Show error message with only the OK button.
    MsgBox "No item is open"
  End If


MacroExit:
  ' Set all objects equal to Nothing to destroy them and
  ' release the memory and resources they take.
  Set objOutlook = Nothing
  Set objInspector = Nothing
  Set objMail = Nothing


  Exit Sub


ErrorHandler:
  ' Display the description and number of the error.
  MsgBox "Error: " & Err.Description & vbCrLf & "Error # " _
    & Err.Number
  ' Clear the error.
  Err.Clear
  ' Exit the macro.
  GoTo MacroExit
End Sub
```

Insert Outlook Data into Word

The DLToWord (Distribution List to Word) macro takes the names of members of an Outlook distribution list and their e-mail addresses and inserts them into a Word table. This macro not only shows a way to get information about the members of a distribution list from Outlook, but it also demonstrates one method of exporting formatted information from Outlook to a Word document. Exporting Outlook data into Word tables, bookmarks, and form fields is a common way to present Outlook data formatted in ways that are impossible from within Outlook.

The Word document and table are created by the macro. Controlling one program from within code in another program is called automation. Automation is very powerful and can be used to control many programs, including most of the applications in the Office 2000 suite. Make sure that a reference is set to the Word object library before you enter or test this macro. You always need to have project references set to any object library you intend to use in your code. See the earlier section "Setting Project References" for more information.

Figure 25-9 shows the sequence of actions the DLToWord macro follows.

Two Outlook Application properties that are new to Outlook 2000 are used in this macro: the Explorer object and the Selection collection. An Explorer object is what is used to view a folder in Outlook. When you view the Inbox, Drafts, Journal, or any other Outlook folder you are doing this in an Explorer object. The Selection collection object is the one or more items currently selected in an Explorer object. Collections are groups of similar objects. When you look at the Outlook object model in the Object Browser, you will see many examples of collections, such as Selection, Explorers, Inspectors, Items, Recipients, and so on. Figure 25-3, shown earlier in this chapter, shows some other Outlook collections, the AddressEntries, AddressLists, and Attachments collections in the Object Browser's Classes window.

Many of these collections have corresponding individual items, such as individual Explorer, Inspector, and Recipient objects. This macro uses a Recipient object, declared as objRecipient, and a distribution list item, objDL. A Recipient is a user or resource, usually the person to whom an e-mail is addressed. Here is the content of this macro:

```
Public Sub DLToWord()
    ' This macro requires references to the Outlook
    ' and Word object models.
    Dim objOutlook As Outlook.Application
    Dim objExplorer As Outlook.Explorer
    Dim objSelection As Outlook.Selection
    Dim objDL As Outlook.DistListItem
    Dim objRecipient As Outlook.Recipient
```

BUILDING OUTLOOK APPLICATIONS

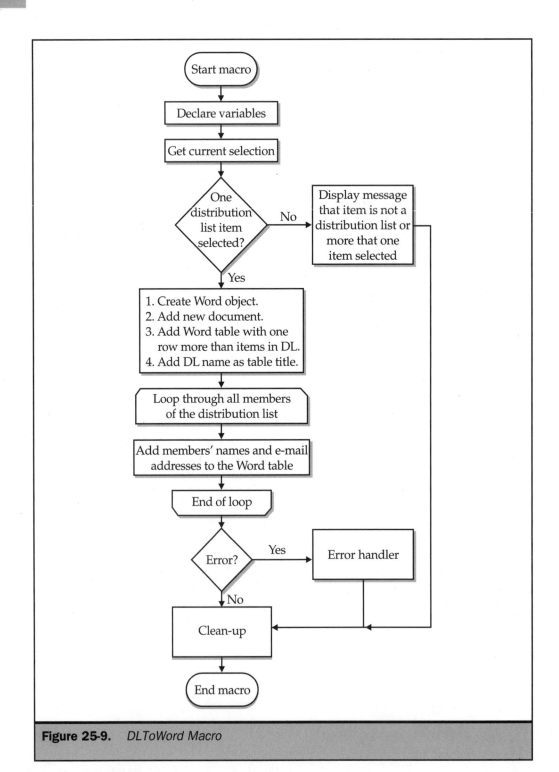

Figure 25-9. *DLToWord Macro*

The DLToWord macro uses automation to control Word, and declares objects for the Word application, including Document, Table, and Range. In addition to the string variables used for the distribution list field values, it also uses two long variables, which can represent numbers ranging from -2,147,483,648 to 2,147,483,647. The long variables are used as counters for the number of items in the distribution list.

```
Dim objWord As Word.Application
   Dim objDoc As Word.Document
   Dim objTable As Word.Table
   Dim objRange As Word.Range

   Dim lngCount As Long
   Dim lngIndex As Long
   Dim strName As String
   Dim strAddress As String
   Dim strListName As String

   On Error GoTo ErrorHandler

   Set objOutlook = CreateObject("Outlook.Application")
```

Similar to the way the currently opened item was instantiated (created) from the ActiveInspector property, the ActiveExplorer property is used to get the current folder. The Selection property is used to get the collection of currently selected items in that folder.

```
' Get the currently active folder window.
   Set objExplorer = objOutlook.ActiveExplorer
   ' Get the selected item(s) in that folder.
   Set objSelection = objExplorer.Selection
```

The macro looks for one and only one distribution list to be selected in the current folder. If those conditions are met, the name of the distribution list is stored in a string variable.

```
' Look for 1 distribution list item to be selected.
   If objSelection.Count = 1 And _
     objSelection.Item(1).Class = olDistributionList Then
       ' Get the selection.
       Set objDL = objSelection.Item(1)
       ' Get the name of the distribution list.
       strListName = objDL.DLName
```

If you use the CreateObject function when Outlook is already open, an instance of that open object is used. With Word and other Office applications, however, a new instance is created if the application is already open. This requires special handling to avoid having multiple instances of an application created. First, the error handler is disabled by the On Error Resume Next statement, which resumes program execution on the line following the one in which an error occurred. The GetObject function returns an instance of an existing application object if one exists. If no instance of Word exists, CreateObject is used to create a new instance of the Word application object.

```
' Go to next line if there is an error.
    On Error Resume Next
    ' See if Word is already open.
    Set objWord = GetObject(, "Word.Application")
    ' If not, create a new Word application object.
    If objWord Is Nothing Then
      Set objWord = CreateObject("Word.Application")
    End If
```

The next lines first re-enable the standard error handler and then add a document to Word. If an existing instance of Word is being used, this prevents the macro from altering any open documents. The new document is then made the active document, and a range is set to the beginning of the document.

```
    ' Now back to the normal error handler.
    On Error GoTo ErrorHandler
    ' Add a new document to Word and activate it.
    Set objDoc = objWord.Documents.Add
    objDoc.Activate
    ' Set the active range to the document start.
    Set objRange = objDoc.range(0, 0)
```

Next, the count of members of the distribution list is acquired, and then a Word table is created at the beginning of the document, with two columns and one more row than the count of distribution list members. The extra row will be used to insert the name of the distribution list.

```
    ' See how many items are in the distribution list.
    lngCount = objDL.MemberCount
    ' Add a Word table, with 1 more row than list members,
    ' use the first row for the list name. Table has 2 columns.
    Set objTable = objDoc.Tables.Add(objRange, lngCount + 1, 2)
```

The With statement is used to allow reference to items using only their properties, in this case properties of the objTable object. With statements not only make your code run faster, they also make it easier to enter common properties in blocks. The Cell property of the Word table is used to insert the name of the distribution list into the first row in the table. The font for the name is set to boldface.

```
' Use With to make the code faster.
With objTable
    ' Insert the list name in the first row, first column.
    .Cell(1, 1).range.InsertAfter strListName
    ' Make the list name boldface.
    .Cell(1, 1).range.Bold = True
```

A For loop is used to get each member of the distribution list, using the GetMember method of the distribution list object. The index counter of the For loop is used to index into the collection of members of the distribution list and get the name and e-mail address of the list member at that index position. Members of distribution lists are Recipient objects.

```
' Now loop through the members of the list.
For lngIndex = 1 To lngCount
    ' Get a list member
    Set objRecipient = objDL.GetMember(lngIndex)
    ' Get the name of the list member.
    strName = objRecipient.Name
    ' Get the e-mail address of the list member.
    strAddress = objRecipient.Address
```

The name and e-mail address of the list member are inserted into the Word table, with the name inserted in column 1 and the e-mail address inserted in column 2. Then the loop is executed again until there are no more members of the distribution list to process. The table is automatically sized to fit the cell contents using the Columns.AutoFit method of the table, and the With block is terminated with the End With statement.

```
        ' Insert the name and e-mail address.
        .Cell(lngIndex + 1, 1).range.InsertAfter strName
        .Cell(lngIndex + 1, 2).range.InsertAfter strAddress
    Next lngIndex
    .Columns.AutoFit
End With
```

Finally, the cursor is moved to the end of the Word document, the document is made visible, and the macro is terminated as usual.

```
        ' Move the cursor to the end of the document.
        objWord.Selection.HomeKey Unit:=wdStory, Extend:=wdMove
        ' Make the document visible.
        objWord.Visible = True
        objDoc.ActiveWindow.Visible = True
    Else
      MsgBox "Not a Distribution List or more than 1 item is selected"
    End If

MacroExit:
    Set objOutlook = Nothing
    Set objExplorer = Nothing
    Set objSelection = Nothing
    Set objDL = Nothing
    Set objRecipient = Nothing

    Set objWord = Nothing
    Set objDoc = Nothing
    Set objTable = Nothing
    Set objRange = Nothing

    Exit Sub

ErrorHandler:
    MsgBox "Error: " & Err.Description & vbCrLf & "Error # " _
      & Err.Number
    Err.Clear
    GoTo MacroExit
End Sub
```

Importing Contacts from Access

Importing and exporting contact information and other data between Outlook and Access or Excel is a common function that often has problems. Outlook cannot import or export items with custom fields and often misses duplicate items. The ContactsFromAccess macro described in this section demonstrates how to import contacts from an Access table, with code that prevents duplicate contacts from being created.

Figure 25-10 shows the sequence of actions the ContactsFromAccess macro follows.

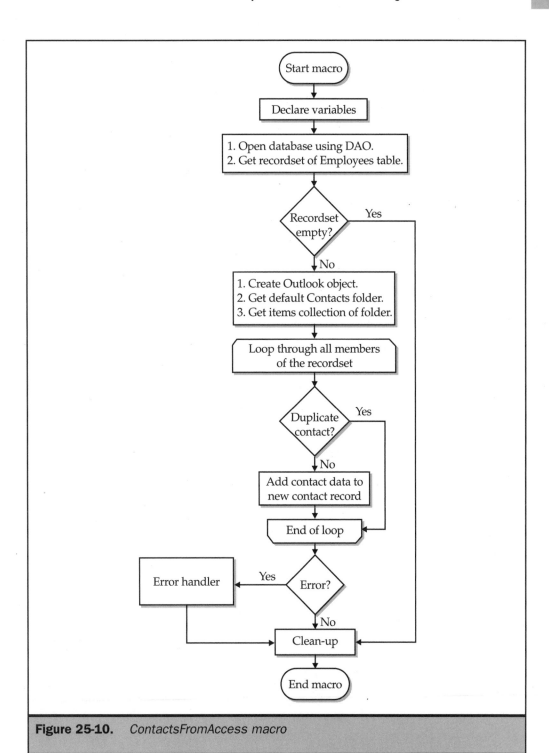

Figure 25-10.   *ContactsFromAccess macro*

This macro makes use of the Outlook NameSpace object, which is used to get direct access to Outlook folders and items. You can think of NameSpace as the window into the Outlook data store, just as Inspectors and Explorers are windows into the Outlook user interface. The only currently available NameSpace for Outlook is the MAPI namespace. Folders in Outlook are MAPIFolder objects, as shown by the objFolder variable.

```
Public Sub ContactsFromAccess()
  ' This macro requires references to the Outlook and DAO
  ' (Data Access Objects) object models.
  Dim objOutlook As Outlook.Application
  Dim objNS As Outlook.NameSpace
  Dim objFolder As Outlook.MAPIFolder
  Dim objContact As Outlook.ContactItem
  Dim objItems As Outlook.Items
```

Data Access Objects (DAO) are used to work with the Access database. ActiveX Data Objects (ADO) is a newer, more universal data access method, but for working with Access databases and tables, DAO is more versatile and easier to use. The next lines declare DAO object variables for a database and a recordset. If you have worked with Access, you are familiar with recordsets as table objects.

```
' Using DAO to work with the Access database.
  Dim dbEmployees As DAO.Database
  Dim rstEmployees As DAO.Recordset

  Dim strFirst As String
  Dim strLast As String
```

Filters are tricky to set up in Outlook. It's often easier to set up a filter that uses variables with a string declared using the string identifier character ($) than using the usual As String clause.

```
' This string is used for a filter.
  Dim ContactToCheck$

  On Error GoTo ErrorHandler
```

The sample Northwind database is opened using the DAO OpenDatabase method. To run this macro, the sample Northwind database must be installed. The path used is the standard installation path—if you installed the samples to another path, change the path string in the OpenDatabase statement.

```
' Open the sample Northwind database.
' If the install path is different, change the path.
Set dbEmployees = OpenDatabase _
   ("C:\Program Files\Microsoft " _
   & "Office\Office\Samples\Northwind.mdb")
```

SQL is a standard database query language, and it is used here to create the recordset of data from the Employees table in the Northwind database. The OpenRecordset method of the database object is used with a SQL statement to get the FirstName, LastName, Address, City, Region, PostalCode, Country, and HomePhone data fields from the Employees table.

```
' Use a SQL statement to get the data from the Employees
' table into a recordset.
Set rstEmployees = dbEmployees.OpenRecordset _
   ("SELECT FirstName, LastName, Address, City, " _
   & "Region, PostalCode, Country, " _
   & "HomePhone FROM Employees;")
```

After the recordset is created, the next statement checks to see if there are any records in it. A newly opened recordset whose record pointer is positioned at EOF (End of File) is an empty recordset. EOF and BOF (Beginning of File) are special locations after and before the records in a recordset. If the recordset is empty, both EOF and BOF will be True. Only one of these conditions needs to be checked, and you can check either one. If the recordset is not empty, the record pointer is moved to the first record in the recordset.

```
' The pointer for a newly opened recordset is EOF
' (End Of File) or BOF (Beginning Of File) only if
' the recordset is empty.
If Not rstEmployees.EOF Then
   ' Set the pointer to the first record
   rstEmployees.MoveFirst
```

After all that housekeeping, Outlook Application, NameSpace, and Contacts folder objects are created with the Set statements. The GetDefaultFolder method is used with the olFolderContacts argument (parameter) to set objFolder to point to the default Contacts folder. The collection of items in the Contacts folder is then assigned to the objItems Items collection object.

```
Set objOutlook = CreateObject("Outlook.Application")
' Outlook has only 1 NameSpace, named MAPI.
Set objNS = objOutlook.GetNamespace("MAPI")
' Get the default Contacts folder.
Set objFolder = objNS.GetDefaultFolder(olFolderContacts)
' Get the collection of items in the Contacts folder.
Set objItems = objFolder.Items
```

The recordset is looped through (iterated) until the EOF condition becomes true. This iterates through the entire contents of the recordset.

```
' Loop through the recordset until the end.
Do While Not rstEmployees.EOF
  ' Extract the first and last names of this entry.
  strFirst = rstEmployees(0)
  strLast = rstEmployees(1)
```

The first and last names of the current record in the recordset are used as part of a filter with the Find method to ensure that no duplicate contacts are created. The first name is compared to the FirstName field in Outlook Contact items, and the last name is compared to the LastName field. The use of quotes in filters or restrictions is tricky; study this filter as an example of how to construct a complex filter string.

```
' Set up a comparison of the first name from the recordset
' and the first name for a Contact item.
ContactToCheck$ = "[First Name] = """ & strFirst & """"
' Add a comparison of the last name from the recordset
' and the last name for a Contact item.
ContactToCheck$ = ContactToCheck$ & " And [Last Name] = """ _
  & strLast & """"
' See if this name already exists in the Contacts folder.
Set objContact = objItems.Find(ContactToCheck$)
```

If no contact is found that matches the first and last names of the current record in the recordset, a new contact item is created using the CreateItem method with the olContactItem argument. The fields from the record are then added to the new contact item. Access database tables may contain Null fields—fields with no value at all. Outlook does not permit Null fields, so a check is made to see if any field is Null before adding it to the contact item. If a Null field is found, that field from the record is not added to the Outlook contact item.

```
If objContact Is Nothing Then
  ' Only add the new contact if it doesn't exist already.
  Set objContact = objOutlook.CreateItem(olContactItem)
  With objContact
    ' Outlook will not accept Null values, so test for that.
    If Not IsNull(rstEmployees(0)) Then
      ' If not Null set the first name.
      ' Repeat for other fields.
      .FirstName = rstEmployees(0)
    End If
    If Not IsNull(rstEmployees(1)) Then
      .LastName = rstEmployees(1)
    End If
    If Not IsNull(rstEmployees(2)) Then
      .HomeAddressStreet = rstEmployees(2)
    End If
    If Not IsNull(rstEmployees(3)) Then
      .HomeAddressCity = rstEmployees(3)
    End If
    If Not IsNull(rstEmployees(4)) Then
      .HomeAddressState = rstEmployees(4)
    End If
    If Not IsNull(rstEmployees(5)) Then
      .HomeAddressPostalCode = rstEmployees(5)
    End If
    If Not IsNull(rstEmployees(6)) Then
      .HomeAddressCountry = rstEmployees(6)
    End If
    If Not IsNull(rstEmployees(7)) Then
      .HomeTelephoneNumber = rstEmployees(7)
    End If
```

The new contact item has no permanent existence until the Save method is used to save it to the Contacts folder. The MoveNext method of the recordset is then used to move to the next record until the recordset has been traversed.

```
        ' Save the new Contact item.
        .Save
      End With
    End If
    ' Go to the next row in the recordset.
    rstEmployees.MoveNext
  Loop ' Until the pointer is at the end of the recordset.
End If
```

The remainder of the macro closes the recordset and database if they exist, and then uses the standard code from the macro template to set all objects equal to Nothing. The rest of the code is the standard exit statement and error handler.

```
MacroExit:
  ' Closing the recordset or database if they do not exist
  ' causes an error.
  If Not rstEmployees Is Nothing Then
    rstEmployees.Close
  End If
  If Not dbEmployees Is Nothing Then
    dbEmployees.Close
  End If

  Set objOutlook = Nothing
  Set objNS = Nothing
  Set objFolder = Nothing
  Set objContact = Nothing
  Set objItems = Nothing
  Set dbEmployees = Nothing
  Set rstEmployees = Nothing

  Exit Sub

ErrorHandler:
  MsgBox "Error: " & Err.Description & vbCrLf & "Error # " _
    & Err.Number
  Err.Clear
  GoTo MacroExit
End Sub
```

Figure 25-11.   *New contacts created by the ContactsFromAccess macro*

Figure 25-11 shows the results of running the ContactsFromAccess macro, with the newly created contacts shown at the top of the Contacts folder window.

Summary

In this chapter, you learned how to create and use Outlook macros. It's a good idea to study the Object Browser to become familiar with the object models for Outlook and other applications you want to automate. There are also many books that teach you about Outlook programming, one is recommended earlier, and there is a list of other Outlook programming books at: http://www.slipstick.com/books/dev.htm. There are also peer-to-peer newsgroups sponsored by Microsoft that specialize in Outlook programming problems and questions. A newsgroup that specializes in Outlook VBA questions is msnews.microsoft.public.outlook.program_vba.

Programming Outlook enables you to unleash the true power of Outlook and Exchange as a development platform. Complex routing, workflow, and contact management systems (to name a few) can be created. There are very few limits to your uses of Outlook when you work with its programming interface.

The Complete Reference

Part VIII

Appendixes

Appendix A

Becoming a Microsoft Office User Specialist

The Microsoft Office User Specialist (MOUS) program is the best way for you to prove to yourself and to prospective employers that you have mastered one or more programs in the Microsoft Office 2000 suite. The program is a reliable way for you to measure your strengths and identify your weaknesses. And by following the prescribed coursework and preparing for the exam, you will improve your skills at using programs in the Office suite.

Three levels of MOUS certification are available:

- **Core** Becoming a Microsoft Office User Specialist at the Core level indicates that you have a comprehensive understanding of the core computer tasks. This certification is available for Word, Excel, PowerPoint, Outlook, and Access.

- **Expert** The holder of an Expert certificate can handle more complex assignments. This certification is currently available only for Word and Excel.

- **Master** This is the highest level of certification. A Master is a person who has passed all five of the required exams in Word, Excel, PowerPoint, Access, and Outlook.

How to Become Certified

To become a certified MOUS specialist in Outlook 2000, you need to prepare for the exam, register to take the test, take the test, and get your test results.

1. Prepare for the Exam

As you begin to prepare for MOUS certification in Outlook, figure out what parts of the program you know well and where you need to learn more. The Outlook skills you need to become a Microsoft Office User Specialist are listed in Appendix B of this book. You can also go to the MOUS Web site at **www.mous.net** to see a list of the skills.

MOUS exams are not multiple-choice exams or fill-in-the-blank exams. Instead, you are asked to perform assignments at a computer. For example, you might be asked to refine the results of a query by adding or removing fields, or to show how to ensure data integrity by setting validation rules. To prepare for the exam, focus on Outlook tasks. Review the examples and material in this book's chapters, but don't bother memorizing information—doing so won't help you pass the test.

This book is a comprehensive reference to Microsoft Outlook. All tasks you can do in Outlook are explained in this book. Appendix B shows you where each exam objective is covered in the book. At the end of most chapters is a table that tells you where MOUS exam objectives are covered. The self-test on the CD that comes with this book quizzes you on every skill set objective and activity. By taking the exam on the CD, you can find out how well you know Outlook and where you need to study more.

2. Register for the Test

All exams are administered by an Authorized Testing Center. To find the testing center nearest you, phone (800) 933-4493 or check the MOUS Web site at **www.mous.net.** Many testing centers require advanced registration, but others accept walk-in candidates as well.

3. Take the Test

All the exams take an hour or less. You are judged on your ability to complete all the tasks exactly as specified within the allotted time. As you take an exam, you can use the Help program, but doing so takes time and may result in your not completing the test in the allotted time.

Microsoft provides guidelines for taking MOUS exams. Here are some general tips for taking a MOUS exam:

- Carefully read the test instructions. When you begin a test, the instructions are moved to the bottom of the screen.

- Answer each question as if your work will be shown to the test exam administrator. Do nothing extra; do only what is requested.

- Since all questions have equal value, try to answer all of them, including the difficult questions.

- Pay close attention to how each question is worded. Responses must be precise. To answer a question correctly, you must do exactly as asked.

- Test scores are based on the end result, not on which technique was used to complete a task or how much time was required. Errant keystrokes and mouse clicks do not count against your score as long as you achieve the correct result. The result is what counts.

- The overall test is timed. Spending a lot of time on one question doesn't matter as far as your test score is concerned, but taking too long on a question leaves less time for completing the remaining questions.

- Answers are either right or wrong. You do not get credit for partial answers.

- If the message "method is not available" appears on the computer screen, try solving the problem a different way.

- *Important:* Make sure you have entirely completed each question before clicking the Next Task button. After you click the Next Task button, you cannot return to that question. A question will be scored as wrong if it is not properly completed before moving to the next question.

4. Get Your Test Results

Each candidate sees his or her test results as soon as the test is completed. Test results are completely confidential. If you pass, you will receive a certificate by mail in four to six weeks. If you fail, you will be informed where you need to focus more attention. You can take the test as many times as you want. Refunds are not given if you don't pass the test; you must pay a new fee each time you take the test.

After you pass the test, you have recognized proof that you possess specific, relevant skills in Microsoft Outlook. A MOUS certificate is invaluable in the job market. The certificate proves to prospective employers that you have the skills to succeed.

Appendix B

Microsoft Office
User Specialist
Exam Objectives

743

The table in this appendix is for Outlook users who are preparing for the Microsoft Office User Specialist (MOUS) exams in Microsoft Outlook 2000. In the table, you will find cross-references to chapters and headings in the book where the exam objectives are explained. To prepare for a MOUS exam, read the list of objectives, and if you don't know an objective well, turn to the part of the bok where it is explained.

Note *At the end of most chapters in this book are tables that show where MOUS objectives are explained. You can also look at the end of chapters to find out where to go to learn more about a MOUS objective.*

Objective	Activity	Chapter	Section Title
OL2000.1	**Use Outlook 2000 mail to communicate with others inside and ouside your company**		
OL2000.1.1	Read mail	4	"Opening and Reading E-mail"
OL2000.1.2	Send mail	3	All
OL2000.1.3	Compose mail by entering text	3	"Composing the Message"
OL2000.1.4	Print mail	5	"Printing E-mail Messages"
OL2000.1.5	Address mail by entering text	3	"Composing the Message"
OL2000.1.6	Use mail features (recall)	3	"Recalling Sent Messages"
OL2000.1.6	Use mail features (reply, forward)	4	"Responding to and Forwarding Messages"
OL2000.1.7	Use address book to address mail	3	"Composing the Message"
OL2000.1.8	Flag mail messages	3	"Flagging Outgoing Messages"
OL2000.1.8	Flag mail messages	5	"Flagging Received E-mail for Future Action (or Inaction)"
OL2000.1.9	Navigate within mail	3	"Navigating Outlook E-mail"
OL2000.1.10	Find messages	5	"Locating E-mail Messages"
OL2000.1.11	Configure basic mail print options	5	"Setting Print Options"
OL2000.1.12	Work with attachments	3 4	"Adding Attachments" "Handling Attachments"

Objective	Activity	Chapter	Section Title
OL2000.1.13	Add a signature to e-mail	19	"Adding Signatures to E-mail"
OL2000.1.14	Customize the look of mail	3	"Formatting Messages"
OL2000.1.15	Use mail templates to compose mail	19	"Saving Time with Templates"
OL2000.1.16	Integrate and use mail with other Outlook components	20	"Sending E-mail"
OL2000.1.17	Customize Menu and task bars	23	"Customizing Toolbars" "Using Menus"
OL2000.2	**Use Outlook 2000 to manage messages**		
OL2000.2.1	Create folders	5 18	"Creating Mail Folders" "Creating Folders"
OL2000.2.2	Sort mail	5	"Sorting E-mail"
OL2000.2.3	Set viewing options	4	"Configuring the Inbox"
OL2000.2.4	Archive mail messages	5	"Archiving E-mail"
OL2000.2.5	Filter a view	5	"Applying Filters"
OL2000.3	**Use the Outlook 2000 Calendar**		
OL2000.3.1	Navigating within the Calendar	10	"Navigating the Calendar Window"
OL2000.3.2	Schedule appointments and events	11	"Adding Appointments" "Scheduling Events"
OL2000.3.3	Set reminders	11	"Staying on Schedule with Reminders"
OL2000.3.4	Print in Calendar	10	"Printing the Calendar"
OL2000.3.5	Schedule multiday events	11	"Scheduling Events"
OL2000.3.6	Configure Calendar print options	10	"Printing the Calendar" "Customizing Print Styles"
OL2000.3.7	Customize the Calendar view	10	"Customizing the Calendar"
OL2000.3.8	Schedule recurring appointments	11	"Creating Recurring Calendar Items"
OL2000.3.9	Customize Menu and task bars	23	"Customizing Toolbars" "Using Menus"

APPENDIXES

Objective	Activity	Chapter	Section Title
OL2000.3.10	Add and remove attendees	12	"Adding and Removing Attendees"
OL2000.3.11	Plan meetings involving others	12	"Using the Meeting Planner"
OL2000.3.12	Save a team or personal calendar as a Web page	10	"Publishing Your Calendar as a Web Page"
OL2000.3.13	Book office resources directly (for example, conference rooms and AV equipment)	12	"Scheduling Meeting Resources"
OL2000.3.14	Integrate Calendar with other Outlook components	10	"Integrating Calendar with Other Outlook Components"
OL2000.4	**Navigate and use Outlook 2000 effectively**		
OL2000.4.1	Use Outlook Help and Office Assistant components	1	"Getting Help"
OL2000.4.2	Move items between folders	5	"Moving and Copying Messages"
OL2000.4.3	Navigate between Outlook components	1	"Getting Around in Outlook"
OL2000.4.4	Modify the master category list	9	"Using a Categories Command"
OL2000.4.5	Assign items to a category	9	"Assigning Contacts to Categories"
OL2000.4.6	Sort information using categories	5	"Assigning Messages to Contacts and Categories"
OL2000.4.7	Use the Office clipboard	20	"Using the Office Clipboard"
OL2000.5	**Use contacts**		
OL2000.5.1	Create contacts	8	"Adding Contacts"
OL2000.5.1	Edit and delete contacts	8	"Modifying and Deleting Contacts"
OL2000.5.2	Send contact information via e-mail	8	"Sending Contact Information via E-mail"

Objective	Activity	Chapter	Section Title
OL2000.5.3	Organize contacts by category	9	"Using Categories to Organize Contacts"
OL2000.5.4	Manually record an activity in a journal	14	"Creating Journal Entries Manually"
OL2000.5.5	Link activities to contacts	8	"Linking Activities to a Contact Record"
OL2000.5.6	Sort contacts using fields	9	"Sorting Contacts"
OL2000.6	**Use tasks**		
OL2000.6.1	Create and update one-time tasks	13	"Creating Tasks"
OL2000.6.2	Accept and decline tasks	13	"Responding to Task Assignments"
OL2000.6.3	Organize tasks using categories	13	"Keeping Track of Tasks with Categories"
OL2000.6.4	Assign tasks to others	13	"Assigning Tasks"
OL2000.6.5	Create tasks from other Outlook components	13	"Creating Tasks from Other Outlook Folders"
OL2000.6.6	Change the view for tasks	13	"Using Tasks Views"
OL2000.7	**Integrate Office applications and other applications with Outlook 2000 components**		
OL2000.7.1	Create and use Office documents inside Outlook 2000	20	"Using Contacts to Create Letters with Word"
OL2000.8	**Use notes**		
OL2000.8	Use notes	15	"Using Notes"
OL2000.8.1	Create and edit notes	15	"Creating Notes"
OL2000.8.2	Organize and view notes	15	"Organizing Notes" "Viewing Notes"
OL2000.8.3	Customize notes	15	"Customizing Notes"

APPENDIXES

Appendix C

About the CD

The CD that accompanies this book contains four multiple choice exams that are designed to assess your skills with Outlook 2000. By taking these tests, you can find out how well you know Outlook 2000 and the areas that you need to learn more about. Even if you are not interested in obtaining a MOUS Certificate, the tests offer an excellent opportunity to test your Outlook skills and knowledge (see Appendix A for more details on MOUS certification).

How to Access the Tests on the CD

When you're ready to access the test material on the CD, follow these steps:

1. Insert the CD-ROM into your CD-ROM drive.

2. The CD contains an automatic install sequence, and you will soon see an image of the book's front cover.

3. Next, you'll be presented with a dialog box that asks you to select one of three options relating to the version of Microsoft Access you have on your computer.

Note *You do not have to have Microsoft Access installed on your computer to use the CD. The installation program will install different components depending on if you have Access at all, and on which version you have. If you're not sure which version of Access you have, if any, click on Start | Programs and from the list of programs shown, determine if Access is on this list. If it is, then you know you have Access installed on your computer. To determine which version of Access you have, launch Access from the list of programs that you see. When the Access splash screen shows up, notice whether it says Access 97 or Access 2000. If you don't see the splash screen, select Help | About Microsoft Access, and the version number information will be displayed. Once you have determined which version you have, close Access.*

4. Once you have selected which version of Microsoft Access you have installed, if any, your CD will automatically run an installation program to copy the files from the CD to your computer. (Remember, you do *not* have to have Access installed on your computer to use this CD.) Once the installation process is complete, you can close the program window that appears on your screen. You're ready to begin the tests!

To begin any of the four Test Yourself Exams, select Start | Programs and from the list of programs shown, select Total Seminars Exams, and the Outlook 2000 exam.

The Two Types of Tests You Can Take

Once you have selected the Outlook 2000 exam icon from the Programs list on the Start menu, you'll have the option to take Practice Exams or Final Exams. Both exams provide a score so that you can see how well you know the material.

Practice Exams

The Practice Exam offers 65 multiple choice questions for each exam and provides an Assistance Window that can help you learn as you take the test. Here you will find hints about which multiple choice answers are correct, you can see if the answer you've chosen on a given question is right, you can explore why the correct answer *is* correct, and you'll find a chapter reference to where more information on this topic is found. When you have completed the test, you can find out your test results and assess your knowledge levels. You will see your score for individual MOUS Objective Skillsets and for the entire test to show where you might need specific refresher work.

Final Exam

The Final Exams offer a timed-exam setting with 65 multiple choice questions for each exam. You can take an entire exam at one sitting or you can choose to exit the exam at any point. You do not have access to the Assistance Window in Final Exam mode. Whether you take the complete test, or just a portion of it, you can see your test results grade and assess your knowledge levels. You will see your score for individual MOUS Objective Skillsets and for the entire test to show where you might need specific refresher work.

Index

F

G

H

WARNING: BEFORE OPENING THE DISC PACKAGE, CAREFULLY READ THE TERMS AND CONDITIONS OF THE FOLLOWING COPYRIGHT STATEMENT AND LIMITED CD-ROM WARRANTY.

Copyright Statement

This software is protected by both United States copyright law and international copyright treaty provision. Except as noted in the contents of the CD-ROM, you must treat this software just like a book. However, you may copy it into a computer to be used and you may make archival copies of the software for the sole purpose of backing up the software and protecting your investment from loss. By saying, "just like a book," The McGraw-Hill Companies, Inc. ("Osborne/McGraw-Hill") means, for example, that this software may be used by any number of people and may be freely moved from one computer location to another, so long as there is no possibility of its being used at one location or on one computer while it is being used at another. Just as a book cannot be read by two different people in two different places at the same time, neither can the software be used by two different people in two different places at the same time.

Limited Warranty

Osborne/McGraw-Hill warrants the physical compact disc enclosed herein to be free of defects in materials and workmanship for a period of sixty days from the purchase date. If the CD included in your book has defects in materials or workmanship, please call McGraw-Hill at 1-800-217-0059, 9am to 5pm, Monday through Friday, Eastern Standard Time, and McGraw-Hill will replace the defective disc.

The entire and exclusive liability and remedy for breach of this Limited Warranty shall be limited to replacement of the defective disc, and shall not include or extend to any claim for or right to cover any other damages, including but not limited to, loss of profit, data, or use of the software, or special incidental, or consequential damages or other similar claims, even if Osborne/McGraw-Hill has been specifically advised of the possibility of such damages. In no event will Osborne/McGraw-Hill's liability for any damages to you or any other person ever exceed the lower of the suggested list price or actual price paid for the license to use the software, regardless of any form of the claim.

OSBORNE/McGRAW-HILL SPECIFICALLY DISCLAIMS ALL OTHER WARRANTIES, EXPRESS OR IMPLIED, INCLUDING BUT NOT LIMITED TO, ANY IMPLIED WARRANTY OF MERCHANTABILITY OR FITNESS FOR A PARTICULAR PURPOSE. Specifically, Osborne/McGraw-Hill makes no representation or warranty that the software is fit for any particular purpose, and any implied warranty of merchantability is limited to the sixty-day duration of the Limited Warranty covering the physical disc only (and not the software), and is otherwise expressly and specifically disclaimed.

This limited warranty gives you specific legal rights; you may have others which may vary from state to state. Some states do not allow the exclusion of incidental or consequential damages, or the limitation on how long an implied warranty lasts, so some of the above may not apply to you.

This agreement constitutes the entire agreement between the parties relating to use of the Product. The terms of any purchase order shall have no effect on the terms of this Agreement. Failure of Osborne/McGraw-Hill to insist at any time on strict compliance with this Agreement shall not constitute a waiver of any rights under this Agreement. This Agreement shall be construed and governed in accordance with the laws of New York. If any provision of this Agreement is held to be contrary to law, that provision will be enforced to the maximum extent permissible, and the remaining provisions will remain in force and effect.

For technical support on this CD-ROM, please contact Total Seminars at total@totalsem.com, or visit http://www.totalsem.com